Communications in Computer and Information Science 1844

Rationale

The CCIS series is devoted to the publication of proceedings of computer science conferences. Its aim is to efficiently disseminate original research results in informatics in printed and electronic form. While the focus is on publication of peer-reviewed full papers presenting mature work, inclusion of reviewed short papers reporting on work in progress is welcome, too. Besides globally relevant meetings with internationally representative program committees guaranteeing a strict peer-reviewing and paper selection process, conferences run by societies or of high regional or national relevance are also considered for publication.

Topics

The topical scope of CCIS spans the entire spectrum of informatics ranging from foundational topics in the theory of computing to information and communications science and technology and a broad variety of interdisciplinary application fields.

Information for Volume Editors and Authors

Publication in CCIS is free of charge. No royalties are paid, however, we offer registered conference participants temporary free access to the online version of the conference proceedings on SpringerLink (http://link.springer.com) by means of an http referrer from the conference website and/or a number of complimentary printed copies, as specified in the official acceptance email of the event.

CCIS proceedings can be published in time for distribution at conferences or as post-proceedings, and delivered in the form of printed books and/or electronically as USBs and/or e-content licenses for accessing proceedings at SpringerLink. Furthermore, CCIS proceedings are included in the CCIS electronic book series hosted in the SpringerLink digital library at http://link.springer.com/bookseries/7899. Conferences publishing in CCIS are allowed to use Online Conference Service (OCS) for managing the whole proceedings lifecycle (from submission and reviewing to preparing for publication) free of charge.

Publication process

The language of publication is exclusively English. Authors publishing in CCIS have to sign the Springer CCIS copyright transfer form, however, they are free to use their material published in CCIS for substantially changed, more elaborate subsequent publications elsewhere. For the preparation of the camera-ready papers/files, authors have to strictly adhere to the Springer CCIS Authors' Instructions and are strongly encouraged to use the CCIS LaTeX style files or templates.

Abstracting/Indexing

CCIS is abstracted/indexed in DBLP, Google Scholar, EI-Compendex, Mathematical Reviews, SCImago, Scopus. CCIS volumes are also submitted for the inclusion in ISI Proceedings.

How to start

To start the evaluation of your proposal for inclusion in the CCIS series, please send an e-mail to ccis@springer.com.

Zhongjie Wang · Shangguang Wang ·
Hanchuan Xu
Editors

Service Science

CCF 16th International Conference, ICSS 2023
Harbin, China, May 13–14, 2023
Revised Selected Papers

Editors
Zhongjie Wang
Harbin Institute of Technology
Harbin, China

Shangguang Wang
Beijing University of Posts
and Telecommunications
Beijing, China

Hanchuan Xu
Harbin Institute of Technology
Harbin, China

ISSN 1865-0929 ISSN 1865-0937 (electronic)
Communications in Computer and Information Science
ISBN 978-981-99-4401-9 ISBN 978-981-99-4402-6 (eBook)
https://doi.org/10.1007/978-981-99-4402-6

This Springer imprint is published by the registered company Springer Nature Singapore Pte Ltd.
The registered company address is: 152 Beach Road, #21-01/04 Gateway East, Singapore 189721, Singapore

Preface

This volume contains the papers from the CCF 16th International Conference on Service Science (CCF ICSS 2023). The conference was hosted by Harbin Institute of Technology in China. CCF ICSS is an annual academic event directed by the Technical Committee of Services Computing, China Computer Federation, China. It is also one of the top events of the service science community in China. ICSS features a unique mix of academic, industrial, and cross-discipline topics, and provides a platform for the presentation and exchange of research results and practical experiences as well as educational developments on serviceology. ICSS aims to bridge the perspectives of researchers and the needs of practitioners.

This volume contains a total of 36 papers divided into 8 categories: Serverless Edge Computing, Edge Services Reliability, Intelligent Services, Service Application, Knowledge-Inspired Service, Service Ecosystem, Graph-Based Service Optimization, and AI-inspired Service Optimization. The conference received 71 paper submissions in total, and the acceptance rate was 51.7%. The paper review process followed a single-blind principle. All submitted papers were first reviewed by the committee to confirm whether they met the requirements such as word count and page limit. Only qualified papers entered the subsequent review process. Each paper was reviewed by 3–4 reviewers, and all reviewers needed to reach a consensus and provide a final review score. Finally, papers were accepted in order of review score from highest to lowest.

The proceedings editors wish to thank the dedicated Program Committee members and all the other reviewers for their contributions. We also thank Springer for their trust and for publishing the proceedings of CCF ICSS 2023.

May 2023

Zhongjie Wang
Shangguang Wang

Organization

Steering Committee

Bing Li	Wuhan University, China
Changjun Jiang	Tongji University, China
Hai Jin	Huazhong University of Science and Technology, China
James Spohrer	IBM Global University Programs, USA
Jianwei Yin	Zhejiang University, China
Jie Zhou	Tsinghua University, China
Jun Wei	Institute of Software, Chinese Academy of Sciences, China
Keqing He	Wuhan University, China
Liang-Jie Zhang	Kingdee Research, China
Rong Chang	IBM Research Watson, USA
Sen Su	Beijing University of Posts and Telecommunications, China
Xiaofei Xu	Harbin Institute of Technology, China
Xiucheng Fan	Fudan University, China
Yanbo Han	North China University of Technology, China
Ying Huang	Lenovo Group / Peking University, China
Yushun Fan	Tsinghua University, China
Zhaohui Wu	Zhejiang University, China
Zhi Jin	Peking University, China
Zhiyong Feng	Tianjin University, China
Zhonghai Wu	Peking University, China

Honorary Chair

Xiaofei Xu	Harbin Institute of Technology, China

General Chairs

Ting Liu	Harbin Institute of Technology, China
Jianwei Yin	Zhejiang University, China

Program Chairs

Zhongjie Wang	Harbin Institute of Technology, China
Shangguang Wang	Beijing University of Post and Telecommunications, China

Organization Chairs

Hanchuan Xu	Harbin Institute of Technology, China
Zhicheng Cai	Nanjing University of Science and Technology, China

Panel Chairs

Zibin Zheng	Sun Yat-sen University, China
Pengcheng Zhang	Hohai University, China
Xiao Xue	Tianjin University, China
Li Kuang	Central South University, China
Jiwei Huang	China University of Petroleum, China
Zhiying Tu	Harbin Institute of Technology (Weihai), China
Lizhen Cui	Shandong University, China
Xiaoping Li	Southeast University, China
Ying Liu	Northeastern University, China
Jiajing Wu	Sun Yat-sen University, China

Publicity Chairs

Ying Liu	Northeastern University, China
Shuang Yu	Harbin Institute of Technology, China

Publication Chairs

Yingjie Wang	Yantai University, China
Ruihan Hu	Harbin Institute of Technology, China

Technical Program Committee

Xingjian Lu	East China University of Science and Technology, China
Chunyan Sang	Chongqing University of Posts and Telecommunications, China
Yueshen Xu	Xidian University, China
Xiaolong Xu	Nanjing University of Information Science and Technology, China
Junna Zhang	Henan Normal University, China
Ying Liu	Northeastern University, China
Xiao Ma	Beijing University of Posts and Telecommunications, China
Yingjie Wang	Yantai University, China
Lingyan Zhang	Central South University, China
Zigui Jiang	Sun Yat-sen University, China
Yong Xie	Qinghai University, China
Jifeng Xuan	Wuhan University, China
Quanwang Wu	Chongqing University, China
Yuanlong Cao	Jiangxi Normal University, China
Shi Dong	Zhoukou Normal University, China
Keman Huang	Renmin University of China, China
Deyu Lin	Nanchang University, China
Cong Liu	Shandong University of Technology, China
Jialei Liu	Anyang Normal University, China
Lianyong Qi	Qufu Normal University, China
Xuyang Teng	Hangzhou Dianzi University, China
Yilong Yang	Beihang University, China
Yuyu Yin	Hangzhou Dianzi University, China
Mingwei Zhang	Northeastern University, China
Shenglin Zhang	Nankai University, China
Jing Li	Shandong University of Technology, China
Jianmao Xiao	Tianjin University, China
Ting He	Huaqiao University, China
Tong Mo	Peking University, China
Guiling Wang	North China University of Technology, China
Zhuofeng Zhao	North China University of Technology, China

Contents

Serverless Edge Computing

Edge Services Reliability

Intelligent Services

Service Application

Knowledge-Inspired Service

Service Ecosystem

Graph-Based Service Optimization

Serverless Edge Computing

Scheduling Workflow Instances to Servers and Serverless Functions in Cloud/Edge Data Centers

Jinquan Zhang(✉) and Shuang Wang(✉)

School of Computer Science and Engineering, Southeast University, Nanjing, China
{zhangjq,shuangwang}@seu.edu.cn

Abstract. Functions of serverless computing are paid by real running time, while VMs (Virtual machines) are paid by rented intervals. Rented resources of the former can be fully utilized, whereas those of the latter are hard to utilize fully. Resource requirements of workflow instances are always unbalanced because of complicated precedence constraints. It is a great challenge to rent appropriate numbers of server and serverless resources for scheduling workflow instances with deadline constraints in cloud/edge data centers. In this paper, we consider the workflow scheduling problem in a hybrid setting with server and serverless to minimize the rental cost with deadline constraints, for which WS3 (Workflow Scheduling in Server and Serverless Configuration) is developed. The proposed algorithm is evaluated over a lot of instances. Experimental results show that the proposed algorithm significantly reduces the total rental costs with a hybrid of server and serverless as compared to that with the only server or serverless configurations.

Keywords: Hybrid configuration · Workflow · Deadline · Serverless

1 Introduction

The precedence constraints among workflow tasks are commonly complicated. Some tasks can be executed in parallel, while others can only be executed in serial. In addition, these applications may be constrained by deadlines when they are submitted to cloud/edge data centers. Traditionally, VMs (Virtual machines) are rented by time units, e.g., hours for the on-demand manner, which leads to many idle time fragments and low resource utilization. Recently, serverless

This work is supported by the National Key Research and Development Program of China (No. 2022YFB3305500), the Key-Area Research and Development Program of Guangdong Province (No. 2021B0101200003), the National Natural Science Foundation of China (Nos. 62273089, 62102080), Natural Science Foundation of Jiangsu Province (No. BK20210204), the Fundamental Research Funds for the Central Universities (No. 2242022R10017), and Collaborative Innovation Center of Wireless Communications Technology.

Z. Wang et al. (Eds.): ICSS 2023, CCIS 1844, pp. 3–16, 2023.
https://doi.org/10.1007/978-981-99-4402-6_1

computing has become popular in many fields, e.g., artificial intelligence [5], big data processing [8], and scientific computing [12]. The tasks can be executed by invoking SFs (serverless functions), which are charged according to their actual execution times. The main advantage of serverless computing lies in the fine-grained billing model and full resource utilization, while it is higher priced than servers. Therefore, it is desirable to execute workflows in the edge data center to satisfy the deadline constraints, and hybrid servers and serverless functions to reduce the total rental cost.

In this paper, the workflow scheduling problem with the hybrid server and serverless resources is considered to minimize the total rental cost. The considered workflow instances are constrained by hard deadlines, and the resources are heterogeneous. Since workflow scheduling problems with only server configurations are NP-hard [14], it is natural that the considered problem is also NP-hard with the following challenges: i) Different billing models of server and serverless increase the heterogeneity of computing resources. It is difficult to rent appropriate numbers and types of VMs and serverless functions for unbalanced resource requirements. ii) There are many topological task orders in a workflow instance, which results in different resource utilization of VMs. Determining an appropriate topological task order is challenging in using rented resources fully. iii) How to allocate the workflow tasks to the rented VMs and serverless functions is challenging to minimize the total rental cost.

Resource utilization and the unit cost of computing resources are two significant factors influencing the total cost. In this paper, a heuristic that aims to minimize the total rental cost by reducing the use of high-priced resources and improving the utilization of low-priced resources is developed for the considered problem. The main contributions are as follows:

1. The proposed problem is formally described and mathematically modeled.
2. Several properties of the problem are studied and adopted for designing workflow scheduling algorithms.
3. The WS3 (Workflow Scheduling in Server and Serverless Configuration) algorithm is developed for the studies problem, which can effectively reduce fragments, improve resource utilization, and reduce the total rental cost.

The rest of this paper is organized as follows: Sect. 2 reviews the state-of-the-art of the problem under study. The problem is introduced in Sect. 3. Section 4 describes the proposed algorithms. Experimental results are shown in Sect. 5, followed by conclusions and future work in Sect. 6.

2 Related Works

In server configurations, time and cost are the two most concerns when scheduling workflows. In most cases, time is regarded as a constraint, and the cost is regarded as an objective [1,15], and vice versa [4,13]. In other cases, time and cost are considered at the same time as constraints [11,16] or objectives [2,17]. ICPCP and ICPCPD2 are two algorithms proposed by Abrishami et al. [1] to minimize the cost. For a similar problem, Wu et al. [15] proposed ProLiS which is a list scheduling heuristic algorithm and L-ACO which is a meta-heuristic algorithm. However, VMs in the above works cannot be fully used and fragments cannot be avoided.

In serverless configurations, the available resources are SFs instead of VMs. A performance and billing model is set up in [9] to predict the makespan and cost of workflows, and a heuristic with four greedy strategies is designed to optimize the two indicators. Deadline and budget are set as constraints in [7] and the corresponding algorithm is proposed for this situation. Elgamal et al. [3] analyzed the influence of state transitions, function placement, and memory size of workflow execution and proposed a function fusion and function placement-based method.

In server and serverless hybrid configurations, there are just a few studies. The hybrid of two kinds of resources makes scheduling problems more complicated. Mahajan et al. [10] explored the trade-offs between serverless computing and traditional cloud computing for independent tasks. Jiang et al. [6] designed a workflow execution system mixing SFs and Iaas/clusters. The tasks are allocated to different environments considering the maximum execution duration limitation, memory limitation, and storage limitation into account of SFs. Different from the above existing studies, the above studies ignore the deadline constraint in a server and serverless hybrid configuration, which is considered in this paper.

3 Problem Formulation

For the considered problem, the following assumptions are made:

- Workflow instances are computation-intensive, and communication time between tasks is ignored.
- Cold-start is not considered, i.e., functions could start quickly without consuming time.
- Running time limitation is considered, which means the execution time for each task is no more than hundreds of seconds.

A workflow instance is described as a DAG (directed acyclic graph) $G = (T, E)$ with a deadline constraint D. $T = \{t_1, \ldots, t_N\}$ is the task set. Each task t_i has instructions w_i. E is the edge set in which (t_i, t_j) means task t_j cannot be executed before t_i. The source task t_1 and the sink task t_N are dummy tasks with 0 instructions.

Serverless functions and VMs are provided in a hybrid configuration. In terms of the statement of cloud service providers, such as Amazon, the prices of functions are proportional to their speeds. In this case, the cost of any type of function is the same when executing computation-intensive task t_i. Therefore, we assume that just the fastest function f_i can be selected for t_i. The speed of f_i is p_i and the price of f_i is c_i. There are M types of VMs, which are sorted according to their processing speeds. $v_{m,n}$ is the nth instance of mth VM type. Each instance is configured with speed $p_{m,n}$ and price $c_{m,n}$ and charged by BTU (billing time unit). The instances of the same type have the same speed and price. In this paper, we assume that the speed of f_i is no slower than any type of VM, i.e., $p_i \geq p_{m,n}, \forall i, m, n$. Besides, all VMs have the same PPR (Performance-to-Price Ratio), which is true in the real clouds, i.e.,

$$\alpha = \frac{p_{m,n}}{c_{m,n}}, \forall m = 1, 2, \ldots, n = 1, 2, \ldots, \quad (1)$$

where $\alpha > 0$ is a constant. Similarly, the PPR of SFs is also a constant β, i.e.,

$$\beta = \frac{p_i}{c_i}, \forall i = 1, 2, \ldots, N. \quad (2)$$

SFs are higher priced than VMs, i.e., $\beta < \alpha$. In this paper, function f_i or VM $v_{m,n}$ is called a unit service, i.e., a function is called for once, or a VM is rented for a BTU.

The objective is to minimize the total cost C while satisfying the deadline D. In any schedule, the task set T can be divided into two subsets, i.e., the tasks executed by SFs T_f and the tasks executed by VMs T_{vm}.

$$T_f \cup T_{vm} = T, \quad T_f \cap T_{vm} = \emptyset \quad (3)$$

The objective can be described as follows:

$$\min\ C = \sum_{t_i \in T_f} \frac{w_i}{p_i} \times c_i + \sum_{m=1}^{M} \sum_{n=1}^{|US_m|} c_{m,n} \times BTU \quad (4)$$

where $|US_m|$ is the number of unit services rented with the mth type of VM. Suppose the total instructions of a workflow instance is a constant K. For any schedule, the following equation should be satisfied,

$$K = \sum_{m=1}^{M} \sum_{n=1}^{|US_m|} p_{m,n} \times U_{m,n} \times BTU + \sum_{t_i \in T_f} w_i \quad (5)$$

where $U_{m,n}$ is the resource utilization of unit service $v_{m,n}$. When some tasks are scheduled while others are not, let Q be the set of the unscheduled tasks. For any task t_j has not been scheduled, $EST(t_j)$, $EFT(t_j)$, $LST(t_j)$, $LFT(t_j)$ refer to the earliest start time, the earliest finish time, the latest start time, the latest finish time of task t_j, respectively. For any task t_j that has been scheduled, $AST(t_j)$, $AFT(t_j)$ refer to the actual start time and actual finish time of task t_j, respectively. If t_j has not been scheduled, it cannot start before the EFTs of its unscheduled predecessors and AFTs of its scheduled predecessors, i.e.,

$$EST(t_j) = \max\{\max_{t_i \in pr(t_j) \cap Q} EFT(t_i), \max_{t_k \in pr(t_j) \cap (T-Q)} AFT(t_k)\} \quad (6)$$

where $pr(t_j)$ is the predecessor set of t_j. The earliest finish time $EFT(t_j)$ equals to the sum of $EST(t_j)$ and estimated execution time $ET(t_j)$ of task t_j,

$$EFT(t_j) = EST(t_j) + ET(t_j) \quad (7)$$

$$ET(t_j) = \frac{w_j}{p_j} \tag{8}$$

Similarly,

$$LFT(t_j) = \min\{\min_{t_i \in su(t_j) \cap Q}\{LST(t_i)\}, \min_{t_k \in su(t_j) \cap (T-Q)}\{AST(t_k)\} \tag{9}$$

$$LST(t_j) = LFT(t_j) - ET(t_j) \tag{10}$$

where $su(t_j)$ is in the successor set of t_j. Besides, all tasks should finish within the deadline D, i.e.,

$$\max_{t_j \in T}\{AFT(t_j)\} \leq D. \tag{11}$$

4 Proposed Algorithm

In this paper, a workflow scheduling algorithm The WS3 (Workflow Scheduling in Server and Serverless Configuration) is proposed for the considered problem, as shown in Algorithm 1. The WS3 algorithms generate two effective schedules with low rental costs by improving two initial schedules, and the better one is finally adopted.

Algorithm 1: Workflow Scheduling in Server and Serverless Configuration (WS3)

Input: G=(T, E); D
Output: Total cost C

```
begin
    Generate a schedule SP1 by improving the initial schedule in a serverless
      configuration;
    Generate a schedule SP2 by improving the initial schedule in a server
      configuration;
    return The minimum cost of SP1 and SP2.
```

4.1 The Properties of the Considered Problem

The considered problem is complex due to the hybridization configuration of VMs and SFs. Therefore, some important properties of the problem are studied first, based on which the WS3 algorithm is proposed.

Although VMs and SFs are different in billing model, SFs can be regarded as a particular type of VM with fixed resource utilization, which is proved by Theorem 1.

Theorem 1. *For task t_i, the cost of f_i is equal to that of a unit VM service with resource utilization β/α and speed $\frac{w_i}{BTU} \times \frac{\alpha}{\beta}$.*

Proof. For any VM instance $v_{m,n}$, $p_i/c_i = \beta$, and $p_{m,n}/c_{m,n} = \alpha$. Therefore, $c_i = \frac{\alpha}{\beta} \times \frac{c_{m,n}}{p_{m,n}} \times p_i$. The cost of the function f_i can be calculated as $\frac{w_i}{p_i} \times c_i = \frac{w_i}{p_i} \times \frac{\alpha}{\beta} \times \frac{c_{m,n}}{p_{m,n}} \times p_i = \frac{w_i}{\beta/\alpha \times p_{m,n}} \times c_{m,n} = \frac{w_i}{\beta/\alpha} \times \frac{1}{\alpha}$. The above formula infers that function f_i is equivalent to any type of VM instance with resource utilization β/α without considering BTU, both of them result in the same cost. The equivalence between SFs and VMs is true in cost, while the execution time of task t_i is not changed. In this paper, f_i is regarded as a unit VM service $p_{m,n}$ that executes t_i in one BTU, i.e., $\frac{w_i}{\beta/\alpha \times p_{m,n}} = BTU$, the speed $p_{m,n}$ satisfies the following equation, $p_{m,n} = \frac{w_i}{BTU} \times \frac{\alpha}{\beta}$.

Corollary 1. *For task t_i, the cost of a VM instance with resource utilization β/α is equal to a function, i.e., $\frac{w_i}{\beta/\alpha} \times \frac{1}{\alpha} = \frac{w_i}{p_i} \times c_i$.*

Theorem 2. *For any schedule, if $U_{m,n} \geq \beta/\alpha, \forall v_{m,n}$, then the total cost of the schedule is not greater than that in a single serverless configuration.*

Proof. According to Formula (4), the total cost can be written as $C = \sum_{t_i \in T_f} \frac{w_i c_i}{p_i} + \sum_{m=1}^{M} \sum_{n=1}^{|US_m|} c_{m,n} \times BTU = \sum_{t_i \in T_f} \frac{w_i c_i}{p_i} + \sum_{m=1}^{M} \sum_{n=1}^{|US_m|} \frac{c_{m,n} p_{m,n} U_{m,n} \times BTU}{p_{m,n} U_{m,n}} = \sum_{t_i \in T_f} \frac{w_i c_i}{p_i} + \frac{1}{\alpha} \sum_{m=1}^{M} \sum_{n=1}^{|US_m|} \frac{p_{m,n} U_{m,n} \times BTU}{U_{m,n}}$. As we know, $U_{m,n} \geq \beta/\alpha, \forall v_{m,n}$. Therefore, the total rental cost $C \leq \sum_{t_i \in T_f} \frac{w_i c_i}{p_i} + \frac{1}{\alpha} \frac{\sum_{m=1}^{M} \sum_{n=1}^{|US_m|} p_{m,n} U_{m,n} \times BTU}{\beta/\alpha} = \sum_{t_i \in T_f} \frac{w_i c_i}{p_i} + \frac{1}{\alpha} \frac{K - \sum_{t_i \in T_f} w_i}{\beta/\alpha} = \sum_{t_i \in T_f} \frac{w_i c_i}{p_i} + \frac{1}{\alpha} \frac{\sum_{t_i \in T_{vm}} w_i}{\beta/\alpha} = \sum_{t_i \in T_f} \frac{w_i c_i}{p_i} + \sum_{t_i \in T_{vm}} \frac{1}{\alpha} \times \frac{w_i}{\beta/\alpha} = \sum_{t_i \in T_f} \frac{w_i c_i}{p_i} + \sum_{t_i \in T_{vm}} \frac{w_i c_i}{p_i} = \sum_{t_i \in T} \frac{w_i c_i}{p_i}$.

Theorem 3. *Minimizing the total rental cost C is equivalent to maximizing of the average resource utilization $\bar{U}$ if all SFs are regarded as special unit VMs.*

Proof. Suppose that $w_{m,n}$ is total instruction allocated to $v_{m,n}$, the total cost can be calculated by $C = \frac{1}{\alpha} \sum_{t_i \in T_f} \frac{w_i}{\beta/\alpha} + \frac{1}{\alpha} \sum_{m=1}^{M} \sum_{n=1}^{|US_m|} \frac{p_{m,n} U_{m,n} \times BTU}{U_{m,n}} = \frac{1}{\alpha} \sum_{t_i \in T_f} \frac{w_i}{\beta/\alpha} + \frac{1}{\alpha} \sum_{m=1}^{M} \sum_{n=1}^{|US_m|} \frac{w_{m,n}}{U_{m,n}}$. This formula can be regarded as a Riemann integral with finite discontinuities. According to the integral median theorem, $\exists \bar{U}$ satisfies $C = \frac{1}{\alpha} (\sum_{t_i \in T_f} w_i + \sum_{m=1}^{M} \sum_{n=1}^{|US_m|} w_{m,n}) \frac{1}{\bar{U}} = \frac{1}{\alpha} \times \frac{K}{\bar{U}}$, where $\bar{U}$ is average resource utilization. $\bar{U} \in [min\{min\{U_{m,n}\}, \beta/\alpha\}, max\{max\{U_{m,n}\}, \beta/\alpha\}]$. The above formula indicates that the total cost C is determined by the average resource utilization.

4.2 Schedule Improvement in a Serverless Configuration

Theorem 1–3 provide basic principles for algorithm design. They inspire us that an initial schedule in a serverless configuration can be improved by guaranteeing the resource utilization of each VM instance over a threshold β/α.

HCPCP (Hybrid Configuration based Partial Critical Path Algorithm) is developed and shown in Algorithm 2. The proposed algorithm mainly contains four steps: parameter initialization, PCP (Partial Critical Path) generation, cyclic packing, and parameter update. The definition of PCP is as follows:

1. Critical Parent: The critical parent of task t_i is the unscheduled parent of t_i with the maximal EFT.
2. Partial Critical Path: The PCP of t_i is empty if t_i does not have any unscheduled parents. Otherwise, the PCP of t_i contains the critical parent of task t_i and the critical parent's PCP.

The details are described as follows. Since no tasks are scheduled at the beginning, initial parameters EST, EFT, LST, LFT are calculated for each task (Algorithm 2). Next, a PCP is built from task t_N (Algorithm 3), which is allocated by the cyclic packing algorithm (Algorithm 4), and parameters are updated after each allocation. After the PCP is allocated, new PCPs are built from the last task to the first one based on the last allocated PCP (Algorithm 3).

Algorithm 2: Hybrid Configuration based Partial Critical Path Algorithm (HCPCP)

```
begin
    Mark all tasks as unscheduled;
    Calculating initial parameters;
    Call AssignParent(t_N);
    C ← Calculate the total cost;
    return C;
```

Algorithm 3: AssignParent

```
Input: task t
begin
    while t has unscheduled parents do
        P ← Build a PCP from t ;
        Call CyclicPacking(P);
        foreach ele ∈ reversed(P) do
            Call AssignParent(ele);
```

Algorithm 4 tries to assign tasks in the PCP to suitable unit VM services as many as possible unless the execution time of the first task is more than one BTU. According to Theorem 3, only the VM with the highest resource utilization is adopted to increase the average resource utilization and reduce the total rental cost. The tasks are marked as scheduled after each allocation. If the highest resource utilization is lower than a threshold β/α, a function is adopted to execute the first task in the PCP instead of allocating all tasks to VMs according to Theorem 2, and the allocated task is marked as scheduled. The above allocation process continues until no tasks are left on the PCP.

Algorithm 4: CyclicPacking

Input: PCP P

begin
  while *Exist unscheduled tasks in P* **do**
    $VmSet \leftarrow$ Unit VM services $\{v_1, v_2, \ldots, v_M\}$ with M types;
    for $i = 1$ *to* M **do**
      Attempt to allocate unscheduled tasks of P to unit service v_i as many as possible;
      $U_i \leftarrow$ Resource utilization of v_i;
    $k = \arg\max_{1 \leq i \leq M}\{U_i\}$;
    if $U_k > \beta/\alpha$ **then**
      v_k is adopted for task allocation;
      Mark the tasks allocated to v_k as scheduled;
      Update parameters for all unscheduled tasks;
    else
      $t^* \leftarrow$ The first task in P;
      Allocate t^* to a serverless function;
      Mark t^* as scheduled;
      Update parameters for all unscheduled tasks;

4.3 Schedule Improvement in a Server Configuration

In this section, the initial schedule is generated by the ICPCP algorithm, and improved by HCSI (Hybrid Configuration Schedule Improvement). Suppose that SP is a schedule in a server configuration. If $\forall v_{m,n}$, $U_{m,n} \geq \beta/\alpha$, the cost of SP is less than that in a serverless configuration. However, it is not likely for all unit services to achieve a higher resource utilization than β/α. Therefore, Algorithm 5 is proposed to replace part of unit VM services whose resource utilization is lower than β/α with functions. The above adjustment increases average resource utilization.

While replacing one unit VM service with a group of functions, it is common that several tasks are executed with two adjacent unit VM services, as shown in Fig. 1. Suppose $v_{m,n}$ is a unit VM service. w_{left} and w_{right} are parts of tasks executed on the former or the latter unit service of $v_{m,n}$. The execution time of $w_{m,n}$, w_{left} and w_{right} in SP are $ET_{m,n}$, ET_{left} and ET_{right}, respectively. If the replacement results in a decrease in total cost, the following inequality must be satisfied, i.e.,

$$(w_{m,n} + w_{left} + w_{right}) \times \frac{1}{\beta} < c_{m,n} \times BTU \tag{12}$$

Divide both sides of the inequality by $p_{m,n}$,

$$ET_{m,n} + ET_{left} + ET_{right} < \frac{\beta}{\alpha} \times BTU \tag{13}$$

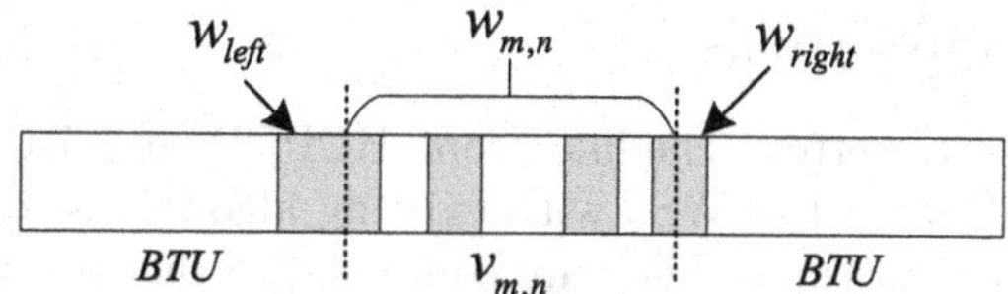

Fig. 1. Unit VM service replacement

Divide both sides of the inequality by BTU,

$$U_{m,n} < \frac{\beta}{\alpha} - \frac{ET_{left} + ET_{right}}{BTU} \tag{14}$$

Formula (14) indicates that the resource utilization of $v_{m,n}$ to be replaced should be equal to or a little smaller than β/α. At the same time, a convenient approach to judge whether a unit VM service should be replaced is provided by the formula (13). The left end of the formula (13) means the total execution time $TET_{m,n}$ of all tasks related to $v_{m,n}$.

Based on the above analysis, Algorithm 5 is proposed. The algorithm checks each unit VM service. If the formula (13) holds for the selected unit VM service, the unit VM service is replaced with functions.

Algorithm 5: Hybrid Configuration Based Schedule Improvement Algorithm

---

Input: *SP* generated by classical algorithms

begin
    foreach *unit VM service* $v_{m,n}$ **do**
        Calculate total execution time $TET_{m,n} \leftarrow ET_{m,n} + ET_{left} + ET_{right}$;
        if $TET_{m,n} < \frac{\beta}{\alpha} \times BTU$ **then**
            Replace $v_{m,n}$ with functions ;
        else
            Continue;
    Calculate the total cost C of the schedule after adjustment using Formula (4);
    return C;

---

5 Experimental Results

To our knowledge, the considered hybrid server and serverless workflow scheduling problem has not been studied yet. A series of experiments are conducted to compare the performance of the proposed algorithms.

5.1 Experimental Settings

Since WS3 adopts a better schedule from HCPCP and HCSI, we compare HCPCP and HCSI instead of WS3 with existing algorithms to verify the effectiveness of the two algorithms. They are compared to the cost of ICPCP [1] and the cost of the schedule in a single serverless configuration. The above algorithms are compared with RPD (Relative Percentage Deviation), which is defined by:

$$RPD(\%) = \frac{C - C_{best}}{C_{worst} - C_{best}} \times 100\% \tag{15}$$

C_{best} is the total cost of the schedule in a server configuration taking full use of VMs. C_{worst} is the total cost of the schedule in a server configuration, allocating each task to a unit VM service with the highest speed. The ANOVA (multi-factor analysis of variance) technique is adopted to analyze results.

All evaluated algorithms are coded in Python and run on an Intel Core i7-7500U CPU @ 2.70 GHZ with 12 GBytes of RAM. All algorithms are implemented with Python in simulation. There are three types of VMs with 1, 2, or 4 cores, respectively, and the functions are configurated with four cores. All the setting of resources origins from AWS EC2[1] and AWS Fargate[2], and the details can be found in Table 1.

Table 1. The configurations of resources in AWS

Type	vCPU	Memory(GB)	Price(USD/h)
a1.medium	1	2	0.0255
a1.large	2	4	0.051
a1.xlarge	4	8	0.102
function	4	8	0.19748

The workflow instances used for algorithm verification are generated using Pegasus Workflow Generator[3]. Four types of workflow applications are evaluated, i.e., Ligo, Montage, Genome, and Cybershake. The estimated execution time of each task is uniformly distributed between 0s and 600s. The number of tasks in a workflow application is selected from {100, 200, 300, 400}. For each workflow application, 20 instances are generated. In addition, the deadline is defined as

$$D = \alpha \times EFT(t_N), \tag{16}$$

where α is a deadline factor that reflects how tight the workflow deadlines are. The deadline factor is valued from {1.2, 1.4, 1.6, 1.8, 2.0}.

[1] https://aws.amazon.com/cn/ec2/pricing/.
[2] https://aws.amazon.com/cn/fargate/.
[3] https://confluence.pegasus.isi.edu/display/pegasus/WorkflowGenerator.

5.2 Comparison and Analysis of Algorithms

The performance of different algorithms is compared through four workflow applications with varying numbers of task and deadline factors. The experimental results for Ligo, Montage, Genome, and Cybershake are shown in Fig. 2(a)–(d), respectively.

Firstly, the performance of different algorithms is compared. Figure 2 indicates in most cases, the RDP of ICPCP is above Serverless, which means that a serverless configuration has cost advantages over a server configuration. The curves of Serverless stay stable in all cases because the costs of workflow instances in serverless configurations are constant. The RPD of the proposed HCPCP is always below Serverless, as it promises to obtain a cost reduction over the serverless configuration. Although there is no guarantee that HCPCP gets a lower cost than that in a server configuration, it can be realized. The proposed HCSI significantly improves the schedule quality in the server configuration. It can obtain a lower cost than the serverless configuration, except for a few cases. That means the schedules in the server configuration generated by the classic algorithms remain a large space for improvement. It is difficult to compare the performance of HCPCP and HCSI, as they have cost advantages over each other in different cases. However, the minimum RPD of HCPCP and HCSI is always below Serverless and ICPCP, which has verified the idea proposed in Algorithm 1.

Next, the influence of the number of tasks on RPD is studied. The curve of ICPCP shows a decreasing trend. The reason is that the increase in task number prevents the VM instances from being occupied by few tasks, resulting in higher resource utilization. Correspondingly, the quality of the initial schedule of HCSI is promoted. However, the promotion may damage the further improvement of HCSI. Therefore, the curve of HCSI shows two different trends of increasing and decreasing in different cases. The increase in task number means an increase in parallel tasks. These tasks result in many short PCPs, which can only be allocated to functions. As a result, the curve of HCPCP shows an increasing trend.

Finally, the influence of deadline factors on RPD is studied. As shown in Fig. 2, the deadline factor has little impact on ICPCP and HCSI. ICPCP attempts to allocate tasks to the cheapest VM, a loose deadline constraint leads to more usage of cheaper VMs. However, all VMs considered in this paper have the same PPR. As analyzed in Theorem 3, the average utilization is the only determinant of the total rental cost instead of price. Therefore, the deadline factor has little impact on ICPCP performance, and the schedule improved from ICPCP. The curve of HCPCP shows a decreasing trend as the deadline factor increases. The reason lies in that HCPCP attempts to allocate tasks to the VM with the highest resource utilization while satisfying the LFT of each task in the current PCP. However, the LFTs may not be satisfied by the VM with the highest resource utilization may not satisfy the LFTs. The slack of deadlines makes the LFTs can be met more easily, which results in higher resource utilization.

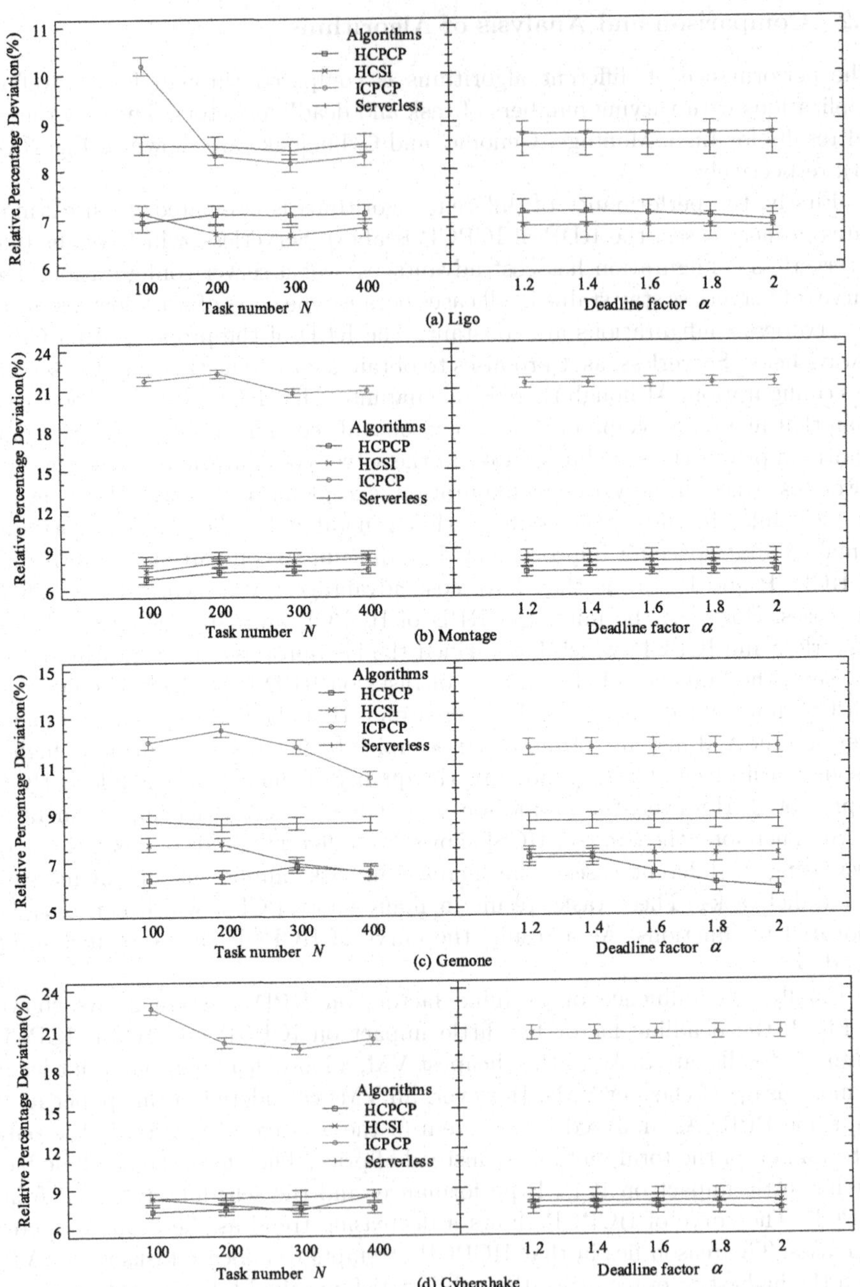

Fig. 2. Interaction plots of the compared algorithms and task number N, deadline factor α on four applications (Ligo, Montage, Gemone, Cybershake) with 95.0% Tukey HSD confidence level intervals.

6 Conclusions

In this paper, a workflow scheduling problem in a hybrid configuration of serverless and server in cloud/edge data centers is studied. The properties of the considered problem are studies, based on which the WS3 algorithm is proposed to select a better schedule from HCPCP and HCSI. Experiments are conducted to evaluate the performance of HCPCP and HCSI on real-world workflow applications. The experimental results show that the proposed HCPCP and HCSI have a cost advantage over single serverless and server configurations, while they have cost advantages over each other in different cases.

HCPCP is conducted without considering allocating tasks across VM instances, which means that the resource utilization of HCPCP can be further improved. Besides, communication time and cold start are not considered in this paper. We will investigate how to promote the utilization further under more complex scenarios.

References

1. Abrishami, S., Naghibzadeh, M., Epema, D.H.: Deadline-constrained workflow scheduling algorithms for infrastructure as a service clouds. Futur. Gener. Comput. Syst. **29**(1), 158–169 (2013)
2. Durillo, J.J., Fard, H.M., Prodan, R.: MOHEFT: a multi-objective list-based method for workflow scheduling. In: 4th IEEE International Conference on Cloud Computing Technology and Science Proceedings, pp. 185–192. IEEE (2012)
3. Elgamal, T.: Costless: optimizing cost of serverless computing through function fusion and placement. In: 2018 IEEE/ACM Symposium on Edge Computing (SEC), pp. 300–312. IEEE (2018)
4. Faragardi, H.R., Sedghpour, M.R.S., Fazliahmadi, S., Fahringer, T., Rasouli, N.: GRP-HEFT: a budget-constrained resource provisioning scheme for workflow scheduling in IaaS clouds. IEEE Trans. Parallel Distrib. Syst. **31**(6), 1239–1254 (2019)
5. Feng, L., Kudva, P., Da Silva, D., Hu, J.: Exploring serverless computing for neural network training. In: 2018 IEEE 11th International Conference on Cloud Computing (CLOUD), pp. 334–341. IEEE (2018)
6. Jiang, Q., Lee, Y.C., Zomaya, A.Y.: Serverless execution of scientific workflows. In: Maximilien, M., Vallecillo, A., Wang, J., Oriol, M. (eds.) ICSOC 2017. LNCS, vol. 10601, pp. 706–721. Springer, Cham (2017). https://doi.org/10.1007/978-3-319-69035-3_51
7. Kijak, J., Martyna, P., Pawlik, M., Balis, B., Malawski, M.: Challenges for scheduling scientific workflows on cloud functions. In: 2018 IEEE 11th International Conference on Cloud Computing (CLOUD), pp. 460–467. IEEE (2018)
8. Kim, Y., Lin, J.: Serverless data analytics with flint. In: 2018 IEEE 11th International Conference on Cloud Computing (CLOUD), pp. 451–455. IEEE (2018)
9. Lin, C., Khazaei, H.: Modeling and optimization of performance and cost of serverless applications. IEEE Trans. Parallel Distrib. Syst. **32**(3), 615–632 (2020)
10. Mahajan, K., Figueiredo, D., Misra, V., Rubenstein, D.: Optimal pricing for serverless computing. In: 2019 IEEE Global Communications Conference (GLOBECOM), pp. 1–6. IEEE (2019)

11. Malawski, M., Juve, G., Deelman, E., Nabrzyski, J.: Algorithms for cost-and deadline-constrained provisioning for scientific workflow ensembles in IaaS clouds. Futur. Gener. Comput. Syst. **48**, 1–18 (2015)
12. Witte, P.A., Louboutin, M., Modzelewski, H., Jones, C., Selvage, J., Herrmann, F.J.: An event-driven approach to serverless seismic imaging in the cloud. IEEE Trans. Parallel Distrib. Syst. **31**(9), 2032–2049 (2020)
13. Wu, C.Q., Lin, X., Yu, D., Xu, W., Li, L.: End-to-end delay minimization for scientific workflows in clouds under budget constraint. IEEE Trans. Cloud Comput. **3**(2), 169–181 (2014)
14. Wu, F., Wu, Q., Tan, Y.: Workflow scheduling in cloud: a survey. J. Supercomput. **71**(9), 3373–3418 (2015). https://doi.org/10.1007/s11227-015-1438-4
15. Wu, Q., Ishikawa, F., Zhu, Q., Xia, Y., Wen, J.: Deadline-constrained cost optimization approaches for workflow scheduling in clouds. IEEE Trans. Parallel Distrib. Syst. **28**(12), 3401–3412 (2017)
16. Zheng, W., Sakellariou, R.: Budget-deadline constrained workflow planning for admission control. J. Grid Comput. **11**(4), 633–651 (2013)
17. Zhu, Z., Zhang, G., Li, M., Liu, X.: Evolutionary multi-objective workflow scheduling in cloud. IEEE Trans. Parallel Distrib. Syst. **27**(5), 1344–1357 (2015)

QoS Accurate Matching Algorithm Based on Service Resource Scheduling on Cloud Platform and Its Application

Xiaodong Zhang, Shenghan Gao, Dianhui Chu(✉), Zhiying Tu(✉), and Junjie Chen

School of Computer Science and Technology, Harbin Institute of Technology, Weihai, China
{zxd,chudh,tzy_hit}@hit.edu.cn, 2201110401@stu.hit.edu.cn

Abstract. Using Quality of Service (QoS) as the standard for resource scheduling is a common method for service resource scheduling on cloud platforms. However, there are both mutually supportive and restrictive multiple technical parameters based on software and hardware resource consumption, and the transparent introduction of a large number of third-party service resources leads to incomplete or even missing QoS attribute values, making service performance evaluation inaccurate and often resulting in problems such as inadequate resource allocation or excessive resource allocation. To address these issues, this paper defines software and hardware QoS attributes and their calculation methods, proposes a dynamic model training method based on FM, and an accurate matching algorithm for service resource scheduling. We design and implement test cases that are the same as the actual operating environment and achieve the expected results after testing.

Keywords: Service resource scheduling · QoS · FM · accurate matching

1 Introduction

Cloud computing is a widely used and cost-effective computing paradigm [1,2]. It integrates cross-domain software and hardware resources to provide virtual service resources to tenants in the form of IaaS, PaaS, and SaaS, on a pay-per-use basis, meeting their needs for scalability, high availability, and reliability. Therefore, resource scheduling for a large number of service requests has become one of the core management tasks of cloud platforms. Service requests have strict requirements for the service instances that respond to them, mainly demonstrated through QoS technical parameters, including response time, availability, success rate, throughput, and so on. These parameters both restrict and promote each other. For example, if the response time is too long, it may be considered a failure (such as in ticket sales), and the availability, success rate, and throughput will all decrease. On the other hand, a shorter response time will increase

Z. Wang et al. (Eds.): ICSS 2023, CCIS 1844, pp. 17–30, 2023.
https://doi.org/10.1007/978-981-99-4402-6_2

the throughput, and an increase in success rate may promote improvements in availability and throughput. Increasing hardware resources is a common means of improving QoS. The more CPU, network I/O, memory, and other resources the service instance obtains, the shorter the response time and faster the execution speed, but the relationship between hardware resource consumption and QoS improvement is not linearly increasing. Due to the limitations of the service components and operating environment, the improvement in QoS may reach saturation, resulting in over-allocation of resources, no significant improvement in QoS quality, and a constantly increasing cost [3].

The article proposes a method for elastic and scalable QoS parameter evaluation to improve the matching accuracy between service request QoS and service response instance QoS, thereby avoiding overallocation of resources. The remaining sections of the article are organized as follows: Sect. 2 introduces related research, Sect. 3 presents the problem, establishes the model, and provides a solution method, Sect. 4 designs test cases and analyzes the results, and Sect. 5 summarizes the research content.

2 Related Work

A cloud platform consists of a large number of virtual nodes, each of which contains both software and hardware service resources. Hardware resources refer to virtual CPU, memory, storage I/O, network I/O, and other service modules that support the operation of software resources. Software resources refer to service systems or components that perform tasks such as computing, storage, and communication. This paper assumes that, under the condition that software functionality can meet service functional requirements, it explores the impact of software and hardware resource service performance on their scheduling. The service performance is exhibited through QoS technical parameters.

Reference [1] proposes a central load balancer technology to avoid virtual machine overload and underload situations, and assigns tasks based on the principle of matching with node priority and status to meet response time requirements. Reference [4] proposes a load balancing algorithm based on bee colony, which regards tasks removed from overloaded nodes as bees and non-overloaded nodes as food sources. It also considers the priority of nodes in the waiting queue, and attempts to achieve minimum response time and improve throughput. References [5–7] predict the service request volume that will arrive at virtual machines in the future time period using prediction methods to guide the system to flexibly allocate hardware resources to meet QoS requirements. References [2, 8–10] directly monitor the usage of relevant hardware resources such as CPU and memory in virtual machines, and formulate corresponding task assignment strategies to ensure that QoS parameter values such as response time and throughput meet requirements. By monitoring and adjusting the state of hardware resources, task assignment and resource scheduling are performed, which often overlooks the impact of service instances themselves, the dependencies between service instances, and the software environment, which may promote excessive allocation of resources, and may not improve the success rate and throughput of service responses, and may even reduce them.

Therefore, there are also some resource scheduling algorithms that study QoS requirements from the perspective of software resources. Reference [11] proposed a universal random coupling structure for obtaining the Halfin-Whitt quality efficiency driven queue diffusion limit, which can dispatch tasks in the best way to shorten the service response time. Reference [12] proposed a trusted optimization resource scheduling algorithm, which takes resource identity, QoS, trustworthy behavior, and feedback trustworthiness as inputs and attempts to optimize service response time and improve resource utilization through corresponding algorithms. Reference [13] analyzed the correlation of cloud platform performance data by using dynamic Bayesian networks and inputted it into a deep neural network module to predict the future state of the system and make the best scheduling decision, thus shortening the response time of requests and reducing the SLA violation rate. However, these algorithms may pose the risk of load congestion, slow response time, and reduced success rate due to a lack of understanding of the remaining load capacity of node hardware resources.

To improve this situation, many scholars have studied QoS matching scheduling algorithms that consider both software and hardware resources. Reference [14] proposed a task scheduling algorithm based on weighted load balancing, which considers parameters such as cost and response time in the cloud environment to determine task priority and uses bee colony optimization to balance the load. Reference [15] established a two-layer metadata load balancing framework embedded with a prefetch-based caching replacement algorithm to solve system performance bottlenecks caused by excessive concurrent requests, such as the rise of average response time and the decline of throughput. Reference [16] optimize resource allocation of various types from the perspective of establishing cloud workflow scheduling models, improve QoS matching, and reduce resource consumption. Such research typically evaluates the leasing cost of computing and storage resources as costs [17], masking the impact of other resources on service performance.

In summary, almost all resource scheduling algorithms that match QoS use related technologies that approximate historical data or predict future resource usage, because the change in node load in a large-scale distributed system has the following characteristics: (1) Self-correlation. The predicted value has some correlation with the past actual measurement value, and the distribution of user access to time is similar at different time scales. (2) Periodicity. The time series of user access exhibits a recurring characteristic on the time axis. (3) Chaos. A deterministic nonlinear system exhibits unpredictable or random phenomena under certain conditions. For the service request load model, its chaos is mainly manifested as a butterfly effect sensitive to minor disturbances macroscopically, and as infinitely nested geometric self-similarity microscopically. Therefore, the change in load can be regarded as a time series process, which has a strong correlation with time.

3 Model

3.1 Problem Description

The QoS of service instances includes multiple attributes, which can be divided into two major categories: the first category is the hardware resource consumption demand, called as "hard QoS", which includes CPU (cpu), memory (mem), network (net), and disk I/O (i/o); the second category is the software performance demand, called as "soft QoS", which includes availability, response time, success rate, and throughput. In this paper, we will also use the following related concepts.

Resource surplus: a comprehensive indicator reflecting the idle state of node hardware resources. Let $ld(h)$ represent the occupancy rate of resource h and $ls(h)$ represent the remaining rate of resource h, then

$$ls(h) = 1 - ld(h) \tag{1}$$

If there is surplus resource in CPU, it can be expressed as:

$$ls(cpu) = 1 - ld(cpu) \tag{2}$$

Expected Value of QoS ($EcVQ$): the service quality parameters committed by the Service-Level Agreement (SLA) before the service instance responds to the service request.

If there is no $EcVQ$ in the SLA or the required $EcVQ$ is worse than the default QoS of the service instance, the default QoS value of the service instance is used as the $EcVQ$.

Experimental Value of QoS($ErVQ$): The QoS value actually detected by the monitoring system after the service instance responds to service requests.

Assuming there are m service instances($S = \{s_1, s_2, \ldots s_i, \ldots s_m\}$) with the same functionality, distributed on different nodes, and running in different environments and consuming different resources, k QoS attributes are selected, that is, $Qos = \{c_1, c_2, \ldots c_k\}$. For the service instance s_i, the detected results of the QoS attributes $ErVQ_i$ obtained after accessing z times are:

$$ErVQ_i = \begin{array}{c} \begin{matrix} c_1 & c_2 & c_3 & \cdots & c_k \end{matrix} \\ \begin{pmatrix} x_{11} & x_{12} & x_{13} & \cdots & x_{1k} \\ x_{21} & x_{22} & x_{23} & \cdots & x_{2k} \\ x_{31} & x_{32} & x_{33} & \cdots & x_{3k} \\ \vdots & \vdots & \vdots & & \vdots \\ x_{z1} & x_{z2} & x_{z3} & \cdots & x_{zk} \end{pmatrix}_i \end{array}$$

in which x_{jj} is the detection result of attribute c_j for the j-th access to service instance s_i. The QoS detection result for accessing the set of service instances S can be expressed as:

$$ErVQ = \{ErVQ_1, ErVQ_2, \ldots, ErVQ_i, \ldots, ErVQ_m\}$$

For service s_i, the average QoS detection result can be expressed as:

$$\overline{ErVQ_i} = (\overline{v_1}, \overline{v_2}, \ldots, \overline{v_l}, \ldots, \overline{v_k})$$

in which,

$$\overline{v_l} = \sum_{i=1}^{z} x_{il}/z$$

Similarly, the expected QoS of service request i can be set as:

$$EcVQ_i = (x_{c_1}, x_{c_2}, \ldots, x_{c_j}, x_{c_k})_i$$

In a cloud platform, components with the same service functionality may be deployed on different nodes as needed. Due to their different compositions, operating environments, and the resources allocated to them by the system, there may be some differences between the $ErVQ$ and $EcVQ$ of the running instances of the same functional service component. The degree of difference can be represented by $\delta = |ErVQ - EcVQ|$, which is called resource suitability. The solution proposed in this paper is to find the service instance that best matches the $EcVQ$ of the service request, which is the service instance with the smallest absolute value of δ:

$$\delta_{min} = \min\{(\overline{ErVQ_i}, EcVQ_i)||\overline{ErVQ_i} - EcVQ_i|, i \in [1, n]\} \tag{3}$$

where i is the service instance number.

Consider that the attributes in QoS may have mutual influence within a certain range, such as larger resource surplus leading to shorter response time and higher success rate. Additionally, during sample collection, QoS attribute values may not be complete or even missing due to the transparent introduction of third-party services. Therefore, this paper uses $ErVQ$ as input and employs Factorization Machine (FM) to train the model $\overline{E}$, which expresses the interrelationships among QoS attributes. Then, by substituting $\overline{ErVQ_i}$ into $\overline{E}$ the value of Er_i is obtained. Similarly, by substituting the expected value of service request $EcVQ_i$, Ec_i is obtained. Formula (3) is transformed into formula (4):

$$\delta_{min} = \min\{(Er_i, Ec_i)||Er_i - Ec_i|, i \in [1, n]\} \tag{4}$$

where n is the maximum number of service instances running in the cloud platform.

All QoS attributes can be included in formula (4) which serves as the basis for precise resource scheduling matching. After further transformation, the optimal matching resources can be obtained by relevant algorithms.

3.2 Dynamic Evaluation Model

This paper uses Factorization Machines (FM) for model training, which unify all QoS attributes as parameters of the model. The model is dynamically adjusted with the continuous accumulation of data to improve the accuracy of matching service requests with service instances.

FM–Establishing the Training Function. FM is a machine learning algorithm based on matrix factorization proposed by Steffen Rendle. Its training equation is shown below:

$$\bar{E} = \omega_0 + \sum\nolimits_{i=1}^{n} \omega_i x_i + \sum\nolimits_{i=1}^{n-1} \sum\nolimits_{j=i+1}^{n} <v_i, v_j> x_i x_j \tag{5}$$

where $\omega_0 \in R, W = (\omega_1, w_2, \ldots w_n)^T, W \in R^n, <v_i, v_j> \in R^{n \times k}, x_i \in ErVQ$, n is the number of variables, $k \ll n$ is the dimension of factorization, $<v_i, v_j>$ represents two vectors v_i and v_j of size k:

$$<v_i, v_j> = \sum\nolimits_{f=1}^{k} v_{i,f} \cdot v_{j,f} \tag{6}$$

Since the model is trained with the measured QoS value ErVQ, x in formula (4) represents CPU, memory, network I/O, availability, response time, success rate, etc. W and $<v_i, v_j>$are the learned parameters.

Obtaining W and $<v_i, v_j>$ with Gradient Descent Method. Loss function f is defined using the difference method. where E represents the actual test values in the FM, and $\bar{E}$ represents the predicted values. The loss function is given by:

$$f(\bar{E}, E) = (\bar{E} - E)^2 \tag{7}$$

In order to solve for the parameters that minimize the loss function, stochastic gradient descent (SGD) is used for optimization learning by introducing it. SGD randomly selects a sample for gradient computation at each step. The formula is as follows:

$$\frac{\partial}{\partial \omega_0} f(\bar{E}, E) = \bar{E} - E$$

$$\frac{\partial}{\partial \omega_i} f(\bar{E}, E) = (\bar{E} - E) x_i$$

$$\frac{\partial}{\partial v_{i,f}} f(\bar{E}, E) = (\bar{E} - E)(x_i \sum\nolimits_{j=1}^{n} v_{j,f} x_j - v_{j,f} x_i^2)$$

To update the weights after computing the gradient, iterate as follows, by descending along the gradient of the objective function:

$$W_0 \leftarrow W_0 + \eta \frac{\partial}{\partial \omega_0} f(\bar{E}, E)$$

$$W_i \leftarrow W_i + \eta \frac{\partial}{\partial \omega_i} f(\bar{E}, E)$$

$$v_{i,f} \leftarrow v_{i,f} + \eta \frac{\partial}{\partial v_{i,f}} f(\bar{E}, E)$$

where, $\eta > 0$ is the learning rate used in the calculation, and its value can affect the convergence speed of the model.

3.3 QoS Accurate Matching Algorithm Baesed on Service Resource Scheduling

When forwarding a service request to a service instance, it is necessary to examine whether the QoS of both the requester and the service provider match. The goal of this paper is to find δ_{min} in formula (4), which is divided into four steps: step 1, substitute $ErVQ$ into the FM trained equation $\overline{E}$. step 2, substitute each $\overline{ErVQ_i}(i = 1, 2, \ldots, m)$ into the equation $\overline{E}$ to obtain all Er_i values in the service set S; step 3, substitute any arriving service request i's $ErVQ_i$ into the equation $\overline{E}$ to obtain Ec_i value; step 4, select the service instances according with δ_{min} in response to the service requests.

Step 1–3 is mentioned above. Although formula (4) accurately expresses the meaning of exact matching, when the number of service requests is large and there are many service instances, the efficiency of solving formula (4) is low and can not meet the requirements of quickly dispatching tasks. Therefore, for step 4, this article establishes a hash service list based on service instances. Each service instance occupies a space of hash service list space according to the size of Er_i value. The service request Ec_i is projected onto the hash service list space to quickly find the best matching service instance. This algorithm is called exact match for services (EMS) and the description is as follows:

Let the service request be $s_y \in S$, and the QoS attributes required in SLA be $C_y = (c_{y_1}, c_{y_2}, \ldots, c_{y_2}, \ldots, c_{y_k})$. We can substitute C_y into $\overline{E}$ to obtain Ec_y and Then, we can use the following method to obtain the access address of the corresponding service:

Sort the Er values of m service instances to form an ordered sequence E:

$$e_1 < e_2 < \ldots < e_m \tag{8}$$

To obtain the difference between adjacent ratings in the ordered sequence E:

$$ed_1 = e_2 - e_1, ed_2 = e_3 - e_2, \ldots, ed_{m-1} = e_m - e_{m-1} \tag{9}$$

Preprocessing. Let the preprocessing results show that difference between any two adjacent scores is greater than a given value ϵ. The preprocessing is as follows: traversing E, if $ed_i > \epsilon$, keep ed_i. If $ed_i < \epsilon$, calculate $ed_i + ed_{i+1}$, if $ed_i + ed_{i+1} > \epsilon$, then nodes associated with ed_i are grouped as a set of nodes, that is $\{node_i, node_{i+1}\}$. Then, the E sequence is modified: remove e_{i+1} from the sequence; if $ed_{i+1} < \epsilon$, then continue to traverse ed_{i+2} onwards until $\sum_{x=i}^{j} ed_x > \epsilon$. Then, group the nodes with $ed_i, \ldots, ed_j$ as a node set $\{node_i, node_{i+1}, \ldots, node_j, node_{j+1}\}$, remove $e_{i+1}, \ldots, e_j, e_{j+1}$ from E.

Assuming that the length of e sequence after preprocessing is n, there is $e_1 < e_2 < \ldots < e_n$. The minimum rating difference is taken as $scale = \min\{ed_1, ed_2, \ldots, ed_n\} / \Delta$, where Δ is subdivision parameter, which is to avoid the difference between any two ordinals s_i and s_j too small.

Set $b_{start} = e_1 - \delta \times scale$ and $b_{start} \geq 0$, where b_{start} is the lower bound of the hash service list value space. Set $b_{end} = em + \delta \times scale$ as the upper bound of the hash service list value space, and $\delta \times scale$ is the lower bound precision constraint.

Construct hash value range segment: $hs = \{hs_1, hs_2, \ldots, hs_n\}$, then we have:

$$hs_1 = [0, \frac{e_1 + e_2}{scale \times 2} - bs), hs_2 = [\frac{e_1 + e_2}{scale \times 2} - bs, \frac{e_2 + e_3}{scale \times 2} - bs), \cdots,$$
$$hs_{n-1} = [\frac{e_{n-1} + e_{n-2}}{scale \times 2} - bs, \frac{e_n + e_{n-1}}{scale \times 2} - bs),$$
$$hs_n = [\frac{e_n + e_{n-1}}{scale \times 2} - bs, \frac{e_n}{scale} - bs + \delta)$$

where $bs = \frac{b_{start}}{scale}$.

If the hash service list is denoted as H, then the length of H is: $(b_{end} - b_{start})/scale + 1$. This shows that any hs_i corresponds to a sequence of consecutive integers of different lengths. Let $p(hs_i)$ denote the upper bound of the i-th interval of the Hash service list, Suppose $p(hs_i)$ is the upper bound of hash service list, then $p(hs_i) = (e_i + e_{i+1})/(scale \times 2) - bs$. If $\lfloor p(hs_i) \rfloor$ is used to represent this expression rounded down to the nearest integer, which is the largest integer less than $p(hs_i)$, then the value range of the hash service list can also be expressed as:

$$hs_1 = [0, \lfloor p(hs_1) \rfloor], hs_2 = [\lfloor p(hs_1) \rfloor + 1, \lfloor p(hs_2) \rfloor], \cdots,$$
$$hs_{n-1} = [\lfloor p(hs_{n-2}) \rfloor + 1, \lfloor p(hs_{n-1}) \rfloor],$$
$$hs_n = [\lfloor p(hs_{n-1}) \rfloor + 1, \frac{e_n}{scale} - bs + \delta]$$

The composition of the hash service list is: $(hs_1, node_1), (hs_2, node_2), (hs_3, node_3), \ldots, (hs_i, node_i), \ldots, (hs_n, node_n)$, where $node_i$ is the access address of the i-th service. If the values are the same, they can be stored in buckets. For example, if the Er of two services s_i and s_j is the same, i.e.,$e_i = e_j (i < j)$, then $(hs_i, node_i, node_j)$. When the service request s_y arrives and gets e_{xy}, then service access address can be obtained by $H[\lfloor (e_{xy} - b_{start})/(scale) \rfloor]$.

Algorithm 1. exact match of services (EMS)

Input: $Input$, $ServicesNodeEwithvaluee$, $threshold$, $subdivision$, $accuracy$, $HashServicesNodeHashE$

Output: $HashServiceNodeHashE$

1: Sort E in ascending order by value e
2: **for** $i = 0$ to $E.length$ **do**
3: record $startE = E_i.e$
4: $i++$
5: merge E_{i-1} and E_i
6: **if** $E_i.e \le threshold$ && $i < E.length - 1$ **then**
7: repeat step 3
8: **else**
9: record $E_i.e = startE$
10: **end if**
11: **end for**
12: Calculate $e = \min(E_{i+1}.e, E_i.e)$

$scale = e/subdivision$
for $i = 0$ to $E.length$ **do**
  $p(hs_i) = (E_i.e + E_{i+1}.e)/(2 * scale) - b_{start}.scale$
end for
for $i = 0$ to $E.length$ **do**
  if $i == 0$ **then**
    $HashE_i = [0, \lfloor p(hs_1) \rfloor]$
  else if $i == E.length - 1$ **then**
    $HashE_i = [\lfloor p(hs_{i-1}) \rfloor + 1, e_n/scale - bs + accuracy]$
  else
    $HashE_i = [\lfloor p(hs_{i-1}) \rfloor, \lfloor p(hs_i) \rfloor]$
  end if
end for

4 Cases and Analysis

To demonstrate the feasibility and effectiveness of the proposed model and algorithm in the paper, we conducted simulation experiments using the WS-DREAM dataset and QWS-E dataset, which are widely recognized by researchers.

We randomly selected 1000 response time records and their corresponding throughput values from the WS-DREAM dataset. Around 2500 Web service invocation records were collected from the QWS-E dataset, which involved 6 QoS attribute information, including response time, availability, success rate, throughput, CPU, and memory. In order to verify the authenticity and randomness of the selected data, statistical analyses were conducted on each QoS attribute value of the two datasets, and the results are shown in Fig. 1 and Fig. 2. The distribution and trend of the selected data are roughly consistent with the overall QoS dataset. It can be seen that the selected data for the experiment has a certain degree of randomness and representativeness. Simulation experiments based on this data can demonstrate the generalizability of the proposed algorithm and model, which can be extended for use on the entire QoS dataset or other datasets.

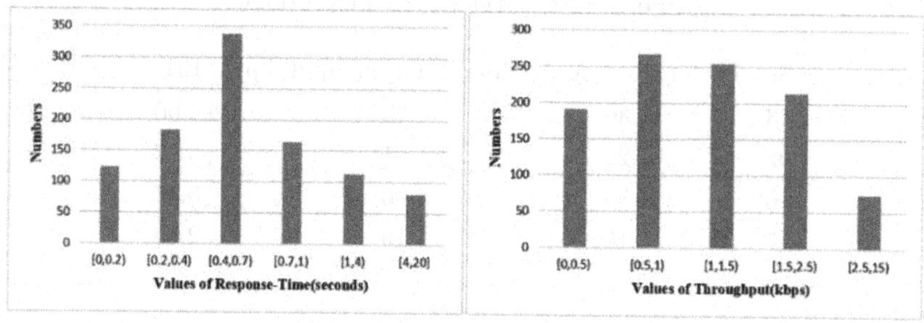

Fig. 1. QoS distribution of WS-Dream data set

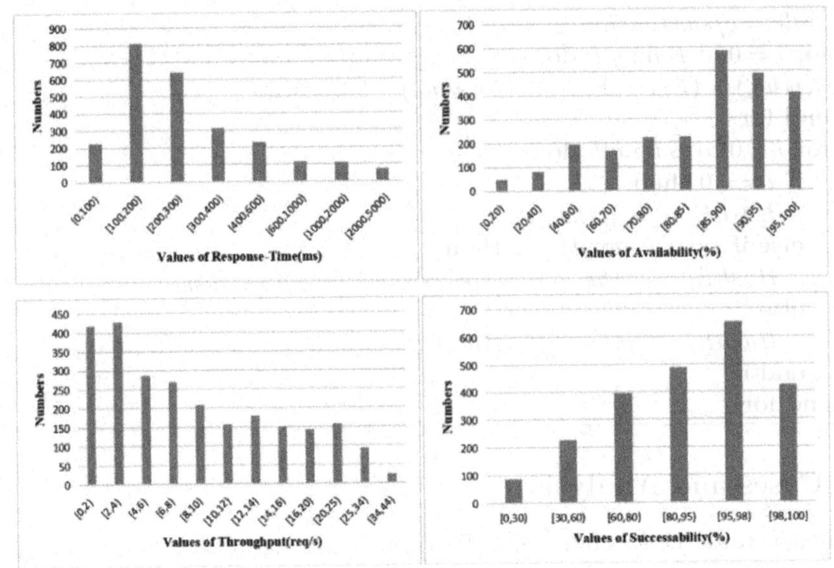

Fig. 2. QoS distribution of QWS-E data set

Service Matching Result of EMS Algorithm. After training the FM model, we obtained the training equation and solved for all Er_i values in the service set S. Based on QoS expectation of the user request, we calculated the $EcVQ$ value and used the EMS algorithm to match the corresponding service node set quickly and accurately. In the WS-DREAM dataset, the hash interval threshold of the EMS algorithm is set to 1. For example, if a user request has a QoS expectation of (response time: 1.8 s, throughput: 0.8 kbps), the corresponding $EcVQ$ value is calculated to be approximately 3.16. The table below shows the service node numbers and their corresponding Er_i values that are close to this satisfaction level in a set of 50 service nodes (Table 1).

Table 1. EMS service matching results.

Service ID	Response Time/s	Throughput/kpbs	Eri
13	1.36	1.45	4.00
02	1.22	1.61	3.87
16	1.59	1.06	3.57
17	1.16	1.19	2.72

Next, we conducted experimental performance comparison between our algorithm and binary search algorithm (BS) which has an average time complexity of $O(\log n)$. The binary search algorithm performed service matching in the sorted service node set based on the Er_i value. In the binary search, we first found the Er_i value node closest to the $EcVQ$ value, and then searched to the left and right for service nodes whose values differed no more than 0.5 from it. Finally, the service nodes that meet the requirements are obtained as shown in the following table (Table 2).

Table 2. BS service matching results BS service matching results BS service.

Service ID	Response Time/s	Throughput/kpbs	Eri
17	1.16	1.19	2.72
16	1.59	1.06	3.57
01	1.84	0.33	2.69

In the QWS-E dataset, there are approximately 2500 service nodes, which is much larger than the number of service nodes in the WS-DREAM dataset, making the distribution of Er_i values more extensive. Therefore, in order to match the corresponding service node set quickly and accurately using the EMS algorithm, the hash interval threshold of EMS was set to 100. At the same time, the left and right search range of binary search was set to service nodes whose Er_i value differed from the $EcVQ$ value by no more than 50. For instance, assuming a user request had QoS expectation of (response time: 180 ms, availability: 80%, throughput: 1.5 req/s, success rate: 80%), the corresponding $EcVQ$ value was calculated as the reference value. Based on it, the service nodes that were close to this satisfaction level in the set were numbered, and the differences between their Er_i and $EcVQ$ values were shown in Fig. 3. The figure indicated that a total of 24 service nodes were found by the EMS algorithm, and 20 service nodes were found by the binary search, all of which were matched in the EMS matching set.

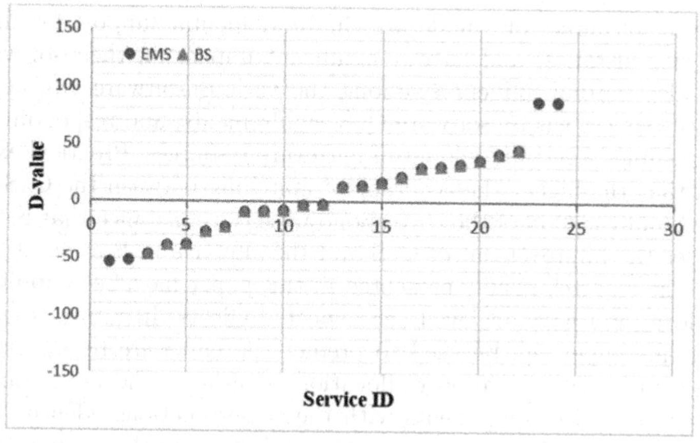

Fig. 3. Sample QWS-E dataset lookup results

Service Matching Efficiency of EMS Algorithm. Simulations were conducted to perform service matching sequentially for 100 and 200 requests respectively, and the search efficiency of EMS and BS were recorded. The experimental results on WS-DREAM and QWS-E datasets were shown in Fig. 4. As can be seen, with the increase of request times, the EMS algorithm was superior to the BS algorithm in terms of execution time.

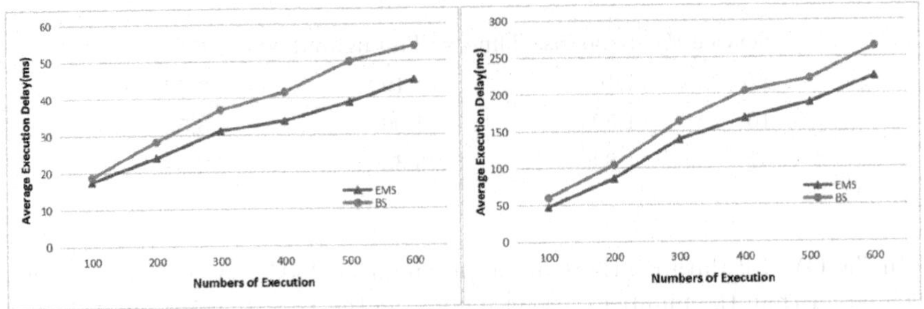

Fig. 4. Comparison of search efficiency

In this section, it was demonstrated through experiments that the proposed model and method in the paper can perform accurate QoS matching based on user's QoS requirements, thus finding service instances that closely satisfy user's expectations. By conducting experiments on two datasets with different QoS attributes, we have shown that our proposed method can be extended to more QoS attributes and consider both hardware and software QoS comprehensively for forwarding service requests.

5 Conclusion

The hardware resources of a node are the fundamental support for the operation of service instances and have a significant impact on their software QoS. There are also mutual influences among the various software QoS attributes. Each service request has its software QoS requirements, and responding to such requests consumes a certain amount of hardware resources. Practical experience has shown that the higher the accuracy of matching between the QoS of a service request and the QoS of the corresponding service instance that responds to it, the better the improvement of QoS and the effective utilization of hardware resources. The research results presented in this paper have been applied in the cloud platform and have achieved the expected effects. In future research, the findings of this paper can be used to predict the hardware resources required for service components, avoid over-allocation or resource shortage, compare the performance of service components with the same functions, identify problematic or improvement-requiring components, and promote the virtuous evolution of the system.

Acknowledgements. This work was supported by the Key R&D Program of Shandong Province (No. 2020CXGC010103).

References

1. Soni, G., Kalra, M.: A novel approach for load balancing in cloud data center. In: 2014 IEEE International Advance Computing Conference, Gurgaon, India, pp. 807–812. IEEE (2014). https://doi.org/10.1109/IAdCC.2014.6779427
2. Wang, P., Huang, Y., Li, K., Guo, Y.: Load balancing degree first algorithm on phase space for cloud computing cluster. J. Comput. Res. Dev. **51**(05), 1095–1107 (2014)
3. Cao, J., Zeng, G.-S., et al.: On-demand physical resource allocation method for cloud virtual machine to support random service requests. J. Softw. **28**(02), 457–472 (2017)
4. Remesh Babu, K.R., Joy, A.A., Samuel, P.: Load balancing of tasks in cloud computing environment based on bee colony algorithm. In: 2015 Fifth International Conference on Advances in Computing & Communications, Kochi, India, pp. 89–93 (2015). https://doi.org/10.1109/ICACC.2015.47
5. Liu, J., Qiao, J., Zhao, J.: FEMCRA: fine-grained elasticity measurement for cloud resources allocation. In: 2018 IEEE 11th International Conference on Cloud Computing (CLOUD), San Francisco, CA, USA, pp. 89–93 (2018). https://doi.org/10.1109/CLOUD.2018.00100
6. Fan, C., Su, R.: Task scheduling optimization algorithm based on load balancing. Comput. Eng. Des. **38**(06), 1532–1535 (2017). https://doi.org/10.1109/CLOUD.2018.00100
7. Hsu, C.-J., Nair, V., Menzies, T., Freeh, V.: Micky: a cheaper alternative for selecting cloud instances. In: 2018 IEEE 11th International Conference on Cloud Computing (CLOUD), San Francisco, CA, USA, pp. 409–416 (2018). https://doi.org/10.1109/CLOUD.2018.00058
8. Ren, X., Lin, R., Zou, H.: A dynamic load balancing strategy for cloud computing platform based on exponential smoothing forecast. In: 2011 IEEE International Conference on Cloud Computing and Intelligence Systems, Beijing, China, pp. 220–224 (2011). https://doi.org/10.1109/CCIS.2011.6045063
9. Saha, A., Jindal, S.: EMARS: efficient management and allocation of resources in serverless. In: 2018 IEEE 11th International Conference on Cloud Computing (CLOUD), San Francisco, CA, USA, pp. 827–830 (2018). https://doi.org/10.1109/CLOUD.2018.00113
10. Mukherjee, D., Borst, S., Leeuwaarden, J., et al.: Universality of load balancing schemes on diffusion scale. J. Appl. Probab. **53**(4), 1111–1124 (2016). https://doi.org/10.1017/jpr.2016.68
11. Deng, X.H., Lu, X.C., Wang, H.: Study on trust evaluation based resource scheduling in iVCE. Chin. J. Comput. **2007**(10), 1750–1762 (2007)
12. Zhang, Y., Hua, W., Zhou, Z., et al.: Sinan: ML-based and QoS-aware resource management for cloud microservices. In: Proceedings of the 26th ACM International Conference on Architectural Support for Programming Languages and Operating Systems (ASPLOS 2021), pp. 167–181. Association for Computing Machinery, New York (2021). https://doi.org/10.1145/3445814.3446693
13. Kaur, R., Khullar, V.: ABC optimized weighted task load balancing algorithm in cloud computing. IPASJ Int. J. Comput. Sci. (IIJCS) **5**(9), 080–090 (2017)

14. Yao, S., Jie, L., Dan, Y., et al.: Load balancing framework for metadata service of distributed file systems. J. Softw. **27**(12), 3192–3207 (2016). https://doi.org/10.13328/j.cnki.jos.00493
15. Fang, B., Sun, L.: Cloud worklow scheduling optimization oriented to QoS and cost-awareness. Comput. Integr. Manuf. Syst. **24**(02), 331–348 (2018). https://doi.org/10.13196/j.cims.2018.02.006
16. Shen, H., Li, X.: Algorithm for the cloud service workflow scheduling with setup time and deadline constraints. J. Commun. **36**(06), 187–196 (2018)
17. Mirhosseini, A., Elnikety, S., Wenisch, T.F.: Parslo: a gradient descent-based approach for near-optimal partial SLO allotment in microservices. In: Proceedings of the ACM Symposium on Cloud Computing (SOCC 2021), pp. 442–257. ACM, New York (2021). https://doi.org/10.1145/3472883.3486985

Environment-Aware Work Load Prediction in Edge Computing

Xing Ma and Zhicheng Cai(✉)

Nanjing University of Science and Technology, Nanjing 210094, China
caizhicheng@njust.edu.cn

Abstract. Computing resources can be brought close to users by mobile edge computing technologies, which can meet users' low latency and computing needs. To address the work load imbalance generated by user movement, most methods focus on time-series prediction. However, no one considers environment information. Based on this, a work load prediction method considering environment information is proposed. The ET-GCN model consists of a graph convolutional network and a gated recurrent unit network, in which the geographic regions covered by the edge servers or base stations are abstracted as nodes in the graph. Then the GCN learns the geospatial features of the city, and the gated recurrent units capture the temporal dependencies. Experiments show that the RMSE of ET-GCN model is 4% less than the existing baseline algorithms.

Keywords: MEC work load · Graph counvolutional network · Spatiotemporal model

1 Introduction

With the advent of the mobile Internet era, user demand and access to various mobile applications such as games and live streaming are increasing day by day [1]. To meet the growing demand of mobile users for quality of service (QoS), multi-access edge computing (MEC) is proposed, providing IT and cloud computing capabilities directly at the network edge to achieve high bandwidth and low latency for mobile services [2]. However, due to the mobility of users and the limited coverage of MEC servers, it is likely lead to the work load imbalance among MEC servers. In this case, the servers cannot adjust the resource allocation in time, which will result in performance degradation and resource waste. Therefore, it is crucial to effectively predict the work load changes due to users' movement.

Traditional time-series prediction models and many RNN-based neural networks do not significantly learn the environmental information that governs work load changes. Traditional time-series prediction methods such as ARIMA, Holt, PropHet et al. [3,4,9] only capture the cyclical pattern of data to make predictions, thus lacking flexibility and having low accuracy. In recent years, with the development of deep neural networks, Seq2Seq models [5] and RNN-based algorithms [6,10,11] have been increasingly used to solve sequence prediction

Z. Wang et al. (Eds.): ICSS 2023, CCIS 1844, pp. 31–42, 2023.
https://doi.org/10.1007/978-981-99-4402-6_3

problems. These models have greatly improved training results because they implicitly learn environmental features. However, environmental features have still not been formally used.

The surrounding environmental factors determine MEC servers' work load variations. However, the environment information under real geography is too large and complex, specifically containing various buildings, areas and road features, which are non-Euclidean data. To better represent spatial features, graph neural networks are [12,13] introduced for spatial modeling. Unlike traditional data-driven approaches, graph neural networks can handle non-Euclidean data and capture road topology information [14]. However, the existing graph neural network models do not focus on the temporal characteristics of the data, which also affects the work load prediction accuracy.

Based on the above background, An environment-aware temporal graph convolutional network is proposed for work load prediction tasks in mobile edge environments. The main contributions of the paper are as follows.

(1) For the complex environment modeling problem under edge computing, the coverage areas of MEC servers are abstracted as nodes of the graph, and the adjacency of servers is abstracted as edges. The graph convolution work is able to be introduced into edge computing.
(2) To solve the dilemma that extracting complex environment information under edge computing, the narrow coverage area of MEC is regarded as an area with specific attributes. Then number of people, area category and activity are extracted as node features.

The rest of the paper is organized as follows. Section 2 reviews related work and developments of work load prediction in edge environments. Section 3 and 4 present the details of our approach. In Sect. 5, experiments are conducted to evaluate the performance of the proposed method compared to baseline algorithms. The contents of this paper are summarized in Sect. 6.

2 Related Work

A class of researches to solve the user mobility problem in MEC are to predict the mobility of users, and the resource allocation strategy of each device can be adjusted after obtaining data like the user's next moment location. With the rapid development of machine learning in recent years, deep neural network models have received widespread attention. Wu et al. [7] used neural networks (NN) to build predictors to minimize disruptions during switching by predicting advance caching of user services, and Lentisco et al. [8] similarly extended this prefetching mechanism based on mobility prediction to improve service latency and service continuity. The M-DRL model proposed by Wu et al. [5] consists of two parts, DRL for supporting multi-user joint training, and glimpse, a seq2seq model tailored for mobility to predict a sequence of locations. However, it is the work load traffic variation that determines the allocation of resources to the edge servers.

Ntalampiras et al. [9] proposed a novel prediction model based on an autoregressive multiple-input single-output (MISO) approach for predicting future traffic conditions, where the input requirements are strongly correlated with a certain mobile service work load in the region. Recurrent neural network (RNN) is a neural network for processing sequential data, and the self-looping mechanism allows this model to learn time dependence well and achieve good prediction results [15,16]. Its variant long short-term memory LSTM and gated recurrent unit GRU can well solve the gradient disappearance and gradient explosion problems during long sequence training. Heng et al. [24] proposed to use LSTM neural networks for time series prediction, thus bringing intelligent mechanisms for processing network resources at the edge of the network. Jiang et al. [11] built a multi-LSTM based algorithm to predict the traffic of small base stations to provide good wireless services.

In recent years, graph convolutional neural network (GCN) has been widely used in classification problems [17,18] and unsupervised learning [19] due to their ability to handle arbitrary graph structures. Zeng et al. [12] proposed an edge-oriented hotspot prediction scheme that uses graph embeddings to represent city-scale edge service capacity through inductive learning of distributed multilayer graph convolutions, and finally predicted edge-oriented hotspots with temporal differences. Deng et al. [13] employed graph neural networks (GNN) in a deep reinforcement model to extract structural features of the graph, and performed computational task transfer among servers to alleviate the resource imbalance problem.

All of the above methods deal with the MEC problem only singularly for time-dependent or spatial dependencies. However, the work load problem involving MEC servers undoubtedly has both temporal and spatial features. Based on this background, in this paper a recurrent neural network approach is proposed based on graph embedding that can capture temporal and spatial features while learning the geographical features of nodes in the graph.

3 Problem Description

An unweighted graph $G = (V, E)$ is used to describe the topology of the network, where V is the set of edge server nodes, $V = v_1, v_2, ...v_N$, and N is the number of nodes. The specific narrow area covered by server is abstracted as the node, because buildings within a smaller geographical area almost have the same characteristics, such as teaching areas, shopping plazas, etc. While E is the set of edges, the adjacency matrix A is used to indicate whether the nodes are physically adjacent, with element values of only 0 and 1. Specifically, it indicates whether the user can travel from the initial node to the target node without going through a third node.

Each node itself represents a specific map area, so it contains specific geographical information that is the feature of the node, denoted as $X \in R^{N \times P}$, where P represents the number of features of the node, and $X_t \in R^{N \times i}$ represents the work load of each node at time i. Features can be any valuable geographical information, so the traffic prediction problem can be considered as learning the mapping function f, and then learning the work load volume at the next T moments under the premise of edge server topology, as shown in Eq. 1.

$$[X'_{t+1}, ..., X'_{t+T} = f(G; (X_{t-n}, ..., X_{t-1}, X_t))] \tag{1}$$

The goal of this paper is to predict the work load of edge servers over time, so X' contains only one value, which is different from X that contains additional geographical attributes. Also, n is the length of the historical time series and T is the length of the time series to be predicted.

In the environment modeling process of MEC, the narrow areas covered by each server are abstracted as areas with specific attribute properties, whcih are realistic entities of the nodes in the graph neural network. As shown in Fig. 1, there are three different types of regions, food area, learning area and sightseeing area. Each area has the number of people at each time period, as well as area's inherent properties. Three characteristics are defined for each node: number of people, area category, activity. The dashed lines between the areas indicate whether the different server zones are adjacent, and this type of data is finally abstracted into the adjacency matrix of the graph.

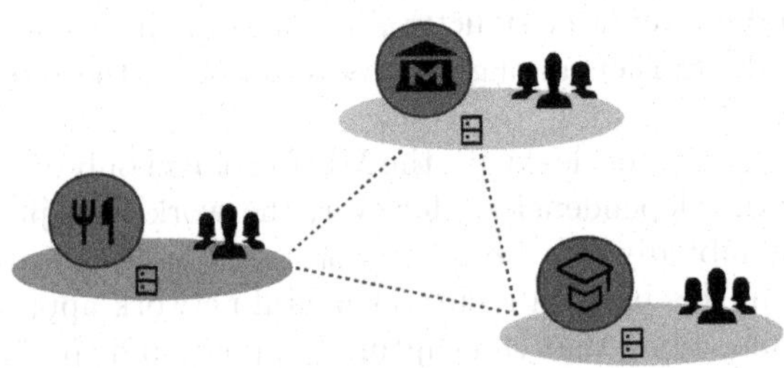

Fig. 1. Graph in Edge Computing

4 Proposed Approach

In the ET-GCN model, the smallest data unit is the nodal feature matrix of a time period. In order to capture the spatial dependencies generated by the topology, unlike the fully connected layer in traditional GRU units, ET-GCN uses a multilayer perceptron and a GCN model for feature learning, and its modeling process is represented as follows.

$$f(E, A) = \sigma(\widehat{A}Relu(\widehat{A}EW_0)W_1) \tag{2}$$

In Eq. 2, E represents the enhanced feature matrix of the node after learning by the multilayer perceptron. A represents the adjacency matrix, $\widehat{A} = \tilde{D}^{-\frac{1}{2}}\tilde{A}\tilde{D}^{-\frac{1}{2}}$ denotes the preprocessing process, $\widehat{A} = A + I_N$ is a matrix that joins the self-connections (unit matrix). D is the degree matrix, W_0 and W_1 represent the network parameters of the first and second layers. σ and $Relu$ represent the activation functions.

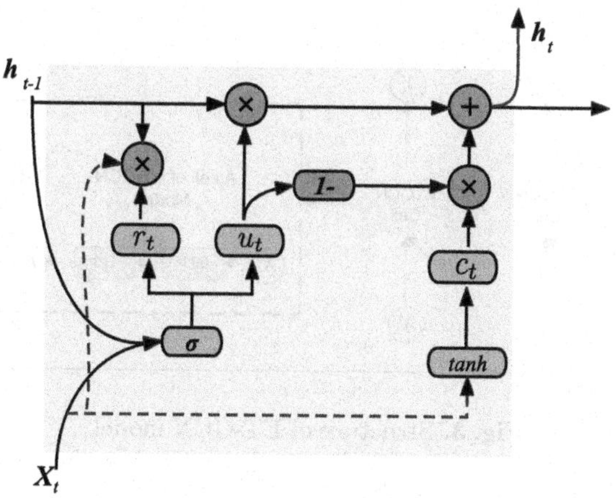

Fig. 2. Structure of GRU model

In addition, the amount of requests which servers receive keep changing over time. In the real world, RNNs have been proposed to capture the time dependence of traffic data. LSTM [20] is a variant of RNN that designs output and forgetting gate units to retain and forget the previous state and the current input and derive the current state through the output gate unit. And GRU [21], builds on the LSTM with an update gate instead of an oblivion gate and an output gate. For the training process of sequence data, ET-GCN follows the design of GRU. Specifically, the GRU model is a combination of update and reset gates, as shown in Fig. 2, where x_{t-1} is the input at moment t − 1, h_{t-k} represents the hidden state at moment t − 1, and σ and $tanh$ refer to the sigmoid and tanh activation functions.

4.1 Environment-Aware Temporal Graph Convolutional Networks

The work load prediction model ET-GCN is shown in Fig. 3. The left side shows the process of spatio-temporal prediction, and the right side shows the specific structure of ET-GCN unit. h_{t-1} represents the output at time $t-1$, MLP is the multilayer perceptron learning, and GC is the graph convolution process. The function f represents the joint learning of MLP and GC, The output of function f and the previous hidden layer state h_{t-1} are learned by the perceptron to get the intermediate states u_t and r_t. Then r_t and h_{t_1} are multiplied and sent to the new cell to get the candidate output c_t, as shown in Eq. 5. As shown in Fig. 2, r_t is the reset gate, which is used to combine the previous state h_{t-1} and the current information X_t to derive the candidate hidden state c_t. u_t refers to the update gate, which decides how much information of h_{t-1} is discarded and which new information of c_t is combined to derive the final hidden state h_t, as shown in Eq. 6.

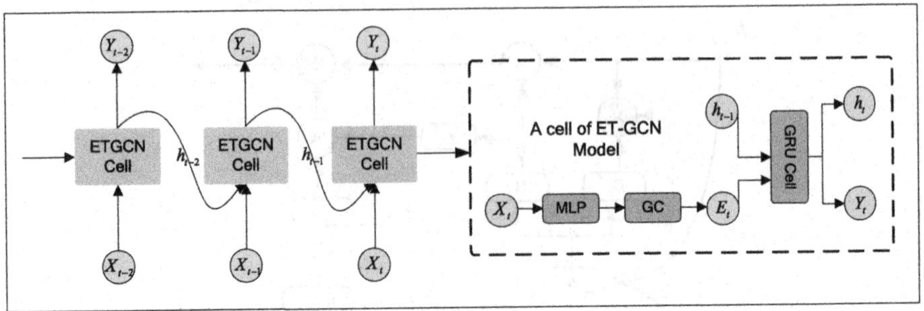

Fig. 3. Structure of ET-GCN model

Algorithm 1 is the formal description of the ET-GCN. For each time slice the node feature matrix X is first learned by a multilayer perceptron to obtain the enhanced feature matrix E. Note that for u and r in Eq. 3 and 4, the parameters W and b are shared. After going through t time slices the predicted values for the next T periods are obtained after passing through the fully connected layer.

In the training process, the goal is to minimize the error between the actual work load Y_t and the predicted value $\widehat{Y}_t$. Equation 7 represents the loss function, the first term is used to minimize the error between Y_t and $\widehat{Y}_t$, the second term reg is an L2 regularization term that helps to avoid the overfitting problem, and λ is a hyperparameter.

$$u_t = \sigma(W_u[f(A, X_t), h_{t-1}] + b_u) \tag{3}$$

$$r_t = \sigma(W_r[f(A, X_t), h_{t-1}] + b_r) \tag{4}$$

$$c_t = tanh(Wc[f(A, X_t), (r_t * h_{t-1})] + b_c) \tag{5}$$

$$h_t = u_t * h_{t-1} + (1 - u_t) * c_t \tag{6}$$

$$loss = ||Y_t - \widehat{Y}_t|| + \lambda L_{reg} \tag{7}$$

Algorithm 1: ET-GCN

Input: $A, X_1,...,X_t$
Output: $X'_{t+1}, ..., X'_{t+T}$
for $i \leftarrow 1$ **to** t **do**
  Obtain Ehanced Matrix E_i by MLP;
  if $i \leq 1$ **then**
    Initialize h_{i-1} with zero;
  end
  GC E_i with Adjacency Matrix A based on Equation 2;
  Chunk the output into Reset Gate r_i and Update Gate u_i;
  Multiply r_i and h_{i-1};
  Calculate Candidate State c_i by GC;
  Obtain h_i based on Equation 6;
end
$X'_t, ...X'_{t+T} \leftarrow Wh_t + b$;

5 Experiments

In this section, the ET-GCN algorithm is compared with three baseline algorithms to verify the importance of learning environment information for work load prediction.

This experiment is conducted on CloudSim-based platform [22], with a total of 500 users' mobile traces initialized for 15 days. The platform collects the number of requests from all servers every 3 min based on the simulation time and records the map information (number of people, area category, activity) of the server as a complete record.

In model training, the collected dataset is divided into two parts, the training dataset and the testing dataset. 80% of the dataset is assigned to the training dataset and the remaining 20% is assigned to the test dataset. For the data pre-processing process, the node feature values are adjusted to between 0 and 1. Each training data contains 13 continuous records, where the first 12 records are unchanged and the 13th retains only the work load as the true value compared to the predicted value.

The hyperparameters of the ET-GCN model mainly include learning rate, training epoch, the number of hidden layers and batch size. They are adjusted to 0.001, 100, 32 and 64 corrspondingly finally.

To evaluate the prediction performance of ET-GCN, five metrics are used to evaluate the prediction results. Specifically, RMSE and MAE are used to measure the prediction error: the smaller the value, the better the prediction. Accuracy is the prediction precision, the R2 and Var calculate the correlation coefficient; the larger these values are, the better the prediction effect is.

(1) Root mean square error (RMSE)

$$RMSE = \left[\frac{1}{n} \sum_{t=1}^{n} (y_t - \widehat{y}_t)^2 \right]^{\frac{1}{2}} \tag{8}$$

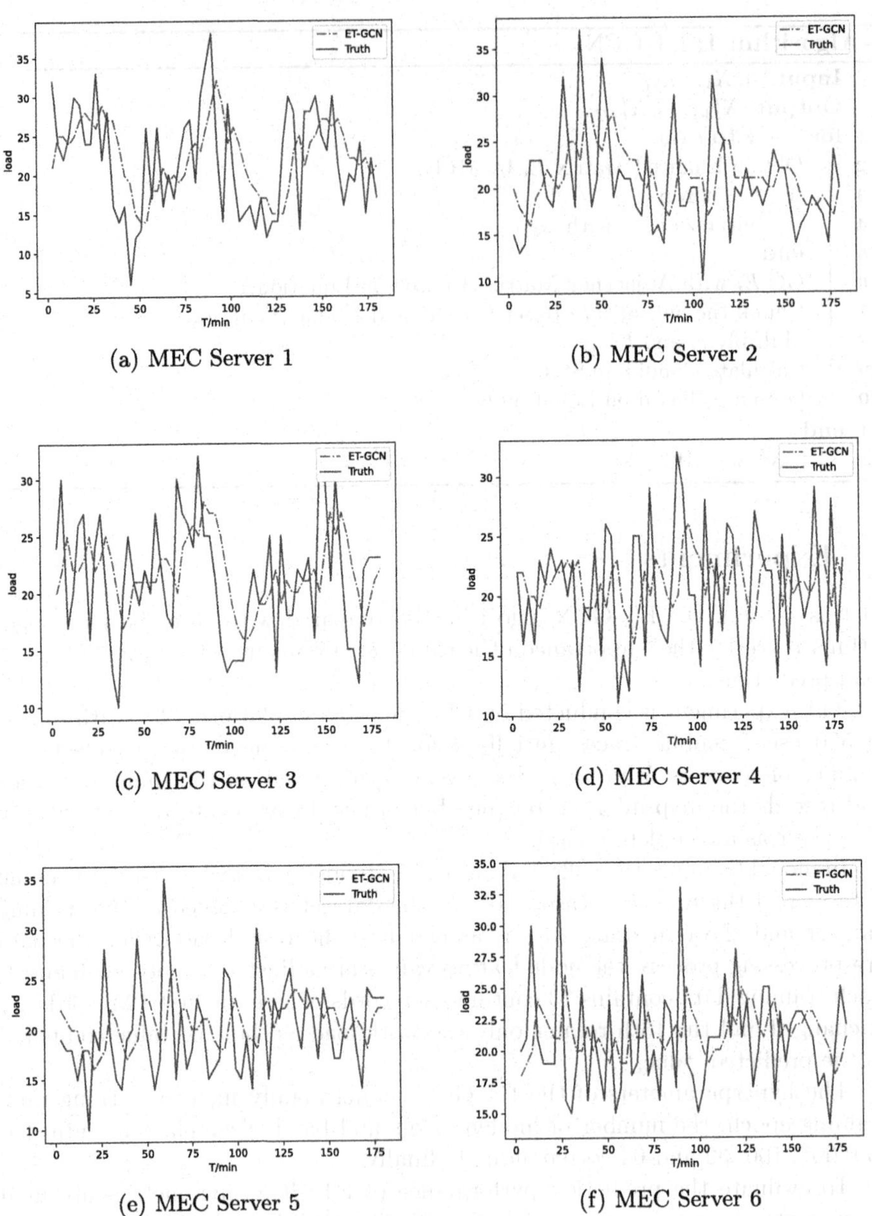

(a) MEC Server 1

(b) MEC Server 2

(c) MEC Server 3

(d) MEC Server 4

(e) MEC Server 5

(f) MEC Server 6

Fig. 4. MEC Servers' work load

(2) Mean absolute error (MAE)

$$MAE = \frac{\sum_{i=1}^{n} |y_t - \widehat{y}_t|}{n} \tag{9}$$

(3) Accuracy

$$Accuracy = 1 - \frac{||y - \widehat{y}||_F}{||y||_F} \tag{10}$$

(4) (R^2)

$$R^2 = 1 - \frac{\sum_{t=1}(y_t - \widehat{y}_t)^2}{\sum_{t=1}(y_t - \overline{y}_t)^2} \tag{11}$$

(5) Explained variation (Var)

$$Var = 1 - \frac{Var(y - \widehat{y})}{Var(y)} \tag{12}$$

5.1 Experimental Results

The performance of ET-GCN is compared with the these baseline methods: Gated Recurrent Unit model (GRU) [21], Joint prediction method for geographically dispersed work loads (JPGDL) [24], T-GCN [23]. Table 1 shows the prediction results of ET-GCN model with other baseline methods for the next 3, 6, 9 and 12 min. It can be seen that ET-GCN obtains the best performance for all the prediction metrics, proving the effectiveness of the ET-GCN model in predicting MEC server work load.

It's clearly see that ET-GCN has better prediction accuracy than the traditional univariate spatio-temporal prediction T-GCN. For example, for the 3-minute work load prediction, the RMSE of the ET-GCN model is reduced by 4.1% compared to the T-GCN model. And for the 6-minute prediction, the RMSE of ET-GCN is reduced by 4%. It indicates that ET-GCN can capture the environmental context information from the data, while the RMSE of ET-GCN model decreases by 6.5% and 6.6% for 3-minute work load prediction compared with GRU and JPGDL which only consider temporal characteristics. Thus, environmental factors and the topology of the graph are helpful in improving the workload prediction.

By observing the changes of RMSE and Accuracy of ET-GCN for different time lengths in Table 1, it can be founded that RMSE always hovered between 3.9 and 4.02, while Accuracy always remained at 0.77. So ET-GCN can obtain the best prediction performance by training regardless of the variation of the prediction range, and the prediction results do not change much. Because of the topology of the graph, the sequential model makes it easier to predict future workload changes.

To better understand the ET-GCN model, three-hour work load predictions for six edge servers are compared with the real values. The visualization results are shown in Fig. 4, respectively. These results show that the ET-GCN model predicts poorly at peak times, and there is some difference between the real traffic information and the prediction results.

Table 1. Predictions of ET-GCN model and other baseline algorithms.

Method	Metric	JPGDL	GRU	T-GCN	ET-GCN
3 min	RMSE	4.257	4.255	4.149	3.976
	MAE	3.341	3.341	3.270	3.109
	Accuracy	0.760	0.759	0.765	0.775
	R^2	0.659	0.661	0.677	0.704
	var	0.659	0.661	0.677	0.704
6 min	RMSE	4.258	4.255	4.163	3.996
	MAE	3.355	3.353	3.295	3.129
	Accuracy	0.758	0.759	0.764	0.774
	R^2	0.658	0.661	0.675	0.700
	var	0.658	0.661	0.675	0.700
9 min	RMSE	4.241	4.237	4.179	4.006
	MAE	3.346	3.340	3.312	3.140
	Accuracy	0.755	0.760	0.763	0.773
	R^2	0.654	0.663	0.672	0.699
	var	0.665	0.664	0.672	0.699
12 min	RMSE	4.226	4.223	4.181	4.020
	MAE	3.332	3.330	3.312	3.156
	Accuracy	0.760	0.761	0.763	0.772
	R^2	0.663	0.665	0.672	0.696
	var	0.663	0.666	0.672	0.697

6 Conclusion

In this paper, a neural network-based server work load prediction method called ET-GCN is proposed. It mainly combines GCN and GRU. In the graph network, edges indicate whether the nodes are directly adjacent to each other, and information about the geographic area where MEC servers are located is described as the features of the nodes. On the one hand, GCN is used to capture the topology of the graph to obtain spatial information. On the other hand, the GRU model is used to capture the dynamic changes of node attributes to obtain temporal information. In addition, the geographical features of the nodes to assist the training are added, and the experiments show that ET-GCN achieves the best results in different prediction ranges compared with the simple temporal model GRU and JPGDL, or the univariate spatio-temporal prediction model T-GCN.

Acknowledgements. This work is supported by the National Natural Science Foundation of China (Grant No. 61972202, 61973161, 61991404), the Fundamental Research Funds for the Central Universities (No. 30919011235).

References

1. Wang, J., Hu, J., Min, G., Ni, Q., El-Ghazawi, T.: Online service migration in edge computing with incomplete information: a deep recurrent actor-critic method. arXiv preprint arXiv:2012.08679 (2020)
2. Guo, F., Tang, B., Tang, M.: Joint optimization of delay and cost for microservice composition in mobile edge computing. World Wide Web **25**(5), 2019–2047 (2022)
3. Benvenuto, D., Giovanetti, M., Vassallo, L., Angeletti, S., Ciccozzi, M.: Application of the Arima model on the Covid-2019 epidemic dataset. Data Brief **29**, 105340 (2020)
4. Elmunim, N., Abdullah, M., Hasbi, A., Bahari, S.: Comparison of GPS TEC variations with holt-winter method and IRI-2012 over Langkawi, Malaysia. Adv. Space Res. **60**(2), 276–285 (2017)
5. Wu, C.L., Chiu, T.C., Wang, C.Y., Pang, A.C.: Mobility-aware deep reinforcement learning with glimpse mobility prediction in edge computing. In: 2020 IEEE International Conference on Communications (ICC), ICC 2020, pp. 1–7. IEEE (2020)
6. Subramanya, T., Riggio, R.: Centralized and federated learning for predictive VNF autoscaling in multi-domain 5G networks and beyond. IEEE Trans. Netw. Serv. Manag. **18**(1), 63–78 (2021)
7. Wu, S., Ren, J., Zhao, T., Wang, Y.: Machine learning based signal strength and uncertainty prediction for MEC mobility management. In: 2021 IEEE 94th Vehicular Technology Conference (VTC2021-Fall), pp. 1–5. IEEE (2021)
8. Lentisco, C.M., Bellido, L., González-Sánchez, D., Martínez-Casanueva, I.D., Fernández, D., Soto, I.: Extending the MEC mobility service to support cache prefetching. In: 2022 18th International Conference on the Design of Reliable Communication Networks (DRCN), pp. 1–4. IEEE (2022)
9. Ntalampiras, S., Fiore, M.: Forecasting mobile service demands for anticipatory MEC. In: 2018 IEEE 19th International Symposium on "A World of Wireless, Mobile and Multimedia Networks" (WoWMoM), pp. 14–19. IEEE (2018)
10. Dlamini, T.: Core network management procedures for self-organized and sustainable 5G cellular networks. arXiv preprint arXiv:1909.09097 (2019)
11. Jiang, H., Peng, D., Yang, K., Zeng, Y., Chen, Q.: Predicted mobile data offloading for mobile edge computing systems. In: Qiu, M. (ed.) SmartCom 2018. LNCS, vol. 11344, pp. 153–162. Springer, Cham (2018). https://doi.org/10.1007/978-3-030-05755-8_16
12. Zeng, Y., Xiang, K.: Edge oriented urban hotspot prediction for human-centric internet of things. IEEE Access **9**, 71435–71445 (2021)
13. Deng, Y., et al.: Resource provisioning for mitigating edge DDoS attacks in MEC-enabled SDVN. IEEE Internet Things J. **9**(23), 24264–24280 (2022)
14. Yu, K., Qin, X., Jia, Z., Du, Y., Lin, M.: Cross-attention fusion based spatial-temporal multi-graph convolutional network for traffic flow prediction. Sensors **21**(24), 8468 (2021)
15. Fu, R., Zhang, Z., Li, L.: Using LSTM and GRU neural network methods for traffic flow prediction. In: 2016 31st Youth Academic Annual Conference of Chinese Association of Automation (YAC), pp. 324–328. IEEE (2016)
16. Van Lint, J., Hoogendoorn, S.P., van Zuylen, H.J.: Freeway travel time prediction with state-space neural networks: modeling state-space dynamics with recurrent neural networks. Transp. Res. Rec. **1811**(1), 30–39 (2002)
17. Defferrard, M., Bresson, X., Vandergheynst, P.: Convolutional neural networks on graphs with fast localized spectral filtering. In: Advances in Neural Information Processing Systems, vol. 29 (2016)

18. Bruna, J., Zaremba, W., Szlam, A., LeCun, Y.: Spectral networks and locally connected networks on graphs. arXiv preprint arXiv:1312.6203 (2013)
19. Kipf, T.N., Welling, M.: Semi-supervised classification with graph convolutional networks. arXiv preprint arXiv:1609.02907 (2016)
20. Hochreiter, S., Schmidhuber, J.: Long short-term memory. Neural Comput. **9**(8), 1735–1780 (1997)
21. Cho, K., Van Merriënboer, B., Bahdanau, D., Bengio, Y.: On the properties of neural machine translation: encoder-decoder approaches. arXiv preprint arXiv:1409.1259 (2014)
22. Beloglazov, A., Buyya, R.: Optimal online deterministic algorithms and adaptive heuristics for energy and performance efficient dynamic consolidation of virtual machines in cloud data centers. Concurr. Comput.: Pract. Experience **24**(13), 1397–1420 (2012)
23. Zhao, L., et al.: T-GCN: a temporal graph convolutional network for traffic prediction. IEEE Trans. Intell. Transp. Syst. **21**(9), 3848–3858 (2019)
24. Heng, Y., Cai, Z.: Multi-application container scheduling approach in edge environments. In: Computer and Digital Engineering in Process (2022)

Hybrid Task Offloading for Serverless Computing in the Multi-edge-to-Cloud Environment

Xin Li(✉) and Long Chen(✉)

School of Computer Science and Engineering, Southeast University, Nanjing, China
{sinlee,longc}@seu.edu.cn

Abstract. Serverless edge computing provides a lightweight and easily scalable new computing model for edge computing. However, its fine-grained tasks, short startup time, and fast execution speed bring new challenges to node caching and task offloading. In this paper, we consider the problems of function-based tasks offloading in a multi-edge environment. We propose a "cloud-edge-end" collaborative three-layer task offloading framework. A new hybrid offloading algorithm (TFHO) is established to offload the randomly arriving tasks. TFHO mainly includes four stages: offloading decision, task sorting, path selection, and function replacement. In the offloading decision, we consider both vertical offloading between edge nodes and the cloud center, and also horizontal offloading between edge nodes themselves. A shortest path method is proposed to select the best offloading path under the multi-hop communication mechanism between edge nodes. In addition, function replacement also solves the problem of which functions to discard by edge nodes when the cache is full. Our experimental results on three real datasets show that the TFHO significantly outperforms the other two baseline algorithms.

Keywords: Hybrid Offloading · Function Cache · Multi-edge · Serverless

1 Introduction

Edge computing is a new paradigm that has gained significant attention in recent years. It refers to the concept of processing data and running applications closer to the source of the data, rather than relying on a centralized cloud. This technology

This work is supported by the National Key Research and Development Program of China (No. 2022YFB3305500), the Key-Area Research and Development Program of Guangdong Province (No. 2021B0101200003), the National Natural Science Foundation of China (Nos. 62273089, 62102080), Natural Science Foundation of Jiangsu Province (No. BK20210204), the Fundamental Research Funds for the Central Universities (No. 2242022R10017), and Collaborative Innovation Center of Wireless Communications Technology.

Z. Wang et al. (Eds.): ICSS 2023, CCIS 1844, pp. 43–56, 2023.
https://doi.org/10.1007/978-981-99-4402-6_4

is especially useful in environments where large amounts of data are generated in real-time, such as IoT devices, autonomous vehicles, and augmented/virtual reality. Task offloading is a key concept in edge computing. It can be used to transfer the computation or data to nearby edge servers or cloud computing centers for processing. It plays a critical role in enabling more efficient edge computing. At the same time, serverless computing is also becoming a novel paradigm for the operation of next-generation cloud data centers. Serverless applications are developed as an ecosystem of microservices, called functions, which are loosely coupled and highly scalable. This approach eliminates the need for developers to worry about server management, scaling, and provisioning, allowing them to focus solely on writing code and building applications.

An urgent problem is how to extend serverless technology from cloud data centers to the edge environment. We all know that edge nodes have limited computation and cache resources compared to the cloud computing center. If we deploy serverless functions in edge nodes, we can only place a relatively small number of function images in the cache, and the total number of function instances that can be opened is also limited. When an edge node is overloaded or receives a request for a function that does not exist in the cache, how to process this request properly to meet its deadline constraint as much as possible becomes particularly important. Secondly, the pattern of function requests of each edge node can be obtained from its historical observations, roughly following a Poisson distribution, and each edge node is also heterogeneous and distributed. Therefore, how to design several feasible offloading methods and make an offloading decision for each simple independent request to minimize the average delay time of the system is also a tricky problem.

Through analysis, there are many challenges to extending serverless technology to the edge. Firstly, there is no way to predict which function requests will arrive in the future, and each edge node has a limited number of functions in the cache, so it is a large challenge to decide which functions to cache and how to replace them when the cache is full. In other words, the existence of the function of the edge node should be seriously considered. Secondly, the edge node has limited computing power and can only open a specified number of function instances. It is also a large challenge to make the best offloading decision for the current state of the edge node with multiple offloading methods available. Thirdly, edge nodes are distributed in different geographical locations, so offloading requests from one edge node to other edge nodes must take into account the transmission costs due to the different locations. Therefore, it is also a large challenge to make the best path selection.

In this paper, we address the aforementioned challenges and make our new contributions. Firstly, we build a three-layer model in the serverless multi-edge environment, namely the cloud center layer, the edge node layer, and the end device layer, which successfully applies serverless functions to the network edge. This provides a substantial extension for edge computing frameworks allowing functions for task offloading. Secondly, we design a horizontal offloading method, which allows the edge nodes to collaborate with each other. On this basis, we design a multi-hop communication mechanism between edge nodes that helps them to offload requests to one another within the shortest distance. This provides a meaningful extension to the existing offloading methods for edge nodes. Thirdly, we propose a hybrid offloading algorithm that divides the task offloading of each request into four stages, namely offloading decision, task sorting, path selection, and function replacement. This achieves fast processing of each function request, which significantly reduces the average delay time of the online system.

The rest of the paper is organized as follows. Related works are described in Sect. 2. Section 3 builds the "cloud-edge-end" three-layer model for the considered problem. In Sect. 4, the proposed hybrid offloading algorithm framework is described. Computational results and evaluations are shown in Sect. 5, followed by conclusions in Sect. 6.

2 Related Works

Edge computing expands the boundaries of cloud computing but also brings new challenges. Task offloading is currently the most popular research direction in edge computing, but most papers focus on the problem of whether end device's requests need to be offloaded and to the cloud or to one of the edge nodes [1–3]. This only considers task offloading in the vertical direction and does not involve any horizontal offloading where edge nodes can collaborate with each other. Some papers consider horizontal collaboration between edge nodes, but they didn't involve offloading to the cloud [4] or getting assistance from the cloud [5]. In [6], the edge node's requests will be offloaded with the assistance of the cloud, but it only solves the burst load problem of the edge nodes without optimizing the average delay time.

FaaS (Function as a Service) is the mainstream direction of Serverless, but there are few papers that combine function with task offloading. Some papers provide a good introduction to the development of serverless applications [7] and on this basis build a platform for the unified management of function services from different cloud providers [8]. However, none of the above practices really apply the functions to the edge. In [9], it considers multiple offloading methods and multi-hop communication between edge nodes, but the function cold-starting process cannot be involved. Only file download requests from edge nodes require pulling configuration and dependency files from the cloud, but it is not really the function cold-starting process [10].

There are many tasks offloading solutions available in the industry now. Mao et al. [11] assume that tasks are processed at the beginning of each time slot, but Xu et al. [12] assume that tasks are accumulated during the time slot and then make decisions at the beginning of the next time slot. Chen et al. [13] consider a multi-user and multi-task offloading scenario and assume that users should pay for the offloading tasks, aiming to minimize this cost. Sen et al. [14] focus on a three-layer offloading model where the key problem is making the offloading decision. Min et al. [15] focus on a one-to-many offloading scenario where users need to decide how much data to offload. We intend to integrate all of the above offloading methods and propose a hybrid offloading algorithm that applies the functions truly to the network edge.

3 System Model

The system model considered here is a typical "cloud-edge-end" collaborative three-layer architecture, as shown in Fig. 1. A single remote cloud computing center connects multiple base stations in a region, and each base station is equipped with an edge server to provide services for the end devices in its coverage area. The base station can communicate with their neighborhoods and cloud computing center through the internet. It is important to note that not all base stations can communicate with each other, but indirect communication can be achieved by relaying through others.

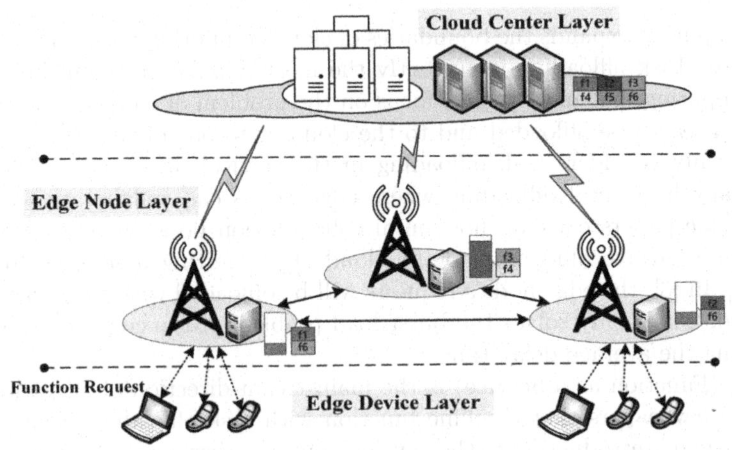

Fig. 1. Three-layer architecture in the serverless multi-edge environment.

The remote cloud computing center has powerful resources such as computation, cache, and network, which can be approximated as unlimited. It also acts as the function registry with a complete set of functions and can not only process all function requests but also send any function configuration and dependency files to the base station. However, the cloud computing center is far away from all base stations and the network delay needs to be seriously considered. The most worthy of study in the three-layer architecture is the edge node layer, they are edge servers equipped in the base stations. Edge nodes have limited resources compared to the cloud computing center, and they are not only geographically distributed, but also heterogeneous in their ability to provide various resources. Edge nodes can only cache a limited number of functions, they can only process function requests that exist in the cache. Additionally, they can pull functions from the cloud computing center (cold-starting) or offload function requests to the cloud computing center and other edge nodes where the function exists. The end devices can send function requests to the surrounding edge nodes to request specific function instances. These requests are independent of each other and expect to get a response as soon as possible.

The arrival of requests at each edge node obeys Poisson distribution, which is a probability distribution used to describe the number of random events that occur per unit of time. In our model, the average number of requests arriving per second at each edge node λ is calculated from the historical observations of that edge node. The formula for the probability of a random event occurring k counts per unit of time is as follows:

$$P(X = k) = \frac{e^{\lambda}\lambda^{k}}{k!} \tag{1}$$

Table 1. Table of task attributes.

Field	Definition
Request_id	Unique primary key of the task
Function_id	Function id requested by the task
Instance_number	Number of function instances required for the task
Deal_time	Expected running time of the task
Data_volume	Data volume carried by the task
Deadline_time	Soft deadline time of the task

The system is an online system that is continuously running. We divide the time of each edge node into time slots, within which requests are accumulated and tasks are scheduled at the beginning of the next time slot. Each request arrives at the system as a pending task t_i, and we impose a soft deadline constraint t_i^d on it, the attributes contained in each independent task t_i are shown in Table 1. If the request arrives at t_i^s and leaves at t_i^e, we formulate the objective function for minimizing the average delay time of the system as follows:

$$T = \frac{\sum_{i=0}^{n} \max(t_i^e - (t_i^s + t_i^d), 0)}{n} \tag{2}$$

4 Hybrid Offloading Algorithm

Once a request arrives at an edge node, in order to minimize the average delay time of the system as much as possible, we first make the offloading decision according to the status of the current edge node, and we set up four feasible offloading methods to determine where this task will eventually be processed. In our model, we propose a hybrid offloading algorithm as shown in Algorithm 1, it considers both vertical offloading from the edge nodes to the cloud computing center and horizontal offloading between the edge nodes in collaboration with each other. We then sort tasks according to one or more attributes of them, such as the closeness to the deadline, this is because some tasks have high requirements for real-time, while others are not sensitive to the completion time. Finally, if the task needs to be offloaded to another edge node, we also need to select the best offloading path between the two nodes. In addition, we allow the current edge node to process this task in a cold-starting mode, which may lead to function replacement in some cases.

Algorithm 1: Task sort and Function cache based Hybrid Offloading Algorithm (TFHO)

Input: System running time τ, average number of requests λ arriving per second in Poisson distribution, tasks set T.
Output: Average delay time of edge node x in τ seconds.

begin
  Initialize Q_x^t, Q_x^w, Q_x^e, F_i, D_x;
  while $i < \tau$ **do**
    Generate tasks set T_i using Poisson distribution with λ;
    $F_i \leftarrow$ *null*;
    $n \leftarrow$ *length*(T_i);
    for $j := 1$ *to* n **do**
      Offload decision for task t_j;
      Add delay time of task t_j to delay set D_x;
      if *Task* t_j *is processed locally* **then**
        Add task t_j to wait queue Q_x^w;
        continue;
      if *Task* t_j *is offloaded to edge node* y **then**
        Add task t_j to transfer queue Q_y^t;
        continue;
      /** Task t_j is offloaded to cloud center can be ignored. **/
      if *Task* t_j *pulls function* f *from cloud center* **then**
        Add function f to functions set F_i;
    Remove completed tasks from execute queue Q_x^e;
    $Q_x^w \leftarrow Q_x^t$;
    Sort tasks in wait queue Q_x^w;
    Replace functions that do not exist in function set F_i;
    $Q_x^e \leftarrow Q_x^w$;
    $i \leftarrow i + 1$;
  return *average*(D_x);

4.1 Task Sorting

Each edge node sorts the tasks accumulated in the previous time slot at the beginning of the current time slot, they include requests newly arrived, accumulated from previous time slots, and transferred from other edge nodes. We set the

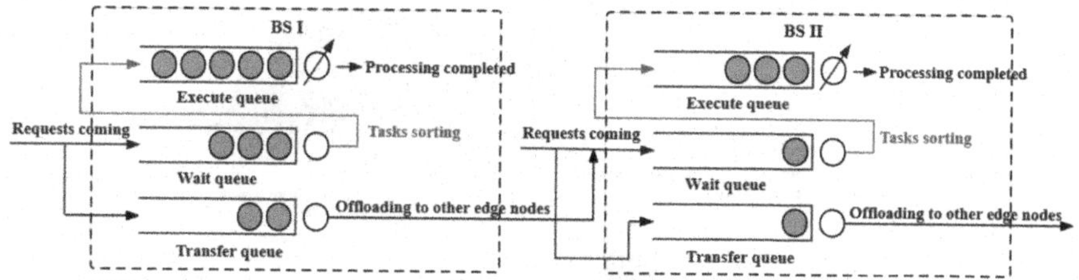

Fig. 2. Three types of queues exist in edge nodes and how they work.

time slot size to one second uniformly and use three queues (not FIFO queue) to describe the task sorting process in detail as shown in Fig. 2. A function request arrives at an edge node and then goes through offloading decision, if it needs to be offloaded to other edge nodes it enters the ***transfer queue***, which sends the request to the target edge node after path selection. If the request decides to process at this node it enters the ***wait queue***. Task sorting means that the tasks in the wait queue are sorted according to a certain attribute and then run sequentially in the ***execute queue***, and return a response to the end device. We finally select the *deadline_time* of the task as the sorting basis and use the *deal_time*, *deal_time/data_volume* as the comparison.

4.2 Offloading Decision

For each function request that arrives at the edge node, an offloading decision will be made to determine how and where it will be processed. In our model, time is divided into fixed time slots, and incoming requests to the edge node are accumulated in the previous time slot, immediately after the offloading decision is made at the beginning of the current time slot. Each request has four options for offloading as shown in Fig. 3, and we calculate the cost of each offloading method and choose the least to process this request.

For a task requesting the function f_1, if the edge node it arrives has the function f_1 in the cache and the node has sufficient computing power, in which case we let the task be processed directly locally and the cost is the expected running time of the task as follows:

$$P_i^1 = t_i^{deal\_time} \tag{3}$$

If the edge node has insufficient computing power and is currently overloaded, it is necessary to consider offloading the function request to another edge node or to the cloud computing center for processing. For a task requesting the function f_3, although the current edge node has function f_3 in the cache and has the ability to process this task, the lack of computing power causes it to offload the task to other edge nodes where the function f_3 exists and is idle to process it. When edge node x decides to offload a task to edge node y for processing, it needs to select the shortest hop $l_{x,y}$ between two edge nodes in the network topology graph. In our model, we assume that the location and number of all edge nodes

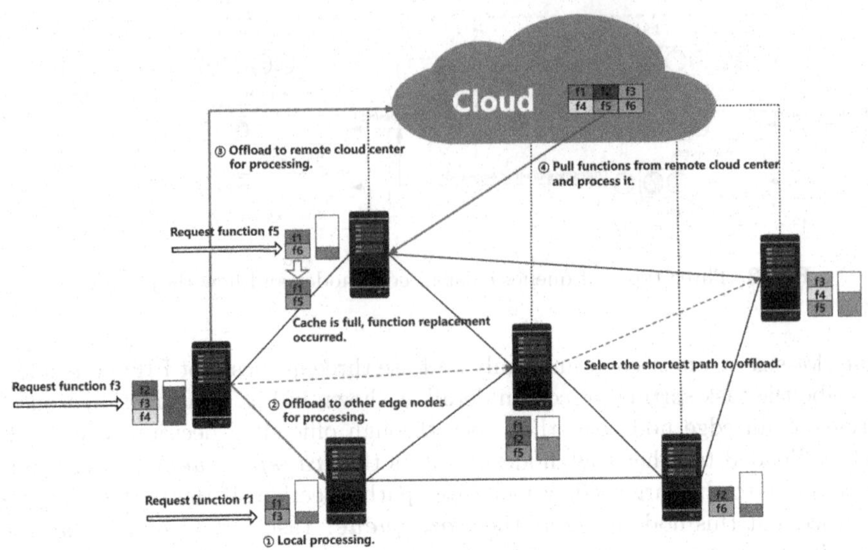

Fig. 3. Four optional offloading methods for each function task.

in a region will not change, so as to construct an undirected graph of the network topology of the edge nodes in the region. The existence of an undirected edge between two edge nodes indicates that they can reach each other within one hop, i.e. they can communicate with each other. If two edge nodes are not reachable within one hop, they can only communicate via the other edge nodes' relay, and multi-hop communication of edge nodes adds additional network delay. Selecting the shortest hop between two edge nodes is a typical shortest path problem that can be well solved using ***Dijkstra*** and ***Floyd*** algorithm. The transmission cost of a task in the edge network is related to the data volume carried by the task and the network bandwidth W, so the total cost when a task is offloaded from one edge node to another is as follows:

$$P_i^2 = \frac{t_i^{data\_volume}}{W} \cdot l_{x,y} + t_i^{deal\_time} \tag{4}$$

In the above scenario, if the edge node decides to offload the task to the cloud computing center for processing, it has to focus on the transmission cost due to the long distance. The cloud computing center has nearly unlimited computing power and all function instances to process arbitrary function requests. In our model, we assume that the cloud computing center is very far away from the region, so the distance to each edge node is the same and the distance between edge nodes is negligible. With the same number of hops L $(\forall x, y \rightarrow L \gg l_{x,y})$ from any edge node to the cloud computing center, the total cost when a task is offloaded from one edge node to cloud computing center is as follows:

$$P_i^3 = \frac{t_i^{data\_volume}}{W} \cdot L + t_i^{deal\_time} \tag{5}$$

In cases where the edge node has sufficient computing power just because the requested function f_5 does not exist in the cache, in addition to offloading the task to another edge node or the cloud computing center for processing, consideration should also be given to pulling the configuration and dependency files for the function f_5 from the cloud computing center so that the edge node could have the ability to process this kind of function request, which is also known as function cold-starting. It is important to note that this paper does not involve any optimizations for function cold-starting, but only considers that edge nodes have the ability to perform function cold-starting. Furthermore, we do not allow the current edge node to perform the function cold-starting when processing requests offloaded from other edge nodes, only the edge node where the native request arrives is allowed to consider this offloading method. If the cold-starting delay time of the function f is S_f, the total cost of processing this task at the current node is as follows:

$$P_i^4 = S_f + t_i^{deal\_time} \tag{6}$$

Finally, based on the load and cache status of the edge node where the request arrives, the realistic and least costly offloading method is selected. The offloading decision method is shown as Algorithm 2 and the expected minimum execution time for this task is as follows:

$$\begin{aligned} P_i = & \ min(P_i^1, P_i^2, P_i^3, P_i^4) \\ & s.t. \ (3), (4), (5), (6). \end{aligned} \tag{7}$$

4.3 Function Replacement

The ability of an edge node to process a function request depends on whether such kind of function exists in its cache, however, the caching capacity of an edge node is limited compared to the cloud computing center and can only cache specified kinds of functions. When the edge node's cache is not full, if a function request triggers a cold-starting process and a new kind of function is pulled from the cloud computing center, it just needs to be put into the cache to serve the request. But when the edge node's cache is full, if a task requests a function that is not in the cache and the corresponding cold-starting process is triggered, function replacement occurs at that point. As shown in Fig. 3, a task requests a function f_5, and after the offloading decision, the system pulls the configuration and dependency files of the function f_5 from the cloud computing center to the local so that the corresponding function instance could be generated to serve it, but the cache of the edge node is currently full, so it is necessary to discard an old function according to the function replacement policy, thus reserving cache space for the new function. This is very similar to the operating system's page replacement algorithm, so we decided to use ***LRU*** and ***LFU*** in practice.

Algorithm 2: Offloading Decision Method (ODM)

Input: A task t, cold start time S_f of function f, for edge node x, the set of functions F_x that exist in cache, the number of function instances C_x that can be opened, the number of hops L from cloud center, and the fixed bandwidth W.

Output: Delay time P for task t after offload decision.

begin
  Construct an undirected graph based on the network topology of the edge nodes;
  $P \leftarrow 0$;
  $f \leftarrow t_{function\_id}$, $c \leftarrow t_{instance\_num}$;
  if $f \in F_x$ *and* $c \leq C_x$ **then**
    return P;
  $d \leftarrow t_{data\_volume}$;
  if $c > C_x$ **then**
    Offload task t to cloud center;
    $P = \frac{d}{W} \cdot L$;
    if $\exists y \rightarrow f \in F_y \wedge c \leq C_y$ **then**
      Offload task t to edge node y with the shortest hop from it;
      $P = \frac{d}{W} \cdot l_{x,y}$;
  if $f \in F_x$ **then**
    return P;
  else
    Pull function f from cloud center;
    $P = min(P, S_f)$;
    return P;

5 Experiments

In this section, the experimental settings are first introduced. After that, we compare the effects of different Poisson distribution λ, task sorting, and function replacement strategies on the system's average delay time. And finally, we verify the efficiency of the proposed TFHO algorithm with the single offloading method algorithm on the system's average delay time.

5.1 Experimental Settings

The tasks set we use is from Alibaba-ClusterData [16]. We pre-process this dataset to filter all simple independent tasks, and then we randomly generate the soft deadline constraint for each task based on the expected running time field. The functions set we use is from Alibaba-FaasNet [17], mainly using the cold-starting time S_f of the function f. We assume that there are 20 kinds of functions in each experiment and each edge node can only cache 5 kinds of functions. For each task, it requests which function is randomly generated from the functions set in each experiment. The distribution of edge nodes is from a real-world base stations dataset EUA-Datasets [18]. We assume that each base station can only communicate with other base stations within 500 m, and then we construct the network topology of edge nodes in the region. It is important to note that each edge node can communicate with all other edge nodes in a direct or indirect way. There are 125 edge nodes in this dataset and we randomly generate the number of function instances $C \in [300, 500]$ that can be opened at each edge node. In addition, the number of hops per edge node from the cloud computing center $L = 20$ and the fixed bandwidth $W = 0.1$ Gbps.

5.2 Experimental Results and Evaluations

We first tested the effect of the average number of requests λ per second on the system's average delay time as shown in Fig. 4(a). We can obtain that the delay time of the system increases slowly as the number of requests increases, but it increases rapidly when $\lambda > 10$. This means that the edge nodes are almost overloaded and have to choose the more time-consuming options of "offloading to the cloud computing center" or "performing a cold-starting process" to process this task, thus increasing the average delay time significantly. If we think that the end devices have a better user experience in getting a response within one second and the throughput of the edge nodes is as high as possible, $\lambda = 10$ is the most suitable choice in our online system.

For task sorting in the edge node's wait queue, we designed a strategy based on the closeness to the deadline. To test the performance of this strategy, we designed four other strategies based on one or more fields in the task attributes Table 1. They are sorted by the task's expected running time and the ratio of expected running time to data volume, respectively. As shown in Fig. 4(b), the closeness to the deadline-based sorting strategy not only achieves the smallest average delay time during the running of the system compared to other strategies but also does not lead to increased delay time as the system continues to run, which is well suited to our proposed online model. For function replacement, we learned from the page replacement algorithm in the operating system, using LRU and LFU. As shown in Fig. 4(c), LRU achieves better function caching results because the area covered by each edge node has a regularity in the kinds of functions it normally processes, and only the most frequently used function types need to be cached.

When we use the closeness to the deadline task sorting strategy, LRU function replacement strategy, and $\lambda = 10$, we compare the proposed TFHO with two algorithms where function requests can be processed locally and with the assistance of the cloud computing center, the result is shown as Fig. 4(d). The function request is processed with the assistance of the cloud computing center, which means that the edge node can process locally, offload to the cloud computing center, and perform a cold-starting process. The experimental results show that the TFHO algorithm is approximately 52.3% faster than local processing and 45.7% faster than processing with the assistance of the cloud computing center. It suggests that if adjacent edge nodes can collaborate horizontally with each

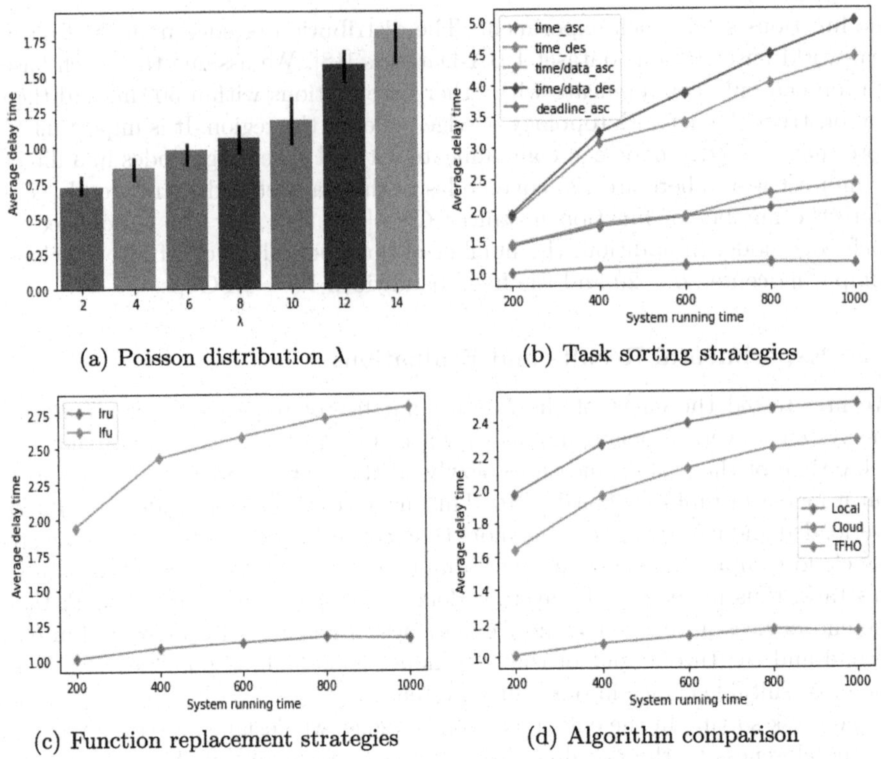

(a) Poisson distribution λ

(b) Task sorting strategies

(c) Function replacement strategies

(d) Algorithm comparison

Fig. 4. Average delay time with different parameters, strategies, and algorithms.

other, the delay time cost of communicating with the remote cloud computing center can be effectively reduced.

6 Conclusion

In this paper, We study the problem of task offloading for function requests in a serverless multi-edge scenario. We build a model for the edge environment that consists of three layers: the cloud center layer, the edge node layer, and the end device layer. We divide the task offloading of each request into four stages: offloading decision, task sorting, path selection, and function replacement, where the latter three stages are optional. Based on the above, we propose a hybrid offloading algorithm, called TFHO, which well solves the task offloading problem for heterogeneous and distributed edge nodes. Our experimental results on three real datasets show that the TFHO algorithm significantly outperforms the other two baseline algorithms by 52.3% and 45.7% respectively. We also find that sorting tasks based on their deadline field and using the LRU function replacement strategy can effectively reduce the average delay time. In future work, we will consider the task offloading strategy when burst loads occur at a single edge node. In addition to this, we will also use reinforcement learning methods to optimize the existing TFHO algorithm.

References

1. Tang, M., Wong, V.W.: Deep reinforcement learning for task offloading in mobile edge computing systems. IEEE Trans. Mob. Comput. **21**(6), 1985–1997 (2022). https://doi.org/10.1109/TMC.2020.3036871
2. Kuang, Z., Ma, Z., Li, Z.: Cooperative computation offloading and resource allocation for delay minimization in mobile edge computing. J. Syst. Architect. **118**, 102167 (2021). https://doi.org/10.1016/j.sysarc.2021.102167
3. Alfakih, T., Hassan, M.M., Gumaei, A.: Task offloading and resource allocation for mobile edge computing by deep reinforcement learning based on SARSA. IEEE Access **8**, 54074–54084 (2020). https://doi.org/10.1109/ACCESS.2020.2981434
4. Wu, J., Lin, H., Liu, H.: A deep reinforcement learning approach for collaborative mobile edge computing. In: IEEE International Conference on Communications, ICC 2022, pp. 601–606 (2022). https://doi.org/10.1109/ICC45855.2022.9839202
5. Hossain, M.D., Sultana, T.: Edge orchestration based computation peer offloading in MEC-enabled networks: a fuzzy logic approach. In: 2021 15th International Conference on Ubiquitous Information Management and Communication (IMCOM), pp. 1–7 (2021). https://doi.org/10.1109/IMCOM51814.2021.9377327
6. Deng, S., Zhang, C., Li, C., Yin, J., Dustdar, S., Zomaya, A.Y.: Burst load evacuation based on dispatching and scheduling in distributed edge networks. IEEE Trans. Parallel Distrib. Syst. **32**(8), 1918–1932 (2021). https://doi.org/10.1109/TPDS.2021.3052236
7. Eismann, S., et al.: The state of serverless applications: collection, characterization, and community consensus. IEEE Trans. Softw. Eng. **48**(10), 4152–4166 (2022). https://doi.org/10.1109/TSE.2021.3113940
8. Jindal, A., Chadha, M., Gerndt, M., Frielinghaus, J., Podolskiy, V.: Poster: function delivery network: extending serverless to heterogeneous computing. In: 2021 IEEE 41st International Conference on Distributed Computing Systems (ICDCS), pp. 1128–1129 (2021). https://doi.org/10.1109/ICDCS51616.2021.00120
9. Sahni, Y., Cao, J., Yang, L.: Multi-hop multi-task partial computation offloading in collaborative edge computing. IEEE Trans. Parallel Distrib. Syst. **32**(5), 1133–1145 (2021). https://doi.org/10.1109/TPDS.2020.3042224
10. Tan, H., Jiang, S.H.C., Han, Z., Li, M.: Asymptotically optimal online caching on multiple caches with relaying and bypassing. IEEE/ACM Trans. Netw. **29**(4), 1841–1852 (2021). https://doi.org/10.1109/TNET.2021.3077115
11. Mao, Y., Zhang, J.: Dynamic computation offloading for mobile-edge computing with energy harvesting devices. IEEE J. Sel. Areas Commun. **34**(12), 3590–3605 (2016). https://doi.org/10.1109/JSAC.2016.2611964
12. Xu, J., Chen, L.: Online learning for offloading and autoscaling in energy harvesting mobile edge computing. IEEE Trans. Cogn. Commun. Netw. **3**(3), 361–373 (2017). https://doi.org/10.1109/TCCN.2017.2725277
13. Chen, W., Wang, D., Li, K.: Multi-user multi-task computation offloading in green mobile edge cloud computing. IEEE Trans. Serv. Comput. **12**(5), 726–738 (2019). https://doi.org/10.1109/TSC.2018.2826544

14. Sen, T., Shen, H.: Machine learning based timeliness-guaranteed and energy-efficient task assignment in edge computing systems. In: 2019 IEEE 3rd International Conference on Fog and Edge Computing (ICFEC), pp. 1–10 (2019). https://doi.org/10.1109/CFEC.2019.8733153
15. Min, M., Xiao, L., Chen, Y., Cheng, P., Wu, D.: Learning-based computation offloading for IoT devices with energy harvesting. IEEE Trans. Veh. Technol. **68**(2), 1930–1941 (2019). https://doi.org/10.1109/TVT.2018.2890685
16. Alibaba cluster trace program. https://github.com/alibaba/clusterdata
17. Alibaba FaaSNet. https://github.com/ds2-lab/FaaSNet
18. EUA datasets. https://github.com/swinedge/eua-dataset

Improving IoT Services Through Business-Process-Aligned Modeling Method

Jianhang Hu[1,2(✉)], Guiling Wang[1,2], Hai Wang[1,2], Wentao Bai[1,2], Junhua Li[1,2], and Jian Yu[3]

[1] Beijing Key Laboratory on Integration and Analysis of Large-Scale Stream Data, Beijing, China
hjh731995@163.com

[2] North China University of Technology, Beijing 100144, China
wangguiling@ncut.edu.cn

[3] Department of Computer Science, Auckland University of Technology, Auckland, New Zealand

Abstract. In recent years, the Internet of Things (IoT) has facilitated the transformation of various traditional systems into a more convenient form of interaction and integration among people, machines, and things. In industry, there exists a significant class of process-oriented information systems, known as Process-aware Information Systems (PAIS), which are supported by business process management (BPM). The aim of business processes is to provide programming paradigms and business logic for IoT, while IoT can facilitate the quick and accurate capture of physical world changes by business processes, enabling them to respond in a timely manner. The heterogeneity in data and protocols among IoT physical entities, along with the continuous nature of their data, poses a challenge for traditional PAIS. These systems lack strict temporal semantics, and their business process event interaction mechanisms only apply to discrete events, making it difficult to efficiently handle continuous events. To address this challenge, this paper proposes a new IoT service model that has the capability to handle and respond to continuous IoT events, and enable the service to be bound to an executable element in a business process. By doing so, the IoT service can become one of the basic programming components for PAIS to respond promptly to changes in the physical world. The proposed model has been validated through case studies and experimental research, demonstrating its effectiveness and efficiency.

Keywords: IoT Service · Business Process · Event Stream · Service Modeling

1 Introduction

In recent years, with the increasing level of informatization, automation, and intelligence in modern society, the IoT industry has become an indispensable part of the new generation of information technology, and has penetrated into

Z. Wang et al. (Eds.): ICSS 2023, CCIS 1844, pp. 57–71, 2023.
https://doi.org/10.1007/978-981-99-4402-6_5

various industries in modern society [1]. IoT technology facilitates the interconnection of physical devices with the virtual world, enabling improved levels of automation. With a multitude of sensors deployed in the business environment, real-time collection of vast amounts of data is possible. This data includes implicitly reflected information on system behavior and external factors, providing a wealth of intermediate information that can be used to optimize responses to dynamic changes in the business process or business process management [2]. As the number of IoT devices continues to increase, enterprises can benefit from the integration of IoT data and BPM to provide new services to customers or improve existing business processes [3]. At the same time, for various IoT applications, there lacks an effective programming paradigm that can improve the business value of massive data and bring value to business processes.

However, there are still some challenges that need to be addressed to ensure that these two fields can benefit from each other. First, IoT and networked physical systems provide a large amount of streaming data in the form of event streams. If BPM directly connects to specific IoT devices, the large amount of data generated by IoT devices may cause too many process instances to be generated, occupying too much memory overhead, and unable to demonstrate the advantageous characteristics of business processes. Therefore, there is an urgent need for a method to transform the data generated by IoT devices into the data that BPM really needs to improve work efficiency. To this end, using service modeling to abstract and provide IoT data to business processes is a promising approach worth exploring.

This paper aims to enhance the current services through business-process-aligned modeling method. Three main contributions are proposed in this paper to address the current issues: 1. Introducing a new IoT service modeling method for encapsulating the processing logic of heterogeneous and continuous IoT device generated event streams. 2. Extending BPMN to enable IoT service model perception, and binding of IoT device generated event streams during the process execution through simplified configuration. This can achieve continuous processing of IoT business event streams without interrupting the normal process execution. 3. Validating the superiority of using IoT services in business processes and the efficiency of encapsulating IoT service processing of business event streams in a physical business process case study.

The rest of this paper is organized as follows: Sect. 2 discusses the related work. Section 3 introduces the IoT service model, and Sect. 4 describes the specific implementation of binding IoT services to business processes. In Sect. 5, a case study on hazardous chemical transportation business process is used to illustrate the feasibility and efficiency of IoT services. Section 6 concludes the article and discusses future directions.

2 Related Work

With the development of the IoT, two key challenges have emerged: communication with things and management of things. The most relevant challenge is integrating different devices for task coordination. Current solutions typically involve a single IoT device, but IoT components from different platforms often lack a unified protocol and standard for data format, communication protocol, and interface definition. The service paradigm is a key means to overcome these challenges. It abstracts IoT devices into IoT services, which, through service mapping, are viewed as unified IoT objects [4].

2.1 IoT Service Modeling Methods

To address the above issues, Service-Oriented Architecture (SOA) has been proven to be suitable [5]. SOA provides a standardized way of describing IoT services and provides service description information for callers. It uses a unified service based pattern to describe IoT devices and implements descriptions of different components at the service level [6].

Subsequently, in the work, the use of traditional service patterns was explored by extending the existing service model OWL-S [7]. However, the protocol stack of SOAP/WSDL services is mainly designed for resource rich infrastructures and is not suitable for resource limited IoT services. Additionally, the model does not involve modeling methods for heterogeneous devices in complex scenarios. Later, some work attempted to extend IoT services on the newer RSETFul, using RESTful web services with lightweight protocols and data formats to reduce service overhead [8]. These methods typically formulate their own private service description patterns, resulting in limitations in their application in the IoT field, with relatively weak capabilities in describing IoT devices and objects.

2.2 Business-Process-Aligned Modeling Methods for IoT Services

It is first noted that a significant barrier to effectively integrating practical resources into business processes is the absence of IoT sensors, actuators, and their local components in business process models.

Deploying IoT based solutions in the business domain requires addressing issues beyond technological complexity. IoT device networks should be properly integrated with BPM infrastructure, allowing the business layer to leverage online and historical data collected by sensors. To handle raw data streams from IoT devices, a method combining IoT sensor data collection with BPM technology is proposed in [9]. The authors emphasize how providing immediate data collected from sensors to BPM tools can help organizations achieve cost savings and efficiency improvements.

The issue of event stream processing is also discussed in [10]. Stefan et al. designed a component model called Eventlets to encapsulate event stream processing functionality for integrating event streams from mobile devices and sensors. Although this approach addresses the issue of event stream processing, the entire engineering process relies on developers designing Eventlets, which inadvertently raises the barrier of entry for this technology, making it less user friendly for business users.

Subsequently, Stefan et al. began applying Eventlets in the BPM field, where they explored the use of event stream processing in BPM. Although this approach can handle IoT device event stream tasks in processes and does not burden business processes with additional workload, it creates an additional process instance for each event stream SPU, which is feasible in non-industrial environments but not suitable for high concurrency scenarios [11].

Overall, current attempts to integrate BPM and IoT do not provide a satisfactory solution, whether from the perspective of event stream processing or from the perspective of new models. In this paper, an IoT service model is proposed that can be perceived by business processes and can handle large scale IoT raw event streams without burdening business processes. The proposed model can also reduce the intrusiveness of BPM, making it easier to use.

3 IoT Service Modeling

This article considers various physical devices, including sensors, tags, and actuators, as physical resources, while IoT services serve as their digital twin representatives and enable access to them. This chapter will first provide a detailed introduction to IoT services from the perspective of the IoT service architecture model, followed by an overview of the components of the IoT service model, and then the six parts of the IoT service model will be introduced.

3.1 IoT Service Architecture Model

This section will introduce the architecture model of IoT services, which is the primary foundation for designing and implementing IoT services. In the initial modeling process of the IoT service model, it is necessary to provide the functionality to encapsulate the ability to read/write the properties of IoT devices and manage their lifecycles. As shown in Fig. 1, there are many steps involved in transforming individual IoT devices in the physical world into a usable IoT service that can be used by BPM.

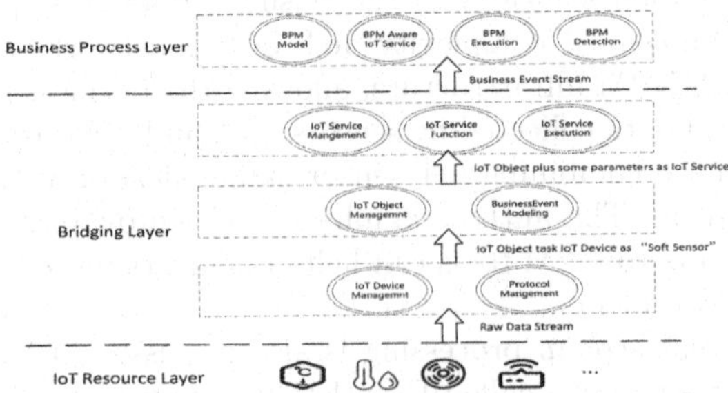

Fig. 1. IoT Service Architecture Model Diagram.

The physical resource layer forms the foundation of the IoT service model by collecting and providing data while supporting hardware and network requirements for data transmission and storage. It consists of IoT devices, sensors, actuators, network devices, etc. These devices come in various types such as sensors, cameras, smart home appliances, and smart medical devices. They collect raw data and store it temporarily on the IoT platform through access gateways.

The bridging layer facilitates data processing and transformation from the physical resource layer for efficient use by the BP layer. The IoT device sublayer models the event stream generated by IoT devices, while the IoT object sublayer combines IoT devices based on common characteristics. The IoT service sublayer is a further abstract combination of IoT objects, supplemented by service interface components for IoT service input and output. These components ensure seamless communication among the layers and optimal performance of the IoT services.

The BP layer is the highest layer in the IoT service model, closely related to user and business needs. In this layer, data is analyzed and processed, and feedback and results required by users are provided. The purpose of the application layer is to meet business needs and help users better understand and manage IoT devices, sensors, and data. The design of the application layer needs to consider factors such as user needs, business process requirements, and data value.

3.2 IoT Service Model

The IoT service model structure is shown in the Fig. 2 below. These submodels together constitute the IoT service model, which can help developers better understand and design IoT systems.

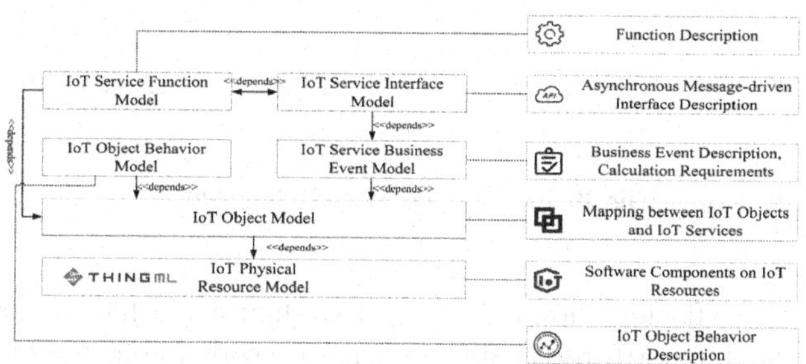

Fig. 2. Physical Resource Model Diagram.

The physical resource model describes the characteristics and properties of various physical devices, sensors, and other hardware resources that serve as IoT data sources. The IoT object model provides an abstract combination of IoT devices involved in the physical resource model, while the IoT object behavior model characterizes the behavior of IoT objects. The business event model not only describes the generation of business events in the entire IoT service but can also be used for the automatic generation of code files on the server side of the IoT service. The IoT service functional model describes the service's features, while the IoT service interface model describes the automatic generation of client side code files and interaction methods for the service. These models can help developers design more efficient IoT systems.

IoT Physical Resource Model. The Physical Resource Model is a specific description and extension of the Physical Resource Layer in the IoT service architecture model. The Physical Resource Model is typically used to describe the hardware resources in an IoT system, such as physical devices, sensors, actuators, as well as their connections and relationships. In this paper, the ThingML model [12] is introduced as a Physical Resource Model and is expanded to be associated with specific IoT devices. ThingML provides a modeling and code generation platform for resource constrained IoT applications. With ThingML, developers can focus on high-level design correctness without spending a lot of time solving many problems related to heterogeneous underlying systems, platform compatibility, and model to implementation correctness. The specific structure of the Physical Resource Model is shown in Fig. 3.

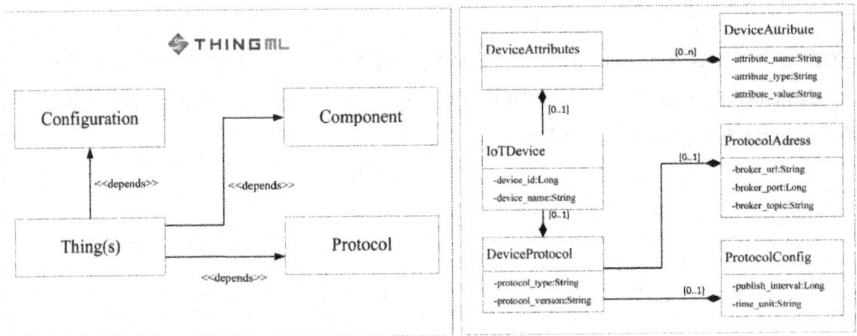

Fig. 3. IoT Service Model Diagram.

In Fig. 3, the left side shows the model configuration file that needs to be written, and the ThingML toolchain can generate code based on this model file. The right side shows the modeling of IoT devices after obtaining the IoT device data source based on the generated code. Firstly, the Things and Configurations on the left side are built based on components and protocols. In ThingML, a Thing can be composed of one or more components and protocols to represent a physical resource or a software component. A Configuration is a combination of Things that represents the composition and configuration of the entire software system. Therefore, Things and Configurations are used to describe the software system level, while components and protocols are used to describe the physical resource model level.

IoT Object Model. This section introduces the IoT object model in the IoT service model. This model is a part of the IoT service model that provides a mapping relationship between physical devices and software sensors. It can be used to allow application developers to represent and manage IoT devices at an abstract level. The model diagram of the IoT object is shown in Fig. 4.

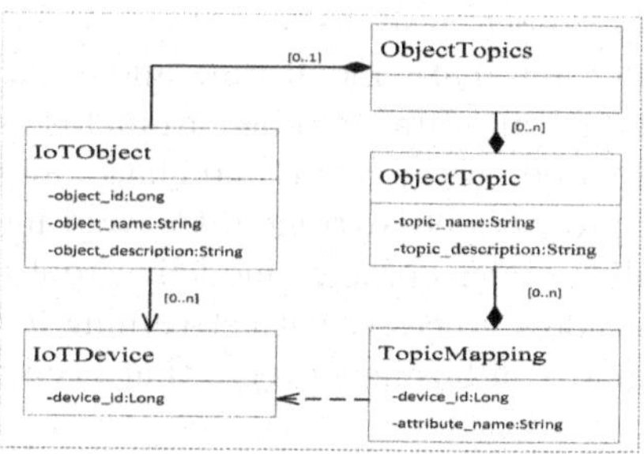

Fig. 4. IoT Objcet Model Diagram.

IoT objects can have different properties and methods that describe the characteristics and functionality of the device. Each IoT object requires a unique identifier for a temperature sensor could be its serial number provided by the manufacturer. The IoT device model corresponding to the IoT object needs to be defined in the IoT object model, that is, which specific physical device the object is mapped to. The specific mapping relationship is implemented using device_id, and each IoT object can contain one or more IoT devices. The IoT object address is an integration of all the addresses of the included IoT devices, and ObjectTopics contains topic information for the IoT object, including multiple ObjectTopics, where each ObjectTopic represents a topic and includes the topic_name and topic_description. TopicMapping represents the mapping relationship of the topic, which can include multiple DeviceIDs and AttributeNames, representing the devices and attributes involved in the topic.

IoT Object Behavior Model. In the IoT service model, the IoT object behavior model is a higher layer on top of the physical resource model and the IoT object model, which is used to describe the behavior of IoT objects. The definition of the IoT object behavior model includes the state of the IoT object and the behavior of the IoT object, where the behavior mainly refers to the actions performed by the IoT object and the interaction between the IoT objects.

In prior work on this topic, it was proposed to aggregate and abstract raw sensor data into higher level business events and bind them to elements in the business process. The article suggested that IoT services should provide the ability to encapsulate the reading/writing of IoT object related properties, and that this should be accomplished using a micro-process approach to model IoT objects. Micro-processes draw on the idea of data-driven process management, using the concepts of objects and object relationships to strengthen the model. Since IoT objects can be easily mapped to these objects, it is reasonable to use micro-processes as modeling elements for IoT sensing business processes [13].

Subsequently, in the research of other students in this project, a deep study was conducted on the IoT object behavior model, and a method for modeling IoT-aware business micro-processes was proposed. The modeling was centered on a single IoT object and integrated the MAPE-K model thinking, mapping the behavior status of the IoT object instance lifecycle to the micro-process instance status, to achieve circular automatic monitoring and adjustment of a single IoT object. Furthermore, based on data obtained from IoT sensing devices, business rules were defined based on the SASE+language, and meaningful business events for the business process were extracted to avoid interference from irrelevant events. Additionally, a micro-process modeling tool prototype system was designed to integrate business processes with streaming IoT sensing data, significantly reducing the number of business events that need to be processed [14].

IoT Service Business Event Model. In IoT systems, business events typically refer to IoT data streams being transformed into events that have business significance. In this process, IoT data needs to be analyzed and processed to extract information that is relevant to the business, ultimately forming a business event. The business event model describes this transformation process and the business events also serve as the output results of IoT services for better utilization. The model diagram is shown in Fig. 5.

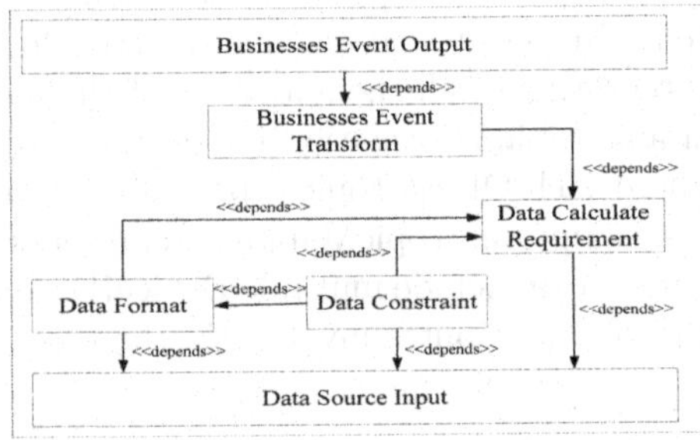

Fig. 5. Business Event Model Diagram.

The role of the business event model in IoT systems is not only to define the process of converting raw data into business events, but also to automatically generate IoT service server code based on the business event model and deploy it for execution. Typically, it includes the following aspects:

Data Source Input: Data enters the stream processing system as a raw data stream through a unified interface into the message middleware. The data source can be data generated by existing production systems or data generated by simulation based on user configurations.

Data Format and Constraint: Based on the user defined data format and range constraints, the multi level structure of raw data is parsed into several single level data items that can be processed by the system, and the value range of the data items is checked. In the generated code, it is responsible for handling abnormal values.

Data Calculate requirement: After the preliminary processing of the data, the requirements are transformed according to the specified calculation requirements and Flink operator specifications.

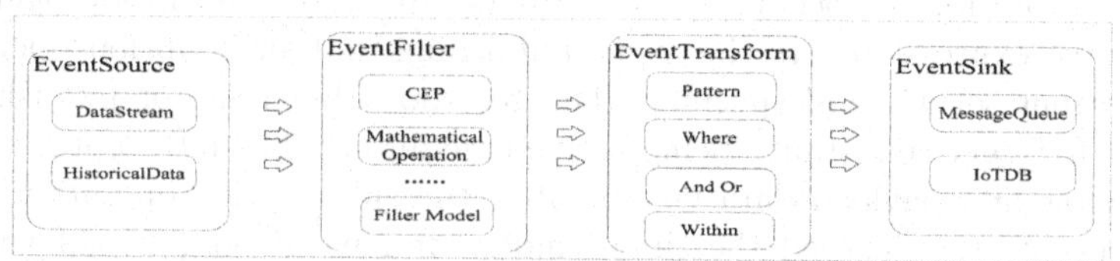

Fig. 6. IoT Service Server Structure Diagram.

Business Event Output: The business event is sent to the business process, or it is persisted to the database for further analysis and mining. The computation results can also be visualized and presented to users. The structure after the IoT service server is automatically generated is shown in the Fig. 6.

IoT Service Interface Model. The IoT Service Interface Model is an important component of the IoT Service Model that describes how the IoT Service Client can be generated and conveniently used. In the IoT Service Interface Model, the service provider can define a set of standard interfaces for client use, as well as customize interfaces to extend the functionality of the IoT service. The automatic generation of the IoT Service Interface Model introduces the standard of AsyncAPI, and some extensions have been made on this basis to comply with the standards of the IoT Service Model, as shown in Fig. 7, where green components represent custom extensions.

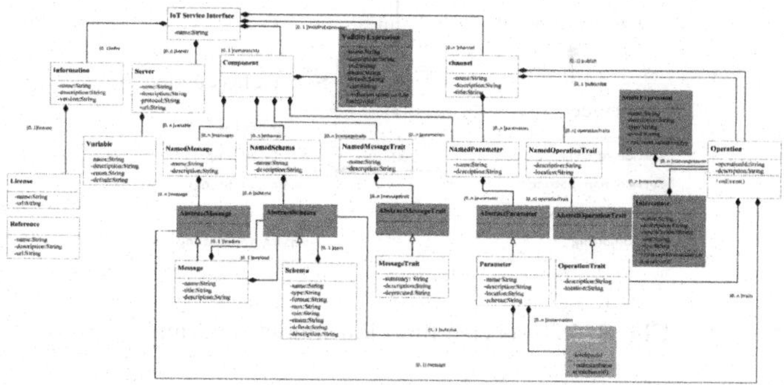

Fig. 7. IoT Service Interface Model Diagram.

The IoT Service Interface Model has been extended based on the AsyncAPI [15] specification, adding relevant class diagrams such as instantiation expression, validity expression, static expression, and interceptor. The instantiation expression can instantiate the IoT object to a specific object, thereby representing the event flow information included in the specified IoT object. The static expression belongs to the subscription level filter, where users can choose to subscribe to specific types of events after the subscription operation. The validity expression sets the event publishing and subscription operations of the current service and specifies when to stop subscribing or publishing to avoid the IoT service instance being active indefinitely. The interceptor sets the time window and payload data volume after the subscription operation occurs to filter events that exceed the time window or have lower payload volumes. These extensions improve the AsyncAPI specification, making the IoT Service Interface Model more applicable to actual application scenarios and enhancing its scalability and usability.

IoT Service Function Model. The IoT service functional model is an important component of the IoT system, which describes the characteristics and properties of the IoT service. It defines the behavior and functionality of the IoT service.

Service description is an important component of the IoT service model, which provides information about the service, including its name, description, input and output parameters, and service invocation method, etc. As shown in Fig. 8, the service description typically includes the following aspects:

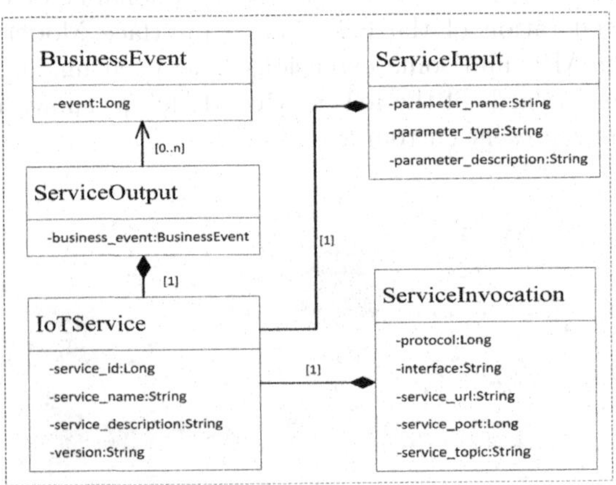

Fig. 8. IoT service function model diagram.

Firstly, the service name and description (IoTService): The service name should clearly express the service's functionality, and should also include descriptive and version information to help users understand the specific features of the service.

Secondly, input parameters (ServiceInput) and output parameters (ServiceOutput): The input and output parameters of the service should be well-defined so that users understand how to use the service and the format of the data that the service outputs. Each IoT service can contain multiple input parameters, and each parameter is unique. In ServiceInput, each parameter is accurately described by defining its name and type, etc. ServiceOutput is mainly associated with the format and content of business events.

Thirdly, service invocation method (ServiceInvocation): The service invocation method should be well-defined, including the service protocol, interface, and port, etc. The invocation of IoT services is asynchronous and uses the AsyncAPI method to connect them through the Kafka message queue middleware.

4 Binding IoT Service to Business Process

This section mainly introduces the way of binding IoT services in BPM processes. The flow engine uses Flowable and BPMN2.0 specifications [16]. Flowable is a lightweight business process engine that can be used to deploy BPMN2.0 process definitions and create process instances for these definitions. This article does not introduce new modeling elements for extension, but combines existing elements. The IoT service is represented in the form of a combination of human tasks and message boundary non-interrupt events in BPMN2.0. Based on the opensource code of Flowable, these two representation elements are merged into one to represent the IoT service. When building a process, this IoT service can be dragged out and associated with the actual IoT service in the IoT service library, and then customized configuration can be performed on this service before deploying and executing the process.

During the execution of the business process, if it reaches the IoT service, the branch of the process is automatically terminated here and the corresponding IoT service is executed. We designed an IoT service helper developing framework to help developers to generate and deploy the corresponding IoT service based on the request received. The business event results generated by the IoT service will be sent to the Kafka topic. The consumer of IoT service, which is called IoT Stub, will subscribe and receive this event stream and bind each event in turn to the message boundary non-interrupt events in the BPM process, thus executing the subsequent process of the message boundary non-interrupt events. At this time, it is equivalent to starting to receive the business events generated by the IoT service and continuously executing the subsequent processes of the IoT service. If the human task at the IoT service is not submitted or does not meet the completion conditions, the IoT service will continue to obtain the business event output of the IoT service to trigger subsequent processes. The core implementation is as follows in Fig. 9.

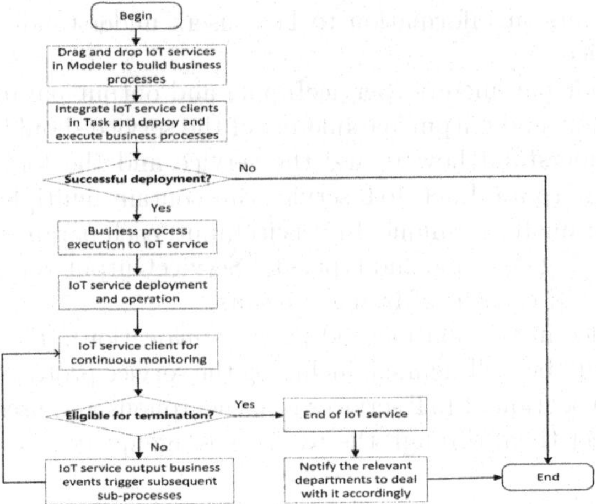

Fig. 9. BPM binding IoT Service.

5 Experiments

In this section, we use a case study of hazardous chemical transportation on the "Yantai-Dalian" route to demonstrate the feasibility and effectiveness of IoT services [17]. A sea transportation process for hazardous chemicals was created using the BPMN2.0 specification, as shown in Fig. 10. After the cargo management department confirms the cargo order and assigns the ship for transportation, the temperature detection IoT service in ship monitoring is activated to monitor the LNG tank containers loaded on the ship. Once cargo that violates temperature conditions is detected during transportation, the corresponding follow operation for handling the cargo is triggered. If the situation is serious, the ship may be notified to return for cargo redistribution. The IoT service continues to run and monitor until the ship reaches its destination, at which point the cargo management department confirms the cargo arrival and terminates the process.

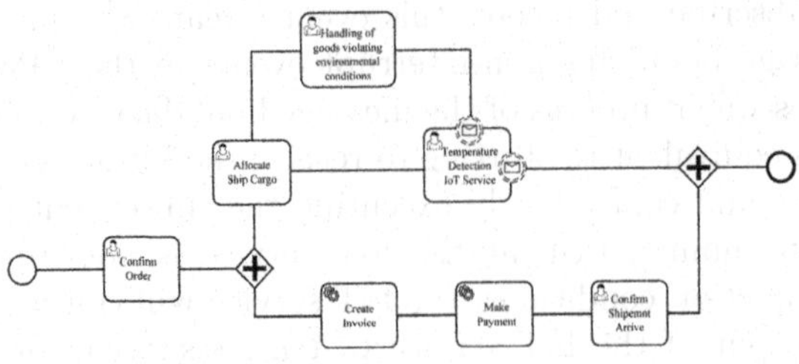

Fig. 10. Hazardous Chemicals Transportation Diagram.

In the above process, we use the output of the business event to continuously trigger the follow process for "cargo violating temperature environmental conditions," in order to monitor the temperature situation of the cargo carried on the ship. The process will stop at the "temperature detection IoT service" until the ship reaches its destination or the task is canceled due to timeout.

5.1 Experimental Environment

Server configuration parameters: Intel i5-6300HQ 2.30 GHz, 16 GB memory, 64-bit operating system. The current testing environment is a simulated event generator, namely a temperature sensor (range: 0 °C–50 °C, testing accuracy: ±0.5 °C).

The experimental procedure involves sending 1000, 3000, 5000, 7000, 9000 simulated event data per second to both the IoT service system and Esper to calculate the corresponding execution time under the same conditions. The execution time in the experiment is calculated based on the time difference between the IoT service and Esper engine's processing of the first and last data.

5.2 Experimental Results

In the execution of the aforementioned process definition in the BPM, the IoT service involves the processing of a large amount of event streams generated by IoT devices. In order to test the efficiency of IoT service execution, a comparison was made with the Esper Complex Event Processing (CEP) engine, which is one of the most common event stream processing applications. The test results showed that the IoT service had faster event stream processing speed, lower overhead, and a simplified programming model for event stream processing components. The Flink engine was used as the core execution engine of the IoT service, and Kafka was used as the JMS proxy. Before the IoT service processing, the original large amount of IoT event streams was filtered based on the filtering conditions in the XML configuration file, thereby further improving the efficiency of IoT service execution.

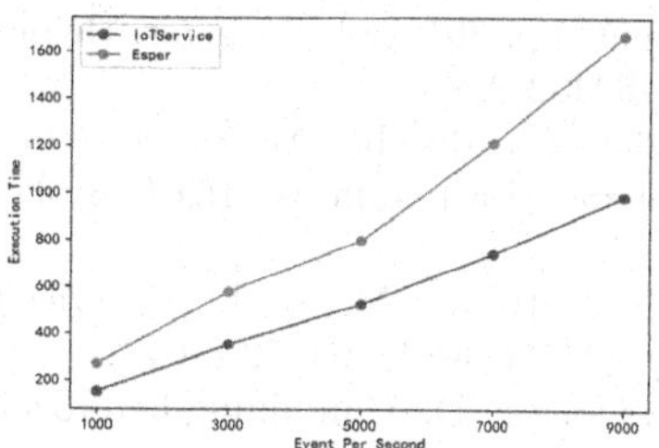

Fig. 11. IoT Service Vs. Esper Execution Time Comparison Diagram.

As a test case, we modeled the triggering factor of the temperature monitoring IoT service as an abnormal event when the temperature is greater than

26 °C, which is also the triggering factor for Esper based on this condition. In order to determine the implementation of the two different solutions of IoT service and Esper, we continuously increased the event rate for comparison. The results, shown in Fig. 11, indicate that as the number of events sent per second increases, the execution time of both IoT service and Esper also increases, but clearly the execution time of IoT service is shorter than Esper, indicating that the efficiency of IoT service in executing event processing is higher than that of traditional CEP engines.

6 Conclusion

This paper proposes a new approach to modeling IoT services, which provides a detailed description of the architecture of IoT services and the components of the IoT service model. It enables the encapsulation of different IoT devices to form IoT objects and, by using business event models, converts the raw IoT data stream into useful business events according to the relevant rules. At the lowest level, the physical resource model, IoT server, and IoT client can all be automatically generated using different methods, which provides convenience for the development and use of IoT services. In order to make IoT services more convenient for BPM usage, this paper also extends BPM to provide a means of binding BPM processes and IoT service resources, making the connection between BPM and IoT services more closely linked.

Acknowledgment. This work is supported by the International Cooperation and Exchange Program of National Natural Science Foundation of China (No. 62061136006) and the Key Program of National Natural Science Foundation of China (No. 61832004).

References

1. Janiesch, C., Koschmider, A., Mecella, M., et al.: The internet-of-things meets business process management: mutual benefits and challenges. CoRR (2017)
2. Weske, M.: Business process management architectures. In: Weske, M. (ed.) Business Process Management, pp. 351–384. Springer, Heidelberg (2019). https://doi.org/10.1007/978-3-662-59432-2_8
3. Janiesch, C., Koschmider, A., Mecella, M., et al.: The internet of things meets business process management: a manifesto. IEEE Syst. Man Cybern. Mag. **6**(4), 34–44 (2020)
4. Bouguettaya, A., Singh, M., Huhns, M., et al.: A service computing manifesto: the next 10 years. Commun. ACM **60**(4), 64–72 (2017)
5. Gama, K., Touseau, L., Donsez, D.: Combining heterogeneous service technologies for building an Internet of Things middleware. Comput. Commun. **35**(4), 405–417 (2012)
6. Fanjiang, Y.-Y., Syu, Y., et al.: An overview and classification of service description approaches in automated service composition research. IEEE Trans. Serv. Comput. **10**(2), 176–189 (2015)

7. Issarny, V., Bouloukakis, G., Georgantas, N., Billet, B.: Revisiting service-oriented architecture for the IoT: a middleware perspective. In: Sheng, Q.Z., Stroulia, E., Tata, S., Bhiri, S. (eds.) ICSOC 2016. LNCS, vol. 9936, pp. 3–17. Springer, Cham (2016). https://doi.org/10.1007/978-3-319-46295-0_1
8. Taherkordi, A., Eliassen, F.: Scalable modeling of cloud-based IoT services for smart cities, pp. 1–6. IEEE (2016)
9. Schönig, S., Ackermann, L., Jablonski, S., et al.: IoT meets BPM: a bidirectional communication architecture for IoT-aware process execution. Softw. Syst. Model. **19**, 1443–1459 (2020)
10. Appel, S., Frischbier, S., Freudenreich, T., et al.: Eventlets: components for the integration of event streams with SOA, pp. 1–9. IEEE (2012)
11. Appel, S., Kleber, P., Frischbier, S., et al.: Modeling and execution of event stream processing in business processes. Inf. Syst. **46**, 140–156 (2014)
12. Harrand, N., Fleurey, F., Morin, B., et al.: ThingML: a language and code generation framework for heterogeneous targets. In: Proceedings of the ACM/IEEE 19th International Conference on Model Driven Engineering Languages and Systems, pp. 125–135 (2016)
13. Gruhn, V., et al.: BRIBOT: towards a service-based methodology for bridging business processes and IoT big data. In: Hacid, H., Kao, O., Mecella, M., Moha, N., Paik, H. (eds.) ICSOC 2021. LNCS, vol. 13121, pp. 597–611. Springer, Cham (2021). https://doi.org/10.1007/978-3-030-91431-8_37
14. Xiaoxuan, W., Guiling, W.: An IoT-aware business micro-process modeling method. J. Zhengzhou Univ. (2023)
15. Gómez, A., Iglesias-Urkia, M., Urbieta, A., et al.: A model-based approach for developing event-driven architectures with AsyncAPI. In: Proceedings of the 23rd ACM/IEEE International Conference on Model Driven Engineering Languages and Systems, pp. 121–131 (2020)
16. Dijkman, R.M., Dumas, M., Ouyang, C.: Semantics and analysis of business process models in BPMN. Inf. Softw. Technol. **50**(12), 1281–1294 (2008)
17. Wang, G., Fang, J., Wang, J., et al.: Service-based event penetration from IoT sensors to businesses: a case study, pp. 72–79. IEEE (2022)

Edge Services Reliability

Research on Cascading Failure of Complex Networks Based on Edge Weight and Capacity Allocation Strategy

Jingmin Yao[1], FanChao Meng[1(✉)], Xuefeng Piao[1], and Xuequan Zhou[2]

[1] School of Computer Science and Technology, Harbin Institute of Technology at Weihai, Weihai 264209, China
fcmeng@hit.edu.cn

[2] School of Economics and Management, Harbin Institute of Technology at Weihai, Weihai 264209, China

Abstract. In real life, complex networks may encounter uncertain attack events at any time, which may lead to large-scale interruption of various services provided by the network. In order to effectively prevent the occurrence of cascading failures in complex networks, this paper studies the impact of edge weight and capacity allocation strategies on complex network attack resistance. By analyzing the dynamic evolution mechanism of edge cascading fault propagation, a complex network edge cascading fault load model with parameters is constructed. Using the failure normalized F index to analyze the network crash threshold under different attack methods, an improved edge remaining capacity allocation strategy is proposed and a simulated annealing algorithm is used to solve the problem. The focus of this paper is to improve the overall resilience of complex networks against cascading failures, by using the strategy proposed in this paper, we observe the change of network invulnerability after attacks on real express networks and scale-free networks. The experimental results show that comparing the five capacity allocation strategies, the improved side residual capacity allocation strategy greatly improves the network crash threshold of the two networks under different attack methods, and enhances the dynamic resistance of the network.

Keywords: Cascading Failure · Capacity Allocation Strategy · Invulnerability · BA Network · Express Network

1 Introduction

In recent years, problems caused by cascading failures have frequently occurred in key infrastructure networks such as transportation networks [1], Internet [2], supply chain networks [3], and communication networks. This has seriously affected

This work was supported by the Natural Science Foundation of Shandong Province in China under grant ZR2020MF032.

Z. Wang et al. (Eds.): ICSS 2023, CCIS 1844, pp. 75–90, 2023.
https://doi.org/10.1007/978-981-99-4402-6_6

people's daily lives and caused huge economic losses to the country. Cascade failure refers to the phenomenon where a small number of nodes or edges fail, leading to consecutive failures in other parts of the network. For example, the large-scale power outages in parts of the Northeast United States and eastern Canada in August 2003 [4], and the internet collapse caused by congestion [2] are considered typical cases of cascading failure. Faced with strong practical needs, this type of cascading failure problem has attracted widespread attention in the academic community.

At present, there are some achievements in the research on cascading failure invulnerability of complex networks. Predecessors proposed a variety of cascading failure models based on the real network structure and characteristics, and studied the performance of different network structures for attack intensity under specific circumstances. In previous studies, many works only focused on the static characteristics of the network, and seldom considered the dynamic characteristics of the load in the real network. In order to have a more in-depth study of the real network, many scholars have further studied the dynamic change process of the load on the network model based on the cascading failure model constructed from the original static point of view of the network. For example, Motter et al. [5] proposed a cascading failure model, and found that when the network load is non-uniform, the high load of the failed node will more easily lead to cascading failures. Later, the research results of Crucitti et al. [6] also showed that the more uneven the flow or betweenness distribution in the network, the larger the range of successive failures in the network. Furthermore, Wang et al. [7,8] studied how edge attacks induce cascading failures in scale-free networks, and studied the general robustness of weighted networks to cascading failures using three different models. Wang et al. [9] studied the problem of successive failures caused by network attacks and edge loads, and proposed a model of successive failures based on overloaded edges with collapse probability. On this basis, a new strategy of "degree and edge double attack" was designed, and verify the effectiveness of the policy. The above research provides a certain reference value for further research on the mechanism of network faults and defense strategies. Later, Sturaro et al. [10] studied a realistic model for the propagation of cascading faults in interacting networks, taking into account the interdependence and complexity between the networks. Wang et al. [11] considered the influence of edge weight and coupling strength between multi-layer networks on the load in the dependent network, and constructed a cascading fault load model with adjustable parameters on the dependent network.

In order to enhance the invulnerability of complex networks under attack, not only the content related to cascading failures must be studied, but also the capacity allocation strategy should be studied and optimized to prevent cascading from spreading throughout the network. To this end, Sun et al. [12] explored considering the dynamics of cascading faults and the uncertainty of capacity allocation, and proposed a capacity matching model based on scale-free networks to defend against cascading faults. Li et al. [13] proposed a scale-free network dynamic invulnerability optimization method based on a limited resource model, and analyzed the influence of different parameters in different models on the network invulnerability performance. This research provides a new idea and method for the optimization of network invulnerability performance. Jin et al. [14] proposed a method to optimize the allocation of resources when the urban rail transit network is maliciously attacked, and verified the effectiveness of the method. In addition, Oded Cats et al. [15] studied the impact of different capacity allocation strategies on the robustness of public transport systems by evaluating the importance of different nodes in the network, and a capacity allocation method based on network structure is proposed to improve the robustness of public transportation system. Liang et al. [16] studied the cascading failure invulnerability of the network structure and operation failure of the express delivery network under the impact of emergencies and demand surges, and compared three capacity allocation strategies. Although the existing research on cascading failures on complex networks has achieved certain results, there are still deficiencies, for example, how to effectively quantify the initial load of real network edges and deeply analyze the impact of network node and edge weights on network invulnerability, is there a better way to optimize the invulnerability of the express network.

Based on this, this paper considers the node degree value and edge weight of the complex network, uses the common network edge initial load definition, and cascades the failure evolution mechanism according to the edge failure, node failure, and load redistribution mechanism on the failed edge. Firstly, a complex network edge cascading failure load model with parameters is constructed. Then compare the influence of random attack and malicious attack on network invulnerability at different attack intensities, and then propose a new capacity allocation strategy, and use multiple strategies to compare to prove the effectiveness of the new strategy. Finally, the express network and scale-free network are used for numerical simulation, and the overall protection strategy of the express network is given, so that the proposed cascading failure model and capacity allocation strategy can be applied to real networks to achieve the purpose of improving the dynamic invulnerability of the network.

2 Cascading Failure Model for Complex Networks

2.1 Edge-Based Cascading Failure Model

After the abstract description, the real complex network is generally represented by a graph composed of edges and nodes. Based on the topological structure of the real express delivery network, this paper describes the real complex network as an undirected weighted graph without considering the flow direction of the load in the network.

Realistic complex network model with dynamic flows represented by an undirected weighted graph $G = (V, E, W, L, C)$. Among them, the set V represents the point set of the graph. The E matrix represents the edge in the network, where e_{ij} is the edge between nodes v_i and v_j, if $e_{ij} = 1$, it means that there is an edge between v_i and v_j, otherwise it means that there is no edge. The W matrix represents the weight value of the edge between v_i and v_j in the network. The L matrix represents the load of the edge in the network, where l_{ij} is the instant load of the edge between nodes v_i and v_j, and we set it as the initial load at a certain time point during the research. The C matrix represents the capacity of edges between nodes in the network.

Edge Weight. This paper introduces the concept of edge weight when constructing the complex network cascading failure model. For complex networks that are common in real life, nodes with large general degrees play a more important role in the network. Therefore, the edge connecting two nodes with large degree is relatively more important. Referring to previous studies on the definition of edge weights in cascading failure modeling [11], it is assumed that the weight $w_{ij}(t)$ of edge ij in a complex network at time t is related to the degree of nodes at both ends of the edge, which is defined as:

$$w_{ij}(t) = (k_i(t)k_j(t))^{\alpha} \tag{1}$$

In formula 1, α is an adjustable parameter, which controls the size and difference of edge weights. The larger the value of α, the greater the weight difference of edges in the network, $k_i(t)$ and $k_j(t)$ represent the degree of i and j at both ends of edge ij at time t, $w_{ij}(t)$ is the degree of edge ij in the weight value at time t.

Initial Load of the Edge. In the model of this paper, it is assumed that the initial load of the edge is based on the weight of the edge, and the initial load $L_{ij}(0)$ of the edge ij in the network is a function of the edge weight $w_{ij}(0)$, then:

$$L_{ij}(0) = \mu w_{ij}(0) \tag{2}$$

In formula 2, μ is an adjustable parameter, and its value affects the intensity of the initial load. In this paper, the value of $\mu = 1$, $L_{ij}(0) = w_{ij}(0)$.

Capacity of Edges. When Moreno et al. [17] adopted the "load-capacity" model to study the cascading failure of the network, the model assumes that information is transmitted between nodes along the shortest path. Referring to previous studies, in the actual network, since the ability of each edge to handle the load is usually limited by the cost, so assuming that the ability of each edge is proportional to the initial load of the edge, the ability of edge ij is:

$$C_{ij} = (1 + \beta)L_{ij}(0) \tag{3}$$

In formula 3, β is the tolerance coefficient of the network, which controls the total amount of redundant resources ΔC, that is, the larger β is, the stronger the ability to handle the load is, and the higher the cost of network investment is, that is to say, if the edge with higher initial load fails, it is more likely to cause cascading failures.

Capacity Allocation Strategy. Since cascading failures occur in real life due to overloading of the load on the side of the crash. Therefore, when an edge ij is overloaded and fails at time t, it is necessary to allocate the capacity carried by this edge to the edge connecting two nodes according to a certain allocation strategy. On the basis of previous research, this paper chooses the following four allocation strategies.

Edge Capacity Allocation Strategy. When the edge ij is overloaded and fails, the load borne by the failed edge should be distributed to the neighbor edges connecting two nodes, and the optimal allocation should be carried out according to the capacity of the neighbor edges. In other words, the larger the capacity of the neighbor side, the higher the load handling capacity, and the more additional load it can receive. That is, the edge capacity allocation strategy:

$$\Delta L_{im}(t) = \frac{L_{ij}(t-1) \times C_{im}}{\sum_{a \in \Gamma_i} C_{ia} + \sum_{b \in \Gamma_j} C_{jb}} \tag{4}$$

Formula 4 means that when the edge im receives additional load, the total load on the edge exceeds the ability of the edge itself to handle the maximum load, that is, when $L_{im}(t) + \Delta L_{im}(t) > C_{im}$, the edge im fails, the load on the edge will be further distributed to other non-failed neighbor edges according to the principle of local redistribution, causing cascading failures to spread on the express network. Where $\sum_{a \in \Gamma_i} C_{ia}$ and $\sum_{b \in \Gamma_j} C_{jb}$ represent the total load of node i and node j.

Average Capacity Allocation Strategy. When the edge ij is overloaded and fails, the load borne by the failed edge is evenly distributed to the neighbor edges connecting two nodes. That is, the average capacity allocation strategy:

$$\Delta L_{im}(t) = \frac{L_{ij}(t-1)}{m} \tag{5}$$

In formula 5, m represents the total number of neighboring edges of node i and node j at time t.

Degree Preference Capacity Allocation Strategy. When edge ij is overloaded and fails, the load to be allocated is first divided based on the degree of connection between the two nodes of edge ij, and then the optimal allocation is made based on the ability of neighboring edges. Degree preference capacity allocation strategy:

$$\Delta L_{im}(t) = \frac{L_{ij}(t-1) \times C_{im} \times E_i(t)}{(E_i(t) + E_j(t)) \times \left(\sum_{a \in \Gamma_i} C_{ia} + \sum_{b \in \Gamma_j} C_{jb}\right)} \tag{6}$$

In formula 6, C_{im} represents the capacity of edge im, $E_i(t)$ and $E_j(t)$ represent the degree value of i and j at time t, $\sum_{a \in \Gamma_i} C_{ia}$ and $\sum_{b \in \Gamma_j} C_{jb}$ represents the total load of the edges connected to ij.

Online Capacity Allocation Strategy. The principle of the online capacity allocation strategy is taken from the online algorithm. When the network is under attack, the capacity redistribution problem is similar to the box packing problem with a known number of boxes. This strategy allocates according to the maximum acceptable side capacity, and the order of allocation is random. When the edge ij is overloaded and fails, randomly select an edge im, compare $L_{ij}(t)$ with the remaining capacity of the edge im, and allocate the capacity to the maximum capacity of the edge im, if there is a surplus, find the next edge until the end. That is, the online capacity allocation strategy model is:

$$\Delta L_{im}(t-1) = C_{im} - L_{im}(t-1) \tag{7}$$

$$\Delta L_{im}(t) = \begin{cases} \Delta L_{im}(t-1) + L_{ij}(t-1), \Delta L_{im}(t-1) \geq L_{ij}(t-1) \\ C_{im}, \Delta L_{im}(t-1) < L_{ij}(t-1) \end{cases} \tag{8}$$

Formula 8 is the online capacity allocation strategy. $\Delta L_{im}(t-1)$ represents the remaining capacity of im before the edge ij is overloaded and fails. If the remaining capacity is greater than $L_{ij}(t-1)$, it will be increased directly, otherwise it will find the next available edge.

In the above four capacity allocation strategies, when the original load plus the additional load on the neighbor side exceeds its maximum capacity, that is $L_{im}(t) + \Delta L_{im}(t) > C_{im}$, a cascading failure is triggered. At this time, the load on the failed edge should be redistributed to other neighbors until the load of all edges in the network is less than the capacity of the edge, and then the network will return to a stable state. In particular, the edge-based cascading failure model has the following basic assumptions:

There may be many different elements in the real complex network due to different judgment criteria, which correspond to nodes and edges in the model of this paper, that is, the real complex network in this paper only has nodes and edges.

There may be multiple redundant paths in real complex networks, so this paper makes clear that redundant paths already exist when constructing the network, and assumes that there is one or more paths between any two points.

The capacity allocation strategy in this paper is studied based on the traffic in the network, the above constructs an edge-based cascading failure model. Assuming that in this model, the traffic arriving at the leaf nodes is much larger than that at the transit nodes, that is, the traffic arriving at the target node partially during the cascading failure is ignored.

2.2 Dynamic Evolution Process of Cascading Failures in Complex Networks

The dynamic evolution process of cascading failures on the complex network is shown in Fig. 1.

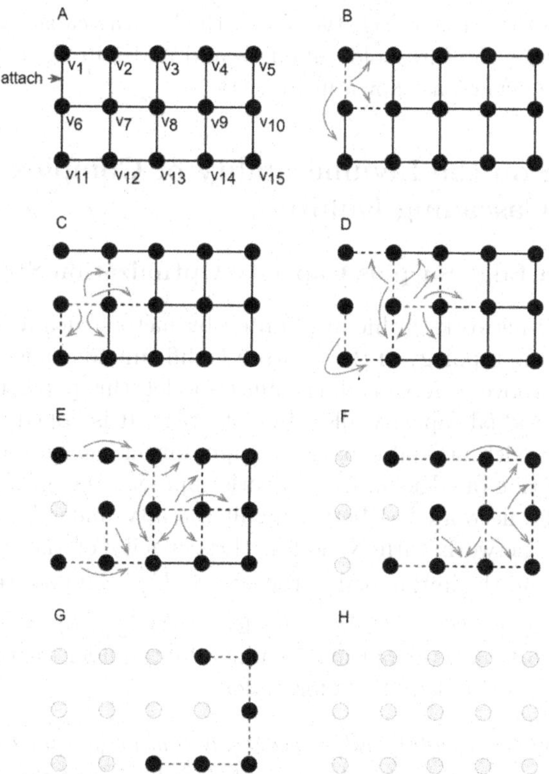

Fig. 1. Dynamic evolution process of cascading failures in complex networks.

The black dots in the figure represent normal running nodes. Black lines represent edges that are functioning normally. White dots represent failed nodes. A dashed red line indicates that the edge has failed. The black dotted line indicates that the edge is about to fail after accepting traffic from the adjacent edge. The yellow arrows indicate the flow direction of the traffic.

In the initial state, the loads on all existing edges in the network are less than or equal to the capacity of the edge, and the network is in a normal operating state, as shown in Fig. 1A. In the actual network, cascading failures are often caused by the failure of some edges in the network. Edge e_{16} in Fig. 1A is attacked, and the traffic on this edge will be allocated to edge e_{16}, e_{67}, e_{6-11} according to a certain capacity allocation strategy, as shown in Fig. 1B. Since the sum of the current flow of edge e_{67} and the flow allocated to this edge by $e_1 6$ is greater than the capacity of edge e_{67}, edge e_{67} fails, as shown in Fig1C. After the edge e_{67} fails, all the traffic undertaken by this edge is distributed to the connected edge, which further leads to the failure of the adjacent edge, as shown in Fig. 1D and Fig. 1E. When the traffic carried by all edges connected to a node in the network is greater than the capacity of the edge, the node also fails, as shown in Fig. 1F and Fig. 1G. When the bearing capacity of all edges in the network reaches the threshold, all edges and nodes in the network fail, and the global failure occurs, as shown in Fig. 1H.

3 Research on the Invulnerability of Complex Networks Against Cascading Failures

3.1 Improved Edge Surplus Capacity Optimization Strategy

Because complex networks in life are limited by factors such as realistic conditions and costs, the topology of the network is difficult to change. Therefore, on the basis of the above edge cascading failure model, this paper proposes a new improved edge residual capacity allocation strategy. It is hoped that a heuristic search algorithm with mutual capacity compensation can be used to make the capacity distribution of edges in the network approach the optimal distribution state, so that the network has better invulnerability under limited redundant resources. For a network with N nodes, the capacity of the network edge is recorded as c_{ij}, and the initial load of the edge is $L_{ij}^{(0)}$. Suppose there is a capacity allocation strategy $\Omega^* = \{L_{ij}^* | ij \in E\}$ to satisfy $\sum_{i,j} L_{ij}^* = \sum_{i,j} L_{ij}^{(0)} + \Delta L$, making the network have the optimal invulnerability under the condition of certain ΔL. Here are some definitions for policies.

Theorem 1. *When cascading failure occurs, assuming that the total failure ratio of the edge reaches t, the load $L_{ij}^{(t)} > C_{ij}$ of the edge ij defines the edge failure, and the edge is recorded as f_{ij}, and the unfailed edge is r_{ij}. Therefore, two sets Right and False can always be determined, satisfying $Right = \{r_{ij} | ij \in E\}$, $False = \{f_{ij} | ij \in E\}$, $Right \cap False = \oslash$,$Right \cup False = E$.*

Theorem 2. *For the improved edge remaining capacity allocation strategy Ω, define two sets of Givers and Receivers, $Givers = \{L_{ij} | L_{ij} \geq L_{ij}^*, ij \in E\}$, $Receivers = \{L_{ij} | L_{ij} < L_{ij}^*, ij \in E\}$, $Givers \cup Receivers = E$.*

Theorem 3. *Define a capacity adjustment operator Θ acting on Givers and Receivers. The calculation process of $Givers \Theta Receivers$ is:*

a. *Take 1 unit of capacity from each side of Givers to form the free capacity $\sigma(L)$:*

$$\sigma(L) = |Givers| \tag{9}$$

b. *Assign $\sigma(L)$ preferences to edges in Receivers. Assuming the edge $e_{ij} \in Receivers$, the capacity increment $\sigma(l_{ij})$ can be obtained to satisfy:*

$$\sigma(l_{ij}) = \sigma(C) \cdot \frac{C_{ij}}{\sum_{e_{im} \in Receivers} C_{im}} \tag{10}$$

According to the above definition, the objective function of the improved edge capacity allocation strategy is as follows:

$$\Omega_{ij}(t+1) = \begin{cases} L_{ij}(t+1), \min\{1, exp(\frac{f(\Omega_s(t))-f(\Omega_f(t))}{T})\} \geq 1 \\ \Omega_{ij}(t), other \end{cases} \tag{11}$$

subject to:

$$L_{ij}(0) = (1+\beta) \cdot w_{ij}^{(0)} \tag{12}$$

$$L = \sum_{i,j=1}^{E} (1+\beta) \cdot w_{ij} \tag{13}$$

$$\sum_{i,j} L_{ij}^{*} = \sum_{i,j} L_{ij}^{0} + \Delta L \tag{14}$$

$$\Delta L_{im} = L_{im} - \sum_{i,j=1}^{E} L_{ij} = \beta \sum_{i,j=1}^{E} L_{ij} \tag{15}$$

The load of any edge ij cannot be lower than the initial load $L_{ij}^{(0)}$, so the remaining capacity ΔL_{im} available for allocation on the network is satisfied, and it is known that the number of remaining allocated resources can be allocated in a linear relationship to each node in the network. When a network node fails, the node is removed. The above capacity allocation strategy is solved using the simulated annealing algorithm, and the goal is to find the optimal classification strategy Ω_{ij}^{*} for the network capacity when the express network is under attack.

The specific steps of the capacity allocation algorithm are as follows:

*Step*0: Given the global initial temperature $\tau_c = \tau_0$, the tolerance factor β and the attack method. Given an initial allocation strategy $\Omega^{(f)} = \Omega^{(0)} = \{L_{ij}^{(0)} | ij \in E\}$, and use formula 12 to calculate the initial capacity.
*Step*1: Calculate the failure edge normalization index F of the network under the current allocation strategy and construct sets $Right^{(f)}$ and $False^{(f)}$.
*Step*2: Define the initial set $Givers = Right^{(f)}$, $Receivers = False^{(f)}$, execute the operation of $Givers \cup Receivers$, and obtain a new allocation strategy $\Omega^{(s)}$.
*Step*3: Calculate the failure edge normalization index F under the current allocation strategy and construct $Right^{(s)}$ and $False^{(s)}$.
*Step*4: If $\Omega^{(s)} > \Omega^{(f)}$, accept $\Omega^{(s)}$ as a better allocation strategy, and define $\Omega^{(f)} = \Omega^{(s)}$, proceed to *Step*1, otherwise, proceed to *Step*5.
*Step*5: Reconstruct $Givers = Givers - Givers \cap False^{(s)}$, $Receivers = False^{(f)}$, execute $Givers \Theta Receivers$, and update the allocation strategy $\Omega^{(s)}$.
*Step*6: Calculate the failure edge normalization index F under the current allocation strategy. If $\Omega^{(s)} > \Omega^{(f)}$, then accept $\Omega^{(s)}$ as a better allocation strategy, update the best allocation strategy, and proceed to *Step*1, otherwise proceed to *Step*7.

*Step*7: Accept the current allocation strategy with a certain probability, and update the optimal allocation strategy, and proceed to *Step*1.
*Step*8: When the simulated temperature control approaches $\tau_c \rightarrow 0$, the algorithm exits.

The above is the optimal capacity allocation strategy proposed in this paper. In order to better compare capacity allocation strategies, this paper compares five capacity allocation strategies. Among them, the edge capacity allocation strategy is the original strategy, the improved edge remaining capacity allocation strategy is the optimization strategy, and the other three strategies are the average capacity allocation strategy, degree preference capacity allocation strategy, and the online capacity allocation strategy is a commonly used strategy in previous papers.

3.2 Metrics

The paper measures the invulnerability of the express network mainly based on the following two indicators.

Normalized Index *F* of Failure Edge. The number of other edges in the network that cause failure after removing edge ij is denoted as F_{ij}, and it can be known that $0 \leq F_{ij} \leq E - 1$, that is:

$$F = \frac{\sum_{ij \in G} F_{ij}}{E - 1} \tag{16}$$

Using the index F, we can intuitively see the strength of the network's overall ability to resist cascading failures. That is to say, when the number of network collapse edges gradually increases, the value of F will also gradually increase. When $F = 1$, the network completely collapses, then the edge deletion ratio at this time is the network crash threshold, so this paper measures the invulnerability of the network mainly to observe whether the network crash threshold increases.

Network Efficiency E. Network efficiency refers to the average value of the reciprocal path weights of all edges in the network:

$$E = \frac{1}{N(N-1)} \sum_{i \neq j} \frac{1}{w_{ij}} \tag{17}$$

In formula 17, w_{ij} represents the weight between edges ij, N represents the number of nodes in the network, and E represents the global efficiency of the network.

3.3 Numerical Simulation

This paper selects two sets of network data, which are scale-free network data and express network data. Among them, the express network data is the data obtained from the Internet, the official website of the express company, etc. The express delivery network has a total of 330 points and 2578 effective edges. The selection of outlets is divided according to city-level districts, and 330 common cities in China are selected, and the association relationship of relevant nodes is crawled to form a network. The data in the scale-free network is a network generated using NetworkX library in Python for comparison with the express network, and the basic parameter settings of the scale-free network have the same number of nodes and the same average degree as the express network, $N = 331$, $\langle k \rangle = 16$.

Crash Threshold Experiment. Select BA scale-free network and express network as the model research objects, and compare and analyze the spread of cascading failures under different attack methods and different attack intensities. According to the network structure and attack methods, four groups of different experimental modes are constructed, namely BA network random attack (BA-RA), BA network deliberate attack (BA-DA), express network random attack (Exp-RA), express network deliberate attack (Exp-DA). The experimental parameters are set as $\alpha = 0.4$, $\beta = 0.3$, $N = 331$, $\langle k \rangle = 16$, $E = 5040$.

Using the two metrics of failure edge normalization F and global network efficiency E, discuss the strength of the BA network and the express network to resist cascading failures under two attacks of different intensities.

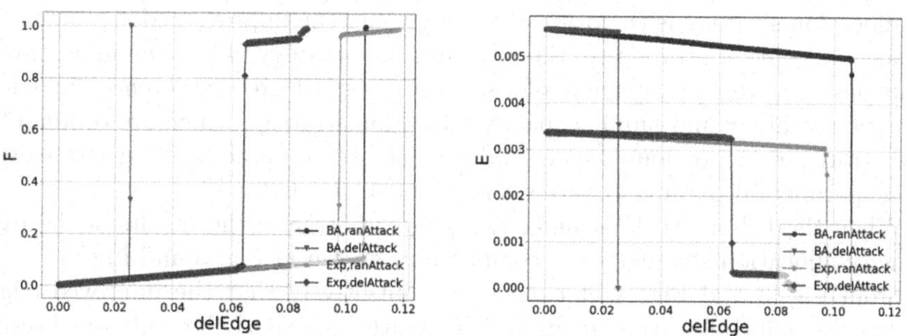

Fig. 2. Experimental results of network Crash Threshold

It can be seen from Fig. 2 that the correlation between the four experimental modes and the two indicators at different attack intensities. For the BA network, the random attack intensity is greater than 10.72% and the network collapses, while the intentional attack is greater than 2.74% when the proportion of deleted edges is greater than the network collapse. For the express network, when the proportion of deleted edges is greater than 6.44%, the deliberate attack will have a huge impact on the network, but there are still available paths in the network, and the threshold of random attacks will increase to 9.77% total breakdown. As the proportion of deleted edges increases, the degree of damage caused by cascading failures to the overall network increases. It can be seen from the right of Fig2 that the number of edges in the BA network with the same number of nodes and the same average degree is much larger than that of the express network, so the global efficiency of the network is also greater than that of the express network. However, the complete collapse threshold of the express network under the two attack methods is better than that of the BA network. This is because of the difference between the topology of the express network and the BA network structure. The hub-and-spoke structure and edge weights of the express network will lead to huge differences in the ability of the network to handle additional loads at different nodes. However, the weight distribution of BA network edges is relatively uniform, so it is more prone to collapse. To sum up, comparing the two attack methods, random attacks have far less impact on the invulnerability of the two networks than deliberate attacks, which means that the express network and BA network are more capable of resisting random attacks, and are more vulnerable to deliberate attacks. Comparing the two networks, with the same number of nodes and the same average degree, the express network has higher invulnerability than the BA network.

Capacity Allocation Strategy Experiment. The BA scale-free network and the express network are selected as the research objects of the model, and the relationship between different capacity allocation strategies and the invulnerability of the network against cascading failures is discussed. In Experiment 2, five capacity allocation strategies were compared, among which the edge capacity allocation strategy is the original strategy, and the improved edge remaining capacity allocation strategy is the optimization strategy. The remaining three strategies are average capacity allocation strategy, degree preference capacity allocation strategy and online capacity allocation strategy, which are commonly used strategies in previous papers and are used to compare existing strategies. The experimental parameters are set as $\alpha = 0.4$, $\beta = 0.3$.

When the BA network is under two kinds of attacks, the results of the five capacity allocation strategies are compared as shown in Fig. 3 and Fig. 4.

From Fig. 3 and Fig. 4, it can be seen intuitively that the improved edge residual capacity allocation strategy has greatly increased the collapse threshold of the BA network and enhanced the network's invulnerability. As can be seen from the above figure, for the improved edge remaining capacity allocation strategy, the random attack crash threshold of BA network increases from 10.72% to 29.89%. The deliberate attack crash threshold increases from 2.74% to 33.45%. The optimization strategy proposed in this paper is obviously better than other strategies. When the BA network is attacked randomly, the edge capability capacity allocation strategy is similar to the average capacity allocation strategy curve, while under deliberate attack, the edge capability capacity allocation strategy has the same threshold as the degree preference capacity

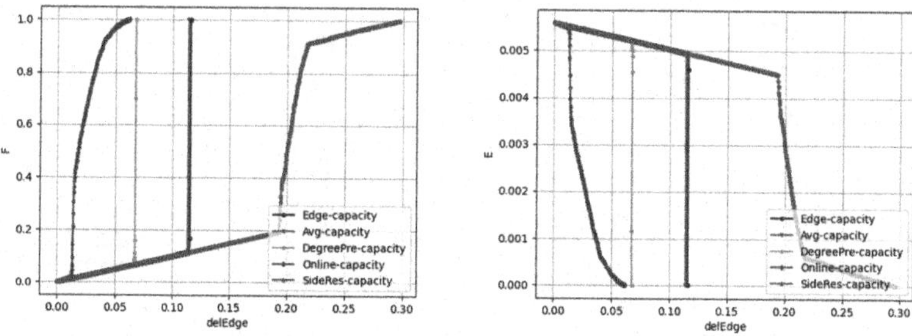

Fig. 3. BA Network Random Attack

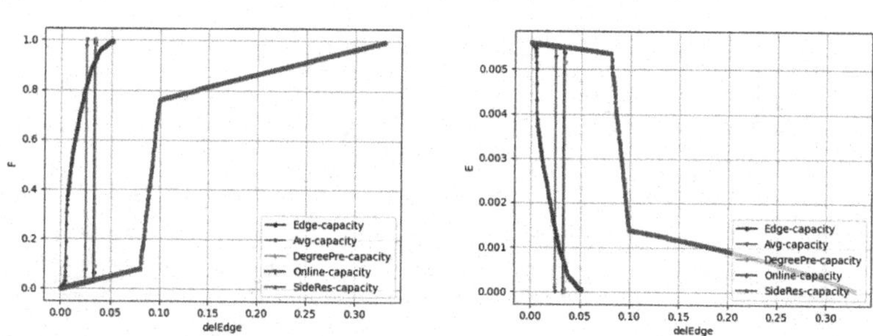

Fig. 4. BA Network Deliberate Attack

allocation strategy. It should be noted that there is a phenomenon in this experiment. After changing the capacity allocation strategy, the crash threshold of the BA network is greater than the crash threshold of random attacks. This is because the improved edge residual capacity allocation strategy is optimized during capacity allocation, and simulated annealing algorithm is used to solve it, and the optimal classification strategy Ω_j^* for network capacity when under attack is found. In turn, the network has higher invulnerability, so the effect on the BA network is more obvious during deliberate attacks. At the same time, the sudden collapse of the network is alleviated. When used in a real network, that is, when a local network suffers a relatively large degree of attack, there is still a path, and the failure edge will no longer suddenly rise to a global collapse.

When the express network is under two kinds of attacks, the results of the five capacity allocation strategies are compared as shown in Fig. 5 and Fig. 6.

From Fig. 5 and Fig. 6, it can be intuitively concluded that the improved edge remaining capacity allocation strategy increases the crash threshold from 11.87% to 37.68% when randomly attacking the express network, greatly improved the impact of the express network on the network during random attacks, enhanced the dynamic invulnerability of the express delivery network. When the express delivery network is deliberately attacked, the five capacity allocation strategies affect the network as a whole. The optimal collapse threshold of the improved residual capacity allocation strategy is raised to 27.54%, followed by the online

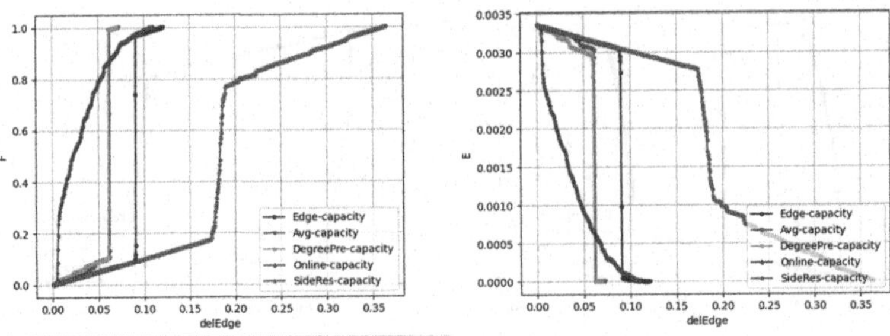

Fig. 5. Express Network Random Attack

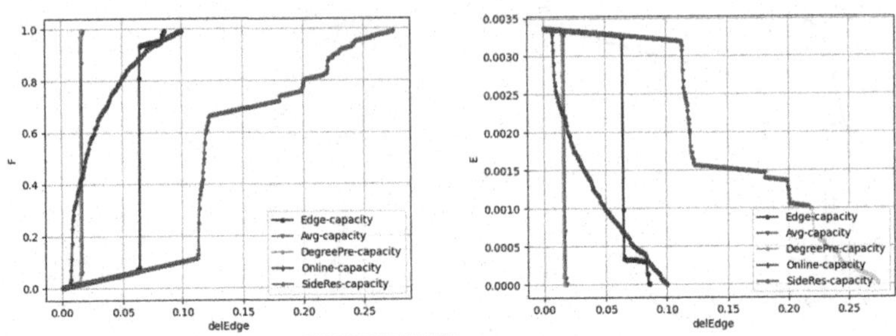

Fig. 6. Express Network Deliberate Attack

capacity allocation strategy. The degree preference capacity allocation strategy and the average capacity allocation strategy are the worst.

When the online capacity allocation strategy and the improved strategy are used, the sudden collapse of the express network is alleviated to a large extent, the improvement strategy changes step by step. Because there are layers of nodes and edges in the express network in reality. When cascading failures occur in the hub lines in the network, the degree of network collapse increases suddenly, but the degree of network collapse becomes slow when the proportion of deleted edges is between 12.23% and 17.45%. Although the central line of the express delivery network fails, in the local network centered on the provincial capital, there are still paths in the network. When the partial network side collapses to a large extent, the network will collapse until the whole network.

4 Conclusion

In order to effectively prevent cascading failures in actual complex networks, this paper studies the impact of edge weights and capacity allocation strategies on complex network invulnerability, proposes a realistic complex network model with dynamic flows, and establishes A cascading fault "load capacity" model with parameters. In order to verify the effectiveness of the model, this paper constructs an actual fast network and a scale-free network with the same basic parameters. On this basis, the influence of random attack and deliberate attack on the indestructibility of the two networks under different attack intensities is studied, and an improved edge residual capacity allocation strategy is proposed to improve the indestructibility of the network, and the simulated annealing algorithm is used to find the optimal allocation strategy.

The main conclusions are as follows: By comparing the network crash thresholds under the two attack methods, it can be seen that both networks have strong anti-random attack capabilities. Comparing the two networks with the same parameters, the express network has higher attack resistance than the BA network. By comparing the five capacity allocation strategies, it can be seen that the improved edge residual capacity allocation strategy greatly improves the network crash threshold of the two networks under different attack modes, and enhances the dynamic resilience of the network.

Based on the above conclusions, we put forward the following suggestions on how to effectively reduce the impact of various attacks on the network: before the impact occurs, optimize the express delivery network layout, strengthen the construction of network infrastructure, and strengthen correlation. Between the network node and the edge, and the application capability of redundant resources, to improve the capacity and processing efficiency of the network edge. Improving the resilience of the network after impacts occur. By sharing information and coordinating resources between networks, the transparency and maximization of network processing capabilities can be achieved. Using an efficient capacity allocation strategy can ensure that network loads can be shifted and evacuated quickly and effectively, thereby improving the survivability of the network. It is recommended that complex networks in reality should learn, self-adjust and adapt to the experience of dealing with shocks, so as to achieve a more resilient network operation state, optimize the emergency mechanism, determine more effective emergency measures, and promote the enhancement of network resilience.

References

1. Sen, Dasgupta, S., Chatterjee, A.: Small-world properties of the Indian railway network. Phys. Rev. E **67**(3), 036–106 (2003)
2. Goh, K.I., Kahng, B., Kim, D.: Fluctuation-driven dynamics of the Internet topology. Phys. Rev. Lett. **88**(10), 108–701 (2002)
3. Montes, C.P., Seoane, M.J.F., Laxe, F.G.: General cargo and containership emergent routes: a complex networks description. Transp. Policy **24**, 126–140 (2012)
4. Motter, A.E.: Cascade control and defense in complex networks. Phys. Rev. Lett. **93**(9), 098–701 (2004)
5. Motter, A.E., Lai, Y.C.: Cascade-based attacks on complex networks. Phys. Rev. E **66**(6), 065–102 (2002)
6. Crucitti, P., Latora, V., Marchiori, M.: Model for cascading failures in complex networks. Phys. Rev. E **69**(4), 045–104 (2004)
7. Wang, W.X., Chen, G.: Universal robustness characteristic of weighted networks against cascading failure. Phys. Rev. E **77**(2), 026–101 (2008)

8. Wang, J.W., Rong, L.L.: Edge-based-attack induced cascading failures on scale-free networks. Physica A **388**(8), 1731–1737 (2009)
9. Jianwei, W., Lili, R.: Research on attack strategy on sequential failure model with overload and collapse probability. Chin. Manag. Sci. **17**(06), 147–156 (2009)
10. Sturaro, A., Silvestri, S., Conti, M.: Towards a realistic model for failure propagation in interdependent networks. In: 2016 International Conference on Computing, Networking and Communications, pp. 1–7 (2016)
11. Jianwei, W., Lin, C., Chen, J.: Research on cascading fault model of interdependent networks considering edge weight and coupling strength. Chin. J. Manag. Eng. **32**(04), 149–157 (2018)
12. Sun, H.J., Zhao, H., Wu, J.J.: A robust matching model of capacity to defense cascading failure on complex networks. Physica A: Stat. Mech. Appl. **387**(25), 6431–6435 (2008)
13. Li Fang, H., Bin, D.P.: Scale-free network dynamic invulnerability optimization based on resource limited model. Syst. Eng. Electron. Technol. **34**(01), 175–178 (2012)
14. Jin, J.G., Lu, L., Sun, L.: Optimal allocation of protective resources in urban rail transit networks against intentional attacks. Transp. Res. Part E: Logistics Transp. Rev. **84**, 73–87 (2015)
15. Cats, O., Koppenol, G., Warnier, M.: Robustness assessment of link capacity reduction for complex networks: application for public transport systems. Reliab. Eng. Syst. Saf. **167**, 544–553 (2017)
16. Liang, H., Li, S.: Research on cascading failure invulnerability of express network under different impacts. J. Fuzhou Univ. **36**(01), 42–50 (2022)
17. Moreno, Y., Gómez, J.B., Pacheco, A.F.: Instability of scale-free networks under node-breaking avalanches. Europhys. Lett. **58**(4), 630 (2002)

IoT Service Runtime Fault Tolerance Mechanism Based on Flink Dynamic Checkpoint

Wentao Bai[1,2](✉), Jun Fang[1,2], and Wei Chang[1,2]

[1] Beijing Key Laboratory on Integration and Analysis of Large-scale Stream Data, Beijing, China
bai_wentao@163.com

[2] North China University of Technology, Beijing 100144, China

Abstract. By integrating Internet of Things (IoT) capabilities to sense real-time conditions in the physical environment, traditional Business Process Management (BPM) has the potential to become more flexible and adaptive. However, the integration of BPM and IoT faces challenges such as programming mechanism mismatches, resource management mechanism mismatches, and adaptive mechanism mismatches. This research considers IoT service-based technology as an effective approach to integrate BPM and IoT. The IoT service must be calculable, composable, bindable, and fault-tolerant. When IoT services run on Apache Flink, the native fault tolerance mechanism may not meet the fault tolerance needs of IoT services due to high-speed fluctuation characteristics of IoT service data sources. Additionally, traditional static checkpoint fault-tolerant mechanisms may not balance runtime overhead and recovery delay optimally. This paper proposes an on-demand dynamic checkpoint fault-tolerant method that calculates the recovery delay in real-time based on data fluctuation rates and actively triggers the checkpoint operation when the user threshold is reached. Experiments show that the proposed method improves system efficiency by up to 11.9% compared to the static checkpoint mechanism.

Keywords: IoT service · fault-tolerance · checkpoint interval · on-demand dynamic checkpoint mechanism

1 Introduction

The development of the Internet of Things has brought about greater connectivity among various industries. Integrating IoT capabilities to sense real-time conditions in the physical environment has the potential to make traditional BPM more flexible and adaptive [1,2], and enable better utilization and programming of the rapidly growing IoT big data through BPM [3]. However, the convergence of BPM and IoT faces several challenges. For instance, BPM requires a specific programming mechanism to support IoT, and traditional predefined process models may not be suitable for processing IoT data. Additionally, the

Z. Wang et al. (Eds.): ICSS 2023, CCIS 1844, pp. 91–105, 2023.
https://doi.org/10.1007/978-981-99-4402-6_7

mismatch between the volume and velocity of IoT big data and the structured data management model of traditional BPM poses a challenge. In response to these challenges, Volker Gruhn et al. proposed the BRIBOT [4] scheme, which highlighted the significance of IoT services for integrating IoT big data and BPM. An IoT service is an independent software organization that abstracts business events from IoT data and possesses five key properties: calculable, composable, bindable, fault-tolerant, and proactive.

Apache Flink has become the preferred medium for running IoT services due to its exceptional streaming data computing capabilities. However, when Flink is used to run IoT services, the static checkpoint fault tolerance mechanism of Flink may not balance the trade-off between recovery delay and throughput adequately. A large checkpoint interval causes long recovery delays, while a small interval reduces the normal running performance of the system. Users can not set the interval parameter intuitively. Furthermore, the high-speed fluctuations of IoT service data sources make checkpointing at data peaks result in significant latency in the system, as shown in Fig. 1. Thus, the static checkpoint interval will reduce the performance and stability of the system when data source inflow rates fluctuate frequently.

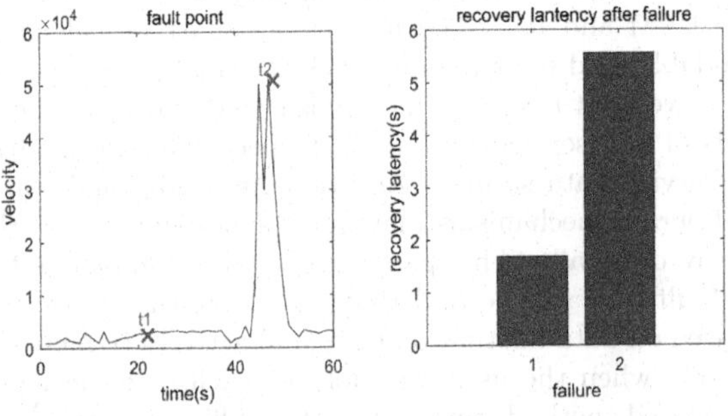

Fig. 1. Comparison of recovery delay at different times

To address these issues, this paper proposes an on-demand dynamic checkpoint fault-tolerant mechanism that limits the system recovery latency within a threshold and ensures that IoT services remain in a stable state. The proposed method defines a checkpoint cost model to predict the time consumption of the checkpoint operation based on the state size, and a recovery cost model to estimate the recovery delay of the current moment based on the amount of data processed since the last checkpoint. The on-demand dynamic checkpoint fault-tolerant method triggers the checkpoint operation actively according to the user's set threshold, and balances the recovery delay and end-to-end latency within the user's requirements. Numerous experiments were carried out to verify the efficiency of our proposed method. The main contributions are as follows:

1) A method of calculating real time recovery delay was proposed.
2) Trigger the checkpoint by real time recovery delay actively, which avoid setting static checkpoint interval unintuitively.

2 Related Work

The traditional fault tolerance strategies for services can be divided into two categories: static and dynamic, based on the stage of adoption [5]. The static fault tolerance strategy is typically implemented during the service design phase and involves adding fault tolerance modules to the service function module. Various service selection methods [6] have been proposed to assist designers in selecting stable services. The FACTS fault-tolerant framework [7] has also been proposed to help developers quickly and easily build fault-tolerant logic. Traditional static fault tolerance strategies are not designed to increase efficiency but rather to improve accuracy.

On the other hand, dynamic fault tolerance policies are enforced when a service fails and can be divided into three modes: forward recovery [8], backward recovery [9], and checkpoint recovery [10]. A substitution tolerance strategy [11] has been proposed to replace the faulty service with another equivalent subset of the service, while a redundant replication fault tolerance strategy [12] ensures that a backup service takes over after a service failure. Backward recovery refers to remedial action for the impact of the failure, and a dynamic calculation method [13] has been proposed to accelerate the speed of backward recovery. However, finding the execution state for backward recovery is a difficult problem, and the checkpoint fault tolerance strategy saves state during the execution phase and can revert to a specific state after a failure [14].

Although the above service fault tolerance strategies have proven effective, they require developers to analyze fault tolerance logic in addition to service function requirements, which increases their workload and the complexity of service design.

When IoT services are deployed on a distributed stream processing system, their fault tolerance mechanisms can be naturally leveraged. Since the invention of the snapshot algorithm by Chandy and Lamport in 1985, the global distributed snapshot algorithm has become the main fault-tolerant mechanism. A considerable amount of research has been done on the problem of optimizing the checkpoint interval. Reference [16] defined the checkpoint interval as a mathematical optimization problem for the first time and proposed using a first-order approximate function to calculate the optimal interval. The optimization goal is to minimize system failure recovery time. Papers [17] proposed a higher-order checkpoint interval estimation function and added a fault recovery cost model, with the optimization goal being to improve the system's efficiency during operation. Reference [18] set different checkpoint intervals for different failure probabilities to ensure system recovery delay. In [19], the data to be processed is evaluated offline first, and the operator expansion capability factor is added to the calculation of the checkpoint interval. Dynamic checkpoints are introduced more comprehensively in [20], but the case of multiple consecutive failures is not considered. Reference [21] derived a checkpoint interval estimation function based on operator utilization and proposed an optimal checkpoint interval model for scenarios where the data source flow rate is constantly changing. However, this approach has two important issues. First, the data needs to be cached in time series prediction algorithms, which can result in a significant memory burden on the cluster when the data flow rate is very high. Second, it is difficult to determine when to merge two fine-grained time segments based on user thresholds, and the algorithm may trigger a checkpoint operation at the highest flow rate. Reference [22] derived an optimal checkpoint interval model based on operator topology utilization, which is not sensitive to data source fluctuations.

In summary, the static checkpoint fault-tolerant method can generally achieve better system performance and can adapt to most types of computing tasks. However, it treats all data equally without considering the characteristics of data distribution and scenarios where the data source flow rate fluctuates.

3 On-Demand Dynamic Checkpoint Fault Tolerance

This paper is primarily concerned with the checkpoint trigger mechanism. The static checkpoint method employs a fixed time to initiate checkpoint operations, while the on-demand dynamic checkpoint method actively triggers checkpoint operations based on the user-defined recovery delay threshold. A higher system efficiency is the purpose of all methods.

3.1 System Efficiency Model

Reference [16] first proposed a model to measure system efficiency, that is, the method of "time proportion of normal logic processing". Reference [21] further refines this measurement efficiency model. Taking checkpoint as intervals, the running time of the entire stream processing system is composed of four segments, as shown in Fig. 2. They are respectively normal processing time (denoted as T_{proc}), checkpoint operation time (denoted as T_{ck}), failure recovery time (denoted as T_{rec}) and invalid processing time(denoted as T_{inv}).

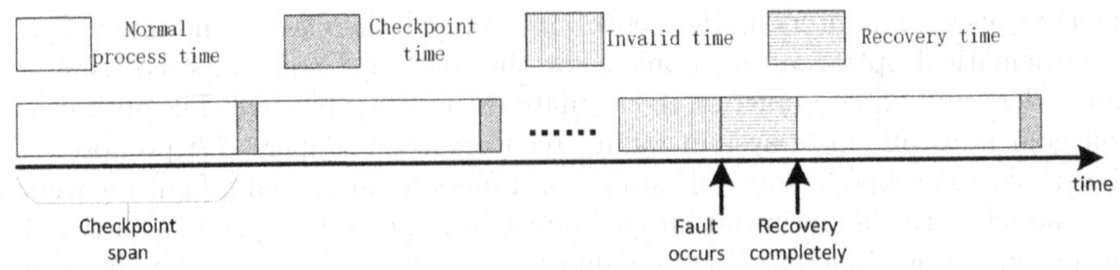

Fig. 2. Time fragments of the runtime processing

In this paper, we continue to use the concept of time proportion as the basis for measuring system efficiency. The efficiency formula for each individual checkpoint cycle is as follows:

$$E = \frac{T_{proc}}{T_{proc} + T_{ck} + T_{rec}} \tag{1}$$

To implement our method, modeling the checkpoint cost and recovery cost is essential.

Checkpoint Cost Model. The actual time required to create a checkpoint is related to the network IO performance and the size of the internal state of the operator. Since the network IO performance of the system is determined by the hardware, the size of the operator's internal state determines the time required for checkpoint creation. Experiments have shown a positive correlation between state size and checkpoint time, as shown in Fig. 3. When cluster software and hardware conditions remain unchanged, an example of the relationship between checkpoint state size and time consumption T_{ck} can be fitted as:

$$T_{ck} = 9.608x + 5.1471 \tag{2}$$

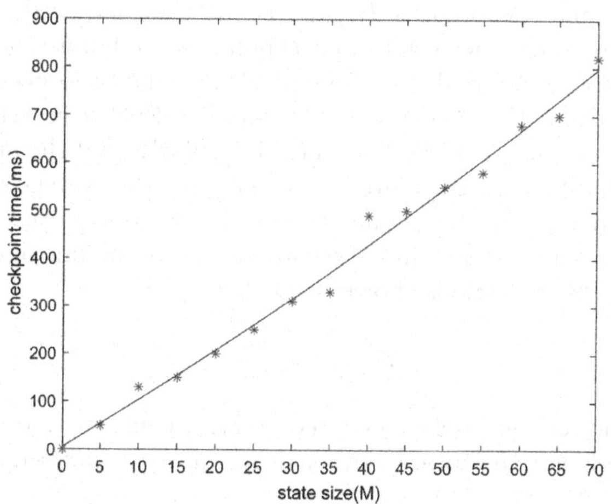

Fig. 3. Relationship between state size and checkpoint time

Recovery Cost Model. The components of each recovery process include four parts: fault detection time, task restart time, state retrieve time, and data replay time [23], as shown in Fig. 4.

The fault detection time (denoted as T_{detect}) represents the time it takes for the system to detect a fault after it occurs. Typically, failures can occur anytime after a heartbeat, which is assumed in this paper to be half the cluster heartbeat interval [21]. The system restart time (denoted as $T_{restart}$) is determined by the performance of the cluster system itself and is set to a constant value. The state recovery time (denoted as $T_{retrieve}$) refers to the time of retrieving state backup data from the remote database and the initialization time.

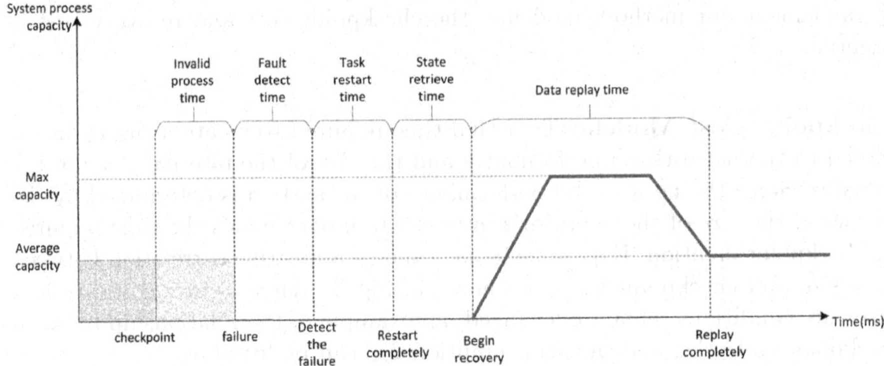

Fig. 4. Time segments of the recovery process

Data replay time (denoted as T_{reproc}) is the time required to replay data that has been processed since the last checkpoint. Since failures occur randomly during the checkpoint interval, the theoretical invalidation processing time can be approximated half the checkpoint interval [24]. Reference [21] pointed out that the flow rate of data sources fluctuates irregularly, and the amount of data replayed after a fault can be calculated by multiplying the average speed since the last checkpoint by half the checkpoint interval. In this paper, we avoid this inaccurate estimation and instead timely record the total amount of data (denoted as w). The reprocessing time is shown in Eq. 3.

$$T_{reproc} = \frac{w}{C_0} \tag{3}$$

In this paper, the recovery delay (denoted as T_{rec}) considers more time factors, then we proposed that the total recovery delay can be expressed as:

$$T_{rec} = T_{detect} + T_{restart} + T_{retrieve} + T_{reproc} \tag{4}$$

3.2 On-Demand Dynamic Checkpoint Algorithm

Different IoT services have different performance requirements. For example, alarm services need to ensure low end-to-end delay and high processing speed. When IoT services run on the Flink system, these indicators are reflected by system efficiency. Therefore, when our algorithm optimizes the maximum efficiency of the system, it needs to consider the limitation of the recovery delay (denoted as α) required by the user. The algorithm goal of this paper can be expressed as:

$$\begin{aligned} &maximize \quad E = \frac{T_{proc}}{T_{proc} + T_{ck} + T_{rec}} \\ &subject\ to \quad T_{reproc} < \alpha \end{aligned} \tag{5}$$

For each individual checkpoint cycle, the On-Demand Dynamic Checkpoint Algorithm (RDCI) determines the timing of the checkpoint operation based on the estimated recovery delay of the current system, ensuring that the recovery delay threshold meets the user's QoS (Quality of Service) constraints. We first define the recovery delay threshold α, the maximum processing speed β, and set the threshold γ (must bigger than α) to enforce the checkpoint. Based on these constraints, we can determine whether to perform the checkpoint operation at a given time. We aim to optimize operator efficiency while ensuring that user QoS constraints are met during each checkpoint cycle. The pseudocode for this algorithm is shown in Algorithm 1.

Algorithm 1: on-demand Dynamic Checkpoint

```
Input: recovery latency α, max processing speed β
Output: checkpoint interval (CI), operator efficiency(E)
Initial speed list, data amount list;
while true do
    Record data amount and speed;
    if recovery latency > α then
        if data source inflow speed < β then
            Trigger checkpoint; Record CI and E;
        else if recovery latency > γ then
            Trigger checkpoint; Record CI and E;
    sleep;
```

The algorithm first receives the thresholds α and β set by the user. After starting, it will always record the total amount of currently processed data, and calculate the current recovery delay every second. If it reaches the threshold α set by the user, it will then judge whether the current data inflow speed is less than β. If the data inflow rate has been greater than β after γ seconds, a checkpoint operation will be forced to be triggered. The algorithm will eventually output and store the current checkpoint interval, and calculate the operator efficiency E within this checkpoint period.

The challenge of this algorithm is how to assist users in specifying the appropriate threshold when running it for the first time. In the subsequent experiments, we will provide recommendations for appropriate threshold ranges based on the flow rates of different data sources. Users can adjust this suggested threshold to achieve a balance between recovery latency and end-to-end latency.

4 Experiment

This experiment mainly answers the following three questions:

1) What are the appropriate threshold α, β and γ under the flow rate of different data sources?

2) Whether the on-demand dynamic checkpoint mechanism can always limit the fault recovery delay within the required range.
3) Whether the operator efficiency is improved compared with the static checkpoint mechanism of native Flink.

4.1 The Overall Efficiency of the System During Long-Term Operation

Based on the evaluation indicators of operator utilization mentioned above, this section demonstrates the overall efficiency of long-term operation. Assuming that over a sufficiently long period of time, there are a total of n checkpoint cycles, during which a total of m failures occurred. Based on practical experience, m is expected to be much smaller than n, i.e., m $\ll$ n. By applying formula 4, the operator efficiency in each period can be calculated.

$$e = \frac{T_{proc}}{T_{total}} \tag{6}$$

$T_{total} = T_{proc} + T_{ck} + T_{rec}$. Then the accumulative efficiency of the system is:

$$E1 = e_1 + e_2 + ... + e_n = (\frac{T_{proc1}}{T_{total1}} + \frac{T_{proc2}}{T_{total2}} + ... + \frac{T_{procn}}{T_{totaln}}) \tag{7}$$

The actual total system efficiency over n checkpoint cycles can be expressed as:

$$E2 = \frac{T_{proc1} + T_{proc2} + ... + T_{procn}}{T_{total1} + T_{total2} + ... + T_{totaln}} \tag{8}$$

Comparing formulas 7 and 8, we can observe that the relationship between E1 and E2 is determined by the threshold α. If α is set to a higher value, RDCI will perform better in terms of efficiency. On the other hand, if α is set to a smaller value, the efficiency of RDCI will be slightly lower compared to the optimization method proposed in the previous paper [21]. Therefore, selecting the appropriate value for α is crucial for the success of the algorithm.

4.2 Experiment Setting

The hardware environment used in this experiment is a cluster consisting of 3 nodes, with one serving as the master node. All nodes have identical configurations and deployment components, as shown in Table 1.

To eliminate the impact of data sources on stream computing throughput, this experiment uses Kafka as the data source and presets two different flow rate fluctuations. The flow rate is stored in the array of the data simulation program and is sequentially sent every second at predetermined intervals. Each data piece is a triplet that comprises a unique GUID, the current time, and a count.

The *WordCount* task is a classic benchmark test task due to its simple structure. The *keyby* operator can simulate an intermediate state of any size. The topology of *WordCount* task is shown in Fig. 5.

Table 1. Cluster configuration information

Config name	value	Config name	value
CPU	2.0 Ghz * 2	OS	Centos7.8
memory	2G	JDK version	1.8.192
disk	40G	Apache Zookeeper	3.14
network	Gb Ethernet network	Apache Kafka	2.14

Source → Flatmap → Keyby → Sum → Sink

Fig. 5. WordCount task topology

In this experiment, faults are manually set up according to different checkpoint intervals to test the recovery performance. For the static checkpoint mechanism, a total of four faults are simulated based on different simulated data flow velocity fluctuations (at least two at fluctuation troughs and at least two at fluctuation peaks). For the RDCI method, faults are simulated in each checkpoint period manually. The fault simulation time points are shown in Table 2.

Table 2. Simulated failures at different checkpoint intervals

Interval	F1	F2	F3	F4	F5
SCI = 20	15 s	35 s	50 s	70 s	95 s
SCI = 30	25 s	50 s	80 s	None	None
SCI = 60	50 s	85 s	None	None	None
RDCI = 3 s	Simulate failure during every checkpoint period				
RDCI = 5 s	Simulate failure during every checkpoint period				
RDCI = 6 s	Simulate failure during every checkpoint period				
RDCI = 10 s	Simulate failure during every checkpoint period				

4.3 Threshold Value Setting

The experiment revealed that the maximum processing capacity of the current Flink cluster is 13333 records per second, i.e., β=13333. After conducting numerous experiments, it was observed that the system restart time is determined by the cluster performance, as depicted in Fig. 6a. Therefore, this paper assumes the system restart time to be $T_{restart} = 1.041$ s.

The relationship between the system recovery time and the amount of data to be replayed is presented in Fig. 6b. The recovery time remains at approximately 1.1 s when the amount of replay data is 10,000 or less, primarily representing the system restart time. As the amount of replay data increases, the recovery time becomes 5990 ms when the replay data reaches 100,000 records, and around 12 s

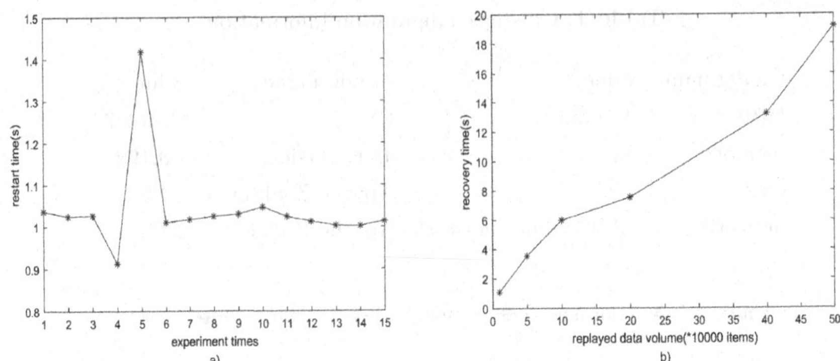

Fig. 6. Statistics of operator restart time and reprocess time after failure

for 400,000 records. Based on the current cluster's maximum processing capacity and recovery time statistics, the initial threshold α can be set to 5 s, which means that the recovery delay should not exceed 5 s under any data fluctuation. In order to accurately verify the recovery delay at different data fluctuation periods, this paper sets $\gamma = \alpha+1$.

4.4 Algorithm Efficiency Verification and Comparison

In this experiment, two types of data flow rate fluctuations were simulated, as shown in Fig. 7. The values of the data fluctuations were determined based on the cluster-related parameters tested in the previous section, in order to minimize measurement errors.

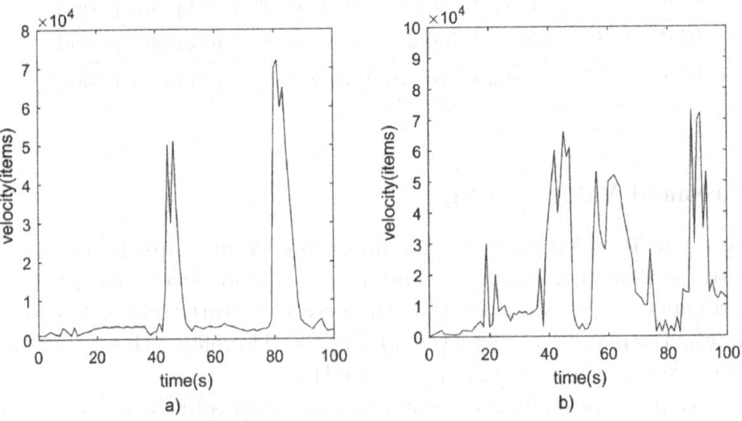

Fig. 7. Two simulations of fluctuating data source inflow velocity

In this experiment, the primary objective of the on-demand dynamic checkpoint method is to ensure the user's QoS requirements. The experiment records the time point when the RDCI method checkpoint is triggered under two flow rate fluctuations, as shown in Fig. 8. The checkpoint interval value is also presented in the figure. It is observed that when the flow rate is low, the checkpoint interval reaches a maximum of 46 s and a minimum of 2 s for testing parameters $\alpha = 3$ s and $\alpha = 5$ s. When the flow rate is high, the maximum checkpoint interval reaches 45 s and the minimum value is 6 s, using parameters $\alpha = 6$ s and $\alpha = 10$ s for testing.

Under two types of flow rate fluctuations, the RDCI method can dynamically trigger the checkpoint operation to restrict the recovery latency according to the flow rate change while maintaining a low end-to-end delay. On the other hand, the static checkpoint method always employs a fixed checkpoint interval, and its recovery delay has reached a maximum of 19.84 s, as illustrated in Fig. 9 and Fig. 10. In contrast, the recovery delay of the RDCI method has consistently remained within the user's set threshold. At the same time, the end-to-end delay of the RDCI method is always similar to the static checkpoint method and more stable, as shown in Fig. 11.

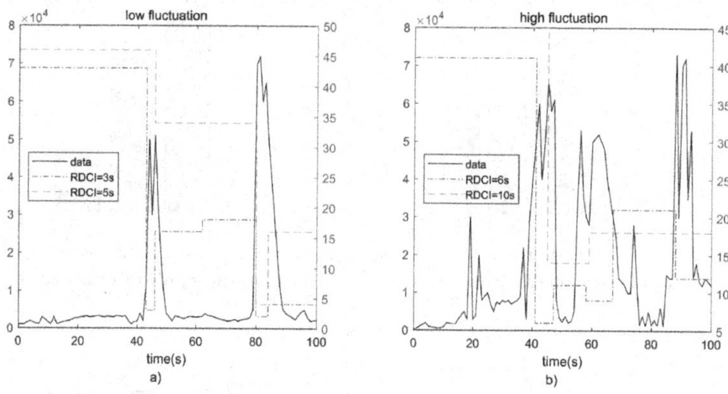

Fig. 8. Dynamic checkpoint trigger time

Operator efficiency is the system performance evaluation index that this paper mainly focuses on. Figure 12a shows the comparison of operator efficiencies under low flow rate fluctuations. When static checkpoint interval is 30 s, the operator efficiency is slightly improved compared with static checkpoint interval is 20 s. However, when the RDCI method with a delay threshold of 3 s is used, the operator efficiency improves by 7.8%. Figure 12b shows the comparison of operator efficiency under high flow rate fluctuations. The operator efficiency of the static checkpoint method increase slightly with the increase of the checkpoint interval. However, when the RDCI method is used with a parameter value of $\alpha = 6$ s, the operator efficiency is significantly improved. Compared to the static

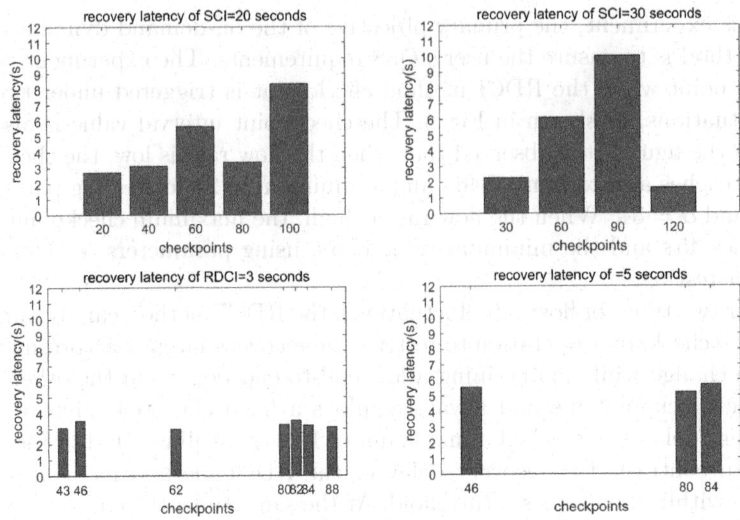

Fig. 9. Recovery latency of low fluctuation

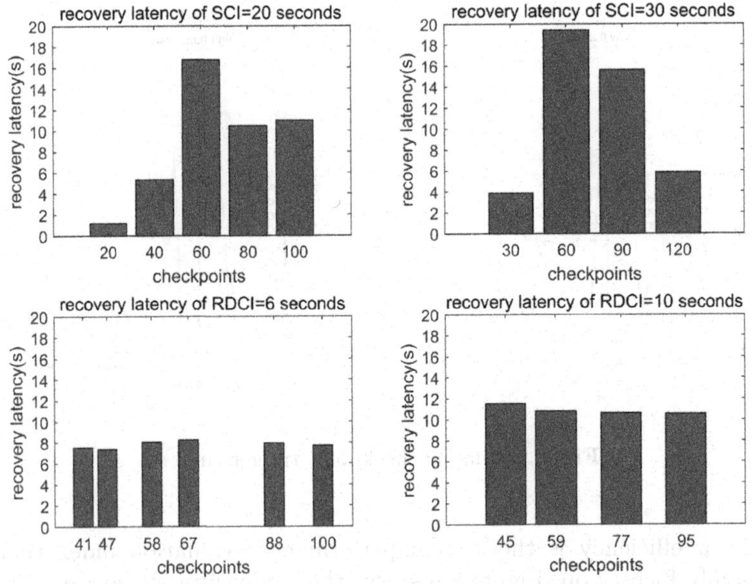

Fig. 10. Recovery latency of high fluctuation

checkpoint interval set to 20 s, the RDCI method improves operator efficiency by 11.9%. Figure 12 shows that different threshold settings of RDCI have varying effects on improving operator efficiency. Hence, appropriate recovery delay thresholds should be set based on specific flow rate conditions in actual scenarios.

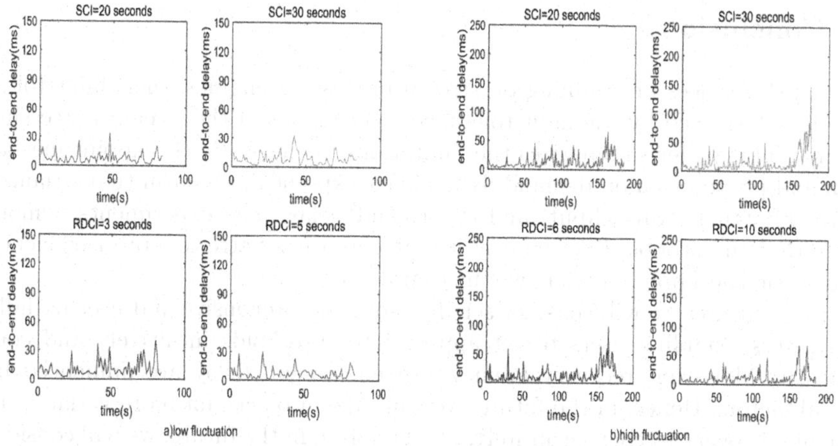

Fig. 11. End-to-end delay of two fluctuations

In summary, the static checkpoint method is unstable when dealing with high-speed data source fluctuations. On the other hand, the RDCI method proposed in this paper dynamically triggers the checkpoint operation adaptively, which can automatically balance the relationship between the recovery delay and the end-to-end delay and keep the recovery delay within the user's set threshold range. The experiment also proves that the RDCI method has better operator efficiency, making it more adaptable in data fluctuation scenarios.

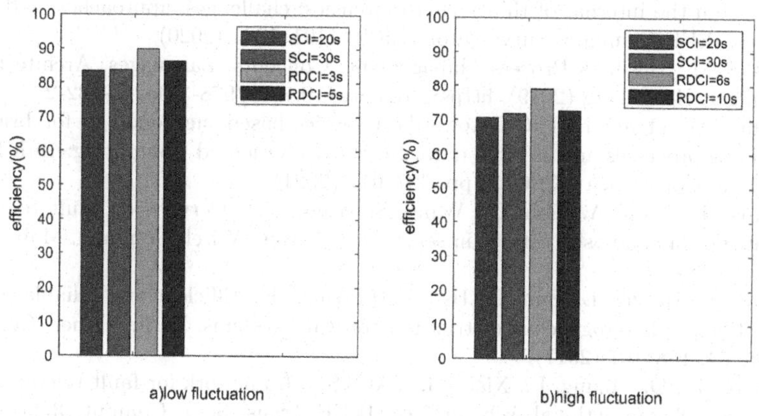

Fig. 12. Comparison of operator efficiency under different fluctuationsn

5 Conclusion

When IoT services are running on stream processing engines, their fault tolerance is constrained by the fault tolerance mechanisms of the stream processing engines. This paper summarizes the limitations of the static checkpoint mechanism and proposes an on-demand dynamic checkpoint mechanism that balances recovery latency, throughput, and end-to-end delay. The experiments demonstrate that the proposed mechanism is stable and has better operator efficiency than static checkpoints under two fluctuation scenarios.

In the future, we will consider setting more comprehensive and user-friendly parameters, enabling users to set appropriate thresholds intuitively and conveniently. Moreover, recovery latency and end-to-end delay are influenced by several factors. Hence, in the future, we will take into account more variables to estimate recovery latency accurately. Furthermore, in the future, we will consider implementing fault-tolerant mechanisms for IoT services that are independent of the stream processing engine.

Acknowledgement. This work is supported by the International Cooperation and Exchange Program of National Natural Science Foundation of China (No. 62061136006).

References

1. Stankovic, J.A.: Research directions for the Internet of Things. IEEE Internet Things J. **1**(1), 3–9 (2014)
2. Stoyanova, M., Nikoloudakis, Y., Panagiotakis, S., Pallis, E., Markakis, E.K.: A survey on the internet of things (IoT) forensics: challenges, approaches, and open issues. IEEE Commun. Surv. Tutor. **22**(2), 1191–1221 (2020)
3. Weske, M.: Business Process Management: Concepts, Languages, Architectures. Springer, Heidelberg (2019). https://doi.org/10.1007/978-3-662-59432-2
4. Gruhn, V., et al.: BRIBOT: towards a service-based methodology for bridging business processes and IoT big data. In: Service-Oriented Computing: 19th International Conference (ICSOC), pp. 597–611 (2021)
5. Zhang, J., Zhou, A., Sun, Q., Wang, S., Yang, F.: Overview on fault tolerance strategies of composite service in service computing. Wirel. Commun. Mob. Comput. (2018)
6. Wang, S., Huang, L., Sun, L., Hsu, C.H., Yang, F.: Efficient and reliable service selection for heterogeneous distributed software systems. Futur. Gener. Comput. Syst. **74**, 158–167 (2017)
7. Liu, A., Li, Q., Huang, L., Xiao, M.: FACTS: a framework for fault-tolerant composition of transactional web services. IEEE Trans. Serv. Comput. **3**(1), 46–59 (2009)
8. Erradi, A., Maheshwari, P., Tosic, V.: Recovery policies for enhancing web services reliability. In: 2006 IEEE International Conference on Web Services (ICWS 2006), pp. 189–196. IEEE (2006)
9. Wang, S., Lei, T., Zhang, L., Hsu, C.H., Yang, F.: Offloading mobile data traffic for QoS-aware service provision in vehicular cyber-physical systems. Futur. Gener. Comput. Syst. **61**, 118–127 (2016)

10. Angarita, R., Rukoz, M., Cardinale, Y.: Modeling dynamic recovery strategy for composite web services execution. World Wide Web **19**, 89–109 (2016)
11. Gupta, S., Bhanodia, P.: A fault tolerant mechanism for composition of web services using subset replacement. Int. J. Adv. Res. Comput. Commun. Eng. **2**(8), 3080–3085 (2013)
12. Vargas-Santiago, M., Hernández, S.E.P., Morales-Rosales, L.A., Kacem, H.H.: Survey on web services fault tolerance approaches based on check-pointing mechanisms. J. Softw. **12**(7), 507–525 (2017)
13. Mansour, H.E., Dillon, T.: Dependability and rollback recovery for composite web services. IEEE Trans. Serv. Comput. **4**(4), 328–339 (2010)
14. Chiu, L.Y., Fan, S., Liu, Y., et al.: Providing a fault tolerant system in a loosely-coupled cluster environment using application checkpoints and logs. U.S. Patent 9,098,439 (2015)
15. Chandy, K.M., Lamport, L.: Distributed snapshots: determining global states of distributed systems. ACM Trans. Comput. Syst. (TOCS). **3**(1), 63–75 (1985)
16. Young, J.W.: A first order approximation to the optimum checkpoint interval. Commun. ACM **17**(9), 530–531 (1974)
17. Daly, J.T.: A higher order estimate of the optimum checkpoint interval for restart dumps. Futur. Gener. Comput. Syst. **22**(3), 303–312 (2006)
18. Chen, N., Ren, S.: Adaptive optimal checkpoint interval and its impact on system's overall quality in soft real-time applications. In: Proceedings of the 2009 ACM Symposium on Applied Computing, pp. 1015–1020 (2009)
19. Jin, H., Chen, Y., Zhu, H., Sun, X. H.: Optimizing HPC fault-tolerant environment: an analytical approach. In: 2010 39th International Conference on Parallel Processing, pp. 525–534. IEEE (2010)
20. Punnekkat, S., Burns, A., Davis, R.: Analysis of checkpointing for real-time systems. Real-Time Syst. **20**(1), 83–102 (2001)
21. Zhuang, Y., Wei, X., Li, H., Wang, Y., He, X.: An optimal checkpointing model with online OCI adjustment for stream processing applications. In: 2018 27th International Conference on Computer Communication and Networks (ICCCN), pp. 1–9. IEEE (2018)
22. Jayasekara, S., Harwood, A., Karunasekera, S.: A utilization model for optimization of checkpoint intervals in distributed stream processing systems. Futur. Gener. Comput. Syst. **110**, 68–79 (2020)
23. Geldenhuys, M.K., Thamsen, L., Kao, O.: Chiron: optimizing fault tolerance in QoS-aware distributed stream processing jobs. In: 2020 IEEE International Conference on Big Data (Big Data), pp. 434–440. IEEE (2020)
24. Salama, A., Binnig, C., Kraska, T., Zamanian, E.: Cost-based fault-tolerance for parallel data processing. In: Proceedings of the 2015 ACM SIGMOD International Conference on Management of Data, pp. 285–297 (2015)

Multi-round Collaborative Task Assignment Under the Edge Cloud in Mobile Crowdsourcing

Xinxiao Zang[1], Yang Gao[1], Xuqiang Qiu[2], and Yingjie Wang[1](✉)

[1] Yantai University, Yantai 264005, China
towangyingjie@163.com
[2] Yantai Chijiu Clock Co., Ltd., Yantai 264000, China
qiuxuqiang@chijiu.com

Abstract. The rapid development of smart mobile devices has further expanded the perceptual scope of mobile crowdsourcing (MCS) in group workers, the popularity of smart terminal devices can help crowd workers complete large-scale tasks. MCS requires crowd workers to move to specific sensing regions to complete assigned tasks. However, the large amount of interactive data makes the traditional cloud computing cannot meet the requirements of MCS. Meanwhile, with the rapid increase the number of tasks and crowd workers, how to allocate crowd workers reasonably to maximize the benefits of the perception system has become a big research problem. Therefore, this paper constructs a framework of MCS system based on edge cloud and proposes a multi-round cooperative task allocation model (MrcWS) under edge cloud. The multi-round task allocation model partitions edge cloud regions according to the density of crowd workers and recommends suitable tasks by predicting the trajectories of crowd workers. After the crowd workers accept the task, this paper makes a second recommendation for the task according to the future movement trajectory. This paper encourages crowd workers to complete unassigned tasks by setting corresponding task rewards and reputation values. Finally, experiments on the real data set Foursquare show that the model can effectively improve the matching degree of tasks and data quality, and maintain the long-term development of the system.

Keywords: Mobile crowdsourcing · Multi-edge cloud · Task assignments · Worker selection

1 Introduction

With the rapid development of wireless communication and sensing technology, mobile devices have more and more sensors integrated. In this situation, MCS has become a hot research topic in mobile computing. In MCS, crowd workers can use mobile devices such as mobile phones or computers as the basic perception unit to

Y. Wang—Supported by organization x.

Z. Wang et al. (Eds.): ICSS 2023, CCIS 1844, pp. 106–120, 2023.
https://doi.org/10.1007/978-981-99-4402-6_8

collaboratively complete large-scale and complex crowd tasks. The current MCS [1] system consists of three main parts: cloud platform, task requester and crowd worker. Task requesters upload tasks to the cloud platform with limitations for each task (e.g., time range, region scope, budget, etc.). The MCS system has the characteristics of low cost and high coverage, so it is widely used.

With the number of sensors and the amount of data growing rapidly, cloud-based Internet of Things (IoT) [2] solutions are increasingly unable to meet the growing demand. Some scholars have begun to study the MCS system involved in edge-cloud. Mobile Edge Computing technology (MEC) [3,4] improves system efficiency. Kan et al. [5] considered the existence of different kinds of tasks in MEC systems with different time requirements. The overall efficiency of the system was improved by allocating computing resources and communication resources. Dab et al. [6] considered the MEC architecture based on Wi-Fi and proposed a method of joint allocation of user tasks and resources, the goal of minimizing the energy consumption of mobile devices under the constraint of meeting the delay constraints of user tasks. Yang et al. [7] considered a resource allocation method for MEC server collaboration. However, few existing studies have considered the problem of task allocation in the edge cloud region.

After the edge-cloud joins the MCS system, the cloud platform delegates the task to the corresponding edge-cloud through task region. Crowd workers in the edge-cloud region select tasks and submit data. However, it is difficult to predict the probability that a crowd worker will accept the task. Crowd workers are affected by their range of movement and where the task is located. Even if crowd worker accept a task, there are some factors such as credibility, data quality and so on which can affect the outcome of the task. Uneven population distribution in different regions can also complicate the problem. Effectively selecting the optimal crowd worker to perform tasks increases the efficiency and credibility of the system as a whole.

Under the constraints, how to dynamically match more and more suitable crowd workers, improve data quality, reduce the cost of crowd workers and platform, maximize social welfare are the main challenges. Aiming at these problems, this paper studies the task allocation problem under dynamic model, and proposes a multi-round task allocation model based on edge cloud. The main contributions of this paper are summarized as follows:

- This paper proposes a method to divide edge cloud according to crowd density, which greatly reduces the number of outages when crowd workers access servers.
- A multi-round task allocation mechanism is proposed. This mechanism improves the matching rate between tasks and crowd workers. It could select the best crowd workers, so that the movement cost of the crowd workers is reduced, and at the same time, the crowd workers are matched to more appropriate tasks.
- The comparison experiments are conducted on real data sets to verify the effectiveness of the proposed algorithm. It could improve the overall social benefits, the income of crowd workers and the completion rate of tasks.

The remaining components of this paper are as follows. In Sect. 2 introduces the related works. Section 3 introduces the system model. In Sect. 5, the experimental results are presented and analyzed to prove the effectiveness of the proposed method. Section 6 summarizes this paper.

2 Related Work

Research of MCS mainly includes three aspects: privacy protection [8–10], quality control [11–13], task allocation [14,15]. Privacy protection [16,17] is used to protect the sensitive information of sensed data uploaded by crowd workers. Quality control [18,19] is a broad field of study determined by the behavior of crowd workers who directly provide data. Task allocation is not only about recruiting crowd workers, but also about how to protect privacy [20,21] and improve data quality [22] during the uploading of sensed data [23].

Crowd workers' preferences, historical records and other information are also important factors in mobile crowdsourcing [24,25]. Different task types have different attractions for crowd workers. Crowd workers choose tasks according to their preferences. M. Gungor [26] considered the task allocation problem related to preference. The preference problem is solved by maximizing the total weighted satisfaction. Satisfaction is defined as the ratio of two linear functions. To solve this problem, a heuristic method based on nonlinear nonconvex programming is proposed. Li et al. [27] proposed a multi-task strategy based on service benefit perception by comprehensively considering the historical task completion, perceptual ability, task completion difficulty and the enthusiasm of crowd workers. Yang et al. [28] designed a crowd worker decision game to improve the matching degree between crowd workers and tasks through the utility, preferences and competitiveness of crowd workers. To improve the satisfaction of crowd workers and increase the revenue of platform, a stable matching algorithm based on extended delay acceptance algorithm was designed to construct the shortest path for each crowd worker. The above work improves the utilization of crowd workers, but it does not take into account that the matching rate of crowd workers and tasks will be reduced, thus affecting the overall benefit of society.

Location attributes of crowd workers are important when it comes to task allocation. In order to reduce the number of crowd workers as much as possible while completing task, Wang et al. calculated the moving distance through the current position of crowd workers and the specific position of task, and assigned tasks to the crowd workers closest which reducing the time consumption of task completion. However, this method cannot effectively stimulate the enthusiasm of workers. For tasks in remote regions or regions with few crowd workers, it is difficult to match suitable crowd workers, which makes the task be difficult to be completed. Lu et al. [29] proposed HySelector framework based on a two-stage hybrid employee recruitment, which not only recruited opportunistic crowd workers, but also encouraged participatory crowd workers to move to specific regions to complete tasks. The initiative of more crowd workers has been mobilized and the space coverage has been increased. Wang et al. [30] combined the offline stage with the online stage, and carried out joint optimization with the total incentive budget constraint. Density and mobility of mobile workers are key elements in the optimization process. However, it does not take into account that the crowd workers can still accept the recommendation task during the moving process of accepting the next task so as to improve the efficiency of the task. It also doesn't give some low-credit crowd workers a chance to improve their credibility.

Edge computing enables data to be preprocessed at the sensed network edge, which reduces the feedback time and improves the sensed efficiency. Existing researches rarely consider the factors of edge-cloud, coupled with unpredictable anthropogenic factors, the following questions still need to be addressed:

- At present, most of the task allocation models use the Voronoi diagram algorithm to divide the edge cloud, without considering that the density of crowd workers will affect the number of outages when data is uploaded to the server.
- Although the proposed task allocation algorithms have achieved a lot in terms of maximizing utility value and the number of tasks allocated, most of them are based on offline scenarios. It does not consider the failure of task matching in the crowdsourcing process and how to redistribute after success.
- Most current assignments do not consider how to deal with low- reputation crowd workers.

Therefore, this paper proposes a multi-round task allocation model based on edge cloud. In this model, the edge cloud region is divided according to the density of crowd workers in task allocation and the hidden Markov model is used to predict the trajectory of crowd workers. The task is recommended according to the location prediction results and the next round of task recommendation is carried out according to the task location accepted by the crowd workers, so as to ensure that the crowd workers have a greater probability to accept the task. In addition, crowd workers with low reputation values are given opportunities to improve their reputation values to maintain long-term stable operation of the system.

3 System Model

In this section, the edge cloud service model is first introduced, and then related issues are expounded.

3.1 Model Description

As shown in Fig. 1, there are four main components in the multi-round task allocation model: center cloud platform, edge cloud platform, task requester and crowd worker. The center cloud screens out crowd workers who may perform tasks and assigns tasks to corresponding edge clouds. Edge cloud platforms match tasks with appropriate crowd workers for a corresponding profit. For tasks in remote regions, crowd workers are inspired to complete the tasks through

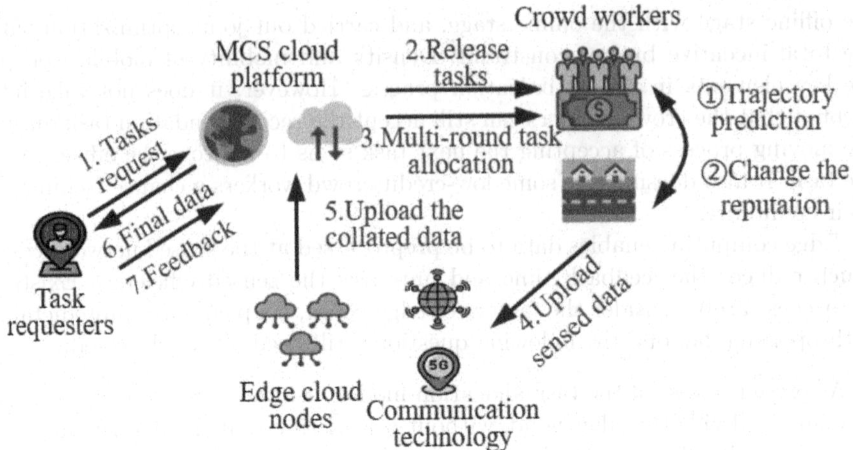

Fig. 1. Multi-round task allocation model in MCS platform.

increasing revenue and credibility. Crowd workers will be paid accordingly after completing tasks, their reputation values, historical trajectory information, perceived data quality and other data will be updated in time. The platform selects the crowd workers with the lowest cost and most likely to complete the task according to the movement track of the crowd workers and the perceived quality of the data, so as to improve the profits of the crowd workers. Through task division on edge cloud, crowd workers in a certain edge cloud region could be more reasonably selected to avoid distribution problems and resource waste on the edge.

Definition 1 (Crowd worker). Let $W = \{W_1, ...W_i, ...W_n\}$, which represents n workers. Each crowd worker W_i $(1 \leq i \leq n)$ is defined as a tuple of six elements $<Loc_{W_i}, Rep_{W_i}, Con_{W_i}, V_{W_i}, C_{W_i}, HInf_{W_i}>$, where Loc_{W_i} is the crowd worker's location. Rep_{W_i} is the crowd worker's reputation. Con_{W_i} is the crowd worker's confidence to complete the task. V_{W_i} is the maximum speed at which crowd workers can move over a period of time. The cost of a crowd worker is related to the distance they move. C_{W_i} is the cost of he distance a crowd worker moves per unit. $HInf_{W_i}$ is for historical information about crowd workers.

Definition 2 (Task). Let $T = \{T_1, ...T_j, ...T_m\}$, which represents m tasks. Each task T_j $(1 \leq j \leq m)$ is defined as a tuple of four elements $< Loc_{T_j}, Rw_{T_j}, R_{T_j}, K_{T_j} >$, where Loc_{T_j} is the location of T_j, Rw_{T_j} is the reward of T_j, R_{T_j} is the spatial coverage radius of T_j, $K_{T_j} = \{Time_s, Time_e\}$ is the start and end time of task T_j.

Definition 3 (The edge cloud). Let $E = \{E_1, \ldots, E_k, \ldots, E_x\}$, which represents x edge clouds. Each edge cloud $E_k (1 < k < x)$ contains the number of the edge cloud coverage region. Edge clouds are randomly divided using a Voronoi diagram.

In order to reduce the migration times, this paper screens the trajectory points of crowd contracted workers in January and then performs DBSCAN clustering to generate several subsets of points closely related to each other. On this basis, the Voronoi diagram of point set subsets is generated. The resulting Voronoi diagram is used to represent the division of edge clouds.

1) Determine the parameter *eps* value in DBSCAN algorithm
eps is generated by k-mean nearest neighbor method and mathematical expectation method. Based on DBSCAN algorithm, DT is defined as the *minpts* data points existing in *eps* neighborhood. DT can be obtained by Eq. 1.

$$DT = \frac{minpts}{\pi * eps} \tag{1}$$

The Euclidean distance is taken as the clustering distance. The distance distribution matrix of the crowd worker trajectory point set D can be calculated by Eq. 2.

$$D_{n*n} = \{D_{distance}(i,j)\,|1 \le i \le n, 1 \le j \le n\} \tag{2}$$

where D_{n*n} is a real symmetric matrix of $n*n$. $D_{distance}(i,j)$ is the distance from the ith object to the jth object in dataset D.
The distance between each data point and its k nearest neighbor data points in the track point set D of crowd workers is calculated, and distance of all data points is averaged to obtain the k-mean nearest neighbor distance of the data set. The elements in the k-th column form the k-nearest neighbor distance vector D_k for all data points. By averaging the elements in vector D_k, the k-mean nearest neighbor distance of vector D_k could be obtained and taken as candidate *eps* parameter. The parameter list of *eps* can be expressed as Eq. 3.

$$eps = D_k \quad 1 \le k \le n \tag{3}$$

2) Generate the *minpts* parameter list
The mathematical expectation method is used to generate the *minpts* parameter list, and the number of *eps* neighborhood objects corresponding to each *eps* parameter is successively calculated. The mathematical expectation of *eps* neighborhood object number of all objects is calculated, as the *minpts* parameter of dataset D. *minpts* can be obtained by Eq. 4.

$$minpts = \frac{1}{n}\sum_{i=1}^{n} P_i \tag{4}$$

where P_i is the number of *eps* neighborhood objects of the i object, and n is the total number of objects in data set D. Finally, the list of clustering categories is solved.
eps candidate items and *minpts* candidate items are extracted which are used to try to use DBSCAN algorithm for clustering. If the number of consecutive candidate clustering categories is the same, the one with relatively large *eps* is selected as the final parameter and input into DBSCAN algorithm.

3) Point set partition processing
   Search for clusters using circles with crowd worker trajectory points as the center of the circle and *eps* as the radius. When the *eps* neighborhood of point P contains more points than *minpts*, a new cluster is created with P as the core point. The clustering algorithm finds all the core points based on *eps* and *minpts*, and then starts at the core points to find new clusters generated by objects with reachable densities. It ends until all the points have been traversed, the final set of points is obtained.
4) Building edge Clouds
   The Voronoi diagram is generated by constructing point sets using Voronoi diagram algorithm, and each region of the Voronoi diagram corresponds to each edge cloud region.

Definition 4 (Quality of service per worker)**.** In our model, the service quality of crowd workers is related to task completion rate P, reputation value $Repw_i$ and task difficulty H(Time required to complete the task) of crowd sensing. First, task completion rate can reflect the probability that superior package workers can successfully complete the new task after receiving the new task. The higher the task completion rate is, the higher the probability that the new task can be completed. Secondly, the credibility of crowd workers varies according to the task completion rate, and the task completion degree in different periods has different effects on the credibility of crowd worker. In this paper, the Ebbinghaus forgetting curve is used to set the weights of task completion rates in different periods. Finally, different tasks have different effects on the service quality of crowd worker. The higher difficulty coefficient of task completion rate, the higher the service quality of crowd worker.

$$QoS_{W_i} = \alpha * Rep_{W_i} * Con_{W_i} * \theta_j^i \tag{5}$$

where α is the ratio of the sum of the difficulty of crowd workers completing tasks to the sum of the difficulty of receiving tasks. The difficulty of the task is given by the platform, Rep_{W_i} is the reputation, Con_{W_i} is the confidence, θ_j^i is the distance function between crowd workers and matching tasks.

The Rep_{W_i} is calculated based on the number of tasks successfully completed and the total number of tasks assigned. Gompertz function and Ebbinghaus forgetting curve function are used to update the reputation value.

4 A Multi-round Collaborative Task Allocation Model

In dynamic task allocation, a multi-round task allocation process is set up. For most crowd workers, tasks are part time and don't interfere with their daily lives. Therefore, in the first round of task allocation, according to the historical movement track of the crowd workers, the next destination of the crowd workers is predicted, so as to make the task recommendation of the current relevant region. In the second round of task allocation, the problem of passing cars is taken into account. After the crowd worker accepts the task, within certain constraints, it recommends the route task between the current position of the crowd worker and the accepted task position to the crowd worker. After two rounds of task assignment, if there is any unassigned task, the third round of task assignment is performed. Wait for new, more suitable crowd workers to join the list of workers, and repeat the first and second rounds of allocation. For example, for tasks in remote regions, few crowd workers will complete the tasks by the way, so it is necessary to find crowd workers who are relatively close to the tasks and whose reputation needs to be improved for reputation and reward incentives.

According to the historical trajectory points of crowd workers, a mobility prediction model is established by comprehensively considering the stay time, visit frequency and transfer probability. Based on the current time and location, the future movement region of the crowd workers and the task preference of the crowd workers are predicted to make task recommendation.

In this paper, the movement model of crowd workers is modeled as a discrete time homogeneous hidden Markov model $(Q_n^{w_i}, T_n^{w_i})$. $Q_n^{w_i}$ represents the n state of crowd worker w_i; $T_n^{w_i}$ represents the start time when crowd worker w_i reaches the n state. From the transition to state $Q_{n+1}^{w_i}$ only the reference state $Q_n^{w_i}$ is needed, so the process is a standard discrete-time Markov chain. A day of crowd workers is divided into 24 time periods on average, and the probability $P_{t_n}^Q$ of crowd workers in a certain region Q in time period T_n on day d is inferred from the trajectory information.

$$P_{t_n}^Q = \frac{\sum\limits_{d=1,2,\ldots,G_i} \sum\limits_{Q} num_Q^{T_n,d}}{\sum\limits_{d=1,2,\ldots,G_i} \sum\limits_{q \in Q_d^{T_n,d}} num_Q^{T_n,d}} \tag{6}$$

where $G_i = \{<Q_1, T_1, D_1>, \ldots, <Q_d, T_d, D_d>\}$ is the trajectory of the crowd workers. Q_d represents the set of arriving regions on day d. T_d represents the set that arrives at the corresponding region on day d. D_d represents the time spent in the corresponding region on day d. $num_Q^{T_n,d}$ is the number of times the crowd worker passes through location Q in time T_n on day d.

Let $P_{(x,y)}$ represent the transition probability of crowd workers from state x to state y, $P_{(x,y)}$ can be calculated by Eq. 7.

$$P_{(x,y)} = P\left(Q_{n+1}^{w_i} = y \,|Q_n^{w_i} = x\right) = \frac{\sum\limits_{d=1,2,\ldots,G_i} \sum\limits_{y} num_y^d}{\sum\limits_{d=1,2,\ldots,G_i} \sum\limits_{Q \in Q_{x.next}^d} num_Q^d} \tag{7}$$

where num_y^d represents the number of times the crowd worker moves from state x to state y on day d. $Q_{x.next}^d$ represents the number of times the crowd worker moves from state x to other states on day d. So w_i is most likely to move to the next state:

$$y = \max_{Y \in Q_{x,next}} (P_{x,y}) \tag{8}$$

In the task assignment, we calculated the *BP* of the crowd workers by linear weighting algorithm. Multiple task objectives are integrated into a single synthesis formula by multiplying points by multiple preferences.

$$BP = a * Rep_{W_i} + b * P_{W_i} + c * DNum_{W_i} \tag{9}$$

where BP is the weighted sum of the reputation value Rep_{W_i}, task completion rate P_{W_i} and total number of completed tasks $DNum_{W_i}$ of the crowd worker W_i. The sum of the weighting coefficients of each part is 1. The stability of the reputation value and service quality of the crowd workers were used to calculate the excellence of the recruited workers. The higher the quality of the tasks performed by the crowd workers, the higher the reputation value of the crowd workers was updated. Reputation value will affect whether the next task assignment is preferentially assigned to the crowd worker. This ensures the quality of the completion of the task.

Algorithm 1. Dynamic multi-round cooperative task assignment algorithm

Input: Task $T = \{T_1, ...T_j, ...T_m\}$, Worker $W = \{W_1, ...W_i, ...W_n\}$,Maximum number of assigned tasks each N_{max}.
Output: Task-Crowd workers successfully matched pairs $FG<t, w>$.
1: **while** not converged or $t \leq$ Max_iter **do**
2: $FG \leftarrow \phi$, $NSW_{T_j} \leftarrow \phi$.
3: Obtain the current location and time of the crowd worker, n is the current location.
4: **if** $\Gamma_n \neq \phi$ **then**
5: Add $F<t, w>$ according to whether the distance calculation meets the task time requirements and threshold requirements.
6: **else**
7: Calculate the time of departure and the most likely area y after departure
8: **if** $\Gamma_y \neq \phi$ **then**
9: Calculate the time of departure and the most likely area y after departure
10: **else**
11: $n = y$
12: **end if**
13: roll-back line 4
14: **end if**
15: **if** crowd workers select tasks in region f that are different from predicted region y **then**
16: $n = f$
17: roll-back line 4
18: **end if**
19: Arrange $F<t, w>$ in descending order according to BP value to obtain the maximum utility matching pair $FG<t, w>$
20: **end while**
21: **return** $FG<t, w>$.

The inputs are the task set T, the crowd worker set W, and the maximum number of tasks assigned by each crowd worker N_{max}. The output is a set of successfully matched task-crowd workers $FG<t,w>$. The first task assignment is to obtain the current location of the crowd worker and determine whether there is a task in this area. Recommend tasks within the area to crowd workers. Crowd workers choose whether or not to accept tasks based on their own needs (lines 1–5). Predict the crowd worker trajectory if there are no executable tasks in the current area. And determine if a task exists in the next area the crowd worker goes to (lines 6–13). After the first round of task assignment, there were three conditions for the crowd workers: 1. The crowd workers accepted the task recommended according to the trajectory prediction; 2. Crowd workers accept tasks they want to complete but are not recommended; 3. Crowd workers are not being matched to the right tasks. After the first round of task assignment, the crowd worker trajectories are iteratively predicted and tasks are recommended based on the updated task locations. And recommend tasks that can be completed along the way according to the task location of successful crowd workers assigned in the first round. In particular, for the second group of crowd workers, success was not predicted, but the task was still matched. Redetermine whether there are executable tasks in the new path. Narrow down the task proposal to avoid repeating incorrect predictions (lines 15–18). In this paper, a linear weighting algorithm is used to calculate the comprehensive evaluation value $BP$of crowd workers. According to BP value, workers in $F<t,w>$ are sorted in descending order to obtain the maximum utility matching pair $FG<t,w>$ (lines 19–21).

5 Experiment and Result Analysis

This section evaluates the effectiveness of the proposed methods by means of comparative experiments.

5.1 Experimental Setup

Dataset. Foursquare is a location-based social networking site where users can share their location via check-in. The Foursquare dataset contains users, places, check-ins, social relationships, and ratings assigned to places by users. Depending on the needs of the experiment, user files from datasets corresponding to the location of crowd workers and site files representing the location of the task are used. In this paper, 400 tasks and 1500 crowd workers were extracted for experiments.

Comparison algorithm. In this paper, two sets of comparative experiments are conducted according to the different divisions of edge clouds. From the four aspects of crowd worker benefit, platform benefit, task completion rate and data perception quality, the proposed method is compared with the other three algorithms, the final evaluation results are obtained. (1) Greedily select the highest data quality crowd workers to complete the task (MDQ) [31]. (2) Randomly recommend tasks around the location of the crowds workers (random) [32].

(3) Recommend crowd workers who can reach the task region through hidden Markov trajectory prediction (HMMTP) [33].

PC Configuration: All experiments run on the PyCharm 2021.1 platform in the Windows 10 operating system. The hardware environment for all experiments is Intel(R) Core(TM) i7-4720HQ with CPU @ 2.60 GHz and 8 GB of RAM.

5.2 Comparison Experiment

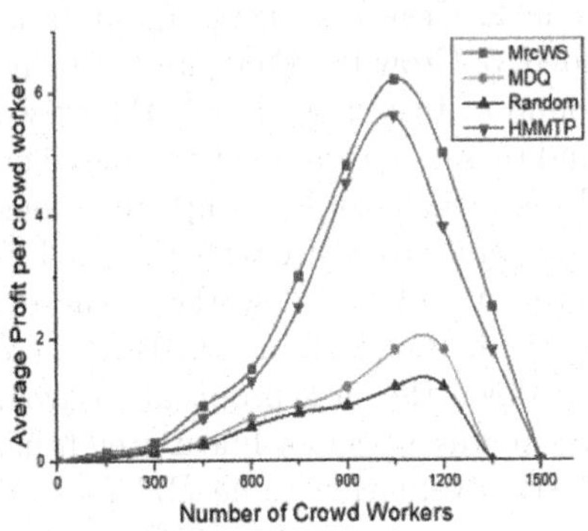

Fig. 2. The average profit per worker after completing tasks.

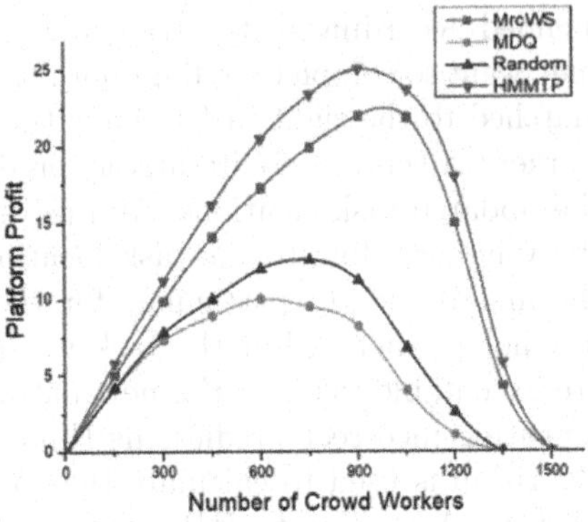

Fig. 3. The profit of the platform after completing tasks.

Figure 2 shows the impact of the increase in the number of crowd workers on the average revenue of crowd workers in the system when the number of tasks is 400. It could be seen that as the number of workers increases, so does the number of tasks on the platform, resulting in a gradual increase on the average profit of crowd workers. When the number of crowd workers is too large, the average profit of crowd workers gradually decreases. The MrcWS algorithm takes into account the trajectory of crowd workers and recommends more appropriate tasks for crowd workers to reduce the mobility costs of crowd workers. The MrcWS algorithm focuses on the mobility of crowd workers and real-time location changes, resulting in better performance than other algorithms. The probability that a task will match the right crowd worker is higher than other algorithms, and the crowd worker will be more profitable.

Figure 3 shows the influence of the increasing number of crowd workers on the average revenue of the platform when the number of tasks is 400. It could be seen that the platform's earnings are not the highest due to the MrcWS algorithm's incentive to compensate crowd workers. However, the MrcWS algorithm attracts more crowd workers to participate in the task, it also has better platform benefits.

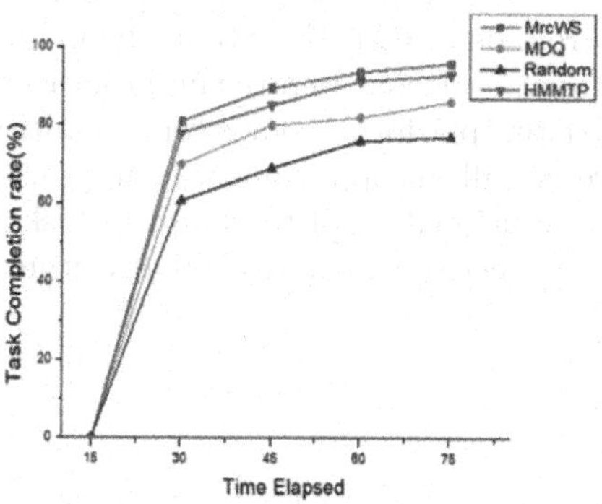

Fig. 4. The average profit per worker after completing tasks.

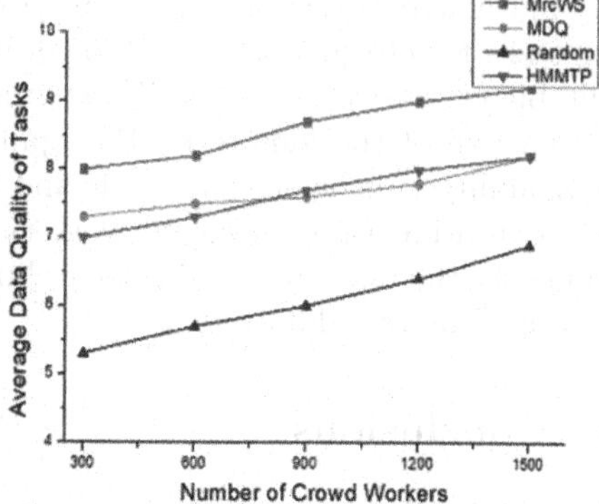

Fig. 5. The profit of the platform after completing tasks.

5.3 Comparison Experiment

It could be seen in Fig. 4, with the increase of time, more and more crowd workers are matched with tasks and the task completion rate gradually increases and tends to be stable. The task completion rate of MrcWS algorithm is higher than that of other algorithms. The MrcWS algorithm considers more factors, not only by predicting the trajectory of crowd workers to recommend more suitable tasks, but also by predicting the location of the next task to be executed. Even if in the first round of task allocation, crowd workers do not choose tasks recommended by trajectory prediction, in the second round of task allocation, they will reasonably recommend other tasks based on the selected tasks. Compared with the HMMTP algorithm, the MrcWS algorithm is better at recommending tasks that have smaller mobile costs and are more suitable for crowd workers. When selecting crowd workers, MDQ algorithm prefers crowd workers with high data quality and does not consider the time limit of crowd workers. The Random algorithm does not consider the data quality of crowd workers when selecting crowd workers, so the task completion rate is low.

Figure 5 shows the average level of submitted data quality as the number of crowd workers increases. As can be seen from the description in the figure, MrcWS algorithm is significantly better than other algorithms in terms of the average data quality of tasks when the number of crowd workers is different. The MDQ algorithm is based on a greedy algorithm that preferentially selects crowd workers with high data quality and high quality task completion. Due to the limitation of the degree of allocation of the MDQ algorithm audience package workers and tasks, the tasks cannot be better completed. The MrcWS algorithm takes into account not only the quality of the crowd worker but also the reputation value of the crowd worker and the task completion rate, resulting in a higher and more stable overall data quality.

Through the results of the above comparison experiments, the MrcWS algorithm performs better. The MrcWS algorithm recommends tasks according to the movement trajectories of crowd workers and reduces the cost of completing tasks for crowd workers. Through three rounds of task allocation, the more suitable crowd workers after linear weighting are selected iteratively. From the perspective of the long-term development of the platform, some workers with poor ability can be screened out, and there is still an opportunity to improve the reputation value of crowd workers who occasionally fail to complete tasks and cause the reputation value to decline. The effectiveness of MrcWS algorithm is verified by real data sets.

6 Conclusions

Most task allocation problems under spatio-temporal crowdsourcing are analyzed based on static models, which do not take into account the mobility of crowd workers and the dynamic entry and exit of crowd workers and tasks. It is difficult to get good results in practical applications. Therefore, this paper proposes a dynamic multi-round cooperative task allocation model under the edge cloud. Firstly, according to the density of crowd workers, the edge cloud region is divided by DBSCAN algorithm and Voronoi diagram segmentation method. Reduce edge users being moved out of the signal coverage of the initial deployment server due to their high mobility. Secondly, the situation where the user service link is interrupted due to the loss of communication connection with the server, thus affecting the service quality perceived by the user. A multi-round task allocation model is designed to select suitable crowd workers for task recommendation by reasonably increasing the trajectory prediction range and linear weighting algorithm. Moreover, according to the task location accepted by the crowd workers, the task assignment rate and task completion rate are recommended. In attention, the incentive mechanism is used to motivate the crowd workers who are difficult to match tasks to complete remote tasks to improve their reputation, eliminate inferior crowd workers, maintain the normal operation of the system and increase the coverage of crowd workers. Finally, the effectiveness of the proposed algorithm is verified by experiments from four aspects of crowd workers' income, platform income, task matching rate and task completion rate. It is proved that the proposed method is effective. In future work, the cold start problem should be considered for dynamic multi-round task allocation of crowd workers without moving trajectories.

References

1. Deb, A., Mi, B., Am, C., Ms, D.: Mobile crowd sensing – taxonomy, applications, challenges, and solutions. Comput. Hum. Behav. **101**, 352–370 (2019)
2. Wang, W., Wang, Y., Duan, P., Liu, T., Tong, X., Cai, Z.: A triple real-time trajectory privacy protection mechanism based on edge computing and blockchain in mobile crowdsourcing. IEEE Trans. Mob. Comput. (2022)
3. Mehrabi, M., You, D., Latzko, V., Salah, H., Fitzek, F.H.P.: Device-enhanced MEC: multi-access edge computing (MEC) aided by end device computation and caching: a survey. IEEE Access **7**(99), 166079–166108 (2019)

4. Xiang, C., et al.: Edge computing-empowered large-scale traffic data recovery leveraging low-rank theory. IEEE Trans. Netw. Sci. Eng. **7**(4), 2205–2218 (2020)
5. Zhao, H., Wang, Y., Sun, R.: Task proactive caching based computation offloading and resource allocation in mobile-edge computing systems. In: 2018 14th International Wireless Communications & Mobile Computing Conference (IWCMC), pp. 232–237 (2018)
6. Dab, B., Aitsaadi, N., Langar, R.: Joint optimization of offloading and resource allocation scheme for mobile edge computing. In: 2019 IEEE Wireless Communications and Networking Conference (WCNC), pp. 1–7 (2019)
7. Yang, Y., Wang, Y., Wang, R., Chu, S.: A resource allocation method based on the core server in the collaborative space for mobile edge computing. In: 2018 IEEE/CIC International Conference on Communications in China (ICCC), pp. 568–572 (2018)
8. Liu, T., Wang, Y., Li, Y., Tong, X., Qi, L., Jiang, N.: Privacy protection based on stream cipher for spatiotemporal data in IoT. IEEE Internet Things J. **7**(9), 7928–7940 (2020)
9. Sun, Z., Wang, Y., Cai, Z., Liu, T., Tong, X., Jiang, N.: A two-stage privacy protection mechanism based on blockchain in mobile crowdsourcing. Int. J. Intell. Syst. **36–5**, 2058–2080 (2021)
10. Wang, W., et al.: Privacy protection federated learning system based on blockchain and edge computing in mobile crowdsourcing. Comput. Netw. **215**, 109206 (2022)
11. Gong, W., Qi, L., Xu, Y.: Privacy-aware multidimensional mobile service quality prediction and recommendation in distributed fog environment. Wirel. Commun. Mob. Comput. **2018** (2018)
12. Chi, C., Wang, Y., Li, Y., Tong, X.: Multistrategy repeated game-based mobile crowdsourcing incentive mechanism for mobile edge computing in internet of things. Wirel. Commun. Mob. Comput. **2021**, 1–18 (2021)
13. Li, F., Wang, Y., Gao, Y., Tong, X., Jiang, N., Cai, Z.: Three-party evolutionary game model of stakeholders in mobile crowdsourcing. IEEE Trans. Comput. Soc. Syst. **9**(4), 974–985 (2021)
14. Lu, Z., Wang, Y., Tong, X., Mu, C., Chen, Y., Li, Y.: Data-driven many-objective crowd worker selection for mobile crowdsourcing in industrial IoT. IEEE Trans. Industr. Inf. **19**(1), 531–540 (2021)
15. Zhang, Q., Wang, Y., Yin, G., Tong, X., Sai, A.M.V.V., Cai, Z.: Two-stage bilateral online priority assignment in spatio-temporal crowdsourcing. IEEE Trans. Serv. Comput. (2022)
16. Zheng, X., Cai, Z.: Privacy-preserved data sharing towards multiple parties in industrial IoTs. IEEE J. Sel. Areas Commun. **38**(5), 968–979 (2020)
17. Cai, Z., Xiong, Z., Xu, H., Wang, P., Li, W., Pan, Y.: Generative adversarial networks: a survey toward private and secure applications. ACM Comput. Surv. (CSUR) **54**(6), 1–38 (2021)
18. Chi, C., Wang, Y., Tong, X., Siddula, M., Cai, Z.: Game theory in internet of things: a survey. IEEE Internet Things J. **9**(14), 12125–12146 (2021)
19. Wang, Y., Gao, Y., Li, Y., Tong, X.: A worker-selection incentive mechanism for optimizing platform-centric mobile crowdsourcing systems. Comput. Netw. **171**, 107144 (2020)
20. Cai, Z., He, Z., Guan, X., Li, Y.: Collective data-sanitization for preventing sensitive information inference attacks in social networks. IEEE Trans. Dependable Secure Comput. **15**(4), 577–590 (2016)
21. Cai, Z., Zheng, X.: A private and efficient mechanism for data uploading in smart cyber-physical systems. IEEE Trans. Netw. Sci. Eng. **7**(2), 766–775 (2018)

22. Qi, L., Zhang, X., Dou, W., Hu, C., Yang, C., Chen, J.: A two-stage locality-sensitive hashing based approach for privacy-preserving mobile service recommendation in cross-platform edge environment. Futur. Gener. Comput. Syst. **88**, 636–643 (2018)
23. Cai, Z., He, Z.: Trading private range counting over big IoT data. In: 2019 IEEE 39th International Conference on Distributed Computing Systems (ICDCS), pp. 144–153 (2019)
24. Shi, C., et al.: Deep collaborative filtering with multi-aspect information in heterogeneous networks. IEEE Trans. Knowl. Data Eng. **33**(4), 1413–1425 (2019)
25. Kou, F.F., et al.: Hashtag recommendation based on multi-features of microblogs. J. Comput. Sci. Technol. **33**, 711–726 (2018)
26. Güngör, M.: A fractional 0–1 program for task assignment with respect to preferences. Comput. Ind. Eng. **131**, 263–268 (2019)
27. Li, Z., Liu, H., Wang, R.: Service benefit aware multi-task assignment strategy for mobile crowd sensing. Sensors **19**(21), 4666 (2019)
28. Yang, G., Wang, B., He, X., Wang, J., Pervaiz, H.: Competition-congestion-aware stable worker-task matching in mobile crowd sensing. IEEE Trans. Netw. Serv. Manage. **18**(3), 3719–3732 (2021)
29. Lu, A.q., Zhu, J.h.: Worker recruitment with cost and time constraints in mobile crowd sensing. Future Gener. Comput. Syst. **112**, 819–831 (2020)
30. Wang, J., Wang, F., Wang, Y., Wang, L., Lv, Q.: HyTasker: hybrid task allocation in mobile crowd sensing (2019)
31. Cheng, P., Lian, X., Chen, L., Shahabi, C.: Prediction-based task assignment in spatial crowdsourcing. In: 2017 IEEE 33rd International Conference on Data Engineering (ICDE) (2017)
32. Sarker, S., Razzaque, M.A., Mehedi, M., Almogren, A., Zhou, M.: Optimal selection of crowdsourcing workers balancing their utilities and platform profit. IEEE Internet Things J. **6**(5), 8602–8614 (2019)
33. Wang, E., Yang, Y., Jie, W., Liu, W., Wang, X.: An efficient prediction-based user recruitment for mobile crowdsensing. IEEE Trans. Mob. Comput. 1 (2018)

A Container Migration Method for Edge Environments Based on Malicious Traffic Detection

Jing Wang[1], Zhangbing Zhou[1,2](✉), and Yi Li[1]

[1] School of Information Engineering, China University of Geosciences (Beijing), Beijing 100083, China
zbzhou@cugb.edu.cn

[2] Computer Science Department, TELECOM SudParis, Evry 91001, France

Abstract. Edge computing reduces network latency and improves service responsiveness by bringing services down to the edge. Compared to servers in the cloud center, edge devices are deployed more decentralized. Also, due to size and resource constraints, edge devices are difficult to manage or update security patches uniformly in real time. It makes it easier for malicious traffic to affect the security of the edge environment. In this paper, we propose a container migration method based on malicious traffic detection. We build a graph using the graph structure features of network flows to instantly detect the attacked nodes in the network and obtain the list of container services to be migrated. Considering energy consumption and network load balancing, a genetic algorithm based on non-dominated ranking is used to generate a strategy for container migration for edge networks.

Keywords: Container Migration · Edge Computing · Multi-Objective Optimization

1 Introduction

Edge devices are widely distributed, flexible in application, and highly intelligent. However, limited by various constraints such as size and version, the resources of edge devices for computing, storage and communication are not sufficient to withstand a complete security defense system [1]. Meanwhile, edge computing nodes have a strong distributed feature, which makes it difficult to use a unified security policy and management mechanism for supervision. Edge IoT devices have thus become a breeding ground for malicious traffic [2]. For example, the Mirai botnet once infected millions of IoT devices, including routers, cameras, and DVRs, and launched distributed denial-of-service (DDoS) attacks against DNS service providers like Dyn, causing widespread disruption and leading to the outage of some prominent websites. Malicious traffic in edge networks can have a negative impact on services, information security, and other related areas.

Z. Wang et al. (Eds.): ICSS 2023, CCIS 1844, pp. 121–137, 2023.
https://doi.org/10.1007/978-981-99-4402-6_9

Containerization is the packaging of an application and its dependencies into a container to form a portable, redeployable unit of software [3]. It enables applications to be deployed and run quickly across different platforms, operating systems, and environments. Running a single service in a container is preferable to running multiple services [4]. Compared to virtualization, which is also a packaged computing environment, containerization can be efficiently deployed anywhere using the same image, without the need to maintain different images for virtualized and nonvirtualized servers. As a result, containerization has become one of the standard practices for modern application development and deployment.

Dynamic edge environments require flexible reconfiguration and load balancing. Container migration enables the need for containers to be hosted on different nodes, improving the resource utilization and flexibility of the system [5]. Traditional container migration techniques usually require the suspension of container services to complete the preservation and recovery of container images and data volumes, and the whole process takes seconds or even minutes. With the container live migration method, the system can perform container migration without service interruption [6]. Container live migration technology greatly reduces downtime and enables capacity adjustment, cross-platform deployment, upgrade and disaster recovery without user awareness. Therefore, for edge networks deployed with containers, we can maintain service stability and information security in the network by promptly migrating containers on nodes that receive malicious traffic.

In this paper, we propose a container migration method based on malicious traffic detection. First, the network flows between nodes are detected to identify the malicious traffic and the attacked nodes. Then, the containers on the nodes under network attack are migrated to other nodes in advance to guarantee the high availability of edge network services under malicious traffic attacks. The main contributions of this work are as follows:

- We first apply the improved GraphSAGE algorithm to malicious traffic detection in edge environments, named MTDG. The graph structure features of a network flow are mapped into a graph to generate edge embeddings for edge classification work. By considering each network flow in the graph, the method aggregates the meta-information of the edges themselves with their graph structure features to generate edge embeddings to perform edge classification.
- We propose a container service migration method based on non-dominated sorting genetic algorithm. The container migration process is modeled as a multi-objective optimization problem. Considering the total energy consumption during the container migration process and the load balancing of the network after container migration, this article uses the NSGA-II algorithm to generate the optimal container service migration strategy.

2 Related Work

2.1 Malicious Traffic Detection

Malicious traffic detection in edge computing environments can ensure the security of network nodes and the reliability of services. In recent years, machine learning methods have played an important role in malicious traffic detection.

Doshi et al. [7] proposed a distributed shared deep learning based IoT attack detection system. They used middleboxes to observe the traffic between devices and the Internet, and exploited IoT-specific network behavior for feature selection to achieve higher accuracy. McDermott et al. [8] use Bidirectional Long Short Term Memory based Recurrent Neural Network (BLSTM-RNN) as an IoT DDoS attack detection scheme, using word embeddings for text recognition and converting attack packets into a tokenized integer format. Su et al. [9] innovatively proposed a lightweight approach based on the idea of image processing. A single-channel grayscale image of the malicious traffic data file transformation is first generated, and then a lightweight convolutional neural network is used to distinguish different classes of IoT malicious traffic.

In practical edge computing scenarios, the resources of containers and user requests are constantly changing. In order to be applicable to dynamic edge network situations, researchers have applied graph neural networks to IoT-related problems. Bekerman et al. [10] studied a session-based network representation using (source IP, source port, destination IP, destination port, protocol) to describe the traffic between two nodes in a specific time frame while the session aggregates the network traffic with the same source and destination nodes. Busch et al. [11] construct a graph using the network traffic between any two nodes in a time period and learn suitable representations from this network flow graph to obtain rich traffic information.

The above research indicates that using graph data structures can better preserve the structural characteristics of the network and improve the accuracy of network traffic classification. Therefore, in this paper, we use graph neural networks to model the edge computing environment. The intention is to capture the complex topological structure information between network nodes for malicious traffic detection.

2.2 Graph Neural Networks

In practical edge computing scenarios, edge devices are usually able to combine advanced technologies such as computer vision to achieve data acquisition and analysis related to images, gas concentration, temperature, etc. At the same time, the location tags and timing tags of the collected data are easily available because of the geographic location and other information possessed by the device itself. The graph neural network model captures the correlation between data by modeling the topology of the edge network. Edge environment graph structure modeling usually includes both geospatial and implicit semantic aspects.

From a geospatial perspective, an IoT device as a node represents its relative location in a certain area, and the edge is the data flow or other traffic information transmitted between devices. Boyaci et al. [12] propose a scalable real-time detection mechanism for spurious data injection attacks by fusing the underlying graph topology of the grid with spatially relevant measurements in the GNN layer. Hamilton et al. [13] proposed a universal inductive framework called GraphSAGE. It uses sampling and aggregation of features from neighboring nodes to generate embeddings, which has been widely applied to the task of representing geographic spatial nodes.

From an implicit semantic point of view, nodes reflect deep features of the current device and edges represent logical associations of nodes. This case is mainly applied to knowledge representation, dynamic linking and other scenarios with potentially learnable associations. Zhang et al. [14] proposed a GNN-based approach for modeling IoT devices by considering both temporal and logical relationships of data. Neural networks are used to simulate sensor networks and generate nonlinear and complex relationships. Shrivastava et al. [15] developed a standardized framework to support different prediction tasks from dynamically increasing IoT network device data.

2.3 Container Migration Strategy

On a macro level, container migration decisions are a form of container scheduling. Major container orchestration platforms, such as Docker Swarm, Google Kubernetes, etc., use schedulers to determine the best location for container services [16]. To achieve better performance, scientists have explored more container migration strategy approaches. The existing migration strategies can be broadly classified into four categories: mathematical modeling approaches, heuristic and meta-heuristics algorithms, and machine learning algorithms [17].

Integer Linear Programming (ILP) is a mathematical modeling approach that uses a set of linear constraints to optimize a linear function objective. Zhou et al. [18] proposed an ILP-based container migration approach that considers the temporal constraints of the task, resource constraints, and execution privileges. Kaur et al. [19] proposed an ILP-based multi-objective formulation that considers parameters in terms of carbon footprint, interference, and energy consumption in the edge network. Get a low-energy application solution while ensuring the best performance for users within the edge computing system.

Heuristic and meta-heuristic algorithms can generate scheduling solutions faster when the problem size is larger. The meta-heuristic algorithm is an improvement of the heuristic algorithm, which is a combination of a stochastic algorithm and a local search algorithm. Wen et al. [20] find a set of devices that need to be consolidated by monitoring the load patterns and thresholds of physical devices and use a genetic algorithm to generate an efficient container migration plan. Fan et al. [21] proposed a PSO-based scheduling algorithm that considers network latency, service reliability, and load balancing factors to determine a containerized microservice deployment strategy in the edge computing paradigm. Vhatkar et al. [22] proposed a multi-objective resource allocation method using the lion algorithm assisted by the whale optimization algorithm. The final optimized resource allocation plan is given by considering objectives such as threshold distance, cluster load balancing, system reliability, and overall network communication cost.

Deep machine learning uses the hierarchical structure of artificial neural networks to learn and make decisions. Machine learning algorithms effectively improve container migration decision performance by detecting network anomalies, predicting request volume, etc. Akhtar et al. [23] proposed a framework called COSE for cost prediction using statistical learning techniques. Configure parameters such as memory, CPU, cloud provider for the user while minimizing cost and meeting latency constraints. Mehta et al. [24] proposed a container scheduling solution called WattsApp, which is based on a neural network power estimation model. If a node violates the power constraint, container migration or resource reduction is performed to ensure the power limit. Liu et al. [25] used a linear regression model for resource utilization prediction to determine the timing of container migration.

3 System Model

3.1 Edge Network Model

A two-layer system model is proposed to measure the impact range of malicious traffic detection, and to describe the container migration problem. The system model is discussed as below:

- Edge layer: This layer consists of n edge devices, which can be represented by the set $D = \{d_1, d_2, \ldots, d_n\}$. Each edge device d can be represented by a tuple $d = \{devId, x, y, ip, cap, hoCon\}$, where $devId$ is the unique numeric identifier of the node, x and y are the position parameters of the node, ip is the IP address of the node, cap is the initialized resource capacity of the node which is related to the type of node device, and $hoCon$ is a list of container deployed by edge devices. All edge devices are evenly distributed in the network.
- Container layer: This layer contains m containers, which can be represented by the set $C = \{c_1, c_2, \ldots, c_m\}$. Each container c can be represented by a tuple $c = \{conId, requ, onDev, ip, cap, hoCon\}$, where $conId$ is the unique numeric identifier of the container, $requ$ is the resource capacity required by the current container, $onDev$ is the edge device where the container is deployed. Each container hosts only one service.

3.2 Performance Model

Energy Model. Considering the wireless sensor network environment at the edge, this paper uses a simplified First Order Radio Model (FORM) [26] to measure the energy consumption during container migration. The energy consumption of the model for sending k bits of data from node i to node j at a distance d is shown below.

$$E_{cmm,ij}(k,d) = E_{Tx}(k,d) + E_{Rx}(k) \tag{1}$$

$$E_{Tx}(k,d) = E_{elec} \times k + \epsilon_{amp} \times k \times d^2 \tag{2}$$

$$E_{Rx}(k) = E_{elec} \times k \tag{3}$$

where $E_{Tx}(k,d)$ is the energy consumption for forwarding data of size k to a node of distance d, $E_{Rx}(k)$ is the energy consumption for receiving k bits of data, E_{elec} is the unit radio dissipates constant and ϵ_{amp} is the transmit amplifier energy dissipates constant.

The size of container c migrating from edge device d_i to d_j can be expressed as

$$S_c = T_c + M_c \tag{4}$$

where T_c denotes the amount of transmission data for container c and M_c denotes the amount of memory resource data.

Hence, the total energy consumption for all containers to be migrated can be represented as

$$E_{total} = \sum_{c \in C_{mig}} E_c \tag{5}$$

where C_{mig} is the set of containers to be migrated and E_c is the energy consumption for migration of container c from edge device d_i to d_j calculated by Eqs. (1) to (4).

Load Balancing Model. Load balancing is a measure of the degree of load on the edge environment. Uneven distribution of resources in the edge environment may cause nodes with higher instantaneous power to become unreliable. In this study, we consider the average resource utilization of nodes [27] as a performance metric for measuring network load balancing to enhance the reliability and flexibility of the system.

The average resource utilization of an edge node device depends on the occupancy of the individual resources of all container services deployed on the node which can be described as

$$R_d = \sum_{r \in Re} \sum_{c \in Con} c^r / d^r \tag{6}$$

where r denotes a certain resource capacity of the device d, Re is the set of all resources. Con is the set of all containers on the device, generated by the $hoCon$ of the device. Depending on the specific situation, different weights can be given to different resource setting parameters in the network, and all parameters should add up to 1.

The total average resource utilization of the edge devices is calculated as follow.

$$RU = \sum_{d \in D} R_d / EM \tag{7}$$

where D is the set of all edge devices in the network. EM denotes the number of edge nodes in the network with running containers deployed, which can be expressed as

$$EM = \sum_{d \in D} \beta_d \tag{8}$$

where β_d is used to determine whether an edge device is being occupied by a running container service and can be computed by a binary function.

$$\beta_d = \begin{cases} 1, & \text{if at least one container is running} \\ 0, & \text{otherwise} \end{cases} \tag{9}$$

After that, the load balancing ratio of each edge device can be calculated as follow.

$$L_d = \begin{cases} (R_d - RU)^2, & \text{if } \beta_d = 1 \\ 0, & \text{otherwise} \end{cases} \tag{10}$$

The average load balancing ratio of all edge nodes in the network can be represented as

$$L_{total} = \sum_{d \in D} L_d / EM \tag{11}$$

4 Proposed Method for Container Migration Based on Malicious Traffic Detection

In this section, we propose a container migration decision framework based on malicious traffic detection. It can support edge networks to maintain high reliability in the face of complex traffic environments.

4.1 Malicious Traffic Detection Method

This paper proposes the use of graph neural networks for detecting malicious traffic due to the significant amount of structural information available in network flow data. The graph structure of edge networks allows for direct exploitation of the information, which can be encoded and learned through nodes and edges.

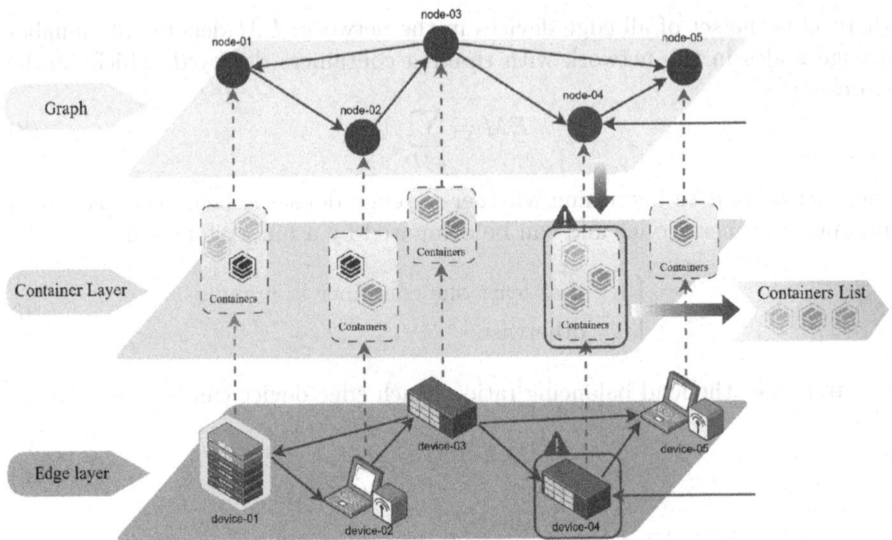

Fig. 1. Mapping structure of edge networks to graphs

Model Mapping. The mapping relationship between the edge network and the graph structure in the proposed construction model is shown in Fig. 1.

The graph mapping structure of the edge network includes three layers: edge layer, container layer, and graph. The edge layer includes real edge devices with network traffic, where devices that receive malicious traffic are marked as dangerous devices. The container layer shows the structure of containers deployed on the edge devices, where all containers hosted by the dangerous devices are added to the list of containers to be migrated. This layer of the graph shows the graph structure generated by the edge network based on traffic mapping. Intuitively, edge devices are mapped as nodes of the graph and network traffic is mapped as edges of the graph.

The GraphSAGE algorithm samples a subset of fixed size uniformly and randomly for each node. The subset consists of nodes and fixed-order neighbors of the nodes. This avoids the node embedding computation with full graph input as in traditional graph neural networks and greatly reduces time complexity of the algorithm. Lo et al. [28] and Chen et al. [29] improved the GraphSAGE algorithm to achieve anomaly detection in the network by considering features such as edges and time series. The graph-based approach for malicious traffic detection in this paper is based on their research implementation, called MTDG.

Malicious Traffic Detection. By combining the GraphSAGE algorithm with the idea of edge embedding, an edge embedding representing the network flow is output to support the downstream edge classification task.

The malicious traffic detection task in this paper is performed based on the previously mentioned graph. The graph is defined as G = (V, E), where V is the set of nodes and E is the set of edges in graph. For a set of network flows, the following four fields distinguish the nodes and edges in the graph in the data: source IP, source port, destination IP and destination port. In this case, the nodes are identified using a binary of IP and port. Other data related to the network flow can be fed into the model as edge information, depending on the specific dataset used.

The node features are initialized with an all-one-vector, and the dimensionality of the node features is the same as the dimensionality of the edge features. For an edge in the graph, its embedding can be obtained by the stitching of two node embeddings. The node embedding obtains the graph structure and edge information of the neighborhood through an aggregation function AGG that considers edge features. The embedding z_v^k of node v at layer k in the graph is calculated by the following equation.

$$h_{N(v)}^k = \mathbf{AGG}_k(\{e_{uv}^{k-1}, \forall u \in N(v), uv \in E\}) \tag{12}$$

$$z_v^k = \sigma(\mathbf{W}^k \cdot \mathbf{CONCAT}(z_v^{k-1}, h_{N(v)}^k)) \tag{13}$$

where e_{uv}^{k-1} is the edge feature of the edge uv of the target node v and its neighbor node u at the level $k-1$. The set $(\{e_{uv}^{k-1}, \forall u \in N(v), uv \in E\}$ denotes the set of edge sampling based on the target node v. $\mathbf{W}^k$ is the trainable weight matrix of the model at the layer k and σ is a nonlinear activation function. In this way, the node embedding z_v^k of the target node v captures the neighborhood topology and edge features.

After obtaining all node embeddings, the edge embeddings in the graph are obtained by connecting the node embeddings at the ends of the edges.

$$z_{uv}^k = \mathbf{CONCAT}(z_u^k, z_v^k) \tag{14}$$

where z_{uv}^k is the edge embedding of the edge uv at layer k between node u and node v, z_u^k and z_v^k are the node embeddings of node u and node v respectively. In this paper, the hidden feature size of each layer is set to 128, so the dimension of the edge embedding generated by concatenation is 256.

The final embedding of all edges in the graph is available by loop training of neighbors of order K. With a softmax layer, the network flow is tagged with a corresponding label. It reflects whether the destination node of the current network flow requires container migration or not.

The complexity of the algorithm mainly lies in the process of node sampling and aggregation. Specifically, the time complexity is related to the actual number of edges p sampled by the current node, which is determined by the specific sampling strategy. Additionally, the feature dimension d of each hidden layer in the node also affects the complexity of the aggregation process. Therefore, the time complexity of node sampling and aggregation is $O(pd^2)$. The number of aggregation operations mentioned above is related to the total number of nodes q in the network and the predetermined number of network sampling layers K. The overall time complexity of the algorithm is $O(pd^2qK)$.

4.2 Container Migration Strategy Method

The NSGA algorithm is a classical genetic algorithm that uses a selection strategy based on non-dominated ranking to select individuals in a population. It constitutes the Pareto front of the population by non-dominated ranking, which represents the set of optimal balancing solutions among multiple objectives. On this basis, the NSGA-II algorithm introduces the crowding distance to evaluate the individual density, which reduces the time complexity of the algorithm.

According to the system model in Sect. 3, the number of target nodes for malicious traffic in the network is assumed to be p. In this paper, the chromosome of the NSGA-II is encoded based on the edge device id as follow.

$$Chromosome = [d_1, d_2, \ldots, d_{n-p}] \tag{15}$$

where the size of Chromosome is q, where d_1 to d_{n-p} is the $devId$ of normal edge device nodes. The element positions 0 to $q-1$ in this matrix represent the q containers to be migrated in ascending order of $conId$. The same $devId$ can appear multiple times in the list, because a single device node in the edge environment may host multiple containers. Ultimately, the genes of the optimal individual are the target devices for all containers that need to be migrated.

In the scenario of this paper, the energy consumption E_{total} during container migration is calculated according to Eq. (5) and the load balancing ratio L_{total} after migration is calculated according to Eq. (11). The MTDG algorithm searches for the global optimal solution by minimizing these two values.

Furthermore, a fundamental QoS constraint needs to be considered during the computation, i.e., the occupied usage of any resource on an edge device should be lower than the maximum amount of that resource. If a solution does not satisfy this constraint, then both E_{total} and L_{total} of that solution are set to infinity.

The time complexity of the NSGA-II algorithm for container migration strategy method is mainly related to the specific algorithm process and parameter settings. This paper considers the following three main aspects. When constructing the non-dominated set, the algorithm needs to calculate the set of individuals dominated by each individual and the set of individuals that dominate it. Suppose the number of individuals in the initial population is p, then the total number of individuals involved in sorting is $2p$. In the first round of non-dominated sorting, each individual needs to compare q objectives with other $2p-1$ individuals. Therefore, the time complexity of this part is $O((2p)^2q)$. When calculating the crowding distance, the time complexity is related to the selected sorting algorithm. Currently, the algorithm with the minimum time complexity is $O(2p\log(2p))$. For each objective, the crowding distance needs to be iteratively calculated, so the total time complexity of crowding distance calculation is $O(2pq\log(2p))$. When sorting the crowding distance, NSGA-II defines a crowding comparison partial order operator. In the worst case, all individuals are in the same front solution set, so the time complexity of constructing the crowding distance sorting for this set is $O(2p\log(2p))$. Therefore, the time complexity of NSGA-II applied to container service migration is $O(p^2q)$.

5 Experiments

5.1 Malicious Traffic Detection

Dataset. In this paper, a new X-IIoTID dataset [30] is used for experimental validation. The dataset provides device-independent network flow intrusion data that can be applied to various heterogeneous and interoperability scenarios. There are 820,834 network flows, each with 3 labels and 65 other features. The three labels differ in perspective and classify the whole dataset into 2, 10 and 19 categories, respectively. It provides sufficient labeling data for both binary and multiclassification experiments.

According to the experimental requirements, we removed two columns of labels from the dataset. The IP and port of the source and target nodes of the flow are separately represented by binary groups. All other 61-dimensional features are input to the model as edge information.

Experimental Metrics. We use five-fold cross-validation to evaluate the performance of the algorithm. The data set is randomly divided into five parts. One of them is selected as the testing set and the others as the training set in turn. The mean of the five experiments in the end is the experimental result. The following metrics were specifically used for the evaluation. Precision describes the actual correct positive prediction rate, recall denotes the fraction of actual positives correctly identified, and the F1 score is a weighted average of precision and recall.

Referring to the implementation in the paper [30], we compare the most commonly used machine learning algorithms and deep learning algorithms, including decision tree (DT), support vector machines (SVM), logistic regression (LR), and deep neural networks (DNN).

Experimental Result. We implemented MTDG and other baseline experiments in the same physical environment. MTDG sets K as 2, indicating that the algorithm samples and aggregates the second-order neighbors of nodes. The model is trained with a epoch of 100, using the Adam optimizer, with ReLU and sigmond as activation functions. Other baseline experiments were set up with the same parameters as in the paper [30].

Analysis of the experimental results shows that both DNN and MTDG algorithms exhibit excellent performance in the precision metric of malicious traffic detection. Meanwhile, MTDG is slightly higher than the comparison algorithm in all three metrics. The reason may be that the network structure formed by the nodes in this dataset has a greater impact on the malicious traffic detection performance compared to other algorithms, especially DNNs, and MTDG captures this feature well. In addition, the F1 score shows that the algorithm results for malicious traffic detection by building graphs are more robust than using features directly for detection (Fig. 2).

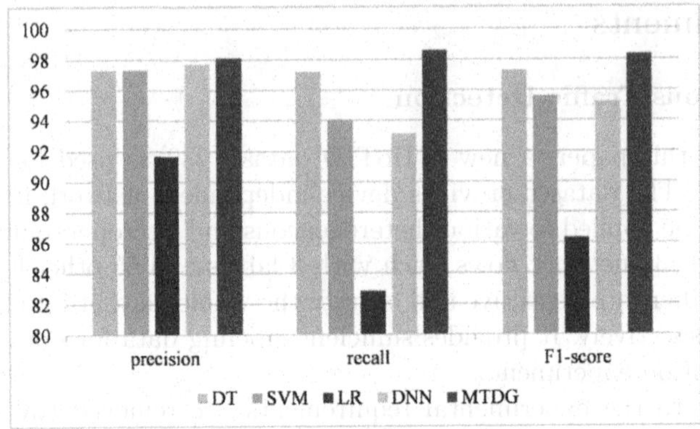

Fig. 2. The precision, recall and F1 score of multiclassification for different experiments

5.2 Container Migration Strategy

Experimental Setup. Since it is costly to build real scenarios, this section uses simulation experiments to simulate the edge network environment. The parameters of the edge devices and containers set in the simulated network are shown in Table 1.

Table 1. Simulation experiment parameters

Parameters	Setup
Simulation grid range	200 m×200 m
Number of edge devices	30
Number of containers	40
Device CPU capacity	8 cores
Device storage capacity	128 GB
Device memory capacity	32 GB
Container CPU requirement	1–2 core
Container storage capacity requirement	1–16 GB
Container memory capacity requirement	1–16 GB

The simulation experiment simulates a network whose range size is 200 m × 200 m. Initially, 30 edge devices and 40 containers are randomly and uniformly distributed in the edge network while satisfying the resource constraints. The edge devices are all homogeneous with 8-core CPU, 128 GB of storage, and 32 GB of memory. The container simulation hosts a variety of different services, where the container service CPU requirement may be 1 or 2 cores, and the storage capacity and memory capacity requirements are randomly generated from 1 to 16.

With experimental exploration, this paper sets the population size of NSGA-II algorithm to 200, the number of iterations to 250, and the distribution indexes of crossover and variation to 40 and 50, respectively.

Experimental Result. In order to verify the optimization of container migration decision method in terms of energy consumption and load balancing, this paper adopts three comparison methods, namely, Random Migration Strategy (RMS), Greedy Migration Strategy (GMS) and the Closest Node Migration Strategy (CNMS).

The RMS algorithm randomly migrates containers to other available nodes. If the node does not meet the resource constraints, the migration options will be recalculated until the target migration node is found or failed. The GMS algorithm processes each container to be migrated sequentially, always migrating a container to the node with the lowest energy consumption and load balancing ratio in the current network. The CNMS algorithm migrates the container to the nearest node that satisfies the QoS constraints.

A comparison of the energy consumption of the three methods with NSGA-II is shown in Fig. 3, and a comparison of the load balancing ratio is shown in Fig. 4. The number of services to be migrated is simulated from 1 to 10 while keeping the number of edge devices at 30 and the number of containers at 40 to verify the energy consumption performance of the algorithms.

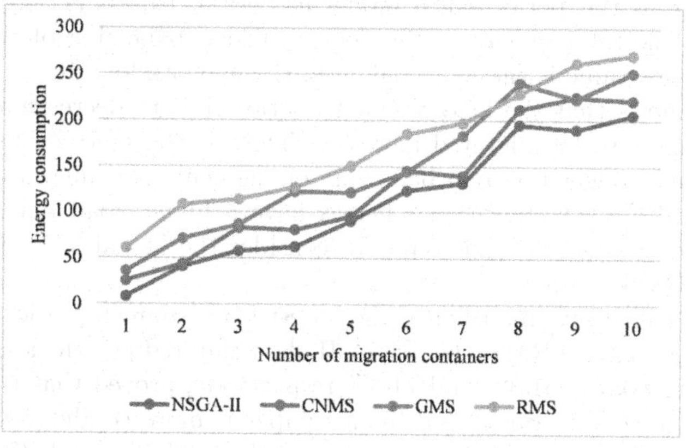

Fig. 3. The impact of the number of container migrations on energy consumption

As can be seen from Fig. 3, the overall energy consumption of all four algorithms grows as the number of migrated containers increases. In particular, the energy consumption of RMS is consistently higher because the random migration decision does not focus on any information about the migration process. The energy consumption of CNMS is relatively low. This is because the algorithm tends to migrate the container service to the nearest normal node that can assume the service, making the migration distance shorter and energy consumption less. The NSGA-II algorithm used in this paper reduces the energy consumption by at least 5.17% compared to CNMS, consistently maintaining the lowest consumption level. It shows that the algorithm is more efficient than others in terms of energy consumption for the container migration decision.

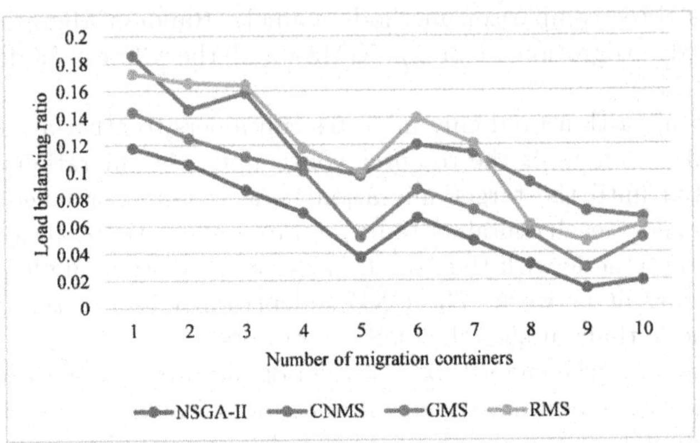

Fig. 4. Impact of the number of container migrations on the load balancing ratio

According to the performance model in Sect. 3, this paper uses the load balancing coefficient to measure the degree of load balancing of the network. The smaller this value is the more balanced the network load is.

Figure 4 shows that the load balancing ratio tends to decrease as the number of containers to be migrated increases. That is, the more containers to be migrated, the stronger the load balancing of the generated migration solution. The RMS and CNMS migration schemes have a higher load balancing ratio. Since neither of these methods tends to consider the global load. The same is true for the GMS method.

NSGA-II has always maintained the lowest load balancing ratio. Comparing with CNMS, GMS and RMS, the NSGA-II algorithm reduces the load balancing ratio by up to 80.5%, 61.8% and 71.3% respectively, proved that the NSGA-II container migration strategy used in this paper is more conducive to ensuring the overall load balancing of the network, and the feasibility and effectiveness of the algorithm are verified.

6 Conclusion

In this paper, we consider the risk of malicious traffic attacks on devices in edge computing environments and propose an MTDG strategy. The strategy uses an improved GraphSAGE algorithm to generate edge embeddings containing flow information by node embedding. With the classification of network flows, the method achieves no less than 98% precision on malicious traffic detection work, proving the feasibility and effectiveness of the method. Subsequently, the strategy models the container migration process as a multi-objective optimization problem. By considering the energy consumption of container migration with network load balancing, the NSGA-II algorithm is used to find the global optimal solution. In comparison with the baseline methods, this method reduces the energy consumption and load balancing ratio by at least 5.17% and 15.48%. Experiments validate the effectiveness of MTDG implementation of container migration policy based on malicious traffic detection.

References

1. Chen, J., Ran, X.: Deep learning with edge computing: a review. Proc. IEEE **107**, 1655–1674 (2019). https://doi.org/10.1109/JPROC.2019.2921977
2. Angrishi, K.: Turning internet of things (IoT) into internet of vulnerabilities (IoV): IoT botnets (2017). http://arxiv.org/abs/1702.03681, https://doi.org/10.48550/arXiv.1702.03681
3. Pahl, C.: Containerization and the PaaS cloud. IEEE Cloud Comput. **2**, 24–31 (2015). https://doi.org/10.1109/MCC.2015.51
4. Resource allocation for edge computing with multiple tenant configurations | Proceedings of the 35th Annual ACM Symposium on Applied Computing. https://dl.acm.org/doi/abs/10.1145/3341105.3374026. Accessed 20 Feb 2023
5. Wang, S., Xu, J., Zhang, N., Liu, Y.: A survey on service migration in mobile edge computing. IEEE Access **6**, 23511–23528 (2018). https://doi.org/10.1109/ACCESS.2018.2828102
6. Govindaraj, K., Artemenko, A.: Container live migration for latency critical industrial applications on edge computing. In: 2018 IEEE 23rd International Conference on Emerging Technologies and Factory Automation (ETFA), pp. 83–90. IEEE, Turin (2018). https://doi.org/10.1109/ETFA.2018.8502659
7. Doshi, R., Apthorpe, N., Feamster, N.: Machine learning DDoS detection for consumer internet of things devices. In: 2018 IEEE Security and Privacy Workshops (SPW), pp. 29–35 (2018). https://doi.org/10.1109/SPW.2018.00013
8. McDermott, C.D., Majdani, F., Petrovski, A.V.: Botnet detection in the internet of things using deep learning approaches. In: 2018 International Joint Conference on Neural Networks (IJCNN), pp. 1–8 (2018). https://doi.org/10.1109/IJCNN.2018.8489489
9. Su, J., Vasconcellos, D.V., Prasad, S., Sgandurra, D., Feng, Y., Sakurai, K.: Lightweight classification of IoT malware based on image recognition. In: 2018 IEEE 42nd Annual Computer Software and Applications Conference (COMPSAC), pp. 664–669 (2018). https://doi.org/10.1109/COMPSAC.2018.10315
10. Bekerman, D., Shapira, B., Rokach, L., Bar, A.: Unknown malware detection using network traffic classification. In: 2015 IEEE Conference on Communications and Network Security (CNS), pp. 134–142 (2015). https://doi.org/10.1109/CNS.2015.7346821
11. Busch, J., Kocheturov, A., Tresp, V., Seidl, T.: NF-GNN: network flow graph neural networks for malware detection and classification. In: 33rd International Conference on Scientific and Statistical Database Management, pp. 121–132. Association for Computing Machinery, New York (2021). https://doi.org/10.1145/3468791.3468814

12. Boyaci, O., et al.: Graph neural networks based detection of stealth false data injection attacks in smart grids. IEEE Syst. J. **16**, 2946–2957 (2022). https://doi.org/10.1109/JSYST.2021.3109082
13. Hamilton, W.L., Ying, R., Leskovec, J.: Inductive representation learning on large graphs (2018). http://arxiv.org/abs/1706.02216, https://doi.org/10.48550/arXiv.1706.02216
14. Zhang, W., Zhang, Y., Xu, L., Zhou, J., Liu, Y., Gu, M., Liu, X., Yang, S.: Modeling IoT equipment with graph neural networks. IEEE Access **7**, 32754–32764 (2019). https://doi.org/10.1109/ACCESS.2019.2902865
15. Shrivastava, N., Bhagat, A., Nair, R.: Graph powered machine learning in smart sensor networks. In: Singh, U., Abraham, A., Kaklauskas, A., Hong, T.-P. (eds.) Smart Sensor Networks. SBD, vol. 92, pp. 209–226. Springer, Cham (2022). https://doi.org/10.1007/978-3-030-77214-7_9
16. Bernstein, D.: Containers and cloud: from LXC to docker to kubernetes. IEEE Cloud Comput. **1**, 81–84 (2014). https://doi.org/10.1109/MCC.2014.51
17. Ahmad, I., AlFailakawi, M.G., AlMutawa, A., Alsalman, L.: Container scheduling techniques: a survey and assessment. J. King Saud Univ. - Comput. Inf. Sci. **34**, 3934–3947 (2022). https://doi.org/10.1016/j.jksuci.2021.03.002
18. Zhou, R., Li, Z., Wu, C.: Scheduling frameworks for cloud container services. IEEE/ACM Trans. Netw. **26**, 436–450 (2018). https://doi.org/10.1109/TNET.2017.2781200
19. Kaur, K., Garg, S., Kaddoum, G., Ahmed, S.H., Atiquzzaman, M.: KEIDS: kubernetes-based energy and interference driven scheduler for industrial iot in edge-cloud eco-system. IEEE Internet Things J. **7**, 4228–4237 (2020). https://doi.org/10.1109/JIOT.2019.2939534
20. Wen, Y., Li, Z., Jin, S., Lin, C., Liu, Z.: Energy-efficient virtual resource dynamic integration method in cloud computing. IEEE Access **5**, 12214–12223 (2017). https://doi.org/10.1109/ACCESS.2017.2721548
21. Fan, G., Chen, L., Yu, H., Qi, W.: Multi-objective optimization of container-based microservice scheduling in edge computing. Comput. Sci. Inf. Syst. **18**, 23–42 (2021)
22. Vhatkar, K.N., Bhole, G.P.: Optimal container resource allocation in cloud architecture: a new hybrid model. J. King Saud Univ. - Comput. Inf. Sci. **34**, 1906–1918 (2022). https://doi.org/10.1016/j.jksuci.2019.10.009
23. Akhtar, N., Raza, A., Ishakian, V., Matta, I.: COSE: configuring serverless functions using statistical learning. In: IEEE INFOCOM 2020 - IEEE Conference on Computer Communications, pp. 129–138 (2020). https://doi.org/10.1109/INFOCOM41043.2020.9155363
24. Mehta, H.K., Harvey, P., Rana, O., Buyya, R., Varghese, B.: WattsApp: power-aware container scheduling. In: 2020 IEEE/ACM 13th International Conference on Utility and Cloud Computing (UCC), pp. 79–90 (2020). https://doi.org/10.1109/UCC48980.2020.00027
25. Liu, J., Wang, S., Zhou, A., Xu, J., Yang, F.: SLA-driven container consolidation with usage prediction for green cloud computing. Front. Comput. Sci. **14**, 42–52 (2020). https://doi.org/10.1007/s11704-018-7172-3
26. Heinzelman, W.R., Chandrakasan, A., Balakrishnan, H.: Energy-efficient communication protocol for wireless microsensor networks. In: Proceedings of the 33rd Annual Hawaii International Conference on System Sciences, p. 10. IEEE Computer Society, Maui (2000). https://doi.org/10.1109/HICSS.2000.926982

27. Peng, K., Huang, H., Zhao, B., Jolfaei, A., Xu, X., Bilal, M.: Intelligent computation offloading and resource allocation in IIoT with end-edge-cloud computing using NSGA-III. IEEE Trans. Netw. Sci. EngD. 1 (2022). https://doi.org/10.1109/TNSE.2022.3155490
28. Lo, W.W., Layeghy, S., Sarhan, M., Gallagher, M., Portmann, M.: E-GraphSAGE: a graph neural network based intrusion detection system for IoT. In: NOMS 2022–2022 IEEE/IFIP Network Operations and Management Symposium, pp. 1–9 (2022). https://doi.org/10.1109/NOMS54207.2022.9789878
29. Chen, C., Li, Q., Chen, L., Liang, Y., Huang, H.: An improved GraphSAGE to detect power system anomaly based on time-neighbor feature. Energy Rep. **9**, 930–937 (2023). https://doi.org/10.1016/j.egyr.2022.11.116
30. Al-Hawawreh, M., Sitnikova, E., Aboutorab, N.: X-IIoTID: a connectivity-agnostic and device-agnostic intrusion data set for industrial internet of things. IEEE Internet Things J. **9**, 3962–3977 (2022). https://doi.org/10.1109/JIOT.2021.3102056

BIFData: A Secure Data Trading Marketplace Platform Based on Blockchain Technology and Smart Contracts

Pei Shang, Ying Liu(✉), Ege Sorguc, and Yuzheng Han

Northeastern University, Shenyang 110000, China
liuy@swc.neu.edu.cn

Abstract. The big data industry is rapidly expanding and the data generated by all kinds of devices is increasingly valuable. However, traditional data markets suffer from data silos and lack effective data security mechanisms, which can easily lead to data theft and misuse. With the emergence of blockchain technology, a solution arises. Blockchain is a decentralized, distributed database that records all transactions occurring in a peer-to-peer network. Its unique characteristics can make data marketplaces more secure and transparent. This paper proposes and implements a data marketplace trading platform that combines blockchain and smart contracts. The platform reduces storage costs by storing metadata on the blockchain, manages data providers using a point system combined with federated learning, and improves the system's operation and storage capacity by using different servers as blockchain nodes. Our implementation is based on the Ethereum platform, and smart contracts are written using the Solidity language. Experimental results confirm the performance of the proposed data trading marketplace platform regarding the security and stability of data transactions.

Keywords: Data marketplace · Blockchain · Smart contracts · Federated learning

1 Introduction

In 2008, Satoshi Nakamoto released a white paper on Bitcoin, which introduced blockchain technology. Bitcoin was the first invention of blockchain cryptocurrency accepted worldwide [21]. Initially, blockchain served as a decentralized electronic cash system that lacked complete automation for transaction execution in the Bitcoin network. Later, Ethereum was developed as an open platform that utilizes blockchain technology. This platform enables developers to design smart contracts. Smart contracts [9,10,17], which operate based on predetermined conditions, are programs that execute tasks like trading, voting, financial coordination, and logistics tracking. Developers can deploy smart contracts via the Ethereum network and Solidity language, effectively executing

Z. Wang et al. (Eds.): ICSS 2023, CCIS 1844, pp. 138–150, 2023.
https://doi.org/10.1007/978-981-99-4402-6_10

conditionally-defined transactions. By utilizing smart contracts in conjunction with the Ethereum network, transactions are automated, resulting in increased efficiency and ease of use.

Marketplace is a platform that connects data providers and consumers to enable reliable data transactions between parties [1]. Traditional transaction methods heavily involve a centralized organization or service provider, which can be inconvenient for both parties and necessitates a trusted third party acting as a guarantor. Concurrently, security and privacy risks arise when sensitive information, such as the personal data of both parties to a transaction, is susceptible to use by third parties. The usage of blockchain technology has become increasingly prevalent in various industries, including data markets. Smart contracts enable both parties engaging in a data transaction to negotiate and encode the transaction terms into executable code within a smart contract. Once a smart contract is deployed on the blockchain, the contained code is executed automatically, automating the transaction process. Figure 1 illustrates the automated trading process for smart contracts. Automating transactions through smart contracts eliminates the need for intermediaries on both sides of the transaction, resulting in more secure and efficient transactions. The automated execution of smart contracts increases transactional reliability and the transactions become irreversible, providing both parties with a more reliable trading environment.

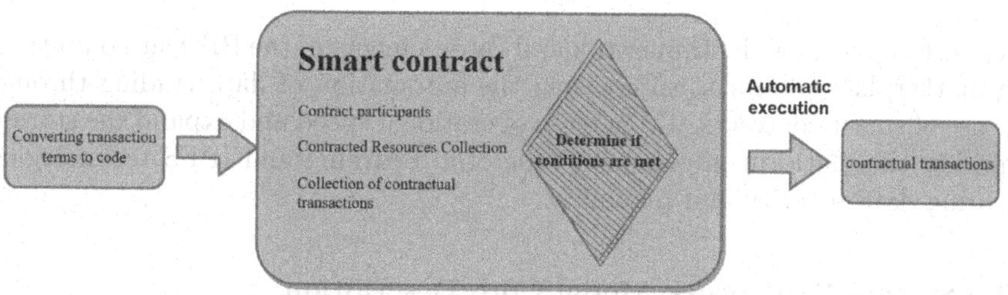

Fig. 1. Data Marketplace Implementation Process.

In this paper, we have developed a marketplace platform for data trading, the BIFData platform. The platform utilizes servers as blockchain nodes to store blocks and participate in consensus protocols, which are more efficient than some data providers due to their superior computing power and storage capabilities. To manage the devices and prevent those with insufficient points from participating in data transactions, we employ federated learning [4,12] to assign appropriate weights for point management. Due to the exorbitant cost of blockchain storage, we decided to utilize IPFS for data storage management. This approach improves distributed fault tolerance, overcomes the blockchain capacity constraint, and lowers the network load. These measures have resulted in a platform that boasts significant improvements in both storage capacity and operational speed. The contributions of this paper mainly include:

(1) To resolve the storage capacity issue faced by IoT devices, servers are chosen as blockchain nodes, with data provider registering as clients behind the corresponding nodes for data transactions.
(2) To mitigate the high costs associated with blockchain storage, IPFS is utilized for data storage management, enhancing distributed fault tolerance and surmounting the blockchain's capacity limitations, thereby reducing network load.
(3) Data provider are managed and malicious attacks are prevented through a points system incorporating federated learning techniques.
(4) We design and implement a decentralized data trading marketplace platform using Solidity smart contracts on the Ethernet platform to automate transactions. In addition, we adopt technologies such as the Truffle framework and web3.js to facilitate the platform's use.

The paper is organized as follows: Sect. 2 outlines the system architecture and delineates the automated process by which data is exchanged through smart contracts. Section 3 presents tests and experiments conducted on the system. Section 4 reviews related work. Finally, Sect. 5 provides conclusions and future directions for research.

2 System Architecture and Process Overview

This section outlines the framework and core elements of the BIFData data trading marketplace platform, showcasing the automation of data trading through the use of smart contracts. To increase operational speed and expand the storage capacity, the platform implements Federated Learning and IPFS technologies, ensuring data security and reliability.

2.1 System Framework Model Core Description

Figure 2 depicts the framework architecture components of the system, which we will describe below.

Data Provider. The data providers, who primarily receive their data from individual data provider, are required to register with the system by selecting the management server. Subsequently, the data providers must complete the corresponding information through the web interface, whereby the data will be uploaded to IPFS [3], while other information will be uploaded to the blockchain as metadata.

Server Node. The server can become a blockchain node by creating an account with an Ether balance in the network, which can connect to their Ether account through the MetaMask. Servers are accountable for the management of data provide who can verify the enlisted servers and designate their management

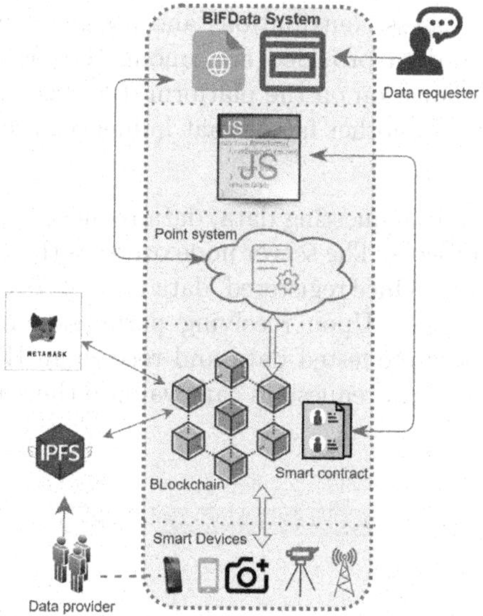

Fig. 2. System framework model.

servers. It is imperative to note that a data provider can only choose one server. Conversely, a server can register multiple data providers within its management domain. Thus, any smart device registration can be executed through a server in its management domain. Servers function as nodes that invoke contracts and contribute to local federated learning while executing the computation and updating of points.

Ethereum Blockchain and Smart Contracts. The core of the application, where all the code and transactions reside, is based on smart contracts. To satisfy the system's functional requirements, we have developed the Euipmentregister contract, Datarecording contract, Datatransaction contract, and Whitelist contract. The Euipmentregister contract is primarily responsible for the registration of data provider. The Datarecording contract is responsible for uploading data information to the blockchain and includes functions such as data query. The Datatransaction contract is responsible for data query, and data transaction, and data provides access to data. The Whitelist contract determines whether there is permission to provide feedback on transactions. Once the smart contracts have been written and tested, they are deployed to the blockchain, where transaction information and metadata are stored.

Point System. The Point system utilizes a reward and punishment mechanism to encourage data providers and data buyers to adhere to the platform's rules, ensuring the stability and quality of data transactions. To monitor and evaluate the behavior of data trading participants, the system employs federal learning techniques to assess contributions and assign points accordingly. The size and quality of the data provided are among the factors that influence a data provider's point allocation on the platform. Likewise, the behavior of data buyers on the platform is another factor that influences their point allocation.

Data Requester. Before requesting data, data requesters are required to complete the registration process. The server node oversees the management of these registered data requesters. Once registered, data requesters can search for desired data and submit a request. Upon receiving permission from the device, the requester can pay for the requested data and receive an IPFS hash to retrieve the data. Post retrieval, data requesters can evaluate the quality of the received data.

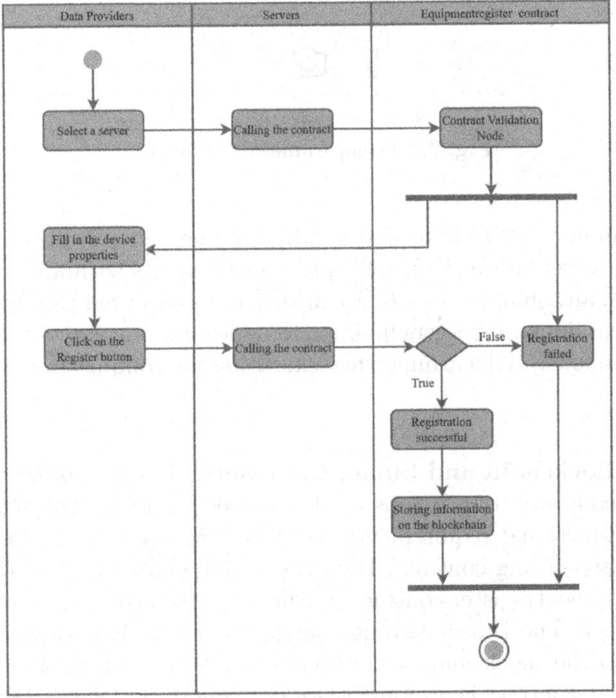

Fig. 3. Data provider registration process.

2.2 Automated Data Trading Through Smart Contracts

Smart contracts enable automated transactions by executing automatically. They can trigger and record transactions automatically based on set conditions. Our analysis of the conditions required for a data transaction scenario resulted in the development of four smart contracts: a device registration contract, a data recording contract, a whitelisting contract, and a data transaction contract. The process of data trading can be demonstrated by describing the purpose and function of the four smart contracts.

Euipmentregister Contract. The device registration contract filters and maps devices to their respective servers during registration. Relevant information is stored after mapping the the data provider to the selected server. During registration, the name, password, network port, MAC address, and IP address fields are filled out, while balance and reset fields are completed automatically(see Fig. 3). Upon completion of each attribute, if the device is unregistered, the registration information is stored on the blockchain through a triggered registration transaction. Registration is prohibited if the device has already been registered before.

Datarecording Contract. The contract's primary function is to store metadata on the blockchain. The data provider must first fill in the metadata information, as shown in Table 1. Before storing metadata, the registration status of the device is checked to ensure that only devices with completed registration can upload data. Additionally, the Daterecording contract allows for data update operations, with updating the hash value of the data being the only necessary action.

Table 1. Metadata record format.

Attribute	Value Type	Example
DataId	Uint	00001
DeviceId	Uint	00001
Dataname	Sring	Tom's picture
Ownername	String	Tom's camera
Datahash	String	QmevTxw... DoJG
Desclink	String	QmTh6N4q... UiPV
Datatype	String	pdf
Tag	String[]	[temperature,scenery]
Size	Uint256	175846
Minpoint	Uint256	10
Price	Uint	5
UploadTime	Uint	161578951
Condition	Enum	Used

Whitelist Contract. The contract serves two main functions. Firstly, it facilitates the validation of data requests by the whitelist contract. This process involves checking whether a data requester has completed registration, and subsequently, the contract adds the data requester to the whitelist, providing permission to request the data. Secondly, the contract manages feedback evaluation permissions. Upon completion of a data transaction, the data requester may provide feedback. To ensure the unique identification of each transaction, the corresponding transaction hash value is stored in the requester's record. The whitelist contract then verifies if the requester has already transacted on the data and grants evaluation rights if so; if not, it denies the requester's evaluation rights.

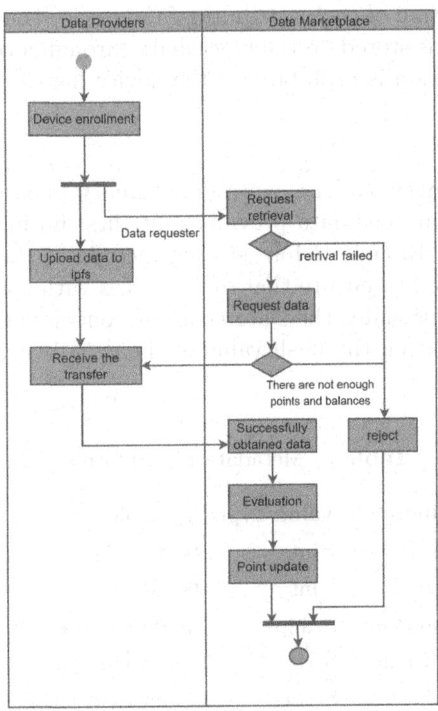

Fig. 4. Data transaction process.

Datatransaction Contract. The Datetransaction contract facilitates data trading, feedback evaluation, and point updates. A requester's identity is verified in a step-by-step process when seeking a data request. Firstly, the whitelist is checked to determine if the requester is authorized to request data, followed by verification of the requester's point score and balance. When these conditions are met, a data transaction is initiated and the relevant transaction information is recorded in the blockchain. Once the transaction is completed, the data requester may evaluate the data, but only if a transaction history for the corresponding data exists. This evaluation will update the requester's point score through a weight update mechanism in federation learning (see Fig. 4).

3 Experiments and Performance Analysis

In this section, we demonstrate the feasibility of implementing the entire framework of our BIFData system, designed for data marketplace trading from data provider in real scenarios. We implemented the blockchain network module using Ethereum as our blockchain platform and Solidity [7,18] as our smart contract development language. Truffle [2] is a set of development frameworks for the Solidity language based on Ethereume [10,11] and we chose to use the Truffle framework when developing the system. Ganache [6] was chosen as our Ethernet test network to test, execute commands, check status, and control how the chain runs. To update points using federated learning, we utilized local federated learning training in Python to transfer training parameters to the corresponding smart contract for point update via JS. Furthermore, we used web3.js to interact with the smart contract and implement a user-friendly front-end interface for the user. The process is shown in Fig. 5: First, install Truffle to generate a DApp development framework and create a project. Secondly, connect to the Ethernet network, which can be simulated by linking Ganache to run in memory and serve externally through RPC. Thirdly, write, test, and deploy smart contracts according to the needs of the system. It is crucial to thoroughly test smart contracts because they cannot be modified once they are deployed, and any loopholes may lead to irreversible consequences. Finally, to interact with the smart contract through the user interface, use the Web3.js library to interact with the blockchain network and smart contracts.

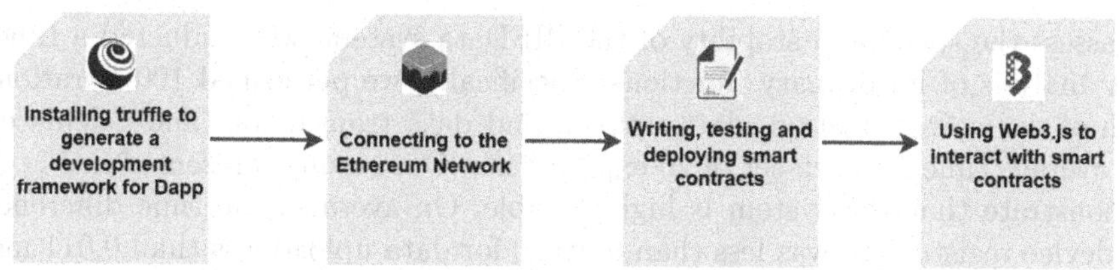

Fig. 5. Data Marketplace Implementation Process.

Table 2. Gas cost.

Invoked function	Average Gas costs for different system functions		Average Gas Cost (USD)	
	BIFData	PATRIoT	BIFData	PATRIoT
AddDevice	343380.4	332479	10.74	10.4
RemoveDevice	28140	23456	0.88	0.73
UploadData	429636.8	471959	13.4	14.7
UpdateData	30828	28946	0.96	0.9

3.1 Gas Cost

To evaluate the efficiency of BIFData, we experimented to measure the Gas used when the user calls the Equipmentregister smart contract functions AddDevice() and RemoveDevice() and the Datarecording smart contract functions UploadData() and UpdateData(). At the same time, we compared the Gas values consumed with the corresponding functions of the PATRIoT [19]system. Currently, 1 Gas costs about 24Gwei (i.e., 25 * 10-9 Ether), and the exchange rate of 1 Ether at the time of writing is $1252.81. We calculate the Gas cost by multiplying the Gas used by each function by the price of gas.

Table 2 illustrates the average Gas usage and cost per function invoked by our system, and also compares it to the PATRIoT function. We can see that our Gas is higher than PATRIoT's when registering and deleting devices. This is because our system uses the server as the node directly for registration and deletion operations, and the Gas usage is related to the computational resources of the function. However, from the results of our experiments, we did not add too many computing resources to increase the cost, we only spent $0.34 more than PATRIoT when registering devices and $0.15 more than PATRIoT when deleting devices. An appropriate increase in Gas consumption can instead make the system run more stable and faster. The experiments prove that the Gas value for the main functions of our system is reasonable and can ensure the proper operation of the system.

3.2 Time Cost

To assess the speed and stability of the BIFData system, we conducted a time-cost analysis of its primary functions. Specifically, we performed 100 iterations each of device registration, data upload, and data transaction, and calculated the average time for each set of 20 experiments. Our results, presented in Fig. 6, demonstrate that the system is highly stable. On average, the time difference for device registration was less than 0.08ms, for data upload less than 0.011 ms, and data transaction less than 0.01 ms. Furthermore, when running the device registration function 100 times, the average running time was 0.08455 ms, for data upload it was 0.1686 ms, and for data transaction it was 0.1450 ms. These results indicate that our system is operating at a reasonable speed, and at a low cost in terms of time expenditure.

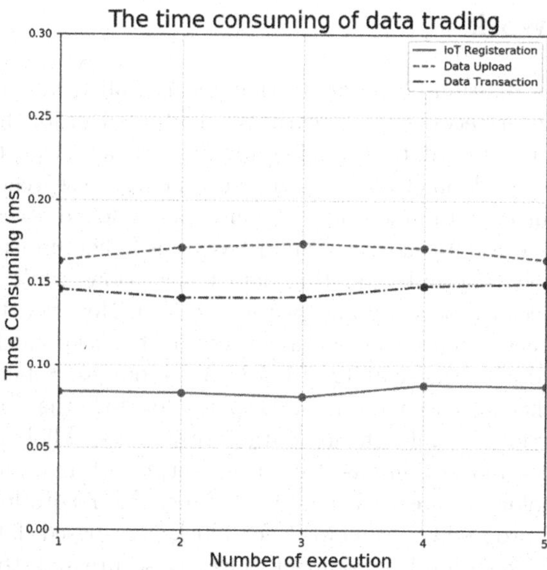

Fig. 6. Average time spent per group for different functions.

3.3 Performance Analysis

Through the use of data marketplace systems, the number of blocks in the blockchain continues to grow. However, the generation time of each block is not fixed and can be influenced by various factors such as network performance, transaction volume, and the number of miners. To evaluate the impact of block increase on the BIFData system, we conducted tests on the system's three main functions while minimizing other influencing factors. Our findings indicate that the system functions remain stable and are not affected by the increase in blocks. Figure 7(a), 7(b), and 7(c) illustrate the change in runtime for the device registration, data upload, and data transaction functions, respectively, with an increase in blocks. The minimal impact of block increase on our proposed system suggests that our system performs well.

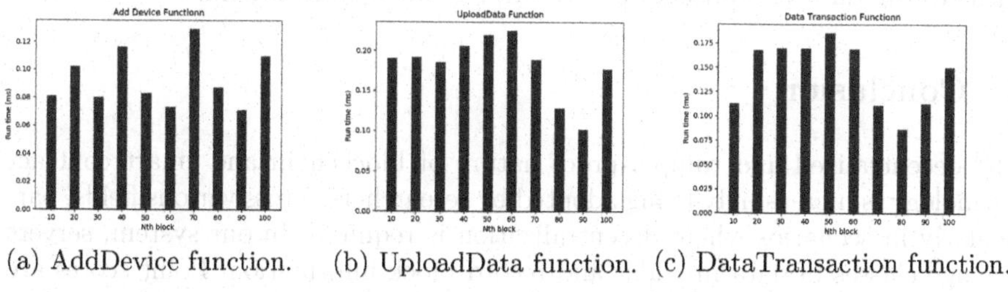

(a) AddDevice function. (b) UploadData function. (c) DataTransaction function.

Fig. 7. Run time for different functions as blocks are added

4 Related Work

A blockchain is a distributed database that records all transactions occurring within a peer-to-peer network [8]. It features a digital ledger for the timely tracking of various transaction data, providing notable privacy protection and transparency.With the development of blockchain technology, researchers can create a trusted, decentralized data marketplace by integrating IoT devices. P. V. Klaine, et al. [16] proposed a data market system based on Ethereum smart contracts, automatically executing and validating data transactions while applying cryptography to protect the security and privacy of data. However, they ignore the potential differences in hardware resource necessity between blockchain systems and IoT devices due to the scarcity of hardware resources. Sober, M. et al. [13] proposed a blockchain-based data marketplace for IoT that uses blockchain technology and Smart Contracts for data transactions. Aljohani, Meshari. et al. [14] proposed a blockchain-based data marketplace framework that utilizes blockchain technology to create a shared, unchangeable record for data trading. G. Su et al. [15] proposed a framework for blockchain-based data transactions that use Trusted Execution Environment (TEE) to secure and store transaction-related data using Intel SGX technology. Blockchain technology also facilitates authentication, data transactions, and payments in the proposed framework, but its implementation requires a substantial investment in computational and storage resources. Consequently, the method ensures that device data is shared while ensuring secure and private sharing. The above solutions have improved some modules of the blockchain system, including reducing energy consumption, improving system efficiency, and facilitating the distribution of blockchain in IoT devices. Most of these articles presume that IoT devices can store blockchains for transaction purposes. However, it is not practical to store blockchains in IoT devices since these devices lack adequate computing power and storage space. S. Fan et al. [20] propose a resource trading system, using a hybrid blockchain and smart contract architecture, that aims to provide secure, efficient, and stable trading transactions between nodes and requesters. C. Li et al. [5] propose a framework for data trading marketplaces based on blockchain technology and federated learning. This framework combines the benefits of blockchain and federated learning to address concerns regarding data privacy and safeguarding the rights of data owners. However, it does not consider the high costs associated with storing data or transaction data directly on the blockchain.

5 Conclusion

The decentralized and tamper-proof nature of blockchain and smart contract technology is increasingly being adopted by researchers across various fields, particularly in scenarios where decentralization is required. In our system, servers manage classes of data provider and record block information. Point scores are calculated via federated learning in a multidimensional manner to ensure their validity. Furthermore, our system offers a user-friendly graphical interface to enhance its ease of use. Our experimental results demonstrate the strong performance of our system. We are currently simulating the real environment and hope to continue to improve the platform.

References

1. Yoo, H., Ko, N.: Blockchain based data marketplace system. In: 2020 International Conference on Information and Communication Technology Convergence (ICTC), Jeju, Korea (South), pp. 1255–1257 (2020). https://doi.org/10.1109/ICTC49870.2020.9289087
2. Truffle: Ethereum development framework (2016). https://github.com/trufflesuite/truffle. Accessed 20 Aug 2020
3. Benet, J.: IPFS-content addressed, versioned, p2p file system (2014)
4. Yang, Q., Liu, Y., Chen, T., Tong, Y.: Federated machine learning: concept and applications (2019)
5. Li, C., Yuan, Y., Wang, F.-Y.: A novel framework for data trading markets based on blockchain-enabled federated learning. In: 2022 IEEE 25th International Conference on Intelligent Transportation Systems (ITSC), Macau, China, pp. 3392–3397 (2022). https://doi.org/10.1109/ITSC55140.2022.9922422
6. Ganache: Personal blockchain for Ethereum development (2016). https://www.truf-flesuite.com/ganache. Accessed 20 Aug 2020
7. Wang, S., Zhang, Y., Zhang, Y.: A blckchain-based framework for data sharing with fine-grained access control in decentralized storage systems. In: IEEE Access, vol. 6, pp. 38437–38450 (2018). https://doi.org/10.1109/ACCESS.2018.2851611
8. Fine-grained access control in decentralized storage systems. IEEE Access **6**, 38437–38450 (2018). https://doi.org/10.1109/ACCESS.2018.2851611
9. Wood, G.: Ethereum: a secure decentralised generalised transaction ledger. Yellow Paper. https://ethereum.github.io/yellowpaper/paper.pdf. Accessed 25 Mar 2018
10. Ethereum Blockchain App Platform. https://www.ethereum.org. Accessed 25 Mar 2018
11. Ethereum Homestead Documentation. https://readthedocs.org/projects/ethereum-homestead. Accessed 25 Mar 2018
12. McMahan, B., Moore, E., Ramage, D., Hampson, S., y Arcas, B.A.: Communication-efficient learning of deep networks from decentralized data. In: Proceedings of the 20th International Conference on Artificial Intelligence and Statistics, AISTATS, vol. 54, pp. 1273–1282. PMLR (2017)
13. Sober, M., et al.: A blockchain-based IoT data marketplace. Cluster Comput. (2022)
14. Aljohani, M., Mukkamala, R., Olariu, S.: A framework for a blockchain-based decentralized data marketplace. In: Haas, Z.J., Prakash, R., Ammari, H., Wu, W. (eds.) WiCON 2022. Lecture Notes of the Institute for Computer Sciences, Social Informatics and Telecommunications Engineering, vol. 464, pp. 59–75. Springer, Cham (2023). https://doi.org/10.1007/978-3-031-27041-3_5
15. Su, G., Yang, W., Luo, Z., Zhang, Y., Bai, Z., Zhu, Y.: BDTF: a blockchain-based data trading framework with trusted execution environment. In: 2020 16th International Conference on Mobility, Sensing and Networking (MSN), Tokyo, Japan, pp. 92–97 (2020). https://doi.org/10.1109/MSN50589.2020.00030

16. Klaine, Y.P.V., Zhang, L., Imran, M.A.: An implementation of a blockchain-based data marketplace using geth. In: 2021 3rd Conference on Blockchain Research & Applications for Innovative Networks and Services (BRAINS), Paris, France, pp. 15–16 (2021). https://doi.org/10.1109/BRAINS52497.2021.9569838
17. Buterin, V., et al.: A next-generation smart contract and decentralized application platform. White paper (2014)
18. Solidity language (2014). https://solidity.readthedocs.io/en/develop/. Accessed 20 Aug 2020
19. Loukil, F., Ghedira-Guegan, C., Benharkat, A.-N.: PATRIoT: a data sharing platform for IoT using a service-oriented approach based on blockchain. In: Kafeza, E., Benatallah, B., Martinelli, F., Hacid, H., Bouguettaya, A., Motahari, H. (eds.) ICSOC 2020. LNCS, vol. 12571, pp. 121–129. Springer, Cham (2020). https://doi.org/10.1007/978-3-030-65310-1_10
20. Fan, S., Zhang, H., Zeng, Y., Cai, W.: Hybrid blockchain-based resource trading system for federated learning in edge computing. IEEE Internet Things J. **8**(4), 2252–2264 (2021). https://doi.org/10.1109/JIOT.2020.3028101
21. Shakila, U.K., Sultana, S.: A decentralized marketplace application based on ethereum smart contract. In: 2021 24th International Conference on Computer and Information Technology (ICCIT), Dhaka, Bangladesh, pp. 1–5 (2021). https://doi.org/10.1109/ICCIT54785.2021.9689879

Intelligent Services

Gait Impairment Assessment Service for Community-Dwelling Older Adults

Xin Hu[1(✉)], Ke Xue[1], Shen Wang[1], Deqiong Ding[2], Yongqing Han[3], Zhao Sun[4], Xiyu Gao[4], Minjun Tian[4], Bo Sang[4], Zhilin Zhang[4], and Dianhui Chu[1]

[1] School of Computer Science and Technology, Harbin Institute of Technology at Weihai, Weihai 264200, Shandong, China
hithuxin@hit.edu.cn

[2] Department of Mathematics, Harbin Institute of Technology at Weihai, Weihai 264200, Shandong, China

[3] Office of Retirement Services, Harbin Institute of Technology at Weihai, Weihai 264200, Shandong, China

[4] Msun Health Technology Group Co., Ltd., Jinan 250000, Shandong, China

Abstract. Older adults want to remain independent with dignity for as long as possible. Gait assessment service plays an essential role in elderly care and rehabilitation by evaluating gait impairment, to provide suitable and continuous treatments. Despite over a decade of research and development in gait assessment, accurate and reliable gait assessment service for older adults in use are few. We propose an automatic gait impairment assessment service, for community-dwelling older adults, by combining multiple LiDAR (Light Detection and Ranging) sensing with 11-meter walking test. Multiple sensors fusion strategy is employed to sense and interpret gaits in a complementary way. Leveraging scan-matching technology and foot tracking method, the gait assessment service can achieve high accuracy with reasonable cost and no privacy issue. The experiment results show obvious differences of disease-specific motor symptoms in comparing groups. The potential merit of gait assessment service in daily use is also explored in this study.

Keywords: Gait impairment · gait assessment · point cloud alignment · foot tracking

1 Introduction

Gait impairments are associated with neurological disorders, stroke and Parkinson's disease for older adults, which are the leading cause of injury, injury-related mortality, and premature institutionalization [1]. Gait impairments caused by neurological disorders appear to be great variety of motor symptoms in temporal and spatial asymmetry [2,3]. Gait analysis service can provide comprehensive understanding of the disease-specific gait impairments, to provide suitable and continuous treatments. A standardized clinical test often used to assess walking

Z. Wang et al. (Eds.): ICSS 2023, CCIS 1844, pp. 153–165, 2023.
https://doi.org/10.1007/978-981-99-4402-6_11

speed is the 11-meter walking test (11MWT) [4], which is well known as Time Up and Go test. However, the 11MWT only provides simple performance measure (stopwatch-based walking speed) and experience-based judgment from clinical workers [5].

Several kinds of sensors are instrumented to the walking path to yield a more comprehensive assessment of gait. In this scenario, RGB-D (RGB-depth) camera based approaches gain enormous interest in the context of gait assessment [6], since the RGB-D camera integrates multiple sensors with reasonable accuracy and cost [7,8]. However, these studies can only analyze a few steps with low accuracy, due to body occlusion caused by field of view limitation [7]. One way to cover a larger volume is to use multiple integrated sensors [8]. Since light changes affect the RGB-D sensors, the registration for multiple sensors is really challenging [9].

Wearable Inertial Measurement Unit (IMU) is another popular sensor instrumented to the walking path [10]. Due to the body-mount manner of the IMU sensors, IMU based approaches are invasive comparing to the RGB-D based methods [11]. The swaying noise of IMU sensor is with high level, even mounted in a close-fitting manner, due to the large Degree of Freedom of limbs [12,13]. Addressing this issue, AI (Artificial Intelligence) based algorithms are proposed by taking the self-adaptive technique [14,15]. However, the IMU sensing data cannot be associated with gait features without field-specific expertise, which makes the IMU sensing data to be invisible for non-specialist [16,17].

Target at privacy, cost, and real-time facility, 2D (two-dimensional) LiDAR (Light Detection and Ranging) is employed for gait analysis. LiDAR can capture foot motions precisel [18], by measuring variable distance on the plane. Continuous recognition method [19], unique deep convolutional network [20], and deep learning architecture [21], are proposed to perform accurate gait analysis. Although research on LiDAR based gait analysis is wide covering and conducted over a period, computational burden and high accuracy remain challenging for the LiDAR based methods.

Targeting at these challenges, we propose an automatic gait impairment assessment service, for community-dwelling older adults, by combining multiple LiDAR sensing and the 11MWT. Spatiotemporal gait parameters are employed to estimate disease-associated gait patterns with quantitative gait information. This study also explores the potential of expanding the gait impairment assessment from clinical test to daily use. The rest of this paper is organized as follows. In Sect. 2, we describe the automatic gait impairment assessment process with experiment setup. More specifically, we introduce a structural feature based iterative closest point (ICP) method for multiple LiDAR scan-matching, a extended Kalman filter (EKF) for foot tracking, and a gait analysis methodology for gait impairment analysis. The experimental results are shown in Sect. 3. Finally, we make discussion on the obtained results and draw conclusion in Sect. 4.

2 Method

Gait assessment in the 11MWT contains two components: generating effective steps and maintaining balance in walking. We would like to address these two

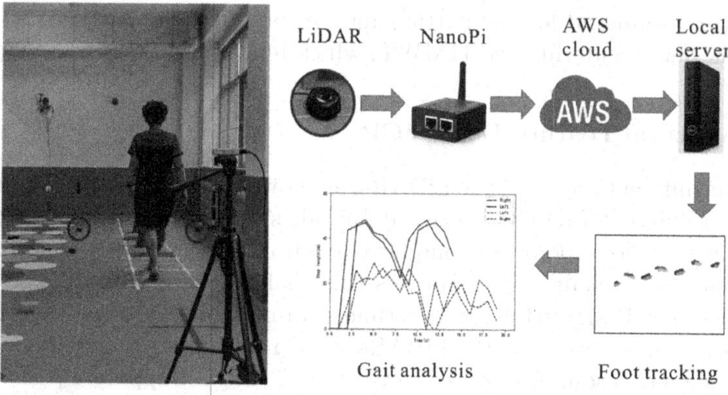

Fig. 1. The gait impairment assessment service setup. The red circles indicate LiDAR sensors. The dots of different colors in foot tracking are the foot silhouettes from multiple LiDAR sensing. (Color figure online)

components in the instrumented 11MWT, to provide a more comprehensive assessment than the standard clinical tests. Moreover, the assessment service should be patient-friendly, easy to use, and no private issue. We design a walking path with multiple LiDAR sensors, as shown in Fig. 1. This walking path based gait assessment system consists one 11-meter walking path, a laser switch, two LiDARs, two NanoPi minicomputers, one AWS cloud, and a local server. The LiDARs are mounted on both sides of the walking path, to capture the foot locomotion. The ranging laser technology embedded in the LiDAR provides a continuous stream of distance data, which takes advantages in wide field of view and consistency of any lighting condition. It gives us the potential to capture the foot locomotion rapidly and measure gait features precisely. Considering the high levels of part self-occlusion in walking, two LiDARs are employed to interpret gaits in different angles simultaneously. The laser switch triggers the assessment process. Subsequently, the gait information along with the environmental information are sensed by the LiDARs, then transferred to the AWS cloud by the two NanoPi minicomputers, and downloaded simultaneously to the local server for assessment in real-time.

2.1 Subjects and Experiment Setting

32 older adults: 5 PD patients, 7 stroke patients, and 20 healthy older adults, age 67.4 ± 6.4 years, height 173.2 ± 5.6 cm, and body mass 69.3 ± 14.3 kg, were recruit into our study from August 2021 to February 2022. This study aims at assessing the gait impairments in PD and stroke, and exploring the potential merit of gait assessment service in daily use.

Participants were asked to walk naturally with comfortable walking speed in the 11MWT. Since the laser switch triggers the assessment automatically, there was no start command for the participants. In practice, the participants took a short walk before entering the 11MWT, which makes the walks more natural.

2.2 Structural Feature Based ICP

Due to the different angles of the LiDARs, as shown in Fig. 2(a), the alignment of scans from different LiDARs is critical for gait simultaneous localization. However, the mussy cloud points of complicate environment make the scan-matching in real-time to be challenging. Address this challenge, we propose a structural feature based ICP algorithm for real-time scan-matching. During the 11MWT, gait information is sensed by the LiDARs as 2D range data (point clouds), 18 Hz with an angular resolution and coverage of 0.5°/270°. Suppose P_1 and P_2 are two frames of point clouds from two LiDARs at the same time, waiting for

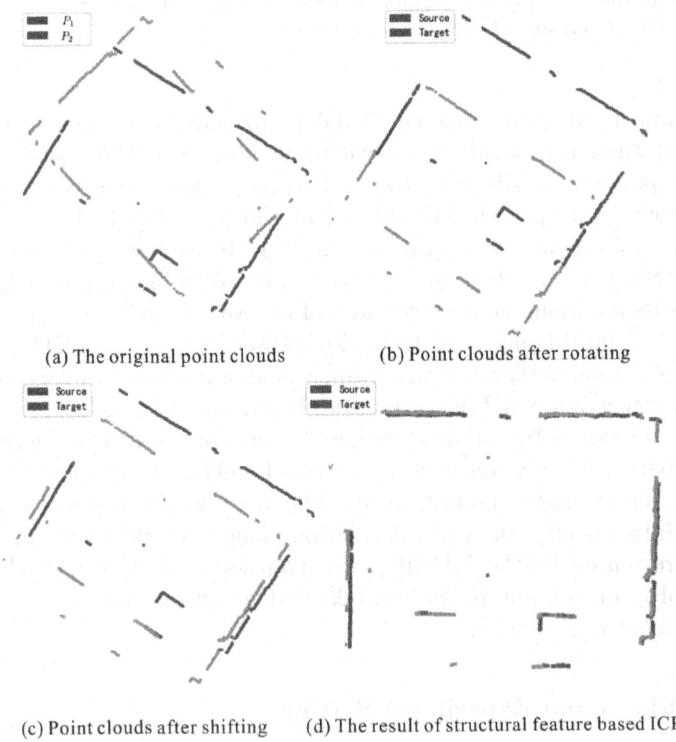

Fig. 2. Point clouds of the structural feature based ICP. (a) Point clouds P_1 and P_2 from two LiDARs waiting for scan-matching. Green and red points are environmental points in the sensing point clouds. (b) Results of rotating in the coarse matching. (c) Results of shifting in the coarse matching. (d) The result of structural feature based ICP. (Color figure online)

scan-matching, as shown in Fig. 2(a). The conventional ICP algorithm can be described as follow:

- Transform P_1 using initial transformation T_0, which is usually set as an identity matrix.
- For each point in P_1, search for a closet point in P_2 as correspondence, with the transformation T_{k-1} in the k-th iteration. For the i-th point in P_1, the index of corresponding point in P_2 is described as $I(i)$:

$$I(i) = \arg\min_{j} ||T_{k-1}P_1(i) - P_2(j)|| \tag{1}$$

- Discover transformation T_k which minimizes the distance between the correspondence:

$$T_k = \arg\min_{T} \sum_{i} ||T_{k-1}P_1(i) - P_2(I(i))|| \tag{2}$$

- Apply transformation T_k to P_1.
- Stop ICP algorithm when the incremental transformation is smaller than the threshold. Otherwise, switch to Step 2.

The accuracy of scan-matching by processing ICP relies on the corresponding relationship between the two point clouds (P_1 and P_2). However, it is challenging to obtain the corresponding point pairs, due to different angles and coverage of the LiDARs. The ICP asks for high overlapping between the two point clouds as initialization. Addressing this point pair issue, we propose a structural feature based coarse matching for ICP.

For indoor environment, LiDAR sensing can obtain obvious structural features, such as walls. Lines of walls are modeled into x-axis associated angles. For each point in point clouds P_1 and P_2, angle feature is calculated as follows:

$$\begin{aligned} &\alpha_i = acos(x_i^*/\sqrt{x_i^{*2} + y_i^{*2}}) \\ &(x_i^*, y_i^*) = (x_{i+1}^*, y_{i+1}^*) - (x_{i-1}^*, y_{i-1}^*) \\ &(x_i, y_i) = (\rho_i \cos\theta_i, \rho_i \sin\theta_i) \end{aligned} \tag{3}$$

where (ρ_i, θ_i) is the range scan of the i-th point p_i in P_1 or P_2; (x_i, y_i) is the coordinate of p_i in rectangular coordinate; (x_i^*, y_i^*) is the direction vector of p_i; α_i is the angle feature at point p_i. After the angle features are calculated, the feature histogram of the two point clouds is shown in Fig. 3 left. The walls appear to be remarkable in the feature histogram, as shown in Fig. 3 left ellipse. The larger the wall captured by LiDAR, the more the points fall into one particular bin. The poses of the point clouds can be estimated according to the wall structural feature. For scan-matching, the walls should overlap each other by rotating and shifting. The rotating operation in point cloud appears to be shifting in feature histogram. The shifting step M can be estimated by minimizing the overlapping error of feature histogram, as follows:

$$M = \arg\min_{m} \sum_{k=1}^{n} (E'_{k+m} - E_k) \tag{4}$$

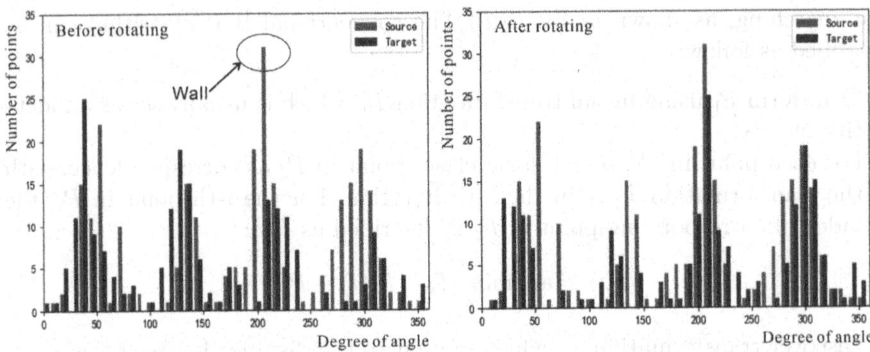

Fig. 3. Feature histogram before and after rotating. In order to meet the real-time scan-matching request, the histogram bin is set to 9°.

where E_k is the number of points fall into k-th bin in the source point cloud; E'_{k+m} is the number of points fall into $(k+m)$-th bin in the target point cloud; n is the number of bins in histogram. After optimizing the shifting step M in histogram, the rotating angle of target point cloud can be calculated as $9°\cdot M$, the rotating result is shown in Fig. 3 right (histogram) and Fig. 2(b) (point clouds).

After rotating, the overlapping error in angle is smaller than 9°. The coarse matching can be obtained by shifting the target point cloud, as follows:

$$\begin{aligned} \Delta x &= \textstyle\sum_{i=1}^{n_1} x_i/n_1 - \sum_{j=1}^{n_2} x'_j/n_2 \\ \Delta y &= \textstyle\sum_{i=1}^{n_1} y_i/n_1 - \sum_{j=1}^{n_2} y'_j/n_2 \end{aligned} \tag{5}$$

where (x_i, y_i) is the i-th point in the source point cloud P_1; (x'_i, y'_i) is the j-th point in the target point cloud P_2; n_1 and n_2 are the point number in P_1 and P_2, respectively. The shifting in coarse matching is calculated as the differences in the mean value of coordinates. The point clouds after coarse matching are shown in Fig. 2(c).

As shown in Fig. 2(c), coarse matching is not precise enough for gait analysis. We employ ICP algorithm to refine the alignment of coarse matching. The structural features are integrated into ICP search, by targeting the corresponding point pair issue of ICP. Since the structural features appear to be obvious on surrounding walls, the wall points are divided into four classes: east, west, north, and south class, to restrain the ICP search and reduce the computational burden.

In the constrained ICP search, the points of same class are easy to match each other with less search. The constraint is enrolled into ICP by giving a penalty to the search in different classes. By combining ICP search with the structural features, the sum of the squared distances $I(i)$, Eq. 1, can be represented as follows:

$$\begin{aligned} I(i) &= \arg\min_j (1 + \lambda(P_1(i), P_2(j)))\|T_{k-1}P_1(i) - P_2(j)\| \\ \lambda(P_1(i), P_2(j)) &= \begin{cases} \beta, & if\ c(P_1(i)) \neq c(P_2(j)) \\ 0, & if\ c(P_1(i)) = c(P_2(j)) \end{cases} \end{aligned} \tag{6}$$

where $\lambda(P_1(i), P_2(j))$ is the penalty item; $c(P_1(i))$ and $c(P_2(j))$ are the classes of point $P_1(i)$ and $P_2(j)$. Two pairing point clouds P_1 and P_2 have the same orientation after coarse matching, as shown in Fig. 2c. The class of each point in the point louds can be easily obtained by using the relative location.

The structural feature based ICP has the capability to provide accurate alignment for gait analysis, as shown in Fig. 2(d). Moreover, the computation time for the proposed matching method is 2 ms, with CPU i3-10100, 4G memory, Python 3, and 15 iterations for ICP search, meets the real-time request.

2.3 Extended Kalman Filter for Foot Tracking

After scan-matching, point clouds sensed by multiple LiDARs are integrated into one whole picture. The scan-matching alignment has 2 mm overlapping error. Since the LiDARs are mounted on both sides of the walking path, the overlapping error will not affect the foot locomotion capture. With the aligned point clouds, EKF is employed to trace foot locomotion during the 11MWT, by extracting the foot silhouettes through the point cloud frames. However, extracting foot silhouettes from 720 points (one frame of sensing) is challenging.

DBSCAN (density-based spatial clustering of applications with noise) method [22] is employed to extract dynamic points, which is a density-based clustering algorithm does not require the specification of the cluster number. Dynamic points of each frame are segmented into several clusters, while the clusters smaller than 5 points are considered as noise. After the DBSCAN based washing process, point clusters are considered as foot candidates.

Due to the dynamic of walking speed comes with trivial foot motion, tracking feet in the 11MWT is challenging. EKF [23] is employed to model this dynamic process for accurate foot tracing. With the obtained foot candidates, the centroids of foot candidates are calculated and fed into the EKF. And each foot candidate centroid has a Kalman tracker, which is modeled as a nonlinear dynamic system. The EKF tracking is broken down into two steps: prediction and update, as following:

- Prediction. The future state of foot is predicted based on the current state.

$$\begin{aligned} X_k &= A_k X_{k-1} + B_k u_k + w_k \\ P_k &= J(X_{k-1}) P_{k-1} J^T(X_{k-1}) + Q_k \end{aligned} \tag{7}$$

  where $X_k = [x_k, y_k, \dot{x_k}, \dot{y_k}]$ is a state vector of centroid $c_k = (x_k, y_k)$ in frame k, $(\dot{x_k}, \dot{y_k})$ is the velocity component, X_{k-1} is the previous state; P_k is the covariance matrix of tracking error, and w_k is the process noise; u_k is the control vector containing acceleration force; A_k is a state transition matrix; B_k is the control matrix of acceleration effect; $J(X_{k-1})$ is the X_{k-1} associated Jacobian matrix; Q_k is the covariance matrix of process noise.

- Update. The update performs state correction by estimating the new state based on the predicted state from the sensor prediction and measurement steps.

$$\begin{aligned} X'_k &= X_k + K_k w_k \\ P_k &= (I - K_k J(X_k))P_k \\ K_k &= P_k J^T(X_k)(J(X_k)P_k J^T(X_k) + R_k)^{-1} \end{aligned} \tag{8}$$

where X'_k is the updated state vector of centroid c_k; I is the identity matrix; R_k is the covariance matrix of sensor noise measurements.

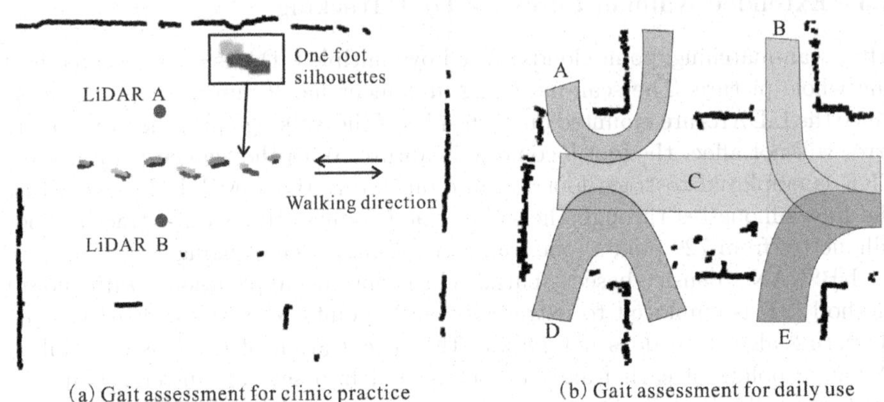

(a) Gait assessment for clinic practice (b) Gait assessment for daily use

Fig. 4. The gait assessment for clinic practice and daily use. (a) The gait assessment for clinic practice. The foot silhouettes captured by the LiDARs (red dots) are shown in different colors, right foot (brilliant blue and pink), left foot (blue and green). For easy viewing, the foot segments are shown every 0.7 s in one direction. One foot point cloud with part self-occlusion is shown in the black rectangle area. (b) The gait assessment for daily use. Area A, B, C, D, and E are five paths estimated based on the foot locations. (Color figure online)

The foot tracking results are shown in Fig. 4(a). It can be easily observed that, the part self-occlusion occurred for the sixth step, the brilliant blue point cloud is much smaller than the pink one. For gait analysis, the two silhouettes for one foot work in a complementary way to gain high accuracy.

2.4 Gait Analysis Methodology

With the foot tracking trajectories, several gait features are employed to look into the gait impairments. The two critical walking components, generating effective steps and maintaining balance in walking, are associated with lower-trunk movements. Generating steps asks the lower-trunk segment to stay stable and provides a reliable platform for vision. And lower-trunk sway should coordinate with the lower-limb motion to maintain the sway angle within a reasonable range, in order to stabilization the head movements.

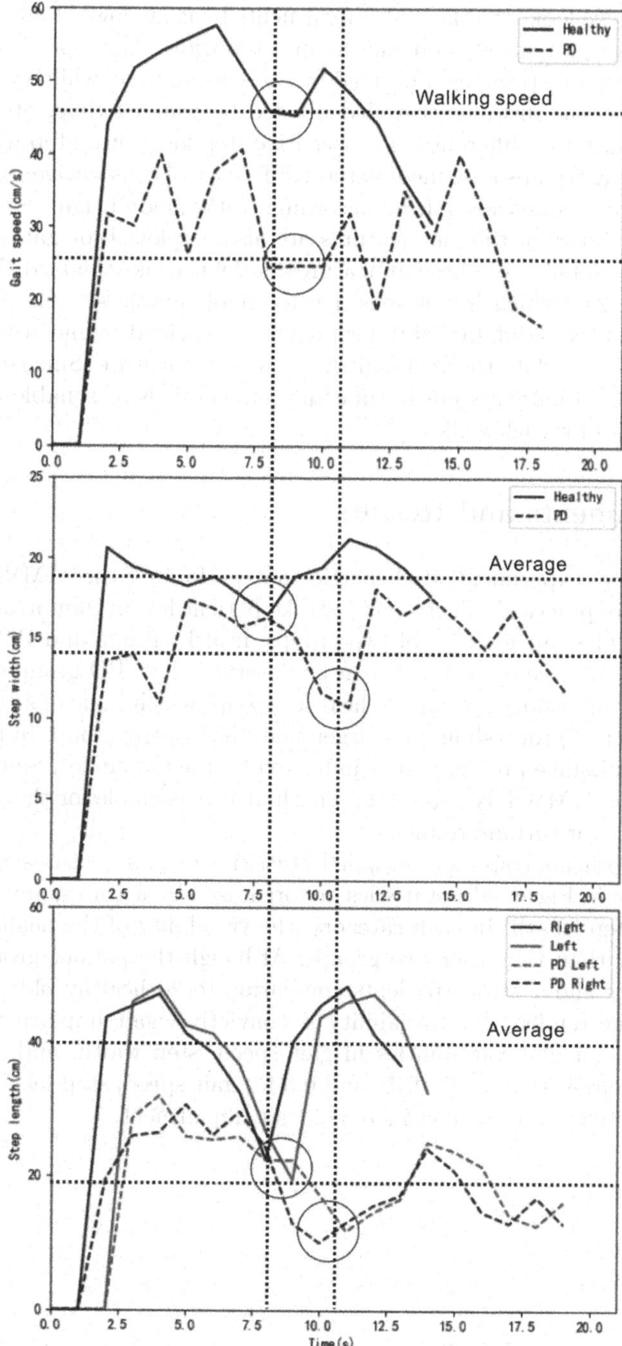

Fig. 5. The gait features of two groups (healthy group and PD group) for comparison. Averages of the features are indicated by horizontal dashed line. The red circles indicate several look-alike problem areas. (Color figure online)

Therefore, we look into the gait impairments by using lower-limb motion features, which are gait speed, step length, and step width. Gait speed is defined as anterior-posterior displacement divided by the sensing time, while walking speed is calculated as the distance travelled divided by walking time. Step length is the anterior-posterior difference of consecutive step locations. Step width is estimated by taking the absolute mediolateral difference of consecutive step location. These gait features are normalized according to the body height.

The variabilities of the gait features are also employed for gait assessment. Traditional variability of the gait features is defined as standard deviation of gait features [24], which is not sensitive to small sample set. Here, we give a novel definition of variability, standard deviation divided by mean value, which is employed to calculate the variabilities of each gait feature. Since each walk in the 11MWT has different steps in time and number, it is reasonable to calculate the variabilities for each walk.

3 Experiments and Results

In the walkway experiment, each participant performed the 11MWT 3 times, after 2 or more practices. There was 1 stroke patient felt uncomfortable to practice 2 times. The gait features of two groups, healthy group and PD group, are shown in Fig. 5 for comparison. It can be observed that, PD group experienced more gait feature changes than the healthy group, which indicates the variabilities of the patient group should be larger than the healthy group. In Fig. 5, there are several look-alike problem areas indicated by the red circles. Since the walking path of the 11MWT is a round trip path, it is reasonable for the participants to walk slowly for turning round.

For in-depth analysis, we compiled statistics of gait features in deviation box, as shown in Fig. 6. The statistics are organized by features, gait speed, step width, and step length. In each category, the variability of the healthy group is much smaller than the other two groups. Although the patient group is small, 5 PD patients and 7 stroke patients comparing to 20 healthy older adults, we insist that the tendency of variability is convictive, gait impairment patients experience larger gait variabilities in gait speed, step width, and step length. Variabilities larger than 0.25, 0.15, and 0.3 for gait speed, step length, and step length respectively, can be considered as gait impairment.

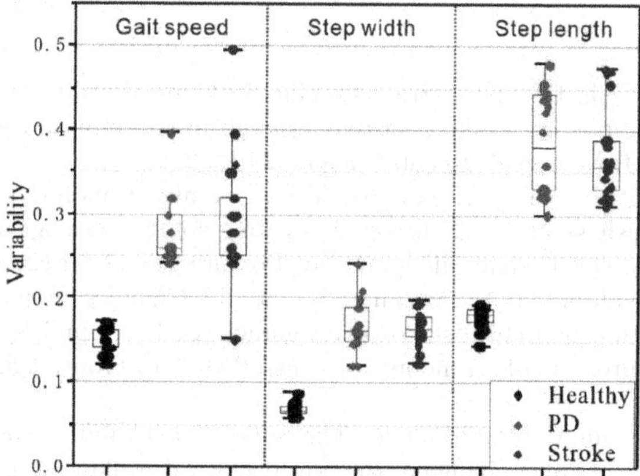

Fig. 6. The variabilities of gait features are summarized in deviation box, and organized in feature groups.

4 Conclusion

Targeting at the challenges in gait impairment assessment, cost, easy deployment, patient-friendly manner, and privacy issue, we propose an automatic gait impairment assessment service, for community-dwelling older adults. A structural feature based ICP method is employed for scan-matching, to synchronize the sensing from different angles. Then, an extended Kalman filter is used to track gaits in ground plane. Gait analysis is processed with gait analysis methodology based on the gait tracking. The comparing results among the three groups show obvious differences in variability.

Due to the small dataset, the quantitative analysis on the degree of gait impairment cannot be reached. We plan to collect a much larger dataset in the future, by using the multiple LiDAR instrumented 11MWT. Moreover, we plan to extend the 11MWT based gait impairment assessment service from clinic practice to daily use, as shown in Fig. 4(b). Several paths are estimated by using the foot locations in daily living situation. Each walking path can be considered as a 11MWT for gait impairment assessment. The walking path estimation shows the potential of the assessment for daily use.

Acknowledgment. This work was supported by the Key Research and Development Program of Shandong Province (Grant 2020CXGC010903), National Natural Science Foundation of China (Grant 62073103), the National Key Research and Development Program of China (Grant 2018YFB1402500), the National Natural Science Foundation of China (Grant 61902090), and Key Projects of Shandong Natural Science Foundation (Grant ZR2020KF019).

References

1. Hedel, H., Rosselli, I., Baumgartner-Ricklin, S.: Clinical utility of the over-ground bodyweight-supporting walking system Andago in children and youths with gait impairments. J. Neuroeng. Rehabil. **18**(1), 29 (2021)
2. Lunardini, F., Malavolti, M., Pedrocchi, A., et al.: A mobile app to transparently distinguish single-from dual-task walking for the ecological monitoring of age-related changes in daily-life gait. Gait Posture **86**, 27–32 (2021)
3. Szturm, T., Kolesar, T.A., Mahana, B., et al.: Changes in metabolic activity and gait function by dual-task cognitive game-based treadmill system in Parkinson's disease: protocol of a randomized controlled trial. Front. Aging Neurosci. **13**, 680270 (2021)
4. Ozden, F., Coskun, G., Bakirhan, S.: The test-retest reliability, concurrent validity and minimal detectable change of the 3-m backward walking test in patients with total hip arthroplasty. J. Arthros. Joint Surg. **8**(3), 288–292 (2021)
5. Yoa, B., Ay, C., Tf, A., et al.: Footsteps and walking trajectories during the timed up and go test in young, older, and Parkinson's disease subjects. Gait Posture **89**, 54–60 (2021)
6. Nunes, J.F., Moreira, P.M., Tavares, J.M.R.S.: Benchmark RGB-D gait datasets: a systematic review. In: Tavares, J.M.R.S., Natal Jorge, R.M. (eds.) VipIMAGE 2019. LNCVB, vol. 34, pp. 366–372. Springer, Cham (2019). https://doi.org/10.1007/978-3-030-32040-9_38
7. Chen, F., Cui, X., Zhao, Z., et al.: Gait acquisition and analysis system for osteoarthritis based on hybrid prediction model. Comput. Med. Imaging Graph. **85**, 101782 (2020)
8. Yorozu, A., Takahashi, M.: Estimation of body direction based on gait for service robot applications. Robot. Auton. Syst. **132**, 103603 (2020)
9. Fo, A., Si, A.A., Ym, A., et al.: RGB-D video-based individual identification of dairy cows using gait and texture analyses. Comput. Electron. Agric. **165**, 104944 (2019)
10. Mao, Y., Ogata, T., Ora, H., et al.: Estimation of stride-by-stride spatial gait parameters using inertial measurement unit attached to the shank with inverted pendulum model. Sci. Rep. **11**(1), 1–10 (2021)
11. Yu, I., Harato, K., Shu, K., et al.: Estimation of the external knee adduction moment during gait using an inertial measurement unit in patients with knee osteoarthritis. Sensors **21**(4), 1418 (2021)
12. Semwal, V.B., Gaud, N., Lalwani, P., et al.: Pattern identification of different human joints for different human walking styles using inertial measurement unit (IMU) sensor. Artif. Intell. Rev. **55**(2), 1149–1169 (2022)
13. Godfrey, A.: Wearable inertial gait algorithms: impact of wear location and environment in healthy and Parkinson's populations. Sensors **21**(19), 6476 (2021)
14. Vh, A., Dd, A., Vb, B., et al.: Lower body kinematics estimation from wearable sensors for walking and running: a deep learning approach. Gait Posture **83**, 185–193 (2021)
15. Piitulainen, H., Kulmala, J.P., Menp, H., et al.: The gait is less stable in children with cerebral palsy in normal and dual-task gait compared to typically developed peers. J. Biomech. **117**, 110244 (2021)
16. Sui, J.D., Chang, T.S.: IMU based deep stride length estimation with self-supervised learning. IEEE Sens. J. **21**(6), 7380–7387 (2021)

17. Nandy, A., Chakraborty, S., Chakraborty, J., et al.: Validation study of low-cost sensors. In: Modern Methods for Affordable Clinical Gait Analysis, pp. 45–55 (2021)
18. Hasan, M., Hanawa, J., Goto, R., Fukuda, H., Kuno, Y., Kobayashi, Y.: Tracking people using ankle-level 2D LiDAR for gait analysis. In: Ahram, T. (ed.) AHFE 2020. AISC, vol. 1213, pp. 40–46. Springer, Cham (2021). https://doi.org/10.1007/978-3-030-51328-3_7
19. Yoon, S., Jung, H.W., Jung, H., et al.: Development and validation of 2D-LiDAR-based gait analysis instrument and algorithm. Sensors **21**(2), 414 (2021)
20. Duong, H.T., Suh, Y.S.: Human gait tracking for normal people and walker users using a 2D LiDAR. IEEE Sens. J. **20**(11), 6191–6199 (2020)
21. Alvarez-Aparicio, C., Guerrero-Higueras, A.M., Rodriguez-Lera, F.J., et al.: LIDAR-based people detection and tracking for home Competitions. In: 2019 IEEE International Conference on Autonomous Robot Systems and Competitions, pp. 1–6 (2019)
22. Latha, S., Samiappan, D., Muthu, P., et al.: Fully automated integrated segmentation of carotid artery ultrasound images using DBSCAN and affinity propagation. J. Med. Biol. Eng. **41**(2), 260–271 (2021)
23. Yang, S., Zhou, S., Hua, Y., et al.: A parameter adaptive method for state of charge estimation of lithium-ion batteries with an improved extended Kalman filter. Sci. Rep. **11**(1), 5805 (2021)
24. Skiadopoulos, A., Moore, E.E., Sayles, H.R., et al.: Step width variability as a discriminator of age-related gait changes. J. Neuroeng. Rehabil. **17**(1), 1–13 (2020)

Named Entity Recognition Service of Bert-Transformer-CRF Based on Multi-feature Fusion for Chronic Disease Management

Diya Chen[1,2], Chen Liu[1,2(✉)], and Zhuofeng Zhao[1,2(✉)]

[1] School of Information, North China University of Technology, Beijing 100144, China
liuchen@ncut.edu.cn, edzhao@ncut.edu.cn

[2] Beijing Key Laboratory of Large-scale Stream Data Integration and Analysis Technology, Beijing 100144, China

Abstract. In chronic disease management, there are many kinds of chronic diseases, the professional terms are complex and diseases have their own characterised disease descriptions, making it difficult for some existing service recommendation methods to make accurate and personalised recommendations for patients with chronic diseases. Therefore, the paper proposes a service recommendation method based on the BERT-Transformer-CRF named entity recognition technology (BTC-SR) to achieve more accurate recommendation services. Firstly, the input disease text data is identified by a BERT (Bidirectional Encoder Representations from Transformers)-Transformer-CRF (Conditional Random Fields) model incorporating radical and pinyin features for named entities, then the relationships between the entities are extracted, and finally an implicit representation of the user is combined to present a recommendation list for the user. Experiments show that the proposed model achieves an F1 value of 60.15 for entity recognition on the CMeEE dataset, which provides better recognition results and lays the foundation for more accurate service recommendations.

Keywords: Chronic diseases · Named Entity Recognition Services · Multi-feature Fusion · Transformer

1 Introduction

With the rejuvenation of chronic diseases, chronic disease management is increasingly becoming a hot topic [1]. A vast amount of services are provided in the chronic disease management system. For example, intelligent interactive follow-up dialogue robots for multiple rounds of dialogue, patient education recommendations, condition assessment, follow-up services such as WeChat; personalised self-management tools for special patients or chronic disease populations,

The Key-Area Research and Development Program of Guangzhou City (202206030009).

Z. Wang et al. (Eds.): ICSS 2023, CCIS 1844, pp. 166–178, 2023.
https://doi.org/10.1007/978-981-99-4402-6_12

intelligent record indicators, medication recommendations; and a collaborative human-machine online communication and service platform. However, there are many types of chronic diseases and complex medical terminology involved, so how to provide accurate services for the chronic disease population is a research hotspot.

Service recommendation is a type of software service that understands user preferences through historical user-project interaction information and recommends services that may be of interest to users based on captured user preferences [2]. In recommendation algorithms, semantic-based recommendation algorithms require a lot of time and human resources in the case of complex service recommendations; keyword-based recommendation methods do not meet the personalised needs of users; content-based recommendation algorithms do not take into account the influence of long distances between texts when learning contextual information about users and are not applicable to service recommendations in the field of chronic diseases with complex terminology. In order to improve the effectiveness of service recommendation for chronic diseases, this paper proposes a service recommendation method (BTC-SR) based on the Bert-Transfer-CRF named entity recognition technique. This method first trains a word vector using Bert, combines the radical features and pinyin features, passes in the Transformer module to extract the features of each character's embedding, saves the flow of information over long distances between texts, decodes the predicted labels using the CRF layer, then extracts the entity-to-entity relationships, and finally combines the patient's implicit behaviour to recommend personalised services for them.

The BTC-SR model integration of radical features and pinyin features, improves the named entity recognition algorithm for long entities and specialized terms, setting epoch to 50, and achieves an F1 value of 60.15 on the CMeEE dataset, an improvement of 1.37 over the base model.

2 Related Work

This article uses Named entity recognition (NER) technology as the basis for service recommendation, so related work is done from recommendation algorithm and NER algorithm.

2.1 Algorithms for Service Recommendation

Recommendation algorithms are divided into traditional recommendation technologies and recommendation algorithms based on deep learning. Among them, traditional recommendation technologies include Semantic-based recommendation, keyword-based recommendation, content-based filtering, collaborative filtering, and hybrid recommendation [3]. Semantic-based recommendation algorithms, which require manual or semi-automatic construction of ontologies. Baidu Encyclopedia and Ding Xiang Yuan use search tools that use keyword-based matching methods that will return the same results to different users searching for the same keywords [4]. The content-based filtering algorithm takes the user's historical selection records or preference records as reference recommendations and mines unknown records and content that are highly relevant to the reference recommendations as system recommendations. Collaborative filtering algorithms obtain dependencies between users and items by analysing the user's rating matrix. Hybrid recommendation techniques incorporate different algorithms into the recommendation system. Nowadays, recommendation algorithms based on deep learning are widely used.

Content-based service recommendation algorithms, literature [5] proposed a service requirement discovery method based on matching the association rules between contextual information and services. The method obtains the association rules between context and service functions, and calculates the similarity of context information to construct a collection of personalised services available in the current application scenario. Based on collaborative filtering for service recommendation algorithms, the literature [6] proposes a cross-domain collaborative filtering model that extends user and item features through the potential factor space of auxiliary domains. The approach uses a Funk-SVD decomposition with an extended two-dimensional location feature vector and a C4.5 decision tree algorithm to predict missing ratings. The algorithm is based on hybrid recommendations, literature [7] proposed an optimal combination prediction idea based on collaborative filtering hybrid recommendation algorithm, which improves the accuracy of rating prediction and enhances the quality of recommendations.

Hansen et al. [8] proposed the CoSeRNN (Contextual and Sequential Recurrent Neural Network) model based on contextual modelling of user preferences. The model models user preferences as an embedding sequence for each conversation (session), and predicts user preferences by adding the user's historical behaviour and context at the beginning of the session.

2.2 Algorithms for NER

Early methods of NER are rule-based and dictionary-based, and later based on machine learning methods and deep learning-based methods. The first method is to develop rule templates by domain experts on the basis of existing knowledge and dictionaries to realize named entity recognition through matching [4]. Yuan J. et al. [6] integrated specific domain entity dictionaries, characteristic character rules and part-of-speech combination rules to identify named entities in the field of power safety, which proved its effectiveness on small sample data, and F1 reached 90. Machine learning-based NER technology uses the labeled training set, manually constructs features and labels words to achieve named entity recognition. Typical machine learning-based NER technologies include the Hidden Markov Model (HMM), the Maximum Entropy Markov Model (MEMM), the Support Vector Machine (SVM) model, and the Conditional Random Fields (CRF) model [7]. Zhai Juye et al. [9]on the basis of CRF, using language, keywords and dictionaries as features and optimizing them using rules. The accuracy, recall and F-value on Chinese electronic medical records have improved significantly, with accuracy increasing to 78.98 and recall and F-value improving to 88.37 and 83.41, which laid the foundation for subsequent NER research in the medical field.

NER technology based on deep learning can automatically discover hidden features in text, does not rely on manual feature selection, and dominates practical applications. Deep learning models mainly include convolutional neural networks (CNN) models, long short-term memory (LSTM) models, and bi-directional long short-term memory models. Sun Z., Li X. [11] after obtaining the Chinese character glyph features and labeling entity types, the fusion vector is sent to Mogrifier GRU, and finally decoded by CRF. It proves the effect of naming entity recognition in electronic medical records. Lian G. combined with the characteristics of network security domain entities, the structure of BI-LSTM-CRF model is improved, so that the model adapts to the recognition of named entities in the network security field, and the F value reaches 87, which provides ideas for the application of BI-LSTM-CRF model to other knowledge fields [12].

3 Service Recommendation Approach Based on NER

Chronic disease service recommendation is intended to provide patients with various chronic diseases with their personalized medication, diet, exercise method guide. Taking hypertension as an example, if the patient is less than 65 years old, simple diastolic hypertension, heart rate is not more than 80 beats per minute, ACEI antihypertensive drugs will be recommended for him, and if it is isolated systolic hypertension in the elderly, CCB is recommended. In terms of diet, patients are recommended with suitable and fasted foods. Before these service recommendations can be provided, firstly, named entities need to be extracted from the disease text, extracting disease symptom entities, drug entities and food entities etc. Secondly, relationships between entities are established so that they can be matched with the user's personalised profile to complete service recommendations. The technical roadmap and NER technology model architecture BERT-Transformer-CRF proposed in this paper are shown as Fig. 1.

The NER technology model architecture BERT-Transformer-CRF proposed in this paper is shown in Fig. 2. First, the input entity features are extracted by fine-tuning the pre-training of the BERT model to fuse the word vector representation sequence with the radical features and the pinyin features. Then, dependency features between long-range texts are obtained by Transformer and features of long entities in the text are learnt. Finally, contextual annotation constraints are learnt in the CRF module and the output entity labels are decoded.

3.1 Transformer Layer

Transformer is a model based entirely on the attention mechanism to improve the speed of model training, using the encoder-decoder architecture. The encoder converts the input sequence $(x_1, ...x_n)$ into a continuous expression $(z_1, ...z_n)$, and the decoder generates the output sequence $(y_1, ...y_n)$ based on that expression. Scaled Dot-Product Attention is an important component of multi-headed attention, which is essentially an attention mechanism that uses dot product

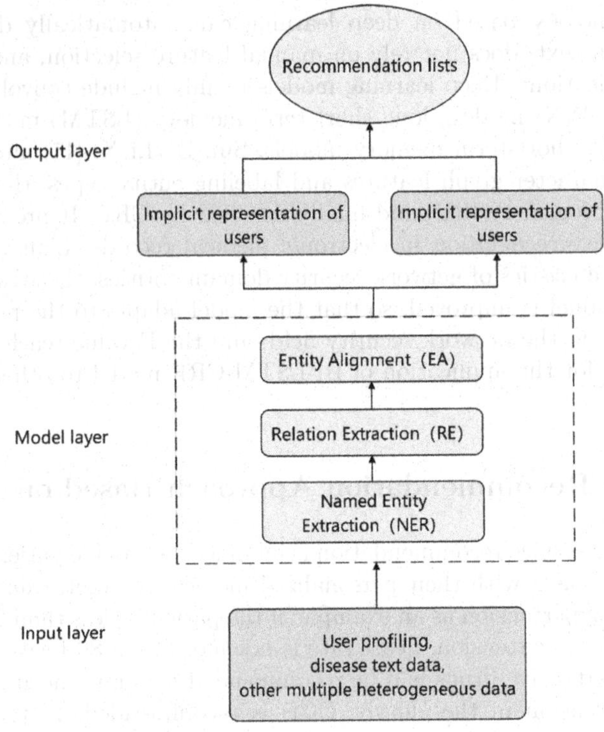

Fig. 1. Process architecture diagram for service recommendations

design to calculate similarity. Figure 3 shows the computation flow of the scaled dot product attention, which is shown in Eq. (1).

$$Attention(Q, K, V) = softmax(\frac{QK^T}{\sqrt{d_k}})V \quad (1)$$

where: $\sqrt{d_k}$ is the dimension of query vector and key vector, and it is the penalty term.

Multi-head attention is composed of multiple self-attention stitching, and the working principle is as follows: After linear transformation of Query and Key-Value, the similarity is calculated using Scaled Dot-Product Attention, and the same operation is performed h times. "h" is the number of layers of multi-headed attention. Finally, the results of each layer are stitched together to obtain feature information from different angles and at different levels. Figure 4 shows the detailed flow of Transformer's multi-headed attention mechanism, and the corresponding calculation formula is shown in Eq. (2) (3). The number of self-attention of the transformer is the number of heads, and each head focuses on different contextual information for each word.

$$head_i = Attention(QW_i^Q, KW_i^K, VW_i^V) \quad (2)$$

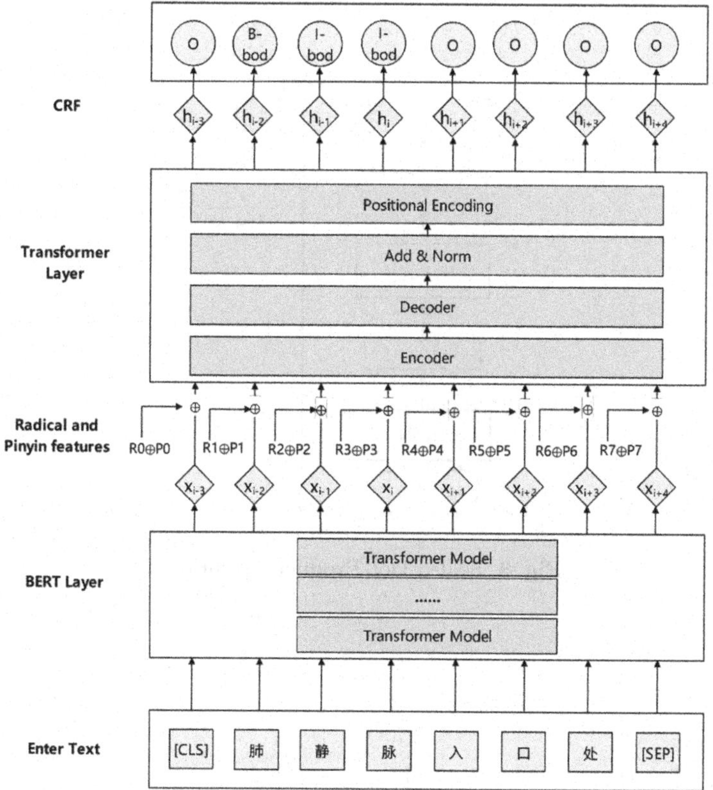

Fig. 2. Model for BERT-Transformer-CRF+radical+pinyin

where: W^Q, W^K, W^V is weight matrixs.

The output matrix of multi-head attention is as follow

$$MultiHead(Q, K, V) = Concat(head_1, ..., head_h)W^O \tag{3}$$

where: Concat means that the results of each layer of the scaled dot-product attention are stitched together.

3.2 CRF Layer

CRF is a basic model for natural language processing and is widely used in scenarios such as word segmentation, entity recognition, and part-of-speech tagging. Through CRF, the model can automatically learn certain constraints to ensure the legitimacy of the predicted label. Secondly, CRF has a transfer feature, considering the order between labels, and automatically learning the constraints of sentences.For example,the entity's start label should be "B-dis", not "I-dis". Therefore, introducing CRF to solve Transformer only considers long distance

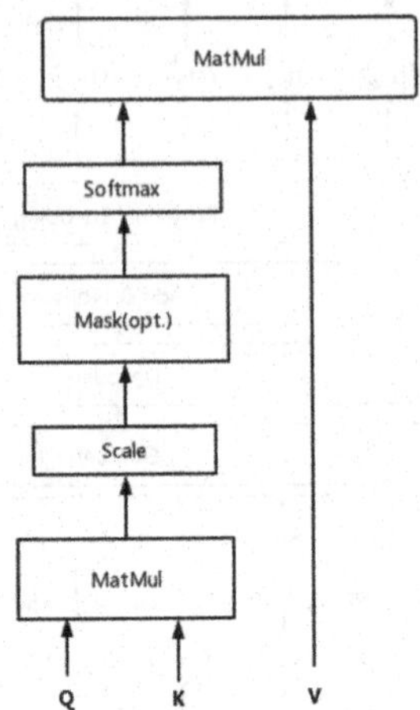

Fig. 3. Scaled Dot-Product Attention

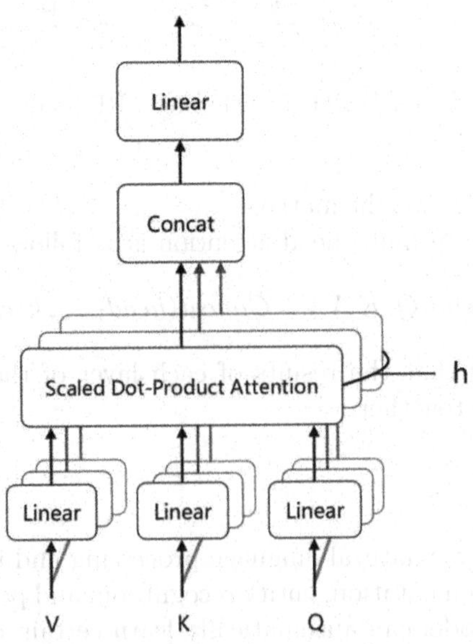

Fig. 4. Multi-head attention structure

dependencies between contexts. For a given input sequence $X = (x_1, ...x_n)$, the sequence probability score predicted by CRF is shown in the following Eq. (4). The normalization formula by the Softmax function is shown in the following Eq. (5) to obtain the probability values of each position of the predicted sequence.

$$score(X, y) = \sum_{i=0}^{n} T_{y_i, y_{i+1}} + \sum_{i=1}^{n} P_{i, y_i} \tag{4}$$

$$p(y|X) = \frac{e^{s(X,y)}}{\sum_{\tilde{y} \in Y_X} e^{s(X,\tilde{y})}} \tag{5}$$

$$Loss = log(p(y|X)) \tag{6}$$

where: $\tilde{y}$ is the real label; Y_X is given disease text all possible label combinations; *score* is the score of the degree of correspondence between the defect text y and the X tag sequence; *Loss* is the loss function.

When the final prediction of the text entity label of medical disease is made by CRF, the global optimal solution is obtained by using the viterbi algorithm, and the solution formula is

$$y^* = argmaxscore(X, \tilde{y}) \tag{7}$$

where: y^* is the sequence of medical disease text labels with the highest score.

4 Experiment and Result

4.1 Dataset Labels

The essence of the NER service based on deep learning is a sequence labeling task, that is, to identify the entity information with specific meaning in the sentence. The following will select the appropriate dataset labeling system to complete the dataset labeling.

Dataset Labels. There are three common methods for sequence annotation, namely BIO, BMES, and BIOSE. BIO annotates the beginning, end and non-entity parts of the entity; BMES, add S as the annotation of a single word entity; The BIOS adds E to the end label of the entity. In this example, the BIO annotation mode is selected. The identification of named entities in the medical field includes 9 types of entities, namely disease names, clinical manifestations, medical procedures, medical equipment, drugs, medical test items, bodies, departments, and microorganisms. The definitions of each category tag are shown in the Table 1, and each label is an abbreviation of the meaning of the entity.

Table 1. Label representations of each entity category

Number	Entity Class	Begin Label	Middle Label	End Label
1	Disease name	B-dis	I-dis	I-dis
2	Symptom	B-sym	I-sym	I-sym
3	Procedure	B-pro	I-pro	I-pro
4	Medical-equipment	B-equ	I-equ	I-equ
5	Drug	B-dru	I-dru	I-dru
6	Medical test item	B-ite	I-ite	I-ite
7	Body	B-bod	I-bod	I-bod
8	Department	B-dep	I-dep	I-dep
9	Microorganism	B-mic	I-mic	I-mic

Dataset Introduction. The data extracted for named entities in this paper is the Chinese medical naming entity recognition data CMeEE in the dataset combination of the previous academic evaluation competitions of CHIP Conference and Aliquark medical search business in 2021, which is rich in corpus and adds medical dialogues, electronic medical records and medical imaging reports written by medical experts, which is more time-sensitive and professional, and the data covers a wide range, and the use of this dataset for named entity recognition research is highly representative.

The dataset includes 15000 pieces of data from the training set, divide the test set by an 8:2,5,000 pieces of data from the validation set, and 3,000 pieces of data from the test set. The total number of words in the annotation data reached 2.2 million, containing 47,194 sentences and 938 files, with an average word count of 2,355 per file. The dataset contains 504 common pediatric diseases, 7,085 body parts, 12,907 clinical manifestations, and 4,354 medical procedures.Table 2 lists the different categories of entity statistics.

Table 2. Statistics of different types of medical entities on CMeEE dataset

Data Set	Training Data	Test Set
Disease name	12673	3170
Symptom	9730	2539
Procedure	4994	1338
Medical-equipment	695	193
Drug	3122	808
Medical test item	2059	522
Body	14178	3519
Department	271	77
Microorganism	1557	351

4.2 Experimental Environment and Evaluation Indicators

The following is an introduction to the experimental environment and evaluation indicators.

Experimental Environment and Parameter Settings. The experiment was carried out in the Linux operating system, developed in Python 3.6 language, the deep learning framework Tensorllow version is 1.15.0, the Bert model is the Bert-Base-Chinese version, and the hardware configuration: CPU model is i5-10400 2.90 GHz, GPU model is GTX2080. The important parameter settings of the model are shown in the Table 3.

Table 3. Model parameter settings

Parameter	Value
batch size	64
dropout rate	0.5
learning rate	1e−05
maxseq length	202
epochs	50

Evaluation Indicators. Evaluate with accuracy, recall, and F1 values. Accuracy is how many of the samples that are predicted to be correct are truly correct; Recall is how many of all the correct samples are correctly identified as positive; The F1 value is the weighted harmonic average of accuracy P and recall R. The higher the evaluation metric data, the better the performance of the entity extraction model. Its calculation formula is as follows:

$$P = \frac{TP}{TP + FP} \tag{8}$$

$$R = \frac{TP}{TP + FN} \tag{9}$$

$$F_1 = \frac{2PR}{P + R} \tag{10}$$

4.3 Comparison of Experiment Results

In order to verify the validity of the proposed method, the following five main named entity recognition algorithms are selected for comparison. Including machine learning algorithm CRF, deep learning and machine learning fusion algorithm BERT-BI-LSTM-CRF, the experimental results are shown in Table 4.

The comparison of CRF and BERT-BI-LSTM-CRF shows the effectiveness of deep learning algorithm, which the P, R, F1 values are increased by 0.71, 2.96, 0.46. The comparison of BERT-BI-LSTM-CRF and BTC shows that Transformer can obtain better feature representation, and the P, R and F1 values are increased by 4.09, 6.31 and 3.57 respectively, which proved the effectiveness of Transformer and was better than other algorithms. It is fully proved that Multi-head attention in Transformer has stronger long-distance dependency representation capabilities. Moreover, By applying pinyin and radical features to the fine-tuned BERT model, the Transformer can obtain richer semantic information, and F1 is improved by 1.37. In addition, the P, R, and F1 of each type of entity are compared. Department and Medical test item recognition is poor, in the Disease name, Drug, Microorganism achieved good results. For example, in disease name, terminology such as "horseshoekidney", "unilateralfusion", "humandiploidcell" are correctly predicted. In drug, predictions for long entities such as "Golden Hamster Kidney Cell (GHKC) and Meriones Gerbil Kidney Cell (MGKC) Inactivated Vaccine" are accurate, indicating that Transformer has a good effect on the identification of long entities. As shown in Table 5.

Table 4. Model parameter settings

Model	P	R	F1
CRF	52.41	54.24	54.75
BERT-BI-LSTM-CRF	53.14	57.20	55.21
BTC	57.23	63.51	58.78
BTC+radical+pinyin	58.43	64.82	60.15

Table 5. Recognition and comparison of different types of entities on CMeEE

Entity Type	P	R	F1
Disease name	69.71	71.7	70.69
Symptom	40.44	46.37	43.21
Procedure	46.05	48.93	47.45
Medical-equipment	53.22	66.31	59.05
Drug	68.28	70.25	69.25
Medical test item	31.41	36.57	33.79
Body	51.97	66.56	58.36
Department	15.97	21.22	16.99
Microorganism	71.73	78.72	75.06

5 Conclusion

Based on personalized recommendation services in the field of chronic diseases, this paper proposes a service recommendation method based on multi-feature fusion Bert-Transformer-CRF named entity recognition technology. First, Bert is used to train word vectors to obtain contextual features. After adding radicals and pinyin features, it is passed into Transformer module to extract embedded features of each character and save remote information flow between texts. The CRF layer decodes the prediction label to obtain the entity classification label. Then the relationship between entities is extracted and the implicit behavior of users is combined with the recommendation. Experimental results show that this method has better named entity recognition effect, which proves its availability in service recommendation, and lays a more solid foundation for improving the accuracy of personalized recommendation service.

References

1. Li, R., Shi, B., Guo, H., Liu, F., Li, T., Li, M.: Research progress of chronic disease management in internet hospitals. Chin. Math. **18**(01), 95–101 (2023)
2. Zhang, M., Zhang, X., Liu, S., Tian, H., Yang, Q.: Review of recommendation systems using knowledge graph. Comput. Eng. Appl. **59**(04), 30–42 (2023)
3. Adomavicius, G., Tuzhilin, A.: Toward the next generation of recommender systems a survey of the state of-the-art and possible extensions. IEEE Trans. Knowl. Data Eng. **17**(6), 734–749 (2005)
4. Li, Y., Wang, R., Nan, G., Li, D., Li, M.: A personalized paper recommendation method considering diverse user preferences. Decis. Support Syst. **12**(07), 49–56 (2021)
5. Zhang, Z., Zhang, X.: Context-aware information service recommendation method for high-speed rail. Comput. Eng. Appl. **57**(12), 231–236 (2021)
6. Yu, X., Jiang, F., Du, J., Gong, D.: A cross-domain collaborative filtering algorithm with expanding user and item features via the latent factor space of auxiliary domains. Pattern Recognit. **94**, 96–109 (2019)
7. Yu Q., Zhao M., Luo Y.: Collaborative filtering hybrid recommendation algorithm based on optimal weight and its application. Oper. Res. Manage. Sci. https://kns.cnki.net/kcms/detail//34.1133.G3.20230227.1815.006.html
8. Hansem, C., Maystre, L.: Contextual and sequential user embeddings for large-scale music recommendation. In: Proceedings of the 14th ACM Conference on Recommender Systems, pp. 53–62. ACM Press, New York (2020)
9. Li, D., Luo, S., Zhang, X., Xu, F.: A review of named entity recognition methods. J. Front. Comput. Sci. Technol. **16**(9) (2022)
10. Yuan, J., Pan, M., Zhang, T., Jiang, Y.: Named entity recognition in the field of power safety based on rules and dictionaries. Electron. Technol. Appl. **48**(12) (2022)
11. Jiang, Q., Gui, Q., Wang, L.: Review of research progress of named entity recognition technology. Electr. Power Inf. Commun. Technol. **20**(2), 15–24 (2022)
12. Zhai, J., Chen, C., Zhang, Y.: Research on entity recognition of Chinese electronic medical record naming based on the combination of CRF and rules. J. Baotou Med. Coll. **33**(11) (2017)

13. Sun, Z., Li, X.L.: Multi-feature fusion Chinese electronic medical record named entity recognition. Comput. Eng. https://kns.cnkinet/kcms/detail//11.2127.TP20221213.1206.005.html
14. Lian G.: Construction of knowledge graph in network security domain based on improved bi-LSTM-CRF. Xinxijishu **12**(2), 130–142 (2022)

Multimodal Intent Recognition Based on Contrastive Learning

Yuxuan Wu, Zhizhong Liu(✉), Zhaohui Su, and Xiaoyu Song

School of Computer and Control Engineering, Yantai University, Yantai 264005, China
lzzmff@126.com

Abstract. Multimodal intent recognition plays a critical role in service science as it enables the achievement of more intelligent and personalized services. Recently, multimodal intent recognition has become a hot topic, and some research has been carried out on this topic. However, most existing research methods focus on exploring intra-modal or inter-modal interactions, which ignore the relationship between multimodal samples. To address this issue, we propose an approach for Multimodal Intent Recognition Based on Contrastive Learning (MIRCL). Firstly, the original samples and augmented samples are separately fed into crossmodal Transformer modules for multimodal feature fusion. The resulting fused multimodal features are then used for contrastive learning. Meanwhile, the fused multimodal features of the original samples are passed into a multimodal information bottleneck (MIB) module for intent recognition. Finally, the contrastive learning task and intent recognition task are jointly trained to optimize the whole model. We carried out comprehensive validation tests based on the publically available dataset MIntRec to prove the superiority of our proposed method.

Keywords: Intent Recognition · Multimodal · Contrastive Learning · Crossmodal Transformer · Multimodal Feature Fusion

1 Introduction

With the proliferation of mobile internet and intelligent IoT devices, a significant amount of digital data is being generated during users' online activities. Intent recognition based on these data can help systems better understand user needs, and provide more efficient service that enhances customer satisfaction and loyalty [1]. Therefore, extensive research has been conducted on intent recognition and have achieved certain good results [2,3]. Typically, these intent recognition tasks are performed on single-modal data (such as text, speech) [4–6].

However, single-modal intent recognition has limitations as a single data source can not provide adequate information to accurately understand the user's intent. Compared to single-modal intent recognition, multimodal intent recognition can utilize multiple modalities of information to identify user intent, thus

Z. Wang et al. (Eds.): ICSS 2023, CCIS 1844, pp. 179–193, 2023.
https://doi.org/10.1007/978-981-99-4402-6_13

providing more features to help the model analyze the intent of data [7]. A series of multimodal intent methods have been proposed in many areas such as conversational intent classification [8], social network intent classification [9,10], identifying action intent [11–13], advertising marketing intent [14,15], etc.

Most multimodal intent recognition works have centered their attention on delving into the intricacies of intra-modal or inter-modal interactions [16,17]. However, learning intra-modal or inter-modal features can produce overfitting as the flexible expression of multimodal data. Therefore, the multimodal intent recognition model should avoid solely focusing on intra-modal or inter-modal interactions and instead allow it to learn common features related to intent. Unfortunately, existing multimodal intent recognition models are unable to learn common features related to intent in multimodal data, as they are unable to address the following two challenges:

- Existing multimodal intent recognition models focus on intra-modal or inter-modal interactions, which ignore the learning of inter-sample resulting in not learning enough intent-related features to form a good feature representation.
- Existing multimodal intent recognition models focus on intra-modal or inter-modal interactions, which generate task-irrelevant noise during multimodal feature fusion. The large amount of noise information greatly weakens the efficacy of the model.

To address these challenges, we propose an approach for Multimodal Intent Recognition Based on Contrastive Learning (MIRCL). Firstly, we generate an augmented dataset based on the original dataset through data augmentation methods. Next, the original samples and the augmented samples are separately fed into the crossmodal Transformer modules for multimodal feature fusion. Then, we calculate the contrast loss based on the fused multimodal features of the original and augmented samples. At the same time, we pass the fused multimodal features of the original samples into the multimodal information bottleneck (MIB) module for intent recognition and calculate the intent recognition loss. Finally, we fit the contrast learning loss and intent recognition loss together for jointly training the whole model. The following is a summary of our main contributions:

- To address the problem that existing models ignore the learning of inter-sample, we propose an approach for multimodal intent recognition based on contrastive learning, which optimizes multimodal fusion through contrastive learning between multimodal samples and helps the model learn sufficiently complete intent features.
- To address the issue of noise information during multimodal feature fusion, we introduced the MIB to improve the multimodal fusion process. The MIB learns the bare minimum necessary representation for the assignment in question by maximising the mutual information between the representation and the target while limiting the mutual information between the representation and the input data.

The rest of this paper is organized as follows: Sect. 2, the related work on intention recognition and contrast learning is reviewed; Sect. 3 is introduced the multimodal intention recognition method based on contrast learning proposed in detail; Sect. 4 reports experimental results; Finally, Sect. 5 concludes this work and discusses some future research activities.

2 Related Work

2.1 Intent Recognition

Intent recognition based on textual modality data is crucial and a subtask that is essential for spoken language understanding [18]. To address the problem of users having multiple intentions in the same utterance in real-world scenarios, Qin et al. [19] proposed an adaptive graphical interaction framework for multi-intent detection, introducing an intent-slot graphical interaction layer that can accurately extract relevant intention information, simulating strong correlations between slots and intentions. In computer vision, Jia et al. [20] proposed an object/context localization loss that enables the model to focus on the key regions of an image for intent recognition behind social media images. Joo et al. [21] proposed a hierarchical model based on syntactic attribute layers to recognize communicative intentions in photos of politicians. In the aspect of multimodal intent recognition research, Zhang et al. [22] demonstrated through numerous experiments that using multimodal models significantly improves performance compared to pure textual modalities, showing the value of multimodal data in the detection of intent. Maharana et al. [23] proposed a multimodal cross-attention model that combines video and textual modalities for intent recognition. Liu et al. [24] used a multi-head cross-attention mechanism and graph neural network to build a hierarchical framework for identifying the sarcastic intent of social network posts from multiple granularities of alignment.

2.2 Contrastive Learning

In computer vision, Han et al. [25] suggested a contrast learning approach that utilized negative cases to address the contrast learning collapse situation by moving the negative cases farther apart to make the distribution of samples more uniform. HE et al. [26] proposed a momentum encoder for contrast learning to increase the number of negative cases using a memory bank to solve the problem of memory limitation on the amount of negative cases. Gunel et al. [27] added contrast loss on top of supervised loss to optimize in the supervised fine-tuning stage. In the area of NLP, Sun et al. [28] have achieved good results with few samples for the same sample, encoded by the teacher model and student model, respectively, as two views of contrast learning, combining task target loss, distillation loss, and contrast loss to train the model together. For multimodal contrast learning research, the research endeavor undertaken by LI et al. [29] has resulted in a novel approach to sentiment detection that employs a multimodal methodology incorporating both contrast learning and multilayer fusion techniques. The study has successfully facilitated the integration of these features within the model's architecture. To the best of our knowledge, we did not find any other work that used contrastive learning in multimodal intent recognition.

3 The MIRCL Modal

The overall architecture of MIRCL is shown in Fig. 1. MIRCL consists of two modules: the multi-task learning module and the multi-modal feature fusion module. Specifically, the multi-modal feature fusion module is shown on the left side of Fig. 1, which combines information from multiple modalities and effectively aligns different modalities to generate a unified representation. The multi-task learning module is on the right side of Fig. 1, which includes two tasks: the contrastive learning task and the intent recognition task. The contrastive learning task optimizes multimodal fusion and helps the model learn sufficiently complete intent features. The intent recognition task first obtains the multimodal features fused from the original samples, and then regularizes them with MIB to eliminate noise and perform intent recognition.

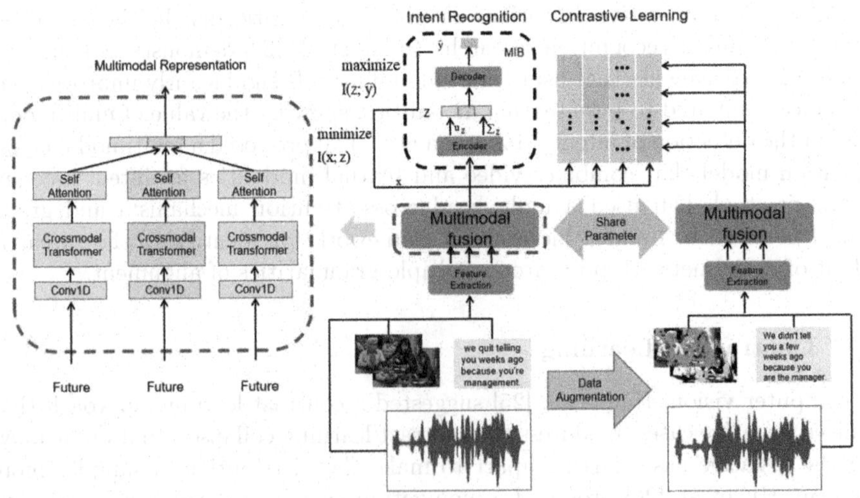

Fig. 1. The Framework Of MIRCL

3.1 Feature Extraction

The feature extraction models are used to extract relevant and meaningful features from raw data, which can then be used as input for downstream tasks. The feature extraction models are not involved in training.

Text Feature Extraction. We use BERT [30] as the text encoder to extract features from text. BERT is built on top of the Transformer and has strong language representation and feature extraction capabilities. Each original text sentence T is transformed into a text feature vector $V_t \in R^{L_t \times D_t}$ through BERT word embedding, where L_t represents the length of the original text sentence T and D_t represents the dimensionality of the feature.

Video Feature Extraction. For video features, first the video is extracted frame by frame into individual images and key frames are selected. Then, pre-trained Faster R-CNN [31] and ResNet-50 [32] are used to extract the features of all key frames and represent them as h. Finally, the target detection method is used to map h to the annotated bounding box area B to obtain the video feature $V_v \in R^{L_v \times D_v}$, as follows:

$$V_v = AvgPool(RoIAlign(h, B)) \tag{1}$$

where $RoIAlign$ is used to transform the feature map of any sized region of interest to a small feature map with a fixed size, so that the obtained small feature map can be more precise and complete. $AvgPool$ refers to the two-dimensional average pooling operation. L_v represents the sequence length of the video segment, and D_{video} represents the dimension of the feature.

Audio Feature Extraction. We use wav2vec [33] to extract audio features. Wav2vec is a pre-training model that can map raw audio samples to a feature space that better represents the data through unsupervised training. Audio features $V_a \in R^{L_a \times D_a}$ are obtained by extracting them using wav2vec.

3.2 Multimodal Feature Fusion

Multimodal fusion is first performed before intent recognition is performed. The overall structure of the multimodal fusion module is shown in the red box on the left of Fig. 1, where the extracted text, video, and audio features are multimodally fused to provide more information for model decision making.

Temporal Convolutions Snd Positional Embedding. First, text features V_t, video features V_v, and audio features V_a are input to a one-dimensional temporal convolutional layer, and each modality feature is reduced dimensionally through Cov1D, mapping the features of the three modalities to the same dimension:

$$\hat{V}_{\{t,v,a\}} = Conv1D(V_{\{t,v,a\}}, n_{\{t,v,a\}}) \in R^{L_{\{t,v,a\}} \times D} \tag{2}$$

where Conv1D represents a one-dimensional convolution operation, $n_{\{t,v,a\}}$ represents the number of convolution kernels in the three modalities, and D represents the feature dimension after convolution. Positional information is encoded with a dimension that is consistent with the mapped features, and then fused with the mapped features:

$$X^{[0]}_{\{t,v,a\}} = \hat{V}_{\{t,v,a\}} + PE(L_{\{t,v,a\}}, D) \tag{3}$$

where $PE(.) \in R^{L_{\{t,v,a\}} \times D}$ computes the (fixed) embedding of each positional index, and $X^{[0]}_{\{t,v,a\}}$ represents the features that contain low-level positional information of different modalities.

Crossmodal Transformers and Self-attention. Through cross-modal transformers, low-level features in other modalities are directly attended to, enabling the fusion of multimodal information and capturing the adaptability knowledge between different modalities in the latent space. Each cross-modal Transformer consists of n layers of cross-modal attention modules. Taking the transfer of information from modality β to modality α as an example, the cross-modal transformers for $i = 1, 2, ..., n$ are as follows:

$$X^{[0]}_{\beta \to \alpha} = X^{[0]}_{\alpha} \tag{4}$$

$$\hat{X}^{[i]}_{\beta \to \alpha} = CT^{[i],mul}_{\beta \to \alpha}(LN(X^{[i-1]}_{\beta \to \alpha})) + LN(X^{[i-1]}_{\beta \to \alpha}) \tag{5}$$

$$X^{[i]}_{\beta \to \alpha} = \int_{\theta^{[i]}_{\beta \to \alpha}} (LN(\hat{X}^{[i-1]}_{\beta \to \alpha})) + LN(\hat{X}^{[i]}_{\beta \to \alpha}) \tag{6}$$

where $\int_{\theta}$ is the position-wise feed-forward sublayer parameterized by θ, CT is the multi-head crossmodal attention module, and LN is layer normalization. After passing through multiple modules, the two modalities obtain the mapping from β to α, and within each module, the input features or the output from the previous module is normalized by layer normalization and then passed through the multi-head cross-modal attention module. CT is specifically defined as follows:

$$Y_{\alpha} = CT_{\beta \to \alpha}(X_{\alpha}, X_{\beta}) \tag{7}$$

$$Y_{\alpha} = softmax(\frac{Q_{\alpha} K^T_{\beta}}{\sqrt{d_k}}) V_{\beta} \tag{8}$$

$$Y_{\alpha} = softmax(\frac{X_{\alpha} W_{Q_{\alpha}} W^T_{K_{\beta}} X^T_{\beta}}{\sqrt{d_k}}) X_{\beta} W_{V_{\beta}} \in R^{L_{\alpha} \times d_v} \tag{9}$$

where $W_{Q_{\alpha}} \in R^{d_{\alpha} \times d_k}$,$W^T_{K_{\beta}} \in R^{d_{\beta} \times d_{\beta}}$,$W_{V_{\beta}} \in R^{d_k \times d_v}$ is the weight. Our approach has three modalities, each of which obtains cross-modal information from the other two modalities through cross-modal transformers. A total of 6 cross-modal transformers are required to obtain 6 feature vectors, and then the feature vectors of the same target modality are concatenated together to obtain the final features through the self-attention mechanism.

$$X_t = transformer(concat(X^{[D]}_{v \to t}, X^{[D]}_{a \to t})) \tag{10}$$

$$X_v = transformer(concat(X_{t\rightarrow v}^{[D]}, X_{a\rightarrow v}^{[D]})) \tag{11}$$

$$X_a = transformer(concat(X_{v\rightarrow a}^{[D]}, X_{t\rightarrow a}^{[D]})) \tag{12}$$

$$X = concat(X_t, X_v, X_a) \tag{13}$$

3.3 Multimodal Information Bottleneck for Intent Recognition

In this paper, we introduce a multimodal information bottleneck [34] to filter the noise in multimodal features. The mutual information of X and Y can be defined as:

$$I(x; y) = KL(p(x, y)||p(x)p(y)) \tag{14}$$

$$I(x; y) = E_{(x,y)} \sim p(x, y)[log \frac{p(x, y)}{p(x)p(y)}] \tag{15}$$

The goal of the MIB is to minimize the mutual information between the original multimodal embedding x and the encoded multimodal embedding z,maximize the mutual information between the encoded multimodal embedding z and the target y. MIB can then be defined as:

$$L = I(y; z) - \beta I(x; z) \tag{16}$$

Since x,y have a high degree of dimensionality, the joint probability distribution and the respective edge distribution cannot be calculated, so it is necessary to fit their probability distributions using neural networks and continuously optimize the lower bound, so that the lower bound of mutual information can be closer to the real mutual information. The lower bound of the objective function is:

$$L = I(y; z) - \beta I(x; z) \geq E_{(x,y)\sim p(x,y),z\sim P(z|x)}[logq(y|z) - \beta KL(p(z|x)||q(z))] \tag{17}$$

where learning the mean and variance of the Gaussian distribution $p(z|x)$ using the respective deep neural networks.

$$p(z|x) = \mathcal{N}(\mu_z, \Sigma_z) \tag{18}$$

The mean u_z and variance Σ_z of a Gaussian distribution are learned by having deep neural networks. The encoded multimodal embedding z is denoted as:

$$Z = \mu_z + \Sigma_z \times \varepsilon \tag{19}$$

where $\varepsilon \sim \mathcal{N}(0, I)$ is a standard normal Gaussian distribution and I is the identity vector whose elements are all equal to 1. kl scatter can be calculated as:

$$KL(p(z|x)||q(z)) = KL(\mathcal{N}(\mu_z, \Sigma_z)||\mathcal{N}(0, I)) \tag{20}$$

where we assume that $q(z)$ is a standard normal Gaussian distribution $\mathcal{N}(0, I)$ and that the choice of reparameterization of $p(z|x)$ and $q(z)$ allows for the computation of an analytic KL-divergence. Finally, the lower bound of the objective function can be simplified as:

$$L_r = \frac{1}{n}\sum_{i=1}^{n}[logq(y_i|z_i) - \beta KL(\mathcal{N}(\mu_{z_i}, \Sigma_{z_i}))||\mathcal{N}(0, I)] \tag{21}$$

where $\beta \geq 0$ is the scalar that determines the minimum information constraint weights in the optimization process, y is the label, n is the batch size, and $logq(y|z) = ylog\hat{y}+(1-y)log(1-\hat{y})$. Here, $maximizeI(y;z)$, which is to maximize $q(y|z)$, is equivalent to minimizing the cross entropy between the prediction and the target y.

3.4 Contrast Learning

Prior to performing contrastive learning, the original data needs to be augmented to obtain contrastive data, as shown in Fig. 1. The data augmentation used in our approach includes text augmentation, video augmentation, and audio augmentation.

Text Data Augmentation. The technique used for augmenting text data in this study is known as back-translation [35], which involves translating the original data into a different language and then translating it back into the original language. Due to differences in language logic and sequence, the back-translation method often generates new data that differs significantly from the original data. Specifically, the original text t is first translated into Chinese t_c and then t_c is translated back into English to obtain the augmented text t_{aug}.

Video Data Augmentation. We extract the video frames and apply colorjitter [36] to each frame for data augmentation. Colorjitter not only allows the model to learn color invariance, but also some contour and spatial structure features. For video data, each frame of the original video is extracted and converted into a sequence of continuous images. Then, the brightness, contrast, saturation, and hue of each frame are randomly adjusted. These operations do not involve image scaling or deformation, which would distort the results.

Audio Data Augmentation. We randomly employ one of three augmentation methods: noise augmentation, time shift augmentation, or pitch shift augmentation. Noise augmentation adds a random noise segment to the original signal with a damping coefficient of P. Time shift augmentation randomly shifts the audio time axis to the left or right. Pitch shift augmentation randomly shifts the pitch of the original audio sample within a range of $\pm 10\%$. Augmented data has higher robustness and improves the model's ability to learn invariant features in the data.

Contrast Loss. In each iteration, a batch size of n is randomly obtained, and the augmented samples of this batch are also obtained, resulting in 2n data points. Each original sample is positively paired with its corresponding augmented sample, and forms a negative pair with the remaining N-1 augmented samples. After obtaining the augmented data, the original sample and augmented sample representations are extracted using a multimodal fusion module. Finally, the contrastive loss L_c is calculated using the NT-Xent loss [26] as the contrastive loss. NT-Xent's objective is to minimize the distance between similar samples and maximize the distance between dissimilar samples. The NT-Xent contrastive loss is defined as:

$$L_c = \frac{1}{n}\sum_{i=1}^{n} -log\frac{exp(sim(X_i, X\_aug_i)/\tau)}{\sum_{j\neq i}^{n} exp(sim(X_i, X\_aug_j)/\tau)} \tag{22}$$

where τ is the temperature coefficient of contrastive learning, and sim is a similarity function that is the cosine similarity between X and X_{aug} after L2 regularization, defined as:

$$sim(X, X\_aug) = X^T X\_aug/ \|X\| \, \|X\_aug\| \tag{23}$$

where $\|\bullet\|$ represents the L2 norm.

3.5 Model Training

The contrastive learning loss and the intent recognition classification loss are combined and weighted together to form the total loss for model training. The total loss for model training is defined as:

$$L = \alpha L_C + \beta L_r \tag{24}$$

where α and β are weight coefficients used to balance the different training losses.

4 Experiment

4.1 Dataset

In this study, we utilized the publicly available MIntRec dataset, which is sourced from the TV show "SuperStore". The MIntRec dataset consists of 2224 multimodal samples, each of which contains audio, video, and text data, and is divided into two coarse-grained intent categories and twenty fine-grained intent categories. The dataset is further partitioned into training, validation, and testing sets with 1334, 445, and 445 samples, respectively. The proportion of different intent categories is consistent across the three subsets, ensuring the validity and fairness of the experiments.

4.2 Parameter Settings

All the models' parameters in this study were updated using the Adam optimizer. The experiments were conducted on a Windows 10 system and implemented in Python language and PyTorch framework with versions 3.8.3 and 1.11.0, respectively. Training was performed on a single GeForce RTX 3090 GPU, with a batch size of 16, a temperature of 0.5, and a learning rate of 0.00003, and lasted for 50 epochs. The F1 score was utilized as the evaluation metric for hyperparameter tuning.

4.3 Baselines

We conducted extensive experiments to evaluate the effectiveness of MIRCL, including the following baselines: (1) Bert: Bert [30] is a pre-trained model using Transformer as an architecture that can be fine-tuned for use in various NLP tasks; (2) Mult: Mult [37] proposes a cross-modal attention model for cross-modal interaction across the entire time sequence in multi-modal non-aligned situations; (3) MAG-Bert: Rahman integrates multi-modal adaptation gate (MAG) into Bert to get MAG-Bert [38], and the MAG structure can help the Bert model receive multi-modal information and use it for fine-tuning. (4) MISA: MISA [39] utilizes a multi-task learning framework to map various modalities to two distinct feature subspaces for learning.

4.4 Results

Analysis of Main Test Results. Table 1 present the performance results of various models on MinRec. We assess the models' performance based on several evaluation metrics, including accuracy, F1 score, precision, and recall, where higher scores indicate superior performance. Models based on multimodal data show significantly improved performance compared to using only text, demonstrating the effectiveness of multimodal data models. The accuracy of MIRCL is 0.61 higher than that of the highest-performing model, MAG-BERT, and its F1 score and precision are 1.81 and 1.04 higher than those of the highest-performing model, MISA, respectively. The recall rate is 1.87 higher than that of MAG-BERT. Table 1 demonstrate that MIRCL outperforms the compared models in terms of performance metrics, indicating that it has better performance than other methods in multimodal intent recognition tasks.

Figure 2 depicts the confusion matrix of MIRCL on MinRec, illustrating the classification results for each intent category. The column and row vectors of the confusion matrix represent the model's predicted and actual intent categories, respectively, and the corresponding values indicate the degree to which the model can correctly recognize each intent category. The model performs well in identifying samples from the advise, complain, and praise intent categories. The confusion matrix in Fig. 2 shows that MIRCL's predicted labels are mainly concentrated on the diagonal, representing true positives without scattered phenomena, which fully demonstrates the superiority and robustness of the model.

Table 1. Quantitative results

Methods	Modalities	F1	ACC	P	R
BERT	Text	67.40	70.88	68.07	67.44
MAG-BERT	Text+Audio+Video	68.64	72.65	69.08	69.28
MulT	Text+Audio+Video	69.25	72.52	70.25	69.24
MISA	Text+Audio+Video	69.32	72.29	70.85	69.24
MIRCL	**Text+Audio+Video**	**71.13**	**73.26**	**71.89**	**71.15**

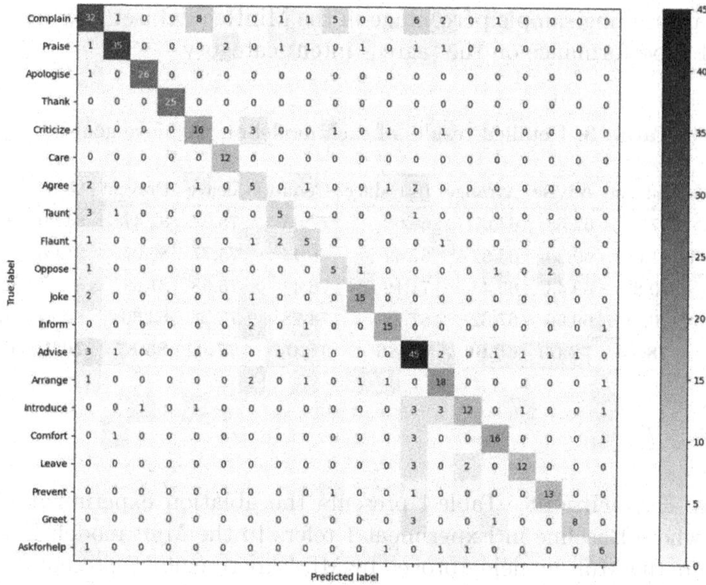

Fig. 2. Confusion matrix of MIRCL on MIntRec

For further validation, Tables 2 and Table 3 illustrate the MIRCL's performance in classifying each fine-grained intent category "Express emotions and attitudes" and "Achieve goals", with F1 scores as the evaluation metric. As evident from the tables, MIRCL has a higher recognition effect than other models in the criticize, taunt, joke, inform, oppose, and leave intent categories, which require the assistance of audio and video information in addition to textual data. Multimodal information can more effectively distinguish these intent categories, demonstrating the advantage of MIRCL in multimodal intent recognition tasks. Notably, the MIRCL model achieved 100% accuracy in the thank intent category. Although the F1 scores of the MIRCL model in the agree intent category are lower than those of other models, they are close to or even surpass those of other models in other intent categories. Based on these experimental results, the MIRCL model performed the best on the public dataset MinRec. The compara-

Table 2. Detailed results of each model on "Express emotions and attitudes"

Methods	Complain	Praise	Apologise	Thank	Criticize	Care	Agree	Taunt	Flaunt	Oppose	Joke
BERT	64.36	85.69	97.93	97.22	47.06	87.42	94.26	15.53	46.12	32.32	27.42
MAG-BERT	67.65	86.03	97.76	96.52	49.02	85.59	91.60	15.78	47.09	33.97	37.54
MulT	65.48	84.72	97.93	96.83	49.72	88.12	92.23	26.12	48.91	34.68	33.95
MISA	63.91	86.63	97.78	98.03	53.44	87.14	92.05	22.15	46.44	36.15	38.74
MIRCL	**60.37**	**85.36**	**96.29**	**100**	**65.30**	**92.30**	**38.46**	**50.00**	**47.61**	**45.45**	**83.33**

tively small training sample percentage in the MinRec dataset may be the cause of MIRCL's performance on the "agree" intent category.

Table 3. Detailed results of each model on "Achieve goals"

Methods	Inform	Advise	Arrange	Introduce	Comfort	Leave	Prevent	Greet	Askforhelp
BERT	67.74	67.68	64.67	68.64	77.05	73.37	82.47	84.90	66.20
MAG-BERT	71.00	69.30	63.82	67.42	76.43	75.77	85.07	91.06	64.44
MulT	70.85	69.43	65.44	71.19	76.44	75.58	81.68	86.65	69.12
MISA	70.18	69.56	67.32	67.22	78.78	77.23	83.30	82.71	67.57
MIRCL	**78.94**	**72.00**	**66.66**	**64.86**	**78.04**	**77.41**	**83.87**	**76.19**	**60.00**

Ablation Experiment. Table 4 presents the ablation experiment results of MIRCL, where Baseline in Experiment 1 refers to the Mult model, Experiment 2 represents the Mult model improved by MI, Experiment 3 represents the model with contrastive learning, and Experiment 4 is the complete model. The results of Experiments 1, 2, and 3 demonstrate the effectiveness of each module as all evaluation indicators of the model have decreased. The table shows that the multimodal intent recognition model improved by the MI module has a positive effect on the classification performance of intent recognition compared to the baseline. Experiment 2 improved the accuracy, F1 score, precision, and recall by 0.29, 1.34, 1.17, and 1.59, respectively. Similarly, compared to the baseline, Experiment 3 improved the accuracy, F1 score, precision, and recall by 0.06, 1.46, 1.92, and 0.96, respectively, indicating that contrastive learning helps optimize the multimodal model during the learning process. By computing similarity and difference properties between the original and augmented samples, our approach can acquire more intention-related features during multimodal fusion. Our feature extraction module has been designed based on existing prior knowledge [22], and it is not the primary focus of our work. Therefore, we have decided not to conduct ablation experiments on the feature extraction module.

Table 4. Results of MIRCL ablation

Num	Methods	F1	ACC	P	R
1	Baseline	69.25	72.52	70.25	69.24
2	Baseline+MI	70.59	72.81	71.42	70.83
3	Baseline+CL	70.71	72.58	72.17	70.20
4	Baseline+MI+CL	71.13	73.26	71.89	71.15

5 Conclusion

We propose an approach for Multimodal Intent Recognition Based on Contrastive Learning (MIRCL). Compared with previous works, we add the learning of inter-sample. We design a contrastive learning tasks based on data augmentation to allow the model to learn enough intent-related features to form a good feature representation. Furthermore, to address the noise issue during fusion, the MIB is introduced in this paper to learn the minimal sufficient representation of the given task. The experimental results demonstrate that the MIRCL model performs significantly better than the baseline model on the public dataset MinRec in terms of accuracy, F1 score, precision, and recall, providing evidence for its effectiveness. In the future, we will improve multimodal fusion methods to further enhance the accuracy of intent recognition.

References

1. Guennemann, F., Cho, Y.C., et al.: The effectiveness of product placement by media types: impact of image and intention to purchase. J. Serv. Sci. (JSS) **7**(1), 29–42 (2014)
2. Akbari, M., Mohades, A., Shirali-Shahreza, M.H.: A hybrid architecture for out of domain intent detection and intent discovery. arXiv preprint arXiv:2303.04134 (2023)
3. Zhang, Q., Wang, S., Li, J.: A heterogeneous interaction graph network for multi-intent spoken language understanding. Neural Process. Lett. 1–19 (2023)
4. Firdaus, M., Ekbal, A., Cambria, E.: Multitask learning for multilingual intent detection and slot filling in dialogue systems. Inf. Fusion **91**, 299–315 (2023)
5. Mei, J., Wang, Y., Tu, X., Dong, M., He, T.: Incorporating BERT with probability-aware gate for spoken language understanding. IEEE/ACM Trans. Audio Speech Lang. Process. **31**, 826–834 (2023)
6. Rafiepour, M., Sartakhti, J.S.: CTRAN: CNN-transformer-based network for natural language understanding. arXiv preprint arXiv:2303.10606 (2023)
7. Huang, Y., Du, C., Xue, Z., Chen, X., Zhao, H., Huang, L.: What makes multi-modal learning better than single (provably). In: Advances in Neural Information Processing Systems, vol. 34, pp. 10944–10956 (2021)
8. Yuan, S., et al.: MCIC: multimodal conversational intent classification for E-commerce customer service. In: Lu, W., Huang, S., Hong, Y., Zhou, X. (eds.) NLPCC 2022 Part I. LNCS, vol. 13551, pp. 749–761. Springer, Cham (2022). https://doi.org/10.1007/978-3-031-17120-8_58
9. Chen, Y.Y., Hsieh, S.K.: An analysis of multimodal document intent in Instagram posts. In: Proceedings of the 32nd Conference on Computational Linguistics and Speech Processing (ROCLING 2020), pp. 193–207 (2020)
10. Kruk, J., Lubin, J., Sikka, K., Lin, X., Jurafsky, D., Divakaran, A.: Integrating text and image: determining multimodal document intent in Instagram posts. arXiv preprint arXiv:1904.09073 (2019)
11. Ignat, O., Castro, S., Miao, H., Li, W., Mihalcea, R.: WhyAct: identifying action reasons in lifestyle vlogs. arXiv preprint arXiv:2109.02747 (2021)
12. Huang, X., Kovashka, A.: Inferring visual persuasion via body language, setting, and deep features. In: Proceedings of the IEEE Conference on Computer Vision and Pattern Recognition Workshops, pp. 73–79 (2016)

13. Fang, Z., López, A.M.: Intention recognition of pedestrians and cyclists by 2D pose estimation. IEEE Trans. Intell. Transp. Syst. **21**(11), 4773–4783 (2019)
14. Hussain, Z., et al.: Automatic understanding of image and video advertisements. In: Proceedings of the IEEE Conference on Computer Vision and Pattern Recognition, pp. 1705–1715 (2017)
15. Zhang, L., et al.: Multimodal marketing intent analysis for effective targeted advertising. IEEE Trans. Multimedia **24**, 1830–1843 (2021)
16. Singh, G.V., Firdaus, M., Ekbal, A., Bhattacharyya, P.: EmoInt-trans: a multimodal transformer for identifying emotions and intents in social conversations. IEEE/ACM Trans. Audio Speech Lang. Process. **31**, 290–300 (2022)
17. Ma, Z., Li, J., Li, G., Cheng, Y.: UniTranSeR: a unified transformer semantic representation framework for multimodal task-oriented dialog system. In: Proceedings of the 60th Annual Meeting of the Association for Computational Linguistics, vol. 1 (Long Papers), pp. 103–114 (2022)
18. Qin, L., Xie, T., Che, W., Liu, T.: A survey on spoken language understanding: recent advances and new frontiers. arXiv preprint arXiv:2103.03095 (2021)
19. Qin, L., Xu, X., Che, W., Liu, T.: AGIF: an adaptive graph-interactive framework for joint multiple intent detection and slot filling. arXiv preprint arXiv:2004.10087 (2020)
20. Jia, M., Wu, Z., Reiter, A., Cardie, C., Belongie, S., Lim, S.N.: Intentonomy: a dataset and study towards human intent understanding. In: Proceedings of the IEEE/CVF Conference on Computer Vision and Pattern Recognition, pp. 12986–12996 (2021)
21. Joo, J., Li, W., Steen, F.F., Zhu, S.C.: Visual persuasion: inferring communicative intents of images. In: Proceedings of the IEEE Conference on Computer Vision and Pattern Recognition, pp. 216–223 (2014)
22. Zhang, H., Xu, H., Wang, X., Zhou, Q., Zhao, S., Teng, J.: MIntRec: a new dataset for multimodal intent recognition. In: Proceedings of the 30th ACM International Conference on Multimedia, pp. 1688–1697 (2022)
23. Maharana, A., et al.: Multimodal intent discovery from livestream videos. In: Findings of the Association for Computational Linguistics: NAACL 2022, pp. 476–489 (2022)
24. Liu, H., Wang, W., Li, H.: Towards multi-modal sarcasm detection via hierarchical congruity modeling with knowledge enhancement. arXiv preprint arXiv:2210.03501 (2022)
25. Han, X.Q., Xu, S.S., Feng, Z., He, R.Q., Lu, Z.Y.: A simple framework for contrastive learning phases of matter. arXiv preprint arXiv:2205.05607 (2022)
26. He, K., Fan, H., Wu, Y., Xie, S., Girshick, R.: Momentum contrast for unsupervised visual representation learning. In: Proceedings of the IEEE/CVF Conference on Computer Vision and Pattern Recognition, pp. 9729–9738 (2020)
27. Gunel, B., Du, J., Conneau, A., Stoyanov, V.: Supervised contrastive learning for pre-trained language model fine-tuning. arXiv preprint arXiv:2011.01403 (2020)
28. Sun, S., Gan, Z., Cheng, Y., Fang, Y., Wang, S., Liu, J.: Contrastive distillation on intermediate representations for language model compression. arXiv preprint arXiv:2009.14167 (2020)
29. Li, Z., Xu, B., Zhu, C., Zhao, T.: CLMLF: a contrastive learning and multi-layer fusion method for multimodal sentiment detection. arXiv preprint arXiv:2204.05515 (2022)
30. Devlin, J., Chang, M.W., Lee, K., Toutanova, K.: BERT: pre-training of deep bidirectional transformers for language understanding. arXiv preprint arXiv:1810.04805 (2018)

31. Girshick, R.: Fast R-CNN. In: Proceedings of the IEEE International Conference on Computer Vision, pp. 1440–1448 (2015)
32. He, K., Zhang, X., Ren, S., Sun, J.: Deep residual learning for image recognition. In: Proceedings of the IEEE Conference on Computer Vision and Pattern Recognition, pp. 770–778 (2016)
33. Baevski, A., Zhou, Y., Mohamed, A., Auli, M.: wav2vec 2.0: a framework for self-supervised learning of speech representations. In: Advances in Neural Information Processing Systems, vol. 33, pp. 12449–12460 (2020)
34. Mai, S., Zeng, Y., Hu, H.: Multimodal information bottleneck: learning minimal sufficient unimodal and multimodal representations. IEEE Trans. Multimedia (2022)
35. Xie, Q., Dai, Z., Hovy, E., Luong, T., Le, Q.: Unsupervised data augmentation for consistency training. In: Advances in Neural Information Processing Systems, vol. 33, pp. 6256–6268 (2020)
36. Wang, P., Wang, J.: Data augmentation method in image retrieval of digital equipment. In: 5th International Conference on Computer Information Science and Application Technology (CISAT 2022), vol. 12451, pp. 312–316. SPIE (2022)
37. Tsai, Y.H.H., Bai, S., Liang, P.P., Kolter, J.Z., Morency, L.P., Salakhutdinov, R.: Multimodal transformer for unaligned multimodal language sequences. In: Proceedings of the Conference. Association for Computational Linguistics. Meeting, vol. 2019, p. 6558. NIH Public Access (2019)
38. Rahman, W., et al.: Integrating multimodal information in large pretrained transformers. In: Proceedings of the Conference. Association for Computational Linguistics. Meeting, vol. 2020, p. 2359. NIH Public Access (2020)
39. Hazarika, D., Zimmermann, R., Poria, S.: MISA: modality-invariant and-specific representations for multimodal sentiment analysis. In: Proceedings of the 28th ACM International Conference on Multimedia, pp. 1122–1131 (2020)

A Dynamic Change Mechanism for Business Process in Science and Technology Service Domain

Shuangyu Lu[1,2], Weilong Ding[1,2](✉), Han Tian[1,2], Kunfeng Yang[1,2], and Zhuofeng Zhao[1,2]

[1] School of Information Science and Technology, North China University of Technology, Beijing, China
dingweilong@ncut.edu.cn

[2] Beijing Key Laboratory on Integration and Analysis of Large-Scale Stream Data, Beijing, China

Abstract. How to successfully implement a dynamic change for business process during execution is a crucial issue that must be resolved in the application of science and technology service. However business process modification research in this domain is insufficient. The traditional approaches redefine the process to adapt to changing business or technical circumstances, the entire procedure takes too long and is inefficient. Aiming at the challenge of business process change in science and technology service application, we propose a business process change mechanism - dynamic change based on BPMN extended language and process validation method. The dynamic change mechanism may realize adding services, rolling back services, and jumping services in business processes. Ultimately, we use three science and technology service cases to verify that the mechanism is feasible in practical application.

Keywords: Science and Technology Service · Business Process Change · BPMN Extension · Process Validation

1 Introduction

With the rapid advancement of science and technology innovation, particularly the extensive application of cloud computing, the internet, big data and other new technologies in science and technology services domain [1], the industry in this domain is presented with unprecedented opportunities for growth. The trend towards integration, specialization, and the fusion of online and offline services is becoming increasingly apparent. Moreover, many new and emerging businesses require science and technology services to collaboratively support their operations. Science and technology service collaboration covers the whole innovation process, which consists of a series of science and technology service activities and involves multiple participants such as Technical Agents and Enterprise users. Technical Agents use business processes to organize various science and technology services to meet the complex business requirements of Enterprise users.

Z. Wang et al. (Eds.): ICSS 2023, CCIS 1844, pp. 194–206, 2023.
https://doi.org/10.1007/978-981-99-4402-6_14

However, in this domain, business processes are in a highly dynamic environment and affected by constantly changing business and technical environment. Technical Agents begin to explore methods to change business processes during execution. Under the current background, business processes present some new challenges as follows.

(1) Collaborative processes too complex to change. In the application of science and technology service, business processes support the collaboration of participants from various domains and organizations to achieve the effective integration of multiple parties resources and knowledge, thus generating a new association relationship of science and technology services. As a result, the change of business processes needs to specify a matching change strategy. This first challenge in such a complex environment is how to modify a task instance without affecting the results of other participants and ensure the stability of the completed part of the business process.
(2) Personalized requirements can not be satisfied during the execution time. Business processes in this domain aim to meet the requirement of Enterprise users, provide customized service collaboration business processes based on Enterprise users' personalized requirements. Because users' requirements may change at any time and from anywhere, then this second most difficult challenge is making business processes adapt to changes in business requirements at any time and in a timely manner.

Based on the challenges of the business process in science and technology service domain, how to design the change mechanism to realize the dynamic change of the business process during execution has become a key problem must be solved. We analyzed three types of change, as well as the requirements-oriented business process verification method after the change, finally designed and implemented the dynamic change mechanism. Three science and technology service cases are used to verify that the dynamic change mechanism can realize three kinds of change operations for the business processes during execution.

2 Related Work

The dynamic change of business process execution is a research hotspot in science and technology service domain. The work dealing with dynamic change of business process is divided into three categories.

2.1 BPMN Extension

According to the literature [2] BPMN extensions are classified into two types according to different uses. The first type of "domain-specific BP" is used to represent or deal with domain-specific process extensions; the second type of "BP improvement" includes extensions aimed at improving BPMN language. The second type of extension is domain-independent and can be used in any domain. The literature [3] proposed a BPMN extension to support the control of the process model's version, so that model changes can be allowed during the execution of the business process, and changes can be achieved at the abstraction level of the business process model with the speed of immediate change. The literature [4] followed a constraint-based modeling approach that supports model abstraction level changes by using rule-enhanced Business Process Modeling Language (rBPMN). RBPMN uses rules to define many alternative paths in BPMN process definitions in a compact manner as a means to address business process flexibility.

2.2 Business Process Dynamic Change Technology

Recent research has stressed the necessity even more for improving the flexibility and dynamics of corporate processes. A company's or organization's business operations must be able to effectively capture and react to external changes if it operates in a highly dynamic environment [5]. According to whether they rely on business process models, current research on dynamic adaptation techniques for business processes can be classified into data-driven and model-driven techniques [6]. Model-driven techniques will be discussed next which is commonly used.

The model-driven approach, a dynamic adaptation method for business processes based on process models. It adopts a variety of techniques to establish variability rules based on process models to satisfy the requirements of business processes for adaptability to changes in the business environment during the execution [7]. Current research on model-driven methods mainly focuses on three aspects: predefined decision points, configurable templates and bottom-up mechanism [8]. Pucher [9] presented a reasonably agile process development approach for the use of predefined decision points in business process, i.e., employing predefined decision points in the modeling phase and allowing business users to adjust the process while the process is being executed. Bizagi [10] introduced an Ad hoc business process that does away with a complete definition of the underlying business logic and consists of a set of activities with decision points. When the Ad hoc business process is executed, the user decides which activities to perform and how to perform them based on business requirements. Predefined decision points has significant drawbacks in actual business process applications since future changes cannot be fully predicted and counted.

Due to the complicated relationships between activities and the changes involved in each business stage of the business process in the actual science and technology service collaboration case. It is challenging to meet the requirements for rapid response and flexible execution of changes in the business process' execution stage when templates and predefined decision points are used. The dynamic change mechanism we proposed offers special benefits for resolving issues involving several tasks and intricate linkages. After the business process has been changed, rapid deployment can be achieved without further exploration.

2.3 Business Process Validation

Validation of business processes is an important aspect of business processes dynamic change. Many process modeling languages have been proposed to address this issue, including the Petri Nets-based YAML modeling language.

However, other process modeling languages, like BPMN, do not have this formal validation. A way of utilizing Petri Nets to validate BPMN processes is suggested in the literature [11]. BPMN models (including their elements, processes, and other components) are first formally defined before the verification is finished by translating BPMN elements into appropriate Petri Nets expressions. Literature [12] introduced a method of mapping BPEL into FSP expressions, combined with MSC diagram to verify the consistency of BPEL. However, there are many semantic differences between BPEL and BPMN, which makes it impossible to apply the method in the literature to BPMN.

3 Dynamic Change Mechanism

The following Fig. 1 shows the overall design of the dynamic change mechanism.

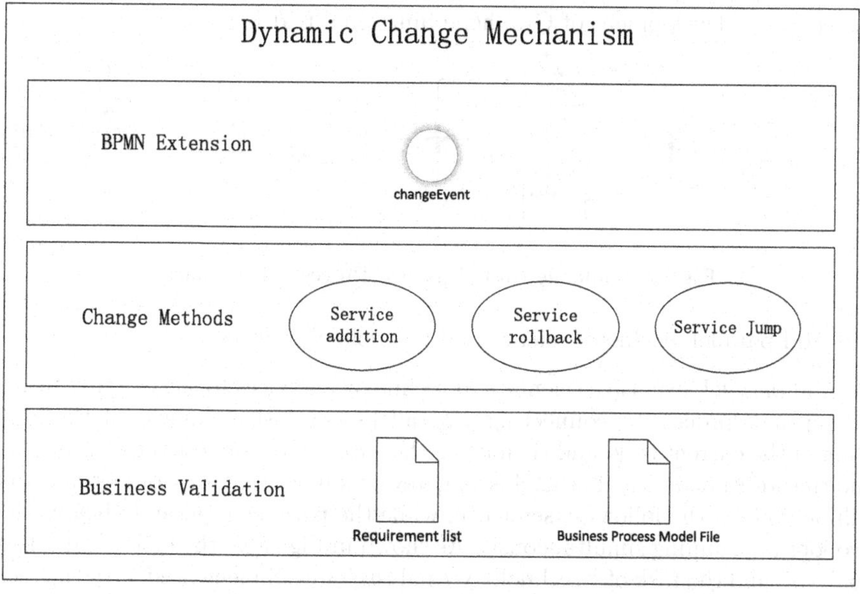

Fig. 1. Dynamic Change Mechanism design drawing

The dynamic change mechanism consists of three parts, which will describe in sectors below.

3.1 Dynamic Change Methods

In this section, we'll analysis change requirements for the business process in science and technology service domain, as well as design concepts and specific processes for the dynamic change approach. Adding services, rolling back services, and jumping services are three change operations that can be performed on the process instance using this method without terminating the current process instance while the business process is running.

Adding Services. The Enterprise users frequently experience a change in demand during the execution of the business process for the application of science and technology service, necessitating the addition of new science and technology service activities to the task set. The task set can be a single or a collection of parallel or branch science and technology service tasks. The following are several scenarios for business process adding services in the science and technology service domain.

(1) Add pre and post sequential science and technology services

The most common scenario for adding services is the precursors and successor science and technology service adding. The following Fig. 2 adds the science and technology service "Waste Water detection" to the business process of "Research and Development of Novel Graphene Textile Materials". This business process aims to organize a variety of scientific and technological services to complete the research and development of Graphene functional textile materials.

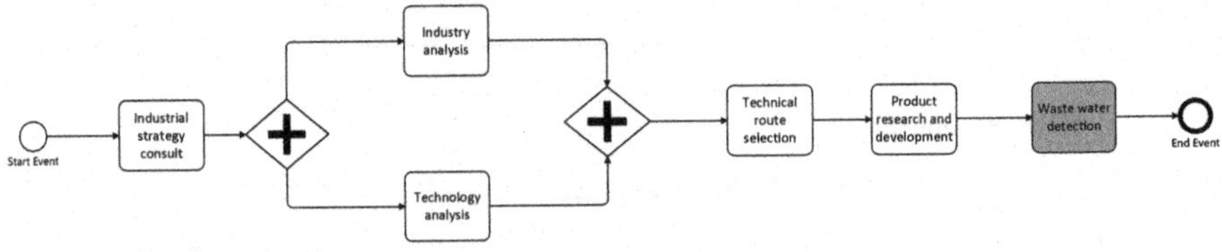

Fig. 2. Graphene R&D Business Process Flow Chart.

(2) Add parallel, exclusive science and technology services

Add parallel, exclusive science and technology services to the existing task in the business process by connecting a parallel or exclusive gateway at the input point of the current task, and then using the gateway to connect the existing task and the additional task. The exclusive gateway implies that only one branch task will be done in the following sequence, while the parallel gateway indicates that two jobs are running simultaneously. As shown in Fig. 3(a), the task of "Industry analysis" and the task of "Technology Analysis" are supplemented with the technical service of "'Data collection". The branch science and technology services adding are depicted in Fig. 3(b).

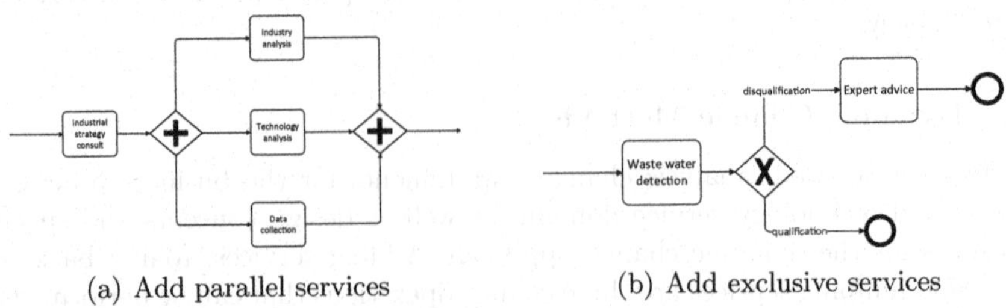

(a) Add parallel services (b) Add exclusive services

Fig. 3. Add parallel, exclusive services

Rolling Back Services. Moreover, execution mistakes or service products from service providers that fall short of expectations are frequently encountered, necessitating the timely reversal of performed tasks in the business process. The analysis of several potential services roll back situations in science and technology domain are as follows.

(1) Sequential branching, exclusive branching and merge rollback

According to the business flow diagram for the "Rare Earth New Materials Industry Science and Technology Consultancy Service Case" which is depicted in Fig. 4, there are numerous branches after the exclusive gateway, only one path can be chosen in the execution process after being processed by the exclusive gateway. As a result, the sequential branch's rollback mode also applies to the exclusive branch and exclusive merge rollback. Without taking into account concerns with process deadlock and data consistency, data restoration is rather simple to achieve. In the historical task nodes, you can immediately roll back to the target node.

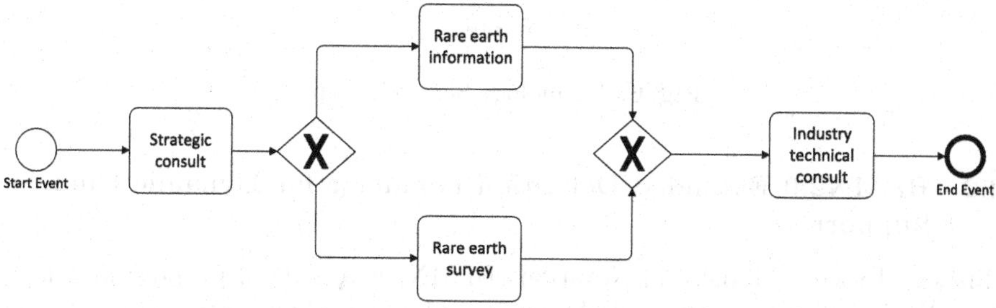

Fig. 4. Rare earth new material business flow chart.

(2) Parallel branch and parallel merge rollback

The task of rolling back a process from a parallel branch task to the task before the parallel gateway is represented as a parallel branch rollback, while the task of rolling back a process from a parallel merge task to the parallel branch is represented as a parallel merge rollback. Fig 5(a) depicts the parallel branch rollback in the Graphene textile new material R&D business process, and Fig 5(b) depicts the parallel merge rollback.

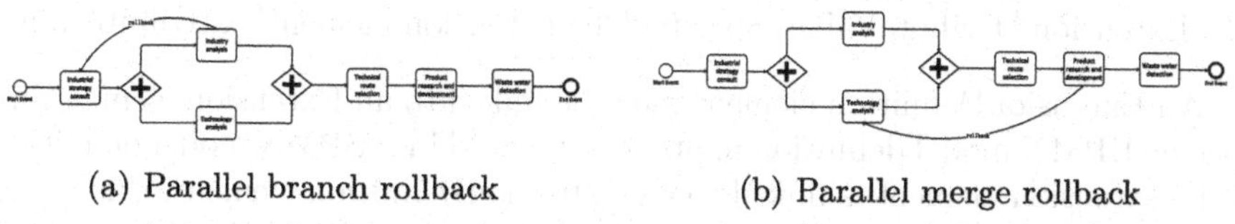

(a) Parallel branch rollback

(b) Parallel merge rollback

Fig. 5. Parallel branch and parallel merge rollback

Jumping Services. The business process of science and technology service application is highly process-oriented. The business process must be executed step by step in strict accordance with the process structure, and the flexibility of executing specific tasks to specific requirements is not high. The dynamic change mechanism implements task jumping to address this issue. As seen in Fig. 6, in the case of the science and technology consulting service for the rare earth new material industry, go directly to the "Industry technical consult service" after finishing the "Strategic consult service," skipping the completion of the middle steps.

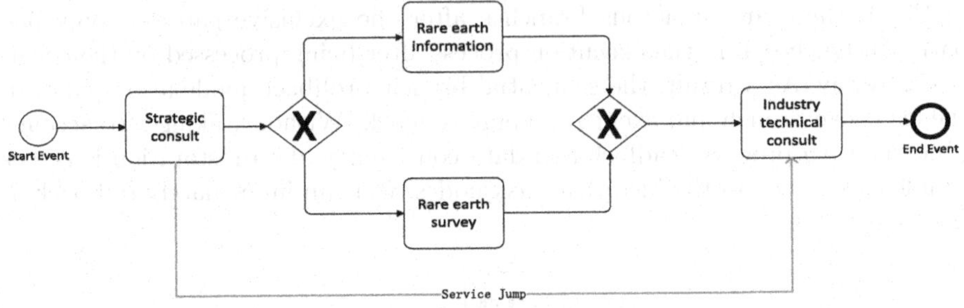

Fig. 6. Technology Service Jump

3.2 BPMN2.0 Extended Definition Language for Dynamic Change Support

Business Process Model and Notation (BPMN) is a general purpose language. The BPMN2.0 meta model includes an extendable mechanism to augment existing BPMN components with non-standard attributes and elements that can be used to process domain-specific processes or to enhance the language itself. The BPMN element is expanded in this article to facilitate dynamic modifications to business processes in science and technology service domain. There are four components to a BPMN extension.

(1) Extension. Link the ExtensionDefinition and its attributes to a particular BPMN model definition by using this element to refer to the extension definition and the extended namespace to represent the extension element.
(2) ExtensionDefinition. To specify a BPMN element's extensible extension element.
(3) ExtensionAttributeDefinition. The attribute in the extension element may have a definition appended to it.
(4) ExtensionAttributeValue. Specifies the extension element's attribute value.

An ExtensionDefinition element must be linked to an Extension element in a specific BPMN model definition in order to be used in a BPMN model definition. If the extension element is linked to an ExtensionDefinition element, this means that any BPMN element that belongs to a subclass of BPMN BaseElement can also be associated with the extension element.

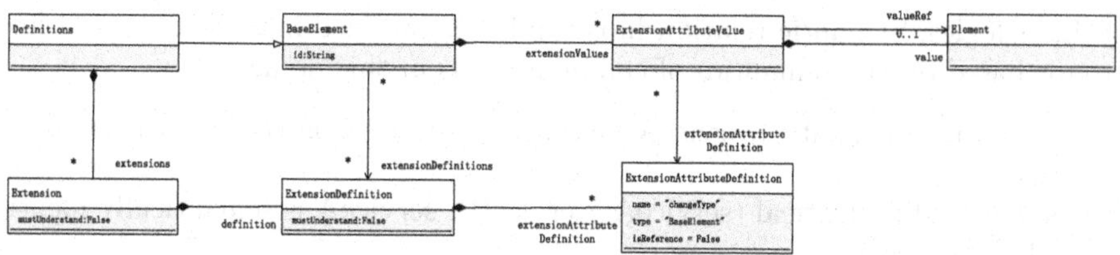

Fig. 7. Extension class diagram of changeEvent element.

In order to abstractly indicate where changes in a business process need to be made and what to do about them, we defined a new subclass "changeEvent" to the event class. This expanded subclass inherits the characteristics and model associations of the event elements and is compatible with the graphical model of the event class. The changeEvent node element has a new custom attribute called changeType to describe various adaptation kinds for various scenarios. The BPMN extended class diagram is displayed in Fig. 7. The ExtensionDefinition attribute name contains a definition for the extension changeEvent. If compatible BPMN tools don't comprehend the extension, they can ignore it since the mustUnderstand attribute of the Extension class has a value of False. The event element "changeEvent", as we proposed, can be represented as follows. changeEvent = <eventID, eventName, changeType, Incoming, Outgoing>. EventID is inherited from event and represents the unique identifier of the event changeEvent, and each changeEvent node element needs a unique identifier ID to distinguish it from other elements. EventName, inherited from event, indicates the name of the changeEvent node element, which depends on the specific change business requirements and can be defined by the technical staff. ChangeType attribute specifies the change type provided by the changeEvent node element. We consider three change types: adding technology service, rolling back technology service and jumping technology service. ChangeType can be "add", "rollback" or "jump", and different change types correspond to different change operations. Incoming, specifies the list of input sides of the change event element. Outgoing, specifies the list of output edges of the change event. Change events are used in the actual process to support dynamic changes to process instances, are triggered by system rules or business logic, and can be set to trigger at a specific time or under specific conditions, and in special cases, can be set to trigger manually.

3.3 Consistency Testing Methods

In real situations, there is no guarantee that a set of modifications will always be successful. To further confirm that the modifications performed appropriately respond to the change criteria, we will offer a post-change business process validation method in this section. The requirements document for the science and technology service domain uses natural language to describe what services the provider needs to perform and what service products to deliver under different business logics. Semantic relationships can be categorized into the following five groups based on the semantics of common needs in this domain.

(1) Semantic continuity (serviceA<serviceB): serviceA is the preorder task of serviceB.
(2) Semantically identical (serviceA=serviceB): serviceA is semantically identical to serviceB.
(3) Semantically opposite (serviceA#serviceB): serviceA is semantically opposite to serviceB.
(4) Semantic parallelism (serviceA||serviceB): there is no clear order of execution between serviceA and serviceB, but subsequent tasks can be performed only after both have been executed.
(5) Semantically unrelated (serviceA * serviceB): serviceA is semantically unrelated to serviceB.

According to the requirement document, BPMN may precisely explain the business logic of the science and technology service domain and express the business process of a science and technology service cooperation case. BPMN has a number of modeling elements, each of which has unique semantics. The mapping between the semantic relationship between the requirements and the BPMN modeling elements is given in Fig. 8 below.

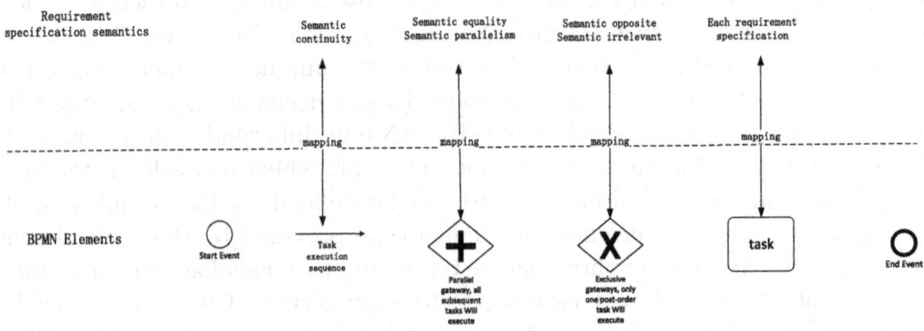

Fig. 8. Requirements specification and BPMN element mapping relationship figure

In order to better check the consistency between requirements documents and business processes, we described the requirements documents required in the algorithm and the related concepts of the processes through formal definitions. A requirement document can be defined by a binary group D< T,R>, where T denotes the set of tasks in the requirement document and R denotes the dependencies between tasks. T and R are defined as follows. T is represented by the binary group T<name, description>, where name denotes the name of this requirement task and description denotes the description of this requirement task. R denotes the set of semantic relations between requirement tasks, which can be represented by R<serviceA, serviceB, type>, and type denotes the semantic relations between serviceA and serviceB. According to the analysis of semantic relations of requirements above, several semantic relations are summarized: sequence, same, contrary, parallel, irrelevant.

A business process can be defined by a binary group P<A,R>, where A denotes the set of activities of the process and R denotes the dependency relationship between activities. A and R are defined as follows. A is represented by the Triad A<id, name, requireDescription>. Id denotes the unique identifier of the activity, name identifies the name of the activity, and requireDescription denotes the requirement description corresponding to the activity. R represents the set of dependencies between activities. It can be represented by R<serviceA, serviceB, access, type>, access means the reachability between serviceA and serviceB, whether there is at least one path from activity serviceA to serviceB, if it is reachable, then access is true, otherwise it is false. Type indicates the type of access between serviceA and serviceB. According to the analysis of several common access types, the following access types are summarized: sequence, parallel and exclusive. We designed the business process validation algorithm for collaborative case requirements based on the definition and description provided above. The algorithm primarily checks that the business process design adheres to the requirements defined in the requirements document.

Algorithm 1. RCCA:Requirements-oriented consistency checking algorithm

```
Input: D<T,Rt>, P<A,Ra>, reqLists, proSteps
Output: messageList
function RCCA(D,P,reqLists,proSteps)
    for i ← 0 to reqLists.length - 1 do
        curActivity ← reqLists[i]
        for j ← i + 1 to reqLists.length - 1 do
            subsActivity ← reqLists[j]
            if proSteps contains curActivity and proSteps contains subsActivity then
                rt ← Rt(curActivity,subsActivity)
                ra ← Ra(curActivity,subsActivity)
                if rt.type == irrelevant and ra.access == true then
                    add "curActivity.name and subsActivity.name does not have relationship" to messageList.    ▷ Make five dependency judgments and return the corresponding modification suggestions.
                end if
            else if ... then
            else
                add "The business process conforms to the requirements definition" to messageList    ▷ If the requirements list is mapped correctly to the business flowchart, the business process meets the business requirements
            end if
        end for
    end for
    return messageList
end function
```

In order to determine whether the requirements and process steps are consistent, the algorithm traverses the list of requirements starting at the index point, maps the semantic relationship between each requirement and all subsequent requirements in the list to the path type between each two activities in the flowchart. If the mapping can be done correctly, returns the business process that satisfies the business requirements, otherwise, it returns a suggestion for changing the process. The length of the reqLists input determines the algorithm's time complexity, whereas the length of the messageList output determines the algorithm's space complexity.

4 Evaluation

In this section, we will take the real science and technology service collab oration case – technology foresight service as an example. Many responsibilities and intricate business procedures are involved in the case. The following cases examined whether dynamic change mechanisms can implement three types of change in complex business processes.

Case 1: The following Fig. 9(a) captures part of the business flow chart in the execution process of technology foresight service collaboration case. The task elements are colored green for "finished" services, blue for "in process" services, and gray for "not started" services in order to record the various execution states of the task. The task of "user opinion feedback" is added to the business process. Figure 9(b) displays the business flow chart following the addition. It is clear that during the addition task, the business process's progress is unaffected, and the completed portion of the business process maintains stability.

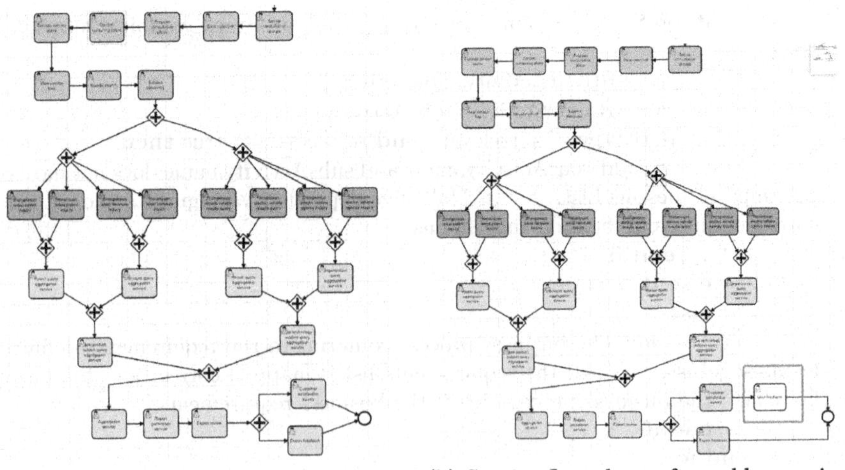

(a) Technical foresight service flow chart (b) Service flow chart after add a service

Fig. 9. Verify the append performance figure

Case 2: The business process of the technical foresight service case is executed to the job of "proposing consulting plan," and the service of "subject discovery"

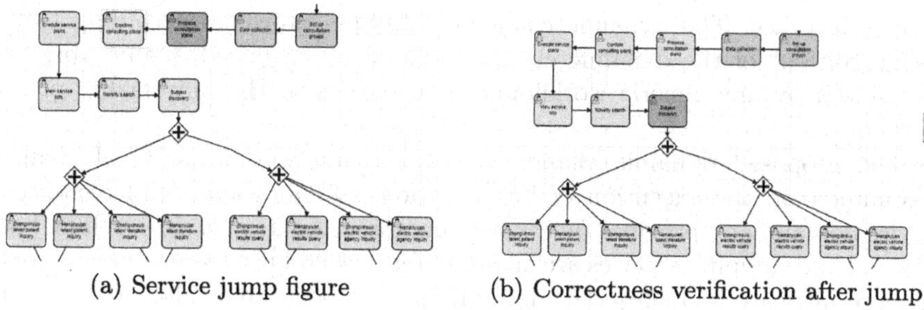

(a) Service jump figure (b) Correctness verification after jump

Fig. 10. Verify the jump performance figure

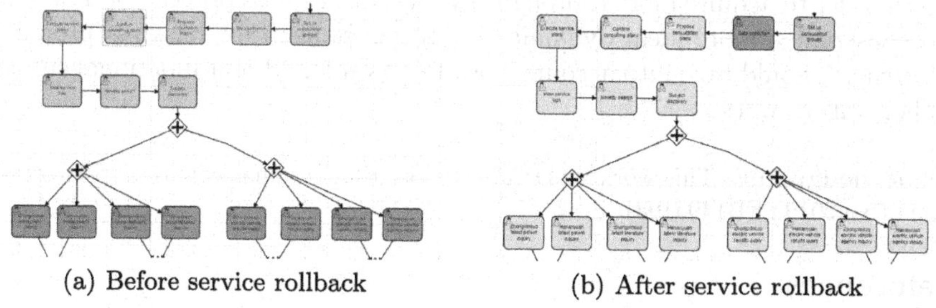

(a) Before service rollback (b) After service rollback

Fig. 11. Verify the rollback performance figure

in the process is selected for jump in order to test the jump performance of the dynamic change mechanism. Figure 10(a) describes the execution progress of the current business process, and Fig. 10(b) depicts the business flow chart after task jump. It can be found that all the intermediate tasks have been skipped and the target task has started to execute.

Case 3: As shown in Fig. 11(a), the technical foresight service business flow chart, the current business process is executed at the parallel gateway, and the subsequent task starts to be executed. Due to the incomplete data collected previously, the business process needs to be returned to the "data collection" task to complete the task again. A fallback from the current business process execution to the Data Collection task is a fallback across parallel branches. Restart after rolling back the Data Collecting service, as indicated in Fig. 11(b). Through the above three cases, it is proved that the dynamic change mechanism can realize three kinds of change operations in the execution of business processes: adding service, rolling back services and jumping services. The entire process requires no termination of the process instance, which is essential in science and technology domain.

5 Summary and Future Work

We proposed a dynamic business process modification method that will allow the workflow engine to quickly adjust to changes without stopping the active process instance. The dynamic change of business processes according to the design concept of the dynamic change mechanism suggested in this work can be realized by any generic workflow engine thanks to the universality of this method.

The proposed dynamic change mechanism analyse the sorts of changes encountered in the execution of business processes in science and technology service domain, and provides functional guarantee. Adding services, rolling back services, and jumping services are allowed. Yet, actual business procedures could be more intricate and subject to more frequent change. It is also important to consider non-functional protections against business process changes, such as whether and how modifications in the context of data associations are permitted. In order to acquire more thorough coverage of business process modifications and construct a more ideal dynamic change mechanism for business processes, researchers should take into account both functional and non-functional support in their future work.

Acknowledgment. This work was supported by the National Key R&D Program of China (No.2019YFB1405103).

References

1. Sun, X.Y.: The advent of a service-oriented society. China Social Science Press (2010)
2. Zarour, K., Benmerzoug, D., Guermouche, N., Drira, K.: A systematic literature review on BPMN extensions. Bus. Process. Manage. J. **26**(6), 1473–1503 (2020)
3. Ben Said, I., Chaabane, M.A., Andonoff, E.: A model driven engineering approach for modelling versions of business processes using BPMN. In: Abramowicz, W., Tolksdorf, R. (eds.) BIS 2010. LNBIP, vol. 47, pp. 254–267. Springer, Heidelberg (2010). https://doi.org/10.1007/978-3-642-12814-1_22
4. Milanovic, M., Gasevic, D., Rocha, L.: Modeling flexible business processes with business rule patterns. In: 2011 IEEE 15th International Enterprise Distributed Object Computing Conference, pp. 65–74. IEEE (2011)
5. von Rosing, M., von Scheel, J., Gill, A.Q.: Applying agile principles to BPM (2015)
6. Gui, S.C., Wang, J.X., Hong, F., Cao, B.: Behavior-based automated process modeling method using recommendation. Comput. Ind. Eng. **26**, 1500–1509 (2020)
7. Vom Brocke, J., Mathiassen, L., Rosemann, M.: Business process management (2014)
8. Zhang, L., Gao, Q., Li, T.: Dynamic adaptation method of business process based on hierarchical feature model. Information **12**(9), 362 (2021)
9. Pucher, M.J.: Agile-, adhoc-, dynamic-, social-, or adaptive bpm. Welcome to the Real (IT) World (2010)
10. Bizagi. Understanding ad hoc processes (2021). https://help.bizagi.com/bpm-suite/en/index.html?understanding_ad_hoc_processes.htm. Accessed 21 Apr 2023
11. Dijkman, R.M., Dumas, M., Ouyang, C.: Formal semantics and analysis of BPMN process models using petri nets. Queensland University of Technology, Technical report, pp. 1–30 (2007)
12. Foster, H., Uchitel, S., Magee, J., Kramer, J.: Model-based verification of web service compositions. In: 18th IEEE International Conference on Automated Software Engineering, 2003. Proceedings, pp. 152–161. IEEE (2003)

User Multi-interest Collaboration for Service Recommendations

Yi Chen(✉), Ting He, and Yongxin Liao

School of Computer Science and Technology, Huaqiao University, Xiamen 361021, China

chenyi@stu.hqu.edu.cn, xuantinghe@hit.edu.cn, lyxin@hqu.edu.cn

Abstract. Traditional recommendation methods solve the user data sparsity problem by collaborative learning and using nearest neighbor information. However, most methods do not specifically analyze multiple interests of users. In fact, it is more likely that there exists a certain common interest preference among users, but their interests in other aspects are completely contradictory. This paper proposes a service recommendation model based on user multi-interest collaboration (UMIC), which takes both user multiple interest preferences and nearest neighbor user information into account during the recommendation. UMIC obtains multiple interest preferences of users through dynamic routing mechanism, considers the features under user's current interest in nearest neighbor construction, and dynamically filters user's nearest neighbors according to the items to be tested, to solve the user data sparsity problem and improve the quality of recommendation. The experimental results show that the evaluation metrics of the proposed model in this paper outperform various advanced sequential models on widely used datasets.

Keywords: Dynamic routing · Multi-interest · Collaborative memory

1 Introduction

Sequential recommendation is an important element in personalized recommendation systems, which models user characteristics based on user-item interaction behavior, captures user preferences, and recommends items that may be of interest to the user. Traditional recommendation methods place user-item interaction records in a two-dimensional scoring matrix, thus achieving prediction by filling the gaps in this matrix. Unlike traditional ones, sequential recommendation treats a user's history as a sequence of items, rather than a collection of items, in order to accurately predict the next item that the user will interact with.

The essence of sequential recommendation is to use the user's historical behavior to make predictions about the next behavior. This is considered a sequential prediction problem, and researchers have borrowed various sequential models from other fields for prediction and applied them to sequential recommendations. From the earliest Markov models to the more recent neural sequence

Z. Wang et al. (Eds.): ICSS 2023, CCIS 1844, pp. 207–218, 2023.
https://doi.org/10.1007/978-981-99-4402-6_15

models, models such as recurrent neural networks and self-attention have been shown to be powerful in capturing complex higher-order features to obtain good recommendation results. However, there is a user data sparsity problem in sequential recommendation. For a single user, modeling his sparse historical behavior sequences is unable to accurately discover the user's true preferences.

To solve the user data sparsity problem, collaborative learning approach is introduced into sequence recommendation. Its basic idea is to use similar user data to address the issue of sparse target user data. For example, Wang et al. [11] used RNN to model the user's behavioral sequences and retrieve the nearest neighbor users based on the potential states of the users learned by RNN. The representation of the target user is then combined with the representation of the retrieved nearest neighbor users for the next term prediction. This type of method not only solves the user data sparsity problem to a certain extent, but also improves the accuracy of recommendation. However, in collaborative learning, how to retrieve the appropriate nearest neighbor users is the key to improve the accuracy of recommendation.

Existing methods always calculate the similarity among users based on their complete historical behavioral sequences, and do not fully consider how users differ under different interest categories. In real life, consumers are more likely to share a common interest preference, while their preferences in other areas are completely contradictory. Based on this, this paper proposes a service recommendation method based on user multi-interest collaboration (UMIC). The method makes it possible to obtain the similarity in retrieving near-neighboring users based on the interest preferences to which the user's item to be tested belongs. First, UMIC uses a multi-interest extraction layer to extract multiple interest capsules from the user's historical behavior sequence through the dynamic routing mechanism of the capsule network. Different interest capsules represent different interest preferences of the user. The attention mechanism is then employed to determine the user's next item to be tested's interest preferences. UMIC uses a memory tensor to store the user's interest preferences through a new collaborative module. For each target user, the collaborative module retrieves the near-neighboring users whose interest preferences are similar to those of the item to be tested, rather than globally similar. Finally, UMIC introduces a fusion gating mechanism that combines the representations generated by target and nearest neighbor users and calculates the recommendation score for each candidate item based on the fused representations. In summary, the main contributions of this work are as follows:

- This paper designs a multi-interest extraction layer that adaptively aggregates different interests of users from their historical behaviors using dynamic routing algorithms of capsule networks.
- In this paper, a new collaborative module is designed, which takes into account the fact that there may be users with similar interests in one domain only and completely contradictory interests in other domains. Therefore, the similarity when retrieving the near-neighbor users is calculated based on the interest preferences of the user's current item to be tested.

- UMIC was evaluated on two real datasets, namely the "Books" and "Health and the Personal Care" from Amazon. The experimental results show that the proposed model significantly outperforms other advanced baseline models.

2 Related Work

2.1 Sequential Recommendation

Sequence recommendation algorithms have been rapidly developed with the improvement of sequence models' ability to capture complex and higher-order features. The Markov models of fixed and variable order assume that the results depend only on the few most recent behaviors. Rendle et al. [9] proposed a combination of decomposition machines and Markov models to improve matrix decomposition by introducing sequences of historical behaviors into the matrix decomposition. However, the assumptions of Markov models also limit its performance, and as the state space grows exponentially with respect to inter-order features, Markov model-based methods have difficulty capturing higher-order features in practice.

Neural sequence models such as recurrent neural networks, long and short-term memory networks, gated recurrent units, and self-attention mechanisms have been used to address the limitations of Markov models. Researchers have used neural sequence models to model the evolutionary process of user behavior sequences. Liu et al. [7] used recurrent neural networks in user behavior sequences to predict the next user behavior. Li et al. [6] used an attention mechanism in a session considering that the next user behavior is not influenced by the historical behavior in the same way. Such methods represent users by modeling a sequence of user behaviors using a fixed-length vector. However, the use of a single fixed-length vector to represent a user suffers from the problem of not being able to adequately represent the multiple interest preferences of the user.

2.2 Collaborative Learning

Collaborative learning has been introduced to solve the user data sparsity problem in sequential recommendation. Song et al. [10] combined users' social networks into a recommendation system to solve the data sparsity problem using friend information. Jannach et al. [4] improved users' social networks by measuring the similarity of users through the degree of overlap between their behavioral sequences. Wang et al. first used RNN to model the user's behavior sequences to obtain the user's representation vector, and then used the user's representation vector to calculate the similarity between users and directly combined the similar user's representation vector with the target user's representation vector. To reduce the search space of similar users, Pan et al. [8] perform initial item recommendation based on the behavior sequence of the target user and then filter irrelevant users using the initial item recommendation. All above-mentioned methods measure the similarity among users based on their complete historical behavioral sequences. However, in real life, consumers are more likely to share a common interest preference, while their preferences in other areas are completely contradictory. Therefore, collaborative learning cannot solve the problem of sparse user data if the differences in multiple interests of users are not fully considered when retrieving near-neighbor users.

2.3 Capsule Network

The concept of Capsule Network [3] was proposed by Hinton in 2011, which uses dynamic routing mechanisms instead of pooling operations to ensure that low-level features can be selectively aggregated into higher-level features. Capsules are used in capsule networks instead of neurons in traditional neural networks. The input and output of a normal neuron is a scalar, called a scalar neuron, while a capsule is called a vector neuron and its input and output is a vector. MIND [5] introduced capsule networks into recommendation systems by using the dynamic routing mechanism of capsule networks to capture multiple interests of users and extract different interests by clustering past behaviors. MDSR [1] is the first neural framework for SR based on end-to-end list generation, which solves the problem of sequential recommendations by considering both accuracy and diversity of recommendations. This type of methods can be used to solve the problem of single user representation. Therefore, this paper uses dynamic routing mechanism to capture multiple interest representations of users and solve the problem of sparse user data through user collaboration.

3 Model Design

3.1 Problem Formulation

Assume there is a user set $u \in U$ and an item set $i \in I$. Each user has a sequence of user historical behaviors $(e_1^u, e_2^u, \cdots, e_n^u)$, sorted by time of the occurrence, e_t^u records the tth item interacted by the user. Given historical interactions, the problem of sequential recommendation is to predict the next items that the user might be interacted in. Notations are summarized in Table 1.

Table 1. Notation.

Notation	Description
u	a user
i	an item
e	an interaction
U	the set of users
I	the set of items
d	the dimension of user/item embeddings
K	the number of interest embeddings

3.2 Framework

This paper proposes a service recommendation method based on user multi-interest collaboration (UMIC), and the model is shown in Fig. 1. First, to address the problem that using one user representation vector cannot adequately represent users' multiple interests, UMIC uses the dynamic routing mechanism of the capsule network to extract multiple interest capsules from users' behavior sequences, and different interest capsules represent different interest preferences of users. Then, the attention mechanism is used to obtain the interest preferences belonging to the user's current item to be tested. Second, to solve the problem of sparse user data, this paper designs a collaborative module, which uses a memory tensor to store the user's interest preferences. For each target user, the collaborative module retrieves the near-neighboring users whose interest preferences are similar to those of the item to be tested rather than globally similar, fully taking into account the differences in users' interests under different item categories. Finally, UMIC introduces a fusion gating mechanism that combines the representations generated by the target user and the nearest neighbor users, and calculates the recommendation score for each candidate item based on the fused representations.

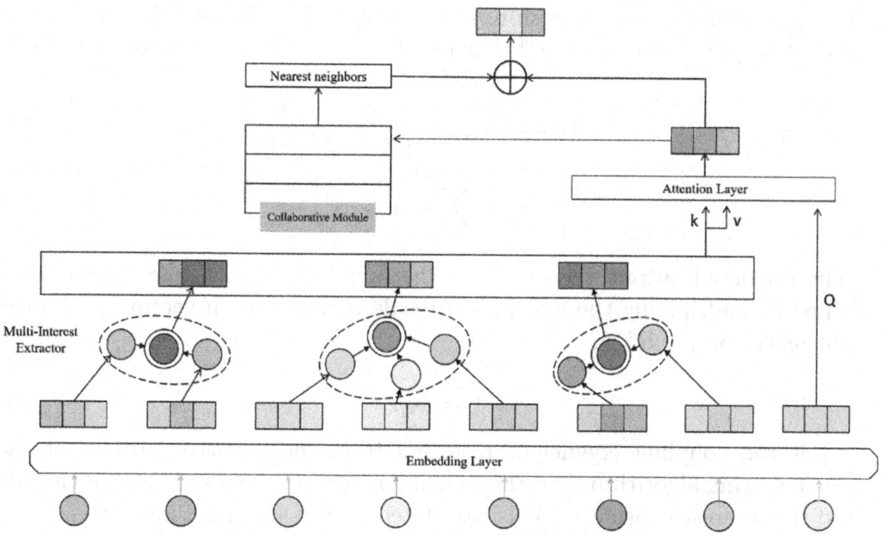

Fig. 1. A framework for user multi-interest collaboration for service recommendations.

3.3 Multi-interest Extractor Layer

This paper uses multiple interest representation vectors of users instead of the traditional single user representation vector to retrieve near-neighbor users. This requires learning multiple representation vectors from the user's historical behavior sequence to represent the different interests of the user separately. To learn multiple representation vectors, this paper designs a multiple interest extraction layer that divides the user's historical behavior into multiple clusters using a clustering algorithm. So that the items from one cluster are closely related and represent a particular aspect of the user's interest, and the representation vector of each cluster is inferred.

Moreover, this paper designs a user interest extraction layer containing a two-layer capsule network to propose multiple interest representations of users from their historical behaviors using a dynamic routing mechanism. The first capsule network is called the user behavior capsule layer and the second capsule network is called the interest capsule layer. Potential relationships are constructed between the user behavior capsule layer and the interest capsule layer through a dynamic routing mechanism. When the input data enters the user behavior capsule layer, the output vector of the interest capsule layer is calculated by the dynamic routing algorithm. In each iteration, the user behavior capsule i is represented as e_i, and the obtained high-level capsule j is represented as v_j. Finally, a user representation vector $V_u = (v_1, v_2, \ldots, v_K)$is obtained by combining multiple interest representation vectors of user u.

The input s_j to the interest capsule j is obtained as an output vector v_j by the activation function squash function, where s_j is the weighted sum of the predicted output vector $\hat{e}_{j|i} \in R^{d \times 1}$ made by the user behavior capsule layer.

$$v_j = squash\left(s_j\right) = \frac{\left\|s_j\right\|^2}{1 + \left\|s_j\right\|^2} \frac{s_j}{\left\|s_j\right\|} \tag{1}$$

$$s_j = \sum_i c_{ij} \hat{e}_{j|i} \tag{2}$$

The predicted output vector $\hat{e}_{j|i}$ of the user behavior capsule layer is then obtained by multiplying the first layer capsule representation vector e_i with the weight matrix $w_{ij} \in R^{d \times d}$.

$$\hat{e}_{j|i} = w_{ij} e_i \tag{3}$$

c_{ij} is the coupling coefficient resulting from the iterative process of the dynamic routing algorithm. It is the weight connecting the user behavior capsule e_i and the interest capsule v_j. It is calculated by the softmax function.

$$c_{ij} = softmax\left(b_{ij}\right) = \frac{\exp\left(b_{ij}\right)}{\sum_k \exp\left(b_{ik}\right)} \tag{4}$$

b_{ij} denotes the prior probability of coupling the user behavior capsule e_i and the interest capsule v_j. By calculating the dot product of the output vector v_j of the interest capsule j with the predicted output vector $\hat{e}_{j|i}$ of the user behavior capsule e_i, and the sum with the original b_{ij} as the latest weight value. the purpose of performing vector dot product calculation is mainly to calculate the similarity of v_j and $\hat{e}_{j|i}$.

$$b_{ij} = b_{ij} + \hat{e}_{j|i} \cdot v_j \tag{5}$$

3.4 Attention Layer

Through multiple interest extraction layers, multiple interest capsules are extracted from the user's historical behavior sequence, and different interest capsules represent different interest preferences of the user. Only the features under the user's current interest should be considered when constructing the nearest neighbor, therefore, during the training process, this paper designs an attention layer based on the attention mechanism to determine the current user's main interest points. Specifically, for the user's target item, this paper calculates the correlation between each interest capsule and the target item, which is used to weight the representation vector of the interest capsule and use it as the final representation vector of the user, where the weight of the interest capsule is determined by the corresponding correlation. In this attention layer, the target item is the query value of the attention mechanism and the interest capsules are the keys and values of the attention mechanism. The representation vector of user u with respect to the item is:

$$v_u^{inner} = Attention\left(e_i, V_u\right) = V_u softmax\left(pow\left(V_u^T e_i, p\right)\right) \tag{6}$$

where pow denotes an exponential operation and p is an adjustable parameter for adjusting attention in steps. When p close to 0, each interest capsule receives uniform attention. When p is greater than 1, the weights are positively correlated with the dot product as p increases.

3.5 Collaborative Module

Since user behavior sequences are sparse, collaborative learning through information of near-neighbor users with similar interest preferences has the potential to alleviate the data sparsity problem. Therefore, in this paper, a collaborative module is designed, and for each target user, the collaborative module retrieves the nearest neighbor users based on the user's current interests rather than based on the user's global behavior sequence.

The collaborative module uses a memory tensor mem to record the representation vector of the target user at the current interest. The collaborative module uses the following read and write operations to access mem.

Read operation: given the representation vector v_u^{inner} of the user's current interest, calculate its similarity to the interests of other users in mem: $sim(v_u^{inner}, v_i^{inner})?\exp(< v_u^{inner}, v_i^{inner} >)$, select the top-k similar users as neighbors, and weight their corresponding similarity as weights and generate the nearest neighbor representation v_u^{outer} of the next item to be predicted by the target user.

$$v_u^{outer} = \sum_0^k sim(v_u^{inner}, v_i^{inner}) v_i^{inner} \tag{7}$$

Write operation: At the beginning of each phase of the experiment, the memory tensor to null values. The memory tensor is updated using the user's current interest representation vector, which always stores the latest m user interest representation vectors. When the memory tensor is written, the oldest user record is deleted from it and the new user interest representation vector is added to the queue. When the memory tensor is not full, it will be added directly.

3.6 Recommendation Decoder

The recommendation decoder evaluates the probability of clicking the next item based on the target user interest representation vector and the nearest neighbor interest representation vector. To selectively combine information from the target user interest representation vector and the nearest neighbor user interest representation vector, in this paper we construct the end-user representation using a fusion gate mechanism that balances the user's own information and collaborates the importance of neighborhood information.

$$v_u = f v_u^{inner} + (1 - f) v_u^{outer} \tag{8}$$

$$f = \sigma(W_i v_u^{inner} + W_o v_u^{outer}) \tag{9}$$

Using the user representation vector v_u and the item representation vector e_i, calculate the probability of user u interacting with item i as:

$$p(i|u) = p(e_i|v_u) = \frac{\exp(v_u e_i)}{\sum_{j \in I} \exp(v_u e_i)} \tag{10}$$

4 Experiments

4.1 Dataset and Experimental Setup

In this paper, two commonly used datasets are selected to evaluate the model recommendation performance. They are Books and Health and Personal Care provided by Amazon, which are widely used public datasets for e-commerce recommendations. The statistics for these two datasets are shown in Table 2.

Table 2. Statistics of the Datasets.

Dataset	users	item	interactions
Amazon Book	459133	313966	8898041
Health and Personal Care	38609	18534	346355

4.2 Evaluation Metrics

In this paper, the following three evaluation metrics are used to assess the performance of the proposed model.

Recall is the ratio of the number of correct positive samples in the recommendation list to the number of positive samples in the test set. For a test case with a recommendation list of size N, Recall is defined as:

$$Recal@N = \frac{1}{|U|}\sum_{u\in U}\frac{\left|\hat{I}_{u,N}\cap I_u\right|}{|I_u|} \tag{11}$$

where $\hat{I}_{u,N}$ denotes the top-N services recommended by the recommendation system, and I_u denotes the services that users have interacted with in the test set.

HR reflects the probability that the generated recommendation list contains positive samples. A higher hit rate indicates a better recommendation. For a test case with recommendation list size N. HR is defined as:

$$HR@N = \frac{1}{|U|}\sum_{u\in U}\delta\left(\left|\hat{I}_{u,N}\cap I_u\right| > 0\right) \tag{12}$$

where $\delta(x)$ denotes the indicator function, but $x > 0$ when $\delta(x) = 1$, otherwise 0.

NDCG@N indicates the evaluation index of the sorting result. NDCG values the sorting order of the recommendation candidate set, and the higher the user's preferred service is in the recommendation candidate set, the larger the NDCG value is, indicating the higher the correctness of the sorting result. NDCG is defined as:

$$NDCG@N = \frac{1}{Z}DCGN = \frac{1}{Z}\frac{1}{|U|}\sum_{u\in U}\sum_{k=1}^{N}\frac{\delta\left(\hat{i}_{u,k}\in I_u\right)}{\log_2(k+1)} \tag{13}$$

where $\hat{i}_{u,k}$ denotes the k-th recommendation term for user u and Z is a normalization constant that represents the value of $NDCG@N$ in the ideal case.

4.3 Competitors

To demonstrate the validity of the model, UMIC is compared with the following model in this paper.

- **PopRec** is a traditional recommendation method that recommends the most popular items to users.
- **YouTube DNN** [2] is one of the most successful deep learning models for industrial recommender systems.
- **GRU4Rec** [12] is the first work that introduces recurrent neural networks for the recommendation.

– **MIND** is a recent state-of-the-art model related with our model. It designs a multi-interest extractor layer based on the capsule routing mechanism, which is applicable for clustering past behaviors and extracting diverse interests.

4.4 Implementation Details

The experiments in this paper are implemented using TensorFlow 1.15. For the parameter configuration, the dimensionality of embedding d is set to 64, the length of user's historical behavior sequence during training m is set to 20, and the maximum number of training iterations is set to 1 million. The number of interest embeddings for the multi-interest model is set to 4 and optimized using the Adam optimizer and a learning rate of lr=0.001.

4.5 Recommendation Performance

UMIC and other advanced models were compared. The performance of each recommended model is shown in Table 3. Among them, MIND obtained better performance compared with the previous models with its inclusion of dynamic routing mechanism. UMIC added a collaborative module to MIND to solve the user data sparsity problem. All models were experimented on two datasets, Amazon Book and Health and Personal Care. The experimental results show that UMIC obtains better performance than the other models on all three evaluation metrics, Recall, HR and NDCG.

Table 3. Recommendation performance.

	Amazon Book			Health and Personal Care		
	Recall@20	HR@20	NDCG@20	Recall@20	HR@20	NDCG@20
PopRec	1.356	3.019	2.258	2.071	4.584	3.315
DNN	4.565	9.328	4.657	4.808	9.116	4.613
GRU4Rec	3.884	8.571	3.934	3.206	8.029	3.768
MIND	4.3591	9.468	3.932	5.532	10.256	5.261
UMIC	**4.957**	**10.633**	**5.017**	**6.426**	**11.576**	**5.791**

4.6 Influence of Hyper-Parameter

Initialization of dynamic routing routes. The random initialization of dynamic routing in the multi-interest extraction layer is similar to the initialization of points in K-means, where the distribution of the initial clustering centers has a significant impact on the final clustering results. Since the routing logarithm is initialized based on a Gaussian distribution $N(0, \sigma^2)$, different values of σ may lead to different convergence and thus have an impact on the performance. To investigate the effect of σ, σ is set to 0.5, 1 and 5 to initialize the learning dynamic routing logs. The results are shown in Fig. 2.

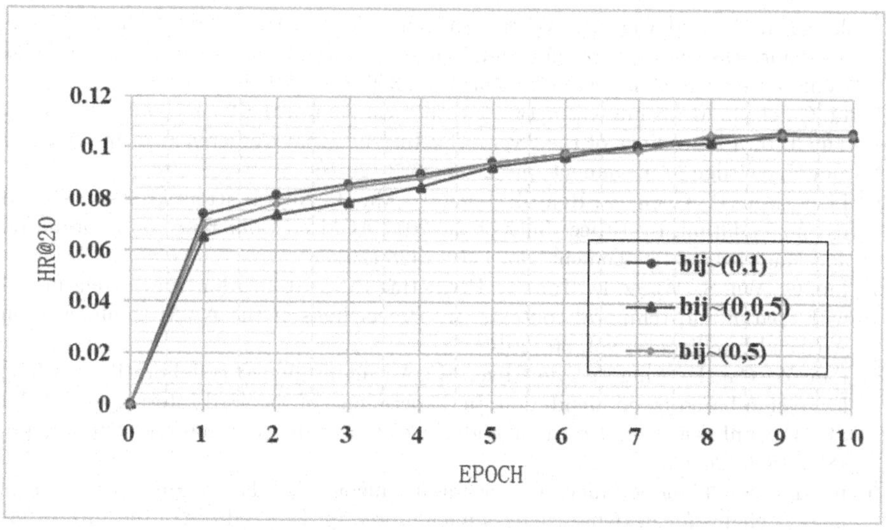

Fig. 2. Effect of initialized dynamic routing on model convergence.

5 Conclusion

In this paper, for the data sparsity problem faced in the recommendation model algorithm, the User Multi-interest Collaboration for service recommendation is proposed, which considers both the similarities and differences of users under different interest categories and models their historical behavior sequences. For each user, UMIC obtains multiple interest preferences of the user through a dynamic routing mechanism, which considers the features under the user's current interest in the nearest neighbor construction, and dynamically filters the user's nearest neighbors according to the items to be tested, thus solving the user data sparsity problem and improving the model recommendation quality. The model in this paper is experimented on widely used datasets. The experimental results show that the present model outperforms other advanced baselines.

References

1. Chen, W., Ren, P., Cai, F., Sun, F., De Rijke, M.: Multi-interest diversification for end-to-end sequential recommendation. ACM Trans. Inf. Syst. (TOIS) **40**(1), 1–30 (2021)
2. Covington, P., Adams, J., Sargin, E.: Deep neural networks for YouTube recommendations. In: Proceedings of the 10th ACM Conference on Recommender Systems, pp. 191–198 (2016)
3. Hinton, G.E., Krizhevsky, A., Wang, S.D.: Transforming auto-encoders. In: Honkela, T., Duch, W., Girolami, M., Kaski, S. (eds.) ICANN 2011. LNCS, vol. 6791, pp. 44–51. Springer, Heidelberg (2011). https://doi.org/10.1007/978-3-642-21735-7_6

4. Jannach, D., Ludewig, M.: When recurrent neural networks meet the neighborhood for session-based recommendation. In: Proceedings of the Eleventh ACM Conference on Recommender Systems, pp. 306–310 (2017)
5. Li, C., et al.: Multi-interest network with dynamic routing for recommendation at Tmall. In: Proceedings of the 28th ACM International Conference on Information and Knowledge Management, pp. 2615–2623 (2019)
6. Li, J., Ren, P., Chen, Z., Ren, Z., Lian, T., Ma, J.: Neural attentive session-based recommendation. In: Proceedings of the 2017 ACM on Conference on Information and Knowledge Management, pp. 1419–1428 (2017)
7. Liu, Q., Wu, S., Wang, L., Tan, T.: Predicting the next location: a recurrent model with spatial and temporal contexts. In: Proceedings of the AAAI Conference on Artificial Intelligence, vol. 30 (2016)
8. Pan, Z., Cai, F., Ling, Y., de Rijke, M.: An intent-guided collaborative machine for session-based recommendation. In: Proceedings of the 43rd International ACM SIGIR Conference on Research and Development in Information retrieval, pp. 1833–1836 (2020)
9. Rendle, S., Freudenthaler, C., Schmidt-Thieme, L.: Factorizing personalized markov chains for next-basket recommendation. In: Proceedings of the 19th International Conference on World Wide Web, pp. 811–820 (2010)
10. Song, W., Xiao, Z., Wang, Y., Charlin, L., Zhang, M., Tang, J.: Session-based social recommendation via dynamic graph attention networks. In: Proceedings of the Twelfth ACM International Conference on Web Search and Data Mining, pp. 555–563 (2019)
11. Wang, M., Ren, P., Mei, L., Chen, Z., Ma, J., De Rijke, M.: A collaborative session-based recommendation approach with parallel memory modules. In: Proceedings of the 42nd International ACM SIGIR Conference on Research and Development in Information Retrieval, pp. 345–354 (2019)
12. Wang, S., Cao, L., Wang, Y., Sheng, Q.Z., Orgun, M.A., Lian, D.: A survey on session-based recommender systems. ACM Comput. Surv. (CSUR) **54**(7), 1–38 (2021)

Service Application

Hardware-Software Co-design for Deep Neural Network Acceleration

Yanwei Wang, Bingbing Li(✉), Lu Lu, Jiangwei Wang, Rengang Li, and Hongwei Kan

Guangdong Inspur Intelligent Computing Technology Co. Ltd., Guangdong, China
{wangyanwei,libingbing02,lulu02,wangjw01,lirg,kanhongwei}@inspur.com

Abstract. Deep neural networks are widely utilized in many fields. However, the extensive requirement of computation is usually difficult to meet to support network inference. Model pruning, a technique to reduce redundant model weights to acceleration, provides a possible way to solve this problem but the improvement is usually limited due to the separation of hardware and software optimization. In this paper, we propose a complete hardware-software co-design framework to support irregular sparse model. Specifically, we prune redundant model weights through iterative pruning by increasing the penalty factor and improve the hardware efficiency through hardware threads control. We achieve significant model efficiency improvement by reducing 64.2% and 86.5% inference latency in vector-multiplication and convolution applications. The experimental results show the significant performance improvement and proves the effectiveness of the proposed method.

Keywords: Deep Neural Network · Acceleration · Hardware-software co-design

1 Introduction

Deep learning has made remarkable advances in data analysis and generation and has been playing an increasingly important role in many different fields. However, the relied deep neural network has extremely high requirements for computing hardware platforms, resulting in the inability to effectively implement the landing of algorithm models in many practical scenarios. This seriously affects the development and application of artificial intelligence.

For the implementation of deep neural networks, most acceleration framework are built based on Nvidia GPU. Since the low-level implement of the driver and acceleration methods are not open-sourced, developers have to use the relatively high-level API for their application implementation, which leads to insufficiency in model usage. Irregular pruning, as an example of model sparsification method for acceleration, is usually not supported in general commercial GPUs. The open-sourced GPU framework by connecting high-level application and low-level computation units provides more freedom for system acceleration and optimization.

Z. Wang et al. (Eds.): ICSS 2023, CCIS 1844, pp. 221–230, 2023.
https://doi.org/10.1007/978-981-99-4402-6_16

As a popular open-sourced GPU framework, Vortex consists of low-level and high-level functions including instruction interface, computation control tools and application developing environment. In Vortex, Portable Computing Language (PoCL) provides a open-source implementation of OpenCL standard and enable the thread control for customized computation arrangement.

In this paper, we propose a novel framework of the acceleration for deep learning networks. Based on irregular heuristic pruning, ADMM, we reduce the number of model parameters significantly without model accuracy loss. By leveraging the process control tool, PoCL, we modify the task scheduler and remove the unnecessary computation sub-tasks by redesigning the "*clEnqueueNDRangeKernel()*" function. Therefore, the latency of the model inference is dramatically reduced.

The contributions of the paper can be summarized as follows:

- We leverage an iterative heuristic irregular pruning based on ADMM strategy to remove redundant model weights without model accuracy drop.
- We propose a computation mission simplification strategy to remove unnecessary computation sub-tasks by redesigning the task scheduler in PoCL in Vortex.
- We propose a complete framework for irregularly sparse network acceleration and provide a potential solution for software-hardware co-design for deep learning acceleration.

2 Related Works

2.1 Model Pruning

Model parameter redundancy is widely recognized and compression is a common step before hardware implementation. Pruning, as a very popular tool for model compression, is widely used since it could remove redundant part of the model without significant model accuracy drop. Irreguler pruning, which prunes redundant model parameters without taking the position into account, is considered a sufficient tool to analyze and reduce the redundancy. However, due to the unfriendliness to hardware, it usually leads to significant computation overhead and is only applied on customized hardware platforms. Regular pruning (e.g. row pruning, column pruning [15], channel pruning [19], head pruning [9]. etc.), which prunes model part according to the designed minimum sub-structure, is considered more hardware friendly and widely used on general-purpose GPUs. However, since the sub-structure is manually chosen and fixed, the compression ratio is usually low due to the loss of freedom of reducing redundancy.

2.2 GPGPU and Hardware Acceleration

General-Purpose GPU (GPGPU) [8,13,17] is a tool for scientific numerical calculations using graphics processing units. Compared with traditional GPUs,

GPGPU can provide higher computing power in scientific numerical calculations due to the removal of computing resources related to image processing. Based on the open-sourced computing architecture RISC-V [1,3], it is a meaningful exploration to develop a computing framework available to all developers, and is committed to establishing an open and unified framework compatible with various platforms [4].

As an open-sourced hardware and software project to support GPGPU, Vortex [4] supports OpenCL [12]/CUDA [11] and runs on FPGA. With a complete open-sourced compiler, driver and runtime software stack, the Vortex platform provides a highly customizable and scalable framework to enable research in GPU architectures.

Vortex accesses the FPGA through the PCIe bus, and the software stack mainly integrates the processing driver kernel interface. It uses OPAE (Open Programmable Acceleration Engine) [2] lightweight C library as a driver to provide the abstraction of FPGA resources, which is a set of functions that can be accessed by software running on the host. It can configure FPGA read/write instructions, and read/write data from RAM on the FPGA. It uses the CCI-P (Core Cache Interface) [16] protocol to allocate a shared memory space. The Accelerator Function Unit (AFU) and the host can share access to memory space for data transfer. Data is read from the shared space and written to FPGA local memory. The Vortex is then reset to begin execution, and once the operation is complete, the results are stored in local memory. The resulting data is then moved from local memory to shared space accessed by the host using MMIO.

OpenCL is the main API supported on Vortex, and the project uses the PoCL [5] open-sourced framework to implement the OpenCL compiler and runtime software. PoCL (Portable Computing Language) is a portable open source implementation of the OpenCL standard, in addition to being an easily portable multi-device (heterogeneous) open-source OpenCL implementation. Its main goal is to improve the interoperability of OpenCL-enabled devices by integrating them into a single orchestration platform; the long-term goal is to use runtime and compiler technology to enhance the performance portability of OpenCL programs on different device types. PoCL currently supports various CPUs: NVIDIA GPU via libcuda, HSA GPU and TCE ASIP. PoCL uses Clang [6] as the C frontend to OpenCL and LLVM [7] as the implementation of the kernel compiler and as a portability layer. If the target platform has an LLVM backend, developers are able to easily get OpenCL support by using PoCL. The functions related to PoCL and Vortex include 1) runtime environment by providing libopencl.so library and header files based on vortex for GCC compilation on the host side; 2) compilation tools to compile kernel.cl file and call clang tool for front-end code analysis, code optimization and back-end executor to call llvm-riskv tools.

The backend of the PoCL compiler was modified to generate a kernel program targeting the Vortex ISA, and the PoCL runtime can directly access the Vortex driver. The communication with FPGA is realized through PCIe. When running Vortex locally, the software stack implements a native runtime that exposes new SIMT functionality and basic resource management APIs provided by RISC-V

ISA extensions to kernel programs running on Vortex. During PoCL compilation, the program statically links the runtime library with the OpenCL kernel. Vortex modifies the PoCL runtime by adding a new device target on its generic device interface to support Vortex. This new device target is basically a variant of the PoCL base CPU target, supports POSIX multithreading (Pthreads), and removes other operating system dependencies for the NewLib interface. Vortex also modifies the single-threaded logic to use Vortex's pocl-spawn runtime API to execute work-item functions.

The PoCL backend compiler is responsible for generating the binary files of the OpenCL kernel. Vortex modifies the PoCL to 1) support for RISC-V by adding new device and compiler support; 2) support for new Vortex instructions; 3) integrate with the Vortex runtime system.

3 Hardware-Software Co-Design for Network Acceleration

In our proposed hardware-software co-design framework, we leverage techniques of pruning and hardware acceleration as shown in Fig. 1. Specifically, we prune the model by reducing the number of model weights through iterative heuristic pruning. Then, we remove unnecessary (the calculation results are known as zero before calculation) submissions accroding to the pruning results. Finally, the inference of the network layers are accelerated.

3.1 Heuristic Irregular Pruning

The objective of irregular pruning is to limit the number of model weights and preserve the model accuracy simultaneously. Specifically, we set constraints for the number of nonzero model parameters and the training process of a N-layer DNN model solves the following problem according to the original ADMM paper [18]:

$$\begin{aligned} &\min_{\{W_i\}} \mathcal{L}_A(\{W_i\}) \\ &\text{subject to: } card(W_i) < l_i, i = 1, ..., N, \end{aligned} \tag{1}$$

where $\mathcal{L}_A$ is the model accuracy loss to update parameters W, $card(\cdot)$ calculates the number of nonzero parameters, and l_i is the desired number of weights in the i-th layer of the DNN model.

The constrained optimization problem can be rewriten as:

$$\begin{aligned} &\min_{\{W_i\}} \mathcal{L}_A(\{W_i\}) + \sum_{i=1}^{N} g_i(Z_i) \\ &\text{subject to: } W_i = Z_i, i = 1, ..., N, \end{aligned} \tag{2}$$

where

$$g_i = \begin{cases} 0, & \text{if } card(W_i) < l_i \\ +\infty, & \text{otherwise.} \end{cases} \tag{3}$$

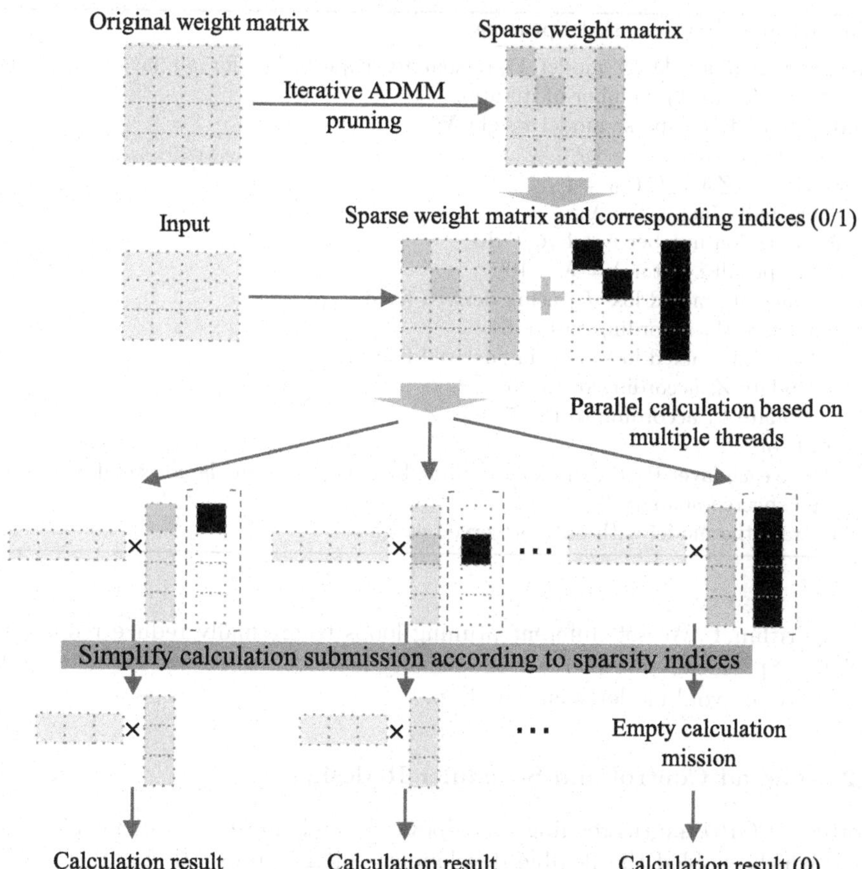

Fig. 1. Hardware-software co-design for DNN acceleration

We follow the solution based on the augmented Lagrangian and the optimal W can be derived iteratively by minimizing the following function:

$$\min_{\{W_i\}} \mathcal{L}_p(\{W_i, Z_i, U_i\}) + \sum_{i=1}^{N} \frac{\lambda_i}{2} \left\| W_i - Z_i^k + U_i^k \right\|^2 - \frac{\lambda_i}{2} \left\| U_i \right\|^2 \tag{4}$$

The above optimization problem can be solved by repeating the following steps:

$$W_i^{k+1} = \min_{\{W_i\}} \mathcal{L}_p(\{W_i^k\}, \{Z_i^k\}, \{U_i^k\}) \tag{5}$$

$$Z_i^{k+1} = \min_{\{Z_i\}} \mathcal{L}_p(\{W_i\}, \{Z_i^k\}, \{U_i^k\}) \tag{6}$$

$$U_i^{k+1} = U_i^k + W_i^{k+1} - Z_i^{k+1} \tag{7}$$

To derive the optimal sparse structure and preserve the model accuracy, we leverage the iterative method to prune the model gradually as expressed

Algorithm 1. Iterative model pruning

Input: pretrained DNN model $\mathbf{D_M}$, sparsity expectation for all layers l_i, initial penalty factor λ_0, number of iteration T
Output: updated sparse model weight $\mathbf{W}$

Set penalty factor $\lambda = \lambda_0$
Set initial $Z_{i0} = I$, $U_{i0} = I$
Set penalty factor $\lambda = \lambda_0$
for iteration number $i = 1$ to T **do**
  Set penalty factor $\lambda = \lambda_0 * 10^{i-1}$
  Calculate mixed loss L_p using derived fixed Z_i
  Update W_i according to Eq. 5
  Calculate mixed loss L_p using derived fixed W_i
  Update Z_i according to Eq. 6
  Update U_i according to Eq. 7
end for
Prune each layer W_i the model according by only preserving larger weights to meet the expected sparsity l_i
Retrain the model with only preserved weights.

in Algorithm 1. We set different pruning loops to gradually reduce redundant weights. Specifically, we increase the penalty factor, λ, to reduce model weights gradually to avoid model accuracy drop.

3.2 Thread Control and Scheduler Redesign

Vortex GPGPU multithreading was a powerful and efficient parallel calculation tool, which enabled the flexible development of the large-scale parallel operation of the modern GPU. It provided a unified program model for the CPU and GPU, allowing the development to write codes that could be executed on two systems. The Vortex GPGPU multithreading is easy to use, provides a comprehensive function, and supports a wide range of languages, including C/C++, OpenCL and CUDA. It also provided a series of functions to help development to maximize the performance of the codes. With the help of Vortex GPGPU multithreading, the development team could quickly and easily create large-scale parallel applications using modern GPU.

The Vortex runtime layer provides three main components: 1) Low-level intrinsic library to interact with new ISA instructions, 2) NewLib stub functions support [14], 3) a native runtime API for launching PoCL kernels.

The Vortex native API offers general purpose utility routines for applications to use. The *poclspawn()* function allows a program to schedule a PoCL kernel to execute on a Vortex. First, the intrinsic layer is able to search all available hardware resources. Then, the calculation mission is divide equally among the hardware resources by the work group dimension and numbers. For each OpenCL dimension, a range of IDs for different available hardware resources are assigned. Then, the warps [10] are spawned and threads are activated using the intrinsic layer. Finally, the kernels are executed with a new OpenCL global id for each warp loop.

PoCL *clEnqueueNDRangeKernel()* function provides a powerful and efficient parallel computing platform that enables developers to take advantage of the massive parallelism of modern GPUs. It provides a range of features to help developers manage their GPU resources, including a task scheduler, a memory manager, and a command queue manager. In our application of network acceleration, we summarize all the necessary calculation submission, divide them into different groups, and control the running loop to take advantage of the massive parallelism of modern GPUs through PoCL *clEnqueueNDRangeKernel()* tool. Specfically, we store the global id of necessary calculations and gather all necessary calculation mission before model inference. In this way, the unnecessary calculation is removed and the whole inference latency is significantly reduced.

4 Experiments

4.1 Irregular Pruning

In our test, we use the LeNet-5 as the base model and do iterative ADMM irregular pruning to reduce redundant model weights. Through iterative irregular pruning by increasing penalty factor gradually, higher model sparsity is expected while preserving the model accuracy. In our test, we initialize the penalty factor, $\lambda = 0.001$, and magnify it by 10 times for each penalty loop. In each penalty loop, we update model weight (W) and parameter mask (Z) separately to reduce redundant weight while preserving model accuracy.

Table 1. Pruning result

Layer	Weights	Weight after Pruning	Sparsity
conv1	0.5K	0.095K	19.0%
conv2	25K	1.83K	7.32%

As shown in Table 1, our proposed iterative ADMM pruning method. LeNet-5 contains two convolution layers, two pooling layers and two fully connected layers. We provide convolution layers pruning as illustration. On convolution layers, our pruning method does not incur accuracy drop and could prune more 92.5% parameters on average as shown in Table 1.

Table 2. Acceleration result while increasing model sparsity for vector multiplication (vecmul) and convolution (conv)

Sparsity	10%	20%	30%	40%	50%	60%	70%	80%	90%
vecmul (ms)	67	61	56	51	45	40	35	29	24
conv (ms)	8504	7970	7379	6782	5650	4519	3392	2282	1149

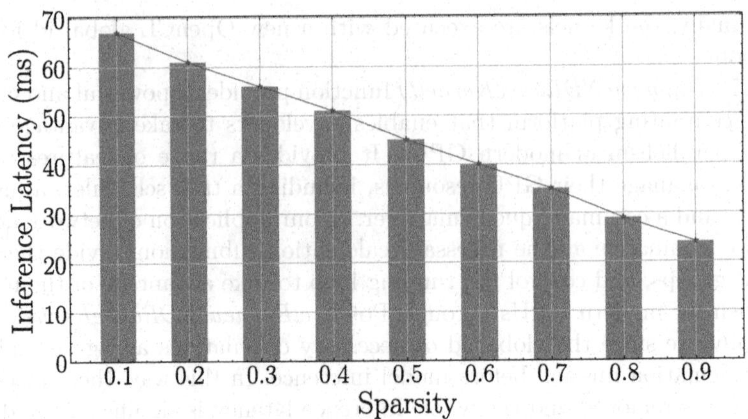

Fig. 2. Acceleration result of vector multiplication

4.2 Redundant Sub-tasks Remove

To test the final performance of hardware-software codesign strategy, we design two tests on vector multiplication and convolution calculation on Vortex platform. The test results are summarized in Table 2 and our proposed method could achieve nearly linear acceleration performance improve while increasing model sparsity.

Vector Multiplication. To verify the actual acceleration performance, we test the sparse vector-multiplication calculation by randomly setting a part to derive the actual process speed. Specifically, we randomly remove redundant calculation mission by: 1) providing a vector-multiplication calculation mission with a fixed vector length (e.g. 640 in our test); 2) randomly setting zeros some (from 10% to 90%) of the values of the input and recording the corresponding specification position; 3) remove redundant calculation missions by skipping corresponding threads. For PoCL in Vortex, we modify the spawn_kernel_callback() function to reduce unnecessary calculation loop according to the parameter mask (Z), through which we skip unnecessary calculation (the results are always zero). As shown in Fig. 2, while increasing the model sparsity from 10% to 90%, the inference latency is reduced nearly linearly. With 90% sparsity, the latency is reduced by 64.2% (from 67 ms to 24 ms).

Convolution Computation Acceleration. For convolution layers, the parameter masks are derived through irregular pruning and utilized to skip unnecessary calculation loop, which is similar to sparse vector-multiplication acceleration. Since the position of the zero weights (weights that are zero out according to pruning) is recorded and compared during convolution layer calculation, computation overhead is introduced. From the test results in Fig. 3,

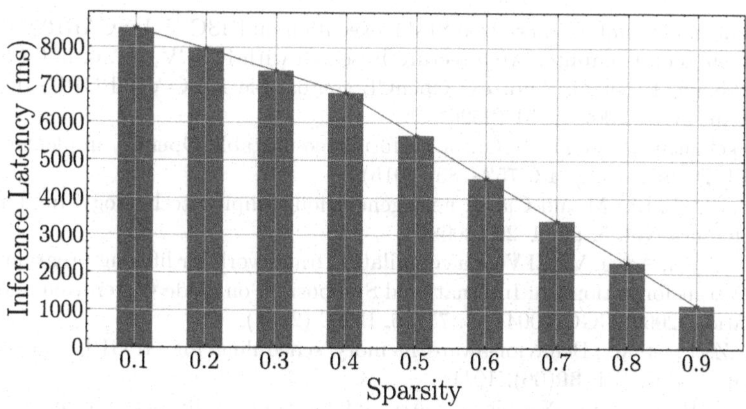

Fig. 3. Acceleration result of convolution

while increasing model sparsity from 10% to 90%, the inference latency is significantly reduced from 8504 ms to 1149 ms (86.5% inference latency is reduced). The results prove that the low-level multithreading control could achieve accurate calculation missions control to support irregular sparse model and achieve significant inference acceleration.

5 Conclusion

In this paper, we propose a complete hardware-software co-design framework to reduce model inference latency. We leverage iterative pruning to reduce redundant weight weights and propose a novel calculation mission simplification strategy through hardware thread control. We achieve significant model efficiency improvement by reducing 64.2% and 86.5% inference latency in vector-multiplication and convolution applications. The test results prove the effectiveness of the proposed method.

Acknowledgements. This research is supported by National Key R&D Program of China Grants No. 2020YFB1805505, and Natural Science Foundation of Shandong Province Grant No. ZR2022LZH017.

References

1. Asanović, K., Patterson, D.A.: Instruction sets should be free: the case for RISC-V. In: EECS Department, University of California, Berkeley, Technical report UCB/EECS-2014-146 (2014)
2. Bragança, L., et al.: Simplifying HW/SW integration to deploy multiple accelerators for CPU-FPGA heterogeneous platforms. In: Proceedings of the 18th International Conference on Embedded Computer Systems: Architectures, Modeling, and Simulation, pp. 97–104 (2018)

3. Collange, C.: Simty: generalized SIMT execution on RISC-V. In: CARRV 2017–1st Workshop on Computer Architecture Research with RISCV, vol. 6, p. 6 (2017)
4. Elsabbagh, F., et al. : Vortex: OpenCL compatible RISC-V GPGPU. In: arXiv preprint arXiv:2002.12151 (2020)
5. Jääskeläinen, P., et al.: PoCL: a performance-portable OpenCL implementation. Int. J. Parallel Prog. **43**, 752–785 (2015)
6. Lattner, C.: LLVM and Clang: next generation compiler technology. In: The BSD Conference, vol. 5, pp. 1–20 (2008)
7. Lattner, C., Adve, V.: LLVM: a compilation framework for lifelong program analysis & transformation. In: International Symposium on Code Generation and Optimization, 2004. CGO 2004, pp. 75–86. IEEE (2004)
8. Liu, Z.-J., et al.: Behavior-aware memory scheduling for GPGPU applications. Comput. Eng. Sci. **39**(06), 1011
9. Michel, P., Levy, O., Neubig, G.: Are sixteen heads really better than one? Adv. Neural Inf. Process. Syst. **32** (2019)
10. Nvidia. Cuda binary utilities. NVIDIA Application Note (2014)
11. Sanders, J., Kandrot, E.: CUDA by Example: An Introduction to General-Purpose GPU Programming. Addison-Wesley Professional, Boston (2010)
12. Stone, J.E., Gohara, D., Shi, G.,: OpenCL: a parallel programming standard for heterogeneous computing systems. Comput. Sci. Eng. **12**(3), 66 (2010)
13. Blaise, T., et al.: Vortex: extending the RISC-V ISA for GPGPU and 3D-graphics. In: MICRO-54: 54th Annual IEEE/ACM International Symposium on Microarchitecture, pp. 754–766 (2021)
14. J. J. Corinna Vinschen. Newlib (2001). http://sourceware.org/newlib
15. Wang, Z., Wohlwend, J., Lei, T.: Structured pruning of large language models. In: Proceedings of the 2020 Conference on Empirical Methods in Natural Language Processing (EMNLP), pp. 6151–6162 (2020)
16. Yan, H., et al.: Constructing concurrent data structures on FPGA with channels. In: Proceedings of the 2019 ACM/SIGDA International Symposium on Field-Programmable Gate Arrays, pp. 172–177 (2019)
17. Yao, Y.: SE-CNN: convolution neural network acceleration via symbolic value prediction. IEEE J. Emerg. Sel. Top. Circuits Syst. (2023)
18. Zhang, T., et al.: A systematic DNN weight pruning framework using alternating direction method of multipliers. In: Proceedings of the European Conference on Computer Vision (ECCV), pp. 184–199 (2018)
19. Zhuang, Z., et al.: Discrimination-aware channel pruning for deep neural networks. Adv. Neural Inf. Process. Syst. **31** (2018)

Red Blood Cell Antigen Typing Based on Image Processing and Machine Learning

Biao Wang[1,2], Lei Wang[2(✉)], Wenchang Xu[2], Shaohua Ding[2], Shengbao Duan[2], and Wenbo Cheng[2]

[1] School of Biomedical Engineering (Suzhou), Division of Life Sciences and Medicine, University of Science and Technology of China, Hefei 230026, China

[2] Suzhou Institute of Biomedical Engineering and Technology, Chinese Academy of Sciences, Suzhou 215163, China

wanglei@sibet.ac.cn

Abstract. Red blood cell (RBC) antigen typing is mainly used in blood group testing, which is critical to providing compatible blood and minimizing the risk of hemolytic transfusion reactions in blood transfusion. This study developed a procedure based on image processing and machine learning, to automatically determinate red blood cell antigen type from the RBC agglutination images. Red blood cell agglutination samples were prepared by mixing blood samples with antibodies in a multi-channel microfluidic device and then captured with a high-speed document scanner. Each image contains 24 blood agglutination sub-areas, which would be automatically cut into 24 sub-images and analyzed in the procedure. HOG (Histogram of oriented gradients), Grayscale Histogram and LBP (Local Binary Pattern) features have been extracted from the sub-images and combined with machine learning algorithms for classification. The machine learning algorithms used in this study included k-Nearest Neighbors (K-NN), Support Vector Machine (SVM), Logistic Regression and Multilayer Perceptron (MLP). Among them, the average accuracy rate of the combination of SVM and histogram reached 93.41% in determining the blood agglutination patterns (agglutination or no agglutination, binary classification), and the accuracy has reached more than 98% on some data sets. Besides, the study adopted a hierarchical classification strategy using different features and achieved an accuracy of 86.57% in detecting blood agglutination degrees (5 classification).

Keywords: RBC antigen typing · image processing · machine learning

1 Introduction

A compatibility test before administering a blood transfusion is necessary to avoid hemolytic transfusion reactions, which might be fatal to the blood

Supported by National Key Research and Development Program of China (No. 2022YFC2503305) and Shandong Province Youth Natural Science Foundation (No. ZR2020QF018).

Z. Wang et al. (Eds.): ICSS 2023, CCIS 1844, pp. 231–246, 2023.
https://doi.org/10.1007/978-981-99-4402-6_17

recipients [1]. RBC antigen typing is the process of determining the type of antigens present on the RBC, while blood type can be detected at the same time. Since blood groups were first discovered in 1901 in Vienna, more than 300 blood group antigens have been categorized among more than 40 blood group systems [2], with varying clinical significance [3]. The main techniques of blood typing are based on agglutination. Agglutination occurs when antibody interacts with specific antigens on RBCs (positive result), or absent when interaction is absent (negative result) [4]. Routine determination methods include slide test, tube test, and microplate agglutination method [5]. Although these methods are reliable, they require manual operation and are not efficient. Currently, the microfluidics-based method has been proposed to improve the RBC typing efficiency [6], the microfluidic method allows the observation of agglutination with the naked eye, which makes it easy for cameras to capture resolvable agglutination images. Therefore, image processing and machine learning algorithms can be combined and applied to the blood agglutination images to realize automatic intelligent typing of red blood cell antigens.

In recent years, blood detection method based on image processing and artificial intelligence algorithm gains great popularity. Tai et al. [7] proposed a hierarchical blood cell image identification and classification method based on multi-class support vector machine (SVM). Thanh et al. [8] applied Convolutional Neural Network (CNN) to distinguish normal and abnormal blood cell images. Ahmet et al. [9] hybrid Alexnet-GoogleNet-SVM to classify lymphocytes, monocytes, eosinophils, and neu-trophils on white blood cells. These automated methods give faster and more precise results. In the field of blood typing, Ana et al. [10] presents an electronic system for automatic blood type determination, which extract the standard deviation value, the minimal and maximal values from the blood images and classify the results by a threshold value. Similarly, Huet et al. [11] calculated the local pixel intensity variance and Castro et al. [12] analyzed the standard deviation of the pixel intensities of background-subtracted images to assess agglutination state. These methods might work well sometimes, but they have high requirements for imaging conditions, and expensive professional imaging equipment is required. Moreover, these algorithms rely heavily on the determination of the threshold value, which might migrate with the experiment environment change, so lack of portability. Another research combine machine learning and image processing in the agglutination images classification. Panpatte et al. [13] extracted the standard deviation and used SVM to detect the agglutination. However, the standard deviation alone is not sufficient to distinguish agglutinated and unagglutinated blood spots since there might be overlapping standard deviation values for both types of images, the usage of the SVM is also not convincing because a threshold value is enough to differentiate single feature.

This study extracts global high-level features from blood agglutination images and use several machine learning algorithms to distinguish agglutination from these features. In the past few years, image recognition methods based on deep learning [14–17] have gained a lot of popularity due to their excellent performance. However, deep learning models are highly dependent on the amount of training data and are computationally intensive, so deep learning is not suitable for application in our case. This study aims to develop a reliable program that integrates user interface, camera control, and red blood cell antigen typing, allowing users to easily operate to obtain the typing results.

Recently, Ding et al. [18] presented a multichannel microfluidic device for parallel analysis of red cell antigen typing. The new device designs a microfluidic chip with zigzag-shaped precise metering channel, each chip is a disc containing four identical microfluidic units, each unit is isolated from each other, which allows four individual blood samples can be run in parallel on a single disc. Each unit contains 6 reaction chambers and each reaction chamber can place different antibodies. In order to distinguish each reaction chamber, the reaction chambers are marked with -A, -B, -D, -C, -E, and -Ctr respectively. Figure 1 shows the structure of the disc, the diameter of it is 110 mm.

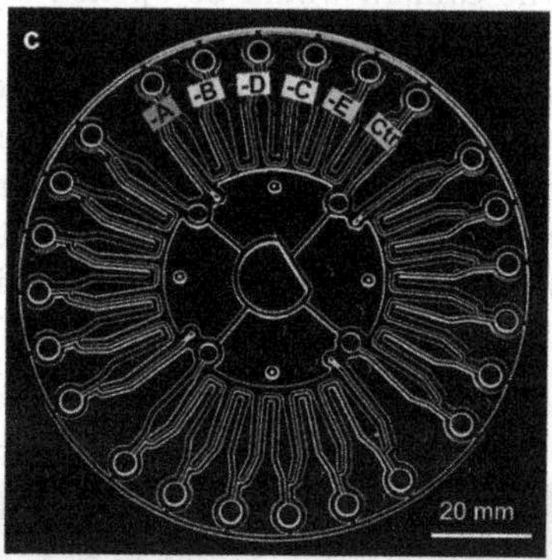

Fig. 1. The structure of the microfluidic disc [18].

A loosely coupled desktop software was developed for the device in this study, which embeds a blood agglutination status determination algorithm, by running it, image acquisition and automatic RBC type determination can be performed. The loosely coupled structure of the procedure enables it to be easily adapted to other systems with simple adjustments.

2 Date Acquisition

2.1 Date Collection

The whole blood samples used in this experiment were collected at the Suzhou Blood Center. All volunteers were informed and consent with the experiments. The blood samples were loaded into the disc [18] described above and mixed with the antibod-ies in it, all operations were completed by experienced laboratory technician. After the blood samples are thoroughly blended with the antibodies, they either agglutinate or do not agglutinate, representing positive or negative results.

The whole blood samples used in this experiment were collected at the Suzhou Blood Center. All volunteers were informed and consent with the experiments. The blood samples were loaded into the disc [18] described above and mixed with the antibodies in it, all operations were completed by experienced laboratory technician. After the blood samples are thoroughly blended with the antibodies, they either agglutinate or do not agglutinate, representing positive or negative results.

The date collection device is a high-speed book scanner, and a white LED back-light panel is coupled to the vertical bottom of the scanner to reduce the impact of ambient light. When collecting images, first place the disc loaded with blood samples on the backlight panel and find suitable position (To achieve this, this position is marked). Then open our program to control the scanner camera, the software operation interface is shown in the Fig. 2 Click the "OpenCamera" button in the interface, the camera would be opened and the real-time images captured by the camera would be displayed in the image frame on the left side of the interface, which prompts the operator to place the disc in the proper position. After adjusting the disc position, click the "Capture" button, the image will be captured and saved to the background for subsequent analysis.

The camera resolution is set to 1920 × 1080 by default, most cameras support this value, we try to test the algorithm capability at this resolution to make it more applicable.

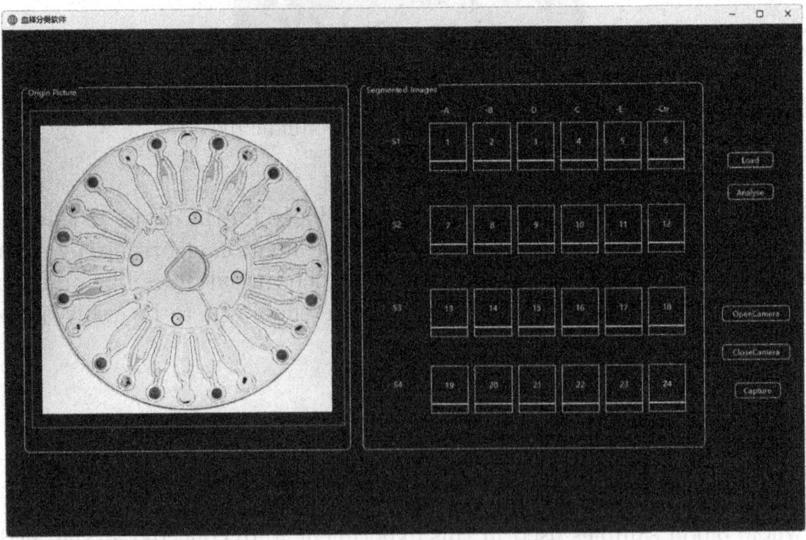

Fig. 2. (a) Overall picture: the interface of procedure. (b) Area surrounded by the red border: the image captured by camera. (Color figure online)

The camera resolution is set to 1920 × 1080 by default, most cameras support this value, we try to test the algorithm capability at this resolution to make it more applicable.

2.2 Date Description

The final data we collected are images containing entire blood sample disc, it can be seen in Fig. 2. As mentioned above, every prepared disc contains four identical microfluidic units and each unit contains six reaction chambers, so each captured image contains a total of 24 blood agglutination spot sub-regions. In each reaction chamber, the blood either reacts with the antibodies and coagulates, or does not react with the antibodies and does not coagulate. Because each reaction chamber can place any antibodies, we do not pay attention to which antibody the blood sample interacts with, but only determinate whether the blood sample is coagulated.

In theory, the blood sample is either coagulated or not coagulated, so this seem to be a binary classification problem. However, there are different degrees of agglutination of blood samples, some are very obvious, while some are of a lower degree, which may be caused by insufficient interaction between blood samples and antibodies. For this lower degree of aggregation, we hope to be able to distinguish it, prompting the operator to decide whether to retest them.

Table 1. The blood agglutination states of different labels.

Label	Blood agglutination state	Positive or negative	number
0		negative	277
1	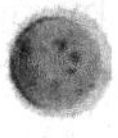	positive	135
2		positive	113
3	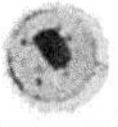	positive	79
4	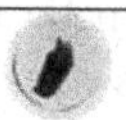 	positive	400
Invalid			4

Finally, these different agglutination patterns are grouped into 5 categories and labeled with number 0–4, with 0 representing no agglutination, and 1–4 representing different degrees of agglutination, the larger the number, the more obvious the degree of agglutination. All labels are marked by professionals. The comparison relationship between labels and blood agglutination states is shown in Table 1.

A total of 42 images were collected in this study, each image contained 24 blood agglutination spots, so a total of 1008 small blood agglutination spot regions were included, among which some invalid data were removed, leaving 1004. The number of blood agglutination state sub-images for each type is shown in Table 1.

3 Method

The blood red cell antigen type determination from the acquired images requires three steps—image preprocessing, feature extraction and classification. The main purpose of image preprocessing is to extract Regions of Interest (ROIs), reducing interference information. Through feature extraction, each image data is represented by a set of vectors, which can be input into the classifier to obtain the final determination result.

3.1 Image Preprocessing

The initial acquired image contains the entire disc with 24 areas of blood agglutination state, which contains too much interference information, it is difficult to directly distinguish each agglutination pattern in a single chamber from the initial image. One of the crucial steps is to extract Regions of Interest (ROIs), each ROI only contains one blood agglutination spot in a single chamber. The extraction of ROIs is performed automatically by our software, which requires the operator to position the disc correctly, there is an indicator mark on the platform where the disc is placed.

This seems to be obtainable by clipping a fixed-size range around the coordinates of each point, however, the camera and disc cannot be guaranteed to be strictly vertical, a slight tilt of the camera will shift the position of the blood spots. Each ROI needs to contain as little interference information as possible, and each blood spot is very small, so it is difficult to simply extract the ROI through fixed coordinates. Three steps are taken by us to achieve it. First, crop a larger area around each blood spot, which is easy to do because the coordinates of the blood point don't shift too much. Second, considering each reaction chamber is circular, a Hough transform [19] is applied to detect circles in each cropped image. However, each reaction chamber is not a strictly standard circle and there are many mis-detected circles, the program filters these circles according to their diameter and takes the average value. Then the extraction of the ROI can be realized by the diameter of the circle and the coordinates of the

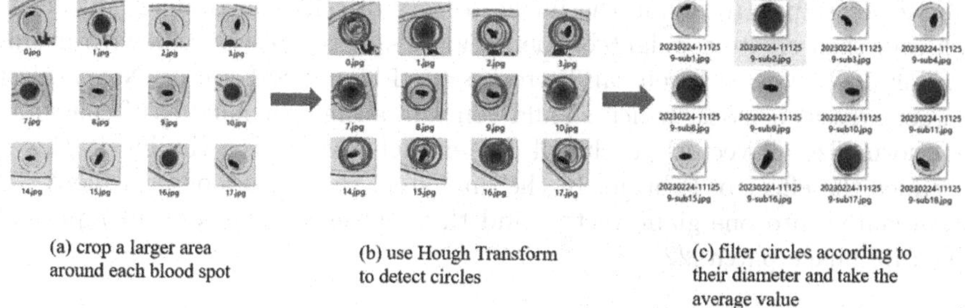

(a) crop a larger area around each blood spot
(b) use Hough Transform to detect circles
(c) filter circles according to their diameter and take the average value

Fig. 3. Schematic diagram of the image segmentation.

center of the circle. Figure 3 illustrates the process of image segmentation. Each ROI was standardized to 54 × 54 pixels.

The results (seen in Fig. 4) have proved that this is a successful strategy. Finally, a median filtering [20] is applied to reduce the noise in the image.

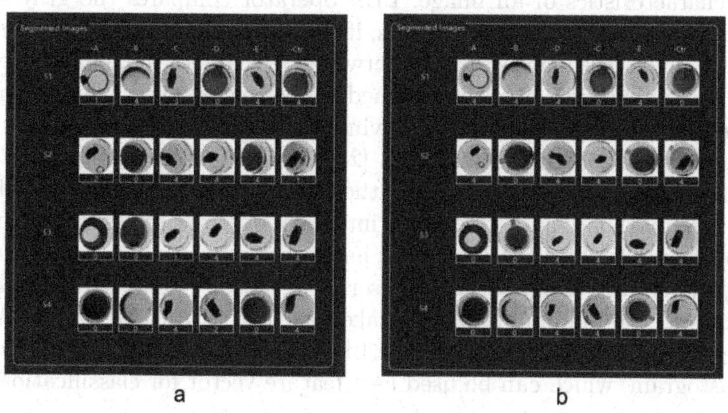

Fig. 4. (a) clip a fixed-size range around the coordinates of each blood spot. (b) clip the blood spots using our strategy.

3.2 Feature Extraction

Feature extraction is crucial to the accuracy of red blood cell antigen typing determination, the features extracted from different agglutination patterns must be distinguishable. This section provides an overview of the feature descriptors used in the study.

HOG. In the HOG feature descriptor [21], the distribution of directions of gradients are used as features. The first step is to calculate the gradient of each pixel in the image, both gradient magnitude and gradient direction are included.

The second step is to divide the image to several cells and count gradients in each cell, then create a weighted orientation histogram of the cells with n bins covering 360°, now each cell can be represented by a n × 1 vector. Next, select a larger area as a block, which should con-tain an integer number of cells, and then normalize all vectors (each cell can extract a vector) in the block, this is to reduce the effect of lighting. In the final step, the vectors of each block are concatenated into one giant vector, and the final feature vector will represent the entire image patch [22].

Image Histogram. The histogram of an image shows the number of pixels in an image at each different intensity value. For an 8-bit grayscale image there are 256 different possible grayscale values. Histograms can also be taken of color images, with the three axes representing the red, blue and green channels, and brightness at each point representing the pixel count. Although the image histogram is simple, it has achieved good results in many classification tasks [23].

LBP. LBP (Local Binary Pattern) [24] is a descriptor used to describe the local texture characteristics of an image. LBP operator compares the gray value of each pixel with their neighboring pixels, if the surrounding pixels are larger than the central pixel, it is marked as 1, otherwise it is marked as 0, finally the binary value of the surrounding pixels is assigned to the central pixel. The original LBP operator is defined as within a 3 × 3 window, so the surrounding pixels form a binary number of 8 digits. Ojala et al. [25] later proposed an improved version of the LBP operator, which changed the original square neighborhood into a circular neighborhood, and adapted to images of different scales by changing the radius of the circle. This LBP operator has rotation invariance. By continuously rotating the circular neighborhood, a series of initially defined LBP values are obtained, and the minimum value is taken as the central LBP value. After all the pixels in an image are labeled, the LBP value of each pixel can be counted into a histogram, which can be used as a feature vector for classification [20].

3.3 Classification Algorithm

In this study, machine learning algorithms are applied to determine the RBC antigen types from the features extracted from blood spot images. We give a brief overview of these algorithms.

SVM. SVM is a supervised learning method often used in machine learning and data mining [26], which can be used for classification, regression and other tasks. SVM constructs a hyperplane or set of hyperplanes in a high-dimensional or infinite-dimensional space to separate samples of each class, and applies an iterative learning process to converge to an optimal hyperplane that maximizes by minimizing the following pa-rameters Separation objective function between two classes of data points.

$$\min_{w,b,\xi} \frac{1}{2} \parallel w \parallel + \frac{c}{n} \sum\nolimits_{i}^{n} \xi_i \quad \text{for } i = 1, 2, ..., N \tag{1}$$

where $C > 0$ is a user specified tuning parameter, and n is the number of training data points.

KNN. K-nearest Neighbors [27] is a memory-based algorithm, which tries to find the K most similar (that is, the closest neighbors in the feature space) samples in the feature space, and predict the label from these. In general, distance can be any metric, commonly used distance measures include Euclidean distance, Mahalanobis distance, Manhattan distance. Despite its simplicity, the nearest neighbor method has been successful in a wide range of classification and regression problems.

Logistic Regression. Although the name of Logistic Regression is regression, the main idea of Logistic Regression is not to regress the target class, but rather to regress the probability of an event occurring [28]. In Logistic Regression, a sigmoid function is applied to simulate the probability and the maximum likelihood estimation (MLE) is used as a loss function.

MLP. MLP refers to Multilayer Perceptron [29], which is a supplement of feed forward neural network. It consists of three types of layers—the input layer, output layer and hidden layer. The input layer receives the input signal to be processed. The output layer performs tasks such as prediction and classification. Each neuron in the hidden layer and the output layer receives a linearly weighted combination of the output of the previous layer, then compares the total input value with a threshold, and finally processes the output of the neuron through the activation function. The activation function is used to generate a nonlinear combination of inputs. Commonly used activation functions include ReLU, Sigmoid, Tanh, etc.

4 Results and Discussion

A total of 42 images were segmented according to the method described in the previous section, 1008 sub-images of 54 × 54 pixel containing single blood coagulation spot were obtained, of which 1004 were valid data. HOG, Grayscale Histogram, LBP were extracted from these images respectively. When extracting the Hog features, each block was specified as 27 × 27 pixels and each cell as 9 × 9 pixels. When extracting LBP features, because LBP value of each pixel is a local feature, all LBP in one image are counted into a histogram as a global feature. When extracting Histogram features, the grayscale histogram was chosen by us because color is noise in this classification problem.

The primary goal of this study is to determine the blood cell antigen type by identifying the agglutination pattern of the blood samples (either agglutinated or not agglutinated). Besides, the study determined different blood agglutination degree, which are divided into 5 classes, marked with numbers 0–4. This study evaluated the algorithm performance on a data set containing 1004 blood agglutination spot sub-images.

Table 2. Blood agglutination patterns determination (binary classification) accuracies (%) of different features and different classifier.

Classifier	Features		
	HOG	Histogram	LBP
SVM	92.01%	93.41%	89.63%
KNN	93.52%	92.32%	91.03%
Logistic Regression	90.22%	92.52%	89.73%
MLP	91.62%	92.81%	86.24%

In order to maintain the objectivity of performance evaluation, a 5-fold cross-validation was used to divide the data set, which randomly divided the entire dataset into 5 parts, each part contains approximately the same percentage of samples of each target class as the complete set. Then uses one of them as the test set each time (including 20% of the data set), and the remaining as the training set. Table 2 shows the accuracy of determining the blood agglutination patterns (binary classification) based on each combination.

Table 3. Blood agglutination degrees determination (5 classification) accuracies (%) of different features and different classifier.

Classifier	Features		
	HOG	Histogram	LBP
SVM	81.09%	83.58%	66.66%
KNN	78.60%	81.59%	69.65%
Logistic Regression	76.12%	80.10%	73.13%
MLP	75.13%	80.59%	65.67%

Selecting different test sets will result in different accuracy rates. The data in Table 2 is the average accuracy rate of five-fold cross-validation, in fact, on some test sets, the highest accuracy rate of more than 98% was obtained. The results have proved that the type of red blood cell antigen can be effectively determined by combining image processing technology and machine learning technology. Among the combina-tion, the effects of Hog and Histogram feature are more stable. SVM and KNN performed best among these classifiers.

The Table 3 shows the accuracy of determining the blood agglutination degrees (5 classification), this is a more difficult classification problem. The result is similar, Hog and Histogram features are more distinguishable, among these combinations, the combination of histogram and SVM achieved the highest accuracy rate, exceeding 83%.

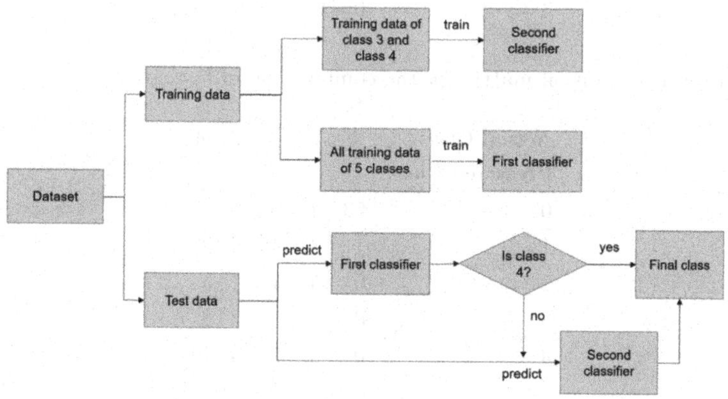

Fig. 5. Schematic illustration of the hierarchical method.

Table 3, 4, 5, 6 and 7 give the confusion matrixes for determining the blood agglutination degrees based on Histogram and SVM, Histogram and KNN, Hog and SVM, Hog and KNN respectively, they are representative in these combinations. It can be observed that errors mostly occur in determining class 2 and class 3, especially in class 3. Overall, the Histogram feature performed slightly better than Hog, and the accuracy rate of the KNN on the class 3 is higher than that of SVM (though both perform poorly).

In order to improve the classification accuracy, this study adopted a hierarchical classification strategy, as shown in Fig. 5 This hierarchical method trains two classifi-ers, one for classifying five class 0–4, another for classifying only class 3 and class 4. The second classifier chooses to classify between class 3 and class 4 because the class 3 has the lowest classification accuracy and is easily classified into the class 4. The first classifier is composed of histogram features and SVM, and the second classifier is composed of Hog feature and KNN, different combinations are beneficial to improve the classification accuracy of the second classifier. When predicting, first use the first classifier to make predictions. If the first classifier prediction value is not 4, take it as the final result. Otherwise, input the corresponding hog feature of this data into the second classifier and take the second prediction value as the final result.

Table 8 shows the confusion matrix of the hierarchical strategy. Table 9 compares the accuracy of different combinations on each class.

Table 4. Confusion matrix for the combination of histogram and SVM.

Actual Class/ Predicted Class	0	1	2	3	4
0	54	1	0	0	0
1	0	21	6	0	0
2	0	2	14	0	7
3	0	0	6	0	10
4	0	0	1	0	79

Table 5. Confusion matrix for the combination of histogram and KNN.

Actual Class/ Predicted Class	0	1	2	3	4
0	53	2	0	0	0
1	1	22	4	0	0
2	0	5	12	1	5
3	0	2	5	3	6
4	0	0	2	4	74

Table 6. Confusion matrix for the combination of Hog and SVM.

Actual Class/ Predicted Class	0	1	2	3	4
0	53	2	0	0	0
1	3	21	1	0	0
2	0	7	12	0	4
3	0	0	1	0	15
4	0	0	1	0	77

Table 7. Confusion matrix for the combination of Hog and KNN.

Actual Class/ Predicted Class	0	1	2	3	4
0	53	2	0	0	0
1	4	23	1	0	2
2	1	13	8	0	1
3	0	0	6	3	7
4	1	4	4	0	71

Table 8. Confusion matrix for determining the blood agglutination degrees based on hierar-chical strategy.

Actual Class/ Predicted Class	0	1	2	3	4
0	54	1	0	0	0
1	0	24	3	0	2
2	0	2	15	2	4
3	0	0	6	4	6
4	0	0	0	3	77

Table 9. Comparison of the accuracy of different combinations.

Method	Label	Accuracy	Average Accuracy
Histogram + SVM	0	98.18%	83.58%
	1	77.78%	
	2	60.87%	
	3	0%	
	4	98.75%	
Histogram + KNN	0	96.36%	81.59%
	1	81.48%	
	2	52.17%	
	3	18.75%	
	4	92.50%	
Hog + SVM	0	96.36%	81.09%
	1	77.78%	
	2	52.17%	
	3	0%	
	4	98.71%	
Hog + KNN	0	96.36%	78.60%
	1	76.67%	
	2	34.78%	
	3	18.75%	
	4	88.75%	
hierarchical strategy	0	98.18%	86.57%
	1	82.76%	
	2	65.22%	
	3	25.00%	
	4	96.25%	

From the results, such a hierarchical strategy is helpful to improve the overall accuracy. However, it doesn't always work because the second classifier may misclassify what the first classifier would have correctly classified. The poor classification effect on some classes is mainly due to the small difference between these classes and other classes, and the boundaries are not clear. Another reason may be that the number of blood samples in each class is unbalanced, some classes only have a small number.

In general, our algorithm has achieved good results, with an average accuracy of 93% (over 98% on some test sets) using 5-fold cross-validation in determining blood coagulation or non-coagulation. The classification accuracy rate of 5 kinds of blood coagulation degree reached 86%. The feature extraction and classification algorithms used in the study are relatively simple and easy to implement, finally, the combina-tion with the best classification effect is embedded in the software. Then the software can classify these blood samples while capturing real-time images or loading existing images, as shown in Fig. 6.

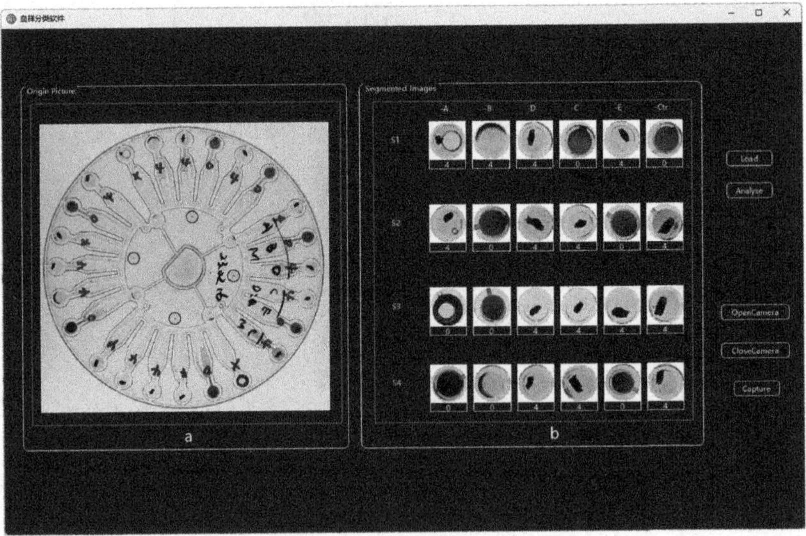

Fig. 6. The interface diagram of the software. (a) the image captured by camera. (b) the segmented images and the corresponding class labels.

5 Conclusions

This study developed a software for automatic red blood cell antigen typing, which based on image processing technologies and machine learning algorithms, achieving reliable determination of red blood cell antigen types. The software is easy to operate, eliminating the need for operators to visually interpret blood sample coagulation patterns and reducing human error.

The study has proved that using image processing and machine learning can effectively determining blood agglutination patterns, especially in determining whether it is coagulated or not. However, it is difficult to accurately distinguishing small differences between some classes. Deep learning may be the way to improve performance in the future. However, how to train a reliable model from a small sample data set and how to reduce the complexity of training and calculation, these are challenges that need to be overcome.

References

1. Daniels, G., Reid, M.E.: Blood groups: the past 50 years. Transfusion **50**(2), 281–289 (2010)
2. Reid, M.E., Oyen, R., Marsh, W.L.: Summary of the clinical significance of blood group alloantibodies. Semin. Hematol. **37**, 197–216 (2000)
3. Malomgré, W., Neumeister, B.: Recent and future trends in blood group typing. Anal. Bioanal. Chem. **393**(5), 1443–1451 (2009)
4. Szittner, Z., Bentlage, A.E.H., van der Donk, E., et al.: Multiplex blood group typing by cellular surface plasmon resonance imaging. Transfusion **59**(2), 754–761 (2019)
5. Li, H.Y., Guo, K.: Blood group testing. Front. Med. **9**, 65 (2022)
6. Chang, Y.J., Ho, C.Y., Zhou, X.M., et al.: Determination of degree of RBC agglutination for blood typing using a small quantity of blood sample in a microfluidic system. Biosens. Bioelectron. **102**, 234–241 (2018)
7. Tai, W.L., Hu, R.M., Hsiao, H.C.W., et al.: Blood cell image classification based on hierarchical SVM. In: 2011 IEEE International Symposium on Multimedia, pp. 129–136. IEEE (2011)
8. Thanh, T.T.P., Vununu, C., Atoev, S., et al.: Leukemia blood cell image classification using convolutional neural network. Int. J. Comput. Theory Eng. **10**(2), 54–58 (2018)
9. Varma, C.G., Nagaraj, P., Muneeswaran, V., et al.: Astute segmentation and classification of leucocytes in blood microscopic smear images using titivated K-means clustering and robust SVM techniques. In: 2021 5th International Conference on Intelligent Computing and Control Systems (ICICCS), pp. 818–824. IEEE (2021)
10. Ferraz, A., Carvalho, V., Machado, J.: Determination of human blood type using image processing techniques. Measurement **97**, 165–173 (2017)
11. Huet, M., Cubizolles, M., Buhot, A.: Real time observation and automated measurement of red blood cells agglutination inside a passive microfluidic biochip containing embedded reagents. Biosens. Bioelectron. **97**, 110–117 (2017)
12. Castro, D., Conchouso, D., Kodzius, R., et al.: High-throughput incubation and quantification of agglutination assays in a microfluidic system. Genes **9**(6), 281 (2018)
13. Panpatte, S.G., Pande, A.S., Kale, R.K.: Application of image processing for blood group detection. Int. J. Electron. Commun. Soft Comput. Sci. Eng. (IJECSCSE) 61–65 (2017)
14. Das, P.K., Nayak, B., Meher, S.: A lightweight deep learning system for automatic detection of blood cancer. Measurement **191**, 110762 (2022)
15. Lamoureux, E.S., Islamzada, E., Wiens, M.V.J., et al.: Assessing red blood cell deformability from microscopy images using deep learning. Lab Chip **22**(1), 26–39 (2022)

16. Bukhari, M., Yasmin, S., Sammad, S., et al.: A deep learning framework for leukemia cancer detection in microscopic blood samples using squeeze and excitation learning. Math. Probl. Eng. **2022** (2022)
17. Sharma, S., Gupta, S., Gupta, D., et al.: Deep learning model for the automatic classification of white blood cells. Comput. Intell. Neurosci. **2022** (2022)
18. Ding, S., Duan, S., Chen, Y., et al.: Centrifugal microfluidic platform with digital image analysis for parallel red cell antigen typing. Talanta **252**, 123856 (2023)
19. Illingworth, J., Kittler, J.: A survey of the Hough transform. Comput. Vis. Graph. Image Process. **44**(1), 87–116 (1988)
20. Gupta, G.: Algorithm for image processing using improved median filter and comparison of mean, median and improved median filter. Int. J. Soft Comput. Eng. (IJSCE) **1**(5), 304–311 (2011)
21. Dalal, N., Triggs, B.: Histograms of oriented gradients for human detection. In: 2005 IEEE Computer Society Conference on Computer Vision and Pattern Recognition, vol. 1, pp. 886–893. IEEE (2005)
22. Lee, K.L., Mokji, M.M.: Automatic target detection in GPR images using histogram of oriented gradients (HOG). In: 2014 2nd International Conference on Electronic Design (ICED), vol. 1, pp. 181–186. IEEE (2014)
23. Wajid, S.K., Hussain, A.: Local energy-based shape histogram feature extraction technique for breast cancer diagnosis. Expert Syst. Appl. **42**(20), 6990–6999 (2015)
24. Ojala, T., Pietikäinen, M., Harwood, D.: A comparative study of texture measures with classification based on featured distributions. Pattern Recognit. **29**(1), 51–59 (1996)
25. Ojala, T., Pietikainen, M., Maenpaa, T.: Multiresolution grayscale and rotation invariant texture classification with local binary patterns. IEEE Trans. Pattern Anal. Mach. Intell. **24**(7), 971–987 (2002)
26. Burges, C.J.C.: A tutorial on support vector machines for pattern recognition. Data Min. Knowl. Discov. **2**(2), 121–167 (1998)
27. Zhang, M.L., Zhou, Z.H.: ML-KNN: a lazy learning approach to multi-label learning. Pattern Recognit. **40**(7), 2038–2048 (2007)
28. LaValley, M.P.: Logistic regression. Circulation **117**(18), 2395–2399 (2008)
29. Gardner, M.W., Dorling, S.R.: Artificial neural networks (the multilayer perceptron)–a review of applications in the atmospheric sciences. Atmos. Environ. **32**(14–15), 627–2636 (1998)

Ethereum Phishing Detection Based on Graph Structure and Transaction Sequence Features Fusion

Yanmei Zhang and Yuwen Su(✉)

School of Information, Central University of Finance and Economics, Beijing 100081, China
2022212372@email.cufe.edu.cn

Abstract. As a kind of cryptocurrency fraud, Ethereum phishing scam poses a serious security threat to the trading environment, hence the urgency of detecting Ethereum phishing scam. Existing research achieved good results by using network embedding methods to automatically extract features, but most of them only use point-in-time transaction information, while ignoring the information of transaction sequences. Based on this limitation, a Graph Structure and Transaction Sequence Features Fusion (GSTSF) method is proposed. Specifically, considering the continuity of Ethereum account transactions, the temporal transaction sequence features contain richer transaction information. The transaction sequence features can be obtained by using the LSTM algorithm and applying a weighted aggregation method. The graph structure features extracted using the Node2vec algorithm are fused with the transaction sequence features using a linear combination. Then the final features fed into the machine learning algorithm for phishing account classification. The experimental results show that the *AUC* of the proposed method are better than those of the previous methods of Ethereum phishing detection.

Keywords: Blockchain · Ethereum · Phishing scams · Sequence feature · Network embedding

1 Introduction

Since Satoshi Nakamoto proposed blockchain in 2008, blockchain technology has undergone a leap forward. The blockchain 1.0 era is the digital currency era represented by Bitcoin, and the blockchain 2.0 era is the smart contract era. The smart contract platform represented by Ethereum propelled blockchain to the blockchain financial era. As blockchain enters the 2.0 era, security threats have increased while blockchain is deeply connected with finance and other fields [1]. Fraud in cryptocurrencies, as one of the security threats in blockchain, includes various types of fraud, such as phishing scams, Ponzi schemes, price manipulation and money laundering, among which phishing scams have caused serious danger to the Ethereum trading environment [2]. Ethereum phishing scams aim to

Z. Wang et al. (Eds.): ICSS 2023, CCIS 1844, pp. 247–262, 2023.
https://doi.org/10.1007/978-981-99-4402-6_18

obtain cryptocurrencies. Phishers send emails with malicious links to direct users to fake websites and then steal cryptocurrencies by collecting critical information from cryptocurrency wallets. On February 21, 2023, a news article posted on Cryptometer reported a fake Ethereum phishing website. More than 2800 wallets have been victimized in the last six months, and this website stole more than $300000 worth of cryptocurrency. This shows that Ethereum phishing scams bring huge economic losses to users, so there is an urgent need for an effective method to detect Ethereum phishing scams.

Based on the transparency of transaction records in Ethereum, extracting information from transaction records is a straightforward way to detect phishing accounts. Some scholars manually extract features such as the number of transactions in transaction records and then input the features into a machine learning classification algorithm for phishing account detection [4–6]. Other scholars have identified Ethereum phishing accounts based on constructed transaction network graphs [7–9]. Feature extraction plays a key role in the process of detecting phishing accounts. Deep learning-based [10–14] and random walk-based [15,16] network embedding methods can automatically extract graph structure features and have achieved great performance. However, the current research has the following problems. First, some of them only use the graph structure features extracted by the network embedding method without adding transaction information, such as transaction amount and time. Second, some of them add transaction information but use only the last moment of transaction information without including the transaction sequence information of the previous time.

Due to the continuity of account trading behavior, the temporal transaction sequences generated by the transactions contain abundant transaction information. Therefore, we fuse graph structure features with transaction sequence features and propose a GSTSF (Graph Structure and Transaction Sequence Features Fusion) Ethereum phishing detection method. Specifically, first, the transaction network graph is constructed based on the collected transaction data using the K-order subgraph sampling method. Second, the graph structure features of the accounts are extracted using the Node2vec algorithm and skip-gram in feature extraction, and the transaction sequence features of the accounts are extracted using the LSTM algorithm and weighted aggregation. Finally, the two types of features are linearly combined and input to the machine learning classification algorithm for phishing account detection. The GSTSF method fuses the graph structure features of accounts with transaction sequence features to obtain a more comprehensive features representation of accounts. Comparative experiments on the real transaction dataset of Ethereum show that the detection performance of the GSTSF method is better than that of previous methods, which proves the effectiveness of the proposed method in this paper.

The main contributions of this paper are as follows.

(1) Considering the transparency of transaction records in Ethereum, we use transaction data to construct the transaction network graph. The random walk sequence is obtained by the Node2vec algorithm and then input into skip-gram to obtain the graph structure features of accounts.

(2) Considering the continuity of transactions in Ethereum, we input the time series information of transaction amount between accounts into the LSTM algorithm. After obtaining the edge representation between accounts, a weighted aggregation is taken to obtain the transaction sequence features of the accounts.
(3) We propose a GSTSF method that fuses graph structure features with transaction sequence features, which provides better performance in detecting phishing accounts than previous methods that use point-in-time transaction information.

2 Related Work

2.1 Ethereum Phishing Scam Related Work

Due to the adverse impact of Ethereum phishing scams on the blockchain environment, scholars have conducted research on how to detect Ethereum phishing scams. Detecting Ethereum phishing scams can be categorized as a two-classification issue. This means that the feature vectors of the accounts should be extracted first and input into the machine learning classification method for two-classification, and then evaluation metrics can be used to measure the classification performance [3]. Existing research can be roughly divided into two categories in terms of extracting account features. One category is manual feature extraction, and the other category uses the network embedding method to extract features automatically based on the transaction network graph. The details of these two categories of extracted features are described below.

Given the visibility of transaction records in Ethereum, the characteristics of a trading account can be extracted visually from the transaction records. For example, the number of transactions, the number of transfers in, the number of transfers out, etc. The literature [4] collects transaction records with phishing addresses from the Ethereum website and extracts features using a cascading feature extraction method. It uses a double sampling integration method to solve the sample imbalance problem and then evaluates the model using a k-fold cross validation method. The literature [5] crawls 992 phishing accounts, 4066 non-phishing accounts and transaction records of first-level neighbors. The 18 manually extracted account features and 7 network features are input into three machine learning models, SVM, KNN and AdaBoost, for phishing account detection. The literature [6] uses a voting-based feature engineering technique to select the most important features and proposes a machine learning-based Eth-PSD method. In the above research, transaction account features are extracted from transaction records by different methods, and machine learning methods are used for phishing account detection.

In recent years, graph-based methods are often used for anomaly detection issues. The constructed transaction network graphs can visualize the transactions between accounts and play a key role in analyzing phishing accounts. The literature [7] constructs a second-order transaction subgraph centered on the target account and proposes an improved Graph2Vec model with added edge direction information. The literature [8] extracts the self-graph on the basis of Graph2vec and proposes a node relabeling strategy based on transaction attributes. A decision tree is then used as a classifier to distinguish phishing accounts. The literature [9] introduces different mapping mechanisms in the original transaction graph and builds multiple TSGN models to enhance the classification algorithm.

Compared with manual feature extraction methods, network embedding is a more efficient and automated feature extraction method. It is mainly divided into deep learning-based and random walk-based network embedding. On the one hand, deep learning methods such as graph convolutional neural network methods (GCN) [10,11], self-supervised incremental deep graph learning methods (SEIGE) [12], temporal transaction aggregation graph networks (TTAGN) [13], and hybrid in-depth neural networks (LBPS) [14] are used to distinguish Ethereum phishing accounts from normal accounts. On the other hand, for the random walk-based approach, the literature [15] proposed the Trans2vec algorithm by adding transaction amount and transaction time to the random walk transfer probability of the Node2vec algorithm. In the literature [16], a transaction network containing 6500 nodes is constructed, and the TA-Struc2Vec algorithm is proposed based on the Struc2Vec algorithm. Then, four classification methods, decision tree, random forest, SVM, and logistic regression, were used for the identification of phishing accounts.

To summarize, existing research partly use manually extracted transaction features and partly use automatically extracted graph structure features, and some scholars add transaction information to the transaction network graph to jointly extract features. However, most of the existing research use only the latest transaction information and do not consider past transaction information. Since there is a certain continuity in the trading behavior of accounts in Ethereum, a sequence of transactions is formed in the time sequence. This temporal transaction sequence contains richer transaction information. Therefore, the features extracted from the temporal transaction sequence play an important role in characterizing the trading accounts.

2.2 Sequence Feature Extraction in Traditional Phishing Scam

The RNN algorithm [17] is a neural network algorithm that can handle sequential data. However, because the RNN network has the problem of 'gradient disappearance' or 'gradient explosion', it cannot obtain more contextual information. The LSTM algorithm [18] can effectively solve the issue of RNN and can capture long-range dependencies. The LSTM algorithm is widely used in traditional phishing website detection. The literature [19] proposed a hybrid algorithmic model of LSTM and Random Forest to detect phishing URLs. It uses the LSTM algorithm to extract the character sequence features of the URLs and combines them with other features for training the Random Forest algorithm. Two hybrid deep learning models based on long and short-term memory and deep neural network algorithms, DNN-LSTM and DNN-BiLSTM models, are proposed in the literature [20]. Both models use manual NLP features and character embedding-based features to detect phishing URLs. In the literature [21], an MCA-LSTM model based on multiscale convolution and an attention mechanism is proposed for time series classification. The model consists of two parallel branches, LSTM and a multiscale convolutional attention module, and incorporates a channel attention mechanism to automatically learn the importance of features.

The above research [19–21] are all applications of the LSTM algorithm in traditional phishing website detection, which provides a reference for this paper in obtaining information on temporal transaction sequences.

2.3 Summary

The existing research lacks consideration of account time transaction sequence information when extracting Ethereum account features. Temporal transaction sequence features play an important role in Ethereum phishing account detection. Therefore, we adopt the sequence feature extraction method from traditional phishing website detection and use the LSTM algorithm to extract temporal transaction sequence features. We fuse temporal transaction sequence features with graph structure features and propose a GSTSF Ethereum phishing detection method.

3 Method

3.1 Overall Framework

The overall framework of the GSTSF method is shown in Fig. 1. Based on the Ethereum transaction data, the framework is divided into three phases: transaction network construction, feature extraction, and node classification. In the transaction network construction stage, we extract transaction subgraphs using the K-order subgraph sampling method for the target accounts to construct the overall transaction network graph. The feature extraction stage is divided into two parts: graph structure feature extraction and transaction sequence feature extraction. Graph structure feature extraction obtains the random walk sequence by the Node2vec algorithm and then inputs it into skip-gram to obtain the graph structure features. Transaction sequence feature extraction means that the transaction information is first sorted by time and then input to the LSTM algorithm, and the output of the LSTM algorithm is the edge representation between two accounts. Then, the different edge representation connected to the same account are weighted and aggregated to that account to obtain the transaction sequence features. In the node classification stage, we linearly combine the graph structure features with the transaction sequence features to form a fused final feature representation. The fused features are input to four machine learning algorithms for classification, and the detection performance of the GSTSF method is evaluated by evaluation metrics.

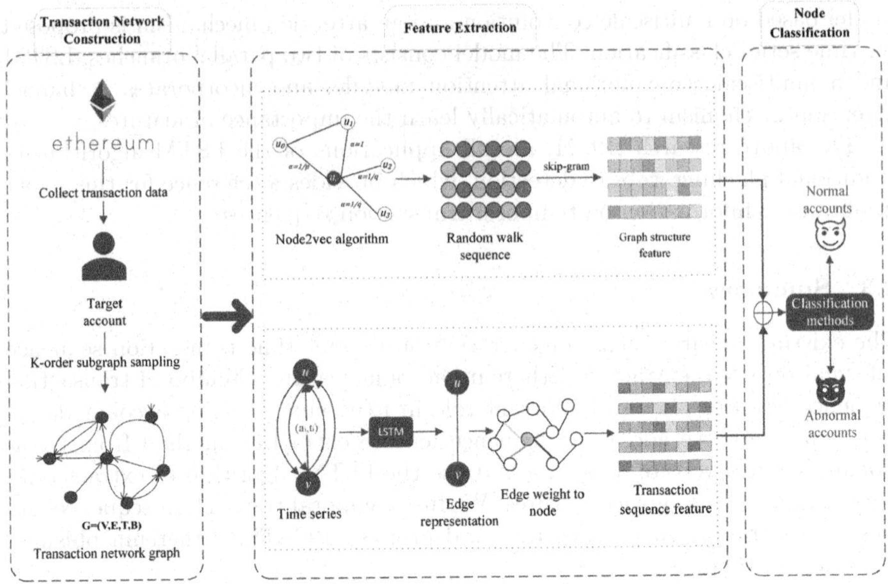

Fig. 1. Phishing account detection framework diagram.

3.2 Transaction Network Construction

This section is based on the transaction data collected at the Ethereum website, and the phishing nodes in the data as well as the randomly selected normal nodes together form the target node set. For the target node set, the transaction subgraph is extracted using the K-order subgraph sampling method, with accounts as nodes and transactions between accounts as edges. The k-order subgraph sampling method means collecting the K-order neighbors of the target node, which is divided into K-in and K-out. K-in that is, the K-order neighbors who transfer in transactions to the target node. Conversely, K-out is the transfer out. Finally, the transaction network graph $G = (V, E, T, B)$ is constructed, where V denotes the node, E denotes the edge, T denotes the transaction time, and B denotes the transaction amount. The whole transaction network graph contains information on transaction amount, transaction direction, transaction time and transaction relationship between accounts, which lays the foundation for the subsequent feature extraction stage.

3.3 Feature Extraction

Graph Structure Feature Extraction. In this paper, we use the random walk-based Node2vec algorithm to extract the graph structure feature representation of nodes. Based on the structure of the graph, the Node2vec algorithm can map nodes into a low-dimensional space and represent them as low-dimensional vectors. The Node2vec algorithm is an algorithm that improves on the DeepWalk algorithm, which combines breadth-first search (BFS) and depth-first search (DFS) for random walks. The BFS searches the nodes in order from closest to farthest away from the starting point. The DFS goes down a path until it can go no further and then backs up to start searching the next path.

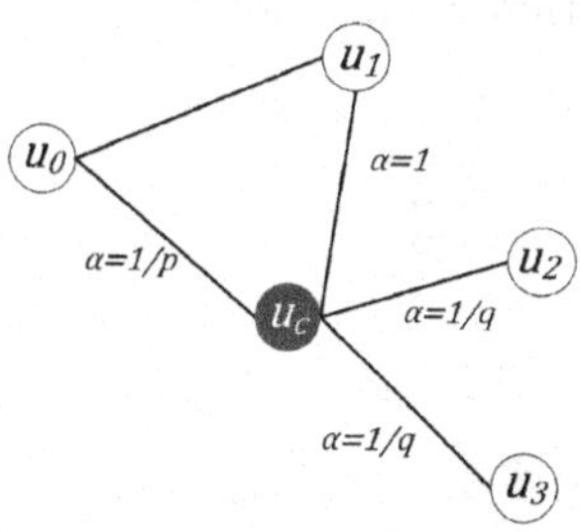

Fig. 2. Node2vec walking process.

Together with the walking process in Fig. 2, the walking strategy of Node2vec is shown in Eq. (1). where $P(u_i = u_t|u_{i-1} = u_c)$ means the transfer probability from node u_c to the next node u_t, and $w_{u_c u_t}$ is the weight on the connected edges.

$$P(u_i = u_t|u_{i-1} = u_c) = \frac{w_{u_c u_t} \cdot \alpha_{pq}(u_0, u_t)}{Z} \tag{1}$$

$$\alpha_{pq}(u_0, u_t) = \begin{cases} \frac{1}{p}, if\ d_{u_0 u_t} = 0 \\ 1, if\ d_{u_0 u_t} = 1 \\ \frac{1}{q}, if\ d_{u_0 u_t} = 2 \end{cases} \tag{2}$$

As shown in Eq. (2), $\alpha_{pq}(u_0, u_t)$ is the parameter that controls the walking trend, u_0 is the previous node of node u_c, and $d_{u_0 u_t}$ represents the shortest path distance between the node u_0 and the next node u_t. If two nodes are the same node, $d_{u_0 u_t}$=0, the probability of jumping back to the previous node is $\frac{1}{p}$. If two nodes are directly connected, $d_{u_0 u_t}$=1, then the probability of jumping to a node that is connected to the previous node u_0 is 1. If two nodes are not connected, $d_{u_0 u_t}$=2, then the probability of jumping to another node farther away is $\frac{1}{q}$. The smaller p is, the easier it is to jump back to the previous node, and the more graph traversal tends to be BFS. The smaller q is, the easier it is to jump to more distant nodes, and the greater the graph traversal tends to be DFS.

The walking sequence of the nodes is obtained by a random walk, and then the sequence is input into skip-gram for training. Therefore, we can obtain the graph structure feature representation of each node.

Transaction Sequence Feature Extraction. To extract the temporal transaction sequence features of the nodes, we sort the transaction amount between nodes in ascending order by timestamp, and the obtained transaction sequence is used as input. The sorted transaction amount sequences are used as input to obtain the edge representation between node pairs through a long short-term memory network (LSTM). Then, the different edge representation connected to the same node are weighted to that node. Finally, we can obtain the transaction sequence feature representation of each node.

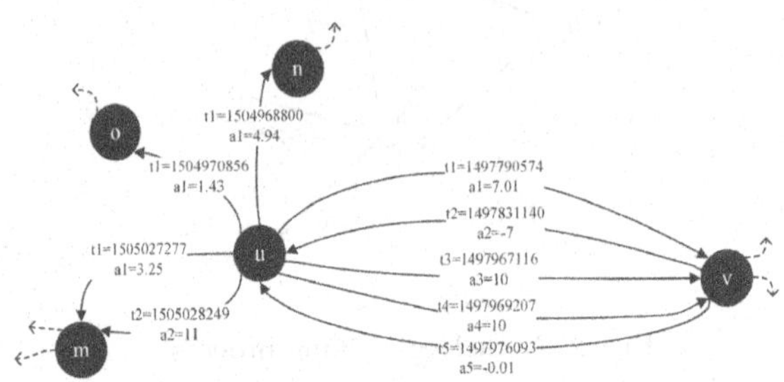

Fig. 3. Time series transaction network.

The transaction information between nodes contains the transaction amount, timestamp and transaction direction. The transaction information generated between two nodes, sorted in ascending order by timestamp, constitutes a time series containing transaction amount and direction. As shown in Fig. 3, $t_i(i = 1, 2, 3...n)$ means the timestamp, $\alpha_i(i = 1, 2, 3...n)$ means the transaction amount at the corresponding timestamp, and the positive or negative value of α_i means the transaction direction, in which α_i is positive when a transaction is transferred from one node to another and negative otherwise.

$$e_{uv} = LSTM(e_1 + e_2 + ... + e_n) = LSTM[(t_1, \alpha_1) + (t_2, \alpha_2) + ... + (t_n, \alpha_n)] \quad (3)$$

We input the transactions between the two nodes sorted by time into the LSTM algorithm. As shown in Eq. (3), taking nodes u and v for example, e_{uv} is the connected edge representation between two nodes, $e_i(i = 1, 2, 3...n)$ represent the n transactions between two nodes. These n transactions are sorted by timestamp in ascending order and then input into the LSTM function provided with the Keras package. Then we can output the vector of time series transaction features between the two nodes u and v.

Through the LSTM algorithm, we can obtain the edge representation of the transactions between nodes. As shown in Fig. 4, taking node u as an example, the feature representation of $e_{uv}, e_{um}, e_{un}, e_{uo}$ and so on edges are obtained. Then, the feature representation of edges are aggregated to node u by weighted averaging to obtain the final features Z_u, $Z_u = \sum \frac{e_{uk}}{j}$, where j means the number of connected edges of node u with other nodes k.

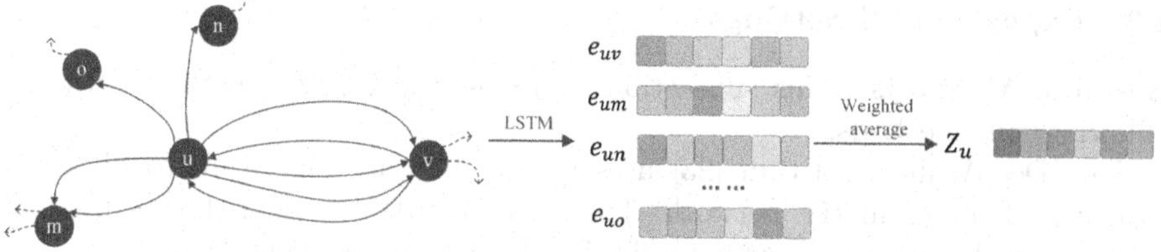

Fig. 4. Transaction sequence feature representation.

3.4 Node Classification

After we obtained the graph structure features and transaction sequence features, we fused them together by direct linear combination as the final feature representation of the nodes. To distinguish phishing nodes from normal nodes, machine learning algorithms are used for classification. Since the data in this paper are labeled data, a supervised classification algorithm is used to distinguish between phishing nodes and normal nodes. In this paper, four classification algorithms are selected, namely, the LightGBM algorithm, Logistic Regression, SVC algorithm, and Random Forest algorithm. The experimental results are obtained by calculating the evaluation metrics as a way to evaluate the detection performance of the GSTSF method.

4 Experiment

The purpose of the experiment is to answer the following three main questions.

RQ1: How to set model parameters for optimal identification of phishing nodes?
RQ2: What is the detection performance of the GSTSF method?
RQ3: What is the difference in the detection performance of GSTSF on different classification methods?

4.1 Dataset

The data in this paper are derived from the publicly available dataset in [22], which collects Ethereum transaction data through the interface provided by Ethereum (etherscan.io). The data contain 445 network phishing nodes, plus 445 randomly selected normal nodes, resulting in 890 target nodes, through which the subgraphs are then collected. The K-order subgraph sampling method is used in collecting subgraphs, choosing K-in = 1 and K-out = 3. The final constructed transaction network contains a total of 86622 nodes and 401176 transaction edges.

4.2 Experimental Settings

Baseline Methods. This subsection compares the GSTSF method with the following four methods.

The DeepWalk algorithm [23] uses a random walk algorithm to obtain a sequence of nodes in the network. Then, the Word2Vec algorithm is used to represent each node as a vector to obtain the feature representation.

The Struc2vec algorithm [24] defines vertex similarity from the perspective of spatial structural similarity and then learns the feature vector of each node by random walk.

The Trans2vec algorithm [15] adds weights containing transaction amount and transaction time to the Node2vec algorithm. The features extracted by this algorithm contain more comprehensive information in the transaction network.

The RioGNN algorithm [25] aggregates all neighbor information to obtain the final node embedding through an enhanced relationship-aware neighbor selection mechanism, which is a new neighborhood selection-guided multi-relational graph neural network architecture.

Evaluation Metrics. The evaluation metrics include $AUC, Precision, Recall$ and $F1-score$, where AUC is the area under the ROC curve formed by calculating $TPRs$ and $FPRs$ under multiple thresholds. As shown in Eq. (4)–Eq. (6), the $Precision$ is the percentage of accounts judged to be suspicious in which phishing nodes truly exist. $Recall$ is the percentage of detected samples of known phishing nodes. $F1-score$ is the score that combines the evaluation of $Precision$ and $Recall$.

$$Precision = \frac{TP}{TP + FP} \tag{4}$$

$$Recall = \frac{TP}{TP + FN} \tag{5}$$

$$F1 - score = \frac{2 \times Precision \times Recall}{Precision + Recall} \tag{6}$$

where TP and FP represent the number of positive and negative samples judged to be positive. TN and FN represent the number of negative and positive samples judged to be negative.

4.3 Parameter Selection

To answer RQ1, this section conducts parameter selection experiments. In this paper, the GSTSF method is used to obtain the node feature representation after fusing the graph structure features with the transaction sequence features. Then, the classification algorithm is used to classify phishing accounts from normal accounts. The classification algorithm used in the parameter selection process is the LightGBM algorithm with parameters set to 15 leaves, maximum depth of the tree set to 6, and learning rate set to 0.1. Using the above four evaluation metrics, a higher value of the evaluation metric indicates that phishing node detection is more effective.

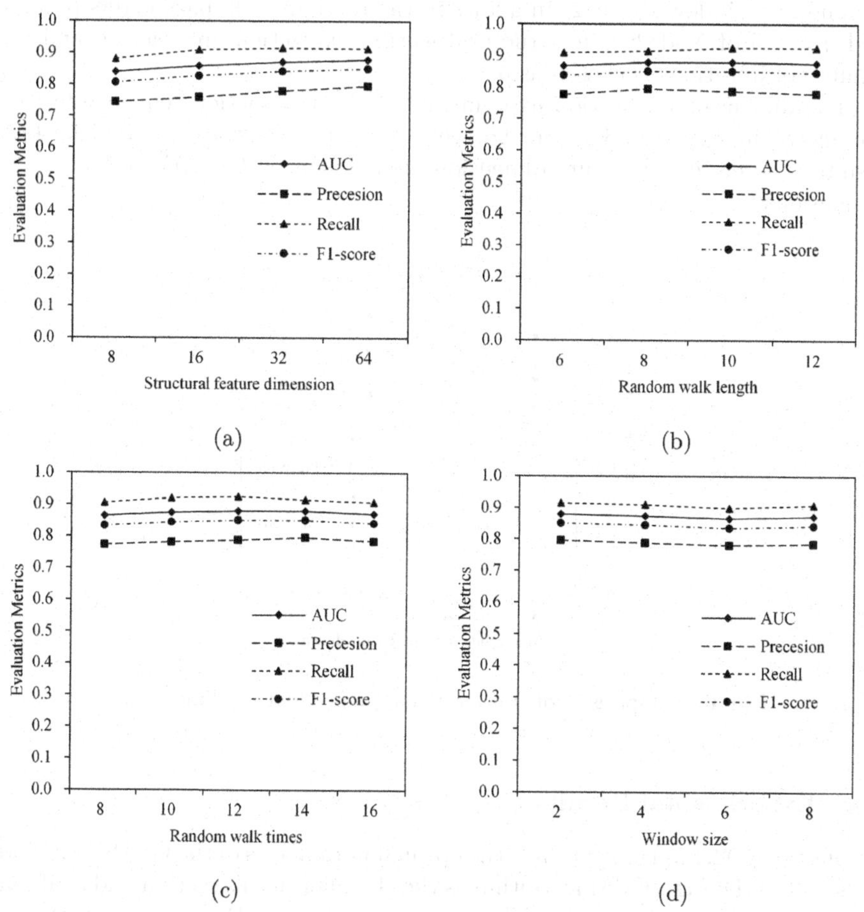

Fig. 5. Comparison of parameters in graph structure feature extraction.

We conduct experiments on the selection of four important parameters in graph structure feature extraction. They are the structural feature dimension d, the random walk length l, the random walk times n, and the window size w. The obtained experimental results are shown in Fig. 5(a)-(d). From Fig. 5(a), we can see that the AUC value keeps increasing as the structural feature dimension increases, which may be due to the fact that longer feature dimensions contain more node information. However, we find that the larger the feature dimension the longer the training time of the model, and 64 dimensions have achieved good results, so the dimension is chosen to be 64. For the random walk length, the AUC value in Fig. 5(b) is high when the length is taken as 8 and 10. However, the *Precision* of the walk length is higher when the length is 8 than when the length is 10, so the random walk length is chosen to be 8. Based on the size of the *AUC* value in Fig. 5(c)and Fig. 5(d), the random walk times is chosen to be 12, and the window size is 2. In addition, the random walk parameters p = 0.5 and q = 0.5 of Node2vec in structural feature extraction are selected and the number of iterations is chosen as 5.

The dimensional selection experiments of the transaction sequence feature are shown in Fig. 6, and it can be seen that 64-dimension achieves the best results. Therefore the feature dimension after fusion by GSTSF method is 128 dimensions.

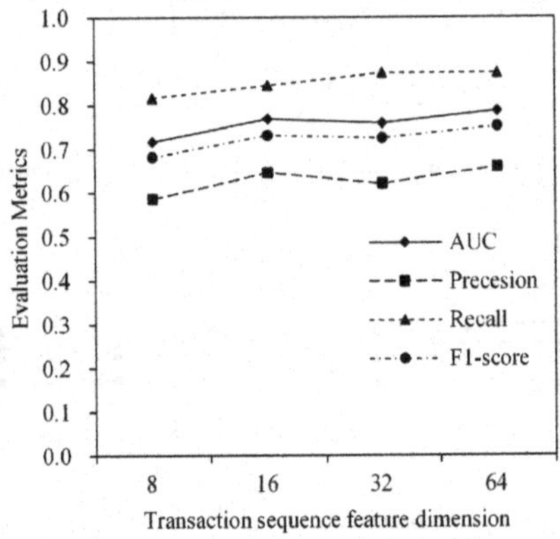

Fig. 6. Comparison of transaction sequence feature dimension.

4.4 Experimental Results

To answer RQ2, after we obtained the optimal parameters of the GSTSF method, we selected the LightGBM algorithm as the classifier in this section and analyzed the performance of the proposed method by comparison. Due to the randomness of the results obtained based on the random walk method, we conducted 10 experiments to take the average, and the experimental results are shown in Table 1.

From Table 1, we can see that the *AUC* value of the GSTSF method reaches 0.879, which is 0.025 higher than that of the Trans2vec method using graph structure features with point-in-time transaction features. GSTSF/GS for using only transaction sequence features and GSTSF/TS for using only structural features, it can be seen that the fused results are higher than these two individual features. Meanwhile, the *Precision* reaches 0.796, the *Recall* reaches 0.914, and the $F1-score$ reaches 0.851, which shows that the GSTSF method can detect phishing accounts well. The detection performance is higher than other methods, which means that time series features make an important contribution.

Table 1. Comparison of detection performance.

Method	AUC	Precision	Recall	F1-score
DeepWalk	0.836	0.742	0.873	0.802
Struc2vec	0.656	0.518	0.817	0.634
Trans2vec	0.854	0.749	0.910	0.822
RioGNN	0.849	0.758	0.892	0.820
GSTSF/GS	0.717	0.586	0.817	0.682
GSTSF/TS	0.845	0.753	0.882	0.812
GSTSF	**0.879**	**0.796**	**0.914**	**0.851**

The details of the 10 experimental results of the GSTSF method are shown in Table 2. The fluctuations in the results of each experiment are from the randomness of the graph structure feature extracted based on random walk. Although there are fluctuations in the results of each experiment, the overall detection performance is still better. This indicates that the fusion of graph structure features and transaction sequence features can better represent account information and thus can detect phishing nodes more accurately.

Table 2. Experimental results of the GSTSF method.

Experiment number	AUC	Precision	Recall	F1-score
1	0.895	0.815	0.930	0.868
2	0.890	0.782	0.958	0.861
3	0.876	0.827	0.873	0.849
4	0.864	0.788	0.887	0.834
5	0.850	0.759	0.887	0.818
6	0.885	0.795	0.930	0.857
7	0.876	0.776	0.930	0.846
8	0.888	0.813	0.915	0.861
9	0.878	0.793	0.915	0.850
10	0.888	0.813	0.915	0.861
Average value	0.879	0.796	0.914	0.851

In addition, different classification methods have an impact on the detection performance of phishing nodes. To answer RQ3, we use the fusion features extracted by the GSTSF method and put them into four classification methods for experiments. They are the LightGBM algorithm, Logistic Regression, SVC algorithm, and Random Forest algorithm. The obtained experimental results are shown in Table 3. From the results of the experiments, it can be seen that the

LightGBM algorithm has the best detection performance, followed by the Random Forest algorithm, and the Logistic Regression and SVC algorithms are less effective. This proves the effectiveness of the LightGBM algorithm on the phishing detection.

Table 3. Comparison of different classification methods.

Method	AUC	Precision	Recall	F1-score
Logistic Regression	0.831	0.769	0.828	0.797
SVC	0.819	0.750	0.818	0.782
Random Forest	0.864	0.771	0.906	0.833
LightGBM	**0.879**	**0.796**	**0.914**	**0.851**

5 Conclusion

In this paper, we extract graph structure features of transaction accounts and transaction sequence features based on Ethereum transaction data and propose the GSTSF method that fuses the two features. First, we collect transaction data from the Ethereum website and construct a transaction network graph. Then, feature extraction is performed based on the constructed transaction network graph. On the one hand, the graph structure features of the nodes are extracted using the Node2vec algorithm based on random walk. On the other hand, the transaction sequence features of the nodes are extracted using the LSTM algorithm and weighted average. Finally, the two types of features are fused by linear combination, and the fused features are input to the machine learning algorithm for node classification. In the experimental process, parameter selection experiments are first performed to determine the optimal parameters, and then the GSTSF method is evaluated by several comparison experiments. The final experimental results show that the detection performance of the GSTSF method has been improved compared with the existing methods, and the AUC value reaches 0.879. The proposed method is a direct linear combination of two types of features, and finding a better fusion method will be the next work.

References

1. Wei, S.J., Lv, W.L., Li, S.S.: Survey on typical security issues of blockchain public chain applications. J. Softw. **33**(01), 324–355 (2022)
2. Trozze, A., Kamps, J., Akartuna, E.A., et al.: Cryptocurrencies and future financial crime. Crime Sci. **11**, 1–35 (2022)
3. Zhang, Y., Yu, W., Li, Z., et al.: Detecting Ethereum Ponzi schemes based on improved LightGBM algorithm. IEEE Trans. Comput. Soc. Syst. **9**(2), 624–637 (2021)
4. Chen, W., Guo, X., Chen, Z., et al.: Phishing scam detection on Ethereum: towards financial security for blockchain ecosystem. In: IJCAI, pp. 4506–4512 (2020)

5. Wen, H., Fang, J., Wu, J., et al.: Transaction-based hidden strategies against general phishing detection framework on Ethereum. In: 2021 IEEE International Symposium on Circuits and Systems (ISCAS), pp. 1–5. IEEE (2021)
6. Kabla, A.H.H., Anbar, M., Manickam, S., et al.: Eth-PSD: a machine learning-based phishing scam detection approach in Ethereum. IEEE Access **10**, 118043–118057 (2022)
7. Yuan, Z., Yuan, Q., Wu, J.: Phishing detection on Ethereum via learning representation of transaction subgraphs. In: Zheng, Z., Dai, H.-N., Fu, X., Chen, B. (eds.) BlockSys 2020. CCIS, vol. 1267, pp. 178–191. Springer, Singapore (2020). https://doi.org/10.1007/978-981-15-9213-3_14
8. Xia, Y., Liu, J., Wu, J.: Phishing detection on Ethereum via attributed ego-graph embedding. IEEE Trans. Circuits Syst. II Express Briefs **69**(5), 2538–2542 (2022)
9. Wang, J., Chen, P., Xu, X., et al.: TSGN: transaction subgraph networks assisting phishing detection in Ethereum. arXiv preprint arXiv:2208.12938 (2022)
10. Chen, L., Peng, J., Liu, Y., et al.: Phishing scams detection in Ethereum transaction network. ACM Trans. Internet Technol. (TOIT) **21**(1), 1–16 (2020)
11. Yu, T., Chen, X., Xu, Z., et al.: MP-GCN: a phishing nodes detection approach via graph convolution network for Ethereum. Appl. Sci. **12**(14), 7294 (2022)
12. Li, S., Xu, F., Wang, R., et al.: Self-supervised incremental deep graph learning for Ethereum phishing scam detection. arXiv preprint arXiv:2106.10176 (2021)
13. Li, S., Gou, G., Liu, C., et al.: TTAGN: temporal transaction aggregation graph network for Ethereum phishing scams detection. In: Proceedings of the ACM Web Conference 2022, pp. 661–669 (2022)
14. Wen, T., Xiao, Y., Wang, A., et al.: A novel hybrid feature fusion model for detecting phishing scam on Ethereum using deep neural network. Expert Syst. Appl. **211**, 118463 (2023)
15. Wu, J., Yuan, Q., Lin, D., et al.: Who are the phishers? Phishing scam detection on Ethereum via network embedding. IEEE Trans. Syst. Man Cybern. Syst. **52**(2), 1156–1166 (2020)
16. Li, R., Liu, Z., Ma, Y., et al.: Internet financial fraud detection based on graph learning. IEEE Trans. Comput. Soc. Syst. **10**(3), 1394–1401 (2022)
17. Yu, J., De Antonio, A., Villalba-Mora, E.: Deep learning (CNN, RNN) applications for smart homes: a systematic review. Computers **11**(2), 26 (2022)
18. Cheng, J., Dong, L., Lapata, M.: Long short-term memory-networks for machine reading. arXiv preprint arXiv:1601.06733 (2016)
19. Fang, Y., Long, X., Huang, C., Liu, L.: Research on phishing website recognition based on LSTM and random forest hybrid framework. Eng. Sci. Technol. **50**(05), 196–201 (2018)
20. Ozcan, A., Catal, C., Donmez, E., et al.: A hybrid DNN–LSTM model for detecting phishing URLs. Neural Comput. Appl. **35**(7), 4957–4973 (2023)
21. Xuan, Y.L., Wan, Y., Chen, J.H.: LSTM time series classification based on multi-scale convolution and attention mechanism. Comput. Appl. **42**(08), 2343–2352 (2022)
22. Lin, D., Wu, J., Yuan, Q., et al.: T-EDGE: temporal weighted multidigraph embedding for Ethereum transaction network analysis. Front. Phys. **8**, 204 (2020)
23. Perozzi, B., Al-Rfou, R., Skiena, S.: Deepwalk: online learning of social representation. In: Proceedings of the 20th ACM SIGKDD International Conference on Knowledge Discovery and Data Mining, pp. 701–710 (2014)

24. Ribeiro, L.F.R., Saverese, P.H.P., Figueiredo, D.R.: struc2vec: learning node representation from structural identity. In: Proceedings of the 23rd ACM SIGKDD International Conference on Knowledge Discovery and Data Mining, pp. 385–394 (2017)
25. Peng, H., Zhang, R., Dou, Y., et al.: Reinforced neighborhood selection guided multi-relational graph neural networks. ACM Trans. Inf. Syst. (TOIS) **40**(4), 1–46 (2021)

Performance Curve Profiling and Gated Recurrent Unit Based State Detection for Cloud Native Microservices

Xu Jiang and Zhicheng Cai(✉)

Nanjing University of Science and Technology, Nanjing 210094, China
caizhicheng@njust.edu.cn

Abstract. Cloud-native technologies have been widely adopted by practitioners and companies with various needs to ensure quality of service by deploying cloud-native applications in cloud servers and using resource auto-scaling techniques to meet changing demands. Although resource auto-scaling techniques in cloud platforms usually maintain the stability of microservices, sometimes they still fail. In this paper, a hybrid performance curve profiling and gated recurrent unit based state detection method (PGS) is developed for identifying the states for cloud-native microservices and provide a basis for resource auto-scaling. Because the microservice states arenot able to identified from transient performance indicators, a performance curve profiling method (PCP) is proposed in PGS to assist identifying microservice states from a global perspective. For constantly changing microservice states, a gated recurrent unit based state detection method (GSD) is proposed to improve the accuracy of states recognition. GSD divides microservice states into three categories based on the slope of the performance curve. The experimental results show that PGS achieves an accuracy of 96.09% for microservice state detection by PCP assisting GSD to judge from a global perspective, which is higher than other methods.

Keywords: Cloud native · State detection · Kubernetes · GRU

1 Introduction

Cloud native technologies, including microservices, containers, and service grids, are gradually being used to develop applications to take full advantage of the features of the cloud [1–3]. These cloud native applications are deployed as microservices on the cloud platform and rely on the cloud platform's auto-scaling engine, scheduler and cloud resource provisioning software to achieve elastic expansion of resources. Resource elasticity scaling based on cloud native technology maintains stability of service quality by increasing or reducing the number of VMs, but does not provide a specific microservice states [4–12]. When resource allocation errors occur, manual adjustments cannot be made. Service states are the important indicators of cloud service resources, which determine the timing

Z. Wang et al. (Eds.): ICSS 2023, CCIS 1844, pp. 263–275, 2023.
https://doi.org/10.1007/978-981-99-4402-6_19

of auto-scaling. Accurate state detection of cloud microservices is beneficial to improve performance and reduce resource costs by allocating reasonable amount of resources.

Due to the microservices performance indicators are transient, it is difficult to judge the states. Many open source platforms have state detection mechanisms that use performance threshold at a single moment to detect states. Threshold-based methods rely entirely on metrics at that moment, such as CPU utilisation, Memory utilisation, etc. and does not take into account resource changes over time [13]. This includes state detection methods used by VM-based commercial cloud providers such as Microsoft Azure and Amazon EC2, as well as open source container orchestrators such as Kubernetes and OpenShift Origin [14–16]. Although threshold-based state detection methods can identify the states of a single moment, competition among resources and different thresholds for different microservices in real platforms can affect the accuracy of state detection.

The classification of microservice states is a key point in state detection. Microervice states can be divided into three categories: resource scarcity, resource adequacy, and resource waste. The HPA in Kubernetes defines the states of microservices by setting CPU thresholds or memory thresholds [17], but thresholds are typically user specified configurations. In the absence of professional knowledge, these configurations are often not optimal, which make threshold-based state detection methods less accurate. At the same time, HPA adjusts the amount of resources through sliding windows, which has a certain lag. Although SLAs are met and service quality is guaranteed, this increases the cost for cloud providers [18].

In this paper, a hybrid performance curve profiling and gated recurrent unit based state detection method is proposed to identify microservices states from a global perspective. The main contributions are: (1) For transient performance indicators, a performance curve profiling method (PCP) is designed in PGS to describe the overall change process of microservice performance indicators. It is necessary to identify the states of microservices from a global perspective. (2) For microservice state recognition, a gated recurrent unit based state detection method (GSD) is designed in PGS to improve the accuracy of state recognition. Combine transient performance indicators and performance curves to more accurately identify the states of microservices.

The rest of this work is organized as follows: Sect. 2 discuss related work. The problems are described in Sect. 3. Section 4 introduces PGS and Sect. 5 shows experimental results. Conclusions and future work are depicted in Sect. 6.

2 Related Work

Resource auto-scaling is a technique for scaling the number of resources in cloud environment based on demand and performance. It allows cloud service providers or subscribers to utilise resources more efficiently, save costs and improve availability and resilience. Data-based auto-scaling refers to the decision to increase or decrease resources based on real-time monitoring data, such as CPU utilisation, memory utilisation, network traffic, etc. Different cloud service providers have different approaches to resource auto-scaling. For example, Amazon Elastic Compute Cloud (EC2) can add or remove instances through auto-scaling groups, Microsoft Azure can control scaling through virtual machine scale sets and Google Cloud Platform can auto-scale in its Compute Engine.

State detection is one of important foundation for auto-scaling of cloud-native microservices, the microservice states determine the timing of resource auto-scaling. Traditional state detection algorithms are used in many fields of daily life [19], including anti-fraud detection and unusual transaction detection in the financial industry, as well as rare disease detection in medicine, such as early-onset Alzheimer's disease, chronic stroke, and cancer [20,21]. Traditional state detection algorithms are primarily data-driven methods used to identify data that is different from other data in the dataset, including clustering algorithms [22], reconstruction algorithms [23], and multi-classifiers [24]. However, when faced with high-volume and high-speed data, traditional state detection algorithms cannot maintain sufficient accuracy [25].

Deep learning-based state detection algorithms are constantly evolving. Compared to traditional state detection techniques, Deep neural networks can perform fast, automated and intelligent analysis and judgement of large amounts of data, saving manpower. At the same time, the deep neural networks can adapt to different scenario requirements through continuous learning and optimisation to improve the flexibility and robustness of detection. Models based on Recurrent Neural Network (RNN), Long Short-Term Memory (LSTM) Network and other neural networks are widely used. Montanari et al. [26] combine rule-based state machines and RNN to improve state detection accuracy through state machines. Sadasivuni et al. [27] use bidirectional LSTM to learn long-term time dependence, reducing the consumption of traditional state detection. Zhang et al. [28] combined CapsNet and RNN to enhance the part-whole relationship.

The most common approach to state detection in open source platforms is the threshold-based approach, where a certain performance threshold is set for a microservice to determine its state, monitoring the health of microservices [29, 30]. However, the threshold-based approach in open source platforms does not provide detailed identification of the states, while a single moment threshold cannot take into account resource changes over time. In contrast, PGS combines the performance curve of microservices with the resource situation at a given moment and divides the states categories according to the gradient of the curve to detect the states from a global perspective.

3 Problem Description

Cloud service providers typically offer a variety of different services, which are divided into microservices with different functions and collaborate through RESTful APIs to form a mashed service system. This system usually provides several different types of services with different access sequences (access paths). Considering the trade-off between cost and user experience, a divide and conquer strategy is adopted to determine the overall SLA for each service type by setting a fixed sub-SLA for each microservice. Since VM are usually paid for in small intervals (such as seconds or minutes), assigning resources separately for each level helps to expand the resources available based on real-time requests for each level. State detection is an important basis for resource scaling, and the resource auto-scaling algorithms scale resources based on the state of each level to ensure the service quality.

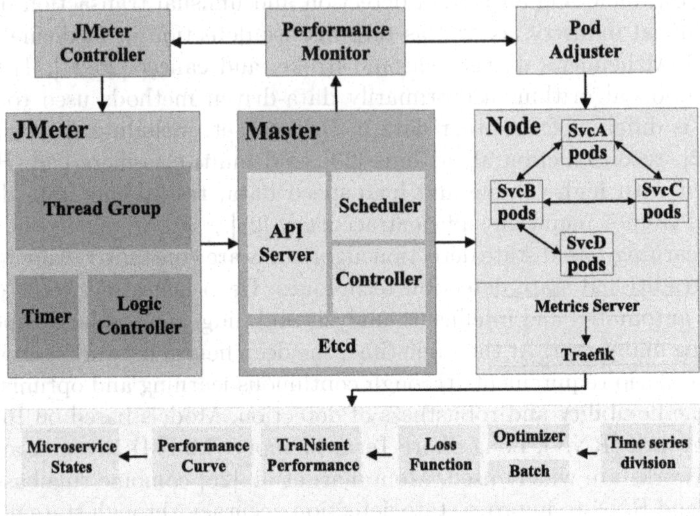

Fig. 1. A Kubernetes-based testing platform

The goal is to design a cloud-native microservice state detection algorithm in this paper which can detect the runtime states of various layers of microservices and provide a basis for resource auto-scaling, making it more accurate. The deep learning model training requires collecting performance change curves from multiple cloud-native microservices ranging from resource scarcity to resource abundance. Considering that applications are deployed as services on cloud platforms, consisting of multiple microservices, a Kubernetes-based testing platform is designed. A containerized network application based on Spring Boot is deployed on the testing platform, consisting of multiple microservices forming a directed acyclic graph (DAG). Adjust the entire platform through performance monitor, and detect performance indicators through a deep learning model to identify microservice states (see Fig. 1).

4 Proposed State Detection Method

In cloud platforms, resources are scaled based on transient performance indicators, but no specific microservice states are given, and transient performance indicators cannot be used to identify the states. Therefore, a performance curve profiling method (PCP) has been developed to consider the states of microservices from a global perspective. In order to identify the microservice states, a gated recursive unit based state detection method (GSD) is developed. The hybrid of PCP and GSD is called performance curve profiling and gated recurrent unit based state detection method (PGS).

4.1 Performance Curve Profiling

Performance curve profiling considers performance indicators from a global perspective to solve the problems of transient microservice performance indicators that cannot identify states. The deployed microservices are subjected to stress testing by sending HTTP requests through the tool JMeter. The number of HTTP requests req_{num} increase monotonously, and the log collection tool Traefik collects log information according to the scheduling cycle s_c and calculates the average response time $\overline{rep}$. Use the performance monitor to judge the collected information, adjust the amount of resources when the critical point c_p is true, and restart the stress test.

$$c_p = \begin{cases} True & \overline{rep} \geq rep_{cp},\ \widetilde{a_r} \geq \alpha \times p_{num},\ s_c \geq s_{cp} \\ False & other \end{cases} \tag{1}$$

where rep_{cp} is the response time threshold. $\widetilde{a_r}$ is the arrival rate, α is the processing capacity of a single pod and p_{num} is the number of pods. s_{cp} is the scheduling cycle threshold.

Algorithm 1: Performance Curve Profiling(PCP)

Initialize p_{num}, s_{cp}
while *True* **do**
    Initialize s_c, req_{num}, c_p
    while c_p *is False* **do**
        Send requests
        Collect performance indicators
        if $\overline{rep} \geq rep_{cp},\ \widetilde{a_r} \geq \alpha \times p_{num},\ s_c \geq s_{cp}$ **then**
            $cp \longleftarrow True$
        end
        Increase the number of requests req_{num}
    end
    Increase pods number p_{num}
end

Algorithm 1 is the formal description of the proposed PCP. When c_p is False, initialize req_{num}, and send requests to the test platform. Collect performance indicators through the Traefik. After a certain period of time, increase req_{num}. When c_p is True, stop sending Http requests, increase p_{num}, initialize s_c and req_{num}. Perform the stress test again.

4.2 Gated Recurrent Unit Based State Detection

The states detection algorithms in open source platforms are part of threshold-based auto-scaling methods, and do not provide specific microservice states. Therefore, a gated recurrent unit based state detection method (GSD) is proposed to detect the microservice states which based on the performance curves collected before the microservices formally runs to improve accuracy.

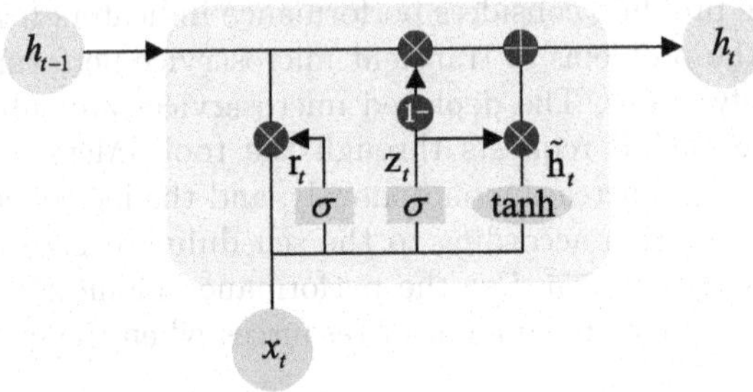

Fig. 2. A neural unit of GRU

Figure 2 shows one of the neural unit structures of the gated recurrent unit (GRU). As shown, the reset gate r_t and update gate z_t are the two most important structures and together determine the output of the neural unit.

$$z_t = \sigma(W_z x_t + U_z h_{t-1}) \tag{2}$$

$$r_t = \sigma(W_r x_t + U_r h_{t-1}) \tag{3}$$

where x_t is the input vector at the current moment, h_{t-1} is the output vector at the previous moment, W, U are the weight matrix, σ is the sigmoid function. z_t controls the degree of updating of the input information at the current moment, r_t controls the degree of forgetting of the input information at the current moment.

$$\tilde{h}_t = tanh(W_h x_t + U_h(r_t \circ h_{t-1})) \tag{4}$$

$$h_t = (1 - z_t) \circ h_{t-1} + z_t \circ \tilde{h}_t \tag{5}$$

where $tanh$ is the tangent function and $\circ$ denotes the element-by-element multiplication operation. $\tilde{h}_t$ is the candidate memory cell at the current moment, obtained by forgetting the contents of h_{t-1} with r_t and then splicing it with x_t. h_t is the memory cell and the output of the current moment, obtained by forgetting the contents of h_{t-1} by $1 - z_t$ and saving the contents of $\tilde{h}_t$ by z_t.

Algorithm 2 is the formal description of the proposed GSD. The performance curve as dataset and cut into sequences $D = [d_1, d_2, ..., d_n]$. The D is divided into different batches B and trained by the z_t and r_t. Finally the classification is performed through the fully connected layer. In the test, the performance curve C of the microservices under test needs to be collected first, mainly using the average response time from the performance curve. Find the time series corresponding to the average response time $\bar{R}_t$ at the current moment in C, splicing the two together to obtain a new time series $\hat{S}_t$ and use it as input to the model to get the states of microservices s_t.

Algorithm 2: Gated Recurrent Unit based State Detection (GSD)

Input: $D, \bar{R}_t$
Output: s_t

Initialize $W_r, W_z, W_h, U_r, U_z, U_h$
for *episode* $= 1, N$ **do**
    Get sequence d_1 from D
    for $b = 1, B$ **do**
        for $t = 1, T$ **do**
            Splice matrix from $d_{i,t}$ and h_{t-1}
            Calculate r_t, z_t
            Non-linear calculate $\sigma(z_t)$ and $\sigma(r_t)$
            Forget memory and get $\tilde{h}_t$ from r_t, d_{i_t} and h_{t-1}
            Get output h_t from z_t, h_{t-1} and $\tilde{h}_t$
        end
    end
    Calculate loss and optimize result
end
Collected performace(average respose time) curve C
Get time series $\hat{S}_t$ from $C[\bar{R}_t]$
Detect s_t from $model(\hat{S}_t)$
return s_t

5 Results and Analysis

In open source platforms, the existing methods are to directly adjust resources, without defining and identifying the microservice states. During the resource adjustment process, the microservice states will not be given. Therefore, PGS is compared with the same type of RNN and LSTM.

The experiments are performed on a platform built on Kubernetes [31]. The resources of each microservice are composed of pods. The Kubernetes cluster is deployed on four physical nodes, including one master node and three worker nodes. The configuration of physical machine is as Table 1.

To obtain the performance curve profile, the deployed microservices are stress tested by loading the testing tool JMeter, which sends 6 requests per second, increasing by 5 requests every 30 s to a maximum of 150 requests per second, and using the deployed log collection tool Traefik to collect log information in a 15 s scheduling cycle. Each uniform resource locator (URL) in Traefik is treated as a request and the response times for all requests in a scheduling

Table 1. The configuration of physical machine

machine	CPU (core)	Memory (G)
Master	4	4
node1	15	20
node2	48	33
node3	40	30

cycle are summed and averaged, with the average response time stored in json format. Each microservice has a manager which can manage multiple pods, each containing 1 core of CPU and 521M of memory, with an initial number of 2 pods and a maximum of 24 pods. When the average response time of the microservice exceeds 1s, the request arrival rate is greater than 5 times the number of pods and the scheduling cycle exceeds 10, increase the number of pods, initialise the scheduling cycle and restart JMeter for stress testing.

For model training, the collected dataset is divided into two parts: the training dataset and the testing dataset, with 60% of the dataset allocated to the training dataset and the remaining 40% allocated to the testing dataset. During data preprocessing, the average response time of the microservices are normalized, adjusting the numerical values to between 0 and 1.

The parameters of the GSD model are as follows. For the input layer, a dense layer of 30 cells is used. The first hidden layer contains 64 units, the second hidden layer contains 32 units and another dense layer is added to the output layer. Softmax and Cross Entropy are used as activation and loss functions. Batch size is set to 10. The learning rate is initially set to 0.1 and MultiStepLR is used to adjust the learning rate to 0.1 times the previous value at epochs of 10, 50 and 80. The Adam function was used as the optimiser. In addition, a dropout layer of 0.3 was added to reduce overfitting. Finally, the model was trained for 100 epochs.

Table 2. The confusion matrix

	Positive	Negative
Positive	TP	FN
Negative	FP	TN

There are several ways to measure the strengths and weaknesses of a deep neural network model such as accuracy, precision, recall and F1-score. The confusion matrix can assist in the calculation of accuracy, precision, recall and F1-score (see Table 2). Where TP is the number of positive samples successfully determined as positive, TN is the number of negative samples successfully determined as negative, FP is the number of negative samples incorrectly determined as positive, and FN is the number of positive samples incorrectly determined as negative.

The formulae for Accuracy, Precision, Recall and F1-score are as follows:

$$Accuracy = \frac{TP + TN}{TP + TN + FP + FN} \tag{6}$$

$$Precision = \frac{TP}{TP + FP} \tag{7}$$

$$Recall = \frac{TP}{TP + FN} \tag{8}$$

$$F1\text{-}score = \frac{2 * Precision * Recall}{Precision + Recall} \tag{9}$$

Accuracy is a measure of the overall quality of the algorithm model, high accuracy means high quality. However, in the case of unbalanced samples, accuracy will fail, so F1-score is needed to assist in validation. F1-score takes into account precision and recall to evaluate a model comprehensively. The larger the F1-score, the higher the quality of the model.

5.1 Experimental Results

Figure 3, Fig. 4 show the variation curves of accuracy, precision, recall and F1-score for RNN, LSTM and PGS. The fluctuation of curves of the three algorithms are dramatic when Epoch is in the interval (0,10), which is due to the initial value of the learning rate is set to 0.1, causing the model to ignore what is learned directly at one stage for the next stage. In the interval [10,50), the fluctuations of curves of the three algorithms decreased as the learning rate was updated, but still failed to converge. In the interval [50,80), the learning rate is updated again and the results of the algorithms hover around the optimal value. When the epoch reaches 80, the learning rate is updated to 0.0001 and the curves of the three algorithms gradually converge with the best results.

Based on Fig. 3 and Fig. 4, it can be observed that the LSTM and PGS gradually converge before the learning rate reaches 0.0001, while the RNN continues to suffer from large fluctuations due to gradient explosion and gradient disappearance. Table 3 shows the final results of the three algorithms. The precision of PGS is 0.27% lower than RNN, which means that PGS is more likely to incorrectly identify the states of microservices. However, the recall of PGS were 0.76% and 0.38% higher than RNN and LSTM respectively, indicating that RNN and LSTM are more likely to miss some results during microservice states identification compared to PGS. The accuracy and F1-scores of PGS were 96.09% and 95.66% respectively, outperforming RNN and LSTM, which means that in terms of overall performance, the model quality of PGS is higher than RNN and LSTM.

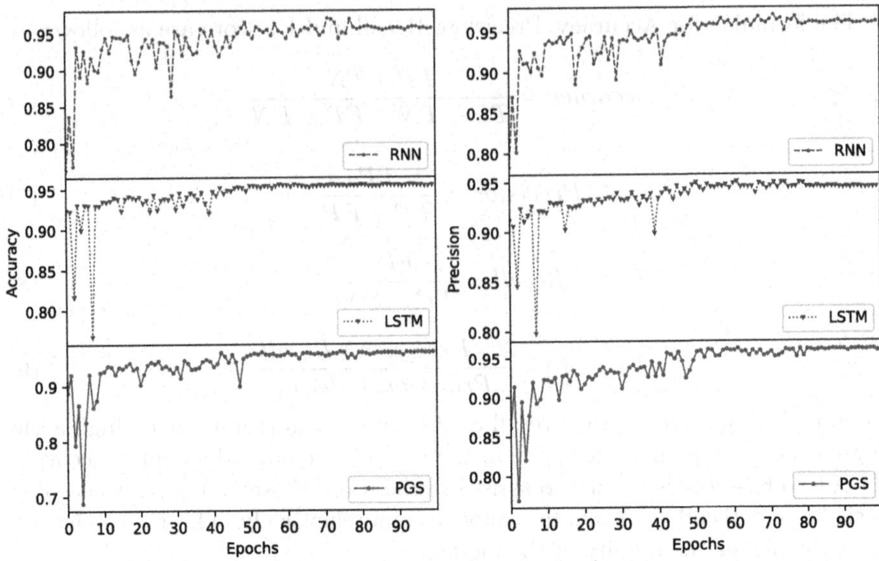

Fig. 3. (a) is the comparison chart of accuracy among three algorithms, and (b) is the comparison chart of precision among three algorithms.

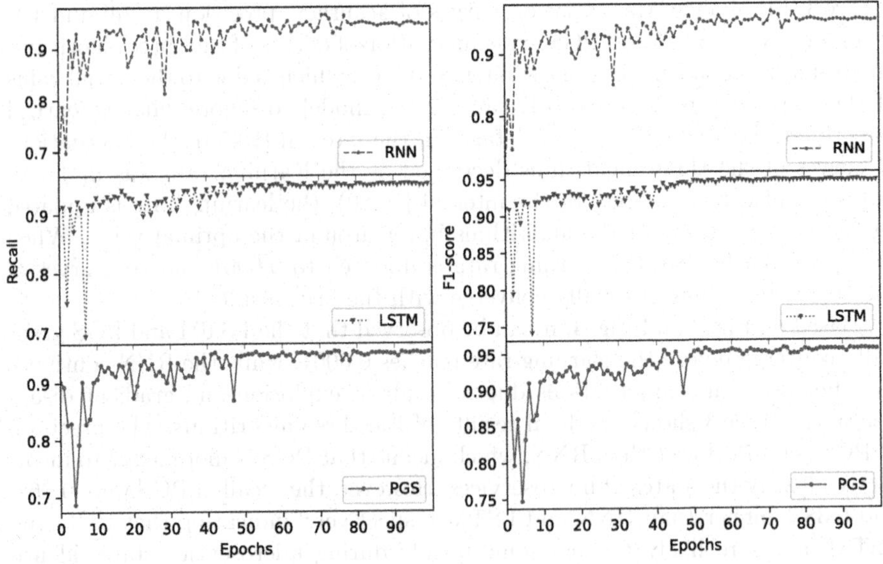

Fig. 4. (a) is the comparison chart of recall among three algorithms, and (b) is the comparison chart of F1-score among three algorithms.

Table 3. The evaluation results of algorithms

algorithms	accuracy (%)	precision (%)	recall (%)	F1-score (%)
RNN	95.62	96.18	94.65	95.41
LSTM	95.46	94.5	95.03	94.76
PGS	96.09	95.91	95.41	95.66

6 Conclusion

In this paper, a microservice state detection method PGS is proposed to identify state from a global perspective in order to improve the effectiveness of state detection. Experimental results show that performance curve profiling can improve the global perspective and the gated recurrent units can provide identification of the states of microservices. Compared to other algorithms, PGS can provide more accurate microservice state identification, providing a basis for auto-scaling. At the same time, PGS can also provide a basis for human intervention when auto-scaling methods fail. The development of predictive cloud-native microservices state models to overcome the shortcomings of reactive approaches is promising future work.

Acknowledgements. This work is supported by the National Natural Science Foundation of China (Grant No. 61972202, 61973161, 61991404), the Fundamental Research Funds for the Central Universities (No. 30919011235).

References

1. Qian, L., Luo, Z., Du, Y., Guo, L.: Cloud computing: an overview. In: Jaatun, M.G., Zhao, G., Rong, C. (eds.) CloudCom 2009. LNCS, vol. 5931, pp. 626–631. Springer, Heidelberg (2009). https://doi.org/10.1007/978-3-642-10665-1_63
2. Kapil, D., Tyagi, P., Kumar, S., Tamta, V.P.: Cloud computing: overview and research issues. In: 2017 International Conference on Green Informatics (ICGI), pp. 71–76. IEEE (2017)
3. Abdelbaky, M., Diaz-Montes, J., Parashar, M., Unuvar, M., Steinder, M.: Docker containers across multiple clouds and data centers. In: 2015 IEEE/ACM 8th International Conference on Utility and Cloud Computing (UCC), pp. 368–371. IEEE (2015)
4. Taherizadeh, S., Jones, A.C., Taylor, I., Zhao, Z., Stankovski, V.: Monitoring self-adaptive applications within edge computing frameworks: a state-of-the-art review. J. Syst. Softw. **136**, 19–38 (2018)
5. Al-Sharif, Z.A., Jararweh, Y., Al-Dahoud, A., Alawneh, L.M.: ACCRS: autonomic based cloud computing resource scaling. Clust. Comput. **20**, 2479–2488 (2017)
6. Islam, S., Keung, J., Lee, K., Liu, A.: Empirical prediction models for adaptive resource provisioning in the cloud. Futur. Gener. Comput. Syst. **28**(1), 155–162 (2012)
7. Jamshidi, P., Sharifloo, A.M., Pahl, C., Metzger, A., Estrada, G.: Self-learning cloud controllers: fuzzy q-learning for knowledge evolution. In: 2015 International Conference on Cloud and Autonomic Computing, pp. 208–211. IEEE (2015)

8. Arabnejad, H., Pahl, C., Jamshidi, P., Estrada, G.: A comparison of reinforcement learning techniques for fuzzy cloud auto-scaling. In: 2017 17th IEEE/ACM International Symposium on Cluster, Cloud and Grid Computing (CCGRID), pp. 64–73. IEEE (2017)
9. Tsoumakos, D., Konstantinou, I., Boumpouka, C., Sioutas, S., Koziris, N.: Automated, elastic resource provisioning for NoSQL clusters using tiramola. In: 2013 13th IEEE/ACM International Symposium on Cluster, Cloud, and Grid Computing, pp. 34–41. IEEE (2013)
10. Khaleq, A.A., Ra, I.: Intelligent autoscaling of microservices in the cloud for real-time applications. IEEE Access **9**, 35464–35476 (2021)
11. Baresi, L., Guinea, S., Leva, A., Quattrocchi, G.: A discrete-time feedback controller for containerized cloud applications. In: Proceedings of the 2016 24th ACM SIGSOFT International Symposium on Foundations of Software Engineering. pp. 217–228 (2016)
12. Zhao, H., et al.: Cloud-cluster hierarchical dispatch for large scale demand-side distributed resources. In: 2021 IEEE 5th Conference on Energy Internet and Energy System Integration (EI2), pp. 272–276. IEEE (2021)
13. Tseng, F.H., Tsai, M.S., Tseng, C.W., Yang, Y.T., Liu, C.C., Chou, L.D.: A lightweight autoscaling mechanism for fog computing in industrial applications. IEEE Trans. Ind. Inf. **14**(10), 4529–4537 (2018)
14. Lee, H., Satyam, K., Fox, G.: Evaluation of production serverless computing environments. In: 2018 IEEE 11th International Conference on Cloud Computing (CLOUD), pp. 442–450. IEEE (2018)
15. Lloyd, W., Ramesh, S., Chinthalapati, S., Ly, L., Pallickara, S.: Serverless computing: an investigation of factors influencing microservice performance. In: 2018 IEEE International Conference on Cloud Engineering (IC2E), pp. 159–169. IEEE (2018)
16. Wang, L., Li, M., Zhang, Y., Ristenpart, T., Swift, M.: Peeking behind the curtains of serverless platforms. In: 2018 {USENIX} Annual Technical Conference ({USENIX}{ATC} 18), pp. 133–146 (2018)
17. Nguyen, T.T., Yeom, Y.J., Kim, T., Park, D.H., Kim, S.: Horizontal pod autoscaling in Kubernetes for elastic container orchestration. Sensors **20**(16), 4621 (2020)
18. Li, M., Su, J., Liu, H., Zhao, Z., Ouyang, X., Zhou, H.: The extreme counts: modeling the performance uncertainty of cloud resources with extreme value theory. In: Troya, J., Medjahed, B., Piattini, M., Yao, L., Fernández, P., Ruiz-Cortés, A. (eds.) ICSOC 2022. LNCS, vol. 13740, pp. 498–512. Springer, Cham (2022). https://doi.org/10.1007/978-3-031-20984-0_35
19. Feng, Q., Li, H., Zhou, Y., Feng, D., Wang, Y., Su, Y.: Review of electric vehicles' charging data anomaly detection based on deep learning. In: 2022 Power System and Green Energy Conference (PSGEC), pp. 337–341. IEEE (2022)
20. Hilal, W., Gadsden, S.A., Yawney, J.: A review of anomaly detection techniques and applications in financial fraud. Expert Syst. Appl. **193**, 116429 (2021)
21. Alvi, A.M., Siuly, S., Wang, H.: Neurological abnormality detection from electroencephalography data: a review. Artif. Intell. Rev. **55**(3), 2275–2312 (2022)
22. Bolzoni, D., Etalle, S., Hartel, P.H.: Panacea: automating attack classification for anomaly-based network intrusion detection systems. In: RAID. vol. 9, pp. 1–20 (2009)

23. Bovenzi, A., Brancati, F., Russo, S., Bondavalli, A.: A statistical anomaly-based algorithm for on-line fault detection in complex software critical systems. In: Flammini, F., Bologna, S., Vittorini, V. (eds.) SAFECOMP 2011. LNCS, vol. 6894, pp. 128–142. Springer, Heidelberg (2011). https://doi.org/10.1007/978-3-642-24270-0_10
24. Thudumu, S., Branch, P., Jin, J., Singh, J.J.: A comprehensive survey of anomaly detection techniques for high dimensional big data. J. Big Data **7**(1), 1–30 (2020). https://doi.org/10.1186/s40537-020-00320-x
25. Yin, N., Zhang, L.: Research on application of outlier mining based on hybrid clustering algorithm in anomaly detection. Comput. Sci. **44**(5), 116–119 (2018)
26. Montanari, F., Ren, H., Djanatliev, A.: Scenario detection in unlabeled real driving data with a rule-based state machine supported by a recurrent neural network. In: 2021 IEEE 93rd Vehicular Technology Conference (VTC2021-Spring), pp. 1–5 (2021). https://doi.org/10.1109/VTC2021-Spring51267.2021.9449032
27. Sadasivuni, S., Chowdhury, R., Karnam, V.E.G., Banerjee, I., Sanyal, A.: Recurrent neural network circuit for automated detection of atrial fibrillation from raw ECG. In: 2021 IEEE International Symposium on Circuits and Systems (ISCAS), pp. 1–5 (2021). https://doi.org/10.1109/ISCAS51556.2021.9401666
28. Zhang, L., et al.: Polyphonic sound event detection based on CapsNet-RNN and post processing optimization. In: 2020 7th International Conference on Information Science and Control Engineering (ICISCE), pp. 1015–1020 (2020). https://doi.org/10.1109/ICISCE50968.2020.00208
29. Balla, D., Maliosz, M., Simon, C.: Towards a predictable open source FaaS. In: NOMS 2022–2022 IEEE/IFIP Network Operations and Management Symposium, pp. 1–5. IEEE (2022)
30. Zhang, X., Li, L., Wang, Y., Chen, E., Shou, L.: Zeus: improving resource efficiency via workload colocation for massive Kubernetes clusters. IEEE Access **9**, 105192–105204 (2021)
31. Bernstein, D.: Containers and cloud: from LXC to docker to Kubernetes. IEEE Cloud Comput. **1**(3), 81–84 (2014). https://doi.org/10.1109/MCC.2014.51

Knowledge-Inspired Service

Stock Market Prediction Based on BERT Embedding and News Sentiment Analysis

Hanlin Yang, Chunyang Ye(✉), Xiaoyu Lin, and Hui Zhou

School of Computer Science and Technology, Hainan University, Haikou, China
{hanlinyang,cyye,linxy,huizhou}@hainanu.edu.cn

Abstract. Stock market trend forecasting has attracted significant interest from investors and researchers. However, due to the high volatility of the stock market and its sensitivity to news events, it is difficult to accurately predict the market trends. Existing studies have confirmed that news events have a great impact on the stock market. However, previous studies focus on the news events only, and lack the exploration of its inner emotional meaning, which is also important to the prediction of stock market trend. To address this issue, we propose a novel method, BERTNSF, to predict the stock market trend concerning both the news information and its inner emotional meaning. By using the pre-trained model BERT as a news text feature extraction tool, BERTNSF can extract the feature of news headlines effectively. BERTNSF also extracts the inner emotional meaning of the textual content in the news articles, and represents them as sentiment vectors. These features are combined with historical prices and technical indicators to predict the stock market trend. We conduct extensive experiments on real-world data to evaluate our proposal. The experimental results show that our method greatly improves the accuracy of stock market trend prediction.

Keywords: Stock movement prediction · Natural language processing · Data mining · Feature fusion

1 Introduction

The stock market broadly implicates a lot of complex financial lore and can be seen as an organic combination of investing, trading and other financial activities. It is the barometer of a country or region's economic and financial activities. The stock market is changing all the time, and it is easily affected by many factors such as the expectations of investors and investment institutions, news media reports, market dynamics and other factors. Therefore, the stock market trend is usually non-linear, volatile and unstable. Since the stock market is susceptible to many events, how to effectively combine influencing factors and make reliable predictions based on them is an interesting yet challenging task.

Nowadays, more and more news articles are published on the Internet, and investors' investment preferences are guided by the emotional polarity in the

Z. Wang et al. (Eds.): ICSS 2023, CCIS 1844, pp. 279–291, 2023.
https://doi.org/10.1007/978-981-99-4402-6_20

articles. [1] have demonstrated the effectiveness of public sentiment in forecasting stock market trends. Although market information is considered to be infinite and growing in practice, it is worth studying how to integrate as many data as possible effectively and make reliable forecasts. Previous studies mainly focused on one single information source. For example, [2] used the Harvard IV-4 dictionary to process reports from The Wall Street Journal, and extracted and quantified the optimistic and pessimistic dimensions of the report after the report was published to help analyze the relationship between trading volume and price trends. [3] analyzed the word frequency of intraday news to quantitatively estimate and predict the short-term stock price. [4] showed that using event embeddings to represent structured events can achieve better performance than the word features of the above methods because they can capture structured relations. On the other hand, [5] incorporated external information from knowledge graphs into the learning process to generate better event representations. [6] used TextCNN neural network to extract text features and integrate other external features to predict main indices of China's stock market, and achieved a certain improvement in the prediction performance. However, the emotional expressions in news content are ignored in above studies.

To address these issues, we propose a novel model, BERTNSF, to predict the stock market trend based on multi source of stock market information, including the news headline text features, the sentiment of the news contents, and the historical prices. The mian challenges lie in how to effectively extract useful information from financial news and how to fuse news-related features and historical price series features to predict the stock market trends. To address these challenges, we first use the pre-trained BERT model to generate a contextual embedding expression with a higher accuracy for major financial news in the stock market. We then analyze the sentiment expressions in financial news articles using a sentiment dictionary, and construct the sentiment representation of the news vector. Next, we design a bidirectional long short-term memory (Bi-LSTM) neural network to fuse text features, encode the contextual dependencies of different features, and learn the sequence information of news text embedding expressions and news sentiments. We also design a LSTM model to extract the features from the historical stock prices and technical indicators commonly used in financial markets. The features of the two networks are fused with the attention mechanism to make the prediction.

The major contribution of this paper is two-folded: First, we propose a novel model BERTNSF to predict the stock trends concerning both the news information and its inner emotional meanings. By fusing multi source information of the stock market such as the news contents, the emotional representation and historical stock prices, our model can predict the stock trends more accurately. Second, we conduct extensive experiments to evaluate our proposal. The experimental results demonstrate that BERTNSF outperformans existing state-of-the-art models in terms of nearly 10% higher accuracy. In particular, the incorporation of news emotions contributes to 1% to 4% improvement in the prediction accuracy.

The rest of this article is organized as follows. Section 2 reviews related work. Section 3 introduces our method. Section 4 uses experiments to evaluate our proposal. Section 5 summarizes the work of this paper and highlights some future research directions.

2 Related Work

The stock market generates a huge amount of trading data every day, which provides a huge amount of data for deep neural networks to train and improve their predictive performance. [7] used historical price data to predict the stock's future return ranking through a novel stock selection model based on deep neural networks. [8] used a deep neural network trained on price data to predict the daily volatility of stocks in the Chinese A-share market.

Most of the models predict the stock market from a fixed time window of the historical stock prices using LSTM networks or gated recurrent units (GRU) networks. [9] used a convolutional neural network model based on LSTM and CNN to combine time-series features and graph features to predict stock prices on pre-treatment stock charts to gain more time sequence features. However, methods based on price time series can learn the changing laws within a period, but cannot deal with the impact of unexpected events and market conditions. Fluctuations in stock prices are susceptible to short-term factors. It is difficult to capture changes in stock prices with one feature only. Therefore, the fusion of multi-sourced financial information is needed.

On the other hand, some researchers use statistical methods to predict stock price changes based on the text of financial news. [10] used Twitter news text and lexical expressions to predict stock returns. [11] used data disclosed by the US Securities and Exchange Commission to forecast future short-term and long-term indices. The proposed text mining approach selects ad-hoc announcements from publishing service providers and integrates machine learning techniques under a decision support system to predict major indices such as DAX, CDAX, and STOXX. However, these work usually used one-hot embeddings, Word2Vec or GloVe. to encode words without concerning their contexts.

In addition, many studies have been conducted to analyze the sentimental meaning in text, for example, mining the sentiment in news articles and social media to predict the stock trends. [12] predict stock movements based on public sentiment tags on Yahoo message boards (a community for investor discussion). The results show that stock movements are strongly correlated with sentiment on message boards. [13] used Google domestic trends, a dataset of daily search volume related to various aspects of macroeconomics, as indicators of public sentiment and macroeconomic factors, and used LSTM to predict daily S&P 500 volatility. [14] used a simple naive Bayesian classification method to classify public sentiment as positive or negative for stock trend prediction.

The sentiment dictionary provides a powerful tool to analyze the sentiment of various texts. [15] used the Opinion Finder and Google-Profile of Mood States (GPOMS) lexicon to analyze the sentiments of investor on Twitter. They predicted the Dow Jones Industrial Average by training a fuzzy neural network with emotion. Their research shows that using a specific dimension of public sentiment can significantly improve the accuracy of predictions. [16] used an LSTM model to allocate portfolios based on stock returns and public sentiment. [17] used the Harvard IV-4 Dictionary and the Loughran-McDonald Financial Dictionary to construct a sentiment space to represent news, and made predictions by training a classification model based on the news representations. The results show that the sentiment analysis model outperforms the bag of words model at the individual stock level, industry level and index level.

3 BERTNSF Model

The BERTNSF model predicts the stock market trend based on multiple source of stock market information, including the news headline text features, the sentiment of the news contents, and the historical prices. This can be formalized as $BERTNSF : \{P, N, S\} \rightarrow \{R\}$, where $\{\boldsymbol{R}\}$ is the prediction result, $\{\boldsymbol{P}\}$, $\{\boldsymbol{N}\}$, and $\{\boldsymbol{S}\}$ are the information of past price of the stock, news text features, and news sentiment representations, respectively. Figure 1 illustrates the overview of our proposed model, which consists of two parts handling past stock prices and news articles (with sentiment), respectively. The first part extracts text features with the pre-trained model BERT, and uses the Chinese financial sentiment dictionary published in the Journal of Management Science by [18] to extract news sentiment representation features. The second part uses LSTM to learn stock price time series to predict future price movements. The details of each part of the model are explained in the following subsections.

3.1 BERT Contextual Embedding

BERT is a Transformers-based bidirectional encoder representation model pre-trained on large-scale datasets (WikiBooks and Wikipedia) to learn basic features of a language [19]. BERTNSF uses the pre-trained BERT model to generate a contextual embedding expression with a higher accuracy for major financial news in the stock market, as illustrated in Fig. 1. The model consists of L layers where each layer has N nodes (each node is a Transformer model). The first layer takes the tokenized content as input, and the BERT model generates $N \times L$ hidden vectors, denoted by $T_{i,j}$. The first token of the first layer is a special [CLS] token to represent the integrated semantics of all nodes, often used for fine-tuning models or text classification tasks. Since the price of the stock market is affected by many factors, and the strength of the impact of news on the stock market is uncertain, fine-tuning the model for a single element of news text may overfit the model. Therefore, we use a pre-trained BERT model (bert-base-chinese) to embed the news text without fine-tuning the model.

[20] showed through comparative experiments that news article summarization is more effective for maintaining prediction performance than using full-length articles. Inspired by this, we use the news headline to generate contextualized news embeddings. We first tokenize the news headline text (if the number

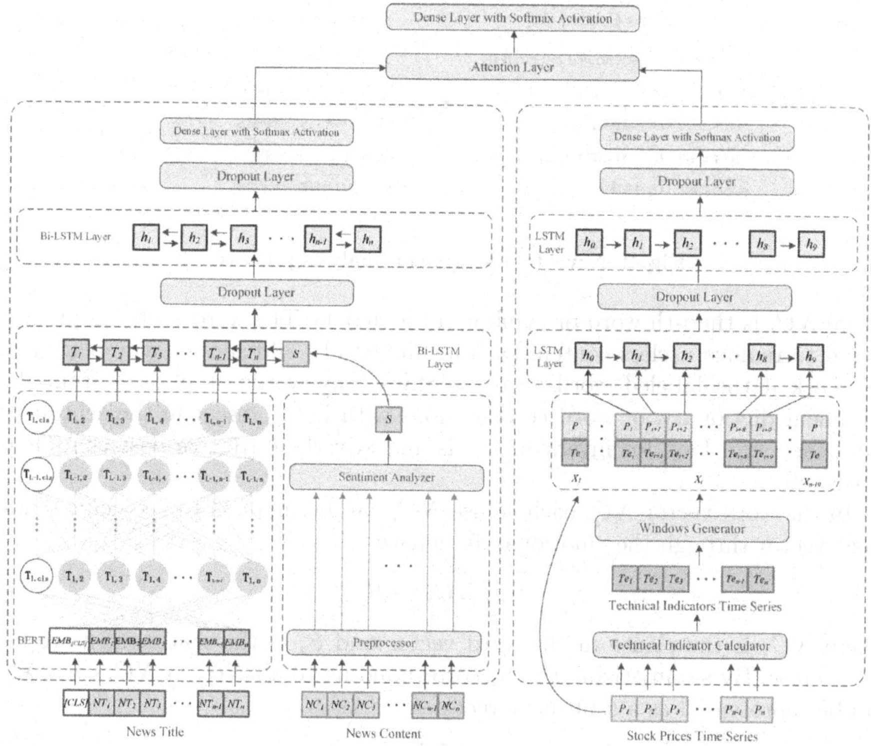

Fig. 1. The architecture of our BERTNSF.

of tokens is less than N, we fill it by adding an empty token at the end of the headline text to N tokens). Then, we input the label sequence into the pre-trained BERT model, as shown in Fig. 1. Since the BERT model has L layers, L different embedding sequences are generated, represented by $Emb_{base,l}$:

$$Emb_{\text{base },l} = [T_{l,2}, T_{l,3}, \ldots, T_{l,N}] \tag{1}$$

The title headline is represented by $Emb_{base,l}$, and l is the hidden embedding layer generated by the intermediate process. and its number is represented as $1 \leq l \leq L$. where $Embase, l$ is a $size\,(T_{l,i}) \times (N-1)$ matrix.

3.2 News Sentiment Analysis

The news content processing module in Fig. 1 contains a preprocessor and a sentiment analyzer. It converts news articles into representations that can be analyzed for sentiment by using a sentiment dictionary.

As shown in Fig. 2, the news full-length articles are first tokenized. For each news article, it is first vectorized and converted to a word vector:

$$NC = [NC_l, NC_2, \ldots, NC_n] \tag{2}$$

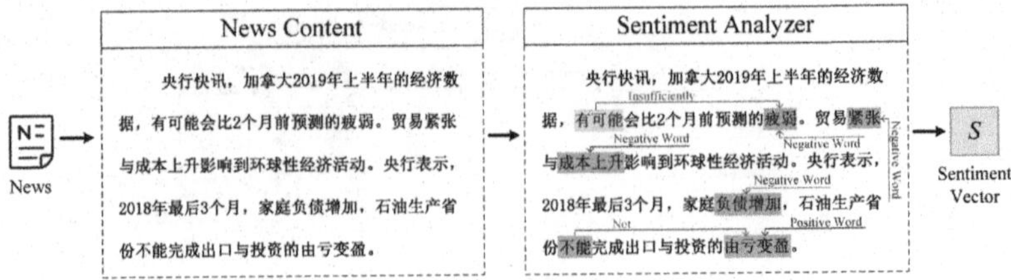

Fig. 2. News text sentiment analysis process.

where NC_i is the i-th word or symbol in the article. The word vector is preprocessed to remove useless content such as line breaks and special symbols. Then we check if the labeled word vector contains any words or phrases from the sentiment dictionary, or word combinations with keys present in the sentiment dictionary, and look for inversion words and adverbs of degree near sentiment words, etc.

In the word vector NC, each clause NC_j can be mapped to a specific sentiment vector through the emotional dictionary,

$$f_D : NC_j \rightarrow S_j \tag{3}$$

where NC_j is the clause in the word vector and S_j is the sentiment score for that clause. By summarizing the S_j corresponding to all NC_j in NC, each NC can be represented as a sentiment vector S:

$$S = \sum_{NC_j \in NC} S_j \tag{4}$$

The embedding token sequence T_i and the sentiment vector S express the features of a given news text from different perspectives. We connect two Bi-LSTM networks to obtain the above and following information of the input features, respectively. Each Bi-LSTM network is connected by a Dropout layer to avoid overfitting. The calculation formula of the dropout layer is as follows,

$$\text{dropout}\ \left(h_t^{l-1}\right) = \text{Bernoulli}(p) \cdot h_t^{l-1} \tag{5}$$

where h_t is the input at time step t, l is the number of layers, where $\text{Bernoulli}(p)$ is a discrete probability distribution of a random variable which takes value 1 with probability p and value 0 with probability $1 - p$.

3.3 Stock Price Time Series

Stock price time series includes transaction data in two dimensions: the price data and trading volume of the stock's daily opening, high, low, and closing prices, among which the closing price and trading volume are the most commonly used, which can be expressed as follows, where i represents the trading day:

$$P_i = \{[\text{ Close }_i, \text{ Volume }_i], i = 1, \ldots, n\} \tag{6}$$

Besides the price P, we also use several commonly used investment technical indicators in the prediction process, as shown in Table 1. Through the configuration of different parameters such as time step length, different technical indicators can be generated to reflect the trend or volatility of the stock from different angles. In Fig. 1, we denote the technical indicators of the trading day i as Te_i, which provides the LSTM neural network with ample market signals. We integrate the features of technical indicators and price series and generate snapshots of the series as input to the LSTM neural network. First, the price vector P_i and the technical indicator vector Te_i are linked in units of each trading day, and the linked vector is defined as h_i. After that, the sequence of h_i is divided into a sliding window with τ as the window size and one day as the time step, the split window is represented as $h_i^{\tau} = [h_i, \cdots, h_{i+\tau-1}]$. Then a Dropout layer is connected to two LSTM networks to avoid overfitting.

Table 1. Technical indicators for stock prices.

Indicator	Meaning	Formula
MA2	2-day close price moving average	2-day close price sum/2
MA3	3-day close price moving average	3-day close price sum/3
MA5	5-day close price moving average	5-day close price sum/5
DIF	Difference between EMA12 and EMA26	EMA12 - EMA26
DEA	Exponential moving average of DIF	i-1-day DEA × 8/10 + i-day × 2/10
MACD	Moving average convergence and divergence	(DIF-DEA) × 2

3.4 Model Fusion

To combine the advantages of different models for stock market prediction, we use an attention mechanism to fuse the outputs of each model, as shown in Fig. 1. The formula is defined as follows:

$$u_i = \text{sigmoid}\left(W_n d_i + b_n\right) \tag{7}$$

$$\alpha_{ti} = \frac{\exp\left(\theta_i u_i\right)}{\sum_j \exp\left(\theta_j u_j\right)} \tag{8}$$

$$V = \sum_i \alpha_i d_i \tag{9}$$

where u_i is the latent feature vector representation, α_{ti} is the attention weight value of the feature, W_n and b_n are the weight and bias, respectively, d is the input value, V is the output of the attention layer. Then, V is input to a binary classification to predict the stock market trends.

4 Evaluation

4.1 Experimental Setup

Dataset. We use three types of datasets in our study. The first dataset includes the news texts from January 1, 2010 to January 1, 2022, a total of 11 years of financial news in China's major news articles, as illustrated in Fig. 3. The second dataset is the time series data of major Chinese stock market indices, including: Shanghai Composite Index (SC Index), CSI 300 Index (CSI300 Index), SZSE Ingredients Index (SI Index), GEM Index, and GEM 50 Index. The third dataset is the sentiment dictionaries. We use the Chinese financial sentiment dictionary published in the Journal of Management Science by [18] to calculate the sentiment vectors of news articles. In addition to this, we also use the adverb word table from HowNet's sentiment dictionary for our sentiment evaluation in news content.

Data Preprocessing. Since the headline of the news is concise and contains the main information of the news, we check the number of the news headline in the dataset and set the maximum length of the headline sentence to 35 tokens (if there are less than 35 tokens, we fill it with 35 blanks mark). To clean the news content and improve the performance of sentiment analysis, we use regular expressions to delete special symbols, English words, numbers and stop words in the stop word list (i.e., Harbin Institute of Technology and Baidu stop word list). We assign two types of labels based on index information. That is, the category whose closing price today is greater than yesterday's closing price is set to "1", and "0" conversely. Also, we split the training and test sets 7:3.

Parameter Settings. We use a pre-trained 12-layer, 768-dimensional, 12-head bert-base-chinese model to generate embeddings for news article titles. According to past research experience, the BERT layers used as embeddings should not be too close to the previous layers, otherwise the contextualized embeddings will be too similar to static embeddings. The empty token$[CLS]$ is often less effective than all hidden vectors in the last layer in various downstream tasks. Therefore, we use hidden layer embeddings of $l = L$ layers.

For sentiment evaluation of news content, we first count a positive unit for positive words or phrases present in the news content that match the sentiment dictionary, and a negative unit for negative words or phrases. Then we look for words with reversed meanings or degree adverbs near the positive or negative emotional keywords to modify the emotional polarity. Since news reports are often based on the reporter's subjective narrative, excessive emotional words and descriptions of events can introduce too much artificial noise into the news events themselves. We selected the daily news from January to June 2018 as the test case, and several sets of sentiment score calculation criteria from the statistical methods commonly used in sentiment dictionaries. We calculated the normal distribution of the daily average score of news for each set of criteria, and selected the criterion that best conforms to the normal distribution as our calculation criterion. The specific modification parameters are shown in Table 2, where i represents the original emotional polarity word score, $Word\ types$ and $modify$ denote the type of degree adverbs and the modification to the original sentiment polarity word score. The Probability-Probability (PP) diagram of the normal distribution of its test cases is shown in Fig. 4. Since the data volume of the test samples is greater than 50, we use the Kolmogorov-Smirnov test to obtain a p value of 0.676, which shows that the test results are not significant and conform to the characteristics of normality. That is, we effectively extract news sentiment features without introducing interference.

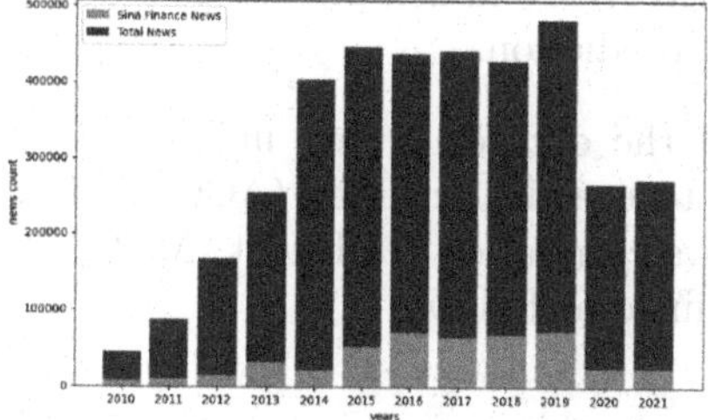

Fig. 3. Statistics of financial news

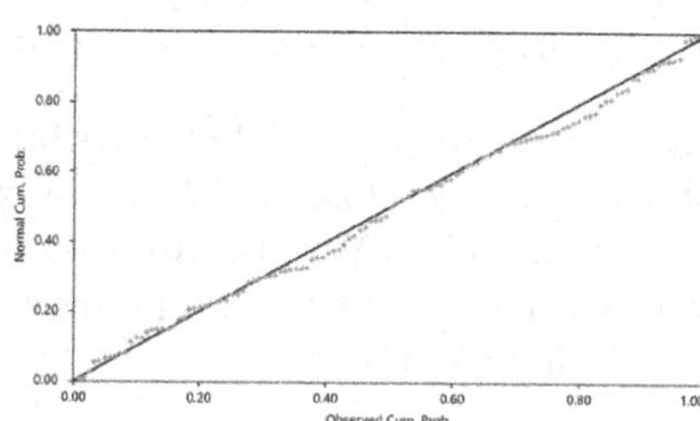

Fig. 4. Sentiment score P-P of daily news

Table 2. Emotional vector calculation formula.

Word Types	Ish	Inverse	Very	More	Most	Not	Over	Insufficiently
Modify	0.8i	−1i	1.8i	1.5i	2i	−1i	−0.5i	0.5i

To follow the principle that the headline features and content features of news are context-dependent and interact with each other, we use the Bi-LSTM method to connect the front and back features. Take the vector embedding sequence $[T_i \ldots T_n]$ of the pre-trained model BERT and the vector S representing the sentiment output as the input of Bi-LSTM, and the hidden neurons of Bi-LSTM are set to 128. Set the Dropout rate to 50%. Finally, the features output by Bi-LSTM through the Dense Layer with Softmax as the activation function are input to Attention for weight distribution.

In our experiments, we set the batch of the LSTM neural network to 32. We choose the Root mean square prop (RMSProp) as the optimizer for the LSTM and set the initial learning rate to 0.001. There are two LSTM layers in our LSTM neural network. Each LSTM layer is connected by a Dropout layer to avoid overfitting. The Dropout rate is set to 50%. At each time step, the first LSTM layer updates the hidden state in the layer and outputs the state value to the next layer. The dense layer following these LSTM layers is used to map the output hidden state of the LSTM layer to a category vector.

Baseline Models. The following models, including the classic event embedding method and state-of-the-art (SOTA) method HAN_SPL, are chose as the baseline models.

- **Event Embedding (EB)**: A prediction method based on event embedding. It uses event embedding to extract news events with influence of different periods, and then makes predictions based on the similarity of events.
- **HAN_SPL**: A prediction method that uses two attention mechanisms to calculate the different impacts of daily news and weekly news, and uses Bi-GRU as a learner.

- **BERT**: THe model has achieved the best results in various competitions and NLP tasks. We directly use the [CLS] label as the final prediction, as proposed by the original authors.
- **BERTF (BERT Fusion)**: Similar to BERTNSF model, but the news content sentiment indicators are not used for prediction.

Metrics. Since the label distribution of the dataset is very uniform (i.e., both 0 and 1 are close to 50%), we choose to use the accuracy (ACC) as the main metric index. We also use the Matthews correlation coefficient (MCC) as the second metric. These two metrics are defined as follows:

Accuracy (ACC):

$$\frac{tp + tn}{tp + tn + fp + fn} \tag{10}$$

Matthews Correlation Coefficient (MCC):

$$\frac{tp \times tn - fp \times fn}{\sqrt{(tp + fp)(tp + fn)(tn + fp)(tn + fn)}} \tag{11}$$

where tp, tn, fn, fp refer to the number of correctly predicted positive samples, the number of correctly judged negative samples, the number of falsely predicted positive samples, and the number of mispredicted negative samples, respectively.

Table 3. ACC comparision of baseline models and BERTNSF.

Index	SC Index	CSI300 Index	SI Index	GEM Index	GEM 50 Index
Model	ACC	ACC	ACC	ACC	ACC
EB	0.575	0.594	0.612	0.618	0.610
HAN_SPL	0.634	0.612	0.641	0.642	0.637
BERT	0.658	0.646	0.656	0.638	0.649
BERTF	0.710	0.709	0.717	0.713	0.709
BERTNSF	**0.735**	**0.741**	**0.722**	**0.725**	**0.712**

Table 4. MCC comparison of baseline models and BERTNSMF.

Index	SC Index	CSI300 Index	SI Index	GEM Index	GEM 50 Index
Model	MCC	MCC	MCC	MCC	MCC
EB	0.151	0.191	0.227	0.235	0.219
HAN_SPL	0.268	0.229	0.283	0.284	0.273
BERT	0.316	0.294	0.312	0.274	0.297
BERTF	0.420	0.420	0.434	0.425	0.418
BERTNSF	**0.471**	**0.485**	**0.444**	**0.450**	**0.424**

4.2 Result Analysis

The detailed results of the experiments are shown in Table 3 and Table 4. We can observe that our BERTNSF outperforms all other baseline models, both in terms of accuracy and Matthews correlation coefficient. In particular, compared with BERT, EB and HAN_SPL, the accuracy of our model is improved. The results also show that BERT-based contextualized embeddings can extract text features better than static embeddings. We also observe that BERTF improves the accuracy by at least 6% compared to BERT results, suggesting that using model fusion to fuse time-series features and textual features in news documents is more effective in improving results than using only a single feature.

Furthermore, we observe that our model BERTNSF has a 1% to 4% improvement in accuracy compared to BERTF, and the MCC correlation coefficient is also improved. This indicates the necessity of adding emotions expressed in the news in the embedding. That is, the integration of news content sentiment can make the expression of news more accurate.

It should be noted that although our method has the best performance, the accuracy still does not exceed 75%, which shows that the accuracy, recall and precision of our method need to be further improved. We speculate that there may be two main reasons: (1) The characteristics that affect the stock market are far more than those studied by our model, and we still have not considered comprehensive influencing factors. (2) News can only represent news events themselves, and with the development of self-media and social networks, uncertain factors affecting people's judgment on news have increased.

5 Conclusions

In this paper, we propose a novel model BERTNSF to predict the stock trends concerning both the news information and its inner emotional meanings. The model adopts a pre-trained model BERT to extract the text feature of news events, and analyzes the emotional polarity of news contents via the emotion dictionary. A two-layer LSTM neural network is also built to learn the time series of the price and technical indicators of stocks. An attention-based model fusion method is designed to integrate these multi-source features to predict the stock market trends. We conducted extensive experiments to evaluate our proposal. The experimental results show that our model is effective, and the accuracy of stock market prediction has been greatly improved.

In the future work, we plan to train some sentiment models to replace the sentiment dictionary to make more accurate predictions. In addition, we also plan to adapt our model to the individual stock level for quantitative transactions.

Acknowledgement. This work was supported in part by the National Key Research and Development Program of China under Grant No.2018YFB2100805, the Key Research and Development Program of Hainan Province under grant No. ZDYF2020008 National Natural Science Foundation of China under the grant No.61962017, 61662019, and grants from State Key Laboratory of Marine Resource Utilization in South China Sea and Key Laboratory of Big Data and Smart Services of Hainan Province.

References

1. Shleifer, A.: Inefficient Markets: An Introduction to Behavioural Finance. Oup, Oxford (2000)
2. Tetlock, P.C.: Giving content to investor sentiment: the role of media in the stock market. J. Financ. **62**(3), 1139–1168 (2007)
3. Schumaker, R.P., Chen, H.: A quantitative stock prediction system based on financial news. Inf. Process. Manag. **45**(5), 571–583 (2009)
4. Ding, X., Zhang, Y., Liu, T., Duan, J.: Deep learning for event-driven stock prediction. In: Twenty-Fourth International Joint Conference on Artificial Intelligence (2015)
5. Ding, X., Zhang, Y., Liu, T., Duan, J.: Knowledge-driven event embedding for stock prediction. In: Proceedings of Coling 2016, the 26th International Conference on Computational Linguistics: Technical Papers, pp. 2133–2142 (2016)
6. Lai, S., Jiang, H., Ye, C., Zhou, H.: Chinese stock market prediction based on multifeature fusion and TextCNN. In: 2021 International Conference on Service Science (ICSS), pp. 59–64. IEEE (2021)
7. Zhang, X., Tan, Y.: Deep stock ranker: a LSTM neural network model for stock selection. In: Tan, Y., Shi, Y., Tang, Q. (eds.) Data Mining and Big Data (DMBD 2018). LNCS, vol. 10943, pp. 614–623. Springer, Cham (2018). https://doi.org/10.1007/978-3-319-93803-5_58
8. Chen, K., Zhou, Y., Dai, F.: A LSTM-based method for stock returns prediction: a case study of China stock market. In: 2015 IEEE International Conference on Big Data (Big Data), pp. 2823–2824. IEEE (2015)
9. Kim, T., Kim, H.Y.: Forecasting stock prices with a feature fusion LSTM-CNN model using different representations of the same data. PLoS ONE **14**(2), e0212320 (2019)
10. Oliveira, N., Cortez, P., Areal, N.: Some experiments on modeling stock market behavior using investor sentiment analysis and posting volume from twitter. In: Proceedings of the 3rd International Conference on Web Intelligence, Mining and Semantics, pp. 1–8 (2013)
11. Feuerriegel, S., Gordon, J.: Long-term stock index forecasting based on text mining of regulatory disclosures. Decis. Support Syst. **112**, 88–97 (2018)
12. Nallapati, R., Ahmed, A., Cohen, W., Xing, E.: Sops: stock prediction using web sentiment. In: Seventh IEEE International Conference on Data Mining Workshops (ICDM Workshops) (2007)
13. Xiong, R., Nichols, E.P., Shen, Y.: Deep learning stock volatility with google domestic trends. arXiv preprint arXiv:1512.04916 (2015)
14. Zhang, G., Xu, L., Xue, Y.: Model and forecast stock market behavior integrating investor sentiment analysis and transaction data. Clust. Comput. **20**(1), 1–15 (2017)
15. Bollen, J., Mao, H., Zeng, X.: Twitter mood predicts the stock market. J. Comput. Sci. **2**(1), 1–8 (2011)
16. Malandri, L., Xing, F.Z., Orsenigo, C., Vercellis, C., Cambria, E.: Public mood-driven asset allocation: the importance of financial sentiment in portfolio management. Cogn. Comput. **10**(6), 1167–1176 (2018)
17. Li, X., Xie, H., Li, C., Wang, J., Deng, X.: News impact on stock price return via sentiment analysis. Knowl.-Based Syst. **69**, 14–23 (2014)
18. Yao, J., Feng, X., Wang, Z., Ji, R., Zhang, W.: Tone, sentiment and market impacts: the construction of Chinese sentiment dictionary in finance. J. Manag. Sci. China **24**(5), 21 (2021)

19. Devlin, J., Chang, M.W., Lee, K., Toutanova, K.: BERT: pre-training of deep bidirectional transformers for language understanding. arXiv preprint arXiv:1810.04805 (2018)
20. Li, X., Xie, H., Song, Y., Zhu, S., Li, Q., Wang, F.L.: Does summarization help stock prediction? A news impact analysis. IEEE Intell. Syst. **30**(3), 26–34 (2015)

Chinese Medical Named Entity Recognition Based on Label Knowledge Enhancement

Shengyu Li[1,2], Lei Wang[2(✉)], Wenchang Xu[2], Xiaonan Si[1,2], Biao Wang[1,2], Hanbin Ren[2], and Wenbo Cheng[2]

[1] University of Science and Technology of China, Hefei 260026, China
[2] Suzhou Institute of Biomedical Engineering and Technology, Chinese Academy of Sciences, Suzhou 215163, China
wanglei@sibet.ac.cn

Abstract. To solve the problem of text complexity in Chinese medical text named entity task, a model BERT-Label-Span based on label knowledge enhancement had been proposed, which can improve the accuracy of medical information system in Chinese medical named entity recognition task. The model decomposes the problem-text joint coding into two independent coding modules and performs the joint coding based on the BERT pre-training model. Then the semantic fusion module based on the attention mechanism explicitly uses the label knowledge to enhance the representation of medical text. Finally, the span of the named entity is predicted based on the heuristic matching principle. The experiment on the CCKS2019 Chinese medical text dataset shows that the F1 value of the named entity recognition task of the model reaches 85.554, which is higher than the existing main-stream methods and proves the effectiveness of this method.

Keywords: Label Knowledge · Named Entity Recognition · Attention Mechanism · BERT

1 Introduction

With the wide application of information technology in medical treatment, relevant AI technology is gradually integrated into the medical industry, and a large amount of text data has been accumulated in the medical field, most of which are stored in the form of electronic medical records [1]. Electronic medical records, also known as computer-based patient records, are health information systematically collected from patients and people in a digital format and stored electronically. Medical text named entity recognition is a basic task of text mining in the medical field. This task aims to automatically identify valuable medical

Supported by National Key R&D Program of China (NO. 2022YFC2503305) and National Science Youth Foundation of Shandong Province of China (NO. ZR2020QF018).

Z. Wang et al. (Eds.): ICSS 2023, CCIS 1844, pp. 292–304, 2023.
https://doi.org/10.1007/978-981-99-4402-6_21

entities from massive medical text data, and store the extracted medical entities in a structured form. It is of great significance to the standardization and follow-up research of texts such as electronic medical records.

Chinese medical text data is often information-intensive, and contains a large number of semi-structured and unstructured data. The use of abbreviations or abbreviations, synonyms and other phenomena often occur in the text. These characteristics lead to the complexity and ambiguity of the named entities in Chinese medical texts, which increases the difficulty of the named entity recognition task. The existing models used for Chinese medical named entity recognition tasks inevitably have problems such as low efficiency of data utilization and weak data mining ability, and there is still a certain gap between them and the named entity recognition models in the general field. The research purpose of this paper is to combine natural language processing technology with medical professional fields, and propose a Chinese medical named entity recognition method that makes full use of the prior knowledge of named entity labels.

2 Related Work

Chinese medical named entity recognition is the key task of medical information extraction, and plays an important role in medical relationship extraction, medical text abstract, machine translation and medical health question answering system. Chinese medical named entity recognition methods can be roughly divided into four types: rule-based method, unsupervised learning, feature-based supervised learning method and deep-learning method.

Rule-based method often requires experts in the medical field to manually build dictionaries and rule templates based on specific corpus content [2]. The selected features include statistical information, keywords, indicators and head words, and the string matching is the main means. Hanisch [3] et al. proposed an algorithm to identify proteins and potential genes in medical texts with a preprocessing synonym dictionary.

Feature-based supervised learning transforms named entity recognition tasks into multi-classification or sequence marking tasks. This method requires standard annotated data sets and carefully designed features to represent each training example, and then uses machine learning algorithms to learn a model, and recognize similar patterns from data that has never been seen before. As the key of supervised learning named entity recognition system, the feature vector is the abstract representation of text, in which a word is represented by one or more Boolean values, numerical values or nominal values [4]. Based on these features, many machine learning algorithms are applied in the supervised named entity recognition task, including hidden Markov model [5], decision tree [6], maximum entropy model [7], support vector machine and conditional random field [8].

The method based on deep learning uses the word vector as the input and learns the expected features through the deep learning framework. This method has three core advantages. First, thanks to nonlinear transformation, the model based on deep learning can learn complex features from data through nonlinear activation function. Secondly, deep learning saves a lot of work in designing named entity features, and can effectively automatically learn useful representations and potential factors from the original text data. The deep learning neural network can be trained in the end-to-end paradigm through gradient descent, which allows us to design complex systems. The language model embedding using Transformer pre-training is becoming a new paradigm of named entity recognition task. These embedding combined with context features can be used to replace traditional word embedding, such as Word2Vec [9] and ELMo [10]. Some researches have achieved good performance by combining traditional embedding with pre-training model embedding [14]. Moreover, researchers can further fine-tune the embedding of these language models through an additional output layer to solve the problem.

3 Machine Reading Comprehension

MRC (Machine Reading Comprehension) [11] model extracts the answer span from the text data paragraphs of a given question, so that the start and end positions of the answer can be predicted. Through this method, the task of named entity recognition and information extraction can be transformed into a multi-round question and answer task.

For a named entity recognition task, it is equivalent to giving an input medical text sequence $X = \{x_1, x_2, ..., x_n\}$ of gout EMR, where n represents the length of the text sequence. We need to find a label $y \in Y$ for each medical entity, where Y is a predefined list of all possible label types (such as surgery, medicine, etc.). The model mainly includes two steps: data set construction and problem generation: 1) First of all, we need to convert the annotated Chinese medical text dataset into a group of (question, answer, text) triples. For each label type $y \in Y$, it is associated with the question list $q_y = \{q_1, q_2, ..., q_m\}$, where m represents the length of the generated question. The annotated medical entity $x_{start,end} = \{x_{start}, x_{start+1}, ..., x_{end-1}, x_{end}\}$ is a substring of X that meets the requirements of *start* < *end*. By generating natural language questions based on tags, we can obtain triples $(q_y, x_{start,end}, X)$, which is exactly what we need (question, answer, text). 2) In the machine reading comprehension model, the generation of natural language problems is a very critical step, because natural language problems encode prior knowledge related to labels, which has a significant impact on the final result of medical entity recognition. At present, the mainstream method is to use the annotation of annotation guidance as a reference for construction problems, and the annotation of annotation guidance refers to the criteria provided by the text dataset to the annotation doctor of the dataset, that is, the description of label categories. The annotation as a guideline should be as accurate as possible in the medical field related to the text, so that the annotated doctor can annotate the concepts in the text without ambiguity.

The MRC model has two advantages. First, it naturally solves the problem of nested entities by transforming the named entity recognition task into multiple rounds of question answering tasks [15]. Second, the query statements in the model encode the prior knowledge of the medical entity to be extracted, and increase the ability of the medical entity recognition of the electronic medical record text.

4 BERT-Label-Span Model

After transforming the Chinese medical named entity recognition task into the named entity span prediction task, we proposed BERT-Label-Span model structure based on label knowledge enhancement in this paper. The model is divided into three parts: semantic joint coding layer, semantic fusion layer and decoding layer. The structure of the model is shown in Fig. 1. The Chinese medical text and the label of the named entity category are used as input, and they are jointly encoded through two BERT pre-trained networks with shared weights. After that, the Chinese medical text embedding generated by the encoder and the named entity class label embedding are combined through the semantic fusion layer based on the attention mechanism, and then we can obtain the embedding of the Chinese medical text enhanced by the named entity category label knowledge. Finally, based on the heuristic matching principle, the text embedding enhanced by label knowledge is used to predict whether each index is the start index or the end index of the entity category. This model makes better use of label knowledge in the named entity recognition task of Chinese medical text, and can obtain more ideal accuracy in the experiment.

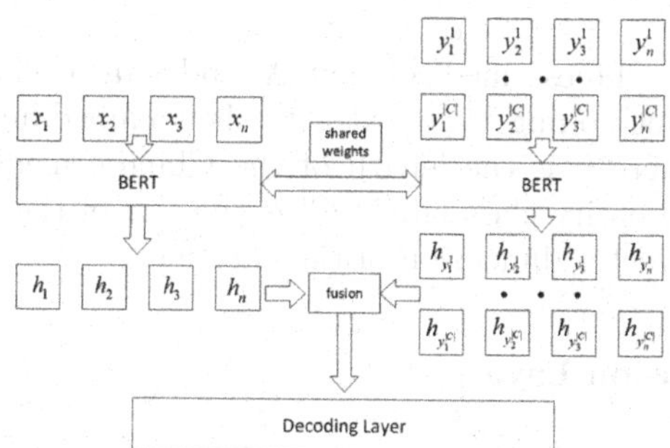

Fig. 1. Structure diagram of BERT-Label-Span model.

4.1 Semantic Joint Coding Layer

The purpose of the semantic coding layer is to encode Chinese medical text and the labels of entity categories into the embedding layer. BERT pre-training model [12], as a deep bidirectional language representation model pre-trained in large-scale corpus, can maximize the semantic features of the output text and conduct efficient finetuning. It uses masking language model and next sentence prediction to capture context semantics at word and sentence levels. The structure of BERT is shown in Fig. 2. The coding layer of the proposed model uses BERT pre-trained model as the encoder. In addition, considering that the number of labels of named entity categories is relatively small compared with the whole Chinese medical text, it is not necessary to build an encoder for them from scratch. By sharing weights, the encoder can be shared between the two without introducing additional parameters. Given the input Chinese medical text and named entity category label, the semantic joint coding layer extracts their embedding $h_x \in R^{n \times d}$ and $h_y \in R^{|C| \times m \times d}$.

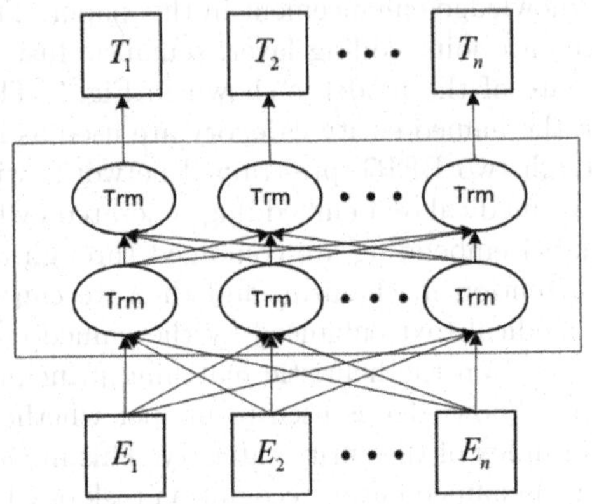

Fig. 2. Structure diagram of BERT.

Given the input Chinese medical text X and named entity category label Y, the semantic joint coding layer extracts their embedding $h_x \in R^{n \times d}$ and $h_y \in R^{|C| \times m \times d}$, where n is the length of the Chinese medical text X, is the length of the named entity class label, $|C|$ is the size of the named entity class set C, and d is the vector dimension of the encoder.

4.2 Semantic Fusion Layer

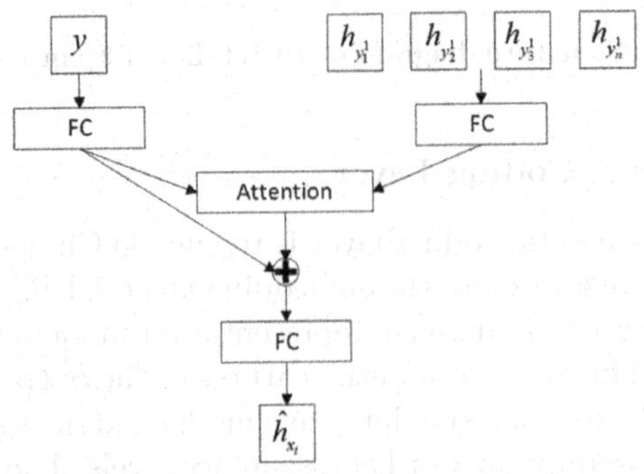

Fig. 3. Structure diagram of semantic fusion layer.

Considering that adding the two embeddings directly will lose important details, we design a semantic-guided attention mechanism to explicitly use tag knowledge to enhance text representation. According to the papers of Vaswani et al. [13], the core idea of attention mechanism is to learn weights for different features through neural networks, and then enhance the expression of features with higher relevance to the task according to the size of the weights, and suppress the parts of features that are not related to the task. The structure of semantic fusion layer is shown in Fig. 3. In order to better calculate, first input the Chinese medical text embedding h_X and label embedding h_Y into a fully connected layer respectively, and map their representation to the same feature space:

$$h'_X = F_1 \cdot h_X \tag{1}$$

$$h'_Y = F_2 \cdot h_Y \tag{2}$$

where F_1 and F_2 are the learnable parameters of the fully connected layer. Then, the attention mechanism is applied to the label of each character named entity category in Chinese medical text. For any $1 \leq i \leq n$ make x_i to be the i th token of the text X and $h'_{x_i} \in R^d$ to be the ith row of h'_x. Similarly, for any $1 \leq j \leq m$ and category $c \in C$, make y_j^c to be the j th token of the named entity category label $c \in C$ and $h'_{y_i^c}$ to be the embedding of h'_Y. The attention score is obtained by calculating the dot product of h'_{x_i} and $h'_{y_i^c}$ before using the softmax function:

$$a_{x_i,y_j^c} = \frac{\exp(h'_{x_i} \cdot h'_{y_i^c})}{\sum_j \exp(h'_{x_i} \cdot h'_{y_i^c})} \tag{3}$$

Finally, the fine-grained features obtained by the attention mechanism are embedded into the token through the addition operation:

$$h^c_{x_i} = h'_{x_i} + \sum_j a_{x_i,y_j^c} \cdot h'_{y_i^c} \tag{4}$$

$$\hat{h}^c_{x_i} = tanh(U \cdot h^c_{x_i} + b) \tag{5}$$

where $\hat{h}^c_{x_i}$ is the code related to the named entity category, and $U \in R^{d \times d}$, $b \in R^d$ are the learnable parameters. By repeating this calculation, the embedding expression of each token x_i related to the named entity category will be obtained.

4.3 Decoding Layer

Different from the classical sequence annotation model, the decoding layer of this model is based on the span prediction named entity prediction framework, including label representation, span representation and span prediction. Each span prediction system can be conceptualized as a system combiner, which can reidentify named entities from different system outputs. The decoding layer is mainly used to mainly calculate the boundary embedding, and use the start and end tag patterns to represent the target span to be extracted. Specifically, the vector shown below is calculated for each token x_i:

$$start_{x_i} = sigmoid(f_o(M_s o \hat{h}_{x_i} + b_s)) \tag{6}$$

where $M_s \in R^{|C| \times d}$ and $b_s \in R^d$ are the learnable parameters, o is element wise multiplication, and f_o is the function that sums the rows of the input matrix. This vector indicates that for any category $c \in C$, x_i is the probability of the beginning of the category span. Likewise, we can also get end_{x_i} through similar calculation, which means that x_i is the probability of the end of a span.

Since this study is mainly aimed at NER tasks without nested entities, the heuristic matching principle is followed in the decoding process to avoid overlapping span prediction in the decoding calculation and determine the span from the perspective of probability. This method contains a finite state machine, which has three states: 1) Start and end are not detected; 2) Only start is detected; 3) Start and end are detected. Specifically, when the current token is at the beginning, state 1 changes to state 2; When the current token is at the end, state 2 changes to state 3; When the current character is a new start, state 3 changes to state 2. If there are two start signs at the same time, choose the one with the higher probability. If there are two end flags at the same time, the operation is the same as above. In this way, the span with the highest prediction probability is reserved for those overlapping spans.

4.4 Loss Function

For the input Chinese medical text $X = (x_1, x_2, ...x_n)$ containing n tokens and named entity category $c \in C$, only if x_i is the real starting position of c, the $STA^c_{x_i}$ value of the ith element of the definition vector $STA^c \in 0, 1^n$ is 1. Similarly, define the vector $END^c \in 0, 1^n$ to represent the real end position. In this way, the span start position loss function and end position loss function of this model can be obtained. Add the two to get the final loss function of this model:

$$L_{start} = \frac{1}{n} \sum_{1 \leq i \leq n} \sum_{c \in C} CE(start^c_{x_i}, STA^c_{x_i}) \tag{7}$$

$$L_{end} = \frac{1}{n} \sum_{1 \leq i \leq n} \sum_{c \in C} CE(end^c_{x_i}, END^c_{x_i}) \tag{8}$$

$$L = L_{start} + L_{end} \tag{9}$$

where CE represents cross entropy operation.

5 Experiment Design and Result Analysis

5.1 Chinese EMR Text Data Set

The Chinese medical text used in the model experiment in this paper uses the data set of CCKS2019, which contains six predefined named entity categories:

disease and diagnosis, examination, examination, surgery, medicine and anatomical site. This dataset contains six predefined named entity categories: disease and diagnosis, medical examination, medical laboratory science, operation, drug and anatomical site. An example of the dataset is shown in Table 1: When preprocessing the data, in order to facilitate the experiment, the BIO three-digit labeling method is used, where B-X represents the beginning of the named entity, I-X represents the end of the named entity, and O represents that it does not belong to any type.

Table 1. Experimental environment.

Label	Example
Corpus	患者于入院前20+年，常于受凉后出现喘累、气促，时感咳嗽、咳痰，咳出白色泡沫痰，呈阵发性发作,常自服抗炎药或于附近门诊输液治疗后下述症状可缓解(具体治疗方案不详)，下述症状逐渐加重，需住院治疗。入院前3天，患者受凉后再次出现喘累、气促，伴咳嗽、咳痰，痰呈白色泡沫痰，无端坐呼吸，无咯粉红色泡沫痰，无胸痛咯血，无发热，无胸闷、无恶心、呕吐,无两上肢水肿，无潮热、盗汗，无畏寒、寒战，无腹泻、腹痛，无尿频、尿急，无意识障碍等。今日到我院门诊就诊，为进一步诊治，门诊以”慢支炎、肺气肿，高血压”收入我科住院治疗。患者此次起病以来精神、食欲、睡眠一般，大小便正常，体力体重无明显变化。
Disease and diagnosis	慢支炎[233,236] 肺气肿[237,240] 高血压[241,244]
Anatomical site	胸[149,150] 胸[159,160] 两上肢[170,173] 腹[191,192]腹[194,195]

The Chinese electronic medical record text is quite different from the Chinese text in the general field, and the traditional natural language processing method is difficult to achieve good results. There are the following unique difficulties: (1) The language characteristics of Chinese electronic medical records are very obvious, with rich medical terminology and strong professionalism, and the definition and use of terms vary among different medical fields. (2) The diversity of language expression also increases the difficulty of text processing. (3) Due to non-standard writing by doctors and inaccurate data entry, there is a large amount of noise in medical texts that requires cleaning and error correction.

5.2 Experimental Environment and Parameters

In the experiment, we used the Chinese pre-training model BERT-wwm-ext released by Joint Laboratory of Harbin Institute of Technology and iFLYTEK Research. The sequence length of the sentence is set to 512, the dimension of the hidden layer is set to 768, and the learning rate of the BERT pre-training model is set to 2e−5. In addition, because the network of BERT pre-training model is large, considering the problem of video memory, batchsize is set to 6. In the training process, the optimization strategy uses the AdamW optimizer. The environment used in this experiment is shown in Table 2:

Table 2. Experimental environment.

Configuration	Specification and model
Operating system	Linux
CPU	Intel(R) Xeon(R) Gold 6330 CPU @ 2.00 GHz
GPU	RTX3090
Memory	45G
Python	3.8
CUDA	11.3
Pytorch	1.10.0

5.3 Evaluation Indicators

The overall performance of the model is evaluated by three evaluation indicators: precision rate (P), recall rate (R) and F1 value (F_1). The calculation formula is as follows:

$$P = \frac{T_P}{T_P + F_P} * 100\% \tag{10}$$

$$R = \frac{T_P}{T_P + F_N} * 100\% \tag{11}$$

$$F1 = \frac{2PR}{P + R} * 100\% \tag{12}$$

For the category of each named entity in the formula, T_P indicates that the actual positive sample forecast is positive, F_P indicates that the actual negative sample forecast is positive, and F_N indicates that the actual positive sample forecast is negative. Since the experiment in this paper is a named entity recognition task of Chinese medical text, the macro-average of accuracy rate(P), recall rate (R) and F1 value(F_1) is used as the evaluation index. The macro-average calculation method is to calculate the accuracy rate, recall rate and F1 value of each category to obtain the arithmetic average.

5.4 Influence of Decoding Strategy

After the joint encoder with BERT as the backbone, the model proposed in this paper adopts the decoding strategy of heuristic matching principle different from the traditional nearest distance matching strategy. We have done comparative experiments on these two decoding strategies, and the experimental results are shown in the following Table 3:

Table 3. Experiment of decoding strategy.

Strategy	Accuracy rate	Recall rate	F1 value
Nearest distance matching principle	85.187	84.572	84.878
Heuristic matching principle	87.223	83.948	85.554

According to the experimental results, the F1 value of the heuristic matching decoding strategy is 0.676% points higher than that of the nearest distance matching decoding strategy, which shows that the heuristic matching principle can better use the calculated probability information and improve the accuracy of named entity recognition.

5.5 Comparative Experiment of Different Models

In order to verify the effectiveness of the model proposed in this paper, we set up a comparative experiment, which uses the following models for comparison:

(1) BERT-CRF model [16]: connect the CRF layer under the BERT pre-training model, and learn the transfer rules between adjacent entity labels in the dataset through conditional random fields.
(2) BERT-SPAN model [17]: span prediction model is used to replace the classical sequence annotation model.
(3) BERT-MRC model [11]: Transforms the task of entity extraction into the task of extraction reading comprehension.
(4) BERT-BiLSTM-CRF model [18]: Based on BERT-CRF, the context features in two directions are obtained through the BiLSTM layer.

In order to prevent the influence of accidental results and ensure the reliability of experimental results, each model passed ten experiments and finally took its average value. The macro average of the accuracy rate, recall rate and F1 value is calculated as the validation index. The experimental results are shown in Table 4 below: The above experimental results show that the F1 value of the model proposed in this paper reaches the highest among several models.

Table 4. Experiment of different models.

Model	Accuracy rate	Recall rate	F1 value
BERT-Span	81.711	81.367	81.538
BERT-MRC	80.187	80.572	80.379
BERT-CRF	80.575	80.248	80.413
BERT-BiLSTM-CRF	83.458	84.696	84.072
BERT-Label-Span	87.223	83.948	85.554

The BERT-CRF model uses conditional random fields to model the dependence between the prediction results of the network. BERT-BILSTM-CRF improves the recognition ability of named entities of the model by acquiring context features through the BiLSTM layer on the basis of the model. The F1 value of the model proposed in this paper is 1.482% points higher than that of the BERT-BILSTM-CRF model. The former model needs to predict boundary words and internal words simultaneously in the named entity recognition task, which is often very difficult. Especially for Chinese medical texts, there are many categories of named entities. Entity texts have both single characters and long phrase combinations. However, our proposed model relies on the span-dependent decoding strategy. It only needs to predict the boundary of the entity span when performing the named entity recognition task by predicting the start and end tags for position matching, which has better performance than traditional methods.

BERT-Span model uses span prediction to replace the traditional sequence labeling model, and the decoding strategy in the experiment also uses the heuristic matching principle to transform decoding into a multi-label classification problem to predict the span boundary. But considering the complexity of Chinese medical text, we introduce label information through attention mechanism and extract the span of named entities by reading and understanding tasks. In this way, the model can learn the label semantic information of the named entity category and make full use of the prior knowledge. The experimental result shows that the F1 value is increased by 4.016% points.

The core idea of the BERT-MRC model is to transform the named entity recognition task into an extraction reading comprehension, and splice the label of the named entity as a problem and the initial Chinese medical text. This method can also enable the model to learn a part of the semantic knowledge of the label of the named entity. However, Li et al. [11] conducted a visual analysis of the attention part, and found that the high score attention corresponding to the named entity of the model is not concentrated in the core part of the problem as expected, but scattered in some irrelevant information. The F1 value of the model proposed in this paper has increased by 3.681% points, indicating that the semantic fusion module based on the attention mechanism designed based on this model is better than the implicit fusion based on the self-attention mechanism. We can better learn its knowledge enhancement representation through the prior knowledge in the medical named entity label, so that our attention can be fully focused on the label of the named entity. In addition, the BERT-MRC model needs to splice each text to be predicted and the label of each Chinese medical named entity category as the input of the model when reasoning, and also needs to do so many forward calculations. The model in this paper decomposes this problem-text joint coding into two independent coding modules. All named entity labels need to be coded only once, which theoretically has a higher efficiency of inference.

6 Conclusion

In order to solve the problem that there are many kinds of named entities in Chinese medical text and the length of entity text is different, we propose a BERT-Label-Span model based on label knowledge enhancement to improve the accuracy of named entity recognition. The model encodes label annotations of Chinese medical text and named entity categories separately, and integrates the prior knowledge of labels into Chinese medical text embedding through semantic fusion module based on attention mechanism. Through this method, we can not only solve the difficulties of the traditional sequence annotation model in dealing with nested and discontinuous entities, but also overcome the problems of distraction and low efficiency of inference of the traditional extraction reading comprehension method. The experiment shows that the accuracy, recall and F1 value of the model in the Chinese medical text dataset are higher than the mainstream algorithm model.

References

1. Kim, E., Rubinstein, S.M., Nead, K.T., et al.: The evolving use of electronic health records (EHR) for research. In: Seminars in Radiation Oncology. WB Saunders, vol. 29, no. 4, pp. 354–361 (2019)
2. Sekine, S., Nobata, C.: Definition, dictionaries and tagger for extended named entity hierarchy. In: LREC, pp. 1977–1980 (2004)
3. Hanisch, D., Fundel, K., Mevissen, H.-T., Zimmer, R., Fluck, J.: ProMiner: rule-based protein and gene entity recognition. BMC Bioinform. **6**(1), S14 (2005)
4. Nadeau, D., Sekine, S.: A survey of named entity recognition and classification. Lingvist. Investig. **30**(1), 3–26 (2007)
5. Eddy, S.R.: Hidden Markov models. Curr. Opin. Struct. Biol. **6**(3), 361–365 (1996)
6. Quinlan, J.R.: Induction of decision trees. Mach. Learn. **1**(1), 81–106 (1986)
7. Kapur, J.N.: Maximum-Entropy Models in Science and Engineering. Wiley, Hoboken (1989)
8. Lafferty, J.D., McCallum, A., Pereira, F.C.N.: Conditional random fields: probabilistic models for segmenting and labeling sequence data, pp. 282–289 (2001)
9. Mikolov, T., Sutskever, I., Chen, K., Corrado, G.S., Dean, J.: Distributed representations of words and phrases and their compositionality. In: Advances in Neural Information Processing Systems, pp. 3111–3119. MIT Press (2013)
10. Peters, M.E., et al.: Deep contextualized word representations. arXiv:1802.05365 (2018)
11. Li, X., et al.: A unified MRC framework for named entity recognition. arXiv preprint arXiv:1910.11476 (2019)
12. Devlin, J., et al.: BERT: pre-training of deep bidirectional transformers for language understanding. arXiv preprint arXiv:1810.04805 (2018)
13. Vaswani, A., et al.: Attention is all you need. In: Advances in Neural Information Processing Systems, pp. 5998–6008. MIT Press (2017)
14. Tripathy, J.K., et al.: Comprehensive analysis of embeddings and pre-training in NLP. Comput. Sci. Rev. **42**, 100433 (2021)
15. Kwiatkowski, T., et al.: Natural questions: a benchmark for question answering research. Trans. Assoc. Comput. Linguist. **7**, 453–466 (2019)

16. Souza, F., Nogueira, R., Lotufo, R.: Portuguese named entity recognition using BERT-CRF. arXiv preprint arXiv:1909.10649 (2019)
17. Fu, J., Huang, X., Liu, P.: SpanNER: named entity recognition as span prediction. arXiv preprint arXiv:2106.00641 (2021)
18. Gao, W., Zheng, X., Zhao, S.: Named entity recognition method of Chinese EMR based on BERT-BiLSTM-CRF. In: Journal of Physics: Conference Series, vol. 1848, no. 1. IOP Publishing (2021)

Multi-convolutional Attention Networks for Dialogue Q&A Extraction

Yuying Zhu, Chunyang Ye(✉), Hui Zhou, Taizheng Wang, and Lei Wang

Hainan University, Haikou, China
{yuyingzhu,cyye,zhouhui,taizhengwang,leiwang888}@hainanu.edu.cn

Abstract. To help software engineers find useful information, it is desirable to extract Q&A from developer dialogue to build software engineering virtual assistant (Chatbots). One of the challenges is how to extract and learn deep features of developer conversations from complex information to improve the diversity and coherence of Chatbot conversations. Existing Q&A extraction methods usually focus on the text only, and ignore the code snippets, which however contains useful contextal information in the developer conversations. As a result, the extracted Q&A may be inaccurate or even wrong. To address this issue, we propose a deep learning model MCADDL to extract distributed representations of developer dialogue for Q&A extraction concerning both the text and the code snippets. By capturing the features of Q&A context data in the form of digital vectors encoding text and code snippets separately, MCADDL learns the higher-order feature interactions of text and code snippets through multi-convolutional attention to identify potential joint features. In this way, our MCADDL can effectively extract the Q&A from developer conversations. Experimental results demonstrate that our MCADDL approach outperforms the baseline solutions in terms of a higher Precision (74%), Recall (60%) and F-measure (66%).

Keywords: question-answering extraction · deep learning · attention mechanism · code embedding

1 Introduction

Question and answer (Q&A) systems have received much attention in both software engineering (SE) academic and industrial communities due to their usage in many SE tasks. For example, many methods have been proposed to build Q&A systems for SE virtual assistants (Chatbots) [7,10,16,30]. The extraction of Q&A plays an important part in Q&A systems. In particular, deep learning models are used to learn the mapping between input and output to generate more accurate and natural Q&A. For example, ChatGPT, a general AI base model, and models such as GPT4+ are able to provide powerful language processing and generation capabilities in multiple domains. However, due to the different knowledge structures in different domains, models need to be tuned to better fit their respective application scenarios. Therefore, by collecting Q&A,

Z. Wang et al. (Eds.): ICSS 2023, CCIS 1844, pp. 305–320, 2023.
https://doi.org/10.1007/978-981-99-4402-6_22

Table 1. A Question-Answer Pair

Question	Answer
hi, all! I have dict with oldstring as key and newstring as value. I need replace strings in file according to that dict. What is the best way to do that?	Yeah, the simplest: *with open(my_file) as f:* *content = f.read()* *for k, v in dict.items():* *content = re.sub(k, v, content)* *with open(my_file, 'w') as f:* *f.write(content)* Though there probably is a "better" way.

this thesis can provide enough available data to improve the performance and effectiveness of GPT4+ models.

Existing studies usually adopt methods from NLP domains to extract the Q&A from the SE online developer chats based on the text informaiton only [15,20,28]. This however is incompetent to effectively understand the content of the dialogue because the SE online developer chats contain not only the texts, but also the code snippets. The ignorance of the codes will lose some semantics and make the extraction of Q&A pairs inaccurate. It may be difficult for single-dimensional textual information to fully reflect the full and detailed meaning of a dialogue utterance. Therefore, considering the information in code snippets is crucial for Q&A to predict and build SE virtual assistants.

Let us illustrate this issue using the example in Table 1, where there are two components in a conversational utterance of a scenario: text and code snippets. First, a segment of text provides a brief description of the subject of the question\answer. Interlocutors typically communicate their main concerns and key messages in the textual subject of the dialogue statement. Then, they provide detailed examples of code snippets about the question\answer, seek help, or explain the demonstration in the body of the dialogue. A fundamental challenge with Q&A extraction from online developer chats is the implicit relevance between the high-level intent reflected in the text and the low-level implementation details in the code snippet. Texts and code snippets are heterogeneous and may not share common lexical tokens, synonyms, or linguistic structures. Rather, their semantic relationship may be the only commonality between them. For instance, the relevant fragment in this question "*I have dict with oldstring as key and newstring as value. I need replace strings in file according to that dict.*" does not contain keywords such as *dict, key(k) and value(v)* or their synonyms. Existing methods thus cannot match the question with the answer after removing the code snippet. Therefore, an effective extraction of Q&A pair requires a higher-level semantic mapping between the codes and texts.

To address this issue, we propose a novel approach to extract the Q&A pairs from SE online developer chats concerning both the texts and codes. The main challenge of using both the texts and codes for Q&A matching lies in how to extract and fuse them effectively, because the textual features and code snippets have different impacts on the Q&A. To do so, we design a novel Multi-Convolutional Attention Networks based Developer Dialog Learning(MCADDL) framework for Q&A extraction. The MCADDL framework uses separate neural network models to learn distributed representations for text and code snippets, treating them as distinct components. In particular, with the help of existing programming language processing and natural language processing pre-trained models, code snippets and text are embedded into a high-dimensional vector space. In this way, the code snippets and text information in a conversation have similar vectors and can be perceived jointly. The goal is to effectively extract the semantics of the texts and codes into the feature vectors. Next, we design an approach to select and fuse the features based on the attention mechanism. In this way, our approach can well exploit the semanatics of texts and codes to understand the content of the dialogue and extract the Q&A pairs effectively.

The main contributions of this work are three-fold: First, we propose a novel method to represent the semantics of text and code snippets effectively for Q&A pair extraction from SE online developer chats. Our goal is to use the combination of code snippets and text to generate Q&A representations which can be used for multiple downstream tasks. Second, we propose a novel multi-convolutional attention network-based developer dialogue learning (MCADDL) framework for Q&A pair extraction. The framework integrates multiple convolution neural networks with the attention mechanism to select and fuse the features more effectively. Third, we conduct extensive experiments using datasets from real-world scenarios. The experimental results demonstrate that MCADDL outperforms several state-of-the-art models significantly. In particular, MCADDL can automatically extract Q&A in SE developer chat conversations with a better performance (accuracy 74%, recall 60%, and F-measure 66%).

The rest of this paper is organized as follows. Section 2 reviews state-of-the-art research efforts on Q&A pair extraction. Section 3 presents the design details of MCADDL. Section 4 evaluates our approach via experiments. Section 5 concludes the work and highlights some future directions.

2 Related Work

2.1 Online Developer Chats

Online chat platforms like IRC, Slack, and Gitter are gaining popularity in open source software development as they enable geographically dispersed teams to communicate easily. This is particularly useful for discussing issue reports and facilitating the bug-fixing process.

Prior studies on the developer conversations mainly focused on learning about developers' opinions and insights on APIs, programming tools, and extracted archival information [8,11] or analyzing developer behaviors and interactions [22,25]. Recently, a study shows that machine learning can be leveraged to automatically identify post-hoc-quality developer conversations [9]. Pan et al. also proposed an automatic classification approach to reveal the characteristics of information types, primary intents, and possible applications [24]. In contrast to prior research, our aim is to acquire distributed representations for Q&A in conversations, rather than mining opinions or APIs. One benefit of our approach is that it provides a directly usable database for the creation of SE virtual assistants (Chatbots).

2.2 Representations of Software Artifacts

Distributed representation is a method for acquiring vector representations of entities, such as words, sentences, and images. Recently, various models have proposed to learn the distributed representation of source codes to capture their semantics. The billions of tokens of code and millions of instances of metadata have spawned a field of study called "big code". The usability of "big code" can be developed by analyzing thousands of well-written software projects to find a reliable, readable, and maintainable pattern to develop tools for software development and program analysis [1]. For example, Gao et al. proposed an approach to fix recurring crash bugs via analyzing Q&A sites [18]. Hellendoorn et al. used language models(n-gram) to accurately capture stylistic aspects of codes [21]. Allamanis et al. used machine learning modeling of source code to learn semantics of programs [2]. Dam et al. constructed a deep learning-based Long Short Term Memory architecture that was capable to learn the representation of software code [13]. Different from many previous works [5,10,11] (which removed code snippets from the preprocessing step), we propose in this paper an approach to learn the feature representation of the code snippets as well as the texts for Q&A extraction.

2.3 Embedding of Programming Language

Programming language embedding learning is an emerging field that aims to extract semantic information from code and represent it in a way that can be used for various downstream tasks such as code completion, code similarity, and code generation [1,4]. In recent years, several language models have been developed that leverage large-scale pre-training on code corpora to learn effective representations for programming languages.

CodeBERT [17] is a transformer-based model that is trained on a large corpus of code and natural language to learn a joint representation of both. It uses a masked language modeling (MLM) objective to predict missing code tokens and a next sentence prediction (NSP) objective to learn the relationship between code and natural language. GraphCodeBERT [19] represents code as a graph where nodes represent tokens and edges represent syntactic and semantic relationships between them. It uses a combination of MLM and graph-level contrastive objectives to pre-train the model. The graph-level contrastive objective encourages the model to learn similar representations for code that have the same functionality but different syntactic structures. CodeT5 [32] is a variant of T5, a transformer-based language model, that is trained on a large corpus of code and natural language to perform various code-related tasks, including code completion, code summarization, and code translation.

3 Multi-convolutional Attention Networks Based Developer Dialog Learning

To effectively improve the accuracy of Q&A pair extraction for online developer chats, the MCADDL framework takes text and code of online developer chats as input. The MCADDL model acquires distributed representations of Q&A in the form of vectors, and combines them to accurately capture the semantic content of questions and answers. Figure 1 depicts the general architecture of MCADDL. Further details on each component of MCADDL are presented in the following subsections.

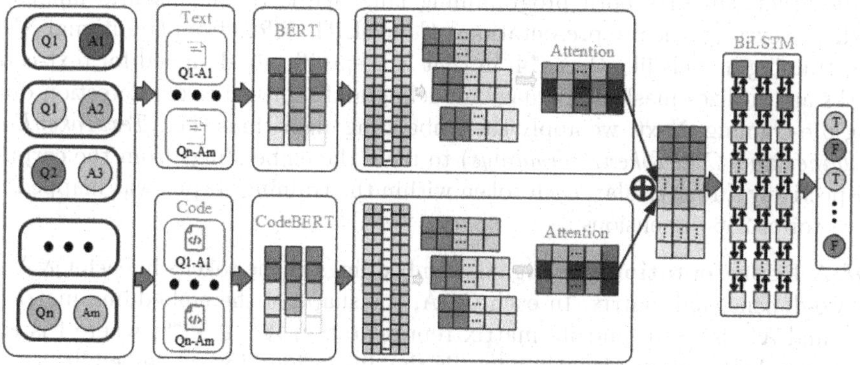

Fig. 1. The Framework of MCADDL

3.1 Preprocessing

From the obtained dataset, we take the first sentence of each dialogue thread (n sentences in the thread) as the question, the remaining n-1 sentences as candidate answers. We identify the Q&A pair by checking whether the candidate answer can be matched with the question. To do so, we first preprocess code snippets and the text of Q&A by using the subsequent actions.

Normalization. We first extract the text and code snippets in each conversation. Since code snippets in the content of a Q&A pair are retained in [''' '''], we use a regular expression to extract the code snippets. Finally, we collect code snippets in a Q&A pair into one composition and the rest portions of the Q&A pair into another composition. To focus on the semantics of the chat sentence, we remove URL, username, and emojis that appear in the text documents. We also replace the English abbreviated form with their original terms. Then we convert the texts to lowercase, tokenize the texts and code snippets, and segment them into a sequence of tokens based on NLTK [29]. The output of the preprocessing are two sequences of tokens for the texts and code snippets of each Q&A, respectively.

Indexing and Padding. To deal with varying sequence lengths in Q&A pairs, we remake each output element into a fixed-length sequence N of token indices using padding and truncation. This involves replacing each token S = $[w_1,..., w_N]$ in the sequence with its corresponding index in the vocabulary (or zero if it doesn't exist), and convert S to $[index_1, \ldots, index_{|N|}]$.

Construction of Software-Specific Token Embedding. Since the codes in software development is different from regular English text, we build two token embeddings to capture their semantics independently: *TextTokenEmbeddings* and *CodeTokenEmbeddings*. We first use the existing public corpus of Chatterjee [10] to obtain the word vector of the texts through BERT. To train the word vectors of the code, we utilize CodeBERT [17], one state-of-the-art. pre-trained model that supports both programming language (PL) and natural language (NL), to extract token representations. CodeBERT differs from traditional NLP pre-training models like Bert [14] in that it is specifically designed for text-code tasks and utilizes masked language modeling and replaced token detection during pre-training. Next, we apply the embedding algorithms (i.e., *TextTokenEmbeddings* and *CodeTokenEmbeddings*) to train the embeddings from the corpus, respectively. In particular, each token within the training corpus was mapped to a vector of 256-dimensions.

Q&A Representation. We organize embeddings of the tokens in each Q&A as a two-dimensional matrix. In each Q&A, the shape of the embedding matrices $\mathcal{X}^T$ and $\mathcal{X}^C$ is fixed, and its matrix representation $\mathcal{X}^T \in \mathbb{R}^{l*d}$, where l is the (zero-padded) sentence length, and d is the dimension of word embedding.

3.2 Semantic Extraction

Semantic extraction is a crucial procedure in Q&A extraction. We propose semantic extraction method based on multiple convolutional attention networks, that is, we use Neural Network Models to extract Q&A features. Particularly, two independent NN models $\mathcal{X}^T$ and $\mathcal{X}^C$ are used as input for the embedding data of text and code in Q&A, respectively. We conducted an study of the dataset and found that the code snippets in the developer's conversations were short, poorly structured, and written in different programming languages. Therefore, most of code representation methods are not suitable for all programming languages [12,23], or require complete functions/methods within the code, limiting their applicability [3,6,27]. To simply the code representation, MCADDL processes code snippets in the same way as the text, in the sense that the code and text are treated uniformly as token, but they have different corpus and semantic features.

Note that different kinds of neural networks models can be utilized for feature extraction. In this paper, we use multiple CNNs as feature extractors and the attention mechanism for feature selection. Note that CNNs are a promising solution for classification tasks when supervised learning classification is usually confined by some critical phrases [33].

In this paper, we choose CNN to handle the context of developer dialogue data because the semantics of dialogue sentences are usually determined by some key phrases containing technical terms so that key code blocks containing different programming languages can be effectively identified [31]. As shown in Fig. 1, the feature matrix of the prior layer is convolved by a set of convolution kernels in the convolutional layer. The output of the convolution operator improved by the bias forms the feature matrix of the next layer through the activation function. Formally, in each of the CNN, the jth feature matrix at the ith layer is also a matrix, and the value at the kth row is represented as $\mathcal{X}_{i,j}^{k}$, which is described as below:

$$\mathcal{X}_{i,j}^{k} = f_{ReLu}(f_{conv2d}(\mathcal{X}_{i-1}^{k+p})) \tag{1}$$

where p is the value at the part of the convolution kernel, f_{ReLu} is the activation function that substitutes all negative values in the feature map by zero, and f_{conv2d} is the convolution function of the CNN.

3.3 Multi-feature Attention Fusion

In order to more effectively extract features from text and code snippets, we suggest selecting and categorizing them based on their significance in relation to question answering. This is achieved through the use of an attention mechanism, which determines the relevance of specific parts of the input by assigning them a weight based on their importance in generating the output. By employing this approach, we can identify the most significant features and enhance the accuracy of our feature extraction process.

$$Attention(Q, K, V) = softmax(\frac{QK^T}{\sqrt{d_k}})V \tag{2}$$

Since the ambiguity of tokens in software engineering is not as common as in natural languages (due to the determinism of programming languages), we use a self-attention mechanism for text and code snippets respectively to select the main features. For example, the attention weight for text is calculated as follows:

$$\alpha_{text} = Attention(QW^Q, KW^K, VW^V) \tag{3}$$

where W^Q, W^K, and W^V are the weight matrices in attention. We then integrate them into the inputs through their interconnected attention weight. That is, This involves concatenating them and passing them through a one-layer linear network, expressed as:

$$\mathbf{x} = W[\sum_i \alpha^{text} h^{text} : \sum_i \alpha^{code} h^{code}] \tag{4}$$

The resulting semantic representation, denoted as x, is obtained by concatenating the text and code snippet inputs using their attention weights, which are represented by W. The concatenation operation is denoted by [:].

3.4 Identifying Q&A

LSTM networks consist of memory blocks that contain a memory cell and are controlled by three gates: an input gate, an output gate, and a forget gate. The network forgets and memorizes information to pass on useful information to future calculations and discard unnecessary information. The gates are calculated based on the previous hidden state h_{t-1} and the current input X_t, with the forget gate f_t, input gate i_t, and output gate o_t being controlled by the sigmoid activation function σ. The equations for one memory cell can be expressed as follows:

$$\begin{aligned} f_t &= \sigma(W_f \cdot [h_{t-1}, x_t] + b_f) \\ i_t &= \sigma(W_i \cdot [h_{t-1}, x_t] + b_i) \\ C_t &= f_t * C_{t-1} + i_t * tanh(W_C \cdot [h_{t-1}, x_t] + b_c) \\ o_t &= \sigma(W_o \cdot [h_{t-1}, x_t] + b_o) \\ h_t &= 0_t * tanh(C_t) \end{aligned} \tag{5}$$

The use of memory cells in LSTMs allows for the retention of information over long periods and facilitates modeling of context at the feature level. To improve 1D sequence recognition, the input signal is processed in both forward and backward directions by separate hidden layers, which are then combined as a feature map in the next layer.

While typical LSTMs only consider past context, bidirectional LSTMs [34] use both past and future context by processing the input in both directions with separate hidden layers. This is especially useful in natural language processing, where word order is closely related to sentence semantics.

For identifying Q&A pairs from the semantic representation of texts and code snippets, MCADDL employs a Bidirectional LSTM that consists of both forward and reverse LSTMs. Although they are structurally the same, they accept input with different word orders, resulting in a hidden layer vector that captures sentence context and better extracts semantic information. Finally, the sigmoid classifier is used to predict the semantic relation labels for the final identification of Q&A.

3.5 Parameters Learning

MCADDL minimizes an objective function that includes the correct activity label y_i and the predicted label $\tilde{y}_i$ for the input vector $\mathcal{V}^{s*n}$.

$$\begin{aligned} loss = &- \sum_i (y_i \cdot log(\tilde{y}_i) + (1 - y_i) \cdot log(1 - \tilde{y}_i)) \\ &+ \frac{\lambda}{2} ||\theta||_2^2 \end{aligned} \tag{6}$$

To prevent overfitting during the training process, all model parameters θ are included in the objective function. Additionally, the dropout technique is employed to improve the robustness of MCADDL. Adam is used to minimize the objective function, as it is computationally efficient and has low memory consumption compared to other optimization techniques.

4 Evaluation

This section presents the extensive experiments performed to evaluate the performance of MCADDL. Specifically, we aim to answer the following questions:

RQ1: Is MCADDL effective in Q&A extraction?
RQ2: What is the impact of code snippets on the performance?
RQ3: What is the impact of processing texts and codes seperately?
RQ4: What is the effects of different pre-trained code representation models?

4.1 Experimental Setup

DataSet. In the experiment, we use two real world datasets to evaluate our proposal: The first one is from Chatterjee et al. [9] (referred to as OriginalDataset). The OriginalDataset contains only 2001 conversations, 23,972 utterances, and 3160 users. 1,601 conversations are used for training and 400 conversations are used for testing. To further evaluate the robustness of MCADDL, we created a larger dataset (referred to as LargeDataset) from Slack Chat dataset[1] following the same principle of the OriginalDataset. The statistics of both datasets are shown in Table 2.

The process of creating the LargeDataset includes four main steps: First, we leveraged DECA[2] to identify the developer chat threads with opinion-based questions from the Slack Chat dataset[3]. Similar to OriginalDataset, only opinion-asking questions and answers are considered in LargeDataset. Second, we randomly sampled 606 threads based on opinion-asking questions and manually excluded low-quality threads that contain too much-unformatted source code, as well as those with too many spelling and grammatical errors or written in nonEnglish languages. Third, we used the ChatEO [9] to predict Q&A, because it has an accuracy of 87% on the extract of opinion-based Q&A from online developer chats. Forth, we manually annotated the set of 606 conversations. We hired 2 master students with (3+ years) of experience in programming to analyze and annotate conversation threads purely for opinion-based questions. We extracted the obtained data and converted it into a dialogue dataset, each utterance includes the thread id, the user name of the interlocutor, and the content of the dialogue. The sample size of the newly added 606 dialogues is sufficient to calculate the consistency measure with high confidence. The two students then went back and forth and resolved any conflicts to create the final dataset. We generated the LargeDataset in Table 2 by integrating the OriginalDataset and the newly annotated dataset containing code snippet dialogues. More specifically, the new dataset(LargeDataset) contains 2607 conversations which is 1.3

[1] https://www.zenodo.org/record/3627124.
[2] https://www.ifi.uzh.ch/en/seal/people/panichella/tools/DECA.html. DECA is a tool for automatically identifying natural language fragments in emails related to the software engineering domain.
[3] https://www.zenodo.org/record/3627124.

Table 2. Charateristics of Dataset

Source	Conversation	Utterance	User	Percentage of Code Snippet
OriginalDataset	2001	23972	3160	1%
LargeDataset	2607	31467	4236	30%

Table 3. Proportion of conversations with code snippets

Source	Conversations	Conversations*Code	Proportion
SlackChat	38956	11558	30%
LargeDataset	2607	795	30%

times the size of OriginalDataset. OriginalDataset only holds 10% of conversations with code, but LargeDataset contains 30%. In LargeDataset, the proportion (Table 3) of conversations with code snippets is comparable to the Slack Chat dataset.We randomly divide the dataset into the training set, validation set and test set with a proportion of 6:2:2.

Evaluation Metrics. The evaluation of the models in the experiments is based on three metrics: precision, recall, and F-measure [26].

Parameter Setting. The hyperparameters of the models are set as shown in Table 4, with the aim of optimizing the performance of the models through a linear search of the hyperparameters.

4.2 Result Analysis

Comparison of Different Prediction Methods (RQ1): To the best of our knowledge, ChatEO is the only one targeted for Q&A extraction of developer chat artifacts. Hence, we use ChatEO [10] as the baseline for performance comparisons. We also compare our model with the following two models in the software engineering neighborhood.

QA-LSTM: Using deep learning (DL) framework to build a model of the question and answer, and measure their closeness via cosine similarity.

QCN: Aggregating information according to the similarity and difference of different components of community Q&A for Q&A extraction.

The comparison results of different models are shown in Table 8. We can observe that MCADDL outperforms ChatEO significantly. In particular, the Precision, Recall, and F-measure of MCADDL are about 27.5%, 49.9%, and 39.9% higher than that of ChatEO, respectively. We can also observe that the performance of QA-LSTM is better than that of QCN because QA-LSTM because it uses deep learning to extract text semantics more effectively. Among these models, MCADDL performs the best. This is because the text vectors are only randomly initialized in QA-LSTM and QCN, whereas MCADDL adopts Bert to

Table 4. Hyperparameters setting

Parameter	Value	Parameter	Value	Parameter	Value
word_embedding	256	cnn_filters	50	$BiLSTM_{num\_units}$	200
kernel_size_1	2 * 200	kernel_size_2	5 * 200	dropout	0.5
kernel_size_3	8 * 200	FC	1024	learning rate	0.001

Table 5. Performance of MCADDL and the baselines

Approach	OriginalDataset			LargeDataset		
	Precision	*Recall*	*F-measure*	*Precision*	*Recall*	*F-measure*
QA-LSTM	0.30	0.19	0.23	0.31	0.19	0.23
QCN	0.13	0.32	0.18	0.15	0.32	0.20
ChatEO	0.63	0.40	0.49	0.58	0.40	0.47
MCADDL	**0.72**	**0.53**	**0.61**	**0.74**	**0.60**	**0.66**

effectively learn contextual semantic information from the text and reduce the instability of token unstructured vectors.

Impact of Code Snippets Information (RQ2): We evaluated whether the inclusion of code snippets improves the prediction accuracy by constructing a sub-model called MCADDL/CODE, which excludes code snippets from the dataset[4], and compared it with the original MCADDL model. The experiment results are presented in Table 6, and we observed a decrease in the prediction accuracy when code snippets were excluded. Therefore, we can conclude that code snippets are indeed useful for improving the prediction accuracy in our model (Table 5).

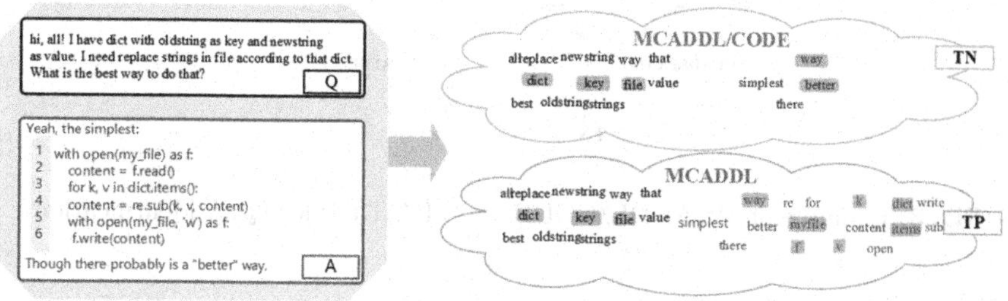

Fig. 2. Example of MCADDL/CODE and MCADDL for Q&A identification

Figure 3 and Fig. 2 present a case study for MCADDL/CODE and MCADDL for Q&A identification from our evaluation dataset. To further investigate why code snippets are helpful, We examize specific examples of the predicted results

[4] https://www.zenodo.org/record/3627124.

of both MCADDL/CODE and MCADDL models. Figure 2 shows the prediction of a Q&A on the first thread. Both models have the same training lexicon and network model, but have different components (whether they contain code snippet information.). It is difficult to match the question and answer directly using the texts only. Therefore, MCADDL/CODE marks the pair as true negative. Differently, MCADDL learns the semantics of texts and codes with a unified vector represenation. Therefore, MCADDL can correctly mark the pair as true positive. The ability to understand semantics allows MCADDL to perform more robust searches. Its search results are more influenced by the keywords in the token in the Q&A. For example, MCADDL/CODE removes the code fragment from the answer sentence, resulting in less semantic information in the answer sentence, so the prediction result of MCADDL/CODE is False.

Table 6. Results for MCADDL/CODE and MCADDL

Approach	OriginalDataset			LargeDataset		
	Precision	*Recall*	*F-measure*	*Precision*	*Recall*	*F-measure*
MCADDL/CODE	0.68	0.55	0.60	0.68	0.52	0.59
MCADDL	**0.71**	**0.55**	**0.62**	**0.74**	**0.60**	**0.66**

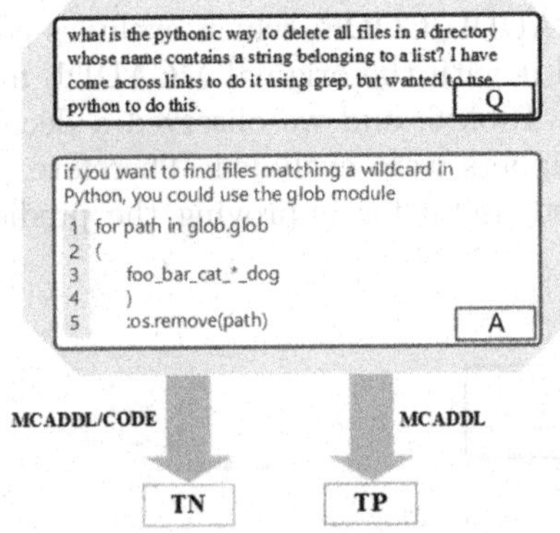

Fig. 3. Example of MCADDL/CODE and MCADDL for Q&A identification

MCADDL demonstrates its ability to identify and fuse semantic information from both text and code snippets (as shown in Fig. 2), enabling it to successfully detect different types of keywords. This is one of its key advantages. Additionally, MCADDL's semantic relevance feature enables it to match fragments of keywords that are semantically related to code snippets, expanding the search scope and providing developers with a wider selection of code snippets to learn from. This is particularly important when the prediction base is small. Furthermore, the ability to associate text and code snippets enables developers to obtain more specific answer demonstrations, which can be highly beneficial. The other example (Q: what is the pythonic way to delete all files in a directory whose name contains a string belonging to a list? I have come across links to do it using grep, but wanted to use python to do this. A: "if you want to find files matching a wildcard in Python, you could use the glob module *'''for path in glob.glob (foo_bar_cat_*_dog) :os.remove(path)'''*) is shows that "delete" in the question sentence clearly has a high semantic relevance to "remove" in the code snippet in the question. MCADDL/CODE removes the code fragment from the answer sentence, resulting in a false negative in the prediction.

Effects of Handling Texts and Code Snippets Separately (RQ3): To assess the impact of separate handling of texts and code snippets in MCADDL on Q&A extraction, we conducted an experiment where we replaced the two independent neural networks in MCADDL with a single neural network to process the texts and code snippets together. This modified model is denoted as MCADDL-COM. Table 7 shows that MCADDL and MCADDL-COM achieve the same result in the OriginalDataset. The reason is that OriginalDataset has very little data containing code fragments (1%, in comparison with LargeDataset 30%), therefore MCADDL cannot learn high-order code representations to achieve accurate Q&A excavation. However, MCADDL outperforms MCADDL-COM in the LargeDataset. This suggests that the separate NN networks in MCADDL is more effective in extracting the semantics of contents in the dialogue with rich codes. This finding is consistent with previous studies that have shown the power of neural networks in learning features from multiple sources [35], making them more suitable for learning interactions between multi-source content.

Effects of Code Representation (RQ4): To investigate the effects of different code representations on the performance, we compare CodeBERT [17], GraphCodeBERT [19] and CodeT5 [32] for code representation in the experiment, as shown in Table 8. We can observe that CodeBERT outperforms the

Table 7. Results for MCADDL-COM and MCADDL

Approach	OriginalDataset			LargeDataset		
	Precision	*Recall*	*F-measure*	*Precision*	*Recall*	*F-measure*
MCADDL-COM	0.68	0.55	0.62	0.70	0.52	0.60
MCADDL	**0.68**	**0.55**	**0.62**	**0.74**	**0.60**	**0.66**

Table 8. Effects of Code Representation

Approach	OriginalDataset			LargeDataset		
	Precision	*Recall*	*F-measure*	*Precision*	*Recall*	*F-measure*
CodeT5	0.53	0.48	0.50	0.71	0.55	0.62
GraphCodeBERT	0.55	0.48	0.51	0.74	0.58	0.65
CodeBERT	**0.63**	**0.40**	**0.49**	**0.74**	**0.60**	**0.66**

other code represenation methods. This might be due to the fact that the code snippets in the Q&A pair are very short and few Token types and dataflow features can be explored in CodeT5 and GraphCodeBert in both the extraction tasks of the Q&A. Considering that the structure of code in the dataset predicted by the Q&A and the integration with text semantics makes MCADDL more oriented towards semantic analysis of code, while CodeBERT is more suitable for syntactic token representation. CodeBERT's performance is attributed to its higher complexity (i.e., large number of trainable parameters, over 124M) and pre-trained dataset. Overall, our results show that the semantic program feature CodeBERT can improve the performance of code representation Q&A extraction.

5 Conclusions

This paper introduced the MCADDL model for effectively extracting Q&A pairs from SE online developer chats by representing the semantics of text and code snippets using a multi-convolutional attention network. The model outperformed state-of-the-art solutions in terms of Precision, Recall, and F-measure, as shown in the experimental results on two benchmark datasets.

For future work, potential features such as integrating the contexts of each sentence in the dialog and code snippets summary could be explored to further improve Q&A pair extraction. Additionally, testing the model in more software environments would help verify its generalization capability.

Acknowledgement. This work was supported in part by the Key Research and Development Program of Hainan Province under grant no. ZDYF2022GXIS230 and ZDYF2020008. This research was also supported by the State Key Laboratory of Marine Resource Utilization in South China Sea, and the Key Laboratory of Big Data and Smart Services of Hainan Province.

References

1. Allamanis, M., Barr, E.T., Devanbu, P., Sutton, C.: A survey of machine learning for big code and naturalness. ACM Comput. Surv. (CSUR) **51**(4), 1–37 (2018)
2. Allamanis, M., Brockschmidt, M., Khademi, M.: Learning to represent programs with graphs. arXiv preprint arXiv:1711.00740 (2017)
3. Alon, U., Brody, S., Levy, O., Yahav, E.: Code2seq: generating sequences from structured representations of code. arXiv preprint arXiv:1808.01400 (2018)
4. Alon, U., Zilberstein, M., Levy, O., Yahav, E.: Code2vec: learning distributed representations of code. In: POPL 2019, vol. 3, no. POPL, pp. 1–29 (2019)
5. Arya, D., Wang, W., Guo, J.L., Cheng, J.: Analysis and detection of information types of open source software issue discussions. In: ICSE 2019, pp. 454–464. IEEE (2019)
6. Ben-Nun, T., Jakobovits, A.S., Hoefler, T.: Neural code comprehension: a learnable representation of code semantics. Adv. Neural Inf. Process. Syst. **31** (2018)
7. Bradley, N., Fritz, T., Holmes, R.: Context-aware conversational developer assistants. In: ICSE 2018, pp. 993–1003. IEEE (2018)

8. Chatterjee, P.: Extracting archival-quality information from software-related chats. In: ICSE 2020, pp. 234–237 (2020)
9. Chatterjee, P., Damevski, K., Kraft, N.A., Pollock, L.: Automatically identifying the quality of developer chats for post hoc use. TOSEM **30**(4), 1–28 (2021)
10. Chatterjee, P., Damevski, K., Pollock, L.: Automatic extraction of opinion-based Q&A from online developer chats. In: ICSE 2021, pp. 1260–1272. IEEE (2021)
11. Chatterjee, P., Damevski, K., Pollock, L., Augustine, V., Kraft, N.A.: Exploratory study of slack Q&A chats as a mining source for software engineering tools. In: MSR 2019, pp. 490–501. IEEE (2019)
12. Ciniselli, M., et al.: An empirical study on the usage of transformer models for code completion. TSE **48**, 4818–4837 (2021)
13. Dam, H.K., Tran, T., Pham, T.: A deep language model for software code. arXiv preprint arXiv:1608.02715 (2016)
14. Devlin, J., Chang, M.W., Lee, K., Toutanova, K.: BERT: pre-training of deep bidirectional transformers for language understanding. arXiv preprint arXiv:1810.04805 (2018)
15. Di Sorbo, A., Panichella, S., Visaggio, C.A., Di Penta, M., Canfora, G., Gall, H.C.: Development emails content analyzer: intention mining in developer discussions (t). In: ASE 2015, pp. 12–23. IEEE (2015)
16. Eberhart, Z., Bansal, A., McMillan, C.: A wizard of OZ study simulating API usage dialogues with a virtual assistant. TSE **48**, 1883–1904 (2020)
17. Feng, Z., et al.: CodeBERT: a pre-trained model for programming and natural languages. arXiv preprint arXiv:2002.08155 (2020)
18. Gao, Q., Zhang, H., Wang, J., Xiong, Y., Zhang, L., Mei, H.: Fixing recurring crash bugs via analyzing Q&A sites (t). In: ASE 2015, pp. 307–318. IEEE (2015)
19. Guo, D., et al.: GraphCodeBERT: pre-training code representations with data flow. arXiv preprint arXiv:2009.08366 (2020)
20. Guzman, E., Maalej, W.: How do users like this feature? A fine grained sentiment analysis of app reviews. In: RE 2014, pp. 153–162. IEEE (2014)
21. Hellendoorn, V.J., Devanbu, P.T., Bacchelli, A.: Will they like this? Evaluating code contributions with language models. In: MSR 2015, pp. 157–167. IEEE (2015)
22. Lin, B., Zagalsky, A., Storey, M.A., Serebrenik, A.: Why developers are slacking off: understanding how software teams use slack. In: CSCW 2016, pp. 333–336 (2016)
23. Oda, Y., Fudaba, H., Neubig, G., Hata, H., Sakti, S., Toda, T., Nakamura, S.: Learning to generate pseudo-code from source code using statistical machine translation (t). In: Automated Software Engineering, pp. 574–584 (2015)
24. Pan, S., Bao, L., Ren, X., Xia, X., Lo, D., Li, S.: Automating developer chat mining. In: ASE 2021, pp. 854–866. IEEE (2021)
25. Sahar, H., Hindle, A., Bezemer, C.P.: How are issue reports discussed in Gitter chat rooms? J. Syst. Softw. **172**, 110852 (2021)
26. Sasaki, Y., et al.: The truth of the f-measure. Teach Tutor Mater **1**(5), 1–5 (2007)
27. Silva, D., Silva, J., Santos, G.J.D.S., Terra, R., Valente, M.T.O.: RefDiff 2.0: a multi-language refactoring detection tool. TSE **47**, 2786–2802 (2020)
28. Sinha, V., Lazar, A., Sharif, B.: Analyzing developer sentiment in commit logs. In: MSR 2016, pp. 520–523 (2016)
29. Thanaki, J.: Python Natural Language Processing. Packt Publishing Ltd. (2017)
30. Tian, Y., Thung, F., Sharma, A., Lo, D.: APIBot: question answering bot for API documentation. In: ASE 2017, pp. 153–158. IEEE (2017)

31. Upadhyaya, S., Parajuli, A., Shakya, S.: Predictive use cases of CNN based multi label classification for programming languages. In: ICCCIS 2019, pp. 375–380. IEEE (2019)
32. Wang, Y., Wang, W., Joty, S., Hoi, S.C.: CodeT 5: identifier-aware unified pre-trained encoder-decoder models for code understanding and generation. arXiv preprint arXiv:2109.00859 (2021)
33. Yin, W., Kann, K., Yu, M., Schütze, H.: Comparative study of CNN and RNN for natural language processing. arxiv 2017. arXiv preprint arXiv:1702.01923 (2021)
34. Zhang, S., Zheng, D., Hu, X., Yang, M.: Bidirectional long short-term memory networks for relation classification. In: PACLIC 2015, pp. 73–78 (2015)
35. Zhang, S., Yao, L., Sun, A., Tay, Y.: Deep learning based recommender system: a survey and new perspectives. ACM Comput. Surv. (CSUR) **52**(1), 1–38 (2019)

Knowledge Graph Construction for Healthcare Services in Traditional Chinese Medicine

Zhiwei Yi[1], Bolin Zhang[1], Xingpeng Deng[1], Jiahao Wang[1], Zhiying Tu[1(✉)], Dianhui Chu[1], Xin Hu[1], Deqiong Ding[1], Yong Guan[2], and Zhao Sun[3]

[1] Harbin Institute of Technology, ICES Center, Harbin, China
22S030149@stu.hit.edu.cn,
{brolin,tzy_hit,chudh,hithuxin,mathddq}@hit.edu.cn
[2] Qingdao Municipal Center for Disease Control & Prevention, Qingdao, China
[3] Msun Health Technology Group Co., Ltd., Gansu, China
sunzhao@msunhealth.com

Abstract. Traditional Chinese medicine (TCM) is a bright pearl in the treasure house of healthcare applications that has attracted increasing attention due to its huge applying potential, especially in the prevention and intervention of COVID-19 Pandemic. Such applications for healthcare decision-making are powerful tools to help provide actionable and explainable medical services to patients, but they are a knowledge-driven system and rely on knowledge graphs. However, most of TCM-related materials and guidebooks are preserved in the form of documents, lacking structured information and conceptual knowledge. To facility the study of domain-specific knowledge graphs in TCM, we define the ontology of knowledge graph in TCM with 29 types of entities and 32 types of relations, and then annotate a high-quality dataset (TCM-ERE) for Entity and Relation Extraction (E&RE) aligning with the concepts of the TCM-ontology. More than 40% of relations can only be inferred from multiple sentences in TCM-ERE, thus it can also be used for Chinese document-level E&RE research. The baseline models trained on the TCM-ERE are used to extract fact triples from TCM medical records for the enriching scale of the TCM-related knowledge graph (TCM-KG). TCM-ERE, TCM-KG and the baseline models are publicly available at https://gitee.com/yi_zhi_wei/acup1.git.

Keywords: Knowledge graph · Knowledge extraction · Traditional Chinese medicine · Healthcare services

1 Introduction

Traditional Chinese medicine (TCM) shines on the world medical stage and has been included in the 'list of representative works of human intangible cultural heritage' by United Nations Educational, Scientific and Cultural Organization (UNESCO). Thus, the TCM-related healthcare applications has received

Z. Wang et al. (Eds.): ICSS 2023, CCIS 1844, pp. 321–335, 2023.
https://doi.org/10.1007/978-981-99-4402-6_23

increasing attention. Existing works mainly focuses on TCM diagnosis of diseases [9], medical record management [12] and TCM-drug discovery [18], all of which downstream applications rely on the management of domain-specific knowledge.

In recent years, knowledge graph has become an emerging technology in the field of knowledge management. The construction of knowledge graph will play a key role in the integration of various TCM-related knowledge (e.g. clinical guidelines, medical records, and classical prescriptions, excavates), sorts out clinical experience and academic ideas, and implement intelligent and personalized knowledge services in TCM.

However, the construction of such a domain-specific knowledge graph arouses the following issues: Constructing TCM knowledge graph manually is time-consuming and labor-intensive, while automatic construction of TCM knowledge graph depends on the entity and relation extraction models and the related training datasets.

To this end, we propose a complete construction process of TCM knowledge graph, and open sourced our audited graph (TCM-KG) to facilitate related research in the field of TCM: i) We first define the ontology of TCM-KG by fusing the existing ontologies in TCM, which contains 29 types of entities, 32 types of relations. ii) Based on the concepts in our TCM-ontology, we annotate a high-quality dataset (TCM-ERE) for TCM-related entity and relation extraction tasks, which contains 4500 sentences and 4000 entities, and 20000 relations. iii) Then, we trained different NER models and relation extraction models based on the pre-trained language models (e.g. BERT [5], ERNIE [11], Roberta [8], and Albert [6]). iiii) The best models on each task will be used to extract triples from the crawled documents in TCM online forums[1]. All the triples auto-extracted by models are checked by TCM experts and the fact triples are stored in Neo4j to expand our graph (TCM-KG).

The main contributions are summarized as follows:

- To support the conversational services for healthcare applications, we model the ontology for the domain of traditional Chinese medicine and release a large knowledge graph, including 4000 entities, 20000 relations and 33750 triples.
- To construct the knowledge graph automatically, we annotate a TCM-related knowledge extraction dataset and train the baseline models on the task.
- To facility the study of TCM-related healthcare services, the knowledge graph, extraction dataset, baseline models will be publicly available at https://gitee.com/yi_zhi_wei/acup1.git.

The rest of this paper is organized as follows. Section 2 summarizes the related work about knowledge extraction dataset and knowledge graph construction method. Section 3 outlines the overall process for constructing the knowledge graph, encompassing ontology modeling, dataset construction, and the knowledge extraction models. Section 4 presents statistical information about the constructed dataset and the knowledge graph. The detail of the experimental envi-

[1] http://www.gjmlzy.com:83/ and https://www.ayskjaj.com/.

ronment, baseline results, and analysis of the outcomes for knowledge extraction is described in Sect. 5.

2 Related Work

Knowledge graph refers to a type of knowledge representation, where knowledge is structured in the form of facts, also known as triples. These triples are formulated as (head, relation, tail), which model the connections between various entities. This system of knowledge is extensive and capable of capturing intricate relationships among domain concepts. It is a novel technology in the big data era, widely used for large-scale knowledge management and intelligent services. Knowledge graph plays a crucial role in numerous applications, including knowledge retrieval, question-answering, knowledge recommendation, and knowledge visualization [1].

Building a medical knowledge graph involves extracting concepts, entity relationships, and attributes from a vast amount of structured, semi-structured, and unstructured medical data [7]. Jia et al. [4] discussed the data sources, research content, and application prospects of the TCM knowledge graph. Yu et al. [17] proposed a technique for constructing a TCM knowledge graph with a traditional Chinese medicine language system. Ruan et al. [13] presented a semi-automatic construction process for a TCM knowledge graph using a multi-strategy learning method, which was applied in intelligent assisted prescription applications. Miao et al. [10] analyzed a large amount of data from different sources, combining existing traditional Chinese medicine knowledge bases to build a Chinese herbal prescription knowledge graph.

Furthermore, we collected knowledge graphs from the domains of Western and traditional Chinese medicine, including Nephrology and traditional Chinese medicine Health Preservation and so on. The statistical information regarding the entities and their relationships present in these knowledge graphs can be found in the Table 1.

Table 1. Statistics of relevant medical KG information

KG	Entities	Relations	Entity types	Relations types
Lin [15]	About 20000	Unknown	18	7
Chang [2]	22050	6980	18	15
Yu [14]	<10000	<10000	22	23
Liu [3]	524	1097	18	17

Nevertheless, the research on constructing knowledge graphs in the domain of traditional Chinese medicine is still limited. There is a lack of in-depth knowledge graphs for specific areas of traditional Chinese medicine, such as knowledge graphs for the moxibustion domain. Additionally, there is a scarcity of relevant traditional Chinese medicine domain ontologies and knowledge extraction datasets.

3 Knowledge Graph Construction

3.1 Overall Construction Process

The overall steps for constructing a knowledge graph for traditional Chinese medicine are illustrated in Fig. 1. It involves several steps, starting with ontology modeling that defines the concepts and relationships relevant to traditional Chinese medicine. The next step is manual annotation of unstructured data, where we assign entity types and relationship types based on the ontology model. This annotated dataset is then used to train a model to extract knowledge from more unstructured text. We evaluate the trained model on a new dataset of unannotated text and review the predicted results to verify their accuracy with human experts. Then we repeat this iterative process to create a more comprehensive and extensive knowledge graph for traditional Chinese medicine.

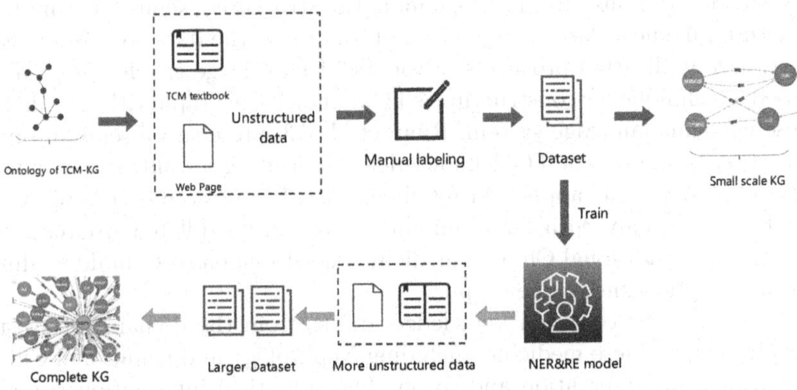

Fig. 1. Process of TCM KG Construction

3.2 TCM-Ontology Modeling

To construct an ontology for the Traditional Chinese Medicine domain, several steps need to be followed. First, it is crucial to identify the ontology's domain and scope, specifying the types of TCM knowledge to be represented and the intended users. Second, relevant TCM literature, including textbooks, research articles, and clinical practice guidelines, should be collected to identify key concepts, relationships and their attributes. Additionally, it is necessary to consult with experts in the TCM domain to verify the accuracy of the information and gather their feedback.

Our TCM-ontology comprises of approximately 29 relationship types and 32 entity types, which include commonly found entities like diseases, symptoms, prescriptions, Chinese medicine, acupuncture points, moxibustion methods, and other entities relevant to Traditional Chinese Medicine (TCM). The accuracy and completeness of the TCM-ontology were verified by experts in the field. A partial view of the ontology layers can be seen in the Fig. 2, and the details of some entities and relationships are shown in Table 2.

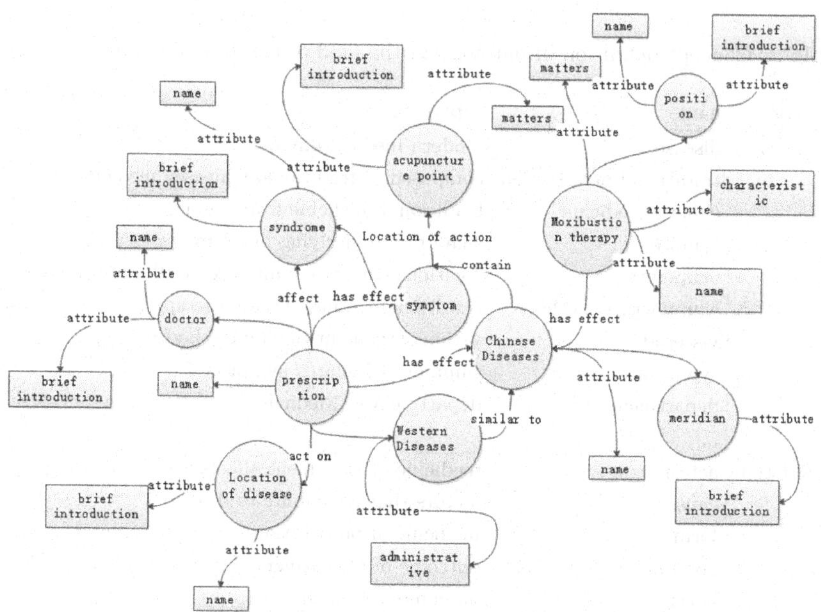

Fig. 2. TCM-ontology

3.3 Dataset Collection

Our initial dataset was derived from a book on moxibustion, which broadly covers various aspects of traditional Chinese medicine moxibustion. The book provides fundamental knowledge on moxibustion, operational methods, and specific applications of moxibustion in common diseases. The process involves establishing precise data annotation formats and selecting traditional Chinese medicine texts as sources of knowledge. The annotation format of the dataset was based on the DocRED dataset proposed in [16].

In order to ensure the quality of our dataset, we conduct automatic validation using two methods: entity automatic validation and relation automatic validation. The entity automatic validation algorithm is employed to check for any missing or mislabeled entities in the document. On the other hand, the relation automatic validation algorithm is used to verify the presence of entities involved in a relation within the evidence sentence, and to check for any mislabeled or out-of-bounds relations. Specific validation process can not be shown as the details are too lengthy.

Table 2. Concept definition of ontology in the field of traditional Chinese medicine.

Type	name	explain
Entity	disease	modern medical illnesses
	traditional prescription	composed of traditional Chinesev medicine
	chinese medicine	traditional medicine from China
	symptom	sign of an underlying problem
	acupoints	locations where acupuncture needles are inserted
	acupuncture method	traditional Chinese needle therapy
	viscerad	various organs in the human body
	syndromes	summary of related symptoms
	department	department of Medicine
	...	...
Relation	act on	medicine or treatment affects the body
	cause	factors that contribute to disease
	form	medicine of preparation
	good at	outcome of a treatment
	effect	outcome of a medicine
	...	...

3.4 Knowledge Extraction

The knowledge extraction process aims to extract entity-relation triples that conform to the facts from the document and is divided into Named Entity Recognition (NER) and Relation Extraction (RE) tasks.

NER. The task of Named Entity Recognition (NER) entails identifying entities within a given text, where the input/output format usually comprises the text and corresponding entity labels. To tackle this task, we employed a model that integrates a pre-trained language model (PTML), a Bi-LSTM layer, a SPAN prediction layer, and a custom loss function named focal loss. The model architecture is shown in Fig. 3.

The model consists of three layers. The first layer is the sentence representation layer, which employs a pre-trained language model to generate sentence vector representation. The second layer is a bidirectional LSTM layer, which uses the output of the first layer to learn interdependencies between neighboring tokens. The final layer is a span prediction layer, which addresses the challenge of nested entity recognition by converting sequence labeling tasks to start and end index predictions for entities within the text. This technique involves assigning a label to each token in the text, indicating if it is the beginning, inside, or outside of an entity, and predicting the start and end indices of the entity. This approach has been found to improve the accuracy of entity recognition, particularly for languages with complex syntax and rich morphology. The focal loss implemented in the above code can be represented by the following formula:

$$FL(p_t) = -(1 - p_t)^{\gamma} \log(p_t) \tag{1}$$

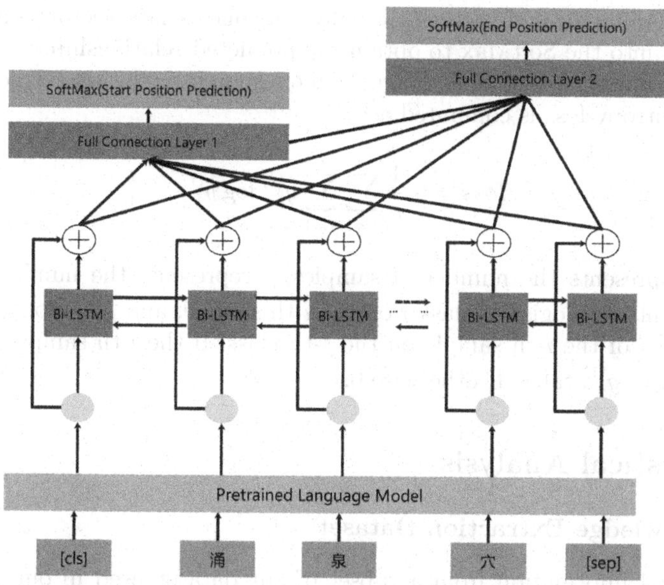

Fig. 3. NER Model. The model takes a sequence of words as input and produces a sequence of entity tags for each word. To accomplish this, the pre-trained language model is utilized to create contextualized word embeddings, which are then fed into the Bi-LSTM layer to capture the sequential information. Finally, the output of the Bi-LSTM layer is passed through the SPAN prediction layer to obtain the entity tags.

In NER task, the focal loss is used to train a neural network model to predict named entities. By introducing the focal loss, the model can be trained to pay more attention to hard examples that are initially misclassified with high confidence, which can lead to improved performance in NER task. Here, p_t represents the predicted probability of the true label for a given sample, and γ is a hyperparameter that determines the degree of focusing on hard examples.

RE. Relation extraction (RE) is an essential text classification task that entails identifying and classifying semantic connections between entities in text. This task has significant applications in fields such as information retrieval, knowledge discovery, and question answering. RE models generally take unstructured or semi-structured text data, such as scientific papers or news articles, as input. The output of the model is a structured representation of the relationships between the identified entities, often categorized by labels such as "is-a", "part-of", or "causes". The model architecture is shown in Fig. 4.

First, We concatenate the sentences related to the evidence into a single input for the model, then we input the concatenated sentence into the pre-trained language model to obtain encoded vector e. We then concatenate the text of the head and tail entities and input them into the pre-trained language model to obtain encoded vector h. Finally, we concatenate vectors e and h and input them into the SoftMax to obtain the predicted relationship.

To fine-tune the pre-trained language models on the relation extraction task, the cross entropy loss is computed as:

$$loss = -\frac{1}{n}\sum_{i=1}^{n}\sum_{j=1}^{c} g_j^{(i)} \log \hat{y}_j^{(i)}, \tag{2}$$

where n represents the number of samples, c represents the number of class, $\hat{y}_j^{(i)}$ represents the logist of class j on the i-th sample, and $g_j^{(i)}$ represents a the ground truth of the i-th sample on the j-th class. If the i-th sample is true on the j-th class, $g_j^{(i)}$ takes 1, otherwise 0.

4 Statistical Analysis

4.1 Knowledge Extraction Dataset

We analyzed information from a subset of our dataset used in our study. We counts the distribution of the number of sentences in each document in the dataset, and the statistical results are shown in Fig. 5(a). The average number of sentences in each document is 5.93. And we counts the distribution of the number of entities in each document in the data set. The statistical results are shown in Fig. 5(b). Each sentence has an average of 18.23 entities. Furthermore, more detailed statistical information about this subset can be found in the Table 3.

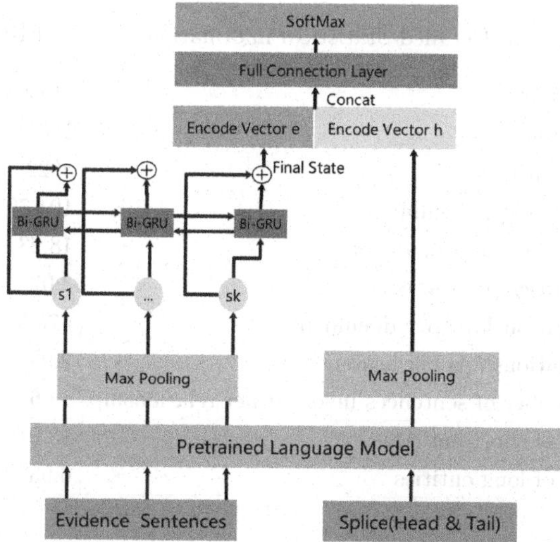

Fig. 4. RE Model. This model is designed to capture both local and global contextual information from the input text, allowing it to accurately identify complex relationships between entities.

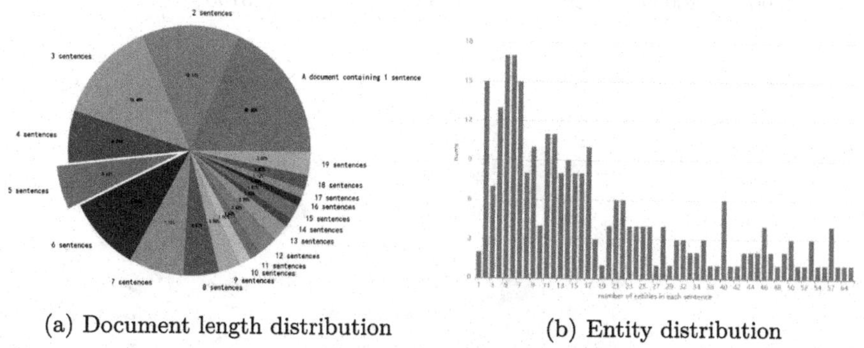

(a) Document length distribution (b) Entity distribution

Fig. 5. Statistical information of TCM-ERE.

4.2 TCM-Related Knowledge Graph

Based on the knowledge extraction dataset in the field of traditional Chinese medicine, using the written knowledge extractor, the knowledge graph of the field of TCM constructed through knowledge extraction and knowledge alignment contains nearly 33750 triples. The construction results are shown in Table 4 and a 3-hop subgraph in TCM domain KG is shown in Fig. 6.

Table 3. Detailed Statistical information of TCM-ERE

Statistical Item	Statistical Value
Number of sentences	1601
Number of entities	4922
Average words per document	101.79
Average entities per document	18.23
Average entities per sentence	3.07
Average relationships per document	17.35
Average relationships per sentence	2.93
Average number of sentences involved per relationship	1.66
Percentage of short entities	93.07
Percentage of long entities	6.93

Table 4. Statistical information of our TCM-KG

Entities	Relations	Entity types	Relations types	Number of triples
4000	20000	29	32	33750

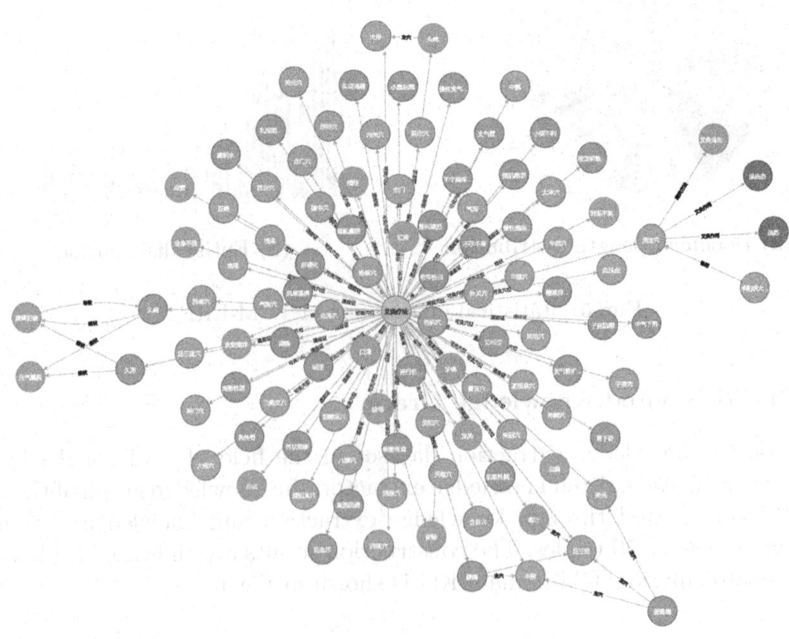

Fig. 6. A 3-hop subgraph in TCM-KG stored in Neo4j.

5 Experiments and Results

5.1 Experimental Setup

Experimental environment: Windows 10 Professional operating system, Intel(R) Core(TM) i9-9750H 2.60 GHz CPU, NVIDIA RTX 2060 (6 GB) GPU, 16 GB RAM, and deep learning framework PaddlePaddle 1.7.

In NER and RE task, Precision, Recall, and F1 Score are commonly used as evaluation metrics. They can be calculated as the following formulas:

$$Precision = \frac{TP}{TP + FP} \tag{3}$$

$$Recall = \frac{TP}{TP + FN} \tag{4}$$

$$F1 = 2 \cdot \frac{Precision \cdot Recall}{Precision + Recall} \tag{5}$$

where TP denotes the number of true positives, FP denotes the number of false positives, and FN denotes the number of false negatives. Precision measures the proportion of predicted positive samples that are actually positive, while Recall measures the proportion of actual positive samples that are correctly predicted as positive. F1 Score is the harmonic mean of Precision and Recall, which balances both metrics and provides an overall evaluation of the model's performance.

In addition, we conducted a comparative analysis of various parameter values for the model and ultimately selected the following parameter settings for NER and RE tasks: For NER task, we set the batch size to 32, the initial learning rate to 9e−5, the optimizer to AdamW, the warmup to 0.1, and the epoches to 80, the max sentence length to 256. For RE task, we set the batch size to 32, the initial learning rate to 5e−5, the optimizer to AdamW, the warmup to 0.1, and the epoches to 50, the max sentence length to 256.

5.2 Results Analysis

We have selected several model combinations as baselines, as shown in the Table 5 below, using the model architecture introduced in Sect. 3.4 as a framework. From the table and the corresponding Fig. 7 and Fig. 8, it can be observed that the model combination Ernie-Health+Bi-LSTM+SPAN-Predict achieved the best scores and performance for the NER task, while the model combination Ernie-tiny+GRU+MLP achieved the best scores and performance for RE task.

Based on experimental results, we analyze the possible reasons for the performance differences and explain why certain model combinations lead to improved results For NER task:

- BERT-WWM+LSTM+CRF: This combination has the lowest F1 score. BERT-WWM (Whole Word Masking) is a variation of the original BERT

Table 5. Experiment Results

Task	model	precision	recall	F1
NER	BERT-WWM+LSTM+CRF	0.66	0.82	0.74
	Ernie-Health+MLP	**0.76**	0.83	0.80
	ALBERT+Bi-LSTM+SPAN_predict(focal loss)	0.75	0.82	0.79
	Chinese-ELECTRA+Bi-LSTM+SPAN_predict(focal loss)	0.71	0.87	0.81
	Ernie-Health+Bi-LSTM+SPAN_predict(focal loss)	0.75	**0.89**	**0.84**
RE	BERT-WWM+GRU+MLP	0.73	0.80	0.77
	ALBERT+GRU+MLP	0.75	0.82	0.79
	RoBERTa-WWM+GRU+MLP	0.77	0.82	0.80
	Ernie-tiny+GRU+MLP	**0.80**	**0.86**	**0.83**

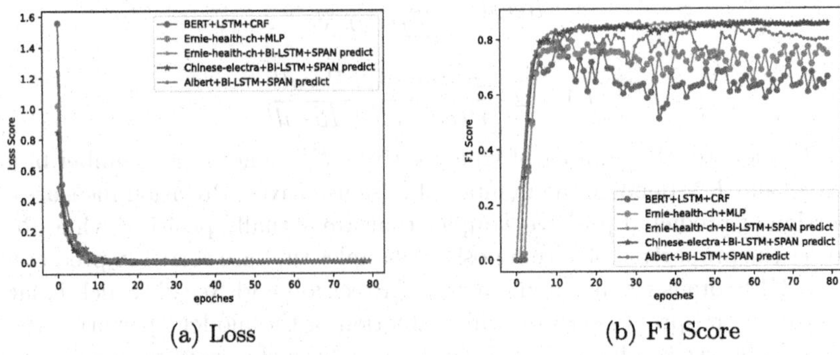

(a) Loss (b) F1 Score

Fig. 7. The performances of different models on NER task.

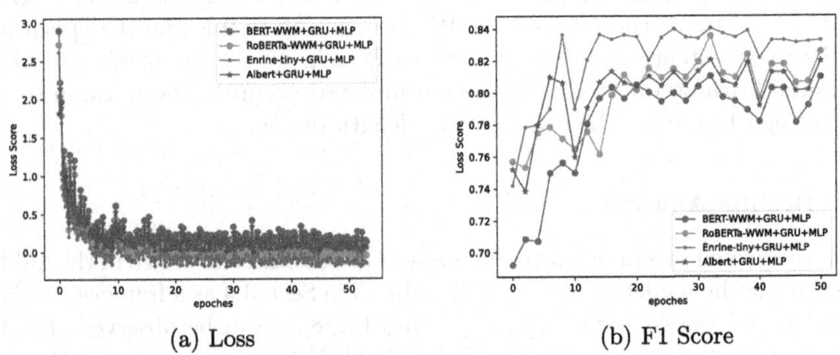

(a) Loss (b) F1 Score

Fig. 8. The performances of different models on RE task.

model, which uses whole word masking during pre-training. However, its performance might be limited by the structure of the LSTM and CRF layers. LSTMs might not be able to capture long-range dependencies effectively, while CRFs only model local dependencies between adjacent tags.

- ALBERT+Bi-LSTM+SPAN-Predict: ALBERT is a lightweight version of BERT, which can learn more efficiently. The combination of ALBERT and Bi-LSTM captures both contextual information and long-range dependencies better than the BERT-WWM+LSTM+CRF model. The SPAN-Predict method models the start and end positions of the entities, which could be more effective in identifying entities compared to CRF.
- Chinese-ELECTRA+Bi-LSTM+SPAN-Predict: Chinese-ELECTRA is a pre-trained model based on the ELECTRA framework and fine-tuned on the Chinese corpus. It is known to have better performance and efficiency than BERT. The combination with Bi-LSTM and SPAN-Predict allows the model to better capture contextual information, dependencies, and accurately predict entity boundaries, resulting in improved performance compared to the ALBERT+Bi-LSTM+SPAN-Predict model.
- Ernie-Health+Bi-LSTM+SPAN-Predict (focal loss): This model combination achieves the best performance and F1 score stability with increasing training epochs. The use of Ernie-Health provides domain-specific knowledge, while the Bi-LSTM layer captures dependencies in the data effectively. The SPAN-Predict method identifies entities more precisely. Additionally, the focal loss function addresses the issue of class imbalance in the dataset, which helps the model to focus on hard-to-classify examples and improves overall performance.

In summary, the improvements in model performance can be attributed to domain-specific pre-trained models, better context capture with Bi-LSTM, more accurate entity identification using SPAN-Predict, and the use of focal loss to address class imbalance issues. Additionally, the analysis of the RE task is similar to the analysis summarized in NER. Due to space constraints, we will not elaborate further.

6 Conclusion

Traditional Chinese medicine has a significant effect in healthcare services such as the prevention, diagnosis, treatment, amelioration or cure of disease, while these kind of services depends on the domain-specific knowledge graph. To support the study of TCM-related knowledge graph, this paper propose a semi-automatic construction method and the related materials. In the future, we will continuously enhance our dataset and knowledge graph, and leverage them for more intelligent healthcare services.

Acknowledgment. This work is partially supported by the National Key R&D Program of China (Grant 2022YFF0903100), the Key Research and Development Program of Shandong Province (Grant 2020CXGC010903), the National Natural Science Foundation of China (Grant 62073103), the Leading Benefiting People Fund Of Qingdao Science and Technology (21-1-4-rkjk-16-nsh), and the Mount Taishan Scholar Project Special Fund.

References

1. Bollacker, K., Evans, C., Paritosh, P., Sturge, T., Taylor, J.: Freebase: a collaboratively created graph database for structuring human knowledge. In: Proceedings of the 2008 ACM SIGMOD International Conference on Management of Data, pp. 1247–1250 (2008)
2. Chang, D., et al.: DiaKG: an annotated diabetes dataset for medical knowledge graph construction. In: Qin, B., Jin, Z., Wang, H., Pan, J., Liu, Y., An, B. (eds.) CCKS 2021. CCIS, vol. 1466, pp. 308–314. Springer, Singapore (2021). https://doi.org/10.1007/978-981-16-6471-7_26
3. Fan, L., Ming-Qiang, W., Ling-Xiang, L., Li-Yun, H.: Exploration on construction method of knowledge graph of veteran TCM physicians' clinical experiences. Chin. J. Tradit. Chin. Med. Pharm. (2021)
4. Jia, L., et al.: Construction of traditional Chinese medicine knowledge graph. J. Med. Inform. 51–53 (2015)
5. Kenton, J.D.M.W.C., Toutanova, L.K.: BERT: pre-training of deep bidirectional transformers for language understanding. In: Proceedings of NAACL-HLT, pp. 4171–4186 (2019)
6. Lan, Z., Chen, M., Goodman, S., Gimpel, K., Sharma, P., Soricut, R.: Albert: a lite BERT for self-supervised learning of language representations. arXiv preprint arXiv:1909.11942 (2019)
7. Liu, Q., Li, Y., Duan, H., Liu, Y., Qin, Z.: Knowledge graph construction techniques. J. Comput. Res. Dev. **53**(3), 582–600 (2016)
8. Liu, Y., et al.: Roberta: a robustly optimized BERT pretraining approach. arXiv preprint arXiv:1907.11692 (2019)
9. Mao, H., Zhang, B., Xu, H., Gao, K.: An end-to-end traditional Chinese medicine constitution assessment system based on multimodal clinical feature representation and fusion. In: Proceedings of the AAAI (2022)
10. Miao, F., Liu, H., Huang, Y., Liu, C., Wu, X.: Construction of semantic-based traditional Chinese medicine prescription knowledge graph. In: 2018 IEEE 3rd Advanced Information Technology, Electronic and Automation Control Conference (IAEAC), pp. 1194–1198. IEEE (2018)
11. Sun, Y., et al.: Ernie 2.0: a continual pre-training framework for language understanding. In: Proceedings of the AAAI Conference on Artificial Intelligence. vol. 34, pp. 8968–8975 (2020)
12. Tian, Y., et al.: Research and implementation of real world traditional Chinese medicine clinical scientific research information electronic medical record sharing system. In: Proceedings of the BIBM (2022)
13. Tong, R., Sun, C.l., Wang, H.F., Fang, Z., Yin, Y.: Construction of traditional Chinese medicine knowledge graph and its application. J. Med. Intell. **37**(4), 8–13 (2016)
14. Tong, Y., Jing-hua, L., Qi, Y.: The construction and application of knowledge mapping of health preservation of traditional Chinese medicine. Chin. Digit. Med. **12**(12), 3 (2017)
15. Yan-Rong, L., Yi, Z., Di, L., Dong-Ping, Q., Hai-Yan, S.: Constructing a medical knowledge graph of nephropathy based on the electronic medical records of nephropathy specialists. J. Southwest Univ. (Nat. Sci. Ed.) **42**(11), 52–58 (2020)

16. Yao, Y., et al.: DocRED: a large-scale document-level relation extraction dataset. In: Proceedings of the 57th Annual Meeting of the Association for Computational Linguistics, pp. 764–777 (2019)
17. Yu, T.: Knowledge graph for TCM health preservation: design, construction, and applications. Artif. Intell. Med. **77**, 48–52 (2017)
18. Zhang, L.X., et al.: TCMSID: a simplified integrated database for drug discovery from traditional Chinese medicine. J. Cheminformatics **14**(1), 1–11 (2022)

Service Ecosystem

Building Community Service Ecosystem Models

Kunkun Deng, Yuan Wan, Yuhe Qu, Xiao Wang, Hanchuan Xu(✉), Tonghua Su, and Zhongjie Wang

Harbin Institute of Technology, Harbin, China
xhc@hit.edu.cn

Abstract. The digital age has led to new resource sharing mechanisms, which require a corresponding adjustment in community governance. Constructing community service ecosystem is not only the adjustment of community governance to the new resource sharing mechanism, but also the reform and innovation of community development to adapt to the new situation. Therefore, a scientific and in-depth understanding of community service ecosystem is the key to improve the quality of community governance. However, the existing researches are only limited to the governance measures and improvement paths in some areas of the community, ignoring the overall systematization of the community, failing to put the elements of the community into the overall consideration of the ecosystem, and lacking the analysis of the structural relations, resources and environment of the community ecosystem. Therefore, we propose a community service ecosystem model (CSEM), which covers multiple subjects such as stakeholders, services, resources, and their relationships. To describe the occurrence and concerns of the evolution of the community service ecosystem, we introduce "evolutionary events", "features", and "values". Finally, we provide an approach to construct CSEM from POI data.

Keywords: Community service ecosystem · Multiple subjects · POI data · Approach

1 Introduction

The emergence of information technology has revolutionized the production and consumption of public services. This has led to the introduction of concepts such as smart cities and smart communities [8], which have significant impacts on current community models and services. However, these concepts have also brought complex challenges, such as the diversification of subjects and services, which have resulted in uneven levels of various services in the community and inadequate community infrastructure.

To address these challenges, it is crucial to develop a community service ecosystem model (CSEM) that integrates a community digital ecosystem theory and a smart service research platform [2]. The CSEM is based on the summary of the elements of the current community, including stakeholders, services, and

Z. Wang et al. (Eds.): ICSS 2023, CCIS 1844, pp. 339–350, 2023.
https://doi.org/10.1007/978-981-99-4402-6_24

resources [12], and is extracted to describe the composition of the community and their relationships to satisfy the macro-level description of community service.

The literature on the topic of digital ecosystems is sparse and the areas of focus vary. Valdez [14] proposed a framework for building a digital ecosystem model, but there are still several problems in building a digital ecosystem model for community services:

- Lack of a community service ecosystem model describing the community domain. In reality, the research on community service is not deep enough and lacks advanced concepts.
- There is a lack of corresponding computer technology route to realize the construction and example verification of the community service ecosystem model. Most of the ecosystem models are ideas or frameworks, and there is a lack of specific model building platforms.
- Lack of reliable data sources to support model validation and application. In actual construction, it is difficult to collect complete community composition data in various regions. Due to the differences in development and living habits in different regions, the community structure varies greatly, and the collected community data is also diverse.

In our research, we summarize the macroscopic model of community service ecosystem through research, and use the model as a guide to combine knowledge map-related technologies to construct a community service ecosystem graph. The community service ecosystem graph is an instance of the CSEM, including various entity instances and their relationships in the community service ecosystem model.

To gather data for the construction of the CSEM and ecosystem graph, we propose using POI data in conjunction with knowledge extraction from various community articles. This approach will enable us to extract various knowledge and relationships and refine the different components and relationships of the CSEM.

The main contributions of this paper are summarized as follows:

- The community service ecosystem model is summarized and constructed, which describes the community at the macro level, and guides the generation of community service ecosystem graph.
- Proposed an approach for constructing CSEM. Using knowledge map related technologies to extract knowledge and relationships from various community data to build community service ecosystem graph, and obtain an instance of CSEM.
- Developed a platform to realize model design and a process to generate the instance of CSEM.

The remainder of this paper is organized as follows. In Sect. 2, we provide an in-depth discussion of the relevant technologies of the digital ecosystem model. Next, we introduce the CSEM in detail in Sect. 3, highlighting its key components and relationships. In Sect. 4, we describe the construction process of our

CSEM, providing a step-by-step breakdown of our methodology. To illustrate the functionality of our system, we present a case study in Sect. 5. Finally, we briefly summarize and look forward to future research in Sect. 6.

2 Related Work

The term "ecosystem" originated from the field of biology [15]. The concept of "ecosystem" has been applied to many other fields, resulting in different types of ecosystem models, such as industrial ecosystem [6], digital ecosystem [7], and business ecosystem [1] and so on. In the context of the above, the concept of the service ecosystem originates from the integration of services and ecosystem concepts.

Numerous service ecosystem models have been proposed in different fields. For example, Gui et al. [4] introduced the evolution of the e-commerce service ecosystem (ECSEM), which forms through resource sharing, advantages complementation and synergistic innovation among all system subjects. The ECSEM is influenced by the flow of commodities, information, and capital through the e-commerce platform. Alistair et al. [3] discussed the rise of the web service ecosystem model (WSEM), which is a logical collection of web services subject to constraints that are characteristic of business service delivery. Zheng et al. [16] introduced the Smart Product Service Ecosystem (SPSE), defined as an ICT-based dynamic ecological smart PSS network which integrates customers, smart product service systems, smart service platforms, and product service suppliers for value co-creation and customer experience improvement through smart interaction, mutual cooperation, resource sharing, and optimal configuration. Liu [9,10] proposed a subgraph of historical interaction between stakeholders and services from a Multilayer network-based Service Ecosystem Model (MSEM) [11]. The MSEM comprehensively covers the interconnections between stakeholders, service delivery channels, service functional features, and non-functional features, and business domains. Additionally, Zhou et al. [17] proposed a cloud manufacturing service ecosystem (CMSE) that meets complex customization needs through a dynamic collaborative network between cloud manufacturing services. It describes the dynamic evolution process of the CMSE through three layers: individual, organization, and society.

However, there is a noticeable gap in the field of community services, as there is a lack of relevant service ecosystem models and supporting technologies that can describe ecosystem community instances under ecosystem models. To address this gap, our paper proposes a Community Service Ecosystem Model (CSEM), which integrates various community entities, including community residents, community services, community resources, and community organizations. Moreover, we use knowledge map and other relevant technologies to realize the process of generating CSEM instances based on our model. CSEM comprehensively depicts the relationship between community entities, and the community instance provides an intuitive representation of the ecosystem of a community.

Model	Type of Service	Distinctive Layer
MSEM	General Service	Event Layer Domain Layer
ECSEM	E-commerce Service	Environmental Layer
WSEM	Web Service	Application Layer Middleware Layer
SPSE	Smart Product Service	Smart Technologies Layer
CMSE	Cloud Manufacturing Service	Social Layer Organizational Layer
CSEM	Community Service	Feature Layer Event Layer

3 Community Service Ecosystem Model

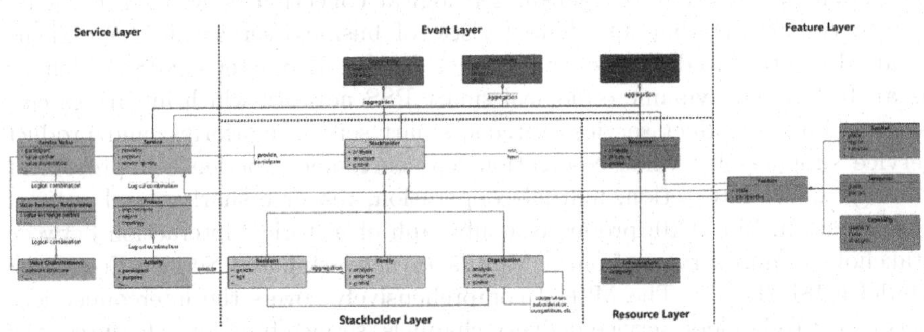

Fig. 1. Illustration of the community service ecosystem model(CSEM)

A community is a living network of various social relationships composed of people living in a certain region. In this context, a community service ecosystem refers to a series of organized and purposeful systems aimed at promoting community development by matching the needs of community residents and their environment, while optimizing the allocation of community resources, guiding energy flow, ensuring sustainable development, and promoting diversity. The main actors in this ecosystem include government, market, community, and residents (Fig. 1).

Based on the above definition and description, we propose a Community Service Ecosystem Model (CSEM) that consists of five layers: the event layer, the stakeholder layer, the service layer, the resource layer and the feature layer. The elements of each layer form a network structure, and the interlayer relations connect the network of five layers into an overall layered network.

3.1 Stackholder Layer

Stakeholder refers to any stakeholder in the economic activities of production, exchange, distribution and consumption in the community. Its object can be individual or group. There are three types of stakeholders:

- Resident: members who live in the community for a long time and engage in production and consumption.
- Family: refers to the marriage, blood relationship or adoptive relationship, on the basis of relations of social life between units.
- Organization: the combination of mutual coordination of collective or group, such as property, government agencies, service providers, etc.

They all inherit from stakeholders. Residents pay attention to their age and gender attributes, and residents exist in social structures, including families, organizations and other social networks, so families are formed by aggregation of residents. Community division of labor will form a variety of community organizations, and then constitute a variety of dependence between individuals and groups, and form the organizational structure of the community. The organization is formed by the aggregation of residents, and there are various relations among the organizations, such as cooperation, subordination and competition.

At this point, we can see that individuals aggregate into groups. Although we give some information about the attributes of individuals, this information is not enough to explain the group information to which individuals belong, which may lead to the atomic fallacy, that is, group information is incorrectly inferred from individual information. It is necessary to consider the sociological differences in attributes between clusters and members. So we define the analysis properties, structure properties, and global properties of the cluster. The analysis attribute is obtained by collecting individual information in the group, such as the ratio of male to female in an organization. The structural attribute is based on the relationship among cluster members, while the overall attribute is the characteristic of the cluster itself, which is not affected by individual members. For example, the service content provided by the organization is the overall attribute of the cluster.

3.2 Service Layer

Service refers to the public services and other material, cultural, and life services provided to the community. The attribute of service emphasizes the service provider and the service receiver, who can be individuals or groups, making service provision dependent on stakeholders. Additionally, we also emphasize the attribute of service quality, which is measured by the satisfaction of service recipients. This satisfaction is generated from the comparison between the expectation of the service receiver and their actual service experience. Therefore, to carry out service activities, the needs of service recipients should be defined firstly, and then the service needs should be transformed into corresponding service attributes, which can be called "quality of service". The service activities are organized into processes, which are a series of regular human activities or operations with a specific object, implementer, and logical relationship between activities. Therefore, we introduce the concepts of activity and process, where activities are associated with residents, and the aggregation of activities forms processes. These processes, in turn, form services. The relationship between stakeholders and services is characterized by engagement and provision.

The Community Service Ecosystem is a complex and vast system that involves numerous service participants engaged in intricate value exchange relationships. Within this system, the diverse service operations, service values, and value exchange relationships constitute a large value network. Thus, we introduce the concepts of service value, value exchange relationship, and value chain/network to capture the essence of this network. Service value is generated by service activities and is shared by both the service provider and the service recipient. The aggregation of service values and service participants forms the value exchange relationship, which, in turn, becomes part of the larger value chain/network. Incorporating the value system elements into the community ecosystem model enhances the value modeling of community ecosystem, promotes the identification and resolution of value conflicts, and facilitates the optimization of resource allocation.

3.3 Resource Layer

Resources are the general term of material resources, financial resources, human resources, information and other materials within the community. The operation of the community can not be separated from the support of resources. Resources are essential for the production activities of community members in the community. Community resources have a wide range of meanings. For example, human resources and natural materials are all resources. Stakeholders inevitably engage with resources when participating in services, and this relationship between stakeholders and resources is characterized by ownership and use.

3.4 Feature Layer

In the real world, every community element exhibits its unique features, including basic capability features and temporal and spatial features. The capability features highlight the intrinsic attributes of each entity. The units of capability vary depending on the entity, and can include quantity, quality, and strength, among others. Spatial features emphasize the scale and perspective of the element. Different scales exhibit different perceptions of space, and spatial features take different forms in various perspectives. For instance, position or location is emphasized in the perspective of place space, space scope is emphasized in the perspective of regional space, and path and interaction are emphasized in the perspective of network space. The temporal feature focuses on a point in time or a specific period. Therefore, we define the concepts of feature, spatial, temporal, and capability. Moreover, the concepts of spatial, temporal and capability inherit from feature. Additionally, feature aggregates with the three elements of community, service, resources and stakeholders.

3.5 Event Layer

A service and resource-related event is initiated by stakeholders and may result in changes in the elements and evolutionary relationships within the community service ecosystem. The evolution of the community service ecosystem is typically triggered by various events, such as policy changes, emergencies, etc. For instance, if the government plans to build a high-tech institute in a particular area, the community's structure may undergo evolution with the influx of more highly educated individuals, more infrastructure development, and enhanced community services. The entities involved in this evolution are service, stakeholder, and resource evolution. Therefore, we introduce the concept of an evolutionary event, which is linked to service, resource and stakeholders. Additionally, we emphasize the evolution of apartments and resources that are human-dominated. Thus, we propose the concept of apartment and infrastructure, where apartments are aggregated in the community, and infrastructure inherits from resources.

4 An Approach for CSEM Construction

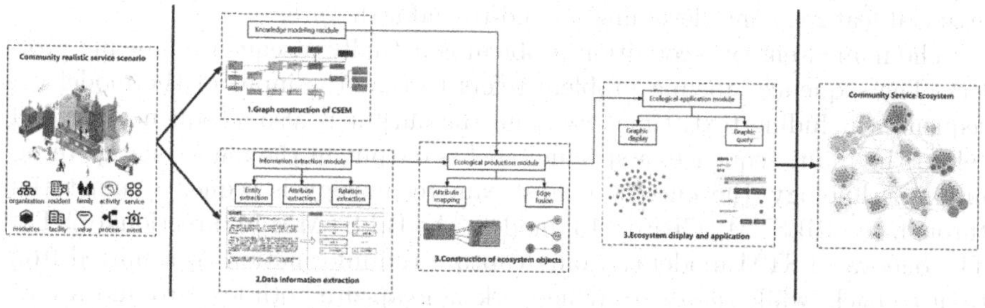

Fig. 2. An approach for constructing a community service ecosystem model (CSEM)

Figure 2 illustrates the process of our method to build a community service ecosystem model, which includes the following four steps. The first step is graph construction of community service ecosystem model (CSEM), building a community service ecosystem model through graph model. The second step is data information extraction which uses deep learning technology to extract the information we need from the data, mainly including entities, relationships and attributes. The third step is to build the community service ecological objects according to the results of the first and second step, and then align the data field with the graph model and its attribute field mapping. Finally, we provide applications of CSEM,including graphic display and graphic query.

4.1 Graph Construction of CSEM

The knowledge modeling module aims to organize relevant information and knowledge of entities using a specific knowledge representation language or data structure. The knowledge expressed thereby can be interpreted and processed by the computer system. In this paper, we use a graph model to construct the community service ecosystem model. We describe the node types and edge types of the graph model, as well as the attribute list and attribute types on the nodes/edges. Furthermore, we support the dynamic expansion of multiple attributes. In our system, we have manually drawn a preset community service ecosystem model.

4.2 Data Information Extraction

The ecological production module can directly use and transform structured data, and map it to build a community service ecosystem model. However, unstructured data requires the information extraction module to extract relevant information such as entity recognition, relationship extraction, and attribute extraction. The methods include feature template-based methods, supervised learning based on kernel functions, and deep learning-based methods. In this study, a Named Entity Recognition (NER) method based on deep learning is used to identify entity classes in the text. The benefits of using deep learning for NER include the ability to learn more complex features from data through nonlinear transformation, avoiding the need for constructing a large number of artificial features, and designing an end-to-end structure.

The named entity recognition problem is actually a sequence labeling problem. The sequence labeling problem refers to that the input of the model is a sequence, including text, time, etc., and the output is also a sequence For each cell in the input sequence, a specific label is output in the named entity recognition technology, the current mainstream technology is sequence annotation through the BiLSTM+CRF [5,13] model. The BiLSTM is bi-directional LSTM. The one-way LSTM model can only capture the information transmitted from front to back, while the two-way network can capture both forward and reverse information, making the use of text information more comprehensive and effective. The CRF layer can add some constraints to ensure that the final prediction result is valid (the CRF layer can learn the constraints of the sentence). These constraints can be automatically learned by the CRF layer when training data. With these useful constraints, the wrong prediction sequence will be greatly reduced.

4.3 Construction of Ecosystem Objects

The ecological production module aims to establish the corresponding relationship between the graph elements and data in the graph model and import them into the graph database. In this paper, we primarily employ the technology of knowledge graph to achieve this task. For various elements defined in the graph model, including the identification of nodes, attributes on nodes and edges, the corresponding fields in the data are specified respectively. Then the edge is built between the source node and the target node through the identification of nodes. Finally the data is loaded for mapping into the Neo4j database.

4.4 Ecosystem Display and Application

The ecological application module consists of two components: graphic display and graphic query. The graphic display component supports node/edge data search and filter. The platform incorporates an information window function that provides an intuitive view of node/edge data. Under different perspectives and layouts of each diagram ecosystem model, the relationship diagram will show different patterns and behaviors, and the content presented will also be different. Our system supports multiple layouts, which are implemented through algorithms or strategies based on the coordinates of data computer points on the canvas.

The system also supports OpenCypher query language for graphic query. OpenCypher is a declarative graph database query language that is expressive and efficient in querying and updating graphs. It meets the needs of developers and operation experts at the same time. Although OpenCypher language is simple in design, it is powerful in function and can easily express highly complex database queries. This enables professionals from diverse fields to focus on their core tasks while minimizing the time and cost spent on database access.

5 Case Study and Future Works

The 2km range of a community in Shanghai is taken as the research object. The data comes from the POI data of the downtown communities in Shanghai and contains a variety of labels. The specific information is shown in the Fig. 3. Based on the POI data, we focus on data areas that reflect relationships between community elements, like name, resource, type, location, and so on. Entity matching is then done based on the POI's name, type, and so on.

ID	address	adcode	cityname	type	resource	typecode	adname	citycode	name	location	business.opentime_today
0	622-624 Yuanshen Road	310115	Shanghai	Healthcare Services	Psychiatric Hospital	090210	Pudong New Area	021	Shanghai Pudong New Area Mental Health Center (Yuanshen Road)	121.534538,31.230315	08:00-21:00
1	No. 2-23, Lane 355, Weifang Road	310115	Shanghai	Serviced Apartment	Residential District	120302	Pudong New Area	021	Yuanzhu Community	121.534114,31.229411	无
2	Floor 2, Natatorium East, Yuanshen Stadium, No. 655, Yuanshen Road	310115	Shanghai	Catering Services	Cafe	050500	Pudong New Area	021	Dianju Cafe	121.535354,31.231123	无
3	Next to the South 1st Gate in the North District of Yuanzhu Community	310115	Shanghai	Shopping Services	Aquatic and Seafood Market	060706	Pudong New Area	021	XINMENG, Xinmeng Supermarket	121.535171,31.228768	06:00-24:00
4	377 Weifang Road	310115	Shanghai	Life Services	Laundry	071500	Pudong New Area	021	Polyester laundry	121.535066,31.228745	09:00-23:00

Fig. 3. Part of POI types information in a Shanghai community

First, we build a community service ecosystem model through the graph model or directly use our preset graph model in the system, as shown in the Fig. 4.

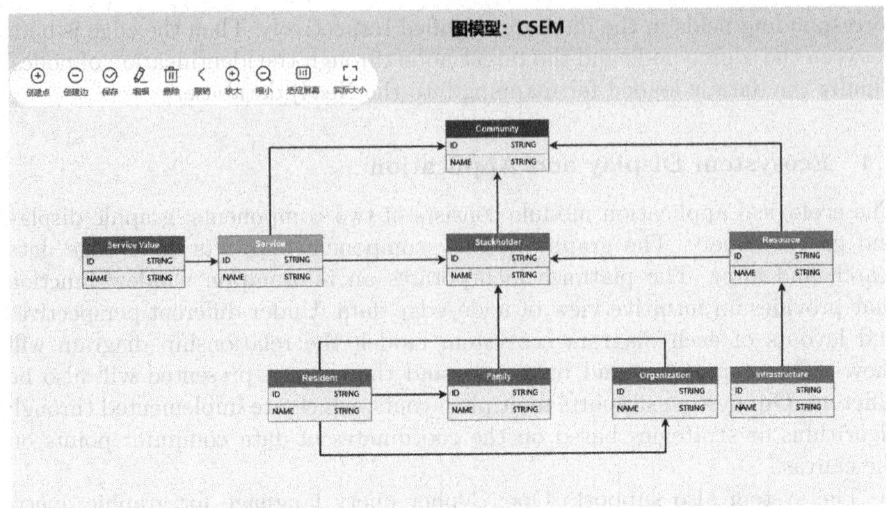

Fig. 4. Partial graph model of community service ecosystem

Then the graph model is saved as schema.json as shown in the Table 1, which is divided into four parts: version, graphName, nodes and edges. schema.json defines the graph version, graph name, node set and edge set respectively. The property is defined inside nodes and edges.

Table 1. The field name of the schema

Field_Name	Description
version	The version information records the schema changes. The value is long and not less than 0
graphName	The name of the graph, which is globally unique.
nodes	Records all nodes' information of the graph. The node is stored in map format. key is the type name of the node, and value is the basic information about the node.
edges	Records all edges' information of the graph. The edge is stored in map format. key is the type name of the edge, and value is the basic information about the edge.
property	It is the attribute information of nodes and edges, stored in the form of Json Array, each Json object corresponds to a property

Next, because POI data is of a semi-structured type, we fused its mapping directly into the community service ecosystem. Finally, we use the gForce layout to show part of the community service ecosystem diagram, as shown in the Fig. 5, the organizations in the community form associations with the services they provide, and at the same time, the organizations either occupy or use the corresponding resources.

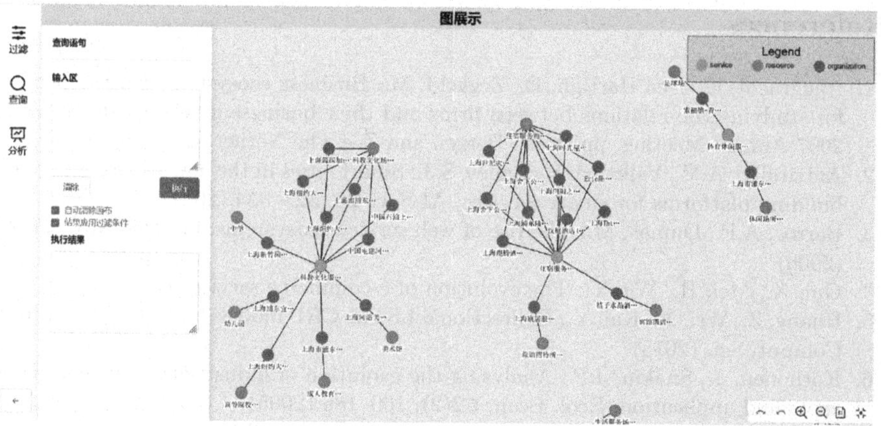

Fig. 5. Partial instance of community service ecosystem model (CSEM)

However, this paper has the following deficiencies:

1. The defects of POI data will bring certain uncertainties to the research results. Although POI data is large and accessible, covering spatial and attribute information of geographic entities, residents, relationships and other information are still missing. In order to improve the universality and robustness of the research, the establishment of multi-source data fusion method is a positive direction.
2. The complexity of community service ecosystem needs to be further studied. Our study only describes the community service ecosystem as a whole at a certain moment, and selects time series data to analyze the spatio-temporal change features and evolution process to be further revealed.

6 Conclusions

We have developed a community service ecosystem model (CSEM), which offers significant advantages due to its broad applicability across multiple fields. It not only puts constituent elements into the ecosystem for overall consideration, but also introduces values, resources and evolutionary events into the model, fully demonstrating the characteristics of community service ecosystem. In addition to CSEM specifications, we have proposed a method for constructing it. The theoretical and practical significance of our study is noteworthy for the community service ecosystem. However, given the complexity of the real environment, there is still room for further expansion. While we have demonstrated an example of CSEM using POI data, the model's universality can be enhanced through in-depth expansion and coverage by integrating multi-source data in empirical studies.

Acknowledgements. The research in this paper is partially supported by the National Key Research and Development Program of China (No.2021YFF0900900).

References

1. Anggraeni, E., Den Hartigh, E., Zegveld, M.: Business ecosystem as a perspective for studying the relations between firms and their business networks. In: ECCON 2007 Annual Meeting, pp. 1–28. Bergen aan Zee The Netherlands (2007)
2. Anttiroiko, A.V., Valkama, P., Bailey, S.J.: Smart cities in the new service economy: building platforms for smart services. AI Soc. **29**, 323–334 (2014)
3. Barros, A.P., Dumas, M.: The rise of web service ecosystems. IT Prof. **8**(5), 31–37 (2006)
4. Gui, X., Mei, H., Wu, Y.: The evolution of e-commerce service ecosystem (2018)
5. Huang, Z., Wei, X., Kai, Y.: Bidirectional LSTM-CRF models for sequence tagging. Comput. Sci. (2015)
6. Korhonen, J., Snäkin, J.P.: Analysing the evolution of industrial ecosystems: concepts and application. Ecol. Econ. **52**(2), 169–186 (2005)
7. Li, W., Badr, Y., Biennier, F.: Digital ecosystems: challenges and prospects. In: Proceedings of the International Conference on Management of Emergent Digital EcoSystems, pp. 117–122 (2012)
8. Lindskog, H.: Smart communities initiatives. In: Proceedings of the 3rd ISOneWorld Conference, vol. 16, pp. 14–16 (2004)
9. Liu, M., Tu, Z., Wang, J., Wang, Z.: A novel multi-layer network model for service ecosystems. In: 2020 International Conference on Service Science (ICSS), pp. 23–30. IEEE (2020)
10. Liu, M., Tu, Z., Xu, H., Xu, X., Wang, Z.: Community-based service ecosystem evolution analysis. Serv. Oriented Comput. Appl. **16**(2), 97–110 (2022). https://doi.org/10.1007/s11761-022-00333-9
11. Liu, M., Tu, Z., Xu, X., Wang, Z., Wang, Y.: A data-driven approach for constructing multilayer network-based service ecosystem models. Softw. Syst. Model. **22**, 1–21 (2022)
12. O'Sullivan, J., Edmond, D., Ter Hofstede, A.: What's in a service? Distrib. Parallel Databases **12**, 117–133 (2002)
13. Peng, Z., Wei, S., Tian, J., Qi, Z., Bo, X.: Attention-based bidirectional long short-term memory networks for relation classification. In: Proceedings of the 54th Annual Meeting of the Association for Computational Linguistics (Volume 2: Short Papers) (2016)
14. Valdez-De-Leon, O.: How to develop a digital ecosystem: a practical framework. Technol. Innov. Manage. Rev. **9**(8), 43–54 (2019)
15. Willis, A.J.: The ecosystem: an evolving concept viewed historically (1997)
16. Zheng, M., Ming, X., Wang, L., Yin, D., Zhang, X.: Status review and future perspectives on the framework of smart product service ecosystem. Procedia Cirp **64**, 181–186 (2017)
17. Zhou, D., Xue, X., Zhou, Z.: SLE2: the improved social learning evolution model of cloud manufacturing service ecosystem. IEEE Trans. Industr. Inf. **18**(12), 9017–9026 (2022)

AI Technology Adoption, AI Knowledge Integration and AI Product Development Performance

Lingyun Yin, Siqi Zhu, and Jianming Zhou(✉)

Guangdong University of Finance & Economics, School of Business Administration, Luntou Road. 21, Guangzhou 510320, People's Republic of China
jmzhou@gdufe.edu.cn

Abstract. This paper studied how artificial intelligence (AI) technology adoption affected AI product development performance through promoting AI knowledge integration, and took 113 AI product R&D teams from China as studied samples for empirical study. Structural equation modeling tested results suggest that (1) AI technology adoption has direct positive effect on R&D team's AI knowledge integration including AI internal knowledge integration and AI external knowledge integration, and AI product development performance significantly; (2) AI knowledge integration including AI internal knowledge integration and AI external knowledge integration has direct positive effect on AI product development performance significantly, and mediates the relationship between AI technology adoption and AI product development performance.

Keywords: AI Technology Adoption · AI knowledge Integration · AI Product Development Performance

1 Introduction

Artificial intelligence (AI) refers to the intelligence exhibited by machines manufactured by humans, trying to simulate human thinking processes and behaviors through computers (Chen et al., 2020) [1]. The development of AI has brought great opportunities to human society, and can even cause changes no less than the industrial revolution (Gruetzemacher and Whittlestone, 2022) [2]. AI has brought about changes in people's lifestyles (e.g., face recognition technology, GPS navigation system), changes in enterprise production methods (e.g., machine learning, deep learning technology), and changes in the world's economic structure (e.g., ChatGPT technology). The great convenience that AI brought to human has made AI receive widespread attention. How to promote

Supported by Guangdong Soft Science Project (Grants No. 2020A1010020045), Innovative Team Project of Guangdong Universities (Grants No. 2019WCXTD008), and Guangdong "13th Five year" Project for Education and Scientific Research (Grants NO. 2020LY104).

Z. Wang et al. (Eds.): ICSS 2023, CCIS 1844, pp. 351–359, 2023.
https://doi.org/10.1007/978-981-99-4402-6_25

AI technology to help organizations to achieve high-performance goals for AI product development has become a topic that enterprises must pay attention to (Korteling et al., 2021) [3].

Previous research on AI product development performance has mostly focused on technical and consumer perspectives, such as AI sensors (Kubosawa et al., 2022) [4], AI image analysis (Rutter et al., 2021) [5], AI recommendation (Duan et al., 2019) [6]. However, few studies have considered the AI technology adoption from the perspective of users or organizations. The research of Ibrahim and Obal (2020) pointed out that AI technology adoption is an important way to improve product development performance [7]. It can help enterprises integrate a large amount of AI knowledge, thereby improving product development performance and bringing enterprises a competitive advantage. Therefore, this paper pays attention to the mechanism by which AI technology adoption affects AI knowledge integration and AI product development performance.

2 Literature Review and Research Hypotheses

Technology adoption theory evolved from information adoption theory (Li and Tao, 2022) [8]. Sussman and Siegal (2003) developed a theoretical model of information adoption and defined information adoption as the process by which people form a decision about a need based on the perception of usefulness through the "peripheral route" or "central route" [9] . Xu (2012) combined the theory of Sussman et al. (2003) to regard technology adoption as a dynamic process, and employee adoption is regarded as a constituent element of organizational adoption. In turn, it penetrates and affects individual organizations, and manifests as a process of overall adoption by the organization [10]. Knowledge integration is divided into internal integration and external integration. However, due to the "recessive attributes" of professional knowledge, it is difficult for knowledge integration to cross organizational boundaries. The adoption of AI technology is not only beneficial to the internal communication of the organization, but also promotes tacit and explicit knowledge to transfer from each other, so that knowledge integration can cross organizational boundaries, which is conducive to external knowledge integration (Forman and Van Zeebroeck, 2019) [11] .

That is to say, the AI technology adoption can create an environment conducive to the transfer and transformation of explicit and tacit knowledge for organizations, thereby effectively promoting the knowledge integration process that is conducive to the integration of AI internal knowledge and AI external knowledge integration. In addition, the research of Ibrahim and Obal (2020) further showed that technology adoption will bring "resources with competitive advantage" to the organization, thereby improving new product development performance [7]. Based on this, this paper argues that AI technology adoption will also have a direct and positive impact on AI product development performance. Therefore, we propose the following assumptions:

H1a: AI technology adoption has direct positive effect on R&D team's AI internal knowledge integration significantly.

H1b: AI technology adoption has direct positive effect on R&D team's AI external knowledge integration significantly.

H2: AI technology adoption has direct positive effect on R&D team's AI product development performance.

Hou et al. (2009) distinguished knowledge integration into "knowledge internal integration" and "knowledge external integration" according to different sources, and promoted the success of product development through the combination of inter-departmental integration within the organization and inter-organizational integration outside the organization [12]. Knowledge integration is a part of knowledge management. Therefore, AI knowledge integration includes AI internal knowledge integration and AI external knowledge integration. For the needs of AI product innovation, the organization integrates internal and external AI knowledge, eliminates useless AI knowledge, improves the efficiency and effectiveness of AI knowledge utilization, and makes the AI product development process more efficient, and then improves the performance of AI product development [13]. In other words, AI knowledge integration includes AI internal knowledge integration and AI external knowledge integration, which has a direct and positive impact on AI product development performance. Therefore, based on the above research, this paper proposes the following hypotheses:

H3a: AI internal knowledge integration has direct positive effect on R&D team's AI product development performance.

H3b: AI external knowledge integration has direct positive effect on R&D team's AI product development performance.

According to the mediating effect principle of Baron and Kenny (1986) [14] and combines the previous hypotheses, we believe that AI knowledge integration including AI internal knowledge integration and AI external knowledge integration may mediates the relationship between AI technology adoption and AI product development performance. Hence, we propose the following hypotheses:

H4a: AI internal knowledge integration mediates the relationship between AI technology adoption and AI product development performance.

H4b: AI external knowledge integration mediates the relationship between AI technology adoption and AI product development performance.

3 Research Design

3.1 Research Framework

According to the previous literature review, this paper's research framework and hypotheses are presented in Fig. 1.

3.2 Measurement

In this paper, the format and content of the questionnaires of AI technology adoption (AITA), AI internal knowledge integration (AIIKI), AI external knowledge integration (AIEKI), AI product development performance (AIPDP) are

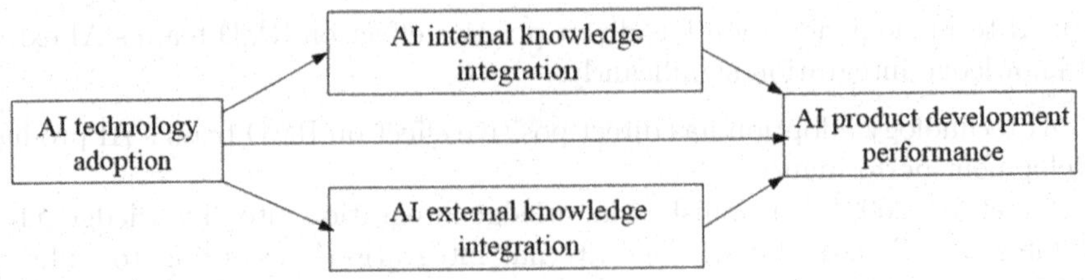

Fig. 1. The research framework

initially developed from literature review with five-point Liker Scale. The measuring scale of AI technology adoption was development by Davis (1989) which comprised 3 items [15]. The measuring scale of AI knowledge integration with two dimensions of AI internal knowledge integration and AI external knowledge integration was development by Iansiti and Clark (1994) which comprised 3 items respectively [16]. And the measuring scale of AI product development performance was development by Zhou et al. (2014) which comprised 4 items [17].

3.3 Sampling

This study adopted a questionnaire survey method for data collection, and took the Chinese AI product R&D team as the research object. The respondents of the questionnaire were limited to executives or project managers who understand the company's product development situation. A total of 150 questionnaires were sent out by means of telephone contact, door-to-door investigation and mailing of questionnaires. After 3 months, a total of 124 questionnaires were recovered, of which 113 were completed and the effective recovery rate was 75.3%. Judging from the background information of the respondents who answered the questionnaire, the majority of the respondents were men, with 83 people accounting for 73.5%, the average age was 32 years old (standard deviation = 4.16), 53 people with a master's degree, accounting for 46.9%, and 41 people with a doctorate degree, accounting for 36.3%.

4 Data Analysis

4.1 Reliability and Validity Analysis

We used SPSS19.0 to do alpha test for ensuring the reliability of measuring scales, and the tested results indicated that all Cronbach's α value were greater than the standard value of 0.7 which presented in Table 1, showing that the measuring scales of AI technology adoption, AI internal knowledge integration, AI external knowledge integration, and AI product development performance have good reliability.

Table 1. Cronbach's α value of measuring scales.

Variables	α value
AI technology adoption	0.805
AI internal knowledge integration	0.791
AI external knowledge integration	0.920
AI product development performance	0.938

And the validity test of AI technology adoption, AI internal knowledge integration, AI external knowledge integration, and AI product development performance is used CFA method. The results presented in Table 2 indicated that the four-factor model fitted the data was better than any other alternative models, suggesting that all measuring scales have good validity.

Table 2. Results of validity analyzing with CFA

Model	Factors	CFI	TLI	RMSEA	$\chi2$/df
Four-factor	AITA, AIIKI, AIEKI, AIPDP	0.948	0.932	0.088	1.866
Three-factor -1	AITA, AIIKI+AIEKI, AIPDP	0.845	0.805	0.149	3.480
Three-factor -2	AITA+AIIKI, AIEKI, AIPDP	0.856	0.819	0.143	3.295
Three-factor -3	AITA+AIPDP, AIIKI, AIEKI	0.826	0.781	0.158	3.785
One-factor	AITA+AIIKI+AIEKI+AIPDP	0.525	0.430	0.254	8.238

4.2 Test of Overall Theoretical Model

Structural equation modeling (SEM) was used to test hypothesis. Most scholars believed that the overall model fitness of SEM should be measured from absolute fitness, asymptotic fitness and summarized fitness aspects. Results of the direct and indirect SEM fitness presented in Table 3 indicated that most of the indicators were higher than the accepted criteria.

4.3 Test of Hypothesis

We summarized the direct and indirect SEM model test results can be seen in Table 4. It can be seen that, H1a, H1b, H2, H3a, H3b were all supported.

Meanwhile, the direct and indirect SEM model with path coefficient and error value could be seen in Fig. 2 and Fig. 3.

Path coefficients in Fig. 2 and Fig. 3 found that when the direct SEM model was added with AI knowledge integration including AI internal knowledge integration and AI external knowledge integration, the direct effect of AI technology

Table 3. The overall model fitness results of direct and indirect SEM

Overall model fitness		Ideal criteria	Accepted criteria	Direct SEM	Indirect SEM
Absolute fitness	GFI	≥0.90	≥0.80	0.919	0.847
	RMR	≤0.05	≤0.08	0.025	0.064
	RMSEA	≤0.08	≤1.00	0.115	0.102
Asymptotic fitness	AGFI	≥0.90	≥0.80	0.825	0.768
	RFI	≥0.90	≥0.80	0.907	0.827
	NFI	≥0.90	≥0.80	0.943	0.867
	CFI	≥0.90	≥0.80	0.964	0.923
Summarized fitness	$\chi 2/\text{df}$	1.00 2.00	2.00 3.00	2.469	2.158
	PNFI	≥0.50	≥0.50	0.583	0.667
	PGFI	≥0.50	≥0.50	0.427	0.559
	AIC	<Satu. AIC (62)	<Indp. AIC (56)	572.584	1001.214

Table 4. Path coefficient and hypothesis test results

Paths	Estimate	P-value	Hyp	Result
AITA→AIIKI	0.377**	0.002	H1a	✓
AITA→AIEKI	0.625**	0.000	H1b	✓
AITA→AIPDP	0.375**	0.000	H2	✓
AIIKI→AIPDP	0.257*	0.019	H3a	✓
AIEKI→AIPDP	0.312*	0.015	H3b	✓

Notes: *Significant at P<0.05; ** Significant at P<0.01;

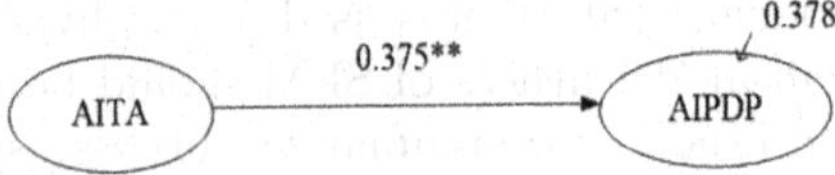

Fig. 2. The direct SEM model with path coefficient

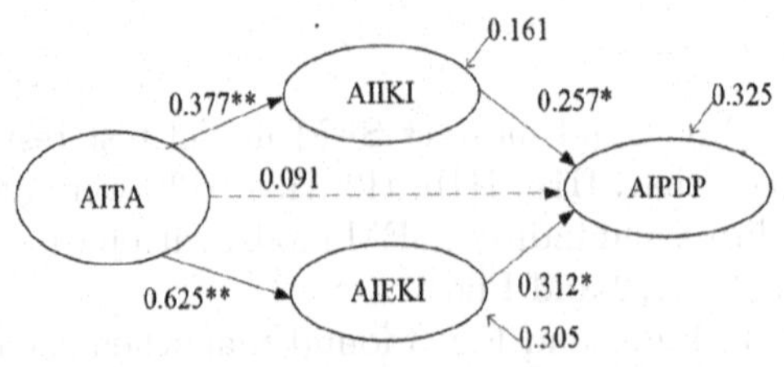

Fig. 3. The indirect SEM model with path coefficient

adoption on R&D team's AI product development performance became insignificant from 0.375** to 0.091. According to Baron and Kenny's suggestion [14], AI knowledge integration including AI internal knowledge integration and AI external knowledge integration was likely to mediate the relationship between AI technology adoption and R&D team's AI product development performance.

In order to test the mediating effect, we used Bootstrapping methods recommended by Hayes (2013) to do analysis [18]. Bootstrapping results in table 5 showed that the mediating effect of AI internal knowledge integration and AI external knowledge integration were 0.075 and 0.195, between 95% confident interval of [0.001, 0.231] and [0.068, 0.395]. As 95% confident interval of AI internal knowledge integration and AI external knowledge integration both include no zero, which indicated that the mediating effect of AI knowledge integration including AI internal knowledge integration and AI external knowledge integration were significant. Hence, H4a and H4b were supported.

Table 5. Bootstrap testing results for the mediating effect of AI knowledge transfer

Direct path	Indirect path	Mediating effect	95% confident interval
AITA→AIPDP	AITA→AIIKI→AIPDP	0.075	[0.001, 0.231]
AITA→AIPDP	AITA→AIEKI→AIPDP	0.195	[0.068, 0.395]

5 Conclusions and Discussion

This paper study whether and how AI technology adoption can help increasing R&D team's AI product development performance through improving AI knowledge integration including AI internal knowledge integration and AI external knowledge integration with 113 AI product R&D teams from China as studied samples. The results have theoretical and practical significance.

Firstly, this study confirmed that AI technology adoption was an antecedent variable of AI knowledge integration, which had a direct and positive impact on AI internal knowledge integration and AI external knowledge integration. Therefore, in the era of knowledge economy, R&D teams should create more efficient communication channels for enterprises by introducing AI technology and using AI platforms, which can effectively promote the interaction and transformation of knowledge among R&D teams, help integrate AI knowledge, and better connect with the outside world Interaction promotes the absorption and integration of external knowledge, thereby helping enterprises create stronger competitive advantages.

Secondly, this study confirmed that AI knowledge integration, including AI internal knowledge integration and AI external knowledge integration, will significantly improve the AI product development performance. Therefore, enterprises should build an effective knowledge integration mechanism, and use it as a part of knowledge management, embed it in the product development process of the enterprise, and even widely apply it as part of the corporate culture, so as to improve the efficiency and effectiveness of corporate knowledge utilization and continue to help enterprises create high performance in AI product development, so that enterprises can always stand firm in the fierce market competition.

Finally, this paper confirmed that AI knowledge integration, including AI internal knowledge integration and AI external knowledge integration, plays a significant mediating role between AI technology adoption and AI product development performance. This research result uncovers the "black box" between AI technology adoption and AI product development performance, suggesting that AI technology adoption can promote AI product development performance by promoting the AI knowledge integration process of enterprises. This conclusion has positive significance for our indepth understanding of the positive impact of AI technology adoption on enterprises.

References

1. Chen, L., Chen, P., Lin, Z.: Artificial intelligence in education: a review. IEEE Access **8**, 75264–75278 (2020)
2. Gruetzemacher, R., Whittlestone, J.: The transformative potential of artificial intelligence. Futures **135**, 102884–102885 (2022)
3. Korteling, J.H., van de Boer-Visschedijk, G.C., Blankendaal, R.A., et al.: Human- versus artificial intelligence. Front. Artif. Intell. **4**, e622364 (2021)
4. Kubosawa, S., Onishi, T., Tsuruoka, Y.: Soft sensors and process control using AI and dynamic simulation. Arxiv preprint (2022)
5. Rutter, R.N., Barnes, S.J., Roper, S., et al.: Social media influencers, product placement and network engagement: using AI image analysis to empirically test relationships. Ind. Manage. Data Syst. **121**(12), 2387–2410 (2021)
6. Duan, C., Xiu, G., Yao, F.: Multi-period E-closed-loop supply chain network considering consumers' preference for products and AI-push. Sustainability **11**(17), 1–32 (2019)
7. Ibrahim, S., Obal, M.: Investigating the impact of radical technology adoption into the new product development process. Int. J. Innov. Manage. **24**(4), 1–25 (2020)
8. Li, Y.P., Tao, N.N.: A Multi-layer dynamic impact model of employee artificial intelligence technology adoption: a literature review. China Hum. Res. Dev. **39**(1), 35–56 (2022)
9. Sussman, S.W., Siegal, W.S.: Informational influence in organizations: an integrated approach to knowledge adoption. Inf. Syst. Res. **14**(1), 47–65 (2003)
10. Xu, F.: Research on Organizational Information System Adoption Based on Integrated TOE Framework and UTAUT Model. Shandong University, Jinan (2012)
11. Forman, C., Van Zeebroeck, N.: Digital technology adoption and knowledge flows within firms: can the internet overcome geographic and technological distance? Res. Policy **48**(8), 1–16 (2019)
12. Hou, J.G., Liu, Y., Zhang, C.L.: Research on new product development based on knowledge integration. Sci. Technol. Prog. Countermeasures **26**(12), 105–108 (2009)
13. Chen, L., Lu, R.Y.: Research on enterprise knowledge integration. Sci. Res. Manage. **24**(3), 32–38 (2003)

14. Baron, R.M., Kenny, D.A.: The moderator-mediator variable distinction in social psychological research: conceptual, strategic, and statistical considerations. J. Pers. Soc. Psychol. **51**(6), 1173–1182 (1986)
15. Davis, F.D.: Perceived usefulness, perceived ease of use, and user acceptance of in-formation technology. MIS Q. **13**(3), 319–340 (1989)
16. Iansiti, M., Clark, K.B.: Integration and dynamic capability: evidence from product development in automobiles and mainframe computers. Ind. Corp. Chang. **3**(3), 557–605 (1994)
17. Zhou, J.M., Chen, M., Liu, Y.F.: Analysis on the relationship between knowledge leadership, team knowledge sharing and product innovation performance. Enterp. Econ. **9**, 120–125 (2015)
18. Hayes, A.F.: An Introduction to Mediation, Moderation and Conditional Process Analysis: A Regression-Based Approach. Guilford Press, New York (2013)

Enhancing IoT Service Interface Through AsyncAPI with Extensions

Hai Wang[1,2], Guiling Wang[1,2](✉), Jing Gao[1,2], Jianhang Hu[1,2], Junhua Li[1,2], and Haoran Zhang[1,2]

[1] School of Information Science and Technology, North China University of Technology, Beijing 100144, China
wangguiling@ict.ac.cn

[2] Beijing Key Laboratory on Integration and Analysis of Large-Scale Stream Data, Beijing, China

Abstract. In recent years, various Internet of Things (IoT) applications have penetrated into various areas of human life. In the IoT environment, various IoT service systems perform task collaboration by integrating with a large number of heterogeneous software and hardware devices in an open environment, providing intelligent services to the outside world. However, traditional service applications, when facing IoT with massive data, cannot meet the high real-time requirements of modern applications by relying on a pull-based response method, which also increases system operation pressure. Therefore, an event-driven architecture is adopted to provide IoT services, and service users only need to focus on how to determine the subsequent process based on event content. In this paper, we propose an IoT service interface model based on AsyncAPI, which provides a static expression of service for service subscribers, effectively expresses various operations, and makes IoT service usage more flexible. Secondly, we extend AsyncAPI to define a unified IoT service interface specification, solved the problem of protocol heterogeneity in event transmission. And complete the related code generation mechanism for the transmission of event information between systems. Finally, we apply this interface model to IoT service usage and conduct experimental verification, demonstrating the effectiveness of the IoT service interface model in event-driven communication.

Keywords: IoT service · Event Driven Architecture · Service modeling · AsyncAPI

1 Introduction

IoT is an open and comprehensive network of intelligent objects that have the capacity to auto-organize, share information, data, and resources, react, and act in the face of situations and changes in the environment. It enables communication between humans, things, and things by providing a unique identity to each and every object in the world [1,9]. IoT services apply the service-oriented thinking to the Internet to solve the issues of resource integration, resource reuse,

Z. Wang et al. (Eds.): ICSS 2023, CCIS 1844, pp. 360–372, 2023.
https://doi.org/10.1007/978-981-99-4402-6_26

and interoperability among heterogeneous components in IoT. By extending the sensor network to the physical world, various heterogeneous physical facilities and traditional web services are able to call each other, exchange information, and thus seamlessly integrate the physical world and the virtual network world [7].

However, with the continued growth of IoT services and sensors, the traditional request-response architecture model is insufficient to meet the demands for efficient handling and real-time interaction of IoT data, and may bring serious system stress and burden [8]. IoT service systems can use an event-driven architecture model to handle massive amounts of data in IoT and coordinate IoT services using event sessions [13]. The use of an asynchronous communication model in the event-driven architecture(EDA) pattern can immediately respond to events occurring in IoT services without waiting for requests to be initiated and responses to be received. AsyncAPI[1] is a specification for defining and documenting event-driven APIs. This specification provides a mode that can be read by both humans and machines and has high readability. Moreover, the specification is agnostic to transport protocols and applicable to various protocols such as MQTT, Kafka, and HTTP, which satisfies the requirements of event transmission in IoT services across multiple protocols. However, AsyncAPI is still insufficient to meet the current characteristics of IoT service usage, lacking operations for IoT service instantiation and the executions available to service subscribers.

This paper proposes an IoT service interface model based on AsyncAPI and implements it. The IoT service interface model is primarily utilized to construct the usage for IoT services, connecting service publishers and subscribers through an event-driven architecture. Firstly, we extend AsyncAPI to instantiate IoT services during event transmission and provide service consumers with operations including service static expression, validity expression, and event interception. This approach enhances the flexibility of utilizing IoT services. Secondly, based on the extended definitions, we define a unified IoT service interface specification and provide a standard format for IoT service usage. We also complete a relevant code generation mechanism to facilitate event information transmission between systems. Finally, we apply this interface model to a business scenario that combines IoT services with BPM and conduct experimental verification to prove the effectiveness of the IoT service interface model in event-driven architecture communication and evaluate service usage efficiency.

The rest of this paper is structured as follows: Sect. 2 reviews previous work related to IoT service interface models in EDA. Section 3 describes the basic structure and usage specifications of the IoT service interface model, including the workflow to generate event-driven architecture using the model. Section 4 Apply the IoT service interface model in the IoT service system and business process through a scenario of maritime transportation of hazardous chemicals. Finally, Sect. 5 provides a summary of the paper and outlines possibilities for future work.

[1] https://github.com/asyncapi.

2 Related Work

2.1 Construction of IoT Service

In previous works, Guiling Wang et al. proposed a new IoT service modeling method for encapsulating the processing logic of event streams generated by heterogeneous IoT devices from multiple sources, expanding the perception of IoT service models in a way that complements BPM [12]. IoT services are composed of IoT devices, IoT objects, and a business event layer in Fig. 1. IoT devices belong to the physical resource layer, collecting various environmental sensing states in real-world scenarios and transmitting data resources through gateways. IoT objects record a certain category of IoT devices and can combine multiple IoT devices for data processing based on business rules. The business event layer has IoT data sources included in IoT objects as its input and generates business events based on different scenario rule requirements as its output. This paper constructs IoT services based on IoT service modeling and applies them in accordance with the IoT service interface model specification.

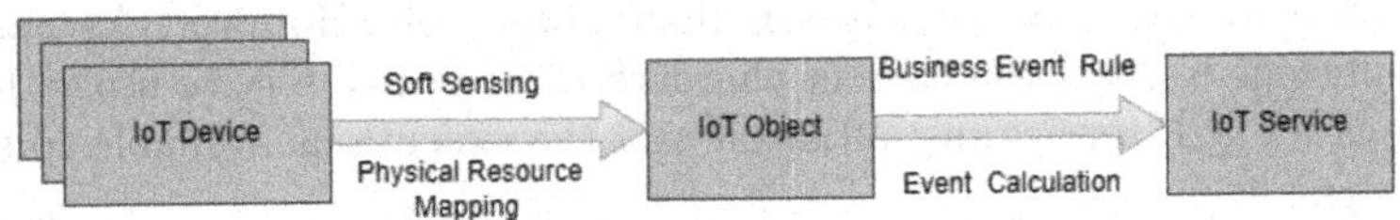

Fig. 1. IoT Service Modeling Process

2.2 IoT Service Usage

To solve the issue of IoT service usage, SOA provides a standard way to describe IoT services and offer service description information to callers, uses a unified service-based pattern to describe IoT devices, and implements the description of different components at the service level [4]. However, SOA still needs to address some problems in the application of IoT services, such as most IoT services are provided by devices with limited resources, so a more lightweight service is needed. Subsequently, some work attempted to extend IoT services on newer RESTful protocols, using lightweight protocols and data formats in RESTful Web services to reduce service overhead and develop their private service description mode [10,14]. As a result, their application in the IoT field was limited, and their ability to describe IoT devices and IoT objects was relatively weak.

In addition, with regard to the massive IoT data, the reactive request method is unable to satisfy the load demands of IoT services. Therefore, an EDSOA architecture for IoT services has been proposed in literature, which aims to decouple services in the behavior layer using an event-driven architecture execution model for IoT services in a distributed environment [13]. To integrate the event flow generated by mobile devices and sensors, Stefan et al. designed a component model, Eventlets, to encapsulate event flow processing functions [2]. Although this resolves the issue of event flow processing, the entire project is designed by developers, which increases the technology's usage barrier and is not user-friendly to business users. To effectively describe event-driven architecture specifications, Abel Gómez et al. proposed a syntax and code generation template that relies on AsyncAPI with a uniform standard in event-driven architecture [6]. This generates an internal DSL based on Java to support the architecture of event-driven systems. Although this approach effectively describes event-driven architecture and generates client and server systems, it still poses challenges for IoT service demands for event flow processing and subscription operations.

2.3 Code Generation

Automatic code generation based on specification-based service description formats is of great significance for service usage. By manually implementing a DSL interpreter that can automatically convert into a code generator and harbors considerable portability [3], DSL can be utilized across a broad range of target environments and programming languages. The authors [11] developed a model-driven software tool that supports the specifications and code generation related to the REST software architecture style and development of text-based and graphical concrete syntax using the Xtext and Sirius frameworks, respectively, in a distributed system environment. A series of code generators were implemented using the Xtend programming language, which enable the generated code to run in cloud software architecture.

3 IoT Service Interface Model

3.1 IoT Service Interface Model Structure

In an IoT service system, communication between IoT services is carried out through events. Within service communication, operations such as publishing, subscribing, and transmitting events are carried out. In the IoT service interface model, we define the usage specifications for IoT services. This specification is a documented description of services based on IoT service interface model structures. Such descriptions can be read by both humans and machines and use JSON/YML file formats for describing IoT services. Next, we will introduce the basic structure of the IoT service interface model, its working principles, and a description of service specifications. Our expanded components are shown in the green section of the Fig. 2.

The Info: Records the basic information of the IoT service interface, which can be used to declare the IoT service name, version, and description information.

The Server: The server represents a message broker, server, or any other type of computer program object that is capable of sending or receiving data. This section includes information such as the server URI, communication protocol, and security configuration used for business event transmission. For example, protocols such as MQTT or Kafka can be configured, including account and permission information for the communication protocol server.

The Channels: A channel consists of a topic name and information used for subscription and publication, and is used to store information on each channel and its corresponding operations. This information includes the description of the topic, the type of the topic, and the data structure used for the topic. The type information can describe the message details of each topic, including message format, and whether the published messages need to be guaranteed to be ordered.

An Operation: Used to describe the publish and subscribe operations of business events, mainly including fields such as operationId and description. The publish operation defines the events that the application consumes from the channel, while the subscribe operation generates and sends events to the channel. For IoT service consumers and producers, the role of the operation is to define the message format of the communication, so that producers and consumers of the IoT service can parse and process events.

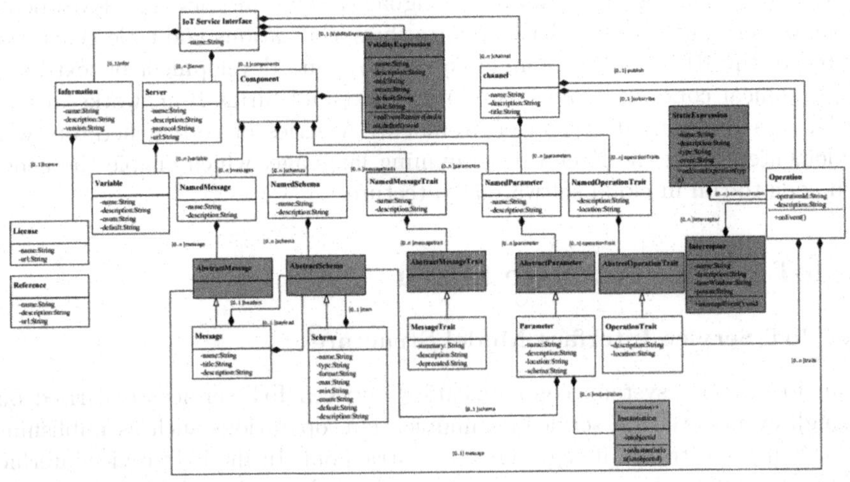

Fig. 2. IoT Service Interface Model.

A Message: The role of a message is to transport data from an IoT service producer to an IoT service consumer. Exchange of information between consumers and producers is achieved through messages. By defining a consistent message format and using message namespaces to differentiate between different messages, the data exchange between IoT service consumers and producers can be guaranteed to be correct and effective.

A Component: Components are used to define and store reusable objects, and elements defined in the Components object can be referenced using a Reference object. Reusable objects are mapped by name in their corresponding fields and include Schema, message, messageTrait, Parameter, and OperationTrait.

A Reference: A Reference is used to reference another position in the specification from one location in order to reuse redundant information such as duplicate definitions or descriptions. By employing $ref, the readability and maintainability of the IoT service interface specification can be improved.

The Schema: Schema is used to define the event body that is transmitted by IoT services in terms of data type, structure, and rules, including all the properties, data types, and formats of requests and responses. Key fields include type, which represents the field type, and max, min, and default, which respectively set the maximum value, minimum value, and default value of each property.

A Instantiation: Instantiation enables instantiation of IoT objects on specific entities, representing the event flow information included in the specified IoT object. An IoT object is the most basic unit that can be instantiated in IoT services, designed to provide an abstract mapping of physical IoT devices. By using instantiation, the event flow in IoT services can be split into sub-flows, each of which includes events that are relevant to the specified IoT object. Relevance is established by obtaining the IoT object ID and properties. For example, in a monitoring service for an LNG(Liquefied Natural Gas) transport ship, the IoT service can be instantiated to the storage tank 1 on the ship, and the temperature and pressure event information of the tank can be obtained.

A ValidityExpression: ValidityExpression is employed in IoT service subscriptions. IoT service subscribers cannot rely on a fixed event flow or notifications from service providers who leave the system. To prevent IoT service subscribers from remaining active indefinitely, Validity Expression provides an expression of validity targeting different IoT objects to manage the lifecycle of service subscriptions. The onEventRemove() method is employed to complete all resource clean-up tasks when a service subscription lifecycle ends.

The StaticExpression: StaticExpression is necessary because service subscribers may not require all of the event information provided by IoT service providers and may only be interested in certain types of events. Static Expression is a subscriber level filter. When a subscription occurs, users can select the specified types of events they need to subscribe to. This type of filter verifies whether the events subscribed in the IoT service interface meet the expected criteria and whether the event types are the same. Users can configure their interests in events at the subscription phase. If the event flow does not match, no further event processing is necessary. Key fields include name and type, which identifies the event type.

An Interceptor: Interceptor allows service providers and consumers to add custom logic during transmission, including service authorization, addition, and interception of events. Service authorization binds secure authentication to the event transmission to increase inter-service security. Event interception enables interception of events during transmission according to specific rules.

As shown in the Fig. 3, on the basis of IoT service interface model, we propose a unified specification of IoT service interface. A use case of transporting hazardous goods by ship in heavy fog is declared according to this specification. Firstly, the IoT service interface protocol is declared following the 2.0.0 specification, and the description information of the IoT service is stored in the info section.

```
IoT Service Interface: 2.0.0
info:
  title: descripe iot service
  version: 1.0.0
servers:
  production:
    url: 'localhost:{port}'
    protocol: mqtt
    description: Test broker
    variables:
      port:
        default: '1883'
        enum:
          - '1883'
          - '8883'
valityexpression:
  eventend:
    description: set service end time
    end: '1'
    unit: hour
channels:
  'iot/iotservice/{iotobjectid}/monitor':
    parameters:
      iotobjectid:
        $ref: '#/components/parameters/iotobjectid'
    publish:
      operationId: publishiotservice
      message:
        $ref: '#/components/messages/iotservice'
    subscribe:
      operationId: subscribeiotservice
      message:
        $ref: '#/components/messages/iotservice'
        staticexpression:
          filterEvent:
            description: subscribe other type event
            type: string
            event: 'fog'
        interceptor:
          interceptorTimeOut:
            description: set event out window
            timeWindow: '500'
            param: 'ServiceUser'
components:
  messages:
    iotservice:
      payload:
        $ref: '#/components/schemas/iotservice'
  schemas:
    iotservice:
      type: object
      properties:
        id:
          type: string
        fogwarning:
            $ref: '#/components/schemas/fogwarning'
    fogwarning:
      type: object
      properties:
        id:
          type: string
          description: identifier of the event
        timestamp:
            $ref: "#/components/schemas/timestamp"
        event:
          type: string
          description:  fog warning  information
        fogvalue:
            $ref: '#/components/schemas/value'
    timestamp:
      type: string
      format: date-time
      description: Date when the message was sent
    value:
      type: string
      description: event value when the message was sent
  parameters:
    iotobjectid:
      description: the instantiation of the  iotservice
      schema:
        type: string
```

Fig. 3. Application of IoT service interface specification in the scenario of shipping hazardous chemicals.

The service information is described in the server section, and local MQTT communication server is used for event transmission with the address and port number of the server specified. The ports connected to the server are enumerated in the variables section, which are '1883' and '8883' respectively. The former is set as the default for subsequent connection configuration. The valityexpression section sets the configuration information to prevent the subscription business events from being active indefinitely. In the channel section, the topic name of the IoT service event transmission is set as iot/iotservice/iotobjectid/monitor, where iotobjectid is used for instantiating and associating IoT object information in the scenario. There are two operations under this topic, publish and subscribe. The publish operation ID is publishiotservice, which is used for unique identification, and the message sent references the iotservice event defined in the message section. The subscribe operation ID is subscribeiotservice, and the information subscribed to is the iotservice event defined in the message section. The interceptor is used to filter out event information that exceeds the specified time window and obtain the specified service authorization information during subscription. The staticexpression section selects the fog attribute event of interest among many IoT service events. The interceptor is configured with a time window and service authorization, and only events that meet the requirements can be accurately subscribed. In the component section, the message component encapsulates the basic event attributes defined in the schema using the payload. The message is divided into iotservice and fogwarning, with the event attribute information in iotservice being id, and that in fogwarning being id, timestamp, event description, and fog intensity value. Finally, the iotobjectid in the parameter section corresponds to the parameter in the topic and can be instantiated as an IoT object. This constitutes an example of using IoT service specification.

3.2 Event Driven Code Generation Mechanism

After defining the IoT service interface specification, we developed a code generation module using a model-driven approach. The Eclipse Modeling Framework (EMF) and Ecore metamodel are widely used in academia as model-driven software development platforms. It follows a simple, intuitive, and practical modeling method that includes the core concepts of object-oriented modeling, and can directly map the IoT service interface specification to Java code. Modelers use an Ecore class diagram to describe the structure of the IoT service interface, and the code generator provided by EMF maps the class model to a corresponding set of Java interfaces and implementation classes. To achieve the transformation from the Ecore model to the IoT service interface metamodel and the IoT service interface specification, we use Xtend technology. Xtend is a Java-based domain-specific language (DSL) that enhances Java syntax, provides code templates and template operations. The project is built using Xtext, which can create an IoT service interface DSL, including syntax rules, parsers, validators, and code generators. In contrast, Xtend is used to write code generators for the service interface.

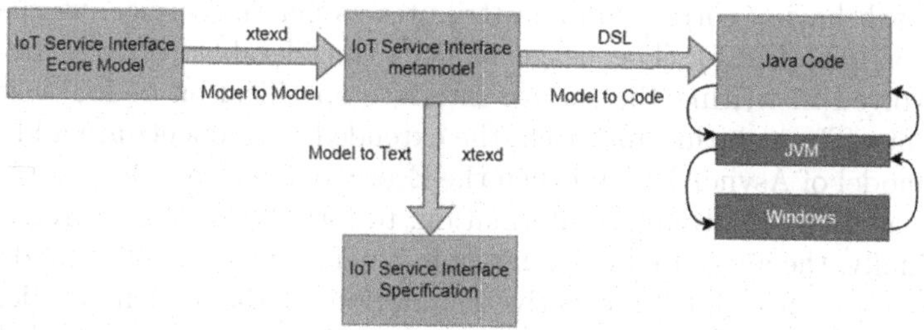

Fig. 4. IoT service interface model code generation

The workflow for IoT service interface model generation and model transformation is specifically described below. As shown in the Fig. 4, we first construct an Ecore model describing the IoT service, which includes the data information of the IoT service. After creating the Ecore model, the IoT service interface model and the IoT service structure code are generated based on a pre-defined IoT service interface specification template. This involves converting the IoT service Ecore model to the IoT service interface metamodel (Model to Model transformation). Once we have the IoT service interface metamodel, we use the template expression of Xtend to convert the IoT service interface metamodel to the IoT service interface specification Model to Text transformation. Finally, we convert the IoT service interface metamodel according to the IoT service interface specification pre-defined using Xtext to Java executable code.

```
ValityExpression:
    {ValityExpression} name=AnyString ':' '{'(
        ( '"description"' ':' description=AnyString ','?  )?
        &('"end"' ':' end=AnyString ','? )?
        &('"unit"' ':' unit=AnyString ','?)?
        &('"default"' ':' degfault=AnyString ','?)?
        & ( '"enum"' ':' '[' ^enum+=AnyString (',' ^enum+=AnyString)* ']' ','? )?
    )'}';
StaticExpression:
    {StaticExpression} name=AnyString ':' '{'(
        ( '"description"' ':' description=AnyString ','?  )?
        &('"type"' ':' type=AnyString ','? )?
        &('"event"' ':' event=AnyString ','?)?
    )'}';
Iotobject:
    {Iotobject} name=AnyString ':' '{'(
        ( '"description"' ':' description=AnyString ','?  )?
        &('"iotobjectid"' ':' iotobjectid=AnyString ','? )?
        &('"iotobjectname"' ':' iotobjectname=AnyString ','?)?
    )'}';
```

Fig. 5. IoT service interface specification based on xtext.

This passage describes the language rules of a DSL built using Xtext, which is employed to describe the service interface specification of IoT. The DSL code encompasses the Variable, Validation Expression, and Static Expression objects, each having corresponding attributes as per the service interface specification of IoT (Fig. 5). The usage of DSL considerably reduces the manual effort involved in writing the service interface specification of IoT customized components. Through this approach, the extended components are added to the original model of AsyncAPI, and then the Ecore model is used for standard editing, such as filling in attribute information, to form validation expressions, and so on. Finally, the annotated data model is generated through the model engine transformation, providing an effective foundation for the implementation of IoT service interfaces. This work contributes a simple and extensible modeling approach to support the construction and implementation of IoT service interface specifications while reducing manual workload.

4 Experiments

4.1 Experimental Scenarios

In our research scenario [12], IoT sensing data is monitored and modeled in real-time, and transformed into IoT services that are transmitted through event transmission to the business process system. The system retrieves actual sensor status and executes or adjusts the business event accordingly. To verify the effectiveness of the IoT service interface model, a maritime transportation scenario involving heavy fog will be used. As shown in the Fig. 6, the process diagram of Boyuan vessel's transportation in heavy foggy weather is shown below. Once the vessel sends a report request, the regulatory department begins monitoring the transportation processes by subscribing to IoT services through non-interruptive activity boundaries. These IoT services are used to monitor vessel operation in heavy foggy environments, to ensure that navigation lights are compliant with the navigation light specifications for vessels in fog, and to monitor vessel whistle regulations for foggy weather. If severe foggy weather is detected, the navigation light and whistle status monitoring services will be activated, and normal transportation or decision-making such as adjusting the route will occur. In this business scenario, the IoT service interface model is introduced to complete the event transmission task from the IoT service published to the business process subscription.

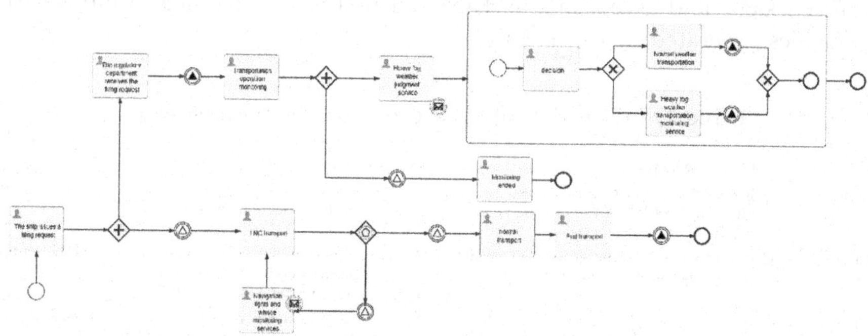

Fig. 6. IoT service interface model code generation flowchart.

4.2 Experimental Result

As shown in the Fig. 7, this is the experimental process of the IoT service interface model. The heavy fog environment monitoring service for ships, fog navigation light specification monitoring service, vessel whistle monitorina service in foggy weather services are obtained from the IoT service library, and the services are described using the IoT service interface specification (Expanded on the basis of Fig. 3).

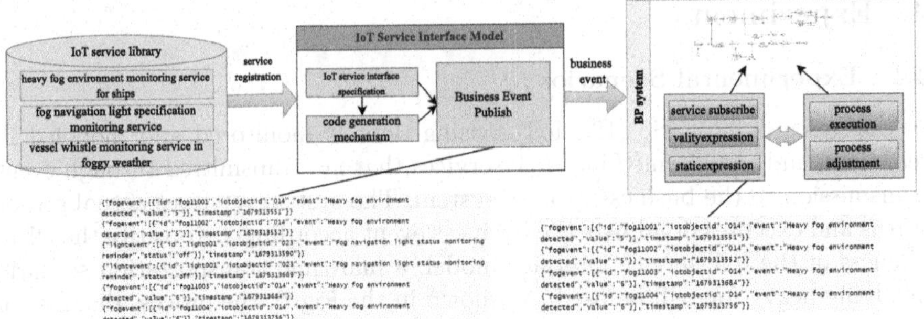

Fig. 7. IoT service interface model code generation flowchart.

Based on the IoT service interface specification, the file describing the IoT service interface specification is used with a plugin tool to generate the code for an IoT business event-driven architecture, and multiple tests are conducted for instantiation, validity, static expressions, and interceptor functions, the test is shown as Table 1. It can be proved that the IoT service interface specification is effective when the BP system successfully subscribes to the IoT service event stream and performs subsequent process decisions and adjustments. The corresponding code generated based on the pre-defined IoT service interface specification includes schema package, message package, infra package, monitor package, server package, and extensions package. The extensions package comprises the source files generated by extensions.

Table 1. IoT service interface extension function test case.

Function	Operating steps	Expected results	Actual results
Instantiation	IoT service provider specifies the information of IoT objects when transmitting business events	The business flow subscriber receives the business event information included in the IoT object	reach exception
ValityExpression	the subscription duration for the business process subscription client	the business process subscriber stops receiving business events from the IoT service publisher after a specified time	reach exception
StaticExpression	the IoT service publisher transmits ship maritime navigation warning events, including navigation lights, whistling, ship fog monitoring, and other events. At the business process subscription end, it specifies the receiving range of interested fog environment events and events	the business process only receives attribute information of dense fog events	reach exception
Interceptor	add event interception time information to the business process subscription end	the business process subscription end stops subscribing to business event information that exceeds the specified receiving time	reach exception

Table 2 includes the package name and lines of code (LOC) of the generated code files corresponding to the source file codes generated by the DSL. According to literature [5], the individual average productivity is 14.4LOC per hour. The 1650LOC generated by the IoT service interface model would take approximately 114.58 h, or 4.77 days. The specification document for generating the IoT service

Table 2. Automatically generated event driven architecture code directory.

Package	Class name	LOC
schema	Fogewarning.java Iotservice.java Timestamp.java Lightwarning.java Value.java	372
message	iotservice.java	73
infra	Ichannel.java IJdonSerializable.java IMessage.java IOperation.java IParameter.java IServer.java	309
monitor	MonitorChannel.java PublishOperation.java SubscribeOperation.java	342
server	IoTServiceExampleServer.java	248
extensions	IoTObject.java StaticExpression.java ValityExpression.java Interceptor	306
	total.	1650

event-driven architecture system is approximately 96 lines, and the automation rate is approximately 17.19:1.

5 Conclusion

This paper proposes an IoT service interface model for constructing event-driven architectures in IoT service usage. The model is detailed in terms of its structure and code generation workflow. The IoT service model provides a documented interface usage specification, expands the logical processing capabilities of subscribed event streams, and provides a code generation mechanism for quickly constructing the event-driven architecture used in IoT services. To verify the effectiveness and superiority of the IoT service model, we applied it in a real case by using the interface specification to construct business event transmission channels, integrate IoT services into the business process, and successfully subscribe to business event streams while executing subsequent logical operations on the event stream. In future work, we will continue to expand the service model and compatibility with more communication protocols to meet the diverse needs of event transmission. At the same time, we will optimize the code generation process and provide more ways to generate event-driven source code based on IoT service specifications.

Acknowledgements. This work is supported by the International Cooperation and Exchange Program of National Natural Science Foundation of China (No. 62061136006) and the Key Program of National Natural Science Foundation of China (No. 61832004).

References

1. Aggarwal, R., Das, M.L.: RFID security in the context of "internet of things". In: Proceedings of the First International Conference on Security of Internet of Things, pp. 51–56 (2012)
2. Appel, S., Frischbier, S., Freudenreich, T., Buchmann, A.: Eventlets: components for the integration of event streams with SOA. In: 2012 Fifth IEEE International Conference on Service-Oriented Computing and Applications (SOCA), pp. 1–9. IEEE (2012)
3. Birken, K.: Building code generators for DSLs using a partial evaluator for the xtend language. In: Margaria, T., Steffen, B. (eds.) ISoLA 2014. LNCS, vol. 8802, pp. 407–424. Springer, Heidelberg (2014). https://doi.org/10.1007/978-3-662-45234-9_29
4. Fanjiang, Y.-Y., Syu, Y., Ma, S.-P., Kuo, J.-Y.: An overview and classification of service description approaches in automated service composition research. IEEE Trans. Serv. Comput. **10**(2), 176–189 (2015)
5. Gómez, O.S., Rosero, R.H., Cortés-Verdín, K.: CRUDyLeaf: a DSL for generating spring boot rest APIs from entity CRUD operations. Cybern. Inf. Technol. **20**(3), 3–14 (2020)
6. Gómez, A., Iglesias-Urkia, M., Belategi, L., Mendialdua, X., Cabot, J.: Model-driven development of asynchronous message-driven architectures with AsyncAPI. Softw. Syst. Model. 1–29 (2021)
7. Hang, S.: Research on quality of service optimization methods for internet of things systems. Ph.D. thesis, Northeastern University (2019). (in Chinese)
8. Liu, Y.: Design and implementation of a data fusion module in an internet of things resource access and intelligent processing platform. Master's thesis, Beijing University of Posts and Telecommunications (2017). (in Chinese)
9. Madakam, S., Lake, V., Lake, V., Lake, V., et al.: Internet of things (IoT): a literature review. J. Comput. Commun. **3**(05), 164 (2015)
10. Taherkordi, A., Eliassen, F.: Scalable modeling of cloud-based iot services for smart cities. In: 2016 IEEE International Conference on Pervasive Computing and Communication Workshops (PerCom Workshops), pp. 1–6. IEEE (2016)
11. Terzić, B., Dimitrieski, V., Kordić (Aleksić), S., Milosavljevic, G., Luković, I.: Microbuilder: a model-driven tool for the specification of rest microservice architectures (2017)
12. Wang, G., Fang, J., Wang, J., Yu, J., Zhang, L., Han, Y.: Service-based event penetration from IoT sensors to businesses: a case study. In: 2022 International Conference on Service Science (ICSS), pp. 72–79. IEEE (2022)
13. Zhang, Y., Duan, L., Chen, J.L.: Event-driven SOA for IoT services. In: 2014 IEEE International Conference on Services Computing, pp. 629–636. IEEE (2014)
14. Zhao, Yu., Zou, Y., Ng, J., da Costa, D.A.: An automatic approach for transforming IoT applications to RESTful services on the cloud. In: Maximilien, M., Vallecillo, A., Wang, J., Oriol, M. (eds.) ICSOC 2017. LNCS, vol. 10601, pp. 673–689. Springer, Cham (2017). https://doi.org/10.1007/978-3-319-69035-3_49

A Composite Service Selection Approach Based on Functionality Folding and Reinforcement Learning

Weijie Chu(✉), Yun Chen, YiFeng Xiang, Tong Mo, and Weiping Li

School of Software and Microelectronics, Peking University, Beijing, China
{chuwj,motong,wpli}@ss.pku.edu.cn, cloud_chen@pku.edu.cn,
xiangyifeng@stu.pku.edu.cn

Abstract. The current service composition approaches usually assume that the candidate services among different abstract tasks are independent, and they select the optimal candidate service sequentially for each abstract task based on the constraints. However, such solutions are not suitable for the situation that the coarse-grained services implement multiple abstract tasks. In this paper, we propose an approach to model task correlation for service composition as set cover problem and using the DQN algorithm to find the optimal solution.

Keywords: Constraint-Satisfied Service Composition · Folding of service functionality · reinforcement learning

1 Introduction

The constraint-satisfied service composition problem is to select the appropriate services for each task in the customer's business requirements, so as to meet the customer's functional and non-functional requirements as much as possible. So far, many research efforts have been devoted to solving the constraint-satisfied service composition (CSSC) problem [1,3,4]. These methods divide the service composition process into two stages: first, modelling the user's functional requirements into a set of abstract tasks. For each abstract task, candidate services with the same functionality are gathered into a candidate services collection. Then, finding the appropriate service in each candidate services set to form an optimal composite service. These methods assume inter-independence between the candidate services of the different abstract tasks. However, from the perspective of service provider, associated functions are folded into a coarse-grained service in order to improve their competitiveness in the market. Taking the description specification (WSDL) of web service as an example, the function represented as a set of operation tag definitions, which is the smallest unit of task description. Since the coarse-grained service may be bound to one or more fine-grained abstract tasks, there will be an extra step that several related task nodes should be bound together. As the number of the services may be very large, any type

Z. Wang et al. (Eds.): ICSS 2023, CCIS 1844, pp. 373–379, 2023.
https://doi.org/10.1007/978-981-99-4402-6_27

of combination for any services may appear and be part of the best composited service. It is necessary to arrange and combine the services in the candidate service set, and select the specific service with the best QoS among all possible combination methods for binding.

2 Problem Formulation

This paper focuses on the composite service selection problem, so as to best meet the user's functional requirements and QoS constraints. User's functional requirements are represented as a task set. Here we give the formal definition of composite service selection problem:

1. Abstract tasks set: {t1, ..., tm} represents the set of abstract tasks that compound to meet the user's functional requirements.
2. User's constraints Set C: {cAtt1, cAtt2, ..., cAttl}. Each 'cAttri' in set representing user's constraints on different QoS non-functional attributes. A 'cAttri' can be expressed as a pair (cAttrName, operator, value). (i.e., execution time and price).
3. Candidate Service:{ CS1,CS2,...,CSi... } that implement one or more abstract tasks defined in task set. CSi can be formalized as a 3-tuple { ServiceID, FuncTaskSet, cAttrValue }, where:
   - ServiceID is the identifier of a candidate service.
   - FuncTaskSet = {TaskID1, TaskID2, ...,TaskIDl}, represents one or more functional tasks that the service implements. l is the length of the set.
   - cAttrValue contains multiple constraints.
4. Given a task set T with finite number of elements. A collection$\{T_i\}_{i\in I} \subseteq 2^T$of subsets of T indexed by I. For each candidate service S, we denote a function$\varphi(s)$ to express tasks covered by S, denote by$\varphi(s) : S \rightarrow \{T_i\}_{i\in I}$

The functionality-related CSSC problem concerns how to select optimal candidate services $Sl = s1 \bigcup s2 \ldots \bigcup sn$ with satisfying $T = \bigcup_{(si\in Sl)} \varphi(si)$and the given constraints.

3 Composite Service Selection Model

The composition service selection approach is to select a group of optimal candidate services for covering all the abstract tasks of user's requirements to form the optimal composite service, meanwhile, all the constraints should be satisfied. As shown in Fig. 1, we describe the process as follow:

Step1: User's requirements and constraints representation. The service request from the user is proposed including the functional and non-functional requirements. According to functional requirements, a workflow is built, which represents the set of abstract tasks t1, ..., tm. According to user's constraints on non-functional attributes, a constraint set is built, which represents the set of all

Algorithm 1. Composite Services Selection Algorithm.

Input: The set of user's requirement tasks and constraints
The set of candidate services;
Output: The DQN model;
indexing tasks correlated candidate services;
indexing candidate services correlated tasks;
preprocess the DQN model
for(int i=1 to episodeNumberMax)
Initial stateActionspacesNumber with tasks $n \leftarrow n^2$
For every state (code_state, qos_left, candidate_ services) in state_action_space:
Code_state indicate tasks status that covered or not
Qos_left indicate the available constraints values
Services indicate the available candidate services set
Act and training process of DQN model

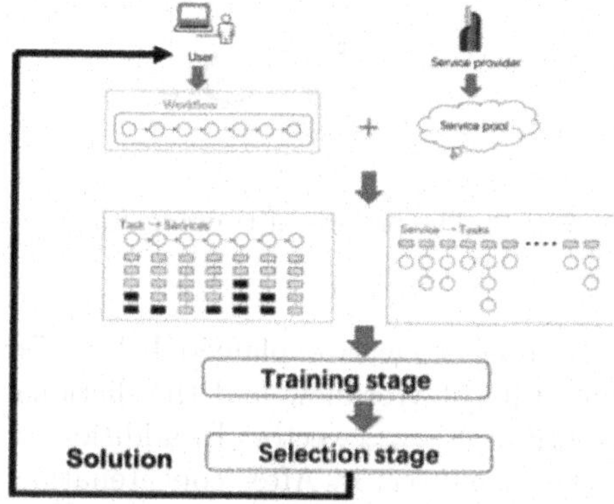

Fig. 1. The process of composite service selection.

constraints {cAttr1, cAttr2, ..., cAttrN}. A constraint in set models as a triple (attribute, operator, value).
Step2: Service's description. Service provider describe services as 3-tuple ServiceID, CorrespondingTasks, cAttrValues according to the definition in step 1.
Step3: Candidate service's set of abstract tasks. By service discovery, the candidate services which can fulfill specific function of an abstract task gather into a candidate service set {CS1, CS2,...,CSn}. A service may fulfill one or more functions which describe as different abstract tasks, therefore it may appear more than one abstract task set below.
Step4: During the training stage and selection stage, optimal candidate services are selected to form the composite service. According to the abstract task set and QoS constraints, a dynamic service composition solution is formed to meet both the functional and the user's constraint requirements.

The training stage of model is shown in the Fig. 2. After the process mentioned above, we get the Workflow and two kinds of dictionary. The blue node in Workflow mains that the task has been finished, and the white node means it hasn't finished.

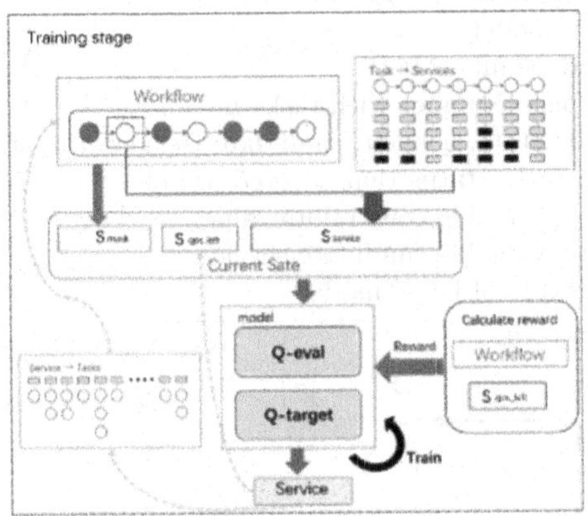

Fig. 2. The process of training stage.

One step during training stage is explained below. Firstly, combining the information of current state of Workflow and the dictionary mapping Task to Services, we get the current $S_{service}$ vector. In addition, according to the sate of Workflow, we get the $S_mask$vector. After concatenating S_{mask}, S_{qos_left} and $S_{service}$, the whole current state is formed. Then our algorithm input the state into the DQN model. The DQN model will output a selected service. And by referring to the dictionary mapping Service to Tasks, all task nodes influenced by the selected service will turn into blue in the Fig. 3. Then the state of Workflow will be updated. Besides, our algorithm will calculate the reward. And the DQN model will get trained with the reward information. The selection stage is similar to the training stage. The main difference is that only Q-eval network in DQN model will be used. And the selection stage is shown in Fig. 3.

As shown in Fig. 3, the algorithm first carries out some preprocessing to make the problem model convenient for subsequent processing. After that, the experience pool and DNN are initialized. In each loop, the state value is initialized first, and then a head is randomly selected. The Q function represented by the head is used to complete the whole episode, realize the deep exploration, and sample each step. In the training process, the data set is sampled according to the weight, and the generated mask is used to filter the head, so that the sample data is given to the corresponding head for learning. Update target Q network regularly.

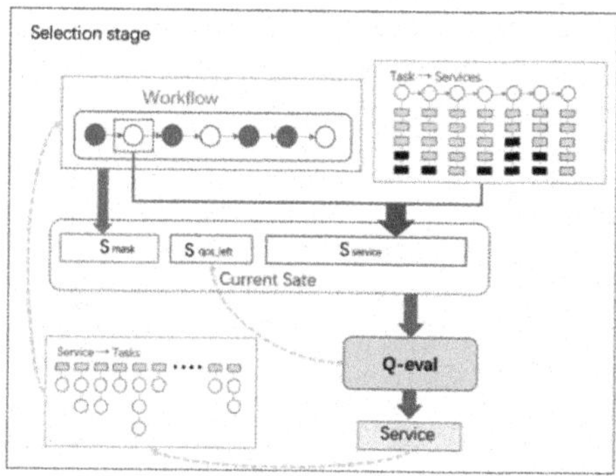

Fig. 3. The process of selection stage.

4 Experiment

In order to test the performance of the model better, the experiment simulate data illustration as below, a user's functional requirements and non-functional requirements as follow:
Functional requirements: 6 parallel abstract tasks including task1, task2, task3, task4, task5, task6
Non-function requirements: (price≤5000) and (time≥14)
The candidates services set contains 11 types of task node collections:
$\{1\}, \{2\}, \{3\}, \{2,3\}, \{4\}, \{5\}, \{6\}, \{4,5\}, \{4,6\}, \{5,6\}, \{4,5,6\}$
For the candidate service that containing equal kinds of abstract task, the price and time are simulated as (250,9), (500, 7), (750, 5), (1000, 3), and (1250, 1). Moreover, 10% evenly distributed random perturbation is applied to each attribute value of each candidate's service. The optimizer uses RMSprop and the size of the experience replay pool was set to a power of two, including 512, 1024, 2048, 4096, 8192, 16384, and 32768. The number of iterations is 2000. The experimental results are as follows:

After 2000 rounds of iterative training, probability sampling is used for the results. Firstly, all the behavior scores in each state are normalized, and then the softmax value is selected randomly as the selection probability. In this paper, precision @ K is used as an index to evaluate the model, which represents the proportion of model discovery services. Figure 4 shows that the model has 80% discovery rate for the top 60 composite services, while for the lower ranking services, although limited by the number of samples and probability, it also remains above 70%. The precision of exhaustive method is 1, and the random sampling, which is equal to the ratio of the number of samples and the total number of combination schemes, is about 0.3%.

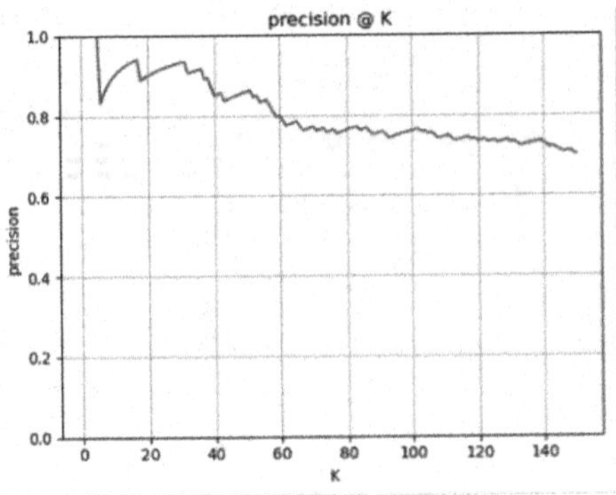

Fig. 4. Proportion of model discovery services

5 Related Work

In the field of service computing, service composition has attracted attention in recent years and vast quantities of approaches are proposed [1,3,4] to resolve varied business needs. These approaches from different perspectives in different domain to resolve different service composition problems. Many works focus on building service-based systems (SBSs) by composing existing services. The authors of paper [10] propose a data-driven approach for web APIs recommendation that integrates web API discovery, verification and selection operations based on keywords search over the web API correlation graph. The paper [11] designs DAWAR, a diversity-aware Web APIs recommendation approach that finds diversified and compatible APIs for mashup creation.

There is a stream of research focusing on constraint-satisfied service composition that select candidate services for each task in the workflow with sequential structure to form the optimal composition service meeting the QoS constraints [3,4]. The relevant researchers considered reinforcement learning technology that used for planning and optimization in dynamic environments as a key component and aim at optimize the execution plan. The major limitation to that approach is that it only considers modeling candidate services set for each task in workflow. As for the scenarios that coarse-gained service related multiply tasks, the above approach cannot handle with that.

To address the above issue, based on our previous work [2], we propose a candidate services correlation model in selection strategy processing, which support coarse-grained services representation.

6 Conclusions

In this paper, we propose a service composition approach to model task correlation of coarse-gained services. The proposed approach based on an MDP model and used a DQN algorithm to solve the model. In the future, we will develop an extend version to service-based system building domain further improve its efficiency.

Acknowledgement. This work was supported in part by National Key R&D Program of China under Grants No. 2022YFF0902703.

References

1. Zhang, Y., Cui, G., Deng, S., Chen, F., Wang, Y., He, Q.: Efficient query of quality correlation for service composition. IEEE Trans. Serv. Comput. **14**(3), 695–709 (2021). https://doi.org/10.1109/TSC.2018.2830773
2. Chu, W., Wang, Y., Mo, T., Li, W.: A constraint satisfaction service composition method supporting one to many task pattern. In: 2021 IEEE International Conference on Services Computing (SCC), Chicago, IL, USA, pp. 382–387 (2021). https://doi.org/10.1109/SCC53864.2021.00054
3. Ren, L., Wang, W., Xu, H.: A reinforcement learning method for constraint-satisfied services composition. IEEE Trans. Serv. Comput. **13**(5), 786–800 (2020). https://doi.org/10.1109/TSC.2017.2727050
4. Yu, X., Ye, C., Li, B., Zhou, H., Huang, M.: A deep Q-learning network for dynamic constraint-satisfied service composition. Int. J. Web Serv. Res. (IJWSR) **17**, 55–75 (2020)
5. Chenghua, L., Jisong, K.: Multi-attribute decision making and adaptive genetic algorithm for solving QoS optimization of web service composition. Comput. Sci. **46**(02), 187–195 (2019)
6. Song, C., Jingquan, Z., Ruiyun, C.: Investigation on optimization of web service composition employing chaos ant colony algorithm. Comput. Technol. Dev. **27**(02), 178–181+186 (2017)
7. Wang, H., Gu, M., Yu, Q., Fei, H., Li, J., Tao, Y.: Large-scale and adaptive service composition using deep reinforcement learning. In: Maximilien, M., Vallecillo, A., Wang, J., Oriol, M. (eds.) ICSOC 2017. LNCS, vol. 10601, pp. 383–391. Springer, Cham (2017). https://doi.org/10.1007/978-3-319-69035-3_27
8. Gavvala, S.K., Jatoth, C., Gangadharan, G.R., Buyya, R.: QoS-aware cloud service composition using eagle strategy. Futur. Gener. Comput. Syst. **90**, 273–290 (2019)
9. Wang, Z., Cheng, B., Zhang, W., Chen, J.: Q-Graphplan: QoS-aware automatic service composition with the extended planning graph. IEEE Access **8**, 8314–8323 (2020). https://doi.org/10.1109/ACCESS.2019.2963548
10. Qi, L., He, Q., Chen, F., Zhang, X., Dou, W., Ni, Q.: Data-driven web APIs recommendation for building web applications. IEEE Trans. Big Data **8**(3), 685–698 (2022). https://doi.org/10.1109/TBDATA.2020.2975587
11. Gong, W., et al.: DAWAR: diversity-aware web APIs recommendation for mashup creation based on correlation graph. In: Proceedings of the 45th International ACM SIGIR Conference on Research and Development in Information Retrieval (SIGIR 2022). Association for Computing Machinery, New York, NY, USA, pp. 395–404 (2022). https://doi.org/10.1145/3477495.3531962

Graph-Based Service Optimization

Proactive Perception of Preferences Evolution Based on Graph Neural Networks

Lixin Pang, Zhizhong Liu(✉), Lingqiang Meng, Linxia Li, and Xiaoyu Song

School of Computer and Control Engineering, Yantai University, Yantai 264005, China
lzzmff@126.com

Abstract. User preferences play an important role in intelligent services, smart recommendations, and so on. Unfortunately, user preferences are dynamic and always evolving. How to proactively perceive users' preferences evolution has become a critical issue. Recently, some wonderful research results about preference learning or preference prediction has been achieved. However, existing works can only perceive the change of preferences implicitly, cannot present users' preferences change explicitly. To tackle this issue, we propose an approach for proactive perception of preferences evolution based on graph neural networks (PPGNN). Firstly, PPGNN constructs a directed sequence graph based on the user's historical item interaction sequence, and learns the embedded vector representation of nodes in the directed sequence graph with the gated graph neural network (GGNN). Secondly, PPGNN learns the complex correlation between users and items in the interaction sequence using attention networks to obtain users' long-term preferences. Meanwhile, PPGNN uses the location-aware network to preserve the location information in the sequence, and extracts user's short-term preferences from the sequence with the attention network. Thirdly, PPGNN combines the user's long-term and short-term preferences through a gated-fusion network and recommends an item that the user is most interested in. Finally, PPGNN perceives the evolution of user preferences by comparing the recommended items with the items that the user was previously interested in. Extensive experiments have been conducted to validate the proposed method and demonstrate its effectiveness.

Keywords: Preferences Evolution · Graph Neural Networks · Attention Network

1 Introduction

With the rapid development of e-commerce platforms, users' consumption behaviors are becoming diverse and complex [1]. To facilitate users' lives and work, intelligent services and recommendation systems have emerged, which can provide users with better personalized experiences [2]. Users' preferences are the key

Z. Wang et al. (Eds.): ICSS 2023, CCIS 1844, pp. 383–398, 2023.
https://doi.org/10.1007/978-981-99-4402-6_28

foundation of many intelligent services, and are important factors for achieving user satisfaction and improving business conversion rates [3]. However, users' preferences are always evolving with changes in the environment. Therefore, how to proactively perceive the evolution of users' preferences is critical for the development of personalized recommendations, intelligent services, and so on.

Let's consider a scenario where Tom is planning to go to a nursing home after retirement. A nursing service company NS constructs a composite service that can meet Tom's demands and preferences. However, Tom's preferences may change in daily life. For example, Tom's preference for meat products may shift towards vegetarianism, or his interest in traditional Chinese medicine may shift to Western medicine. In this scenario, NS should proactively perceive the evolution of Tom's preferences, which helps to provide him with services that meet his new preferences to replace the previous services, so as to improve user satisfaction. Predictably, problems caused by preference changes like the above example will increase rapidly in the future. Therefore, it is urgent to need a method for proactive perception of preferences evolution.

In recent years, although some scholars have conducted extensive research on preferences learning [4–9] and preferences prediction [10–15], and have achieved certain wonderful results, there are still some shortcomings:

(1) Most existing research just learns users' preferences in some recommendation models, which do not establish the mapping relationship between preferences and items, and can only perceive the change of preference implicitly, but cannot explicitly present users' preferences change.
(2) Most existing research has ignored the relative positional relationship of items in the interaction sequence, when learning users' preferences for items from the session sequences.

To tackle the above issues, we propose an approach for proactive perception of preferences evolution based on graph neural networks (PPGNN). Firstly, based on the user session data, PPGNN converts the user's historical interaction sequence to a directed sequence graph, and applies the gated graph neural network (GGNN) to learn the nodes' embedded vector representation in the directed sequence graph. Secondly, PPGNN uses the attention network to learn the complex relationship between users and items in the interaction sequence, which is helpful to obtain the user's long-term preferences. Meanwhile, the location information in the sequence is preserved based on the location-aware network, and the user's short-term preferences are extracted from the sequence with the attention network. Thirdly, PPGNN uses the gated-fusion network to combine long-term and short-term preferences together and recommends the item that the user is most interested in. Finally, PPGNN realizes the proactive perception of preferences evolution by establishing a mapping relationship between items and preferences, and on this basis by comparing the recommended item and the item that the user was previously interested in. The main contributions of this work can be summarized as follows:

(1) To actively perceive the evolution of users' preferences, we propose an approach for proactive perception of preferences evolution based on graph neural

networks. To the best of our knowledge, this is the earliest work on the proactive perception of preferences evolution which can present users' preferences change explicitly.

(2) To mine users' preferences information well, we propose a location-aware network that integrates a learnable location matrix into the item embeddings to preserve the position information in the interaction sequences.

(3) We conduct a large number of experiments on two real-world datasets. The experimental results demonstrate that PPGNN outperforms other baseline models, and prove the validity of our proposed method.

The remainder of this paper is organized as follows. Section 2 discusses the related work. Section 3 presents the problem statement and definitions. Section 4 elaborates our proposed model. Section 5 reports the performance evaluation. Finally, Sect. 6 concludes this work and discusses future research activities.

2 Related Work

Our work is closely related to preferences learning, preferences prediction and Graph Neural Networks. In this section, we will introduce related work to these three areas.

2.1 Preferences Learning

Early preferences learning methods relied primarily on collaborative filtering techniques [4,5], which mainly utilized the historical interactions between users and items to learn user preferences for items. With the development of artificial intelligence and natural language processing, researchers have started to explore the use of user comments and conversations as a new supplementary data to learn user preferences. Xu et al. [6] proposed the FPAN model, which uses the filtering mechanism to aggregate online feedback information of users to learn user preferences. Zhang et al. [7] proposed the NRTEH model, which extracts explicit and latent topic features from news headlines through topic embedding, and mines users' long-term and short-term preferences for them. In order to solve the ambiguity in natural language conversation, Godavarthy et al. [8] proposed a personalized memory transfer model (PMT), which uses key-value memory structure to directly extract user feedback from conversation and learn user preferences online. Yao et al. [9] proposed a recommendation algorithm for multi-turn conversations based on multi-granularity feedback information. The algorithm considers user feedback and analyzes the environment state through DQN algorithm to comprehensively learn user preferences.

2.2 Preferences Prediction

With the development of deep learning, user behavior is one of the most basic features that reflect user preferences. Currently, scholars commonly combine sequence recommendation with research in preferences prediction. Li et al. [10]

designed an attention mechanism network containing time interval gated recurrent unit to associate user dynamic preferences with time and predict user preferences in real time. Ying et al. [11] proposed the SHAN model, which learns the evolution of user preferences and the correlations between different items through multi-level attention mechanisms. This model considers both short-term and long-term preferences to predict items that a user may be interested in. Luo et al. [12] proposed a user dynamic preference model based on user behavior sequence, which combines users' short-term and long-term interests to predict users' dynamic preferences. Lei et al. [13] proposed a two-stage sequence recommendation framework that includes bi-directional self-attention embedding and gated recurrent units, which can better model user interests and predict the next interested item. Wu et al. [14] proposed a Graph-enhanced Capsule Network for next-item recommendation task. It combines long-term and short-term user interest models, utilizes sequential user behavior to capture joint-level and item-level sequential patterns, and achieves good performance. Wang et al. [15] proposed the SURGE model, which integrates different preferences in users' long-term behavior into an interest graph to extract core interests, thus improving the performance of sequence recommendation.

2.3 Graph Neural Network

Graph Neural Network (GNN) [16] is a novel type of neural network inspired by the ideas of graph embedding and Convolutional Neural Network (CNN), which is capable for extracting features from graph-structured data. Currently, existing research works on GNN has achieved remarkable results in different fileds, such as natural language processing [17], text classification [18], feature relation extraction [19], and so on.

Among various graph neural network frameworks, Gated Graph Neural Network (GGNN) [20–22] is a model that extends recurrent neural networks to graph structures. It is suitable for processing sequential information and can be used to analyze entities and their relationships in recommendation systems. Wu et al. [20] proposed the SRGNN model, which converts session sequences into graphs and uses a GGNN layer to learn item transition patterns. Wang et al. [21] proposed a POI recommendation model that uses GGNN to learn node features in sequence graphs and employs a personalized hierarchical attention network to mine user preferences. Li et al. [22] proposed an attention-based spatio-temporal gated graph neural network model, which combines spatio-temporal context information when learning the user check-in sequence graph using GGNN to improve the performance.

3 Problem Statement

In this section, we describe some important definitions and the problem studied in this work. Let $U = [u_1, u_2, \ldots, u_m]$ denotes the set of users, $P = [p_1, p_2, ..., p_s]$ denotes the set of user preferences and $V = [v_1, v_2, ..., v_n]$ denotes the set of items in all interaction sequences. The item interaction data of user u is denoted by a timestamped sequence $S_u = [v_{u,1}, v_{u,2}, ..., v_{u,n}]$, where $v_{u,i} \in V$ is the ith interaction record of the user u in the sequence S_u. The purpose of our model is to perceive the evolution of preferences from sequences of user's items interaction data. Specifically, given the historical interaction sequence S_u of user u, the model can recommend the item that user u is most interested in. Then, the item is compared with the user's previous interested items to perceive the evolution of the user's preference.

4 Our Methodology

To actively perceive preferences evolution, we propose a proactive preference evolution perception method based on graph neural networks (PPGNN). The structure of PPGNN is shown in Fig. 1, which mainly consists of five parts: 1) Item interaction sequence graph construction module, 2) Feature representation learning module, 3) Preference capture module, 4) Prediction module, and 5) Perception of preferences evolution.

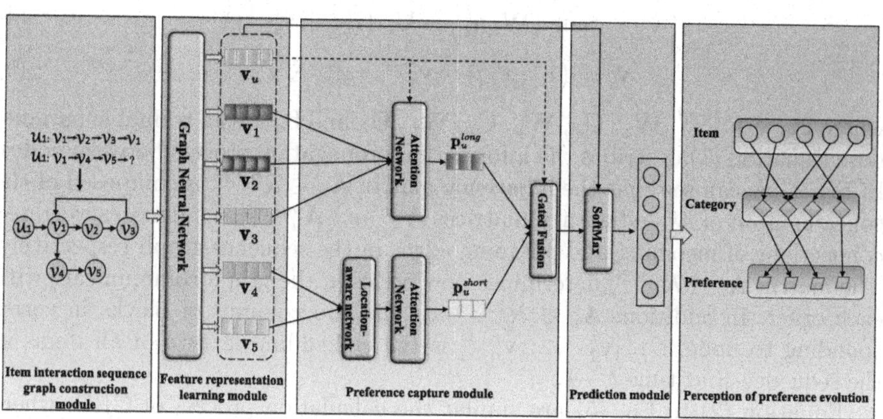

Fig. 1. The structure of the PPGNN model.

4.1 Item Interaction Sequence Graph Construction Module

Since the graph structure can represent the whole sequence of behaviors without cutting the user behavior sequence into a fixed length as in sliding windows, we construct the user interaction sequence graph based on users' items interaction data. The graph can preserve more sequence information, which is helpful to improve preferences learning.

Specifically, we construct each interaction sequence S as a directed graph $G = (\mathcal{V}, E)$, where E denotes the set of edges, $\mathcal{V} = (U, V)$ indicates the vertex set, U represents the set of users, and V represents the set of items. Each user-item edge $e = (u, v)$ represents an interaction record between user u and item v. Each item-item edge $e_{(v_{i-1}, v_i)}$ indicates that the user has visited item v_i after visiting item v_{i-1}. Due to the possibility that users may interact with some items multiple times, we assign a standardized weighted value for each edge, which is determined by the item/user node's in-degree divided by its node's out-degree.

4.2 Feature Representation Learning Module

In the feature representation learning module, we apply Gated Graph Neural Network (GGNN) to learn embedding vectors of users and items. Each user $u \in U$ and item $v \in V$ are embedded in a latent feature space. The node vector $\mathbf{v}$ denotes the item latent feature or the preference vector of the user. Specifically, for the embedding vector $\mathbf{v}_i$ of each node on the interaction sequence graph $G_{V,E}$, the update functions are given as follows:

$$\mathbf{a}_{s,i}^{t} = \mathbf{A}_{u}^{i} \cdot \left[\mathbf{v}_{1}^{t-1}, \ldots, \mathbf{v}_{n}^{t-1}\right]^{T} \mathbf{H}_{o} + \mathbf{b}_{o} \tag{1}$$

$$\mathbf{z}_{s,i}^{t} = \sigma\left(\mathbf{W}_{x}\mathbf{a}_{s,i}^{t} + \mathbf{U}_{x}\mathbf{v}_{i}^{t-1}\right) \tag{2}$$

$$\mathbf{r}_{s,i}^{t} = \sigma\left(\mathbf{W}_{y}\mathbf{a}_{s,i}^{t} + \mathbf{U}_{y}\mathbf{v}_{i}^{t-1}\right) \tag{3}$$

$$\mathbf{v}_{x}^{t} = \tanh\left(\mathbf{W}_{h}\mathbf{a}_{s,i}^{t} + \mathbf{U}_{h}\left(\mathbf{r}_{s,i}^{t} \odot \mathbf{v}_{i}^{t-1}\right)\right) \tag{4}$$

$$\mathbf{v}_{i}^{t} = \left(1 - \mathbf{z}_{s,i}^{t}\right) \odot \mathbf{v}_{i}^{t-1} + \mathbf{z}_{s,i}^{t} \odot \mathbf{v}_{\mathbf{x}}^{\mathbf{t}} \tag{5}$$

where $\mathbf{H_o} \in \mathcal{R}^{d\times 2d}$, $\mathbf{W}_x$, $\mathbf{U}_x$, $\mathbf{W}_y$, $\mathbf{U}_y$, $\mathbf{W}_h$, $\mathbf{U}_h$ and $\mathbf{b}_o$ are all trainable parameters. Equation (1) describes the information propagation process between nodes. In Fig. 2, we can see that the adjacency matrix $\mathbf{A}_u \in \mathcal{R}^{n\times 2n}$ is composed of the concatenation of two adjacency matrices $\mathbf{A}_u^{in}$ and $\mathbf{A}_u^{out}$, which denotes weighted connections of incoming and outgoing edges in the sequence graph respectively. The matrix $\mathbf{A}_u \in \mathcal{R}^{n\times 2n}$ determines how nodes in the graph communicate with each other. In addition, $\mathbf{A}_u^i \in \mathcal{R}^{1\times 2n}$ are the two columns of blocks in corresponding to node $v_{s,i}$. $[\mathbf{v}_1^{t-1}, ..., \mathbf{v}_n^{t-1}]$ is the embedding feature of all items in the sequence S at time $t-1$.

Equation (2) to Eq. (5) are similar the calculation process of GRU, where $\mathbf{z}_{s,i}^t$ controls the forgotten information and $\mathbf{r}_{s,i}^t$ controls the newly generated information. Here, σ denotes the sigmoid function, $\odot$ is the dot product operation. Finally, the embedding representation of all nodes in the sequence graph is learned and the final node vector is obtained.

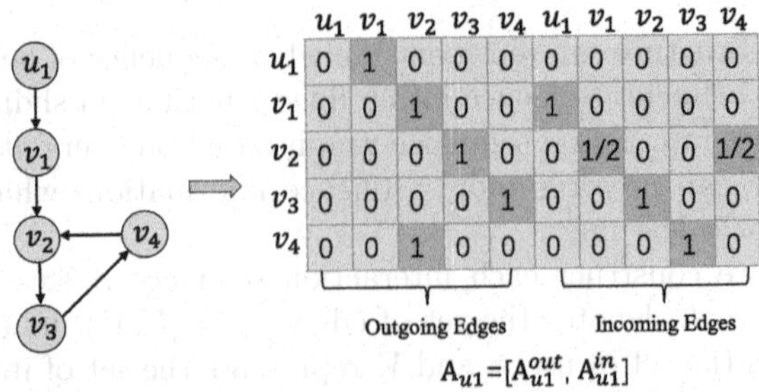

Fig. 2. An example of an interaction sequence graph and the connection matrix A_{u1}.

4.3 Preference Capture Module

Users' long-term preferences are relatively stable and can be inferred from their long-term behaviors. Firstly, according to Eq. (6), the hidden representation $\mathbf{h}_i$ is obtained by transforming the embedding vector of each item $i \in S_u$ with a multi-layer perceptron. Then, the embedding vector $\mathbf{v_u}$ of user u is used as the context vector, and the attention weight $\rho_{u,i}$ between user u and the corresponding item is calculated based on Eq. (7). This weight represents the significance of item v_i to user u. Finally, according to Eq. (8), the item embedding vector and the attention score are weighted and summed to calculate the long-term preference $\mathbf{p}_u^{\text{long}}$ of user u. This process can be illustrated as Eq. (6) to Eq. (8):

$$\mathbf{h}_i = \phi\left(\mathbf{W}_1 \mathbf{v}_i + \mathbf{b}_1\right). \tag{6}$$

$$\rho_{u,i} = \frac{\exp\left(\mathbf{v}_u^\top \mathbf{h}_i\right)}{\sum_{i \in S_u} \exp\left(\mathbf{v}_u^\top \mathbf{h}_i\right)} \tag{7}$$

$$\mathbf{p}_u^{long} = \sum_{i \in S_u} \alpha_{u,i} \mathbf{v}_i \tag{8}$$

where $W_1 \in \mathcal{R}^{d \times 2d}$ and $b_1 \in \mathcal{R}^d$ are trainable parameters, ϕ represents the Relu activation function.

Users' short-term preferences are dynamically changing and can be inferred from their recent interaction behaviors. The positional information of the user interaction sequence is crucial, as the order of interactions indicates the process of preference change over time. Therefore, we propose a location-aware network that introduces a learnable position embedding matrix $L \in \mathcal{R}^{n*d}$ to preserve positional information in the sequence, whici is defined as follows:

$$\begin{bmatrix} \mathbf{x}_1 \\ \mathbf{x}_2 \\ \vdots \\ \mathbf{x}_n \end{bmatrix} = \begin{bmatrix} \mathbf{v}_1 + L_1 \\ \mathbf{v}_2 + L_2 \\ \vdots \\ \mathbf{v}_n + L_n \end{bmatrix} \tag{9}$$

where n denotes the length of the recent interaction sequence, and $L_i \in i_R^d$ represents the location vector information of v_i.

The attention mechanism is used to learn the corresponding weights, which are linearly combined to obtain short-term preference features $\mathbf{p}_u^{\text{short}}$ of user u. This process is shown in Eq. (10) to Eq. (11):

$$\beta_{u,i} = q^T \sigma\left(W_2 \mathbf{x}_n + W_3 \mathbf{x}_i + b_2\right) \tag{10}$$

$$\mathbf{p}_u^{short} = \sum_{i=1}^{n} \beta_{u,i} \mathbf{x}_i \tag{11}$$

where W_2, $W_3 \in \mathcal{R}^{d \times 2d}$and $b_2 \in \mathcal{R}^d$ are trainable parameters, and $\beta_{u,i}$ denotes the attention allocation coefficient in the sequence.

Finally, to effectively integrate both types of preferences, we introduce a gated-fusion network [23] that combines them to obtain the user's final preference $\mathbf{p}_u$. This process is shown in Eq. (12) to Eq. (13):

$$f = \sigma\left(W_4\mathbf{v}_u + W_5\mathbf{p}_u^{long} + W_6\mathbf{p}_u^{short} + b_3\right) \tag{12}$$

$$\mathbf{p}_u = (1-f)\odot\mathbf{p}_u^{long} + f\odot\mathbf{p}_u^{short} \tag{13}$$

where σ denotes the Sigmoid function, f is a weight coefficient, and $\odot$ represents element-wise matrix multiplication.

4.4 Prediction Module

In the prediction module, the softmax layer can be used to calculate the probability of the target user u interacting with the candidate item v_i based on the user's preference $\mathbf{p}_u$ and the item's feature $\mathbf{v}_i$, thus recommending the item that the user is most interested in. Specifically, $\hat{\mathbf{z}}_{u,i}$ represents the score of each candidate item $v_i \in V$, which is described as Eq. (14):

$$\hat{\mathbf{z}}_{u,i} = \mathbf{p}_\mathbf{u}^\mathrm{T}\mathbf{v}_i \tag{14}$$

Then, the Softmax function is used to normalize the calculated scores:

$$\hat{\mathbf{y}} = softmax(\hat{\mathbf{z}}) \tag{15}$$

where $\widehat{\mathbf{z}}$ represents the prediction score of each candidate item and $\widehat{\mathbf{y}}$ represents the probability that the target user will be exposed to the item next. In this work, we utilize the cross-entropy loss function to learn and optimize the objective, which is defined as follows:

$$\mathcal{L}(\hat{\mathbf{y}}) = -\sum_{i=1}^{m} y\log\left(\hat{y}_i\right) + (1-y_i)\log\left(1-\hat{y}_i\right) \tag{16}$$

where y_i is the true value of the next interaction item in the sequence one-hot vector.

4.5 Perception of Preferences Evolution

To perceive the evolution of preferences, we first establish the mapping relationship between preferences and items that users are interested in. Then, according to the preference evolved judgment rule, we compare the item that the model recommended with the item that user previously interested in. Finally, we judge whether the user's preferences are changed. Specifically, assuming that $V = [v_1, v_2, ..., v_n]$ represents the set of items, $C = [c_1, c_2, ..., c_m]$ represents the set of item categories, where n and m represent the number of specific items and categories in the dataset, and usually $n \geq m$. Each item v corresponds to a unique category c, but there can be multiple items under each category. Considering that the category information of items can usually reflect the specific kind of user preferences. For example, when the category of the item predicted by the model is basketball, it implies that the user currently prefers basketball sports; when the category of the item is books, it indicates that the user prefers reading. Here, the mapping relationship between items and preferences is established as in Eq. (17):

$$P_{v_i}^{c_j} =< v_i; c_j > \tag{17}$$

where $P_{v_i}^{c_j}$ represents the preference information corresponding to item v_i. The judgment rule of preference evolution is defined as Eq. (18):

$$\begin{cases} If\left(P_{v_i}^{c_j} = P_o\right) \Rightarrow \text{ Preference does not change} \\ If\left(P_{v_i}^{c_j} \neq P_o\right) \Rightarrow \text{ Preference changes} \end{cases} \tag{18}$$

where $P_{v_i}^{c_j}$ represents the preference information corresponding to item v_i, and P_o represents the user's original preference information. When $P_{v_i}^{c_j}$ is the same as P_o, it means that the user's preference has not changed; when $P_{v_i}^{c_j}$ is different from P_o, it indicates that the user's preference has changed, and the preference has evolved from P_o to $P_{v_i}^{c_j}$.

5 Experiments

In this work, users' preferences evolution is perceived by comparing the recommended item and the item that the user was previously interested in. So, the performance of the item recommendation model is the core of our proposed method. Therefore, we conduct experiments to verify the performance of our proposed recommendation model, and adopt relevant metrics of the recommendation model to evaluate the performance.

5.1 Evaluation Datasets

We conduct extensive experiments based on two public datasets (Gowalla and Foursquare). Gowalla [22] is a check-in dataset collected from the Gowalla website, which allows users to share their location through check-ins. Foursquare [22] is a location-based social platform that enables users to share their locations with others via mobile devices. These two datasets contain a large number of check-in records, each of which contains a unique user ID and POI ID. Data in these two datasets are pre-processed to filter out inactive users and unpopular POIs. Then, 80% and 20% of each dataset are selected as the training and testing datasets, respectively. The processed statistics of the selected dataset are shown in Table 1.

Table 1. Statistics of the evaluation datasets.

Datasets	Gowalla	Foursquare
User	6533	1809
POI	23329	5514
Check-in record	307376	128147

5.2 Evaluation Metrics

We leverage two frequently-used evaluation metrics *Recall@K* and Mean Reciprocal Rank (*MRR@K*) to evaluate the performance of the method, where $K \in \{5, 10, 15, 20\}$. *Recall@K* represents the proportion of test cases in which the correctly recommended item is ranked within the top K in the ranking list. *MRR* is the average of the mutual rankings of correctly recommended items, with higher values indicates that the correct recommended item appears closer to the top of the ranked list.

5.3 Baselines and Parameter Settings

The PPGNN model is compared with the following models to evaluate its performance. FPMC [24]: The model is a sequential prediction method based on Markov chain. HRM [25]: The model uses a two-layer structure to mine and fuse sequential behavior and users' preference representations to make recommendations. CPAM [26]: This model combines Skip-gram interest embedding with logic matrix factorization to recommend items, taking into account contextual influences and users' preferences. SHAN [11]: This model uses a hierarchical attention network structure to capture both the long-term and short-term preferences of users for recommendation. SR-GNN [20]: This model transforms the sequence of items into a structured graph and learns the session representation using GNN. ASGNN [21]: This model uses graph neural networks to model interaction sequences and employs two layers of personalized hierarchical attention networks to capture and integrate users' preferences for recommendation.

In this work, all trainable parameters are initialized using a Gaussian distribution with a mean of 0 and a standard deviation of 0.1. In addition, the Adam optimizer is used to optimize the model. The initial learning rate is set to 0.001, the batch size is set to 100, the number of epochs is set to 30, and the $L2$ penalty is set to 10^{-5}.

5.4 Performance Comparison

We compare the performance of the PPGNN model with the baseline models in terms of *Recall@K* and *MRR@K* on the two public datasets. The experimental results depicted in Fig. 3. From Fig. 3 we can find that:

(1) The performance of FPMC and CPAM models is significantly lower than other models on two datasets. Specifically, FPMC mainly only captures the first-order Markov relation, which simplifies the user behavior characteristics, so the model performance is relatively poor. Since CPAM can only capture users' general interests, it is challenging to model the user's behavior sequence.
(2) HRM and SHAN models show better performance than FPMC and CPAM on both datasets. That's because they consider both long-term and short-term preferences of users. Meanwhile, it demonstrates that both long-term

and short-term preferences play a vital role in recommendation tasks. Specifically, HRM simultaneously mines the sequential behavior and users' preferences for recommendation. SHAN uses hierarchical attention networks to capture users' long-term and short-term preferences from behavioural sequences, and combines them to improve the performance of recommendations.

(3) SRGNN, ASGNN and PPGNN models perform significantly better than other models on two datasets. That's because they introduce graph neural networks to capture the transfer relationship between items, which helps to improve the model's performance. For example, on the Gowalla dataset, the *Recall*@20 of the SRGNN model is 18.41%, the *Recall*@20 of the ASGNN is 21.06% and the *Recall*@20 of the PPGNN is 24.12%. SRGNN uses GNN to model user behavioral sequences and captures users' preferences by learning complex transfer relationships between sequences. But it targets anonymous users and overlooks their personalized needs. ASGNN uses GNN to model the graph of user access sequence, and adopts a personalized hierarchical attention network to capture and integrate users' preferences for recommendation. However, ASGNN ignores the positional information of items in the sequence. The PPGNN model achieves the best performance, because it considers the location of items in the sequence and their relevance to the most recent interaction items, which removes irrelevant items and fully exploits users' preference information. In addition, our model uses the gated-fusion network to combine preferences, which fully considers users' personalized needs.

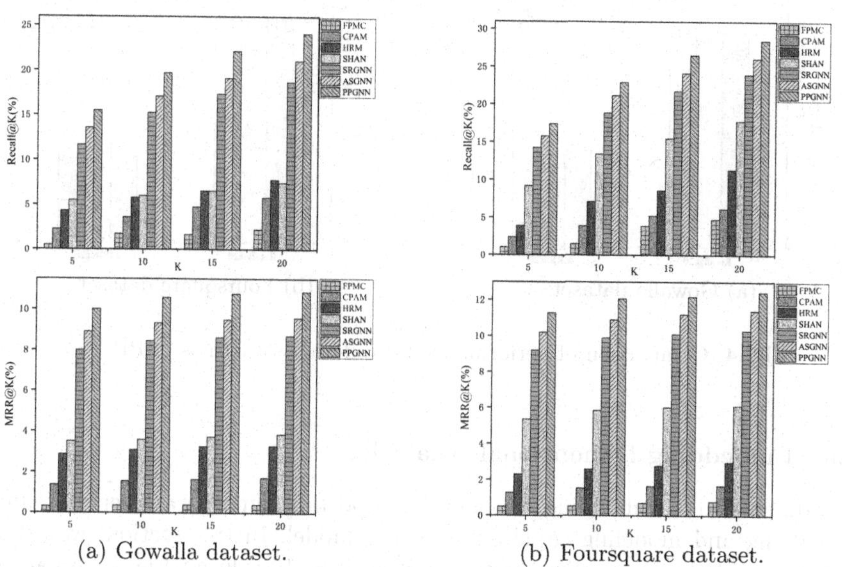

(a) Gowalla dataset. (b) Foursquare dataset.

Fig. 3. Performance comparison of PPGNN with the baseline model.

5.5 Ablation Study

In this section, we conduct further analysis on the model's architecture to demonstrate its effectiveness. We compare the PPGNN model with two variant models, PPGNN-P (without positional information) and PPGNN-C (without gated-fusion network). Specifically, PPGNN-P does not use the location information module, which means it ignores the effect of location on the importance of the item in the interaction sequence. PPGNN-C linearly fuses the long-term and short-term preferences directly. The experimental results are shown in Fig. 4. From Fig. 4 we can find that:

(1) After removing the location information module, the performance of the model decreased, which indicates that embedding location information can improve the effectiveness of the PPGNN model. The embedding of the location matrix can more accurately represent the importance of each item, which is helpful to fully mine users' preference information.
(2) The PPGNN model performs better than PPGNN-C. This is because PPGNN uses gated-fusion network to integrate long-term preferences and short-term preferences, which fully considers users' the personalized needs and behavioral patterns.
(3) The PPGNN model in this paper achieves the best results. This not only confirms the effectiveness of each sub-module but also proves the superiority of our model.

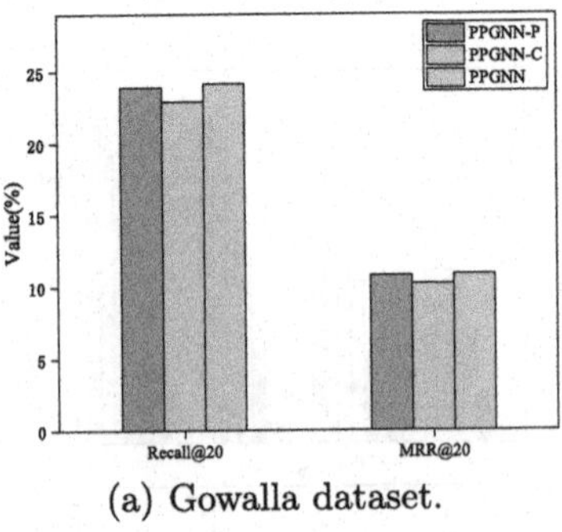

(a) Gowalla dataset.

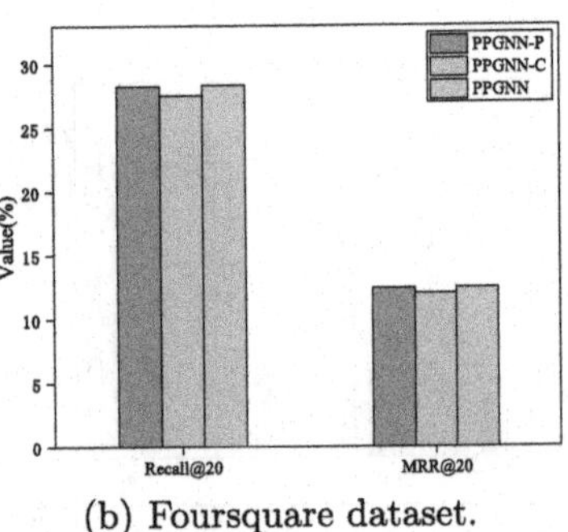

(b) Foursquare dataset.

Fig. 4. Comparison of performance for different structures of PPGNN.

5.6 Embedding Dimensional Analysis.

The dimension of embedding vectors is an important hyperparameter that affects the fitting and modeling capabilities of the model. In this section, we set the dimension of the embedding vectors d from 0 to 100. From Fig. 5 we can find that as the d changes from 10 to 80, the $Recall@20$ and $MRR@20$ of the model increase on both datasets. This is because high-dimensional embeddings are able to fully learn the data features, thus improving the performance of the model. The model achieves the best performance on these two datasets when the d is set to 80. In addition, it can be found that as d gradually increases from 80 to 100, the performance of the model slightly decreases. This may be due to the overfitting problem, which deteriorates the model's generalization ability.

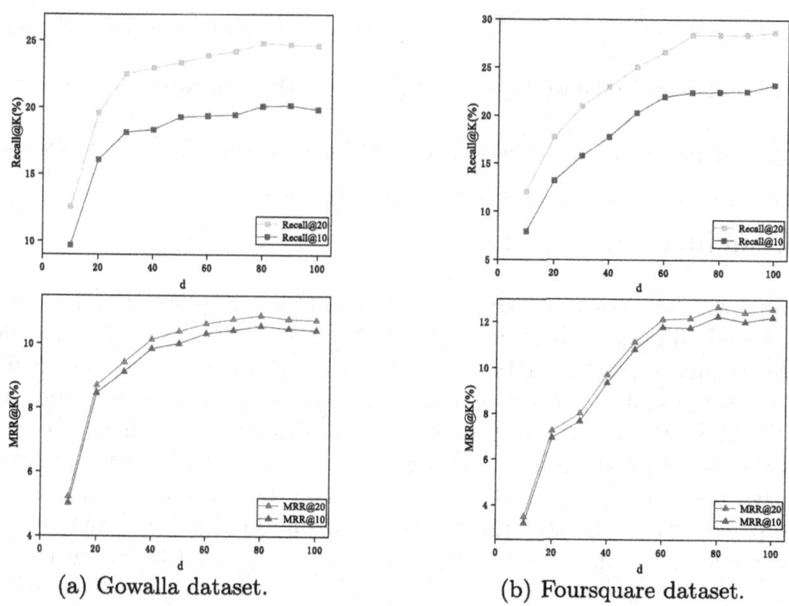

(a) Gowalla dataset. (b) Foursquare dataset.

Fig. 5. Performance comparison of models with different embedding dimensions.

5.7 Analysis of the Number of Layers in Gated Graph Neural Networks

In this section, we further investigate the impact of the number of layers in the gated graph neural network(GGNN) on the performance of the model. We conduct experiments on the Gowalla and Foursquare datasets by setting the number of GGNN layers to 1, 2, and 3, respectively. The experimental results are depicted in Fig. 6. From Fig. 6, we can find that on both datasets, the performance of the model hardly improves or even slightly decreases as the number of GGNN layers increases. This suggests that a single layer of GGNN is adequate for effectively capturing the correlation of interaction sequences.

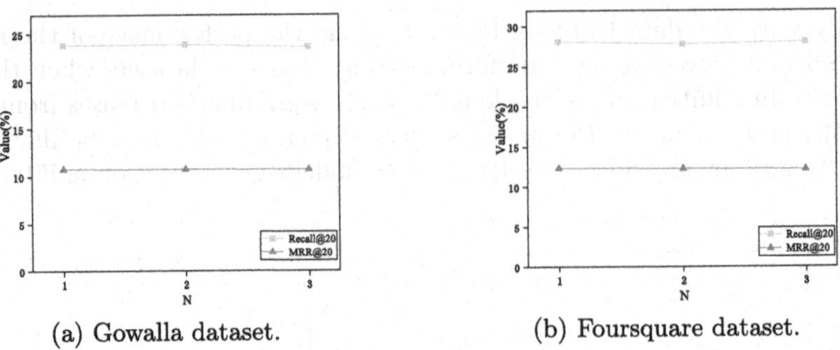

(a) Gowalla dataset. (b) Foursquare dataset.

Fig. 6. Comparison of model performance with different numbers of GGNN layers.

6 Conclusion

In this paper, we propose an approach for proactive perception of preference evolution based on graph neural networks (PPGNN). Firstly, PPGNN constructs a directed sequence graph based on the user's historical item interaction sequence, and learns the embedded vector representation of nodes in the graph. Then, PPGNN captures user's preferences from the interaction sequence to recommend the item that the user is most interested in. Finally, PPGNN realizes the proactive perception of preferences evolution by establishing a mapping relationship between items and preferences, and on this basis by comparing the recommended item and the item that the user was previously interested in. In future work, based on the model in this paper, we will comprehensively consider the influence of the time interval information of item interactions to further improve the performance of the model.

Acknowledgements. This work is supported by: National Natural Science Foundation of China (Grant nos. 62273290), Key projects of Shandong Natural Science Foundation, China (Grant nos. ZR 2020KF019).

References

1. Yang, L., Xu, M., Xing, L.: Exploring the core factors of online purchase decisions by building an e-commerce network evolution model. J. Retail. Consum. Serv. **64**, 102784 (2022)
2. Chiu, M.C., Huang, J.H., Gupta, S., Akman, G.: Developing a personalized recommendation system in a smart product service system based on unsupervised learning model. Comput. Ind. **128**, 103421 (2021)
3. Alzoubi, H., Alshurideh, M., Kurdi, B., Akour, I., Aziz, R.: Does BLE technology contribute towards improving marketing strategies, customers' satisfaction and loyalty? the role of open innovation. Int. J. Data Netw. Sci. **6**(2), 449–460 (2022)
4. Yang, M., Zhou, M., Liu, J., Lian, D., King, I.: HRCF: enhancing collaborative filtering via hyperbolic geometric regularization. In: Proceedings of the ACM Web Conference 2022, pp. 2462–2471 (2022)

5. Li, Y., Liu, J., Jin, Y., Fan, X., Wang, B.: Crowdfunding platform recommendation algorithm based on collaborative filtering. J. Eng. Res. (2022)
6. Xu, K., Yang, J., Xu, J., Gao, S., Guo, J., Wen, J.R.: Adapting user preference to online feedback in multi-round conversational recommendation. In: Proceedings of the 14th ACM International Conference on Web Search and Data Mining, pp. 364–372 (2021)
7. Zhang, H., Shen, Z.: News recommendation based on user topic and entity preferences in historical behavior. Information **14**(2), 60 (2023)
8. Godavarthy, N., Wang, Y., Ebesu, T., Suthee, U., Xie, M., Fang, Y.: Learning user preferences through online conversations via personalized memory transfer. Inf. Retrieval J. **25**(3), 306–328 (2022)
9. Yao, H., Ye, D., Chen, Z.: Multi-round conversational reinforcement learning recommendation algorithm via multi-granularity feedback. J. Comput. Appl. **43**(1), 15 (2023)
10. Li, Z., Zhang, L., Lei, C., Chen, X., Gao, J., Gao, J.: Attention with long-term interval-based deep sequential learning for recommendation. Complexity **2020**, 1–13 (2020)
11. Ying, H., et al.: Sequential recommender system based on hierarchical attention network. In: IJCAI International Joint Conference on Artificial Intelligence (2018)
12. Luo, M., Zhang, X., Li, J., Duan, P., Lu, S.: User dynamic preference construction method based on behavior sequence. Sci. Program. 2022 (2022)
13. Lei, J., Li, Y., Yang, S., Shi, W., Wu, Y.: Two-stage sequential recommendation for side information fusion and long-term and short-term preferences modeling. J. Intell. Inf. Syst. **59**, 1–21 (2022)
14. Wu, B., He, X., Zhang, Q., Wang, M., Ye, Y.: GCRec: graph-augmented capsule network for next-item recommendation. IEEE Trans. Neural Netw. Learn. Syst. (2022)
15. Chang, J., et al.: Sequential recommendation with graph neural networks. In: Proceedings of the 44th International ACM SIGIR Conference on Research and Development in Information Retrieval, pp. 378–387 (2021)
16. Gao, C., et al.: A survey of graph neural networks for recommender systems: challenges, methods, and directions. ACM Trans. Recommender Syst. **1**(1), 1–51 (2023)
17. Liu, B., Wu, L.: Graph neural networks in natural language processing. In: Graph Neural Networks: Foundations, Frontiers, and Applications, pp. 463–481. Springer, Singapore (2022). https://doi.org/10.1007/978-981-16-6054-2_21
18. Ghosh, S., Maji, S., Desarkar, M.S.: Graph neural network enhanced language models for efficient multilingual text classification. arXiv preprint arXiv:2203.02912 (2022)
19. Xue, F.: Refining latent multi-view graph for relation extraction (2021)
20. Wu, S., Tang, Y., Zhu, Y., Wang, L., Xie, X., Tan, T.: Session-based recommendation with graph neural networks. In: Proceedings of the AAAI Conference on Artificial Intelligence, vol. 33, pp. 346–353 (2019)
21. Wang, D., Wang, X., Xiang, Z., Yu, D., Deng, S., Xu, G.: Attentive sequential model based on graph neural network for next poi recommendation. World Wide Web **24**(6), 2161–2184 (2021). https://doi.org/10.1007/s11280-021-00961-9
22. Li, Q., Xu, X., Liu, X., Chen, Q.: An attention-based spatiotemporal GGNN for next POI recommendation. IEEE Access **10**, 26471–26480 (2022)
23. Zhu, G., et al.: Neural attentive travel package recommendation via exploiting long-term and short-term behaviors. Knowl.-Based Syst. **211**, 106511 (2021)

24. Rendle, S., Freudenthaler, C., Schmidt-Thieme, L.: Factorizing personalized markov chains for next-basket recommendation. In: Proceedings of the 19th International Conference on World Wide Web, pp. 811–820 (2010)
25. Wang, P., Guo, J., Lan, Y., Xu, J., Wan, S., Cheng, X.: Learning hierarchical representation model for nextbasket recommendation. In: Proceedings of the 38th International ACM SIGIR conference on Research and Development in Information Retrieval, pp. 403–412 (2015)
26. Yu, D., Wanyan, W., Wang, D.: Leveraging contextual influence and user preferences for point-of-interest recommendation. Multimedia Tools Appl. **80**, 1487–1501 (2021)

Generating Transportation Network Datasets for Benchmarking Maritime Location-Based Services: A Preliminary Approach

Jiali Yao(✉), Yongpeng Shi, and Jiayu Zhang

School of Information Science and Technology,
North China University of Technology, Beijing, China
yaojiali3000@163.com

Abstract. Maritime Location-Based Services (LBS) play a key role in global trade and economic development, with hot research topics such as trajectory prediction, traffic forecasting, abnormal behaviors detection, and so on. However, researchers in this field encounter difficulties due to the limited availability of refined transportation network datasets. Different from the urban traffic network, the road network (or route network) of the ocean is dynamic, complex, and requires mining from massive real-world trajectory data to obtain. This makes it particularly challenging to generate sufficient transportation datasets for benchmarking maritime LBS. To meet this challenge, this paper preliminarily proposes a novel method for generating synthetic maritime transportation networks: the Maritime Degree-Corrected Block Method (MDCBM). Our proposed method builds on the fundamental concepts of stochastic blockmodels (SBMs) to generate synthetic maritime transportation networks with a predefined cluster structure. To address the variation in node degrees found in real-world maritime networks, we incorporate a degree correction term into the edge probability function. Additionally, we modify the degree distribution to follow a power law distribution with a limited numerical range. To further enhance the realism of the synthetic networks, we also introduce attribute information for both nodes and edges. Our experimental results demonstrate that the MDCBM method can generate synthetic networks that better reflect the observed properties of the Bohai maritime network with satisfying effectiveness.

Keywords: Maritime transportation network · Graph generation · Stocatic blockmodels · Benchmark for LBS

1 Introduction

Maritime Location-Based Services (LBS) play a critical role in global trade and economic development, with research topics ranging from trajectory prediction

Z. Wang et al. (Eds.): ICSS 2023, CCIS 1844, pp. 399–413, 2023.
https://doi.org/10.1007/978-981-99-4402-6_29

[2,11] to traffic forecasting [3,20] and abnormal behavior detection. For example, LBS can help shipping companies optimize their routes and reduce fuel consumption, leading to significant cost savings.

However, the lack of access to refined transportation network datasets presents a significant challenge to researchers in this field. Although some datasets exist, they are often limited in number [5], remarkably similar to one another. Additionally, some of these datasets are particularly ill-suited , exhibiting extreme structural characteristics that do not reflect real-world scenarios. These limitations make it challenging for researchers to develop and benchmark models for maritime LBS. The ocean's road network, in contrast to urban traffic networks, is characterized by its dynamic and complex nature, which necessitates extensive data mining of real-world trajectory data. Their different properties, such as topology, network density, hierarchy, and connectivity, making it challenging to apply existing models of land transport networks to the ocean's route network. These differences pose significant challenges for researchers seeking to generate sufficient transportation datasets for benchmarking maritime LBS.

In order to address the limited availability of refined transportation network datasets, this paper presents a preliminary solution for generating synthetic maritime transportation networks, namely the Maritime Degree-Corrected Block Method (MDCBM). The proposed approach involves generating graphs with a predefined cluster structure and utilizing Dijkstra's shortest path algorithm to generate trajectory data for all nodes. By adding a degree correction parameter and attributes and modifying the degree distribution, the method can better reflect the properties observed in the Bohai maritime network, thereby providing researchers with a realistic and reliable dataset for benchmarking maritime LBS.

The main work and contributions of this paper are reflected in the following aspects:

- A novel method for generating synthetic maritime transportation networks based on Stochastic blockmodels is proposed, providing sufficient transportation datasets for benchmarking maritime LBS.
- To address the variation in node degrees found in real-world maritime networks, a degree correction term is incorporated into the edge probability function. The degree distribution is modified to follow a power law distribution, and attribute information is introduced for both nodes and edges to better reflect the observed properties of the Bohai maritime network.
- Extensive experiments are conducted to evaluate the effectiveness of the proposed framework. The results confirm that the framework can generate synthetic networks that better reflect the observed properties of the Bohai maritime network with satisfactory effectiveness.

This paper is organized into five sections. Section 1 defines situational information and related concepts. Section 2 introduces the background and related work, including the differences between land and sea transportation networks, and the key preliminary definition of SBM and its extensions. This section also discusses related work. Section 3 presents the statistical properties of the world-wide marine transportation network and explains the principles of our proposed framework and approach. Section 4 demonstrates the effectiveness of our through specific and experiments. Section 5 concludes the paper.

2 Background and Related Work

2.1 Background

Differences Between Land and Sea Transportation Networks. Maritime transport networks and land transport networks differ significantly in their topology, network density, hierarchy, connectivity, and interdependence [10,12,16]. In terms of topology, maritime networks have a more decentralized structure with smaller ports spread out along coastlines, while land networks tend to have a hierarchical structure with hub cities and smaller connected cities. Additionally, maritime networks have lower network densities with fewer direct connections between ports, compared to land networks which tend to have a higher density of connections. The hierarchy of nodes in maritime networks is not as clear as in land networks. Maritime networks are primarily connected through shipping routes and seaports, whereas land networks have multiple transportation options like roads, railways, and air transport. Finally, the interdependence between land and maritime transport networks can be complex and varies across regions. Therefore, when modeling and analyzing these networks, tailored approaches are needed to capture the unique characteristics of maritime transport networks.

SBM. Stochastic blockmodels (SBMs) [9] are a class of probabilistic models for analyzing the structure of networks. SBMs assume that the nodes in a network can be partitioned into a finite number of groups or communities, and that the probability of an edge between any two nodes depends only on the group assignments of those nodes. We begin by considering the example in Fig. 1 , where the network consists of 100 nodes and 1795 edges. The nodes are divided into 3 groups, where groups 1, 2 and 3 contain 34, 33 and 33 nodes respectively. The nodes within the same group are more closely connected to each other than to nodes in another group.

The adjacency matrix Y of the graph is an $n \times n$ symmetric binary matrix, where $y_{ij} = 1$ if vertices i and j are adjacent and $y_{ij} = 0$ otherwise. The total number of edges in the graph is $m = \frac{1}{2}\sum_{i,j} y_{ij}$. The adjacency matrix for the example is shown in Fig. 2, where black and white represent 1 and 0, respectively.

SBMs have become increasingly popular in recent years due to their ability to identify hidden community structures in various types of networks, such as social networks, biological networks, and transportation networks. One of the main advantages of SBMs is their ability to generate synthetic networks that can be used as benchmarks for network analysis algorithms. However, it ignores the variation in the node degrees in real-world networks. In particular, the objective function uses the same probability for each possible edge, regardless of the

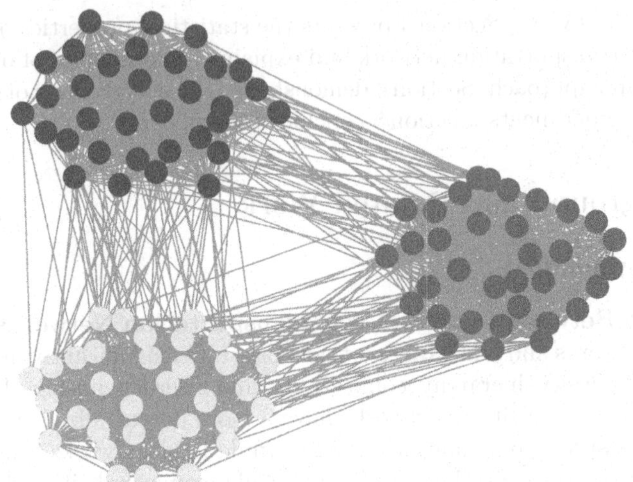

Fig. 1. A simplest stochastic block models.

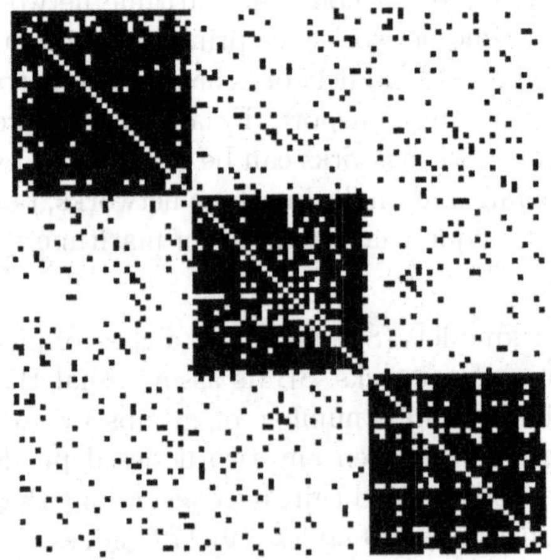

Fig. 2. Adjacency matrix of example in Fig. 1.

nodes' degrees. This can be problematic in networks with heterogeneous degree distributions. For example, in "karate club" network of Zachary [19], the SBM fails to split the network into the known factions because it does not take the degree sequence into account [7].

DCSBM. The Degree-Corrected Stochastic Blockmodel (DCSBM) [7] is an extension of the Stochastic Blockmodel (SBM) that addresses the limitation of the SBM. In DCSBM, each node is associated with a hidden attribute, which is typically interpreted as the node's degree. The model assumes that the probability of an edge between two nodes is a function of the product of their hidden attributes. Specifically, the probability of an edge between nodes i and j is given by: $P_{ij} = \frac{\psi_{g_i g_j}}{\sqrt{d_i d_j}}$, where g_i and g_j are the groups of nodes i and j, respectively, d_i and d_j are the degrees of nodes i and j, respectively, and $\psi_{g_i g_j}$ is the element of the symmetric parameter matrix Ψ that represents the probability of an edge between two nodes in groups g_i and g_j. Compared to SBM, DCSBM adds a degree correction term, $\sqrt{d_i d_j}$, in the edge probability function. This correction term takes into account the fact that nodes with higher degrees are more likely to form edges with other nodes. Therefore, the DCSBM can better capture the variation in node degrees and generate more accurate models for real-world networks.

However, the DCSBM assumes that the community assignments of nodes are independent of each other, which may not be true in some real-world networks. Additionally, the DCSBM assumes that the degree distribution of nodes within each community follows a Poisson distribution, which may not always be an accurate assumption. In maritime networks, the degree distribution follows a power law distribution [6] rather than a Poisson distribution.

2.2 Related Work

Maritime trajectory network generation has been studied extensively in recent years, and various methods have been proposed to generate maritime trajectory networks. One approach is data-driven based automatic maritime routing from massive trajectories in the face of disparity.

The Inverse Reinforcement Learning (IRL) method [21] learns the underlying reward function that governs the vehicle's decision-making process based on observed traffic volume and trajectory data, enabling the generation of synthetic population vehicle trajectories that are consistent with the observed data. It can leverage multiple data sources to enhance link flow estimation and provide a more complete and accurate picture of link flows across the entire network, However, the method relies on the assumption that the observed traffic volume and trajectory data are accurate and representative of the entire population, which may not always be the case. The DPT method [4] generates synthetic trajectory networks by applying privacy-preserving techniques to raw GPS trajectories. It discretizes trajectories using hierarchical reference systems, estimates the distribution of movements using prefix tree counts, and generates synthetic trajectories using direction-weighted sampling. The method improves accuracy and fidelity by capturing individual movements at different speeds. Kim et al. [8] proposes a novel privacy-preserving framework for generating synthetic trajectory data using deep learning methods. The proposed two-phase data collection scheme helps to improve the utility of the collected dataset, and the novel location encoding method captures the probabilistic mapping between true and perturbed locations. It can effectively generate synthetic trajectory datasets whose probability distributions are similar to those of the true dataset. However, the three method above may require significant computational resources and processing time, limiting its practical applicability, especially for large datasets.

The Two-Stage GAN method (TSG) [18] aims to generate large-scale GPS trajectories by considering the trajectory's geographical and sequential features. TSG uses map images to extract road information and generates GPS point sequences using two parallel Long Short-Term Memory networks. The discriminator is conditioned on encoded map images, which helps to ensure the generated trajectories correspond to the road network. The proposed method is able to generate plausible large-scale trajectories. However, TSG requires accurate and available map images, which may not always be feasible. The model's performance is also influenced by the quality of the input GPS data and the accuracy of the extracted road network information. The Hermoupolis trajectory generator [14] uses a two-step approach to generate individual object trajectories that follow mobility patterns. Hermoupolis generates trajectories with a better fit to real-world data and more diverse mobility patterns. However, the generator requires pre-defined mobility patterns or an iterative clustering algorithm, which may not be practical in situations where mobility patterns are not well-defined or available.

Inspired by these methods, our proposed method generates a synthetic network that captures the real-world behaviors of vessels and can be used to expand the maritime trajectory network. MDCBM allows for the generation of complex network structures and enables the analysis of network properties, such as node centrality and clustering coefficient. Additionally, MDCBM can handle missing data and noise, making it a robust method for network generation.

3 Methodologies

This section presents our synthetic graph generator method, MDCBM, designed to capture the distinctive characteristics of maritime transport networks. We begin by analyzing the statistical properties of the World Maritime Network (WMN), and observe that it displays small-world network behavior with power-law characteristics, a hierarchical structure, and a rich-club phenomenon. Based on these properties, we introduce the construction of MDCBM, elucidating the degree-corrected principle and the process for generating trajectory data.

3.1 Statistical Properties of Worldwide Marine Transportation Network

In the following we will present an empirical analysis of worldwide marine transportation network (WMN), considering ports as nodes and container ships as links connecting the ports. Using different network representations such as the L- and P-spaces [17], we study the statistical properties of the network, including degree distribution, degree correlations, weight distribution, strength distribution, average shortest path length, line length distribution, and centrality measures (Fig. 3).

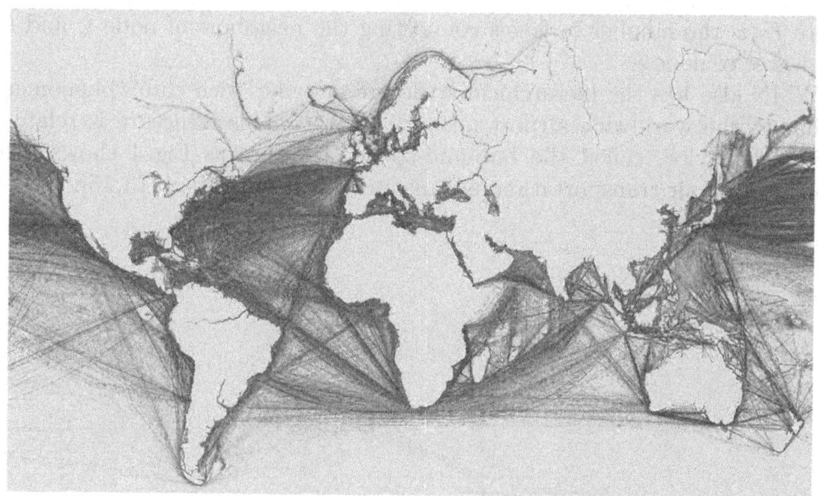

Fig. 3. World maritime route map.

The degree distribution of WMN follows a truncated power-law distribution in the L space and an exponential decay distribution in the P space. The distributions of the in-degree, out-degree and undirected degrees in the space L all follow a truncated power law distribution with almost the same exponents [6]. In- and out-degree obey the function

$$P(k) \sim k^{-1.7} \tag{1}$$

before $k = 20$. For k >20 their distributions bend to

$$P(k) \sim k^{-2.95} \tag{2}$$

The unweighted degree in space L has the same exponents −1.7 and −2.95, but the critical point becomes k = 30. [1] explains that the cost of connectivity prevents the addition of new links to large degree nodes. In space P all three degree distributions follow exponential distributions

$$P(k) \sim e^{-\alpha k} \tag{3}$$

where the parameters are estimated to be $\alpha = 0.0117$ for in-degree and $\alpha = 0.0085$ for out-degree, $\alpha = 0.0086$ for unweighted degree.

The average shortest path length is 3.6 in the space L and 2.66 in the space P. This means generally in the whole world the cargo need to transfer for no more than 2 times to get to the destination. The clustering coefficient is high (0.7) in the P space, suggesting that WMN is a small-world network. The formula for calculating clustering coefficient (C_i) of node i is:

$$C_i = \frac{2E_i}{k_i(k_i - 1)} \tag{4}$$

where E_i is the number of edges connecting the neighbors of node i, and k_i is the degree of node i.

WMN also has the hierarchical structure and the "rich club" phenomenon, similar to the worldwide airport network (WAN). This structure is related to optimal behavior, called the hub-and-spoke structure as Fig. 4 shows, which exists in both air transportation and maritime transportation [13,15].

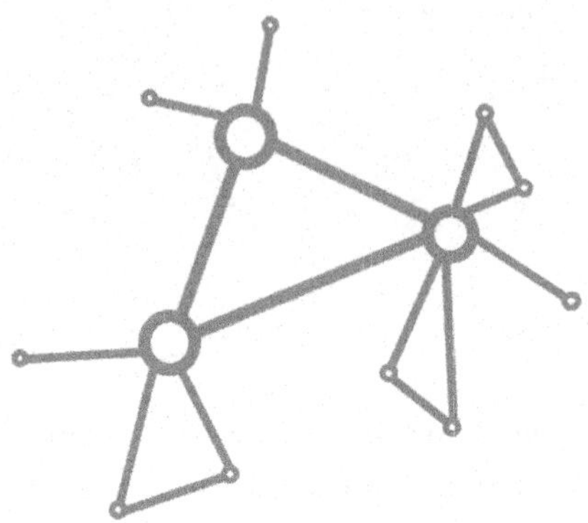

Fig. 4. A classic hub-and-spoke structure in the maritime transport industry. There are three central nodes with very strong links to each other and several nodes with weak links to hubs.

3.2 Construction of MDCBM

In Fig. 5, we outlined the process of generating a synthetic maritime trajectory network. Initially, the node number n and group number k were defined, and nodes were assigned to groups randomly. A Poisson distribution connectivity matrix was then set, and a degree correction parameter list was customized based on a predefined degree sequence. We obtain node list and feature dataframe that are geographically located in the Bohai Sea region. Next, we employed the MDCBM model, which incorporates degree correction parameters and degrees based on the predefined sequence. Attributes were introduced to nodes and edges. Once the road network generation process was complete, we utilized Dijkstra's shortest path algorithm to generate trajectory data for all nodes. In the following, we focus on the processes of generating the road network by MDCBM.

Define *n* and *k*. In the simplest stochastic blockmodel, each of n vertices is assigned to one of K blocks, groups, or communities, and undirected edges are placed independently between vertex pairs with probabilities that are a function only of the group memberships of the vertices. In the context of maritime trajectory events, nodes can represent vessel docking points. Each node can have certain attributes such as longitude and latitude, and the edges represent the route section with distance attributes. Blocks can represent clusters of docking points in the network.

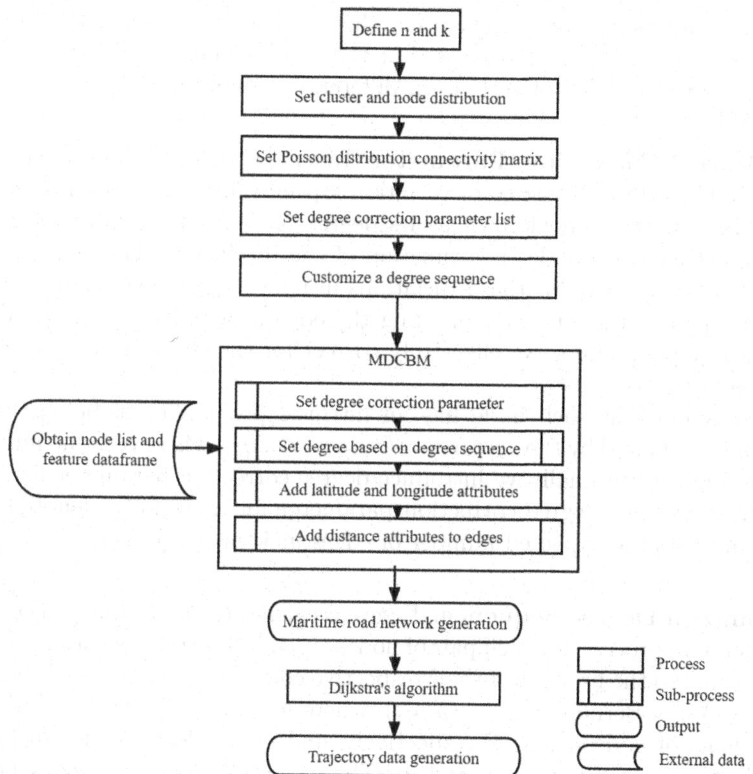

Fig. 5. Flowchart of trajectory generation in MDCBM.

Set Cluster and Node Distribution. If we denote by g_i the group to which vertex i belongs, then we can define a $K \times K$ matrix Ψ of probabilities such that the matrix element $\psi_{g_i g_j}$ is the independent probability of an edge between vertices i and j. We also define a K-vector z of community assignments, where z_g is the number of vertices in community g. We can define a probability distribution over all possible graphs with n vertices and m edges by treating each possible graph as a sample from the distribution. It can help to identify hubs, outliers, or other important nodes in the network. The probability of the observed graph Y is given by the likelihood function:

$$\begin{aligned} P(Y|\, z, \Psi) &= \prod_{i<j} \psi_{g_i g_j}^{y_{ij}} \left(1 - \psi_{g_i g_j}\right)^{1-y_{ij}} \\ &= \prod_{g \in 1,\ldots,K} \left[\prod_{i \in g} \prod_{j \in g} \psi_{gg}^{y_{ij}} \left(1 - \psi_{gg}\right)^{1-y_{ij}}\right] \left[\prod_{i \in g} \prod_{j \in g'} \psi_{gg'}^{y_{ij}} \left(1 - \psi_{gg'}\right)^{1-y_{ij}}\right] \end{aligned} \tag{5}$$

where g' represents a community other than g. The first product in the second line is over all pairs of vertices within the same community, and the second product is over all pairs of vertices in different communities.

Set Degree Correction Parameter List. In real-world networks, node degrees often exhibit a degree of variation. Specifically, each node is associated with a hidden attribute, known as its degree, and the probability of an edge forming between two nodes is a function of the product of their hidden degree attributes. To account for these variations in node degrees, we introduce node-specific degree parameters. By dividing the edge probability by the product of these degree parameters, we effectively correct for the effect of node degrees on the edge formation process.

We assume that each node has an intrinsic probability of belonging to a community, denoted by the vector $\gamma = (\gamma_1, \gamma_2, \dots, \gamma_K)$, where K is the number of communities. Additionally,we introduce degree correction parameter list, which contains power-law degree correction parameter for each node, denoted by p_i, that represents the expected number of edges incident on node i.

Customize a Degree Sequence. Edges are generated according to the following generative process: for each pair of nodes (i, j), an edge exists with probability proportional to the product of their respective community membership probabilities, i.e., $Y_{ij} \sim \text{Bernoulli}(w_{g_i g_j}/(p_i p_j))$, where g_i and g_j denote the community assignments of nodes i and j, respectively, and $w_{g_i\ g_j}$ denotes the edge probability between communities g_i and g_j. The expected number of edges between nodes i and j is then given by $d_i d_j w_{g_i g_j}$. The degree parameter p_i is assumed to be drawn from a distribution $F(p)$ according to Eq. 1, which is estimated from the observed degree distribution of the network. To correct for the effect of node degrees, the edge probability is divided by the product of the degree parameters of the nodes, $p_i p_j$, which acts as a scaling factor to adjust for the tendency of high-degree nodes to have more edges than low-degree nodes. This results in a degree-corrected edge probability of $w_{g_i g_j}/p_i p_j$.

To ensure a controllable degree distribution , we now restrict the range of node degrees according to Eq. 4. For the degrees of nodes, we first set the maximum degree to $d_{max,1} = 8$. We then traverse every node in the entire network and randomly remove $d - d_{max,1}$ edges from any node that has a degree greater than $d_{max,1}$. This process is repeated until all nodes in the graph have a degree of less than or equal to $d_{max,1}$. We then set $d_{max,2} = 20$ and repeat the same process to control the node degrees below $d_{max,2}$. Finally, we divide the degree distribution of all nodes into three segments based on the proportion of nodes with degrees of 8 or less, exactly 8, and between 8 and 20. Specifically, we set the proportions to 40%, 20%, and 20% respectively, based on the degree distribution of all nodes and the total number of nodes.

Generate Road Networks. We retrieved a list of nodes that are geographically located in the Bohai Sea region, along with their corresponding node characteristics dataframe. The MDCBM model was then applied, incorporating degree correction parameters and degrees based on the predefined sequence. Node-specific attributes such as latitude and longitude were added. Distance attributes for edges were introduced based on the location information of adjacent nodes.

Generate Trajectory Data. After road network generation, Dijkstra's shortest path algorithm was used to generate trajectory data for all nodes. By efficiently computing the shortest path between each pair of nodes in the graph, the algorithm connected each node to its closest neighbours.

4 Experiments

We conducted experiments to measure the time required to generate MDCBMs of various sizes using the proposed algorithm. The experiments were carried out on a computer with a 2.9 GHz Intel Core i7 processor and 16 GB of RAM.

Trajectory Generation. In this study, the MDCBM was subjected to varying numbers of nodes, ranging from 100 to 10,000, and the duration of graph generation was meticulously recorded. Three measurements were taken for each specific number of nodes, and the mean value was computed.

The findings indicate that as the number of nodes in the MDCBM increased, the generation time increased almost quadratically. For instance, the generation time for 100 nodes was found to be 0.12 s, while for 10,000 nodes, it was 96.04 s. These results align with the theoretical time complexity, thus confirming the validity of the MDCBM.

For an MDCBM model with n nodes, the time complexity mainly depends on the following factors:

- **generating random parameters:** the time complexity for generating random parameters for the SBM model is typically $O(1)$ or $O(n)$, depending on the complexity of the random number generation method.
- **generating the adjacency matrix:** based on the generated random parameters, an $n \times n$ adjacency matrix is required to represent the graph. Since there can be a maximum of $\frac{n(n-1)}{2}$ edges in a graph, the time complexity for generating the adjacency matrix is $O(n^2)$.
- **graph algorithms based on the adjacency matrix:** the time complexity of graph algorithms based on the adjacency matrix is usually proportional to the size of the adjacency matrix.

For example, the time complexity for graph traversal, shortest path algorithms, connectivity algorithms, etc. Based on the adjacency matrix is usually $O(n^2)$ or $O(n^3)$. In special cases, such as when the graph is sparse (with far fewer edges than $\frac{n(n-1)}{2}$), adjacency list-based algorithms can be used to optimize the time complexity. The time complexity of the MDCBM model mainly depends on the

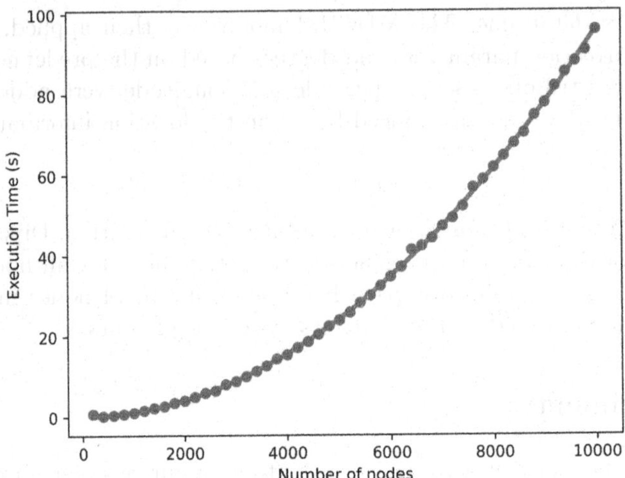

Fig. 6. MDCBM generation time.

size of the graph and the time complexity of the graph algorithms based on the adjacency matrix. If adjacency list-based algorithms or other optimization methods are used, the time complexity can be further improved (Fig. 6).

Properties Verification. The degree distribution of the MDCBM generated graph follows a truncated power-law distribution with a function of $P(k) \sim k^{-1.7}$ (see Fig. 7). The graph has an average shortest path length of 2.66 and a high clustering coefficient of 0.7, indicating that it is a small-world network. In MDCBM, the high clustering coefficient suggests the presence of tightly connected groups of nodes. Furthermore, the degree distribution shows a higher frequency of nodes with higher degrees, which suggests the presence of highly interconnected nodes or "hubs". The combination of these two factors, high clustering coefficient and the presence of highly connected nodes, suggest the presence of the "rich club" phenomenon in the network.

The resulting network is found to exhibit small-world properties. This can be seen from the calculated values of the small-world evaluation metrics, sigma and omega. The sigma value of the generated graph is approximately equal to 1.18, which is greater than 1. This suggests that the graph is a small-world network, as the value of sigma greater than 1 indicates that the network has a higher degree of clustering than a random network. Additionally, the omega value of the generated graph is approximately equal to 0.12, which is close to 0. This indicates that the network has small-world characteristics, as a small value of omega suggests a short average path length between nodes.

In summary, the findings of this study indicate that the algorithm we have proposed is capable of generating maritime trajectory networks with high accuracy and in various sizes. The MDCBM approach exhibits superior performance

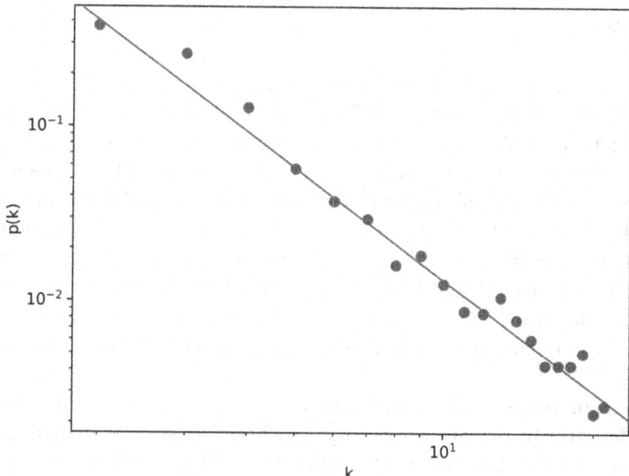

Fig. 7. Degree distribution.

in generating synthetic networks that closely resemble the observed characteristics of the Bohai maritime network. These results hold significant implications for practical applications that necessitate the generation of large MDCBMs, such as the creation of extensive road networks and the prediction of trajectory paths.

5 Conclusion

This paper proposed the Maritime Degree-Corrected Block Method (MDCBM) as a preliminary solution to generate synthetic maritime transportation networks. By incorporating a degree correction term, adjusting the degree distribution, introducing attribute information, and making other modifications, the MDCBM method can reflect the observed properties of the Bohai maritime network more realistically. Our experimental results validate the efficiency of the MDCBM method in generating synthetic networks, thereby providing a reliable dataset for benchmarking maritime LBS.

Acknowledgements. I would like to express my sincere gratitude to my advisor, Professor Wang, for her invaluable guidance, support, and encouragement throughout this year. I am truly grateful for her dedication and patience in helping me navigate through the challenges of my research. I am also deeply grateful to my senior colleagues, Peng and Yu, for their insightful advice and assistance. Their knowledge and expertise have been instrumental in shaping my research and helping me expand my understanding of the field. I would like to acknowledge the unwavering support of my parents, who have consistently encouraged me to pursue my dreams and provided me with unconditional love and care. Their unwavering support has been a constant source of strength and motivation for me. Without their love and support, I would not have been able to achieve my goals. I am forever grateful for their sacrifices and unwavering belief in me.

References

1. Amaral, L.A.N., Scala, A., Barthélémy, M., Stanley, H.E.: Classes of small-world networks. Proc. Nat. Acad. Sci. **97**(21), 11149–11152 (2000). https://doi.org/10.1073/pnas.200327197, https://www.pnas.org/doi/abs/10.1073/pnas.200327197
2. Graser, A., Schmidt, J., Dragaschnig, M., Widhalm, P.: Data-driven trajectory prediction and spatial variability of prediction performance in maritime location based services. In: LBS 2019; Adjunct Proceedings of the 15th International Conference on Location-Based Services/Gartner, Georg; Huang, Haosheng. Wien (2019)
3. Hartigan, P.: Transport and processing of perishable information: essential infrastructure for location based services. In: Third International Conference on 3G Mobile Communication Technologies, pp. 345–349 (2002). https://doi.org/10.1049/cp:20020417
4. He, X., Cormode, G., Machanavajjhala, A., Procopiuc, C.M., Srivastava, D.: DPT: differentially private trajectory synthesis using hierarchical reference systems. Proc. VLDB Endow. **8**(11), 1154–1165 (2015). https://doi.org/10.14778/2809974.2809978
5. Hu, W., et al.: Open graph benchmark: Datasets for machine learning on graphs. In: Larochelle, H., Ranzato, M., Hadsell, R., Balcan, M., Lin, H. (eds.) Advances in Neural Information Processing Systems, vol. 33, pp. 22118–22133. Curran Associates, Inc. (2020)
6. Hu, Y., Zhu, D.: Empirical analysis of the worldwide maritime transportation network. Phys. A: Stat. Mech. Appl. **388**(10), 2061–2071 (2009). https://doi.org/10.1016/j.physa.2008.12.016, https://www.sciencedirect.com/science/article/pii/S0378437108010273
7. Karrer, B., Newman, M.E.J.: Stochastic blockmodels and community structure in networks. Phys. Rev. E Stat. Nonlinear, Soft Matter Phys. **83** 1 Pt 2, 016107 (2010)
8. Kim, J.W., Jang, B.: Deep learning-based privacy-preserving framework for synthetic trajectory generation. J. Netw. Comput. Appl. **206**, 103459 (2022). https://doi.org/10.1016/j.jnca.2022.103459, https://www.sciencedirect.com/science/article/pii/S1084804522001096
9. Lee, C., Wilkinson, D.J.: A review of stochastic block models and extensions for graph clustering. Appl. Netw. Sci. **4**(1), 1–50 (2019). https://doi.org/10.1007/s41109-019-0232-2
10. Levinson, D.: Network structure and city size. PLOS ONE **7**(1), 1–11 (2012). https://doi.org/10.1371/journal.pone.0029721
11. Liu, R.W., et al.: Stmgcn: mobile edge computing-empowered vessel trajectory prediction using spatio-temporal multigraph convolutional network. IEEE Trans. Industr. Inf. **18**(11), 7977–7987 (2022). https://doi.org/10.1109/TII.2022.3165886
12. Notteboom*, T.E., Rodrigue, J.P.: Port regionalization: towards a new phase in port development. Marit. Policy Manag. **32**(3), 297–313 (2005)
13. O'Kelly, M.E.: A geographer's analysis of hub-and-spoke network. J. Transp. Geogr. **6**, 171–186 (1998)
14. Pelekis, N., Ntrigkogias, C., Tampakis, P., Sideridis, S., Theodoridis, Y.: Hermoupolis: A trajectory generator for simulating generalized mobility patterns. In: Blockeel, H., Kersting, K., Nijssen, S., Železný, F. (eds.) ECML PKDD 2013. LNCS, pp. 659–662. Springer, Berlin Heidelberg, Berlin, Heidelberg (2013). https://doi.org/10.1007/978-3-642-40994-3_49

15. Robinson, R.: Asian hub/feeder nets: the dynamics of restructuring. Marit. Policy Manag. **25**(1), 21–40 (1998). https://doi.org/10.1080/03088839800000043
16. Rodrigue, J.P., Notteboom, T.: The geography of containerization: half a century of revolution, adaptation and diffusion. GeoJournal **74**(1), 1–5 (2009). https://doi.org/10.1007/s10708-008-9210-4
17. Sen, P., Dasgupta, S., Chatterjee, A., Sreeram, P.A., Mukherjee, G., Manna, S.S.: Small-world properties of the Indian railway network. Phys. Rev. E **67**, 036106 (2003). https://doi.org/10.1103/PhysRevE.67.036106, https://link.aps.org/doi/10.1103/PhysRevE.67.036106
18. Wang, X., Liu, X., Lu, Z., Yang, H.: Large scale GPS trajectory generation using map based on two stage GAN. J. Data Sci. **19**(1), 126–141 (2021). https://doi.org/10.6339/21-JDS1004
19. Zachary, W.: An information flow model for conflict and fission in small groups1. J. Anthropol. Res. **33**, 452–473 (1976). https://doi.org/10.1086/jar.33.4.3629752
20. Zhao, J., Gao, Y., Bai, Z., Wang, H., Lu, S.: Traffic speed prediction under non-recurrent congestion: based on LSTM method and BeiDou navigation satellite system data. IEEE Intell. Transp. Syst. Mag. **11**(2), 70–81 (2019). https://doi.org/10.1109/MITS.2019.2903431
21. Zhong, M., Kim, J., Zheng, Z.: Estimating link flows in road networks with synthetic trajectory data generation: inverse reinforcement learning approach. IEEE Open J. Intell. Transp. Syst. **4**, 14–29 (2023). https://doi.org/10.1109/OJITS.2022.3233904

Modeling Spatio-Temporal Distribution and Matching of Service Capacity and Customer Demands

Huixin Xu(✉), Hanchuan Xu, Xiao Wang, Tonghua Su, Zhongjie Wang, and Xiaofei Xu

Harbin Institute of Technology, Harbin, China
xuhuixin@stu.hit.edu.cn, {xhc,wxlxq,thsu,rainy,xiaofei}@hit.edu.cn

Abstract. In recent years, the concept of Big Service has been proposed to describe the complex characteristics of cross-world, cross-domain, and cross-network services. The main goal of Big Service is to provide on-demand services to users. Accurately providing services on demand requires a full understanding of the characteristics of service participants. Portrait technology is a useful method for describing various attributes, behaviors, and preferences of service participants to provide personalized services. However, existing methods often overlook the macro spatio-temporal connections between service providers and their customers. To address this issue, this paper proposes a service portrait construction approach based on demand-service capacity spatio-temporal matching. The approach focuses on the characteristics of both customers and service providers and provides a method for constructing demand and service capacity distribution models. Additionally, the approach includes a method for analyzing the supply and demand matching condition. We illustrate the proposed approach through a ride-hailing service case. Analyzing the characteristics of service participants and the status of service provision from the perspective of time and space enables providers to allocate resources reasonably and achieve precise services.

Keywords: Service portrait · Supply and demand matching · Sptio-temporal characteristics

1 Introduction

The development of technologies such as the cloud and the Internet of Things (IoT) has given rise to the concept of servitization, leading to a new phase of service development characterized by cross-world, cross-domain, and cross-network complexity. In response to this phenomenon, scholars have proposed related concepts from different perspectives, including Big Service [15], Internet of Services (IoS) [9], and Crossover Services [14]. The core of these concepts is to provide services to users on demand.

Accurately providing on-demand services requires a full understanding of the characteristics of service participants, which is challenging. User portraits,

Z. Wang et al. (Eds.): ICSS 2023, CCIS 1844, pp. 414–428, 2023.
https://doi.org/10.1007/978-981-99-4402-6_30

which describe users' basic characteristics, social relationships, behavior patterns, interests, and preferences, are widely used to provide personalized and precise services, such as in personalized recommendations [7]. Inspired by this idea, some scholars have carried out research on corporate portraits [3,17], which are used to describe the characteristics of businesses. To abstractly portray different aspects of services, we propose the concept of service portraits. Service regulators can use these portraits to establish a comprehensive understanding of services, analyze the matching condition of supply and demand, and identify existing service weak points, so as to optimize services in a targeted manner.

In service science, a service is considered a collaborative process between providers and customers aimed at creating value [10]. Since both the supply and demand sides are crucial to understanding the status of a service, constructing a service portrait must consider both aspects. As an abstract concept, a service portrait can encompass various aspects of a service, including its spatio-temporal characteristics. Prior research has demonstrated that a service's spatio-temporal characteristics can accurately capture customer demand and service capacity information and provide support for service analysis and optimization [1,6,16]. However, there are still some deficiencies in the literature. Some studies have focused only on the temporal or spatial dimension [1,16], while others have examined only the demand or supply side of services [4,7]. Even the more comprehensive studies have mainly focused on service forecasting from a micro perspective [6]. To our knowledge, there is no research that investigates the matching condition between service supply and demand in the spatio-temporal dimension from a medium- to long-term perspective.

In order to fill the gap in existing research, this paper intends to portray service spatio-temporal characteristics and analyze supply-demand matching condition from a macro perspective. To achieve this goal, we pose the following two research questions:

RQ1 How to characterize spatio-temporal characteristics of both sides of supply and demand?

RQ2 How to analyze supply and demand matching condition of services in spatio-temporal dimension?

RQ1 serves as the basis for RQ2 while characterizing spatio-temporal distribution characteristics of a service. RQ2 helps build an understanding of supply and demand matching condition and weak points. Answers to RQ1 and RQ2 together constitute the content of the service portrait studied in this paper, providing a basis for service optimization over a mid-to-long period of time.

Based on the discussions and research questions stated above, we propose a service portrait construction approach that is based on demand-service capacity spatio-temporal matching. To answer RQ1, we suggest demand-service capacity distribution models that describe the distribution characteristics of demand and service capacity from temporal and spatio-temporal dimensions. For RQ2, we first define the gap measurement criterion between supply and demand and then design an algorithm to analyze service weak points. Our proposed approach can analyze service spatio-temporal characteristics and matching conditions from a mid-to-long term perspective and identify current service weak points, providing support for service optimization and achieving precise services.

Our main contributions are summarized as follows:

- We propose a method for establishing service distribution models, which establishes models from two sides (demand and service capacity) and two dimensions (temporal and spatio-temporal). The method can help to build a more comprehensive and accurate understanding of spatial-temporal distribution characteristics of services.
- We propose a supply-demand matching analysis method. Based on the spatio-temporal distribution models, the method analyzes service supply and demand matching condition and finds out service weak points. This method can help understand the gap between supply and demand and links to be optimized, and provide a strong basis for service optimization.

The remainder of this paper is organized as follows. Section 2 introduces some related work. Section 3 describes the proposed service portrait construction approach in detail. Section 4 evaluates the approach through case study and qualitative comparison. Section 5 gives conclusions and future work.

2 Related Work

The proposed service portrait construction approach involves three research topics, namely, service portrait, service spatio-temporal feature and supply and demand matching analysis. Therefore, this section summarizes related work from the above three aspects.

Regarding the concept of service portrait proposed in this paper, existing research can be divided into two categories: one category describes demand-side objects, such as users and customers; the other describes supply-side objects, such as corporates and service providers. Gu et al. [4] proposed a user portrait modeling method based on posted microblog texts. It portrays the psychological concept of Big Five personality of the users, and can be used to provide personalized products or services. Lee et al. [7] proposed a method to construct user portraits using Tweets posted by users, which portrays users' common words and their frequency, so as to provide personalized news recommendation service. Zhang et al. [17] proposed a corporate portrait construction method. It describes a corporate from three aspects, i.e., financial data, research reports and public opinion, and can reflect the business status of the corporate. However, no research has yet unified the research on different service objects under the same concept of service portrait.

Some scholars have studied service spatio-temporal feature. Asl and Ulsoy [1] used stochastic process and Markov decision theory to establish demand and capacity model in temporal dimension, and formulated a capacity management strategy under stochastic demand. Zhang et al. [16] utilized queuing theory for capacity planning and resource scheduling, so that service capacity can adapt to demand in temporal dimension. Ke et al. [6] used deep learning techniques to capture the spatio-temporal characteristics of supply and demand, thereby predicting demand and the gap between supply and demand. Nonetheless, there is currently a lack of research on spatio-temporal characteristics of services from a macro perspective.

As for supply and demand matching analysis, Cui et al. [2] proposed a supply-demand matching method based on three-way decisions theory, while considering both matching fairness and cooperation stability. Wang et al. [12] used the M/M/s/K multi-sever mixed queuing model to discuss matching degree of supply and demand resources according to four key indicators. The method can be applied in different time and space. Li et al. [5] established a multi-dimensional data index system for computing power network services, and proposed an evaluation method for matching degree of supply and demand. It is valuable for allocating and scheduling computing power network infrastructure. Still, no research has analyzed the matching condition of supply and demand in spatio-temporal dimension.

In order to model and analyze service spatio-temporal condition from a macro perspective and also provide a basis for service optimization, this paper proposes a service portrait construction approach based on demand-service capacity spatio-temporal matching.

3 Methodology

3.1 Overall Framework

Figure 1 illustrates the process of our approach. The first step is to collect and clean demand-service capacity data. Second, build an concept-level service portrait framework. Third, establish demand-service capacity distribution models. Followed by analyzing supply-demand matching condition. At last, we can obtain the complete service portrait. The main steps of the approach are modeling and analysis, which are introduced respectively in Sect. 3.2 and Sect. 3.3.

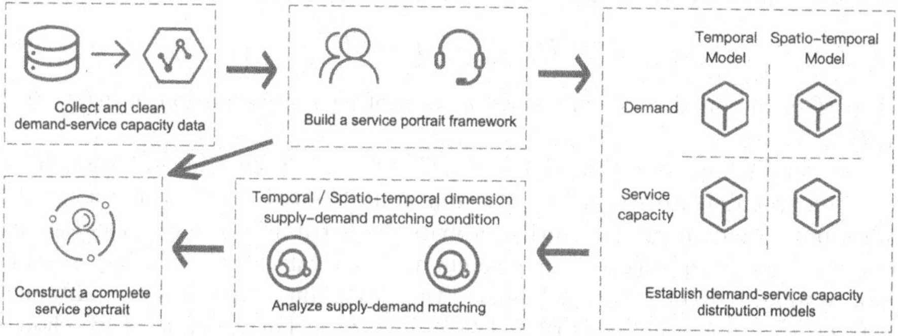

Fig. 1. Illustration of the approach.

The content of proposed service portrait $P_{service}$ in this paper can be expressed as a triplet:

$$P_{service} =< P_{user}, P_{provider}, M > \quad (1)$$

where P_{user} is user portrait, $P_{provider}$ is service provider portrait, and M means supply and demand matching condition. They are respectively expressed as:

- $P_{user} =< D_{des}, \Omega(D)_T, \Omega(D)_{T\times L} >$
  where D_{des} represents demand description, $\Omega(D)_T$ represents temporal distribution model of demand, and $\Omega(D)_{T\times L}$ represents spatio-temporal distribution model of demand.
- $P_{provider} =< C_{des}, \Omega(C)_T, \Omega(C)_{T\times L} >$
  where C_{des} represents service capacity description, $\Omega(C)_T$ represents temporal distribution model of service capacity, and $\Omega(C)_{T\times L}$ represents spatio-temporal distribution model of service capacity.
- $M =< \Omega(\Delta)_T, \Omega(\Delta)_{T\times L}, W_T, W_{T\times L} >$
  where $\Omega(\Delta)_T$ is the supply and demand gap condition in temporal dimension, $\Omega(\Delta)_{T\times L}$ is the supply and demand gap condition in spatio-temporal dimension, W_T is weak point set in temporal dimension, and $W_{T\times L}$ is weak point set in spatio-temporal dimension.

3.2 Demand-Service Capacity Distribution Models

The proposed models are established from two dimensions and two sides. This section will transition from temporal dimension to spatio-temporal dimension. In each dimension, the distribution models of demand and service capacity sides will be introduced.

Temporal Distribution Models. The temporal distribution of demand D is denoted by $\Omega(D)_T$. It is a one-dimensional matrix. Each element in $\Omega(D)_T$ is determined by unit (t), where t is concrete time, and $d(t)$ is the demand value at time t. Therefore, the temporal distribution of demand can be represented as:

$$\Omega(D)_T = \left[d_1 \; d_2 \cdots d_T \right] \quad (2)$$

where T is the number of time slots, d_i is another representation of $d(t_i)$, $\forall i \in [1, T]$.

Demand in any given time slot is considered to be stochastic, and arises from a certain probability distribution. It is important to stress that d_i is not a specific value, but a random variable with a probability distribution. $\Omega(D)_T$ can be seen as a stochastic sequence of independent random variables. By using existing data sensing and collecting techniques, the probability distributions contained in $\Omega(D)_T$ can be easily constructed from real data. For example, if we choose N sample values $d_i^{(1)}, d_i^{(2)}, \ldots, d_i^{(N)}$ at time i, then we can calculate the mean value μ_{d_i}, cumulative distribution function $F_{d_i}(x)$ and other content of demand at time i.

Similarly, we use $\Omega(C)_T$ to denote the temporal distribution of service capacity C. Each element in $\Omega(C)_T$ is determined by unit (t), and $c(t)$ is the capacity value at time t. Therefore, the temporal distribution of service capacity can be represented as:

$$\Omega(C)_T = \begin{bmatrix} c_1 \; c_2 \cdots c_T \end{bmatrix} \tag{3}$$

where T is the number of time slots, c_i is another representation of $c(t_i)$, $\forall i \in [1, T]$.

Since a service may have many service providers, we continue to follow the concepts of *role* and *instance* proposed in previous study [11]. The collection of service providers providing the same type of service is called a role, and each service provider which has its own service time and capacity is called an instance. It is clear that: 1) Different instances have different capacity to provide services. For example, the order quantity that a large restaurant can undertake is greater than that of a small restaurant; 2) Different instances provide services at different time. For example, hot pot restaurants usually open until midnight, while breakfast restaurants may close early. Therefore, service capacity c_i at time i is also a random variable, and its probability distribution can be constructed from real data. Note that service capacity of a role is aggregated from capacity of instances, so the n-th sample value $c_i^{(n)}$ of service capacity can be calculated as:

$$c_i^{(n)} = \sum_{s \in R} g_{s_i}^{(n)} \cdot c_{s_i} \tag{4}$$

where s represents instance, R represents role, $g_{s_i}^{(n)}$ represents whether the instance s provides service at time i in the n-th sample data, its value is 0 or 1, c_{s_i} represents the capacity of instance s at time i. Then the probability distributions contained in $\Omega(C)_T$ can be constructed.

Spatio-Temporal Distribution Models. In temporal distribution model, we discretize time and divide continuous time into discrete time slots. Spatio-temporal distribution model introduces spatial dimension based on the basic concept of temporal distribution model. Similarly, we discretize space, dividing continuous space into discrete regions.

The spatio-temporal distribution of demand D is denoted by $\Omega(D)_{T \times L}$. It is a two-dimensional matrix. Each element in $\Omega(D)_{T \times L}$ is determined by unit (t, l), where t is concrete time, l is concrete location, and $d(t, l)$ is the demand value at time t location l. Therefore, the spatio-temporal distribution of demand can be represented as:

$$\Omega(D)_{T \times L} = \begin{bmatrix} d_{11} & \cdots & d_{1L} \\ \vdots & \ddots & \vdots \\ d_{T1} & \cdots & d_{TL} \end{bmatrix} \tag{5}$$

where T is the number of time slots, L is the number of regions, d_{ij} is another representation of $d(t_i, l_j)$, $\forall i \in [1, T], j \in [1, L]$.

Note that d_{ij} is a random variable. Its probability distribution can be constructed statistically. For example, if we choose N sample values $d_{ij}^{(1)}, d_{ij}^{(2)}, \ldots, d_{ij}^{(N)}$ at time i and region j, then we can calculate the mean value $\mu_{d_{ij}}$, cumulative distribution function $F_{d_{ij}}(x)$ and other content of demand at time i and region j.

Similarly, we use $\Omega(C)_{T\times L}$ to denote the spatio-temporal distribution of service capacity C. Each element in $\Omega(C)_{T\times L}$ is determined by unit (t, l), and $c(t, l)$ is the capacity value at time t. Therefore, the spatio-temporal distribution of service capacity can be represented as:

$$\Omega(C)_{T\times L} = \begin{bmatrix} c_{11} & \cdots & c_{1L} \\ \vdots & \ddots & \vdots \\ c_{T1} & \cdots & c_{TL} \end{bmatrix} \tag{6}$$

where T is the number of time slots, L is the number of regions, c_{ij} is another representation of $c(t_i, l_j)$, $\forall i \in [1, T], j \in [1, L]$.

Each service provider instance has its own location and the scope of providing service. Service scope can be seen as a field that spreads around based on the location. Therefore, the location attribute of instance becomes an important factor in calculating a role's capacity. According to whether the location of a role is fixed, it can be divided into two discussion situations:

- For a role with **unfixed** location (such as a taxi), an instance may only provide service to regions where it is in. Its capacity in the spatial dimension is related to its location. So the n-th sample value $c_{ij}^{(n)}$ of service capacity can be calculated as:

$$c_{ij}^{(n)} = \sum_{s\in R} g_{s_{ij}}^{(n)} \cdot c_{s_{ij}} \tag{7}$$

- For a role with **fixed** location (such as a restaurant), an instance may provide service to its adjacent regions. The farther the distance, the weaker the capacity of an instance to provide service. So the n-th sample value $c_{ij}^{(n)}$ of service capacity can be calculated as:

$$c_{ij}^{(n)} = \sum_{s\in R} g_{s_{ij}}^{(n)} \cdot c_{s_{ij}} \cdot h_{sj} \tag{8}$$

where s represents instance, R represents role, $g_{s_{ij}}^{(n)}$ represents whether the instance s provides service at time i and region j in the n-th sample data, its value is 0 or 1, $c_{s_{ij}}$ represents the capacity of instance s at time i and region j, h_{sj} is the distance attenuation value. The farther instance s is from the region j, the smaller h is, and its value ranges from 0 to 1. Then we can construct the probability distributions contained in $\Omega(C)_{T\times L}$.

3.3 Supply-Demand Matching Analysis

This section proposes a measurement criterion for the gap between supply and demand. It analyzes the gap based on demand-service capacity distribution models established in Sect. 3.2. In addition, an analysis method for weak points of supply-demand matching condition is proposed. It gives the weak points and their mismatching degree according to the gap.

Gap Measurement. The overall gap between supply and demand in temporal dimension and spatio-temporal dimension are represented respectively as:

$$\Omega(\Delta)_T = \begin{bmatrix} \delta_1 \, \delta_2 \cdots \delta_T \end{bmatrix} \tag{9}$$

and

$$\Omega(\Delta)_{T\times L} = \begin{bmatrix} \delta_{11} & \cdots & \delta_{1L} \\ \vdots & \ddots & \vdots \\ \delta_{T1} & \cdots & \delta_{TL} \end{bmatrix} \tag{10}$$

Assuming that the probability corresponding to each unit (t) or (t, l) is independent from others, we propose an measurement method for the gap between supply and demand, which is applicable to a single unit. After unit-by-unit comparison, the overall gap can be obtained. Taking unit (t) of temporal dimension as an example, the gap δ_i is defined as:

$$\delta_i = \delta(d_i, c_i) = \begin{bmatrix} \delta_E(d_i, c_i) \\ \delta_{KS}(d_i, c_i) \end{bmatrix} \tag{11}$$

where $\delta_E(d_i, c_i)$ represents the difference between the mean values of service capacity and demand at time i, which is used to reflect the gap from the average situation, $\delta_{KS}(d_i, c_i)$ represents the Kolmogorov-Smirnov (KS) distance of demand and capacity at time i, which is used to reflect the gap from the overall situation. KS distance can be adopted for evaluating the difference between the two probabilities [8]. Suppose there are two cumulative distribution function $F(x)$ and $F(y)$, their KS distance D_{KS} can be calculated by:

$$D_{KS} = \max |F(x) - F(y)| \tag{12}$$

Its value range is within [0,1]. And as for unit (t, l) in spatio-temporal dimension, calculation of the gap is the same.

Weak Point Analysis. Based on the gap measurement criterion, we propose a method to analyze weak points of supply and demand matching. The method needs to input measurement results of the gap and parameters such as artificially set threshold, and outputs weak points of supply and demand matching. The detailed steps are given in Algorithm 1.

Algorithm 1. Weak point analysis

```
Input: Gap matrix G, Threshold λ, Max size of weak points n, Coefficients a and b
  of gap indicators
Output: Weak points set W
  W ← ∅
  for g ∈ G do
      // Calculate gap severity
      g.severity ← cal_severity(g, a, b)
      if g.severity ≥ λ then
          // Determine gap type
          if g.e > 0 then
              // Oversupply
              g.type ← 1
          else
              // Undersupply
              g.type ← −1
          end if
          W ← W ∪ {g}
      end if
  end for
  if |W| ≥ n then
      // Select the top n weak points
      W ← sort_by_severity(W, n)
  end if
  return W
```

In the algorithm, we combine the two indicators of service gap to get a gap mismatching degree to evaluate the severity of weak points. The severity is calculated as follows:

$$severity = a \cdot \delta_{E'} + b \cdot \delta_{KS'} \tag{13}$$

where $\delta_{E'}$ and $\delta_{KS'}$ are normalized results of δ_E and δ_{KS}, a and b are coefficients of two gap indicators, which subject to $a+b=1$. The severity value ranges from 0 to 1, and the higher the number, the worse the gap. Since the value of δ_E may be positive or negative, it is necessary to take its absolute value when normalizing, the calculation method should be:

$$\delta_{E'} = \frac{|\delta_E| - |\delta_E|_{min}}{|\delta_E|_{max} - |\delta_E|_{min}} \tag{14}$$

After finding weak points of supply and demand matching, platform or service governors can optimize services accordingly, adjust the distribution of demand and service capacity, so as to achieve accurate service provision.

4 Case Study and Comparison

In this section, we illustrate the specific process of proposed service portrait construction approach through a ride-hailing case and compare our approach qualitatively with existing work.

4.1 Case Study

Through data sensing and monitoring technology, platform or service governors can easily get demand and service capacity data. Due to the lack of suitable public datasets, we simulate the data based on a ride-hailing service dataset provided by Didi Chuxing[1], trying to illustrate the construction process of proposed approach under the premise of conforming to real situation.

The dataset provides trajectory data of ride-hailing service in Shenzhen for the whole month of August 2020. In this experiment, we did the following processing on the dataset:

- Since we mainly focus on data fields that can reflect spatio-temporal characteristics of demand and service capacity, only part of the data fields are kept. After being processed, data fields used in this paper can be expressed as (*driver_id*, *order_start_time*, *order_end_time*, *order_start_link_id*, *order_end_link_id*). In addition, road network topology information provided by the dataset is also used.
- It is found that data file size in the first few days was significantly less than data file size in later days. Thereby, only data after August 5th are used.
- For temporal dimension, the dataset uses 5 min as a time slice to record order start time. In order to portray service spatio-temporal characteristics from a macro perspective, we use one hour as a time unit to discretize original data. For spatial dimension, the dataset only provides road link ids and road network topology information, the actual geographic information cannot be obtained. So when determining region unit, we randomly selected 5 regions, each containing 50,000 road links, and the regions do not overlap with each other.
- The dataset records the transaction order, which reflects part of demand and service capacity, so the basic idea of simulating data is to supplement unrecorded demand and service capacity. The total demand can be divided into satisfied and unsatisfied parts, the former is reflected in completed orders, which is given by the dataset, and the latter is mainly reflected in canceled orders. Therefore, we supplement the demand data by referring to the order cancellation rate given by Wang et al. [13]. Similarly, service capacity can be divided into two parts, namely, utilized and unutilized parts. We assume that when a driver completes an order at time i and region j, and does not receive an order at time $i+1$ and region j, there is a chance that he waits to receive the order, which means he may continue to provide service at time $i+1$ and region j. In this case, suppose there is a probability that the driver's service capacity is not utilized at time $i+1$ and region j, then we can supplement service capacity data.
- It can be observed that service capacity of different drivers at the same time is basically the same, and the factors which affect service capacity of a driver are mainly when and in what region he provides services, which is conform with the real situation. Therefore, we use the average order amount of drivers

[1] https://gaia.didichuxing.com.

as individual service capacity of one driver, so as to calculate service capacity of driver role.

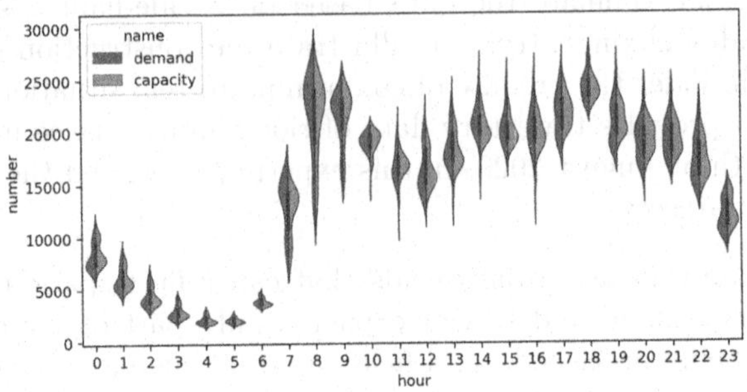

Fig. 2. Temporal distribution of demand and service capacity.

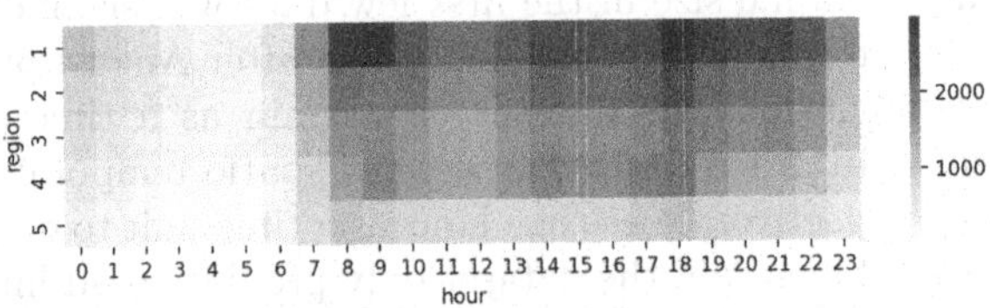

Fig. 3. Spatio-temporal distribution of demand.

By using the simulated demand and service capacity data, we can construct temporal distribution models and spatio-temporal distribution models. In temporal dimension, it can be seen from Fig. 2 that the overall condition of demand and service capacity distribution is basically consistent, with a little gap, but the service require more precise configuration. In addition, it can also be seen that ride-hailing service currently has two periods of peak, 8:00–9:00 and 18:00–19:00, respectively, and the low ebb is 4:00–5:00. In spatio-temporal dimension, for the sake of clarity, only the means of demand and service capacity are shown (see Fig. 3 and Fig. 4). Though demand and service capacity distributions of 5 regions are different, the mainly trend of spatio-temporal distribution is basically consistent with the trend of temporal distribution shown in Fig. 2, which is conform to real situation. Of the 5 regions, region 1 may be so-called hot region, and region 5 may be cold region.

As for gap condition between supply and demand, Fig. 5 indicates that current service has both oversupply and undersupply condition in different time and space units. Overall, some regions (such as region 1) are undersupplied, and some regions (such as region 2) are oversupplied. In temporal dimension, when threshold λ and max size of weak points n are set to 0.7 and 3, weak point analysis result is given in Table 1. In spatio-temporal dimension, when the parameters are set to 0.7 and 5, weak points are listed in Table 2.

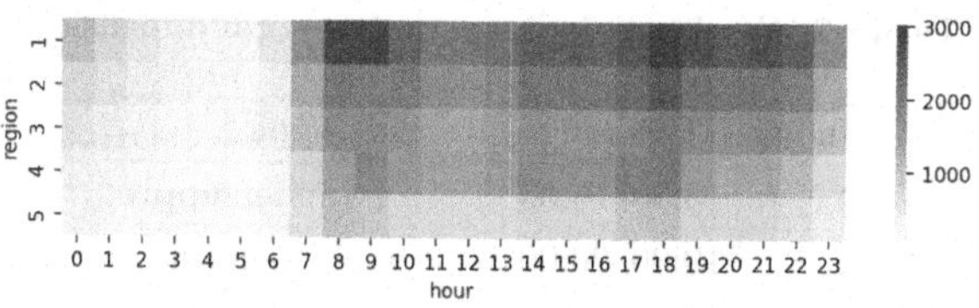

Fig. 4. Spatio-temporal distribution of service capacity.

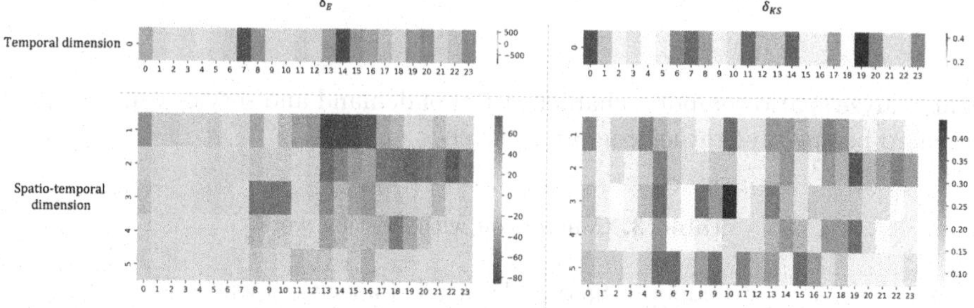

Fig. 5. Gap between supply and demand.

Table 1. Weak points in temporal dimension.

Index	Time range	Type
1	14:00–15:00	undersupply
2	7:00–8:00	undersupply
3	19:00–20:00	oversupply

The above contents together constitute service portrait of the online car-hailing service case, through which we can observe the spatio-temporal distribution characteristics of both supply and demand sides and the matching condition. The weak points in the temporal dimension and spatio-temporal dimension respectively reveal the overall and partial deficiencies of the current service. Platform or service governors can combine the results to make comprehensive decisions, so as to achieve precise services.

4.2 Qualitative Comparison with Previous Work

In Sect. 2, we have introduced some related work, and Table 3 shows qualitative comparison between some of them and our approach. The comparison is carried out in terms of whether the temporal characteristics, spatial characteristics, demands, capacity information of the service are described. Different research questions focus differently, leading to different characterizations of the same concept. Out of this consideration, research tasks are also given in the table for comparison. It can be seen that the approach proposed in this paper can describe

Table 2. Weak points in spatio-temporal dimension.

Index	Time range	Region	Type
1	13:00–14:00	1	undersupply
2	19:00–20:00	2	oversupply
3	14:00–15:00	1	undersupply
4	10:00–11:00	3	oversupply
5	22:00–23:00	2	oversupply

and analyze spatio-temporal characteristics of demand and service capacity from a macro perspective rather comprehensively.

Table 3. Comparison with existing work.

	Temporal	Spatial	Demand	Capacity	Tasks
Asl and Ulsoy [1]	+	–	+	+	Propose an approach to optimal capacity management based on demand
Zhang et al. [16]	+	–	+	+	Adjust both supply and price to meet customers demands
Ke et al. [6]	+	+	+	+	Predict the supply-demand gap
Cui et al. [2]	–	–	+	+	Match demanders and suppliers
This paper	+	+	+	+	Portray and analyze spatio-temporal characteristics of demand and service capacity

5 Conclusion and Future Work

With the development of technologies and the widespread idea of servitization, people are paying more and more attention to how to provide services precisely. As far as we know, no research has yet studied service supply and demand matching condition in spatio-temporal dimension from a mid-to-long term perspective. To fill the gap in existing research, we propose a service portrait construction approach based on demand-service capacity spatio-temporal matching. The approach portrays spatio-temporal characteristics of demand and service capacity, analyzes supply-demand matching condition, and provides evidence for service optimization. The specific process of proposed service portrait construction approach is illustrated through a ride-hailing service case. In future, we plan to conduct subsequent research on service optimization based on weak points between demand and supply, so as to achieve a closed loop from analysis to optimization, which can help the platform or service governors provide precise services.

Acknowledgements. The research in this paper is partially supported by the National Key Research and Development Program of China (No.2021YFF0900900).

References

1. Asl, F.M., Ulsoy, A.G.: Optimal capacity management with stochastic market demand and imperfect information. In: ASME International Mechanical Engineering Congress and Exposition, vol. 37130, pp. 177–184 (2003)
2. Cui, M., Yu, H., Zhang, H., Chen, X.: A novel matching method for supply and demand based on three-way decisions. In: 2019 IEEE 14th International Conference on Intelligent Systems and Knowledge Engineering (ISKE), pp. 82–89. IEEE (2019)
3. Davies, G., Chun, R., da Silva, R.V., Roper, S.: A corporate character scale to assess employee and customer views of organization reputation. Corp. Reput. Rev. **7**(2), 125–146 (2004)
4. Gu, H., Wang, J., Wang, Z., Zhuang, B., Su, F.: Modeling of user portrait through social media. In: 2018 IEEE International Conference on Multimedia and Expo (ICME), pp. 1–6. IEEE (2018)
5. Hongjuan, L., Yan, Z., Jiangong, W., Zhi, G.: A comprehensive evaluation model for the matching degree between supply and demand of the computing power network services. In: 2022 IEEE 2nd International Conference on Electronic Technology, Communication and Information (ICETCI), pp. 270–274. IEEE (2022)
6. Ke, J., et al.: Hexagon-based convolutional neural network for supply-demand forecasting of ride-sourcing services. IEEE Trans. Intell. Transp. Syst. **20**(11), 4160–4173 (2018)
7. Lee, W.J., Oh, K.J., Lim, C.G., Choi, H.J.: User profile extraction from twitter for personalized news recommendation. In: 16th International Conference on Advanced Communication Technology, pp. 779–783. IEEE (2014)
8. Massey, F.J., Jr.: The Kolmogorov-Smirnov test for goodness of fit. J. Am. Stat. Assoc. **46**(253), 68–78 (1951)
9. Schroth, C., Janner, T.: Web 2.0 and SOA: converging concepts enabling the internet of services. IT Prof. **9**(3), 36–41 (2007)
10. Spohrer, J., Maglio, P.P., Bailey, J., Gruhl, D.: Steps toward a science of service systems. Computer **40**(1), 71–77 (2007)
11. Wang, J., et al.: Semi-automatic service value network modeling approach based on external public data. Softw. Syst. Model. **22**, 1–25 (2022)
12. Wang, N., Qi, X., Gao, C., Huang, R., Wang, X.: Vehicle allocation model and its optimization based on supply-demand resources analysis. In: 2021 4th International Symposium on Traffic Transportation and Civil Architecture (ISTTCA), pp. 270–273. IEEE (2021)
13. Wang, X., Liu, W., Yang, H., Wang, D., Ye, J.: Customer behavioural modelling of order cancellation in coupled ride-sourcing and taxi markets. Transp. Res. Procedia **38**, 853–873 (2019)

14. Wu, Z., Yin, J., Deng, S., Wu, J., Li, Y., Chen, L.: Modern service industry and crossover services: development and trends in China. IEEE Trans. Serv. Comput. **9**(5), 664–671 (2015)
15. Xu, X., Sheng, Q.Z., Zhang, L.J., Fan, Y., Dustdar, S.: From big data to big service. Computer **48**(07), 80–83 (2015)
16. Zhang, Q., Zhu, Q., Boutaba, R.: Dynamic resource allocation for spot markets in cloud computing environments. In: 2011 Fourth IEEE International Conference on Utility and Cloud Computing, pp. 178–185. IEEE (2011)
17. Zhang, X., Yu, Z., Li, C., Zhai, R., Ma, H., Liu, L.: Construction of portrait system of listed companies based on big data. In: 2019 6th International Conference on Information Science and Control Engineering (ICISCE), pp. 210–214. IEEE (2019)

A Simulation Model for Proactive Services: A Case Study on Evading Dangerous Areas for LNG Ships

Yongpeng Shi[1,2], Guiling Wang[1,2](✉), Jiayu Zhang[1,2], Zhenyu Li[1], and Jian Yu[3]

[1] School of Information Science and Technology, North China University of Technology, Beijing 100144, China
zjy_9826@163.com, lizhenyu011923@163.com

[2] Beijing Key Laboratory on Integration and Analysis of Large-scale Stream Data, Beijing, China

[3] Department of Computer Science, Auckland University of Technology, Auckland, New Zealand
jian.yu@aut.ac.nz

Abstract. Proactive service is a kind of service that can be automatically provided based on logical judgment without human intervention. The traditional approach to evaluating proactive services involves conducting quantitative analyses through public datasets. However, this method can only evaluate the effectiveness of the specific algorithms and has limitations in evaluating the effectiveness of real-world applications as a whole. Determining a more appropriate evaluation approach for proactive services is a challenging problem. To address this issue, this paper proposes a method to evaluate the effectiveness of proactive services from a simulation perspective with a case of LNG (Liquefied Natural Gas) shipping as an example. Using the multi-agent simulation method, we design and implement a simulation model for LNG ships navigating at sea while avoiding dangerous areas by AnyLogic, which is capable of interacting with the deep learning model for predicting ships' locations. Our simulation model also defines a set of metrics for evaluating the effectiveness of proactive services in the application case. We present a simulation demonstration on evading dangerous areas for LNG ships and conduct simulation experiments. The experimental results show that the simulation model can serve as an effective evaluation method for proactive services. Additionally, the simulation model can also be used to analyze differences in the application effects of proactive services implemented under different prediction algorithms.

Keywords: Proactive Services · Prediction · Multi-Agent Simulation · AnyLogic

1 Introduction

Proactive services typically refers to a type of service that predicts future needs based on data such as object entity behavior, environment, and demand, and

Z. Wang et al. (Eds.): ICSS 2023, CCIS 1844, pp. 429–443, 2023.
https://doi.org/10.1007/978-981-99-4402-6_31

proactively provides personalized services [2]. In recent years, many new methods for proactive services have emerged, and using deep learning models for prediction has become a mainstream approach. However, evaluating the performance of proactive services based on deep learning models poses a challenge. The traditional approach to proactive service evaluation is to use public datasets for quantitative analysis, but this approach can only evaluate the prediction algorithm modules in proactive services, which are actually composed of several different functional modules. Therefore, there are significant limitations in using public datasets for evaluation. For example, the simple proactive service uses later in this paper consists of modules such as the prediction algorithm and the area avoidance service, whose performance is not only affected by the prediction algorithm but is also limited by the area avoidance service. Therefore, it cannot be fully evaluated under this proactive service using the public datasets approach. Simulation technology can simulate various elements in the real world and thus has the potential to be a technical tool for a comprehensive evaluation of the proactive services.

This paper utilizes multi-agent simulation technology [5,7] to create a simulation model that evaluates the actual impact of proactive services. The study focuses on the practical application of proactive services in ensuring the safe navigation and transportation of LNG ships at sea [12]. The sea navigation of LNG ships is simulated using multi-agent simulation technology, and proactive services are incorporated into the simulation environment. The effectiveness of proactive services is determined by analyzing the navigation situation of LNG ships in the simulation environment. The LNG ships and sea navigation simulation software are designed and constructed using AnyLogic simulation software [3]. The main work and contributions of this paper are reflected in the following aspects:

1) A new perspective for evaluating proactive services is proposed, and the application effect of proactive services is evaluated using a simulation model based on the multi-agent simulation modeling method.
2) A simulation model of LNG ship navigation at sea has been designed and implemented using the multi-agent simulation modeling method. The model is capable of interacting with the deep learning model for data.

The remaining part of this paper is organized into several sections. Section 2 discusses related work. Section 3 provides a problem description. Section 4 introduces the simulation model design. Section 5 introduces the experimental content of the simulation model, and Sect. 6 concludes our work.

2 Related Work

Proactive services are data services that can be automatically provided based on logical judgment without human intervention. Yanbo Han et al. [2] advocated a decentralized and service-based approach to dynamically correlating the sensor data and proactively generating higher-level events between sensors and applications. Ohbyung Kwon et al. [11] proposed that depends mainly on the concept of proactive adaptation by the use of reinforcement learning to achieve an autonomous dynamic behavior of web service composition. Hongbing Wang et al. [15] adopted motifs-based Dynamic Bayesian Networks (or m_DBNs) model to perform one-step-ahead time series prediction, and proposed a multi-steps trajectories DBNs (or multi_DBNs) model to further revise the future reliability prediction and a proactive adaption strategy was achieved based on the reliability prediction results. However, proactive services require a specific evaluation and verification process from design implementation to specific application, and current research in this area is still lacking. Therefore, this paper utilizes simulations to improve the evaluation and verification process of proactive services.

With the continuous development and application of science and technology, simulation has become one of the important tools for evaluating and optimizing various systems. Simulations for different tasks are mainly categorized into the following: continuous simulation, discrete event simulation, agent simulation, and hybrid simulation.

1) Continuous simulation is usually used to model continuous physical systems, such as fluid dynamics, thermodynamics, and mechanical systems. E Nkiaka et al. [13] developed an alternative simple continuous simulation model (COSIMAT) using the SIMULINK^{TM} module in MATLAB^{TM} as a means of solving the issue of computational time associated with the detailed models. To perform the continuous simulation of CO2/H2 separation by hydrate-based gas separation (HBGS) process, Li Luling et al. [8] proposed a new multi-phase isothermal flash calculation method.
2) In discrete event simulation, the state of the simulated system changes only at discrete points in time. Giuliana Rotunno et al. [14] proposed a Discrete Event Simulation (DES) model for improving the efficiency of ports with a particular attention to the environmental impact on the surrounding human settlements. Li Yang et al. [9] proposed a discrete numerical method to simulate the vibratory roller compaction of field rockfills.
3) In agent simulation, the system is decomposed into multiple agents, and each agent has its own behavior and decision rules. Jooyoung Kim et al. [7] used multi-agent transportation simulation (MATSim) to find effective evacuation plans at Haeundae Beach, Busan, Korea. Wang Shuai et al. [16] used a digital twin simulation model realized by multi-agent simulation technology to analyze the application in the background of maintenance resource prediction. Inspired by the social behaviors in the biological world, Jiao Li et al. [5] proposed a novel multi-agent coverage path planning algorithm. Hübner M et al. [4] simulated the urban traffic system through multi-agent simulation. Liu J et al. [10] proposed a model to study the ship traffic in a port area by combining cellular automaton (CA) and multi-agent methods.
4) Hybrid simulation combines different simulation methods, such as continuous simulation and discrete event simulation. Ronald Ekyalimpa et al. [1] described a discrete-continuous simulation approach for studying train and pedestrian traffic interactions for purposes of decision support. Karanjkar Neha et al. [6] proposed a framework for mixed discrete-continuous simulations particularly targeted for Digital Twin applications.

3 Problem Description

3.1 Research Problem

Traditionally, proactive services are evaluated using public datasets for quantitative evaluation. However, since such method can generally only evaluate the effectiveness of the specific algorithms and the practical applications may differ from public datasets, the evaluation of proactive services should not be limited to them. The paper aims to explore how to evaluate proactive services from a simulation perspective. The simulation model is designed by taking the example of LNG ships avoiding dangerous areas, and we solve the following problems during the process of designing and implementing the simulation model:

1) How to use multi-agent simulation modeling method to design simulation scenarios for LNG ships avoiding dangerous areas?
2) How to design the evaluation indicators for evaluating proactive services in the simulation scene of LNG ship avoiding dangerous areas?
3) How to evaluate the proactive services in the simulation scene of LNG ship avoiding dangerous areas?

3.2 Basic Assumptions

The logical structure of the proactive services involved in this paper is shown in the Fig. 1.

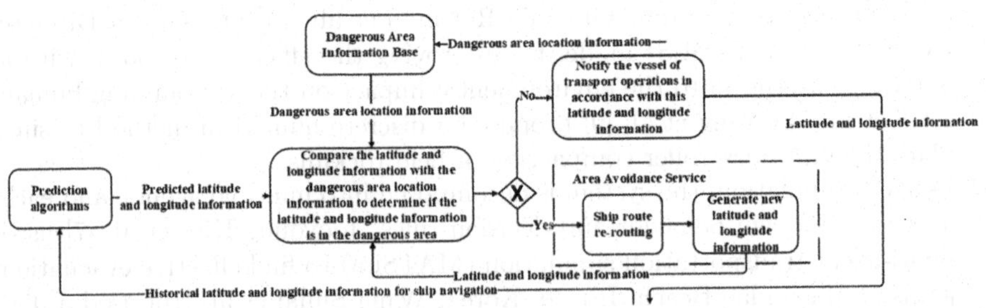

Fig. 1. The logical structure of the proactive services

To simplify the simulation process, the paper set the shape of the dangerous area as a circle with a certain radius in the simulation environment. Although this deviates from the actual shape of the area, it meets the simulation needs. Instead of using a physical motion model of the LNG ship, the paper use a simplified model of uniform velocity, uniform acceleration, or uniform deceleration motion. Moreover, the paper make the navigation time of the LNG ship consistent with the simulation system time in the simulation environment. To ensure the smooth progress of the research, the paper have also set some assumptions for evaluating the proactive services.

4 Simulation Model Design

4.1 Agent Design

This paper focuses on LNG ship navigation and uses an agent model to simulate various elements of the real world. The agent is an important part of the simulation model, and each agent can be given independent parameters and logic. This paper mainly designs agents such as navigation route network, LNG ships, and dangerous areas.

1) Navigation Route Network. The first agent discussed in this paper is the navigation route network, which serves the main function of visual modeling. To construct the navigation route network, we use a GIS map as the foundation and real ship navigation route data to generate the network on the map. In order to ensure the adaptability of the navigation route network, we import and generate external longitude and latitude data and make necessary adjustments based on external data changes. Tables 1 and 2 present the original data of the navigation route network. After merging the data in Table 1 and Table 2, the navigation route network can be generated on the GIS map, as shown in Fig. 2.

Table 1. Node data

Node ID	GIS Latitude	GIS Longitude
4101	121.437045	40.06048029
6	117.7799294	38.98244684
...	...	...

Table 2. Section data

Section ID	Start Node ID	Destination Node ID
1	6	1824
10	802	1894
...	...	...

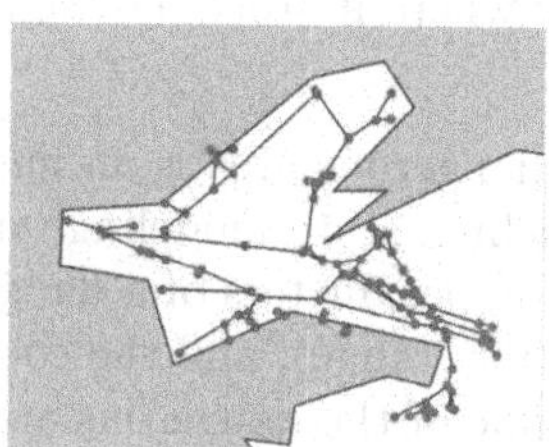

Fig. 2. Route network in Bohai area

2) LNG Ships. This study focuses on conducting visual modeling and state modeling design for LNG ships. The motion state of an LNG ship can be set to three different states: uniform speed, uniform acceleration, and uniform deceleration. The state transition is based on the actual sailing situation. The primary parameters of an LNG ship include serial number, motion state, motion speed, and position information. The ship navigation trajectory data is derived from real ship navigation data in the Bohai Sea area. After processing, the data undergoes motion simulation in the simulation model. Specifically, the paper model the trajectory of an LNG ship based on the data presented in Table 3.

Table 3. Trajectory data

Section ID	Timestamp	GIS Longitude	GIS Latitude	Direction	Ship ID
95	1521564011	122.7037287	36.97140133	4.3943	0
38	1521570324	122.4811517	36.73121	4.0428	0
...	...	...	...	...	...

The state transition of the LNG ship agent is shown in Fig. 3. The ship state model divides the state into three parts: the initial state, motion state, and end state. During the initial state, the ship initializes the trajectory navigation data, which includes the starting point of the ship and the coordinate positions of the destination point at each moment.The motion state consists of three substates: uniform motion state, uniform acceleration motion state, and uniform deceleration motion state. These sub-states are activated by proactive services and converted based on certain conditions. When the ship enters a dangerous area, it will accelerate uniformly until it reaches the maximum speed threshold and then continue to travel at this speed. When the ship leaves the dangerous area, it will decelerate uniformly until it reaches the initial constant speed value and then continue to travel at this speed. Later in this paper, this will show the effect of proactive services. After the initial state, the ship enters the uniform motion state based on the coordinate information and continues to move through the loop structure until it reaches the last coordinate point in the trajectory data. Then, it enters the end state where it stops moving.

3) Dangerous Area. The dangerous area is an important part of this system, mainly involving visual modeling, state modeling, and a database of dangerous area location information. The parameters of a dangerous area include the dangerous area number, radius (i.e., range), and the coordinates of its center point. In this system, the visual shape of the dangerous area is defined as a circle, and its radius is a specified value. The state model of the dangerous area, which is dynamically generated, is shown in Fig. 4.

The state model is divided into two parts: the initial state and dynamic generation. During the initial state, the system acquires information on all position coordinate points within the navigation route network. In the dynamic generation part, a coordinate point from the navigation route network is selected, and the center of the dangerous area is placed on that coordinate point. It should be noted that the center coordinate point of the dangerous area cannot coincide with the center coordinate points of other dangerous areas, and no LNG ships should be within the scope of the dangerous area. A timing loop structure

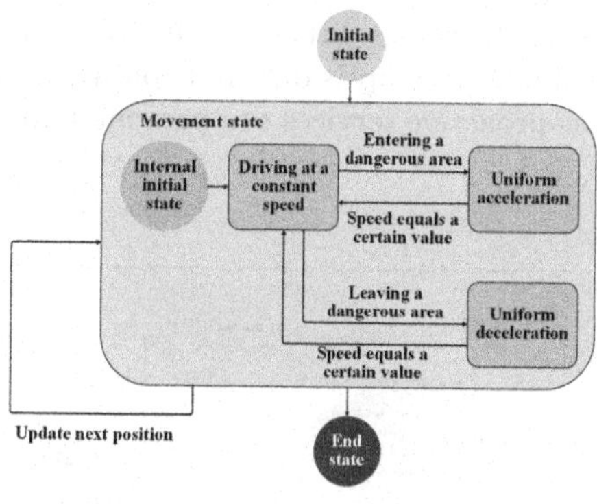

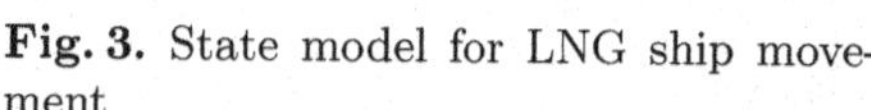

Fig. 3. State model for LNG ship movement

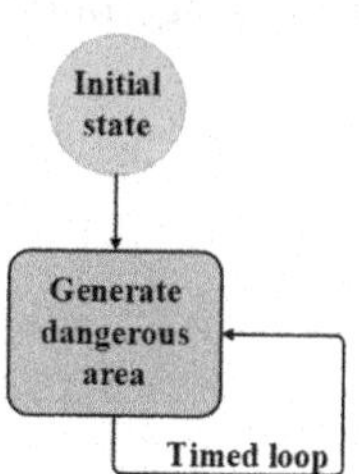

Fig. 4. State model of dynamically generated dangerous areas.

should be set up to periodically update the position of the dangerous area in the navigation route network and store it in the dangerous area position information database.

The dangerous area location information database stores data in a format that includes the ID, time, center point coordinates (latitude and longitude), and radius. This data is used in real-time to determine whether the current position of the ship is within the range of a dangerous area. The data format is shown in Table 4.

Table 4. Dangerous area location information database data format

ID	Time	Center Point Latitude	Center Point Longitude	Radius
95	1521564011	36.97140133	122.7037287	4000
121	1521564112	35.9714122	123.703227	4000
...	...	...	...	...

4) Proactive Services Carrier. The paper implement proactive services in the form of agents and implement its functionality through the agent's events. Figure 5 shows the principle of implementation in the proactive services event. The prediction module is the core component of the proactive services. It performs predictions by calculating the real-time historical coordinate point information of the ship and outputs the predicted results. The location information judgment module determines whether to activate the area avoidance service by evaluating whether the predicted coordinate point is within the dangerous area's range. Within the area avoidance service, a new position coordinate point is generated using the predicted position coordinate point as the center and a specific value as the radius. This new position is then evaluated by the position information judgment module. If the new position coordinate point is within the dangerous area's range, the process repeats until a safe position coordinate point is found. Once a safe coordinate point is found, the ship is directed towards it. By implementing this series of processes, the proactive services can prevent ships from entering dangerous areas.

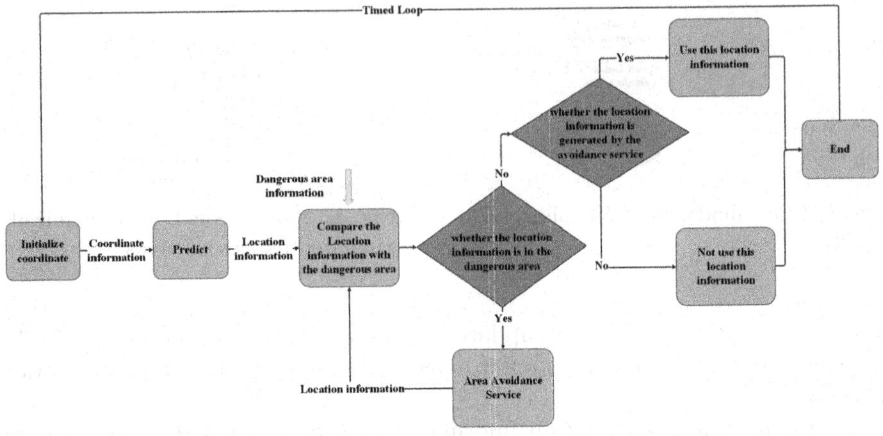

Fig. 5. The principle of implementing proactive services

The data interaction with the prediction model is the key to realize proactive services in the simulation, and this paper uses two timed loop events to complete the data interaction process, as shown in Fig. 6. A data transfer window is constructed in Event 1 for data interaction between the simulation and the prediction model. The window is a $(n, 2)$ data structure, and the size of n is the length of the prediction model input data. Event 1 will complete the following actions at each model time unit: Assuming the length of the data transfer window is n, and all positions have stored the coordinate point information, if there is a need to add a new coordinate point information, the last n-1 data of the window will be moved forward one position, the nth position will be vacated, and the new coordinate point information will be added to the n position. Event 2 indicates that each model time unit sends the data transfer window to the prediction model and receives the results of the prediction model.

4.2 System Design

After establishing the simulation model, the paper load the ship navigation route network data in the Bohai Sea region onto the GIS map and displayed it in the form of points and lines. Based on the user input of the number of LNG ships and the number of dangerous areas, the corresponding ships and dangerous areas are generated on the GIS map. During the ship's movement, it will send real-time latitude and longitude data of its coordinate point to the prediction module of the proactive services. The prediction module will use historical navigation

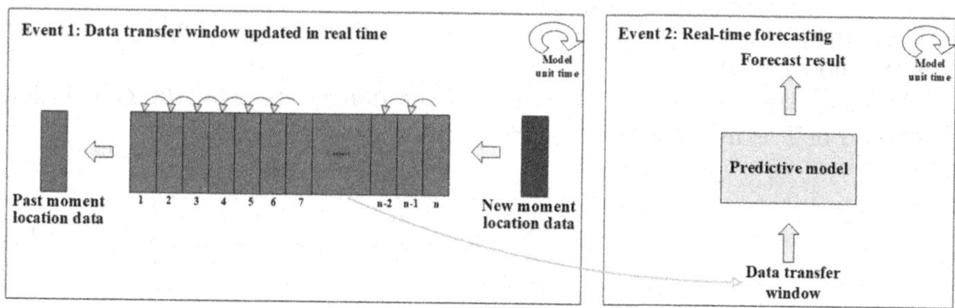

Fig. 6. Data interaction process

data to predict the latitude and longitude position information that the ship will reach in the next moment. Then, the location information judging module will combine the predicted location information with the information in the dangerous area location information database, determine whether the predicted location is within the coverage of the current dangerous area, and decide whether to initiate the area avoidance service. When the location information judging module determines that the predicted location point is within the dangerous range, the area avoidance service will be initiated. The logical structure design of the LNG ship navigation simulation system is shown in Fig. 7.

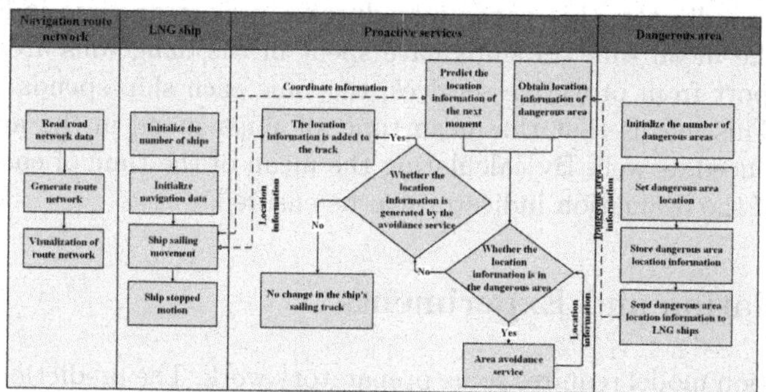

Fig. 7. Design of the overall system

4.3 Evaluation Indicators Design

Indicators. The paper aims to evaluate the effect of proactive services through the simulation environment. Since the proactive services used in this paper will be affected by the trajectory of the ship's navigation, the paper design the following evaluation indicators:

1) The sailing time of each ship is *times* in the dangerous area, and its time unit is the model time unit.
2) The mean time T that all ships sail in the dangerous area, the calculation method of T is as follows:

$$T = \sum_{i=0}^{n} times_i \Big/ n \tag{1}$$

where n is the number of ships in the simulation scene.

Effectiveness Discussion. 1) Discussion of the reasonableness of the sailing time in the dangerous area of each ship: When there is no support from active service, the ship will not judge the dangerous area in navigation, then the ship will definitely travel in the dangerous area. After the proactive services provide support to the ship, the proactive services will start the area avoidance service to avoid the dangerous area. Theoretically, the ship with proactive services support will spend significantly less time navigating in the dangerous area than the ship without proactive services support, and this is verified in the subsequent experimental part. 2) Discussion of the reasonableness of the mean time that all ships sail in the dangerous area: The previous indicator is limited by how well the avoidance service is implemented and the accuracy of the predictions for different ships' routes and proactive services. To overcome the limitations of the previous indicator, this paper introduces a new mean time indicator that calculates the mean time all ships have spent in the dangerous area. As ships receive support from proactive services, the time each ship spends in the area decreases. This means that the mean time all ships spend in the area is theoretically reduced as well. By calculating the mean of the time of each ship, the reliability of the evaluation indicator can be ensured.

5 Simulation and Experiments

The simulation model requires some preparatory work. The prediction algorithm in proactive services used in this paper is based on a deep learning model, so the GRU and Bi-GRU models were pre-trained as prediction models, and the prediction models are evaluated to ensure that they could satisfy the subsequent simulation experiments. Next, the deep learning model should be embedded into the simulation to perform experimental operations. During the simulation model's run, the data changes should be observed and analyzed.

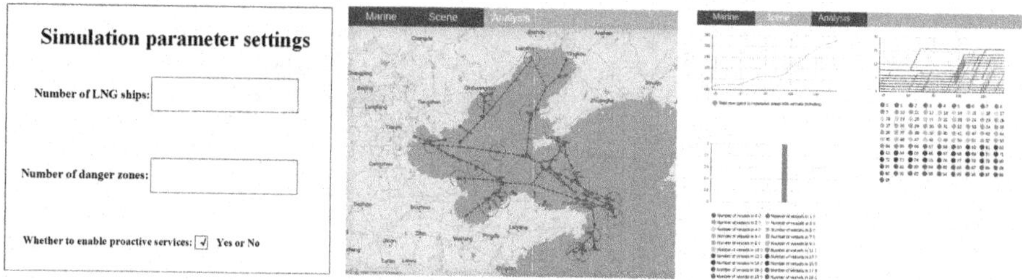

Fig. 8. Interface for setting simulation parameters

Fig. 9. Interface for demonstrating LNG ship navigation

Fig. 10. Interface for analyzing the data on the effects of proactive services

5.1 Simulation Interface

In Fig. 8, users of the simulation model can customize some parameters in the simulation scene, such as the number of ships. The demonstration interface is shown in Fig. 9. In this interface, the user can observe the navigation situation of the ship and the response to the dangerous area. The analysis interface is shown in Fig. 10. In this interface, the data changes of the designed evaluation indicators are output statistically.

5.2 Predictive Model Experiments

To fulfill the business logic of the proactive services utilized in this paper, it is necessary to train a neural network model for predicting location information. The recurrent neural network models GRU and Bi-GRU are utilized as the prediction algorithms for the proactive services in this paper.

Experimental Data. The data samples used for training the neural network model and subsequent prediction are shown in Table 5. The data comes from Table 3.

Table 5. Data sample

Timestamp	GIS Longitude	GIS Latitude
1521564011	122.7037287	36.97140133
1521570324	122.4811517	36.73121
...	...	...

Model Evaluation. To evaluate the performance of the model, the paper use the comparison between the predicted and true values during the testing phase, as evaluation indicators. The results are shown in Fig. 11a, 11b.

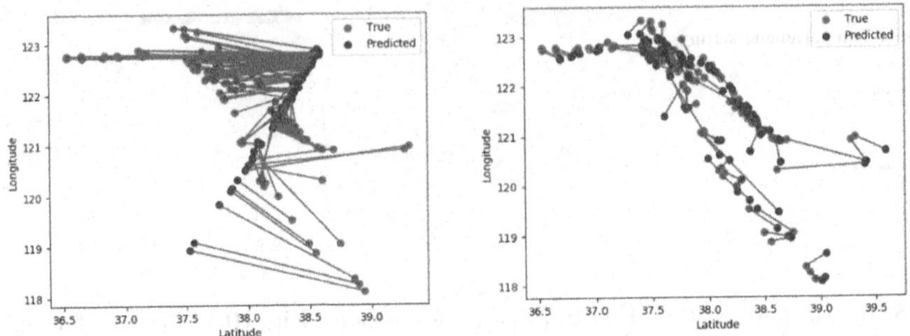

(a) Comparison between predicted and true values of a GRU model

(b) Comparison between predicted and true values of a Bi-GRU model

Fig. 11. Testing the effects of the prediction model

The results indicate that the prediction performance of the Bi-GRU model is better than that of the GRU model. Both models can satisfy the basic requirements for the next simulation model experiment.

5.3 Simulation Model Experiment

Experiment Setup. In order to carry out the simulation experiment smoothly, we need some prerequisite parameter configurations. Set the running unit time of the simulation model as minutes. The basic parameters of the simulation operation are shown in Table 6.

Table 6. Simulation run parameter configuration

Parameter	Configuration
Simulation Model Runtime	200 min
Proactive services	not enabled, by GRU, by Bi-GRU
Number of LNG ships	100 pieces
Uniform sailing speed of LNG ship	10 m/s
Acceleration of LNG ship	0.003 m/s
Minimum Speed Threshold	6 m/s
Speed Threshold	16 m/s
Number of dangerous areas	20
Dangerous area location update time	1 h
Dangerous area radius	4000 m

Analysis of Results. Figure 12 displays the mean time that ships spend in dangerous areas. Based on the results shown in Fig. 12a, 12b, and 12c, it can be observed that the existence time of ships in dangerous areas is significantly reduced after enabling proactive services. Furthermore, the prediction algorithm with high accuracy has the least existence time of ships in dangerous areas under proactive services, indicating that the actual effect of the proactive services is related to the performance of the prediction algorithm. Figure 13 illustrates the sailing time of each ship in the dangerous area. It can be observed that the line segment in Fig. 13a is denser than that in Fig. 13b and 13c. However, some ships have similar sailing times in Fig. 13a and 13b, indicating that the effect of proactive services on each ship may be similar to that without proactive services on predictive models with poor predictive performance. On the other hand, the effect in Fig. 13c is significantly better than that in Fig. 13a and 13b, indicating that proactive services can provide better service for each ship on predictive models with good predictive performance.

In summary, the results show that proactive services can provide a certain degree of safety assurance for ships during navigation, and through the simulation results, it can be analyzed that in the prediction model with higher prediction performance, the safety guarantee provided by the proactive services is better.

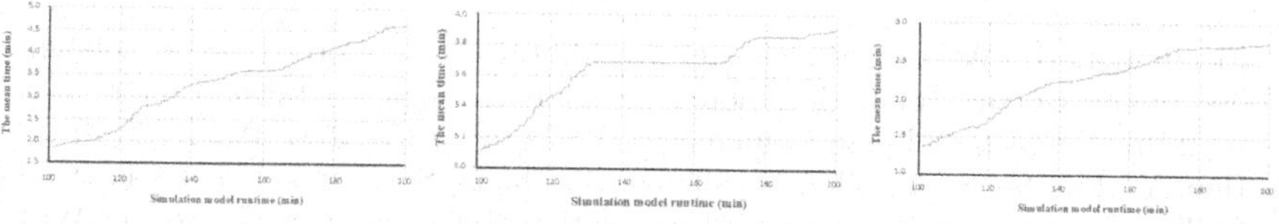

(a) Proactive services not enabled (b) Proactive services based on GRU (c) Proactive services based on Bi-GRU

Fig. 12. The mean time ships are present in the dangerous area

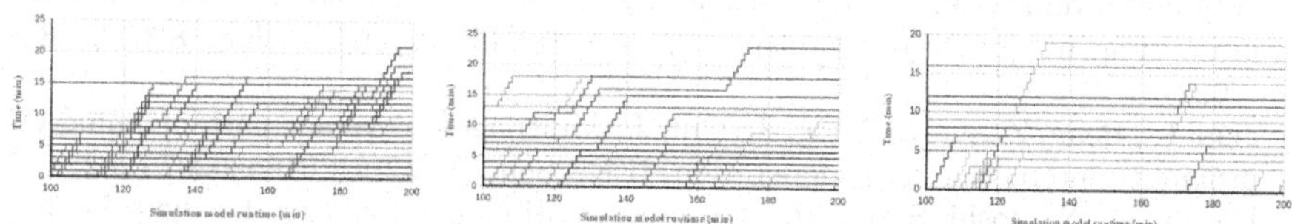

(a) Proactive services not enabled (b) Proactive services based on GRU (c) Proactive services based on Bi-GRU

Fig. 13. The time of each ship's sailing in the dangerous area

6 Conclusion

Traditional methods for assessing proactive services rely on quantitative assessments of publicly available datasets, but this approach has its limitations. To address this issue, the paper propose using simulation methods to verify the effectiveness of proactive services. To demonstrate the feasibility of this approach, the paper design a simulation model based on the scene of avoiding dangerous areas for LNG ships at sea, using the multi-agent simulation modeling method. To implement proactive services in the simulation, the paper also establish data interactions with deep learning models. The simulation experiment demonstrate that proactive services are effective in the avoidance scenarios of LNG ships, and also reveal the impact of different deep learning models on the application of proactive services. In the future, we plan to explore more complex service logic within the simulation model in order to further investigate the effectiveness of proactive services.

Acknowledgements. This work is supported by the Key Program of National Natural Science Foundation of China (No.61832004) and International Cooperation and Exchange Program of National Natural Science Foundation of China (No.62061136006).

References

1. Ekyalimpa, R., Werner, M., Hague, S., AbouRizk, S., Porter, N.: A combined discrete-continuous simulation model for analyzing train-pedestrian interactions. In: 2016 Winter Simulation Conference (WSC), pp. 1583–1594. IEEE (2016)
2. Han, Y., Liu, C., Su, S., Zhu, M., Zhang, Z., Zhang, S.: A proactive service model facilitating stream data fusion and correlation. Int. J. Web Serv. Res. (IJWSR) **14**(3), 1–16 (2017)
3. He, R., Zhao, M., Xiang, W.: System Modeling and Simulation With Anylogic. Chemical Industry Press, Beijing (2020). (In Chinese)
4. Hübner, M., Feierle, A., Rettenmaier, M., Bengler, K.: External communication of automated vehicles in mixed traffic: addressing the right human interaction partner in multi-agent simulation. Transport. Res. F: Traffic Psychol. Behav. **87**, 365–378 (2022)
5. Jiao, L., Peng, Z., Xi, L., Ding, S., Cui, J.: Multi-agent coverage path planning via proximity interaction and cooperation. IEEE Sens. J. **22**(6), 6196–6207 (2022)
6. Karanjkar, N., Joshi, S.M.: Mixed discrete-continuous simulation for digital twins. In: SIMULTECH, pp. 422–429 (2021)
7. Kim, J., Lee, S., Lee, S.: An evacuation route choice model based on multi-agent simulation in order to prepare tsunami disasters. Transportmetrica B: Transp. Dyn. **5**(4), 385–401 (2017)
8. Li, L., Fan, S., Yang, G., Chen, Q., Zhao, J., Wei, N., Meng, W., Fan, J., Yang, H.: Continuous simulation of the separation process of co2/h2 by forming hydrate. Chem. Eng. Sci. X **7**, 100067 (2020)
9. Li, Y., She, C.: Discrete simulation of vibratory roller compaction of field rockfills. Shock. Vib. **2021**, 1–15 (2021)
10. Liu, J., Liu, Y., Qi, L.: Modelling liquefied natural gas ship traffic in port based on cellular automaton and multi-agent system. J. Navig. **74**(3), 533–548 (2021)

11. Moustafa, A., Zhang, M.: Towards proactive web service adaptation. In: Ralyté, J., Franch, X., Brinkkemper, S., Wrycza, S. (eds.) CAiSE 2012. LNCS, vol. 7328, pp. 473–485. Springer, Heidelberg (2012). https://doi.org/10.1007/978-3-642-31095-9_31
12. Nie, X., Liu, Q., Li, G., Dai, R.: Current status and progress of LNG ship maritime transport safety research. China Saf. Sci. J. **27**(5), 87 (2017). (In Chinese)
13. Nkiaka, E., Shrestha, N., Leta, O., Bauwens, W.: Use of continuous simulation model (cosimat) as a complementary tool to model sewer systems: a case study on the Paruck collector, brussels, Belgium. Water Environ. J. **30**(3–4), 310–320 (2016)
14. Rotunno, G., Zupone, G.L., Fanti, M.P., Carnimeo, L.: Discrete event simulation as decision tool for sustainable development in smart cities. In: 2022 IEEE International Smart Cities Conference (ISC2), pp. 1–6. IEEE (2022)
15. Wang, H., Wang, L., Yu, Q., Zheng, Z., Yang, Z.: A proactive approach based on online reliability prediction for adaptation of service-oriented systems. J. Parallel Distrib. Comput. **114**, 70–84 (2018)
16. Wang, S., Wang, Y., Yue, S., Wang, J., Wang, Z., Zhao, J.: Digitally twinned simulation model of self-propelled artillery maintenance and support system. J. Artillery Launch Control, 1–6 (2022). (In Chinese)

AI-Inspired Service Optimization

A Data-Driven Study of Prediction Methods for Coronary Heart Disease

Xu He[1], Xindi Fan[2], Wanxi Zheng[2], Ziming Ti[3], Chunshan Li[1(✉)], Hua Zhang[1(✉)], and Xuequan Zhou[4(✉)]

[1] School of Computer Science and Technology, Harbin Institute of Technology, Weihai, China
lics@hit.edu.cn, zhanghuahit@126.com

[2] School of Science, Harbin Institute of Technology, Weihai, China

[3] School of Information Science and Engineering, Harbin Institute of Technology, Weihai, China

[4] Research Center of Intelligent Computing for Enterprises & Services, Harbin Institute of Technology, Harbin, China
zhouxq@hit.edu.cn

Abstract. Coronary heart disease (CHD) is a globally recognised, highly prevalent disease with a high risk of death and a low cure rate. The World Health Organization estimates that deaths from heart disease will reach 23 million by 2030. Therefore, it is imperative to find a fast and effective method for early diagnosis in order to provide patients with early intervention and improve the effectiveness of treatment. With the in-depth development of machine learning, the function of data analysis and prediction will efficiently help doctors to make a preliminary cluster for a large number of people and detect those who have a dangerous rate of developing coronary heart disease. In this paper, three data pre-processing methods, Smote, Borderline Smote and K-means Smote, were used to construct a risk prediction model for coronary heart disease (CHD) based on an unbalanced data set, combined with four algorithms, Logistic Regression, Random Forest, KNN and SVM. After analysing the data characteristics and adjusting the parameters, different combinations of these methods were compared and a better classification method was selected to predict CHD, achieving higher accuracy, precision, AUC and f1 score. Overall, through experiments, the random oversampling and SMOTE methods can effectively solve the data imbalance problem in most cases.Our final training accuracy could be up to 99%, and the testing accuracy could reach 93%.

Keywords: Random Forest · SVM · SMOTE · machine learning

1 Introduction

1.1 Coronary Heart Disease

Coronary artery disease [1] is a set of clinical symptoms caused by the occurrence of atherosclerosis, stenosis and other conditions in the coronary arteries that supply nutrients to the heart, leading to ischaemia and hypoxia in the heart.

Z. Wang et al. (Eds.): ICSS 2023, CCIS 1844, pp. 447–459, 2023.
https://doi.org/10.1007/978-981-99-4402-6_32

According to the World Health Organization (WHO) [2], cardiovascular disease is the leading cause of death worldwide, killing about 17.9 million people each year, or 31% of all deaths worldwide. Among these, coronary heart disease and stroke are the most common cardiovascular diseases, causing about 8.6 million and 6.1 million deaths, respectively, accounting for 48% and 34% of all cardiovascular disease deaths. China has the highest number of cardiovascular disease deaths, with about 4.2 million cardiovascular disease deaths in 2019, of which about 1.8 million were from coronary heart disease, accounting for 43% of total cardiovascular disease deaths.

Coronary heart disease [3], as a common cardiovascular disease, is generally not easily recognized by patients because the antecedent conditions are not obvious, and the diagnostic accuracy of routine electrocardiogram, haematological examination and nuclear myocardial imaging is not high, which is prone to misdiagnosis. However, the successful application of machine learning techniques to the early diagnosis of disease has significantly reduced the likelihood of misdiagnosis. It is believed that the potential value of this data can be realised by collecting information from patients' clinical visits and laboratory test reports, and then using machine learning to assist in the prevention and early diagnosis of diseases, which can further improve the accuracy of diagnosis and enable patients with coronary disease to enjoy a safe life and healthy body sooner.

1.2 Related Work

Zhu Yue et al. [4] built a prediction model based on Support Vector Model (SVM) and trained according to the data set of physical examination indicators of the southern population. This paper uses Particle Swarm Optimization (PSO) to optimize the parameters of Linear Inner Product Kernel SVM (Liner-SVM), Polynomial Inner Product Kernel SVM (Polynomial-SVM) and Gaussian Radial Basis Inner Product Kernel SVM (RBF-SVM), respectively, which improves the classification accuracy, specificity and sensitivity of SVM. The experimental results show that the optimisation effect of SVM based on radial basis function is the best. Then, the classification and prediction effects of SVM, PSO optimised SVM and BP neural network, linear discriminant analysis (LDA) and logistic regression are compared. The prediction results show that the optimised RBF SVM and Polynomial SVM are the best.

Chen Jianxin et al. [5] based on the 1069 cases of the four diagnostic information of traditional Chinese medicine and the corresponding syndrome differentiation data obtained from the clinical epidemiological survey of coronary disease, used the four data mining methods of Bayesian classification, neural network algorithm, support vector machine (SVM) and decision tree and a statistical method as the prediction model to study and predict them.

Li Jie et al. [6] identified the risk factors for the onset of coronary heart disease by using multiple logistic regression analysis after pre-processing and feature screening of the data of coronary heart disease published by Kaggle, and found that gender, age, average daily smoking, total cholesterol level, systolic blood pressure and blood glucose level were the main risk factors for the onset of coronary heart disease within 10 years.

Idris et al. [7] collected the dataset of acute coronary syndrome (ACS) provided by the National Cardiovascular Disease Database (NCVD) of Malaysia, screened the features using three different principle feature selection methods of embedded decision tree, chi-square test and recursive feature elimination, and used oversampling technique (SMOTE) to process the unbalanced dataset. The specially processed features were input into eight machine learning models for training and prediction, and the AUC value of the best machine learning model is higher than 90%.

Zeinab et al. [8] proposed a hybrid algorithm combining genetic algorithm and neural network based on coronary disease diagnosis dataset. The genetic algorithm gives better neural network weights, which can improve the performance of neural network and effectively improve the diagnosis efficiency of coronary disease.

Kritanawong et al. [9] collected research cases of prediction of coronary disease, stroke and arrhythmia using machine learning (ML) algorithm. The same data uses different algorithms to study the results with heterogeneity, but the idea of meta-statistical analysis improves the statistical efficiency of model prediction, enhances the effect estimation and improves the inconsistency of research results by comprehensively evaluating the results of different research problems with the same algorithm. ML algorithm shows good results, especially SVM and boosting algorithms have strong prediction ability in cardiovascular disease.

The development of machine learning is not long, from the beginning of symbolic machine learning [10] to the hot statistical machine learning in recent years, and then to the emergence of deep learning in recent years. It has a wide range of applications, such as large-scale data mining, computer vision, etc. In recent years, machine learning has been widely appreciated in the medical field, and has been used many times to mine relevant disease information in medical data to help doctors diagnose patients' conditions.

This paper proposes a data-driven coronary heart disease prediction method based on four machine learning algorithms, namely logistic regression, random forest, KNN and SVM. Different algorithms are used to deal with the problem of data imbalance. The effectiveness of the oversampling algorithm to improve the model is verified by experiments.

2 Data Preparation

2.1 Data Source and Dataset Selection

This paper selects a dataset called Cardiovascular Study Dataset on the Kaggle platform to build a predictive model from ongoing cardiovascular studies of residents of the town of Framingham, Massachusetts. The goal of the classification is to predict whether a patient is at risk of developing coronary heart disease (CHD) in the future over 10 years. The datasets provide information on patients. It contains more than 4,000 records and 15 attributes. Each attribute represents a potential risk factor. There are demographic, behavioural and medical risk factors that predict a person's likelihood of developing coronary heart disease within ten years. Some attributes in this dataset have missing data values, which reflects objective reality.

2.2 Data Preprocessing

There are missing values in the dataset; the effective sample size of 'TenYearCHD' in the dataset is 1 (coronary heart disease within ten years) accounts for 15% of the total number, and the effective sample size is small; there is an 'id' attribute that is not relevant to the prediction and is discarded when building the model. The cost of detection is too high, privacy, invalid data, information omissions, etc. will cause the missing attributes of the dataset in actual applications, so the processing of missing values is unavoidable. The method of interpolation filling (mode filling, median filling, mean filling) is used to deal with missing values. Specifically, the properties with missing values are: education, cigsPerDay, BPMeds, totChol, BMI, heartRate, glucose.

3 Methodology

3.1 Logistic Regression

Logistic regression (LR) [11] is a commonly used classification algorithm. It is based on linear regression fitted with a sigmoid logistic function. Logistic regression models are simple, interpretable, easy to implement and widely used.

Linear regression is the construction of a prediction function that represents the linear relationship between the input characteristic matrix and the labels. Linear regression uses the best-fitting straight line, the regression line, to establish a relationship between the dependent variable (Y) and one or more independent variables (X). Linear regression function:

$$y = \omega^T X + b \tag{1}$$

Through the function y, linear regression uses the input feature matrix X to output a set of continuous label values to predict various continuous variables; If the label is a discrete variable, especially a discrete variable that satisfies the 0–1 distribution, you can introduce a link function, transform the linear regression equation y into g(y), and let the value of g(y) be distributed between (0,1), when g(y) is close to 0, the label of the sample is category 0, and when g(y) is close to 1, the label of the sample is category 1, so that a classification model is obtained. For logistic regression, the link function is the sigmoid function.

$$\sigma(x) = \frac{1}{1 + e^{-x}} \tag{2}$$

Bringing linear regression into the sigmoid function, i.e. obtaining the general form of a dichotomous logistic regression model:

$$\sigma(x) = \frac{1}{1 + e^{-\omega^T x - b}} \tag{3}$$

Loss function of logistic regression:

$$J(w) = -\frac{1}{m}\sum_{i=1}^{m}\left[y^{(i)}\log y_{w(i)}\left(x^{(i)}\right) + (1 - y(i))\log\left(1 - y_{w(i)}\left(x^{(i)}\right)\right)\right] \quad (4)$$

This is a continuous convex function, it has only one global optimum, but there is no local optimum, so the extreme point obtained by convergence of the gradient descent method must be the global optimum.

3.2 Random Forest

Random forest [12] is a supervised learning algorithm. As you can see from its name, it creates a forest and makes it somewhat random. The idea is to integrate several weak classifiers so that two minds are better than one.

Random forests take the idea of bagging and do the following:

(1) Taking n training samples from the training set each time to form a new training set;
(2) Using the new training set, M sub-models are obtained;
(3) For the classification problem, the voting method is adopted, and the classification category of the sub-model with the most votes is the final category; for regression problems, a simple averaging method is used to obtain the predicted value.

Random forest takes a decision tree as its basic unit. It is formed by integrating a large number of decision trees. Its tectonic process is as follows:

(1) Decision tree construction
The construction of the tree consists of two parts: sample and feature. Sample: For a total training set T, there are N samples in T, and N samples are randomly selected each time there is a return (because there is a return, it is impossible to traverse all samples despite N). These selected N samples are used to train a decision tree. Features: It is assumed that the number of features in the training set is d, and only k (k<d) are selected each time to construct the decision tree. Construction process:
Step 1: There are N samples in T, and N samples are randomly selected. These selected N samples are used to train a decision tree as samples at the nodes of the decision root.
Step 2: If each sample has M attributes, when each node of the decision tree needs to be split, M attributes are randomly selected from the m attributes to satisfy the condition m << M. Then some strategy (such as information gain) is adopted from the m attributes to select one attribute as the split attribute of the node.
Step 3: As the decision tree is built, each node should be split according to step 2 until it can no longer be split. Note that pruning is not done throughout the decision tree formation.
(2) Generate decision results
Each decision tree will have a vote result, and the category with the most votes will be the final model prediction result (Fig. 1).

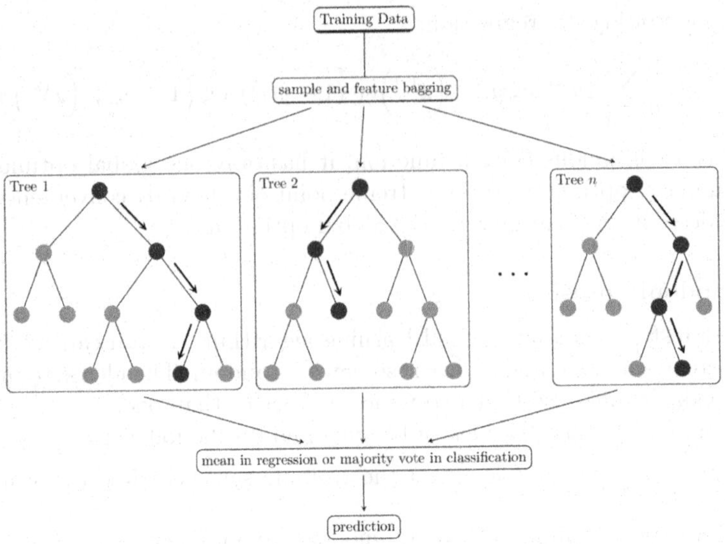

Fig. 1. Random forest prediction process

3.3 KNN

The full name of KNN is K-Nearest Neighbours. The K-nearest neighbour algorithm uses a popular old saying that "birds of a feather flock together". When predicting a new value x, it judges which category x belongs to according to the category of the nearest k points.

Therefore, we can clearly see that the choice of k-value is crucial for the performance of the algorithm: when k is small, the k-nearest neighbour model is more complex and prone to overfitting; when k is large, the k-nearest neighbour model is simpler and prone to underfitting.

The optimal k-value is usually selected by cross-validation:

In many practical applications, data are insufficient. Cross-validation can be used to select a good model. The basic idea of cross-validation is to repeatedly use data, slice the given data, combine the sliced data into a training set and a test set, and then repeatedly perform training tests and model selection on this basis.

3.4 SVM

SVM is a binary classification model [13]. Its basic definition is a linear classifier with the largest interval in the feature space. It contains a kernel function, which makes it a practical non-linear classifier. The learning strategy of SVM is not difficult to understand and can be summed up in one sentence: maximise the distance from the nearest point (support vector) to the hyperplane, i.e. find the most distant hyperplane.

The linear equation of the hyperplane is expressed as

$$\omega^T x + b = 0 \tag{5}$$

In an n-dimensional space, the point $x(x_1, x_2 ... x_n)$ to the straight line distance formula is:

$$\frac{|\omega^T x + b|}{\|\omega\|} \tag{6}$$

The $\|\omega\|$ is $\sqrt{w_1^2 + w_2^2 ... + w_n^2}$.

According to the definition of the support vector, the distance from the support vector to the hyperplane is d, and the distance from other points to the hyperplane is greater than d. The formula can be obtained:

$$\begin{cases} \frac{\omega^T x + b}{\|\omega\|} \geq d, y = 1 \\ \frac{\omega^T x + b}{\|\omega\|} \leq -d, y = -1 \end{cases} \tag{7}$$

Easily convert into $\begin{cases} \frac{\omega^T x + b}{\|\omega\| d} \geq 1, y = 1 \\ \frac{\omega^T x + b}{\|\omega\| d} \leq -1, y = -1 \end{cases}$ additionally,$\|\omega\| d > 0$,for the convenience of derivation,it is denoted as 1 (it has no influence on the optimization of the objective function), so:$\begin{cases} \omega^T x + b \geq d, y = 1 \\ \omega^T x + b \leq -d, y = -1 \end{cases}$ It can be abbreviated as $y(\omega^T x + b) \geq 1$

At this point, the two hyperplanes above and below the maximum distance hyperplane are obtained (Fig. 2).

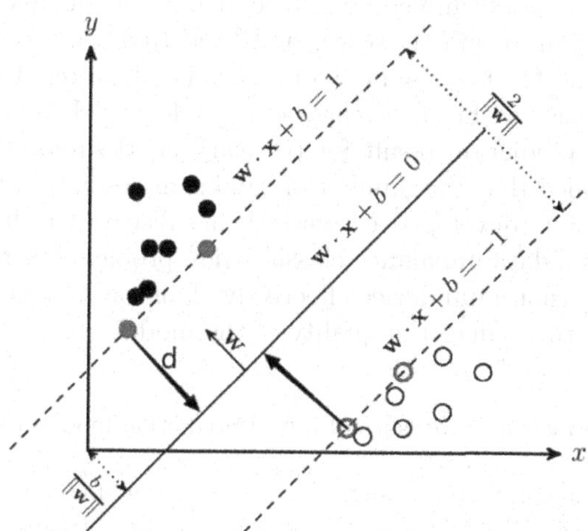

Fig. 2. Maximum spaced hyperplane in SVM

The distance d of each support vector to the hyperplane can be written as $d = \frac{|\omega^T x+b|}{\|\omega\|}$ From the above,$y(\omega^T x + b) \geq 1$,so that $|\omega^T x + b| = y(\omega^T x + b)$,so the d can be transformed to the following form:

$$d = \frac{y(\omega^T x + b)}{\|\omega\|} \tag{8}$$

To find the maximum distance: $max(2\frac{y(\omega^T x+b)}{\|\omega\|})$(multiplication by 2 is convenient for subsequent derivation and has no influence on optimization of objective function). From the above support vector:$y(\omega^T x + b) = 1$, the maximum distance: $max(\frac{2}{\|\omega\|})$ Convert to $min(\frac{1}{2}\|\omega\|)$ For the convenience of calculation, into $min(\frac{1}{2}\|\omega\|^2)$

Finally, the optimization problem is obtained as follows:

$$min(\frac{1}{2}\|\omega\|^2) \quad s.t. \quad y_i(\omega^T x_i + b) \geq 1 \tag{9}$$

3.5 Oversampling Strategy

First, the initial prediction models of logistic regression, random forest, KNN and SVM algorithms were constructed using the data set processed with missing values and the packaged function in sk-learn. In the construction process, the optimal value of parameter C was determined by the cross-validation method in logistic regression in order to select the optimal regularisation intensity. The optimal superparameters "max_depth" and "n_estimators" were determined by the cross-validation method in random forest. In KNN, the optimal hyperparameter "n_neighbours" is determined by grid search. Model quality was determined by accuracy, precision, recall, f1_score, AUC and ROC curve (Table 1).

The recall_1 and f1_1 of the model for the classification of 1, i.e. the risk of coronary heart disease within ten years, are very low, and the model is difficult to make a correct prediction result for coronary heart disease. The underlying data analysis revealed that the number of valid samples within the dataset with a 'TenYearCHD' of 1 (developed coronary heart disease within ten years) was low, and there was a data imbalance classification problem where the model was unable to learn decision boundaries effectively. This can reduce the accuracy of predictions and in turn affect the quality of the model.

Table 1. The performance measure of initial prediction models on the test data

	accuracy	precision_0	precision_1	recall_0	recall_1	f1_0	f1_1	AUC
LR	0.8525	0.8553	0.6667	0.9942	0.0645	0.9195	0.1176	0.7056
RF	0.8456	0.8487	0.3333	0.9954	0.0129	0.9162	0.0248	0.7027
KNN	0.8446	0.8513	0.4	0.9896	0.0387	0.9152	0.0706	0.5970
SVM	0.8496	0.8492	1	1	0.0129	0.9185	0.0255	0.6036

Unbalanced classification is the development of prediction models on highly unbalanced classified datasets to classify datasets with large differences in the number of samples. Many machine learning techniques ignore the performance of a few classes and therefore perform poorly on a few classes.

[14] Currently, methods for solving the unbalanced data classification problem mainly focus on the algorithm level [15,16] and the data level [17,18]. At the algorithm level, mainly combined with the characteristics of unbalanced data to improve the accuracy of minority samples. At the data level, data unbalance is mainly reduced or eliminated by changing the sample distribution of the data sets.

One way to deal with unbalanced datasets is to oversample the minority class [19]: The process of artificially adding or synthesising new samples from a small number of classes in a data set. It can balance the category distribution in the data set and improve the performance of the classifier. The simplest method is to copy samples from a few classes, such as random oversampling, but new samples can also be synthesised from existing samples. This is a type of data enhancement for the minority class called Synthetic Minority Oversampling Technique, or SMOTE

1, Random Oversampling [19]: Randomly select some samples in some classes, and then extend the original dataset by replicating the selected samples. Random oversampling increases the risk of overfitting because a few classes of samples are simply copied, resulting in the model learning information that is too specific and not generalised enough. To avoid overfitting, some other oversampling methods can be used, or some dimensionality reduction or regularisation techniques can be combined.

2, SMOTE [20]: An oversampling method to deal with the class imbalance problem, which can increase the diversity of the data set by producing synthesised minority class samples. The SMOTE oversampling method needs to select an appropriate K-value to determine the nearest neighbour. There is no optimal solution for this parameter. In addition, it cannot change the distribution characteristics of the data set. If some class samples are marginal or noisy, the new samples generated will also tend to be marginal or noisy.

3, BorderlineSMOTE [21] algorithm to deal with the problem of marginalising data samples. BorderlineSMOTE is a method for synthesising new samples using only a few class samples on the borderline. It first classifies the minority class samples into three categories: safe, dangerous and noisy, and then generates the new sample by selecting appropriate majority class neighbours based on the different types of minority class samples. This method can improve the distribution of the borderline and noise regions in the data set and reduce the risk of overfitting. Because BorderlineSMOTE ignores some non-boundary but valuable class samples, some important information in the data set is lost or drowned.

4, K-means clustering algorithm, which is good at preserving the internal structure and distribution of a few class samples: K-means SMOTE [22] is a method based on K-means clustering and SMOTE oversampling, it first performs K-means clustering on a few class samples, then determines how many new samples need to be generated in each cluster according to the number and distance of samples in each cluster, and finally uses SMOTE algorithm in each cluster to generate new samples. This method can effectively deal with the imbalance between and within different clusters, and can also maintain the distribution characteristics of data sets.

4 Experiments and Results

4.1 Experimental Setting and Evaluation Index

In this experiment, four experimental groups were set up, each using LogisticRegression, RandomForest, KNN and SVM to build the prediction model. Each group tested the influence of different over-sampling methods on model performance. Model quality was determined by accuracy, precision, recall, f1_score, AUC and ROC curve.

After processing the data through four oversampling strategies, the relevant performance measure of the new model is obtained (Tables 2, 3 and 4):

Table 2. Performance measure based on Random Oversampling on test dataset

	accuracy	precision_0	precision_1	recall_0	recall_1	f1_0	f1_1	AUC
LR	0.6557	0.6341	0.6710	0.6804	0.6507	0.6473	0.6636	0.7090
RF	0.9340	0.9747	0.9029	0.8850	0.9789	0.9276	0.9394	0.9874
KNN	0.9184	0.9985	0.8656	0.8305	0.9989	0.9068	0.9274	0.9147
SVM	0.6629	00.6478	0.6725	0.6368	0.6829	0.6422	0.6777	0.7091

Table 3. Performance measure based on SMOTE on test dataset

	accuracy	precision_0	precision_1	recall_0	recall_1	f1_0	f1_1	AUC
LR	0.6748	0.6564	0.6923	0.6707	0.6785	0.6635	0.6853	0.7345
RF	0.8761	0.8608	0.8909	0.8837	0.8692	0.8722	0.8799	0.9465
KNN	0.8950	0.9372	0.8632	0.8372	0.9482	0.8844	0.9037	0.9055
SVM	0.6441	0.6288	0.6583	0.6311	0.6561	0.6277	0.6572	0.6989

Table 4. Performance measure based on K-means SMOTE on test dataset

	accuracy	precision_0	precision_1	recall_0	recall_1	f1_0	f1_1	AUC
LR	0.9016	0.8467	0.9680	0.9697	0.8392	0.9041	0.8990	0.9390
RF	0.8993	0.8333	0.9853	0.9866	0.8192	0.9035	0.8947	0.9408
KNN	0.8984	0.8313	0.9879	0.9892	0.8146	0.9034	0.8929	0.9345
SVM	0.8993	0.8325	0.9878	0.9891	0.8163	0.9041	0.8939	0.9305

4.2 Result

The ROC curve and AUC value of the original logistic regression model were not excellent. In the dataset used for analysis, it was found that the number of valid samples with 'TenYearCHD' of 1 (coronary heart disease within ten years) in the dataset was small and the model could not effectively learn the decision boundary. This will reduce the accuracy of the prediction, which will affect the quality of the model (Table 5). Finally, confirm that when using K-means clustering algorithm, you can better maintain the internal structure and distribution of a few class samples, the accuracy, ROC curve and AUC value have been greatly improved, and the model performance has been improved. The prediction accuracy was more than 90 per cent (Figs. 3 and 4).

It can be found that for the initial model built by random forest algorithm, the accuracy of prediction is 85%, but the AUC value is poor. When using the improvement of random oversampling method, you can find that the accuracy of prediction of the AUC value with the training set is very high, but not high in the test set, improved by SMOTE algorithm, The final result is still the optimal random oversampling. This indicates that the number of minority samples is sufficient and representative, and the method of increasing the number of minority samples by repeating them can build an excellent prediction model.

When the K-means algorithm was used to build the initial model, similar to the random forest method, the accuracy was reasonable but the AUC value was low. After dealing with the problem of data imbalance, the AUC of the model and the prediction accuracy of the test set were both around 0.9

Table 5. Performance measure based on BorderlineSMOTE on test dataset

	accuracy	precision_0	precision_1	recall_0	recall_1	f1_0	f1_1	AUC
LR	0.6944	0.6822	0.7055	0.6755	0.7112	0.6788	0.7086	0.7565
RF	0.8843	0.8817	0.8865	0.8753	0.8924	0.8785	0.8895	0.9506
KNN	0.8658	0.9321	0.8678	0.8444	0.9432	0.8862	0.9040	0.9063
SVM	0.6814	0.6914	0.6742	0.6076	0.7495	0.6468	0.7098	0.7449

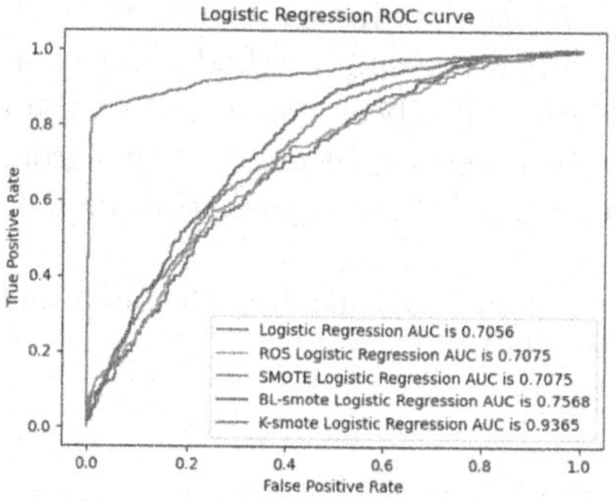

Fig. 3. Logistic Regression ROC curve

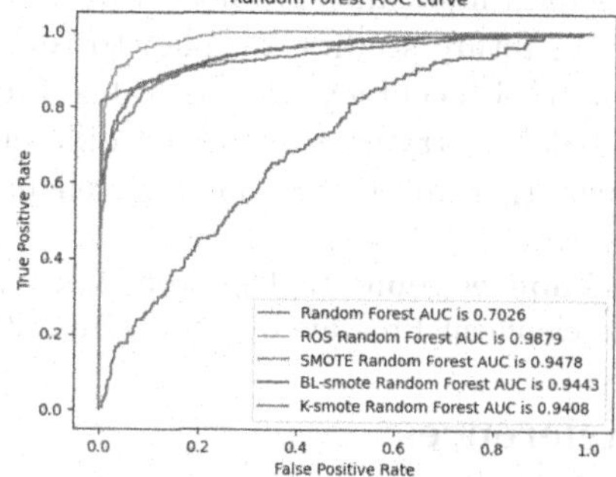

Fig. 4. Random Forest ROC curve

When the SVM algorithm was used, the initially built model still showed a high test set prediction accuracy and a low model AUC. After solving the problem of data imbalance, using K-means SMOTE model performance improved significantly, indicating that there is serious class imbalance in the data set, and a few class samples evenly distributed. An excellent predictive model can be built by K-means clustering and SMOTE oversampling (Figs. 5 and 6).

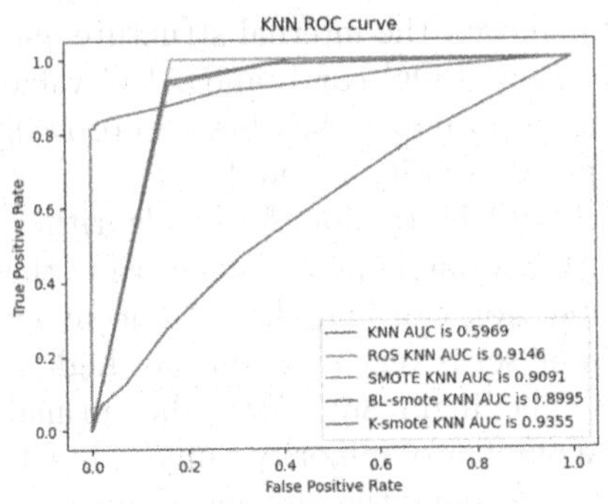

Fig. 5. KNN ROC curve

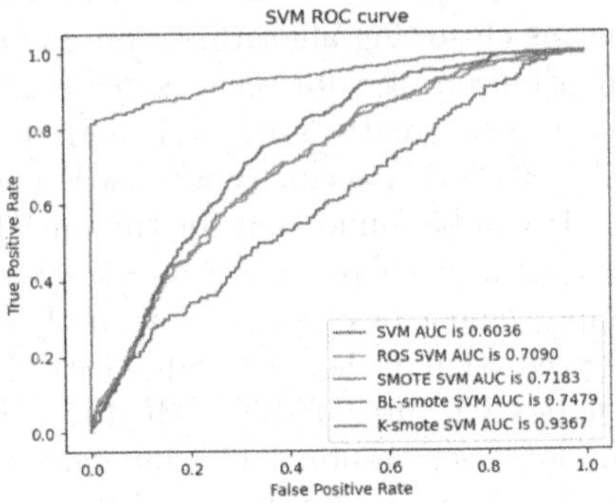

Fig. 6. SVM ROC curve

5 Conclusion

In this study, we used machine learning algorithms to build a data-driven coronary heart disease prediction model to aid in the prevention and early diagnosis of coronary heart disease.

Logistic regression, random forest, KNN and SVM are selected to construct prediction models for comparative experiments. Cross-validation and grid search are used to optimise the parameters. To solve the problem of data imbalance, we use four methods to preprocess the data set: Random Oversampling, SMOTE, Borderline SMOTE and KMeans SMOTE. Finally, the four models are combined to achieve a prediction accuracy of 99% on the training set and 93% on the test set. The experiment shows that the oversampling method can effectively solve the data imbalance problem. Effectively improve the prediction accuracy.

In future studies, we plan to test more data processing methods and compare their accuracy and loss rates; further research has been conducted on data imbalance, trying to combine different oversampling algorithms to learn from each other and build a more excellent coronary heart disease prediction model.

Acknowledgement. This work was supported by the National Key Research and Development Program of China (No.2022YFF0903100)

References

1. Xiaomei, L.: How much do you know about the dangers of coronary heart disease and its treatment? Health All **557**(24), 24–25 (2021)

2. World health statistics 2022: monitoring health for the SDGs, sustainable development goals. World Health Organization, Geneva (2022). Licence: CC BY-NC-SA 3.0 IGO
3. Chang, S.: Research on the application of machine learning algorithm in coronary heart disease prediction. Guilin University of Technology (2021). https://doi.org/10.27050/d.cnki.gglgc.2021.000200
4. Zhu, Y., Wu, J., Fang, Y.: Application of SVM in the classification and prediction of coronary heart disease. J. Biomed. Eng. **30**(06), 1180–1185 (2013)
5. Jianxin, C., Guangcheng, X., Wei, W., et al.: Comparison of data mining classification algorithms for clinical applications in coronary heart disease. Beijing Biomed. Eng. **03**, 249–252 (2008)
6. Li, J., Xiang, F.: Identification of risk factors for coronary heart disease and its prediction model construction. Chin. J. Med. Libr. Inf. **29**(06), 7–13 (2020)
7. Md Idris, N., et al.: Feature selection and risk prediction for patients with coronary artery disease using data mining. Med. Biol. Eng. Comput. **58**(12), 3123–3140 (2020)
8. Arabasadi, Z., et al.: Computer aided decision making for heart disease detection using hybrid neural network-genetic algorithm. Comput. Methods Prog. Biomed. **141**, 19–26 (2017)
9. Krittanawong, C., et al.: Machine learning prediction in cardiovascular diseases: a meta-analysis. Sci. Rep. **10**(1), 16057–16057 (2020)
10. Li, Z.R.: Principles and applications of logistic regression methods. China Strat. Emerg. Ind. 112(28), 114–115 (2017). https://doi.org/10.19474/j.cnki.10-1156/f.001686
11. Hosmer Jr, D. W., et al.: Applied Logistic Regression. Wiley Online Library, Hoboken (2013). https://doi.org/10.1002/9781118548387
12. Breiman, L.: Random forests. Mach. Learn. **45**, 5–32 (2001)
13. Menon, A. K.: Large-scale support vector machines: algorithms and theory (2009)
14. Xu, Z., et al.: A cluster-based oversampling algorithm combining SMOTE and k-means for imbalanced medical data. Inf. Sci. **572**, 574–589 (2021)
15. Lee, S.J., et al.: A novel bagging C4.5 algorithm based on wrapper feature selection for supporting wise clinical decision making. J. Biomed. Inf. **78**, 144–155 (2018)
16. Kavakiotis, I., et al.: Machine learning and data mining methods in diabetes research. Comput. Struct. Biotechnol. J. **15**, 104–116 (2017)
17. Chen, J., et al.: A disease diagnosis and treatment recommendation system based on big data mining and cloud computing. Inf. Sci. **435**, 124–149 (2018)
18. Itani, S., et al.: Specifics of medical data mining for diagnosis aid: a survey. Expert Syst. Appl. **118**, 300–314 (2019)
19. He, H., Garcia, E.A.: Learning from imbalanced data. IEEE Trans. Knowl. Data Eng. **9**, 1263–1284 (2008)
20. Chawla, N.V., Bowyer, K.W., Hall, L.O., Kegelmeyer, W.P.: SMOTE: synthetic minority over-sampling technique. J. Artif. Intell. Res. **16**, 321–357 (2002)
21. Han, H., et al.: Borderline-SMOTE: a new over-sampling method in imbalanced data sets learning. In: International Conference on Intelligent Computing, ICIC 2005: Advances in Intelligent Computing, pp. 878–887 (2005)
22. Last, F., Douzas, G., Bacao, F.: Oversampling for imbalanced learning based on k-means and smote (2018). https://doi.org/10.1016/j.ins.2018.06.056

Verification of IoT-Aware Business Processes Based on Extended Petri Nets

Jiachen Cao, Jing Wang(✉), Shiyi Yang, and Huilong Gong

Beijing Key Laboratory on Integration and Analysis of Large-scale Stream Data, North China University of Technology, Beijing 100144, China

15330052316@163.com

Abstract. With the rapid development of cloud computing and Internet of Things (IoT)technology, the convergence of BPM (Business Process Management) and IoT big data has attracted more and more attention. Integrating IoT services into BPM enables BPM to perceive changes in the physical world more quickly and accurately, but also brings challenges to process verification. The verification method that supports IoT-aware business processes is required. This paper proposes a method to formally represent the Business Process Modeling Notation (BPMN) model with IoT services integrated based on extended Petri nets, and a deadlock detection algorithm for this formaliza-tion method. The case study shows that the method proposed in this paper can effectively detect the deadlock structures in IoT-aware business process-es, and reduce process errors for process modelers.

Keywords: business processes · IoT service · formal verification · Petri nets

1 Introduction

In recent years, with the rapid development of Internet of Things (IoT) technology, IoT has become the common infrastructure and its forefront has shifted from connection of IoT devices to provision of business value and services.

With the widespread application of IoT services, the research on integrating IoT services into BPM has gradually attracted more and more attention [1]. IoT aware business processes apply IoT technology to business processes, extracting events with high value from raw IoT data for use by business processes. Business processes can provide business logic for IoT services. IoT services can help business processes accurately capture changes in the physical world and achieve precise decision-making.

However, integrating IoT services into business processes also brings challenges to process verification. Integrating IoT into business processes requires a special process structure to express the ability of IoT. Because Business Process Modeling Notation (BPMN) [2] do not have clear formal semantics, the process model may have semantic errors, such as conflicts, deadlocks, etc., so it is necessary to convert the built business process into a model with formal semantics for

Z. Wang et al. (Eds.): ICSS 2023, CCIS 1844, pp. 460–474, 2023.
https://doi.org/10.1007/978-981-99-4402-6_33

verification, the special process structure used for integrating IoT has difficulty in formalization.

In current research, the integration of IoT services into BPM was mainly achieved by extending the basic elements of the BPMN standard and adding a class of IoT elements suitable for binding IoT services. Kirikkayis et al. [3] proposes the integration of IoT services through an extended form of IoT elements that employ task elements containing non-interrupting IoT boundary events. For business processes built using such IoT elements, traditional formal verification methods based on Petri nets are not fully applicable.

In the aspect of the mapping from BPMN to Petri nets, there is no mapping rules that can fully express the execution semantics of such IoT elements. And the verification algorithms for the IoT-aware business processes are also lacked.

Aiming at the above challenges, this paper proposes a verification method for IoT-aware business processes based on extended Petri nets. This method includes the mapping rules for interrupting IoT boundary events and non-interrupting IoT boundary events in the business processes and can accurately express the semantics of the IoT elements. In addition, a deadlock detection algorithm is presented based on the reachability graph of the extended Petri nets, and a case study of the maritime transportation is conducted.

The organization of this paper is as follows: Sect. 2 summarizes the related work, Sect. 3 shows the method of formalizing the business process integrated with IoT services into the corresponding extended Petri nets, and Sect. 4 gives the deadlock detection algorithm for the formalized extended Petri net. In Sect. 5, the methods proposed in Sects. 3 and 4 are analyzed and verified through a case study, and Sect. 6 summarizes the paper and gives future research direction.

2 Related Work

Research in recent years has made significant progress in the formal representation and verification of business processes based on Petri nets. To integrate IoT services into business processes, some specific process structures are often required to realize the integration, which poses new challenges about the formal representation and verification of these specific structures.

In the aspect of the formal representation from BPMN to Petri net, Ramadan et al. [4] presents the mapping rules from basic flow elements in BPMN to Petri net structure, and realizes the conversion from simple BPMN process to Petri net. Dechsupa et al. [5] proposes the mapping rules from the task structure with boundary timer events to the extended Petri net in BPMN. Kheldoun et al. [6] proposed the mapping rules for mapping the subprocess structure with boundary cancellation events in BPMN to Petri nets. Dechsupa et al. [7] proposes the mapping rules for mapping the task structure with boundary abnormal events to Petri nets in BPMN. In this mapping, the reading and writing functions of tasks are distinguished, and the impact of different reading and writing errors on task states is described. Li Z et al. [8] proposes the mapping rules for BPMN task structure with message events to extended Petri nets, tasks and message events are respectively mapped to dynamic behavior events with postinternal conditions. At present, there is no research on the interrupting and non-interrupting properties of boundary events in the formal representation of BPMN elements to Petri nets.

In the aspect of the verification of Petri nets, the objectives of the verification are mainly to detect whether the model meets the basic characteristics of Petri nets such as accessibility, security, and activity [9]. Ma Z et al. [10] proposes a compact representation method of Petri net reachability graphs, and a practical algorithm based on the marking reachability problem, which is based on reachability graphs, is used to solve the problem of judging whether a marking is reachable in Petri nets. Aiming at the deadlock problem of Petri nets, Zhong C et al. [11] proposes a decomposition control strategy to judge deadlocks by calculating the reachability graph of subnets of Petri net, which effectively reduces the amount of computation. In addition, various analysis techniques based on Petri nets have been developed as simulation tools. Common Petri net simulation tools include Tina, CPN Tools, Yasper, etc. The current formal verification of Petri nets cannot support verification of processes integrated with IoT services.

3 Formal Representation of IoT-Aware Business Processes

Formal method is a method based on mathematical theory for describing, developing, and detecting computer software and hardware systems. The BPMN process is essentially a directed graph, which can be directly searched to verify the correctness of the BPMN process, but this method has limitations such as poor performance and few verification properties. While the formal method based on Petri nets has powerful Verification and analysis capabilities, as well as mathematical theoretical basis and graphical support, is a great formal verification method. This section introduces the basic elements in BPMN and the mapping rules for formalizing IoT elements for binding IoT services to extended Petri nets.

3.1 Extended Petri Net

This paper uses the extended Petri nets form with the reset arcs [12] added on the basis of the classic Petri nets. Using the extended Petri net can express more behaviors. The definition of extended Petri nets is given as follows:

Definition 1. *A Petri net with reset arcs is a five tuple N=(P,T,F,R,M),where:*

- *(P,T,F) is a classic Petri net;*
- *M:P* $\rightarrow \{0,1,2,3...\}$*is a multiset defined on a place, called a marking or a marking function. For* $p_i \in P$ *,*$M(p_i)=k$*,it means that there are k tokens in place* p_i*,*M_0 *is the initial marking;*
- *R:a subset of*$(P \times T)$*called a reset arcs set,*$R \in P \times T, R \cap F = \emptyset$*;*

- *For* $t \in T$,*if* $\forall p \in P, (p,t) \in F \rightarrow M(p) \geq 1$,*then* t *has the right to occur in the marking* M,*recorded as* $M[t>$;
- *For* $\forall p \in P$, *if* $\forall t \in T$ *and* $(p,t) \in R$, *then* $M[t>$, *it will clear the tokens in the place* p, *recorded as* $M(p) = 0$;
- *If* $M[t>$, *then transition* t *can be triggered in* M. *When* t *is triggered at* M, a· *new marking* M' *will be generated:*

$$M'(p) = \begin{cases} M(p) - 1, if(p,t) \in F \wedge (t,p) \notin F \\ M(p) + 1, if(t,p) \in F \wedge (p,t) \notin F \\ M(p), \ others \end{cases} \tag{1}$$

The elements of the extended Petri nets used in this paper and the explanation of the elements are shown in Table 1:

Table 1. Extended Petri Net Elements

Name	Icon	Explaination
transition	▯	A transition is a modeling unit that represents a processing step.
place	○	The place is a container for storing tokens.
places containing tokens	◉	An arc is an element connecting a transition and a place. An arc can only point from a place to a transition or from a transition to a place. It cannot be from a transition to atransition or from a place to a place.
arc	→	An arc is an elemment connecting a transition and a place. Anarc can only point from a place to a transition or from atransition to a place.
reset arc	→→	The reset arc is a special arc between a transition and a place. If the transition and the place are connected by a reset arc, when the transition is triggered, the tokens in the place will be cleared.

3.2 Formal Representation of BPMN Basic Elements

Formal Representation of Flow Objects. Table 2 shows the formalized mapping rules of Task, Event and Gateways to Petri nets in BPMN. For flow objects in BPMN, tasks and intermediate events are mapped as transitions with one input place and one output place, and the mapped transitions are marked with the names of tasks and events. The start and end events are mapped to a similar structure, except that the start and end events use the form of an additional anonymous transition to represent the start and end of the process. Different types of gateways in BPMN have different mapping rules. At the split of the gateway, the parallel gateway is converted into a transition, which means that all input places jointly control this transition, and each output place is controlled by this transition. Each branch of the exclusive gateway is transformed into a transition, multiple transitions are jointly controlled by the input place, and each transition controls an output place. At the merge of gateways, parallel gateways and exclusive gateways have opposite semantics to splits, so they also have a symmetrical structure with the merge of gateways.

In the transformed Petri net model, the place represented by the dotted line represents the input object or output object of the current node, and the corresponding module after transformation can share the input and output objects with other modules. In general, except for the sequence flow used to connect to the event-based gateway, other sequence flows are mapped to arcs.

Table 2. Mapping of BPMN elements to Petri nets

BPMN object	Petri net model	BPMN object	Petri net model
r Start s	Ps Ts Pr	i r1 r2 Parallel Gateways pg1 (split)	Pi Tpg1 Pr1 Pr2
i End e	Pi Te Pe	i1 i2 r Parallel Gateways pg2 (merge)	Pi1 Tpg2 Pr1
i r Event E	Pi E Pr	i r1 r2 Exclusive Gateways eg1 (split)	Pi Teg1 Teg2 Pr1 Pr2
t Taskt	Pi Tt Pr	i1 i2 r Exclusive Gateways eg2 (merge)	Pi Teg1 Pi Pr1

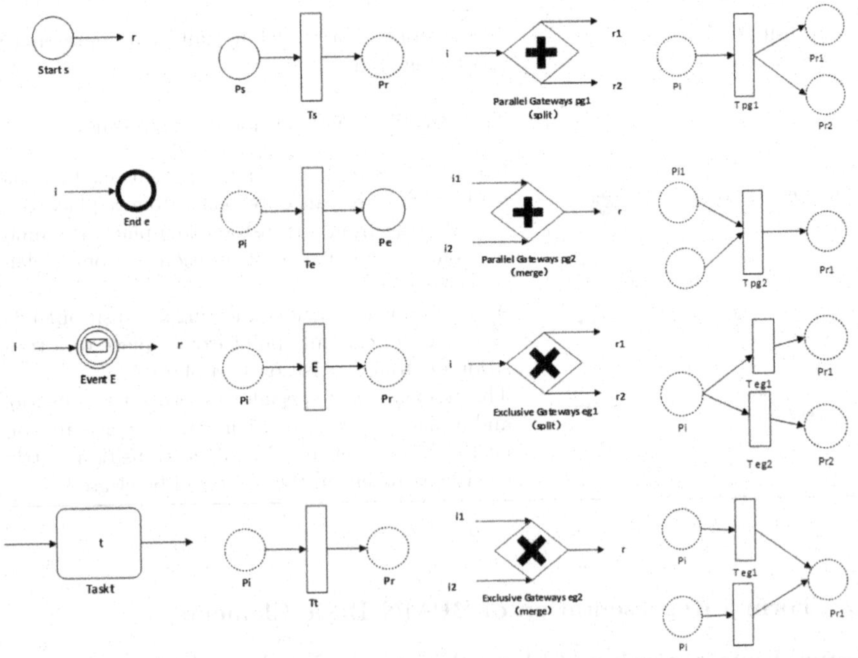

In the transformed Petri net model, the place represented by the dotted line represents the input object or output object of the current node, and the corresponding module after transformation can share the input and output objects with other modules. In general, except for the sequence flow used to connect to the event-based gateway, other sequence flows are mapped to an arc.

Formal Representation of Message Flows. Different process communication and collaboration is usually represented by message flow. Messages are used as the carrier of event interaction between processes. During the process of converting messages into Petri nets, they are mapped to a place with input arcs and output arcs. The message sender is connected to the input arc, and the message receiver is connected to the output arc. The message sender includes the sending task and the event of throwing the intermediate message, and the message receiver includes the receiving task, the message start event, the intermediate message capture event, the boundary message event and the message end event. The message places serve as a link connecting between two process. For the message sender, when a transition is triggered, the message place adds one or more tokens. For the message receiver, the transition enabling conditions are subject to the message place and its contained Influenced by the number of tokens. The following takes the message flow between tasks, the message flow from a task to an intermediate event, and the message flow from a task to a start event as examples to introduce the mapping of message flows from BPMN to Petri nets. The mapping rules are shown in Fig. 1, Fig. 2, and Fig. 3:

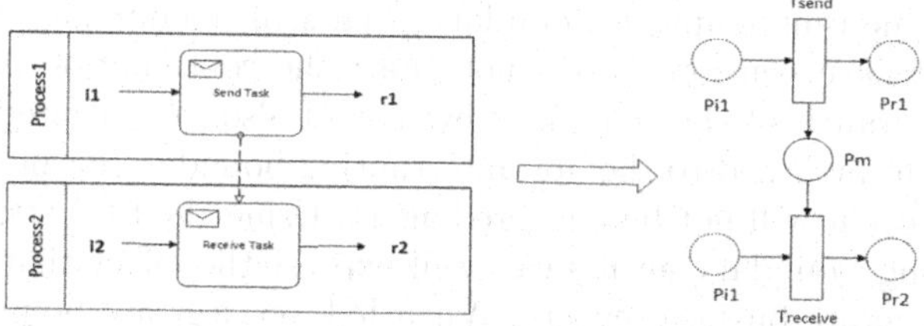

Fig. 1. Modeling of the message flow between tasks

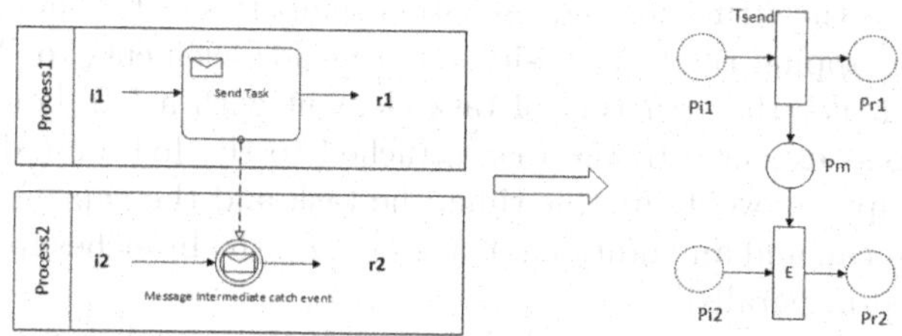

Fig. 2. Modeling of the message flow from a task to an intermediate event

For different processes that cooperate with each other, the extended Petri nets obtained after each process is formalized are connected to each other through message places, and combined into a big Petri net model containing multiple starting nodes.

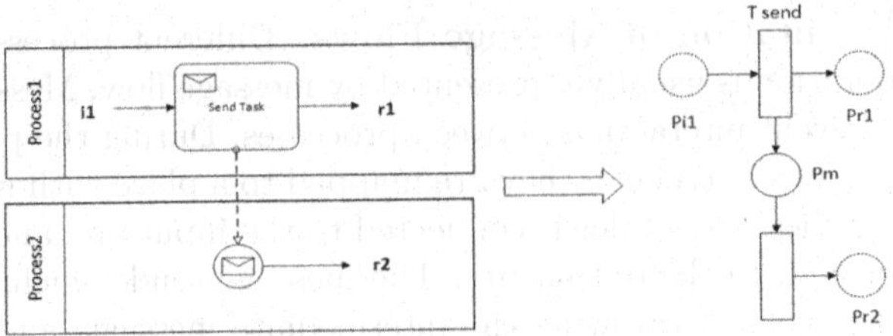

Fig. 3. Modeling of the message flow from a task to a start event.

3.3 Formal Representation of BPMN Extension Elements for Binding IoT Services

To bind IoT services into business processes, the IoT elements which extends BPMN are adopted, which uses the extended form of task elements with non-interrupting IoT boundary events to integrate IoT services. According to the BPMN2.0 standard, for a task element with a boundary event, if the boundary event is triggered during task execution, the executing task will be stopped, and the branch of the boundary event will continue to the next execution. For task elements with non-interrupting boundary events, if a boundary event is triggered during task execution, it will not affect the continuation of the current task, and the branch of the boundary event will also be executed. Only when the task element attached to the non-interrupting boundary event is completed, the boundary event will not be triggered again. Using the task structure with a non-interrupting boundary events can well express the effect that IoT services continue to generate business events. When IoT services are bound to IoT elements, the business process level can continuously obtain the business events generated by IoT services. It avoids the cumbersome use of multiple cycles, and can continuously monitor specific scenes.

According to the structure and execution semantics of non-interrupting IoT elements, the mapping rules of non-interrupting IoT elements to Petri nets are shown in Fig. 4. For the structure of task element with a IoT boundary event, when the process executes to the task attached to the IoT boundary event, it will create a capture event. At this time, the task and the capture event are in parallel, so you can add an additional transition T_3, the branches from transition T_3 are executed in parallel.

For non-interrupting boundary IoT events, business events can be captured multiple times during the life cycle of the attached task and continue to execute along the successor route of the boundary event. Therefore, a loop structure is used from place P_3 to transition E_{IoT} to represent IoT boundary events It can continuously monitor and receive business events for subsequent processing. When the life cycle of the task attached to the IoT boundary event ends, that is, the transition T_1 is triggered, according to the definition of the extended Petri net, the reset arc will clear the tokens in the connected place P_3, which means that the transition E_{IoT} of the boundary event will no longer be is triggered. Using the above mapping rules, the functions of IoT elements can be accurately

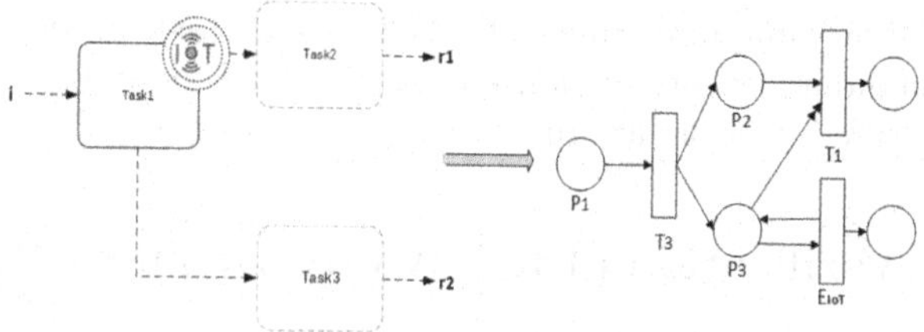

Fig. 4. Mapping of non-interrupting IoT elements to Petri nets

described. It can not only express the scenario where the IoT boundary event can capture business events multiple times, but also express the scenario where there is no need to monitor and receive business events after the task is completed.

In addition, considering that in a specific scenario, a task structure with an interrupting boundary event may be used to integrate IoT services. In this structure, IoT events and attached tasks compete with each other for execution. According to its execution semantics, the mapping rule representation of the task structure with interrupting IoT boundary event to Petri net is shown in Fig. 5.

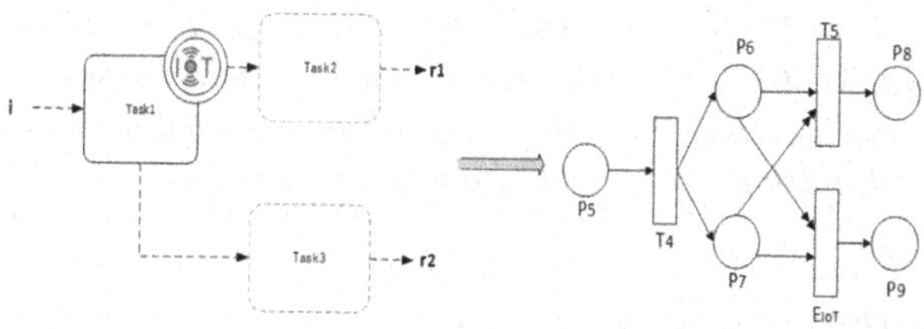

Fig. 5. Mapping of interrupting IoT elements to Petri nets

In Fig. 5, for the structure of task element with a interrupting IoT boundary event, when the process executes to the task attached to the boundary event, there is also a parallel relationship between the boundary event and the task, here an additional transition T_4 is used to implement the branch, indicating during the execution of the task, the event is always monitored. For the interrupting IoT boundary event, the message can only be captured once in the life cycle of its attached task. Once the message is captured, the attached task will be terminated. That is to say, after the transition E_{IoT} of the boundary event is triggered, the transition T_5 of the task will not be triggered. You can use the reset arc to transition the E_{IoT} to the place P_6. When the transition E_{IoT} is triggered, the reset arc will clear the tokens in the place P_6, and transition T_5 will not be triggered. When the life cycle of the task attached to the interrupting IoT boundary event ends, that is, transition T_5 is triggered, the reset arc will clear the tokens in the place P_7, which means that the transition E_{IoT} of the boundary event will no longer be triggered.

Using the above mapping rules, the behavior of task elements with interrupting IoT boundary events or non-interrupting IoT boundary events can be accurately described, this structure have a good expressive effect.

4 Formal Verification of IoT-Aware Business Processes

The analysis and verification of Petri nets is mainly realized by detecting whether the model satisfies some dynamic properties, such as reachability, security, boundedness, liveness, etc. The research of net theory has proposed a variety of analysis methods for Petri nets, mainly including reachability graph and coverable tree, association matrix and state equation, Petri net language and Petri net process, etc. Based on the formal representation of the IoT-aware business process in the previous section, this section further pays attention to whether there is a deadlock in the multi-business process collaboration of the IoT services integration. The deadlock detection problem of the IoT integrated business process collaboration will be discussed below discuss.

4.1 Deadlock Problem

Definition 2. *Liveness: there is a Petri net* $N = (P, T, F, R, M), M_0$ *is the initial marking,* $t \in T$. *If there is any* $M \in R(M_0)$, *there always exist* $M' \in R(M)$ *such that* $M'[t >$, *then the transition* t *is said to be alive. If for any* $t \in T$, *Transition* t *is alive, then the Petri net* N *is called liveness. In this Petri net, the set of all markings reachable from* M_0 *is denoted as* $R(M_0)$, *and agreed* $M_0 \in R(M_0)$.

Definition 3. *Dead markings of Petri nets: there is a Petri net* $N = (P, T, F, R, M)$, *if* $M \in R(M_0)$, *so that for any* $t \in T \rightarrow \neg M[T >$, *then* M *is called a dead marking of* N.

Definition 4. *Dead transitions of Petri nets: there is a Petri net* $N = (P, T, F, R, M)$, *if transition* $t \in T$, *so that for any* $M \in R(M_0) \rightarrow \neg M[T >$, *then* t *is called a dead transitionof* N.

Usually, Definition 3 or Definition 4 can be used to describe deadlock. This paper uses Definition 4 as the concept of deadlock. Deadlocks in IoT-aware process refer to those dead nodes that can never be executed by the process engine. Deadlocks in IoT-aware process mainly include deadlocks within a single process and deadlocks caused by different process interaction and collaboration. The research on deadlock detection inside the process is mature. This paper mainly focuses on the situation of deadlock caused by process message interaction.

4.2 Deadlock Detection Algorithm

The deadlock detection methods of Petri nets include those based on the coverable tree [13], the escape matrix [14] and the reachable graph [15], etc. The deadlock detection of IoT-aware business processes is to detect the Petri nets generated from previous section. This paper chooses the method based on reachability graph to detection the deadlock of process cooperative Petri net. The deadlock detection method based on the reachability graph mainly includes two steps. The first step is to construct the corresponding reachability graph according to the Petri net model, and the second step is to use the deadlock detection algorithm to detect the reachability graph. At present, the deadlock detection algorithm based on the reachability graph is relatively mature. Therefore, the key to deadlock detection of business process for integrating IoT services lies in the construction of the extended Petri net reachability graph. This paper refers to the construction algorithm of the reachability graph in [15], and gives the construction algorithm of the reachability graph of the extended Petri net. The difference from the reachability graph construction algorithm in [15] is that the reset arc of the extended Petri net will affect the tokens in the place connected to the enable excitation, so it is necessary to add the reset arc to the reachability graph construction algorithm. Judgment, if there is a reset arc in the arc set connected to the excitation transition, clear the Token in the place connected to the reset arc. The extended petri net reachability graph construction algorithm is described as follows:

For IoT-aware process deadlock verification, according to the deadlock concept in IoT-aware process and the corresponding relationship between transitions in Petri nets and reachable graph edges, it is only necessary to verify whether the transitions in Petri nets are all in the marker set of reachable graph edges. In this paper, the deadlock verification is carried out according to the reachability graph of the extended Petri net. The deadlock detection algorithm is as follows:

5 Case Study

This section first introduces a scenario of maritime transportation of liquefied natural gas (LNG), and then applies the formal verification method to detect and analyze the IoT-aware business processes.

5.1 Scenario

With the rise of global energy demand, the business volume of LNG marine transportation is growing rapidly, and the number of accidents on LNG carriers on the sea is also increasing every year. There are many factors that cause marine transportation accidents. In addition to factors affected by weather, it is also re-lated to the correctness of the transportation process and the cooperation among transportation related parties. Once an accident occurs, it may cause major losses or disasters in personnel and the environment. Both logistics companies and relevant management departments hope to continuously optimize

Algorithm 1: Reachability graph construction algorithm of extended Petri net

Input: Petri net composed of IoT-aware process formalization $N = (P, T, F, R, M)$

Output: reachability graph $G(V, E)$

```
Initialize the reachability graph G, and use the initial marking M0 as the root
  node of the reachability graph;
Initialize the queue q, and the initial marking M0 enters the queue;
while q is not empty do
    The element at the end of the q queue is dequeued and assigned as the
      current marking M;
    for t in T do
        if t satisfies the transition enable condition in Definition 1 then
            inspire the transition t ;
            for traverse the arc set connected to transition t do
                if arc_i is reset arc then
                    clear the tokens in the place connected to arc_i;
            generate a new marking M';
            if M' is included in G then
                add a directed edge e from M to M' to G;
                associate transition t with e;
            Else
            add the marking M' to G and the directed edge e from M to M';
            associate transition t with e;
            marking M' into the queue q;
```

Algorithm 2: Deadlock detection algorithm based on reachability graph

Input: Extended Petri net $N = (P, T, F, R, M)$ and reachability graph $G(V, E)$

Output: Whether there is a deadlock

```
Initialize the label set of reachable graph edges as Q and Q := E;
for t in T do
    if the name of t does not appear in Q then
        t is a dead transition and output true;
        break;
```

and improve the transportation process with the help of information technology, and improve the risk management ability of LNG transportation at sea. At present, BPM has been widely used in maritime transportation management. With the application of Internet of Things technology, the monitoring ability of LNG carriers in transit has been improved.

Figure 6 shows a simplified scenario of LNG transportation, which includes three processes. The top layer represents the process deployed on IoT device, the middle layer represents the ship transportation process, and the bottom layer represents the transportation management process of the logistics company. The process deployed on the IoT device continuously monitors the real-time pressure information of the LNG tank and sends it to the ship transportation process. The ship transportation process judges whether the tank pressure exceeds the standard based on the received real-time pressure information. In case of an emergency that exceeds the standard, a request for pressure relief will be sent to the shipping company, and the company will make a decision and send the decision result to the ship. If the plan of opening the pressure relief valve is not agreed, the ship will start the circulation pump to mix the LNG in the tank to reduce the pressure. The interactions between processes are carried out through message events.

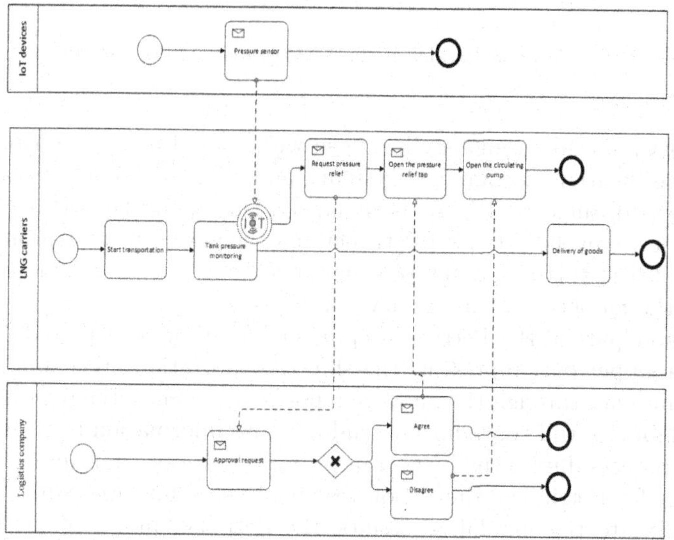

Fig. 6. LNG transportation processes

5.2 Modeling and Verification of LNG Transportation Processes

The three processes in the LNG transportation scenario are transformed into the corresponding Petri net. According to the mapping rules of the message flows, the three Petri nets can be connected into a composite Petri net, as shown in Fig. 7:

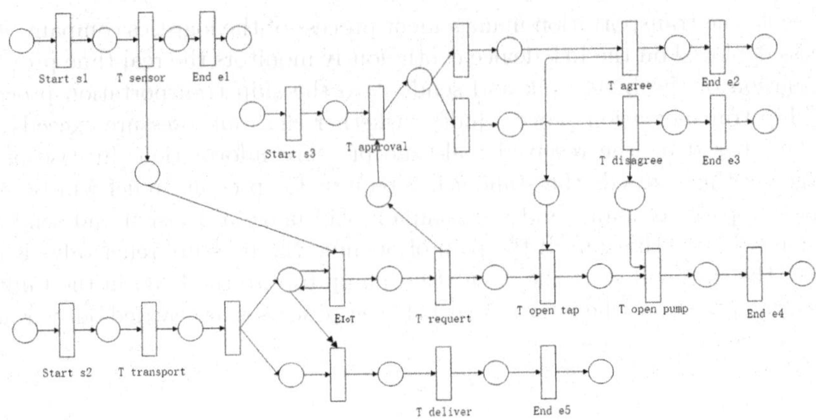

Fig. 7. Petri net model of the LNG transportation scenario

Petri net analysis technology has been widely used in the description, analysis, and verification of computer systems, and Petri net simulation tools have been developed, such as CPN Tools, Tina, etc. Due to the support of CPN Tools for the reset arc in the extended Petri net and the powerful simulation and analysis capabilities, this paper chooses the CPN Tools tool to simulate the Petri nets, and the model structure is shown in Fig. 8-a.

The lower part of the Petri net represents the process deployed on the IoT device, the upper part represents the ship transportation process, and the two processes interact through the message repository p_9. Since the process deployed on the IoT device will continuously send pressure information to the ship transportation process during the LNG transportation process, multiple initial markings are set for Petri. The simulation results are shown in Fig. 8-b:

According to the simulation results, the Petri net model of the IoT-aware busi-ness process didn't change the execution semantics of the original processes, and can accurately express the functions of IoT services.

Deadlocks in IoT-aware process refer to those dead nodes that cannot be executed. This paper adopts the IoT-aware process deadlock detection algorithm in Sect. 4 to perform deadlock detection on the process introduced in the scenario. The detection results shows that the node that starts the circulation pump is a deadlock node. When the process reaches this node, it will wait for the message and cannot end normally, resulting in a deadlock problem. According to the analysis, the structure of the process is adjusted. The adjusted process model is shown in Fig. 9. The deadlock detection of the process is performed again. The detection results show that all transitions can be executed, and there is no deadlock in the process model.

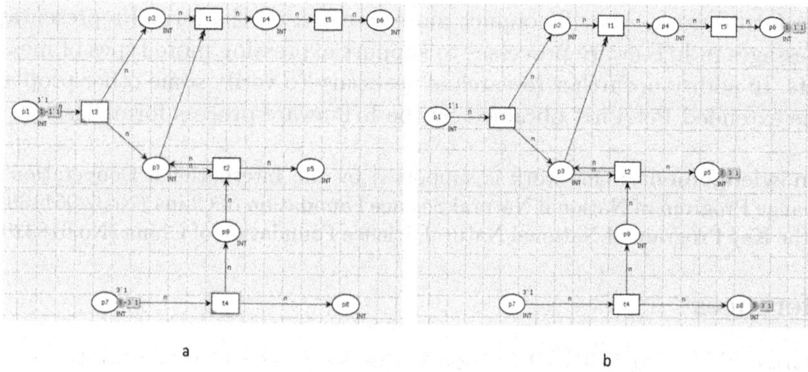

Fig. 8. Petri net model and simulation results in CPN Tools

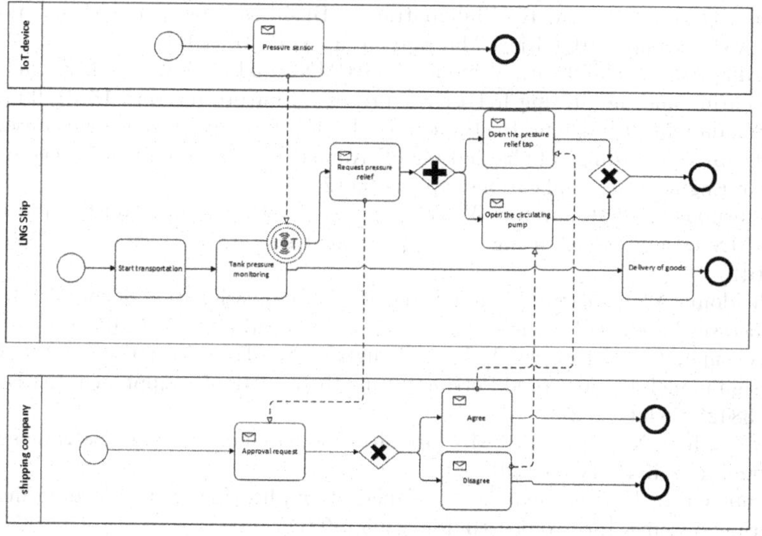

Fig. 9. Adjusted process model

6 Conclusions and Future Work

This paper presents a method for formal verification of IoT-aware business processes The IoT elements used to bind IoT services are formally expressed using the method based on extended Petri nets, and the mapping rules for interrupting IoT boundary events and non-interrupting IoT boundary events are proposed. The validity of the formal representation method is verified by CPN Tools simulation. In addition, this paper provides a deadlock detection algorithm for this formalization method. The case study shows that the method proposed in this paper can effectively detect the deadlock structures in IoT-aware business processes, and reduce process errors for process modelers.

In future work, we will conduct more research on the formal representation of messages in IoT-aware processes to support expressing more types of message events. In addition, further research is necessary to verify some other properties of the extended Petri net obtained by the IoT-aware process formalization.

Acknowledgement. This work is supported by the International Cooperation and Exchange Program of National Natural Science Foundation of China (No.62061136006) and the Key Program of National Natural Science Foundation of China (No.61832004).

References

1. Gruhn, V., et al.: BRIBOT: towards a service-based methodology for bridging business processes and IoT big data. In: Hacid, H., Kao, O., Mecella, M., Moha, N., Paik, H. (eds.) ICSOC 2021. LNCS, vol. 13121, pp. 597–611. Springer, Cham (2021). https://doi.org/10.1007/978-3-030-91431-8_37
2. Omg, O.M.G., Parida, R., Mahapatra, S.: Business process model and notation (BPMN) version 2.0. Object Manage. Group **1**(4), 18 (2011)
3. Kirikkayis, Y., Gallik, F., Winter, M.: BPMNE4IoT: a framework for modeling, executing and monitoring IoT-driven processes. Future Internet **15**(3), 90 (2023)
4. Ramadan, M., Elmongui, H., Hassan, R.: BPMN formalisation using coloured petri nets. In: Proceedings of the 2nd GSTF Annual International Conference on Software Engineering Applications, pp. 83–90 (2011)
5. Dechsupa, C., Vatanawood, W., Thongtak, A.: Hierarchical verification for the BPMN design model using state space analysis. IEEE Access **7**, 16795–16815 (2019)
6. Kheldoun, A., Barkaoui, K., Ioualalen, M.: Formal verification of complex business processes based on high-level petri nets. Inf. Sci. **385**, 39–54 (2017)
7. Dechsupa, C., Vatanawood, W., Thongtak, A.: Transformation of the BPMN design model into a colored Petri net using the partitioning approach. IEEE Access **6**, 38421–38436 (2021)
8. Li, Z., Zhou, X., Wu, K.: BPMN formalization based on extended petri nets model. Comput. Sci. **43**(11), 9 (2016)
9. Grobelna, I., Karatkevich, A.: Challenges in application of petri nets in manufacturing systems. Electronics **10**(18), 2305 (2021)
10. Ma, Z., Tong, Y., Li, Z.: Basis marking representation of petri net reachability spaces and its application to the reachability problem. IEEE Trans. Autom. Control **62**(3), 1078–1093 (2017)
11. Zhong, C., He, W., Li, Z.: Deadlock analysis and control using petri net decomposition techniques. Inf. Sci. **482**, 440–456 (2019)
12. Devillers, R.: Synthesis of (choice-free) reset nets. In: Buchs, D., Carmona, J. (eds.) PETRI NETS 2021. LNCS, vol. 12734, pp. 274–291. Springer, Cham (2021). https://doi.org/10.1007/978-3-030-76983-3_14
13. Reisig, W.: Understanding Petri Nets: Modeling Techniques, Analysis Methods, Case Studies. Springer, Heidelberg (2013)
14. Li, L., Xie, Y., Cen, L., Zeng, Z.: A novel cause analysis approach of grey reasoning petri net based on matrix operations. Appl. Intell. **52**(1), 1–18 (2021). https://doi.org/10.1007/s10489-021-02377-4
15. Liang, H.: The Research and Implementation of Petri Net Based Formal Representation and Verification for Multi-processes. Beijing University of Posts and Telecommunications (2018)

A Cross-Modal Face Reconstruction Method for Service on Blockchains

Zhijie Tan, Xiang Yuan, Siying Cui, Yuzhi Li, Zhonghai Wu, Tong Mo(✉), and Weiping Li

School of Software and Microelectronics, Peking University, Beijing, China
motong@ss.pku.edu.cn

Abstract. The current blockchain systems are suffering the low scalability. In order to improve the scalability and enable the storage of more critical facial data on the blockchain, we propose a novel cross-modal face reconstruction model in this paper. To reduce the huge communication pressure of model synchronization on the blockchain, we use model-independent sketches and natural language texts as intermediate representations of the face. To obtain accurate natural language representations of faces, we designed a precise progressive questioning process to achieve targeted knowledge mining of large multimodal models. The mixed modality intermediate representation of sketches and text greatly reduces the storage volume of faces and increases the visual fidelity. After uploading this mixed modality representation to the blockchain, it effectively reduces the communication and storage pressure of the blockchain. Finally, we used a diffusion generative model that supports mixed modality to reconstruct the face. Experiments have demonstrated the huge potential and application prospects of our method.

Keywords: Blockchain · Face Reconstruction · Cross-Modal Generation

1 Introduction

There has always been an impossible triangle theory in the current blockchain: scalability, decentralization, and security, of which only two can be achieved at the same time [39]. The structure of this impossible triangle is shown in Fig. 1. Specifically, scalability represents the data throughput of the blockchain per second, security represents the reliability of the data on the blockchain, and decentralization represents the number of nodes participating in block generation and data verification in the blockchain. If both decentralization and security are to be met, which requires enough nodes to participate in data verification while ensuring that the majority of these nodes participate in data validation, the concurrency of the blockchain system is inevitably facing the risk of decline. For example, the transaction per second (TPS) of Bitcoin is around 6–7, while that of Ethereum is around 15–20[1]. In contrast, the TPS of the traditional transaction

[1] Data from https://www.ycharts.com/.

Z. Wang et al. (Eds.): ICSS 2023, CCIS 1844, pp. 475–489, 2023.
https://doi.org/10.1007/978-981-99-4402-6_34

network based on VISA bank card system is about 20,000 or more[2].. Therefore, compared with the two characteristics of decentralization and security, scalability has become the Achilles' heel of current large-scale blockchain systems.

To improve the scalability of the blockchain, common technical solutions include super-node technology and sharding technology. Super-node technology has spawned consortium chains, which satisfy both scalability and security but sacrifice decentralization [2]. Super-node technology uses some nodes as data verification nodes, and no longer requires all nodes to participate in the data confirmation and storage process, greatly reducing the concurrency pressure on the blockchain system. However, this technology also gives super nodes unparalleled super privileges, making data tampering actually only require consensus from a few nodes. The representative example of sharding technology is Ethereum [9]. Ethereum uses a shared world state, but transactions in each shard are independently confirmed, and the final shard only needs to upload confirmed transactions. Sharding technology sacrifices security, as it only requires the agreement of the majority of members within a shard to falsify or backtrack data.

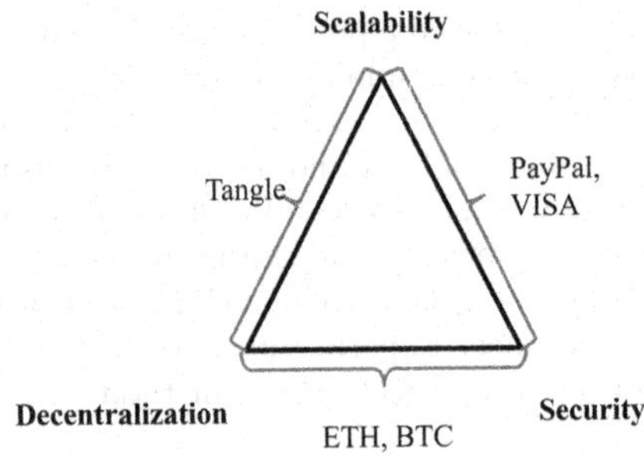

Fig. 1. The impossible triangle theory of blockchain. The three vertices of the Impossible Triangle are decentralization, security, and scalability. Tangle can satisfy decentralization and scalability, VISA and PayPal can satisfy security and scalability, but neither BTC nor ETH, the most popular blockchain systems, can satisfy scalability.

Upon reexamining the impossible triangle theory of blockchain and the current popular routes to improve its scalability, it is evident that current blockchain systems are facing serious communication and storage bottlenecks. In such bandwidth limited environments, blockchain builders and users prefer to store lightweight files such as transaction verifications. However, considering blockchain's role as a communication network in the Metaverse and federated learning algorithms, novel image transmission and storage paradigms are necessary for data with bandwidth and storage requirements. In the 1980s, when the Internet first emerged, users preferred to use lightweight files similar to the current blockchain systems. But soon, a strong demand for visual data resulted in the rapid emergence of new communication protocols, image encoding methods, and specialized

[2] Data from https://www.visa.co.uk/.

image encoding and decoding hardware, and the Internet quickly entered the multimedia era containing a large amount of image and video data. Inspired by [32], in this paper, we propose a new face reconstruction paradigm for government blockchain that strictly satisfies the decentralization and security features of blockchain and does not require introducing additional system support such as external links or cloud storage systems. It achieves secure and high-definition face reconstruction.

Inspired by the current popular pre-trained large models [5,18,21,22] and cross-modal generation methods [1,14–16], we design a hybrid modality data that converts faces into natural language text and sketches, which is uploaded to a blockchain system. The receiver uses a cross-modal generation model that uses multi-modal data to reconstruct the face image. During this process, the blockchain system only needs to verify and store text data, greatly reducing communication and storage pressure. However, at the same time, we also face the following challenges: how to generate accurate intermediate descriptions for a face, and how to ensure that the description can be accurately recognized and generated by the cross-modal model. For face representation generation, methods based on deep learning, such as DeepFace [30] and VggFace [25], provide face representation methods. However, these methods generally face a common restrict in semantic communication: the encoding and decoding ends need to be tightly coupled, or they need to be one-to-one. This requirement leads to a characteristic that the receiver needs to synchronize the decoding model that matches the sender. Downloading and persisting the encoding and decoding models undoubtedly brings enormous communication pressure to the blockchain. Our method no longer requires the sender and receiver to be tightly coupled, with sketches and natural language text themselves are model-independent. Compared to sketches, generating accurate natural language descriptions of faces is a very challenging task. Current popular Visual Question Answering large models lack the ability to accurately describe faces. Therefore, inspired by methods such as InstructGPT [18] and RLHF [4], we design a progressive natural language guidance scheme to achieve deep mining of internal knowledge in large models while generating important natural language descriptions for faces. Finally, we use a hybrid modality data of sketches and instruct prompts to induce the model to generate high-quality face images.

We summarize the contributions of this paper as follows: **(1)** We propose a cross-modal face reconstruction method that is applicable in band width-constrained situations. **(2)** We propose a model-independent hybrid modality representation method for faces while reducing the storage requirements for faces. **(3)** We propose a instruction construction method for knowledge mining in multi-modal large models, avoiding the need for model retraining.

2 Related Work

Multi-modal Large Model. After the success of pretrained large language models in natural language processing, pretrained multimodal models for processing or generating multimodal data quickly became a research hotspot. For image-text inputs, ViLBERT [16] utilizes BERT to extract textual information, Faster-RCNN to extract image features, and a transformer module for fusion. LXMERT [31] is based on ViLBERT but no longer uses pretrained visual or textual feature extractors. ERNIE-ViL [36] introduces an additional scene graph parser outside of image and text, which gets the scene graph as additional information input into the model, thus explicitly injecting the fine-grained correspondence between images and text into the model. Compared to ViLBERT, VLBERT [28] no longer uses a two-stream design and instead inputs image regions and text together into the model. Image-BERT [20] builds on VLBERT and uses the location information extracted by Faster-RCNN as an encoding input into the model. ViLT [11], based on a single-stream model, no longer uses any pretrained image feature extractors and directly inputs image regions using an image encoding method similar to ViT [7]. The BEIT series of methods [1] [19] [34] introduce image latent space encoding from VAE into MMLM. Based on CLIP [21], BLIP [15] introduces a bootstrapping method to obtain more weak-supervised data. BLIP2 [14] treats all multimodal signals as unified inputs, and after unified representation learning, uses PLLM as an indicator to adapt to various downstream tasks, including Visual Question Answering (VQA) and image captioning.

Image Generation Models. Image generation models aim to generate realistic and diverse images from random noise or a given condition. One of the earliest and most popular image generation models is the Generative Adversarial Network (GAN), which consists of a generator and a discriminator competing in a two-player minimax game [10,17]. GANs have been applied in various fields, such as image synthesis [17], image-to-image translation [35], and style transfer [40]. Variational Autoencoder (VAE) [3] is another widely used image generation model that learns a compressed latent representation of the input image and then reconstructs it from the latent space. Conditional versions of GANs and VAEs, such as Conditional GAN (cGAN) [8] and Conditional VAE (cVAE) [26], have been proposed to generate images from a given condition or class label. More recently, flow-based models such as RealNVP [6] and Glow [12] have been proposed to model the probability density function of the data using a sequence of invertible transformations. These models have shown promising results in image generation and have been used to generate high-quality images with controllable attributes. Currently, the Stable Diffusion model based on diffusion models [27,37] has demonstrated unparalleled competitiveness in cross-modal fields such as text-to-image. Combined with technologies such as ControlNet [38] and Dreambooth [23], using mixed-modal data as conditional input to obtain better generated images has become possible.

3 Methodology

This section describes how to use a cross-modal approach for face reconstruction to serve bandwidth limited blockchains. In the first subsection, we formulate the

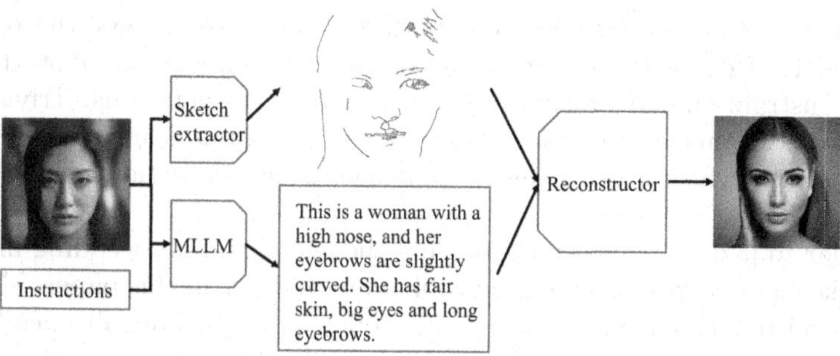

Fig. 2. An overview structure of the algorithm proposed in this paper. The sketch is extracted from the image through the Sketch extractor, and the detailed description of the face information is generated under the guidance of the instructions. Finally, a reconstructor that accepts multi-modal control information generates the image.

problem. In the second subsection, we describe the method for constructing lingual instructions for faces. In the third subsection, we explain the necessity of cross-modal representation for face reconstruction. Figure 2 shows an overview of the proposed model in this paper. To facilitate understanding, the term "instruction" will be used to refer to guidance words directed towards MMLMs, and "prompt" will be used to refer to the intermediate representation of the generated image.

3.1 Problem Formulation

We adopt the problem formulation from [32]. The learning-based face reconstruction process can be defined as:

$$I_o \xrightarrow{f(\theta_1)} X \xrightarrow{g(\theta_2)} I_r \tag{1}$$

In (1), I_o is the original face image, $f(\theta_1)$ is a sampling mapping with parameters θ_1, X is the intermediate representation, $g(\theta_2)$ is a reconstruction mapping with parameters θ_2 and I_r is the reconstructed face image. From the perspective of information bottleneck theory [24,33], $f(\theta_1)$ aims to minimize the mutual information $MI(I_o, X; \theta_1)$ while $g(\theta_2)$ aims to maximize $MI(X, I_l; \theta_2)$. I_l is the lossy compressed face image downsampled from I_o. Therefore, the face image lossy reconstruction problem can be defined as:

$$\arg\min_{\theta_1,\theta_2} MI(I_o, X; \theta_1) - \gamma MI(X, I_l; \theta_2) \tag{2}$$

γ is used to balance f and g. The first term $MI(I_o, X; \theta_1)$ in (2) can be simply understood as the compression rate of the original image, and the second term $MI(X, I_l; \theta_2)$ can be intuitively understood as the distortion rate. The higher the compression rate and the lower the distortion rate of the face, the better the quality of the intermediate representation, and the smaller the optimization objective value calculated by (2). The compression rate and distortion rate jointly constrain the generation of intermediate representations. Trivially, the improvement of image compression rate almost inevitably leads to a decrease in distortion rate, which poses a severe challenge to the generation of intermediate representations.

Similar to [32], to avoid synchronizing the encoding and decoding models in the blockchain network, they are invisible to each other in this paper. Moreover, the transmitted facial images are in the open domain, and all encoders and decoders cannot be fine-tuned according to specific datasets or model structures. The problem is further defined as follows:

$$\arg\min_{P} MI(I_o, X; P) - \gamma MI(X, I_l) \tag{3}$$

P in (3) represents the additional instruct prompt input to the encoder. (3) can be intuitively understood as how to introduce additional control instructions to generate better intermediate representations of faces when the parameters of the encoder and decoder are fixed. The generation and analysis of the control instructions will be elaborated in the following two sections.

3.2 Constructing Lingual Instructions for Face Reconstruction

Inspired by RLHF proposed in InstructGPT [18], we realized that for pre-trained large models like PLLMs and MMLMs with massive parameters, even with fewer parameters, ideal results can be achieved on specific tasks if suitable instructions are provided. From the perspective of data mining, the pre-trained large model itself is a huge knowledge base, but how to mine specific knowledge in such a black-box type of model and design appropriate instructions is crucial. The reconstruction paradigm proposed in [32] focuses more on natural image processing problems defined in the open domain. Discrete instructions (based on natural language) are difficult to fully satisfy the requirements. Therefore, continuous instructing vectors (the output vectors of ControlNet [38]) may be more potential. However, for the facial reconstruction task focused on in this paper, although the number of facial features may be infinite, the semantic dimensions in which facial features exist are finite and countable. These semantic dimensions include facial features such as facial features, skin color, etc.

Before introducing the proposed method for constructing prompts in this paper, Fig. 3 shows the results of naive image caption and visual question answering on an image. The image caption model used is BLIP2_OPT_6.7B, and the visual question answering model used is BLIP2_FlanT5xxl. BLIP2 is currently one of the most powerful MMLMs. From the results shown in Fig. 3, it is clear that it is not feasible to directly ask the MMLMs to provide a detailed description of a face, as MMLMs only focuse on some key information rather than all the facial information. One of the key reasons for this phenomenon is that there are rarely complete descriptions of faces in the training of these large models, only one or two key descriptions. The training data, such as image-text pairs crawled from web pages, often use descriptions like "a woman/man", rather than a complete description of the face. However, when humans browse these web pages, they simultaneously observe the image and text. They spontaneously generate some descriptions of the image, which cannot be discovered from the text and cannot be used as training image-text pairs.

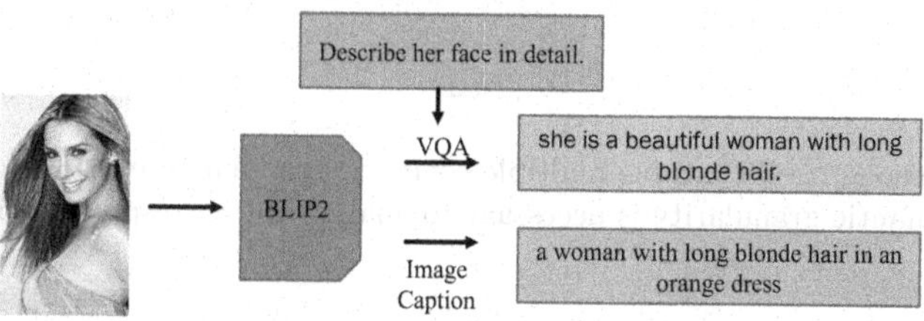

Fig. 3. The results of direct image caption and visual question answering using BLIP2. Both methods pay attention to the blonde hair while ignoring all other facial information.

In addition to the issue with training data, we found that there is a more intrinstic problem here, which is the problem of aligning the semantic granularity levels between images and text. An image often corresponds to multiple fine-grained semantic information, as shown in Fig. 4. Directly asking a MMLM to provide a summary of the image without providing the necessary fine-grained semantic information tends to result in coarse-grained image descriptions rather than detailed descriptions. Therefore, we need to provide MMLMs with fine-grained semantic instructions, mainly focused on relatively local areas such as eyes. The CelebAText-HQ dataset [29] provides fine-grained descriptions of faces. CelebAText-HQ is a subset of the CelebAMask-HQ [13] dataset, consisting of 15,010 images, each of which is manually annotated by ten workers with ten text descriptions of the face, from coarse to fine descriptions of different parts of the face. We use these fine-grained descriptions to construct instructions that are suitable for MMLMs.

We counted the occurrences of nouns and adjectives appearing in all text descriptions in CelebAText-HQ, as shown in Fig. 5. By counting the manually annotated fine-grained facial information, we attempted to restore the most important and common information that humans need to pay attention to regarding a face. The most important information reflects the diversity of faces, such as pink hair, while the most common information reflects the commonality of faces, such as face shape. This paper did not use some pre-defined nouns and adjectives related to facial features to prevent the loss of key facial information due to the author's own cognitive limitations. On the other hand, the labeling of CelebAText-HQ dataset reflects the subjective aesthetic experience of the annotators, and can generate more appropriate instructions for facial standards. The diversity of faces can be reflected through image captioning, while the commonality of faces can be induced by our instructions. The diversity of faces can be

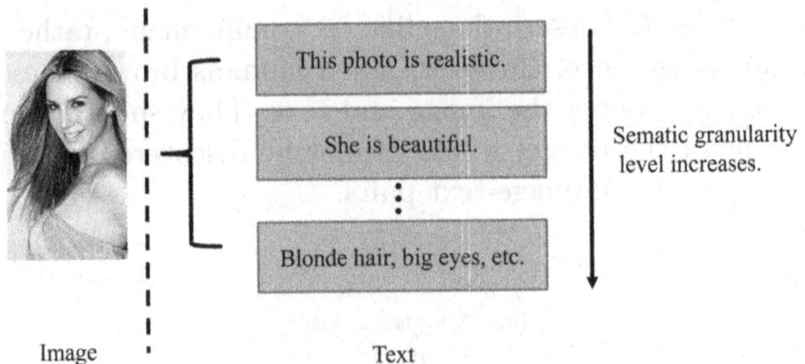

Fig. 4. The image itself contains multiple semantic granularity information, and specifying the semantic granularity is necessary to analyze the corresponding image region.

reflected by image captions, while the common features can be induced by our instructions. Our prompts for face generations consist of two parts: one from image captions and the other generated from instructions. From Fig. 5, gender is the most related feature with faces, which is in line with the annotations in the dataset. Other nouns include fine-grained facial features such as lips and eyes. In the frequency visualization of noun-adjective pairs, double eyelids and large mouths are the most common. To avoid long instructions, we limit the inducing words to the top 10 most common nouns and adjectives, and merge some adjectives. Finally, we design a fully orthogonal set of 21 inducing questions. Some of the instructions are shown in Table 1.

Fig. 5. Image (a) is a visualization of noun frequency, while image (b) is a visualization of noun-adjective pairs frequency. The larger the font size, the higher the frequency of appearance.

3.3 Face Reconstruction Needs Mixed-Modal Data

In computer graphics, the construction of a 3D model typically includes a model skeleton and a mesh. Similarly, for processing a facial image, the face can be considered to be composed of a skeleton and a mesh, with the skeleton representation understood as a sketch, and the mesh as including texture, color, and other image information. Therefore, the intermediate representation X in Eq. (3) can be decomposed as:

$$X = X_s + X_m \tag{4}$$

Table 1. Some examples of our instruction. The first two rows in the table are generative instructions, while the last two rows are discriminative instructions, to prevent the generative instructions from failing to produce any meaningful information in the most extreme cases.

Instructions
What is the hair color of the person?
What is the shape of the person's nose?
Are the person's eyes black?
Is the person's chin double?

In addition to representing information about the size and shape of a face, X_s in (4) also provides crucial pose information for image reconstruction. One challenging issue in semantic reconstruction of images is that the pose of the semantic object is often uncertain. For example, if an image of a tiger lying on the ground is input into the Text-to-Image model, the generated image of the tiger may have an infinite number of poses, such as looking up, looking down, lying from left to right, lying from right to left, and so on. To ensure the fidelity of image reconstruction, the sketch can guarantee the basic position of the semantic object, while the mesh can be generated around this sketch. We will demonstrate the use of single-modal and mixed-modal comparisons in the experimental section.

4 Experiments

In this section, we conducted a variety of qualitative and quantitative experiments around the proposed face reconstruction algorithm in this paper. The quantitative experiments studied the compression efficiency and distortion rate of the proposed algorithm and compared it with various popular image compression algorithms for actual transmission speed on the blockchain. In the qualitative experiments, we focused on the visual effects of face reconstruction using single modality and the mixed modality proposed in this paper.

4.1 Datasets

The faces used in this paper are sourced from CelebAText-HQ. CelebAText-HQ provides multi-level, high-granularity text annotations on top of CelebAMask-HQ, which already contains 30,000 high-resolution images at 512 × 512. Each face contains 19 components, including skin, nose, eyebrows, eyes, ears, lips, mouth, hair, hat, glasses, earrings, necklace, neck, and clothing. 500 images were randomly selected from CelebAText-HQ for the experiments.

4.2 Metrics

Metrics and its descriptions are listed in the following table:

Table 2. Metrics and its descriptions.

Metric	Description
FID	the distance between real and generated imagesusing feature statistics from an Inception network
LPIPS	the distance between images based on perceptualfeatures learned from a deep neural network
PSNR	Peak Signal-to-Noise Ratio measures image quality by comparing the peak signal power to the noise power in the image
SSIM	Structural Similarity Index compares the structural information between two images, taking into account luminance, contrast, and structural similarity

Total Persistence Time (TPT), waiting time (WT), minimun/Maximum waiting time (mWT/MWT), and File Size (F.S.) obey the rule of the smaller the better. Their definitions can be found in [32]. FID, LPIPS, PSNR and SSIM are common visual fidelity metrics. PSNR and SSIM obey the rule of the bigger the better while FID and LPIPS are on the contrary.

4.3 Quantitative Experiments

We use Stable Diffusion as the base generative model and ControlNet [38] as the conditional control network in the following experiments. Canny is chosen to be the sketch extractor. The experiment environment is the same in [32].

Experiments on the Blackchain. As shown in Table 3, the storage format of Canny can also benefit from the progress of image compression methods, and using webp can effectively reduce the transmission volume compared to the jpg storage format. It should be noted that different quality levels of Canny storage formats do not have a decisive impact on the final generated images. It can be foreseen that if a storage format specifically designed for sketches is used, the storage cost will be further reduced. As shown in [32], using only text will continue to exponentially reduce transmission volume, but the finally reconstructed images will have significant pose changes. To ensure the stability of face reconstruction, we recommend using the mixed-modality storage method.

Table 3. In comparison with the traditional image compression method for blockchain transmission experiments. The definitions of TPT, mWT, MWT, and F.S. can be seen in Table 2. We used jpg and webp as the comparison methods and used different compression ratios and fidelity rates. Canny. J. H refers to Canny images stored in high-quality jpg format, Canny. J. L refers to Canny images stored in low-quality jpg format, Canny. W. L refers to Canny images stored in low-quality webp formatand Canny. W. H refers to Canny images stored in high-quality webp format. Canny. J. H+Text represents a mixed modality representation form that combines Canny images and textual content. Bold indicates the best result.

	TPT(s)	mWT(ms)	MWT(ms)	F. S.(MB)
Original	902.48	502.31	1220.21	102
JPG High	331.85	381.44	876.79	47
JPG Low	305.85	361.21	842.62	44
Webp Low	164.18	229.03	581.45	13
Webp High	170.40	240.77	601.27	25
Canny J. H + Text	293.33	317.46	742.02	40
Canny J. L + Text	242.74	282.66	722.34	36
Canny W. L + Text	**137.45**	**175.45**	**474.16**	**10**
Canny W. H + Text	158.19	197.88	408.03	14

Experiments on Visual Fidelity. It should be noted that PSNR and SSIM are rarely used as metrics in text-guided image generation tasks. These two metrics reflect pixel-to-pixel image similarity and are often only used in image compression algorithms. Any change in a pixel will cause a change in these two metrics. For text-guided image generation tasks, the transition from the text modality to the image modality is a dimensionally significant process that includes a lot of uncertainty and randomness. This also results in the generated image structure being uncontrollable, as discussed in Sect. 3.3. For example, it is difficult to control whether a tiger lying on its side is facing left or right in the generated model. The introduction of sketches significantly improves the structural similarity in the process of face reconstruction, thereby improving the performance of PSNR and SSIM. However, we have noticed that although we use a lot of colors as control conditions, these conditions are still not precise enough. In other words, a pair of red eyes can be induced to be generated, but it is still uncertain whether they are rose red or Bordeaux red. Such subtle losses in color can make it difficult to truly improve pixel-to-pixel image fidelity metrics. However, for more detailed color differentiation corresponding to more fine-grained semantic understanding, this is difficult for current multi-modal large models to learn and understand. To improve this type of metric, network structures that store material details or colors, similar to a codebook, can be introduced, but this is beyond the scope of this paper. The similar PSNR and SSIM scores for mixed modality and using only Canny as input are also due to this. Although text introduces additional color information, these colors are not accurate enough to improve the metrics. However, we can see in the quality experiments in the next section that the generated images with only Canny as control conditions are only black and white, while the generated images with mixed modalities as control conditions not only have the same structural details but are also in color. For the human eye, the color red is important, but it is actually difficult to distinguish between Bordeaux red and rose red. For FID and LPLIS, the improvement is expected, which is more in line with human subjective perception (Table 4).

Table 4. Comparison of visual fidelity using different modalities in the experiments. "Canny" represents using only sketch information as a control condition, "Text" represents using only text information as a control condition, and "Canny+Text" represents using a mixed modality of text and sketch as a control condition. Bold indicates the best result.

	PSNR	SSIM	FID	LPIPS
Canny	10.40	0.50	113.95	0.46
Text	8.92	0.40	98.06	0.60
Canny+Text	**10.51**	**0.51**	**91.16**	**0.44**

4.4 Qualitative Experiments

It is evident from Fig. 6 that a sketch with rich structural and positional information can improve the stability of the entire composition. Using only text as a single modality for generation control not only causes displacement of facial position, but also generates multiple faces. It should be noted that we did not use additional prompts such as "a photo of" to induce the model to generate photo-type faces. Using only Canny as a single modality for guidance, the model generates composition effects similar to those of the mixed modality. However, it is evident that, in the case of the first face, using only Canny as the control condition results in gender reversal in the generated image. Even more fatal is the fact that, due to the lack of crucial color information, Stable Diffusion is more inclined to generate sketch-type images, resulting in all images being black and white. We provide an empirical explanation for this phenomenon, namely that when using visual modality as a control condition, Stable Diffusion tends to preserve the color information in the original image. Since Canny only retains black and white information, the generated images are also black and white. Lack of color information is unacceptable in the process of facial reconstruction. Therefore, mixed-modal is need for face reconstruction.

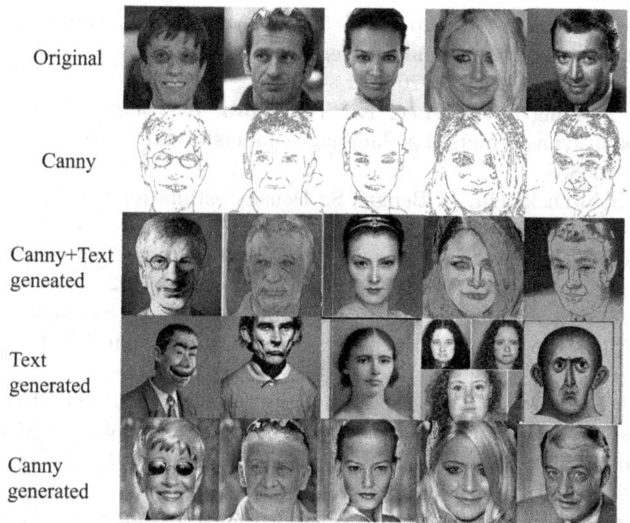

Fig. 6. The comparative experiment on controlling with different modalities. The first row is the original image, the second row is the extracted Canny edge map, the third row is the image generated using the mixed Canny+Text modality, the fourth row is the image generated using only the Text modality, and the fifth row is the image generated using only the Image modality.

5 Conclusion

Improving the scalability of blockchain while ensuring security and decentralization has become a daunting challenge. For the common task of face transmission on the blockchain, this paper proposes a novel cross-modal face generation method. Compared to traditional methods, we design a progressive prompt-based approach to explore the rich knowledge in MMLMs and verify the superior improvement of the cross-modal generation method in transmission efficiency and generated image quality.

Acknowledgement. This work is supported by the Science and Technology Research "JieBangGuaShuai" Program of Liaoning Province, China: Intelligent e-Government System based on Consortium Blockchain under Grant 2021JH1/10400010.

References

1. Bao, H., Dong, L., Piao, S., Wei, F.: Beit: Bert pre-training of image transformers (2021). arXiv preprint arXiv:2106.08254
2. Chen, J., Duan, K., Zhang, R., Zeng, L., Wang, W.: An AI based super nodes selection algorithm in blockchain networks (2018). arXiv preprint arXiv:1808.00216
3. Chen, X., et al.: Variational lossy autoencoder (2016). arXiv preprint arXiv:1611.02731

4. Christiano, P.F., Leike, J., Brown, T., Martic, M., Legg, S., Amodei, D.: Deep reinforcement learning from human preferences. In: Advances in Neural Information Processing Systems, vol. 30 (2017)
5. Devlin, J., Chang, M.W., Lee, K., Toutanova, K.: Bert: Pre-training of deep bidirectional transformers for language understanding (2018). arXiv preprint arXiv:1810.04805
6. Dinh, L., Sohl-Dickstein, J., Bengio, S.: Density estimation using real NVP (2016). arXiv preprint arXiv:1605.08803
7. Dosovitskiy, A., et al.: An image is worth 16x16 words: Transformers for image recognition at scale (2020). arXiv preprint arXiv:2010.11929
8. Gauthier, J.: Conditional generative adversarial nets for convolutional face generation. Class Proj. Stanford Cs231n: Convolutional Neural Netw. Vis. Recogn. Winter Semester (5), 2 (2014)
9. Gencer, A.E., Basu, S., Eyal, I., van Renesse, R., Sirer, E.G.: Decentralization in bitcoin and Ethereum networks. In: Meiklejohn, S., Sako, K. (eds.) FC 2018. LNCS, vol. 10957, pp. 439–457. Springer, Heidelberg (2018). https://doi.org/10.1007/978-3-662-58387-6_24
10. Goodfellow, I.: Nips 2016 tutorial: Generative adversarial networks (2016). arXiv preprint arXiv:1701.00160
11. Kim, W., Son, B., Kim, I.: Vilt: vision-and-language transformer without convolution or region supervision. In: International Conference on Machine Learning, pp. 5583–5594. PMLR (2021)
12. Kingma, D.P., Dhariwal, P.: Glow: generative flow with invertible 1x1 convolutions. In: Advances in Neural Information Processing Systems, vol. 31 (2018)
13. Lee, C.H., Liu, Z., Wu, L., Luo, P.: MaskGAN: towards diverse and interactive facial image manipulation. In: Proceedings of the IEEE/CVF Conference on Computer Vision and Pattern Recognition, pp. 5549–5558 (2020)
14. Li, J., Li, D., Savarese, S., Hoi, S.: Blip-2: Bootstrapping language-image pre-training with frozen image encoders and large language models (2023). arXiv preprint arXiv:2301.12597
15. Li, J., Li, D., Xiong, C., Hoi, S.: Blip: Bootstrapping language-image pre-training for unified vision-language understanding and generation. In: International Conference on Machine Learning, pp. 12888–12900. PMLR (2022)
16. Lu, J., Batra, D., Parikh, D., Lee, S.: Vilbert: pretraining task-agnostic visiolinguistic representations for vision-and-language tasks. In: Advances in Neural Information Processing Systems, vol. 32 (2019)
17. Makhzani, A., Shlens, J., Jaitly, N., Goodfellow, I., Frey, B.: Adversarial autoencoders (2015). arXiv preprint arXiv:1511.05644
18. Ouyang, L., et al.: Training language models to follow instructions with human feedback (2022). arXiv preprint arXiv:2203.02155
19. Peng, Z., Dong, L., Bao, H., Ye, Q., Wei, F.: Beit v2: Masked image modeling with vector-quantized visual tokenizers (2022). arXiv preprint arXiv:2208.06366
20. Qi, D., Su, L., Song, J., Cui, E., Bharti, T., Sacheti, A.: ImageBERT: Cross-modal pre-training with large-scale weak-supervised image-text data (2020). arXiv preprint arXiv:2001.07966
21. Radford, A., et al.: Learning transferable visual models from natural language supervision. In: International Conference on Machine Learning, pp. 8748–8763. PMLR (2021)
22. Radford, A., Wu, J., Child, R., Luan, D., Amodei, D., Sutskever, I., et al.: Language models are unsupervised multitask learners. OpenAI Blog **1**(8), 9 (2019)

23. Ruiz, N., Li, Y., Jampani, V., Pritch, Y., Rubinstein, M., Aberman, K.: Dreambooth: Fine tuning text-to-image diffusion models for subject-driven generation (2022). arXiv preprint arXiv:2208.12242
24. Shwartz-Ziv, R., Tishby, N.: Opening the black box of deep neural networks via information (2017). arXiv preprint arXiv:1703.00810
25. Simonyan, K., Zisserman, A.: Very deep convolutional networks for large-scale image recognition (2014). arXiv preprint arXiv:1409.1556
26. Sohn, K., Lee, H., Yan, X.: Learning structured output representation using deep conditional generative models. In: Advances in Neural Information Processing Systems, vol. 28 (2015)
27. Song, Y., Durkan, C., Murray, I., Ermon, S.: Maximum likelihood training of score-based diffusion models. Adv. Neural. Inf. Process. Syst. **34**, 1415–1428 (2021)
28. Su, W., et al.: VL-BERT: Pre-training of generic visual-linguistic representations (2019). arXiv preprint arXiv:1908.08530
29. Sun, J., Li, Q., Wang, W., Zhao, J., Sun, Z.: Multi-caption text-to-face synthesis: dataset and algorithm. In: Proceedings of the 29th ACM International Conference on Multimedia, pp. 2290–2298 (2021)
30. Taigman, Y., Yang, M., Ranzato, M., Wolf, L.: Deepface: closing the gap to human-level performance in face verification. In: Proceedings of the IEEE Conference on Computer Vision and Pattern Recognition, pp. 1701–1708 (2014)
31. Tan, H., Bansal, M.: LXMERT: Learning cross-modality encoder representations from transformers (2019). arXiv preprint arXiv:1908.07490
32. Tan, Z., et al.: Building a modal-balanced blockchain with semantic reconstruction (2023). https://doi.org/10.48550/ARXIV.2303.02428, http://arxiv.org/abs/2303.02428
33. Tishby, N., Zaslavsky, N.: Deep learning and the information bottleneck principle. In: 2015 IEEE Information Theory Workshop (ITW), pp. 1–5. IEEE (2015)
34. Wang, W., et al.: Image as a foreign language: Beit pretraining for all vision and vision-language tasks (2022). arXiv preprint arXiv:2208.10442
35. Yi, Z., Zhang, H., Tan, P., Gong, M.: DualGAN: unsupervised dual learning for image-to-image translation. In: Proceedings of the IEEE International Conference on Computer Vision, pp. 2849–2857 (2017)
36. Yu, F., et al.: ERNIE-ViL: knowledge enhanced vision-language representations through scene graphs. In: Proceedings of the AAAI Conference on Artificial Intelligence, vol. 35, pp. 3208–3216 (2021)
37. Yu, J., et al.: Vector-quantized image modeling with improved VQGAN (2021). arXiv preprint arXiv:2110.04627
38. Zhang, L., Agrawala, M.: Adding conditional control to text-to-image diffusion models (2023). arXiv preprint arXiv:2302.05543
39. Zhang, S., Liu, Y., Chen, X.: BIT problem: is there a trade-off in the performances of blockchain systems? In: Zheng, Z., Dai, H.-N., Tang, M., Chen, X. (eds.) BlockSys 2019. CCIS, vol. 1156, pp. 123–136. Springer, Singapore (2020). https://doi.org/10.1007/978-981-15-2777-7_11
40. Zhang, Y., Zhang, Y., Cai, W.: Separating style and content for generalized style transfer. In: Proceedings of the IEEE Conference on Computer Vision and Pattern Recognition, pp. 8447–8455 (2018)

LoCom: An Efficient Load-Balanced Concurrency Optimization Method for Bulk-Commodity Regulatory Systems

Hengqi Guo[1], Lianggui Chen[2(✉)], Wenbin Huang[1], Junxiong Lin[1], Zhihui Lu[1], Shijing Hu[1], Gao Zou[2], and Dayao Sha[2]

[1] School of Computer Science, Fudan University, Shanghai, China
[2] Shanghai United Credit Services Co., Ltd., Shanghai, China
chenlianggui@suaee.com

Abstract. To address the lack of effective regulatory measures for the bulk-commodities electronic trading market, a trusted transaction depository system was built using Hyperledger Fabric as a framework to meet the needs of the bulk-commodities regulatory scenario, but the performance of the current Fabric can hardly meet such a large throughput. In this paper, an efficient load-balanced concurrency optimization method (LoCom) for bulk-commodity regulatory systems is proposed. Parallelisation of the endorsement phase is accomplished by transforming the underlying logic of the endorsement phase in this method. For the modified multi-container endorsement scenario, external chain code technology is introduced to manage the endorsement containers, and the transactions are distributed to different containers through dynamic load balancing algorithms. Meanwhile, a multi-threaded approach was adopted to verify the read and write sets of transactions, while parallelising the writing to the historical database and updating the ledger. Through stress testing, the system throughput is increased by nearly two times, close to the limit value in the ideal state, and the number of transactions distributed by the algorithm is basically even.

Keywords: performance optimization · blockchain · bulk-commodities · fabric · containers

1 Introduction

China's imports of bulk-commodities and raw materials have grown exponentially in the last decade and it has become the world's largest importer and consumer of bulk-commodities [1]. In the next 30 years of development, it is foreseeable that China's share of the bulk-commodities industry will remain the unequalled leader in the world. However, due to the wide range of bulk-commodity business areas and the many organisational members involved, there are many drawbacks and redundancies when it comes to trading and circulation [2]. The completion of bulk-commodity transactions is mainly achieved through

Z. Wang et al. (Eds.): ICSS 2023, CCIS 1844, pp. 490–504, 2023.
https://doi.org/10.1007/978-981-99-4402-6_35

the circulation of warehouse receipts, but the lack of guarantee for the mobility of bulk-commodities in China and the long-term lack of authenticity of the existing stock of goods has led to the warehouse receipts in the market in a mostly non-standard form, which cannot meet the risk control requirements of financial institutions in trading, warehousing, circulation and other aspects [3].

The use of blockchain technology can solve the problems of opaque bulk-commodity transactions and inaccurate information in warehousing and logistics [4]. In addition to resistance to repudiation and traceability, the authenticity and validity of the data on the chain can be guaranteed through the mechanism of the blockchain itself, so it can be used as an authoritative channel to provide valid evidence for disputes arising in the course of transactions.

Originally designed for enterprise applications, as is known to all, Hyperledger Fabric is an enterprise-level open source permissioned blockchain [5]. For other popular distributed ledger systems or blockchain platforms in the market, Fabric's own multi-party access architecture fits in with the multiple roles involved in the bulk-commodity trading model. According to statistics, as many as 150,000 transactions are completed daily on a single bulk-commodity trading platform, and the number of transactions is on the rise as the bulk-commodity market expands. In this situation, the performance requirements of the Hyperledger Fabric framework are significant and performance optimisation studies are of great application and practicality.

We have used Hyperledger Fabric as a framework to build a trade custody depository system, which meets the security requirements of the bulk-commodities e-marketplace. However, influenced by the mechanism of Fabric itself, we have optimized the performance of Fabric, proposed and implemented a universal endorsement phase optimization scheme, with the implementation of a multi-container transaction distribution mechanism and a load balancing scheme, and also proposed an optimization of the validation phase for the specificity of the bulk-commodities scenario, our contributions are specified as follows.

1. Optimization of the endorsement phase of Fabric. We have implemented a chain code that can invoke multiple chain code containers to endorse multiple transactions simultaneously, breaking the performance bottleneck caused by a single container.
2. Management and scheduling of multiple chain code containers. A load balancing model is built to schedule different containers, distributing a large number of transactions evenly to a reasonable number of containers for endorsement. External chain code technology is also introduced to manage and schedule multiple containers.
3. Optimisation of the validation phase of the Fabric. The source code was modified to make the validation phase pipelined, and the writing of historical status data and ledgers was also made parallel.

The paper is structured as follows. Section 2 presents the related work. In Sect. 3, we present the optimised design for the endorsement, transaction distribution and validation phases. Section 4 presents the concrete implementation and evaluation results. In Sect. 5, conclusions and future work are summarised.

2 Related Work

In terms of the regulatory service model, there is no regional comprehensive regulatory service platform at home or abroad at the moment. There is a lack of complete analysis of bulk-commodity market quotations to achieve comprehensive risk monitoring and early warning [6], and at present, the trading data of bulk-commodities relies entirely on various trading supporting platforms or third-party depository institutions, making evidence collection and arbitration of trading disputes difficult [7]. Blockchain technology becomes a highly adaptive solution. Bai et al. [8] advocate centralised management of bulk-commodity resources through the establishment of a bulk-commodity electronic trading market to facilitate the formation of domestic resource prices and factors of production. Shi Wenjin et al. [9] proposed a credit management method based on a system prototype. The first case of domestic blockchain application in bulk-commodity trade is the US-China soybean trade [10]. The French company Louis Dreyfus Commodities reached an agreement with Shandong Bohai Industrial Co. to use the ETC blockchain online platform for contract signing and trade qualification. Shanghai Coal Exchange and Shanghai Qikun Information Technology Co., Ltd. jointly develop and operate a blockchain financial services platform for the coal and energy industry based on permissioned blockchain and the "Coal Trade Gold Chain" [11]. In our previous work, we developed a regulatory system for bulk-commodities trading using Hyperledger Fabric as the underlying architecture. This system can potentially address the limitations and challenges associated with current bulk-commodity trading practices.

Since IBM proposed Fabric, both industry and academia have paid considerable attention to its performance optimization efforts, and the widespread use of sharding technology in the blockchain space in recent years has led to significant performance improvements. sharma A et al. [12] proposed to explore Fabric from the perspective of database research, viewing performance in the transaction channel bottlenecks, allowing invalid transactions to be aborted early on by reordering them. Xu Xiaoqiong et al. [13] proposed CATP-Fabric, a permission blockchain system that tolerates conflicting transactions. CATP-Fabric first divides transactions into different groups based on transaction keys, arranges read-only transactions with high priority in the sorting phase, filters out-of-date transactions early, and designs an optimal abort transaction selection algorithm to further minimize the number of aborted transactions. Lu Xu et al. [14] proposed an LMLS approach for write-write concurrency conflicts and a cache-based approach to improve the system for read-write concurrency conflicts. The LMLS approach makes use of a locking mechanism for discovering conflicting transactions at the beginning of a transaction flow.

However, there are fewer studies and gaps in bulk-commodity oriented scenarios, and the technique proposed in this paper is capable of achieving higher performance improvements with the aim of developing more efficient and effective solutions for bulk-commodity trading scenarios, we have conducted further optimization of the entire process at all stages based on our existing regulatory system.

3 System Design

We designed the system to solve the problem of low performance caused by the blockchain technology principle when using Fabric as a transaction deposition system in a large commodity trading scenario.

3.1 Endorsement Phase Performance Optimisation

The core of the endorsement phase of the fabric is simulated transaction execution. When the endorsement policy is satisfied, the client broadcasts the proposal response set to the sorting service node [15]. The most time-consuming phase of the endorsement process is the execution of the chain code in the container, which accounts for nearly 90% of the entire endorsement phase. However, existing technologies limit each node to starting only one endorsement service and one chain code container for executing simulated transactions due to read-write conflict considerations [16]. In the case of a large number of transaction proposals, most transactions need to wait for the chain code container to become free to execute the simulated transactions. The scenario of a trusted depository for electronic bulk-commodity transactions involves a large number of read requests without the need to check the endorsement policy and the read set used in the validation phase. However, when the backing node processes a read transaction, it constructs the data to be used for MVCC and then the backing node sends it to the client. This process takes up the backing container, increasing the latency of the backing phase and reducing overall throughput [17].

Algorithm 1. check_namespace

```
input: namespace
output: namespace
flag := false
length = len(namespace)
if length > 8  &&  namespace[length − 6 :] == "_shard" then
    flag = true
end if
if flag then
    for i = length - 7 to 0 do
        if namespace[i] == '_' then
            return namespace[:i]
        end if
    end for
end if
```

The namespace of the fabric maps directly to the chain code names isolating the different world states, and the namespace is allocated by the Hyperledger Fabric. Even chain codes with the same installation content are assigned to different namespaces [18]. To implement one chain code corresponding to multiple containers on a node, you need to modify the source code to desegregate the namespaces of these same chain codes. We achieve the effect by modifying the namespace deposited during the packaging of the endorsement results, setting the names of the chain codes that need to have the same namespace in the format:

$$XXX\_n\_shard \tag{1}$$

XXX is the uniform namespace of the chain code to be parallelised, n is the number of the chain code, and shard is an additional suffix to distinguish the namespace of the chain code to be parallelised from the namespace of other common chain codes.

The check_namespace method determines whether the incoming name is suffixed with "_shard" and extracts the first part of the incoming name "shard" as the chain code namespace if it conforms to the rules. This ensures that chain codes that do not need to be parallelised are not affected and the original process is maintained. Chain code namespaces that satisfy the rules are modified to the corresponding namespaces. This is shown in Algorithm 1.

Algorithm 2. Modifying the chain code namespace during transaction execution

input: Transaction parameter txParams, namespace, chain code message msg, timeout
output: chain code message ChaincodeMessage, error

```
txParams.CollectionStore = h.getCollectionStore(msg.ChannelId)
txParams.IsInitTransaction = (msg.Type == pb.ChaincodeMessage_INIT)
txParams.NamespaceID = check_namespace(namespace)
txctx, err := h.TXContexts.Create(txParams)
...
return ccresp, err
```

Once the method of checking namespaces has been introduced, apply it where appropriate, as the part involving "ccid" cannot be changed without affecting the communication between the node and the container, so you cannot simply change the "name" or "ccid". We use Algorithm 2 to initiate the process of simulating the execution of a transaction by calling the check_namespace method to replace the namespace of the chain code that needs to be modified. Since each chain code container is identified by a "ccid", the containers are endorsed in parallel before they are deposited into the namespace, and after they are deposited into the world state database, since they share a namespace, they can use any of the containers to query and store data without discrimination.

As can be seen from the comparison in Fig. 1, the two main modifications made to the transaction process are the sharing of namespaces between the containers used to parallelise the endorsement process and the ability for Peer nodes to call multiple chain code containers in order to execute multiple transactions in the transaction proposal in parallel.

3.2 Transaction Load Balancing for Container State

Fabric v2.0 supports the deployment and execution of chain code outside of the Fabric environment. It allows users to manage the running of chain code independent of the node. This solution replaces the need to build and run chaincode on each node. The chaincode can run as a service and its lifecycle will be manageable outside of the Fabric environment [19]. Using external chaincode technology to create parallelised containers, the containers can be deployed or shut down in relation to the current network load, and when the smart contracts in the containers need to be updated, the smart contracts within the containers can be updated without affecting the Fabric network, allowing dynamic management of the number and content of containers [20, 21].

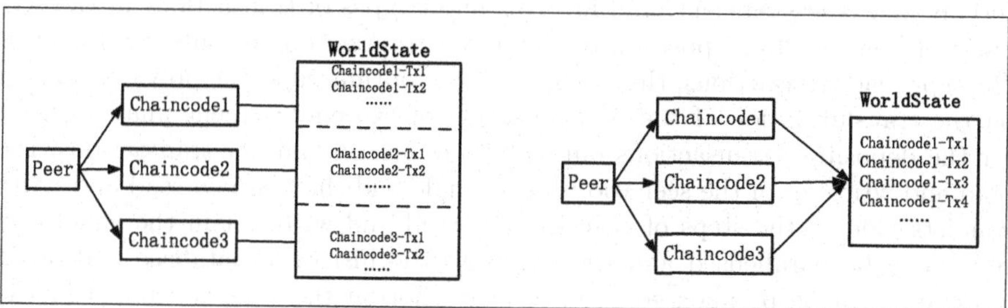

Fig. 1. On the left is the namespace before Fabric's modifications, on the right is the namespace after Fabric's modifications

The number of parallel chain code containers, i.e. service nodes, under the blockchain depository platform for bulk-commodity transactions is limited, and the use of external chain code technology is accompanied by the opening and closing of containers, the number of service nodes will change dynamically, there is no difference in configuration between containers, and the scenario expects that transactions will be distributed to each container as evenly as possible without the influence of container switching, so a consistent Hash algorithm with virtual nodes is suitable for the distribution of transactions [22].

In the consistent hashing algorithm, if a node is added, the only data affected is the data between the new node and the previous node in its ring space, i.e. the data between the first node found counter-clockwise and it, and the rest of the data does not and will not change [23]. The Consistent Hash Algorithm only needs to relocate a portion of the data in the ring space to add or subtract nodes, which provides good scalability and fault tolerance. However, when there are not enough nodes for the Consistent Hash Algorithm, the unequal distribution of nodes can easily result in a situation where the data is skewed and the cached objects are essentially stored on a particular server. To solve this problem virtual nodes can be used, where a number of hashes are calculated for each node and such a node is placed at each location generated by the calculation, such nodes are called virtual nodes, thus solving the problem of skewed data when there are not enough nodes [24].

In the scenario of trustworthy depository for electronic bulk-commodity transactions, each chain code container can be abstracted as a different server, and the names of the parallel chain code containers are dispersed as servers on the hash ring, and each time the transactions are mapped to the ring, the corresponding container is selected by a consistent hash algorithm, so that the effect of automatic distribution of transactions and load balancing can be achieved [25].

3.3 Performance Optimisation During the Validation Phase

The verification phase of the fabric is also one of the bottlenecks in blockchain performance [26,27]. The check of the read and write sets in this phase needs to take into account the double spend problem [28], which is logically executed serially and is less efficient, and involves fewer types of transactions in the scenario of trustworthy deposition of electronic transactions in bulk-commodities [29]. For read transactions, this point has been optimised in the previous section on the transformation of the parallelisation of the endorsement phase, except for the depository transactions only, as there are no transfer transactions, the read and write set of the scenario is very single and there are no read and write conflicts [30], so the steps of checking the read and write set in the validation phase can be parallelised and the writes to the historical database and other databases can be parallelised to effectively shorten the time consumed in the validation phase [13].

In multi-threaded programming, the number of threads needs to be established in relation to the CPU to ensure that new tasks can be assigned to CPU slices in a timely manner when they arise. The Goroutine mechanism allows lightweight threads to automatically allocate CPUs to each task, and if the user allocates enough tasks, the system can automatically allocate them to CPUs for the user, making them run as concurrently as possible. Since the return value of each Goroutine is ignored, channels are introduced as a communication mechanism between routines [31]. A channel is a communication mechanism that allows a Goroutine to send value information through it to another Goroutine. Due to the preference for communication rather than shared memory for resource sharing, Goroutines have created pipelines between them, with swaps to ensure that data is synchronised smoothly. Channels are modelled similarly to queues in that they strictly enforce a first-in-first-out rule to ensure that data is sent and received in order [32].

The fabric is based on a trusted certificate storage scenario for electronic bulk-commodity trading. By modifying the source code, multiple Goroutines can be used to check the read and write sets, and in combination with channels, the order of writing to the ledger can be controlled to achieve the effect of parallelisation of the verification phase [15].

Specifically, the MVCC validation process for a block initially calls EndorserTX to query and validate the read and write sets of transactions, writes the returned validation results to the “updates” set via applyWriteSet, and then uses the updated “updates” set to validate the next transaction in the block until all transactions in the block have been validated or a read/write set conflict has occurred and the block is invalidated. EndorserTX is considered for parallelisation. However, as "updates" are "apply" to the end of the set with the latest result, parallelised writing is not possible and is prone to errors. The "updates" are also the updated values that are eventually written to the ledger and database, so a channel of length of 1 is set to control the writing of the "updates". Only one validated Goroutine can update "updates" at a time, and the final result is a pipelined flow of code [33].

Algorithm 3. validateAndPrepareBatch

```
input: block
output: publicAndHashUpdates,error
if v.db.IsBulkOptimizable() then
    err := v.preLoadCommittedVersionOfRSet(blk)
    if err!=nil then
        return nil, err
    end if
end if
updates := newPubAndHashUpdates()
results := make(chan validateResult)
for _, tx := range blk.txs do
    go v.validateEndorserTX(tx.rwset, doMVCCValidation, updates, results)
    res :=← results
    if res.err !=nil then
        return nil,res.err
    end if
    validationCode = res.validationCode
    tx.validationCode = validationCode
    if validationCode == peer.TxValidationCode_VALID then
        commitTx=version.NewHeight(blk.num,uint64(tx.indexInBlock))
        updates.applyWriteSet(tx.rwset,commitTx,v.db,tx.containsPost)
    end if
end for
return updates, nil
```

We designed Algorithm 3 and Algorithm 4 to mainly modify the use of Goroutine multithreading to call the validateEndorserTx method, adding the channel used to store the results to the list of formal parameters of the calling method, size 1, and constantly removing the results from the pipeline, returning if the error result in the pipeline is not empty, otherwise assigning the result to a value, allowing new data to be deposited only after the previously deposited data has been removed, thus ensuring that the order of writes is not disrupted in the case of check parallelisation. The validateAndPrepareBatch calls the

Algorithm 4. validateEndorserTX

input: Transaction read-write set txRWSet,updates,doMVCCValidation,A pipe that controls the sequence of outcomes results
output: verification result peer.TxValidationCode,error

```
var validationCode = peer.TxValidationCode_VALID
var err error
if doMVCCValidation then
    validationCode, err = v.validateTx(txRWSet, updates)
end if
results ← &validateResult{
validationCode: validationCode,
err: err,}
return validationCode, err
```

validateEndorserTX method, which adds the new channel to the list of incoming parameters. Since the entire validateTx method has been parallelised and a pipeline has been introduced to control the writing of the results, there is no need to consider its internal implementation, just write the results returned by validateTx to the channel in the incoming argument list [34].

The final step in the validation phase of the fabric is the submission of blocks to the ledger that have completed the read and write set checks. First, the entire block is written to the distributed ledger with a valid or invalid flag for that transaction. Then, the write set of the valid transaction is committed to the state database. Finally the history database is updated again to keep track of which keys have been modified by which blocks and transactions [35]. Algorithm 5 parallelises the writes to the history database with those to the state database via the Goroutine method.

Algorithm 5. commit

input: Transaction read-write set txRWSet,updates,doMVCCValidation,A pipe that controls the sequence of outcomes results
output: verification result peer.TxValidationCode,error

```
if l.historyDB != nil then
    if err := l.historyDB.Commit(block); then
        if err != nil then
            panic(errors.WithMessage(err))
        end if
    end if
end if
```

4 Implementation and Evaluation

The Fabric network for this experiment was deployed on a physical machine with a Dell R730 model with 2 Intel(R) Xeon(R) CPU E5-2640 v4 @ 2.40 GHz

CPUs, 32G4 RAM, and 2 500G and 1.2T1 hard disks. The multi-virtual machine simulation crush test real scenario deals with a virtual machine configuration of 8G of RAM, 80G of disk, and an operating system of Ubuntu 16.04, with a total of ten virtual machines participating in the crush test experiment.

Experiments were mainly conducted through the marble chain code, which has the function of new creation and query, meeting the needs of the scenario of trusted depository for electronic trading of commodities. Twelve other chain codes, such as marble_1_shard and marble_2_shard, were installed as parallel chain codes with marble.

The experiment needs to verify five things: whether the namespace segregation is lifted in the endorsement phase, the performance improvement effect before and after the transformation of the endorsement phase, whether the transaction distribution based on the consistency hash algorithm is uniform, the effect of the external chain code invocation, and the performance improvement effect of the verification phase after the transformation.

4.1 Endorsement Phase Performance Optimisation Validation

The namespace was lifted after making changes to the source code. Using the marble chain code to deposit the 01 transaction, the 01 transaction can be looked up using both marble_1_shard and marble_2_shard, and the namespace can be seen to be correctly modified in the log. It can be concluded that the namespace isolation of the query operation has been lifted. In addition to this, using marble to store 0, marble_1_shard to store 1 and marble_2_shard to store 2, all stored successfully, and using marble, marble_1_shard and marble_2_shard to look up 0, 1 and 2 respectively, all successfully queried, we can tell that the chain code conforming to the naming rules is released namespace and the namespace isolation of the stored operation is lifted. Using marble_2 to store data, the namespace is not modified because it does not conform to the naming rules of the parallel chain code, and the stored data cannot be queried by other chain codes, nor can the data stored by marble, marble_1_shard and marble_2_shard be queried using marble_2, and there is data segregation, so we can conclude that other chain codes that are not used for parallelism are not affected.

The performance test was conducted on Fabric after the namespace isolation was lifted and the backing containers were parallelized. The performance test tool tape was used to send a large number of transaction requests to peer nodes, and the results obtained were the overall TPS, combined with the Fabric browser explorer to monitor the outgoing block situation. The number of transactions per experiment was set to 50,000, and the outgoing block size was set to 500 pieces. The number of parallel containers was increased to compare the degree of performance optimisation of Fabric, and the time taken to complete a batch of transactions was recorded to calculate the throughput, and the results are shown in Fig. 2.

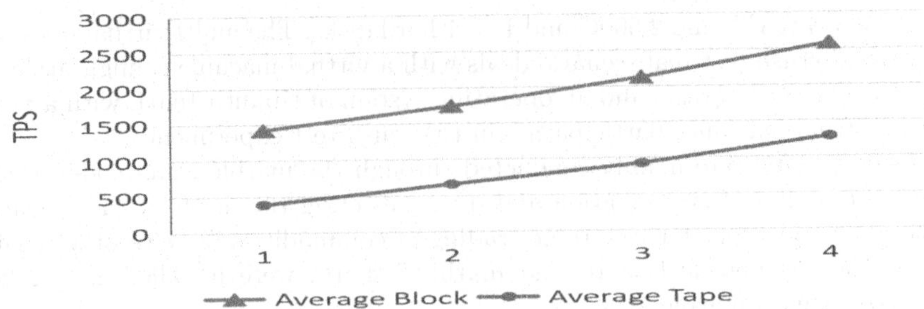

Fig. 2. Comparison of modified Fabric performance tests

4.2 Transaction Distribution Performance Optimisation Validation

After successful installation of the external chaincode, you can see that there are autonomously named containers in the container list, which can be closed or started via the docker-compose file, and when the container is started, the chaincode can be invoked successfully.

To verify the effectiveness of transaction distribution and load balancing, in addition to implementing a consistent hashing algorithm, we wrote a program on which we could simulate the generation of electronic transactions for bulk-commodities, using a multi-threaded, multi-machine approach to initiate transaction requests to Fabric. We simulated a test tool with a producer-consumer model for multi-threading, where the producer generates a certain number of transactions at a time and puts them into the data pool, and the consumer takes them out of the pool to send them to the Fabric network, locking the data pool with a synchronisation mechanism so that only one producer and one consumer can access the data pool at the same time, avoiding the situation of sending duplicate transactions.

The distribution of the consistency hashing algorithm is counted, the number of transactions received by each node, the more the number of virtual nodes, the more even the distribution, when the number of virtual is close to tens of thousands, the distribution is basically even, the number of virtual nodes in the test is set to grow by ten times from 10, the number of real nodes is 5, each node basically distributes about 20% of the transactions (Seen in Table 1).

4.3 Validation Phase Performance Optimisation Validation

The performance of the Fabric after the parallelization of the validation phase of MVCC was tested by sending a large number of transaction requests to peer nodes using the performance testing tool tape. In terms of setting up the experimental control group, since the validation phase has many steps, in order to better observe the effect of reducing the time spent on read/write set checking, in addition to setting up the original version of Fabric without modified source code as the control group, the ideal control group was also set up by modifying the source code, which does not carry out specific read/write set checking and

Table 1. The relationship between the uniformity of hash algorithm distribution transaction and the number of virtual nodes.

Chain code name	10	100	1000	10000	50000
abstore_1_shard	10%	24%	21%	19%	20%
abstore_2_shard	38%	16%	20%	20%	20%
abstore_3_shard	3%	28%	18%	20%	19%
abstore_4_shard	16%	18%	19%	20%	20%
abstore_5_shard	30%	11%	19%	19%	19%

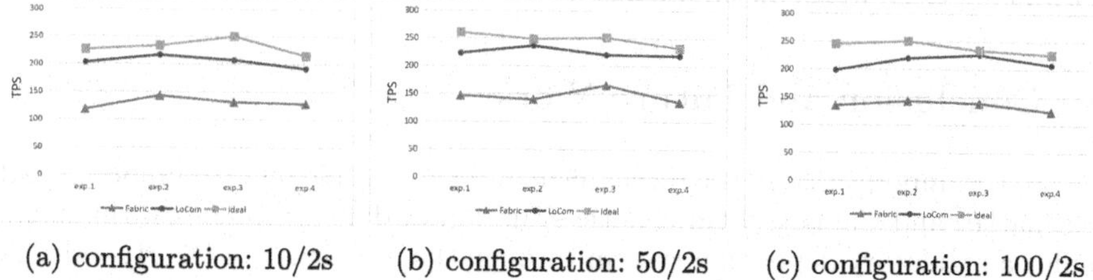

(a) configuration: 10/2s (b) configuration: 50/2s (c) configuration: 100/2s

Fig. 3. Difference in TPS between the three versions when the outgoing block is configured with 10,50,100 transactions as a block with a time interval of 2 s.

sets the checking result to success and returns directly by default, so that the ideal The read/write set check time for the control group is 0.

The number of transactions initiated in one experiment was 4,000, and the time taken to complete this batch of transactions was recorded for each version under a block-out configuration of 10, 50 and 100 for one block respectively, and TPS data was calculated.

From the test results (Seen in Fig. 3), we can see that the namespace is successfully lifted in the endorsement phase, the parallel chain codes can check the deposited transactions before each other, and the non-parallel chain codes do not interfere with each other, there is still namespace isolation, which does not affect the original logic, the LoCom's out block speed is roughly increased by two times, the TPS directly returned by the tape performance test tool is also increased by two times, from the values we can see that the block speed This is due to the fact that there is a sorting and validation phase after the block is released by Fabric, and the time spent in these two phases reduces the overall TPS, and the effect of the increase in exit speed and TPS is basically the same. As the namespace is unsegregated, they can be distributed evenly to different containers for backing, reducing the pressure on single-backed containers and reducing the time taken to issue blocks.

The external chain code deployment is running normally, and normal query and storage functions can also be performed using the external chain code. Statistics on the distribution of transactions distributed through the consistent hash algorithm show that the load is basically even, and when the number of virtual nodes is large enough, the more even the mapping on the hash ring is, and therefore the distribution is even.

The validation phase does not look like the optimisation has achieved more than twice and three times the TPS value, but the control group shows that a large improvement has been achieved. The reason for this is that the read/write set check in the validation phase is parallelised, which improves the speed, but as the writing is done by append and the sequence needs to be controlled, the writing phase after the check is still serialised, resulting in an improvement that is not as significant as that achieved in the endorsement phase by a factor of two. Adjusting the outgoing block settings, the effect is not significantly different, both being close to the desired effect.

5 Conclusion and Future Work

Due to the imperfection of the mechanism of the electronic bulk-commodity trading market and the long-term chaotic situation of difficult forensics, this paper builds a regulatory deposition system through the framework of the Hyperledger Fabric, and achieves parallelization of all phases of transactions by modifying the source code of Fabric, with the distribution of transactions and load balancing of container resources to create a high-throughput deposition platform. We have optimised the endorsement, distribution transaction and validation sessions respectively. And we wrote a pressure testing tool for the trusted depository scenario of electronic commodity trading. After performance testing, the TPS improvement is close to the ideal state.

In future research, we will look into pre-slicing the read and write sets of transactions, where read and write sets can be checked in parallel between different slices and serially within the same slice. When there is an intersection of the read and write sets involved in a particular two transactions, they need to be placed within a single slice, otherwise they can be verified as parallel slices.

Acknowledgement. The work of this paper is supported by the National Key Research and Development Program of China (No. 2019YFA0709502), National Natural Science Foundation of China under Grant (No. 61873309, No. 92046024, No. 92146002) and Shanghai Science and Technology Project under Grant (No. 22510761000) and Shanghai Promotion of High Quality Industrial Development Project (No. 213202).

References

1. Shi, W.B.: Study on the import trade of bulk commodities and its impact on China's economy. Ph. D. Dissertation. Capital University of Economics and Business (2012)
2. Qiao, J.: Discussion on integrated management of risk control, finance and business - based on the perspective of commodity trading enterprises. Economist **03**, 104+106 (2021)

3. Guo, H.: An Empirical Study on the function of Chinese Electronic Commodity Trading Market. Ph. D. Dissertation. Shanghai Academy of Social Sciences (2015)
4. Li, Y.: Economic analysis of blockchain technology to solve credit problems in e-commerce. MS thesis. Beijing Jiaotong University (2018)
5. Xu, L.: Study on Transaction Concurrency and prototype system development based on Hyperledger Fabric. MS thesis, Soochow University (2020)
6. Zhixian, Z.: Research on the development problems and countermeasures of China's bulk commodity e-commerce. China Collect. Econ. **30**, 88–89 (2017)
7. Wang, J., Zhai, W.: Risk Management of Commodity e-commerce platforms in the context of Big Data. Comput. Prod. Distrib. **11** (2019)
8. Bai, X., Wang, J.: Transaction pattern and development trend of bulk commodity e-commerce in China. China Logist. Procurement **11**, 70–71 (2014)
9. Shi, W., Yu, P., Shi, Z.: Methods and Systems of credit Management in Bulk Commodity Trading. CN108921671A (2018)
10. Zou, D., Jia, Q.: Review on the application progress of blockchain in the field of commodity trade. J. Bus. Econ. **10**, 4 (2020)
11. Jiang, L.: Solving international trade credit problems with blockchain. Spec. Zone Econ. **1**, 71–74 (2017)
12. Sharma, A., et al.: Blurring the lines between blockchains and database systems: the case of hyperledger fabric. In: Proceedings of the 2019 International Conference on Management of Data, pp. 105–122 (2019)
13. Xu, X., et al.: Mitigating conflicting transactions in hyperledger fabric-permissioned blockchain for delay-sensitive IoT applications. IEEE Internet Things J. **8**(13), 10596–10607 (2021)
14. Xu, L., et al.: Solutions for concurrency conflict problem on hyperledger fabric. World Wide Web **24**, 463–482 (2021)
15. Kwon, M., Yu, H.: Performance improvement of ordering and endorsement phase in hyperledger fabric. In: 2019 Sixth International Conference on Internet of Things: Systems, Management and Security (IOTSMS), pp. 428–432. IEEE (2019)
16. Maffiola, D., et al.: GOLIATH: a decentralized framework for data collection in intelligent transportation systems. IEEE Trans. Intell. Transp. Syst. **23**(8), 13372–13385 (2021)
17. Lin, J., et al.: A blockchain-based evidential and secure bulk-commodity supervisory system. In: 2021 International Conference on Service Science (ICSS), pp. 1–6. IEEE (2021)
18. Du, X., et al.: A novel data placement strategy for data-sharing scientific workflows in heterogeneous edge-cloud computing environments. In: 2020 IEEE International Conference on Web Services (ICWS), pp. 498–507. IEEE (2020)
19. Li, R., Asaeda, H.: DIBN: a decentralized information-centric blockchain network. In: 2019 IEEE Global Communications Conference (GLOBECOM), pp. 1–6. IEEE (2019)
20. Hewa, T.M., et al.: Survey on blockchain-based smart contracts: technical aspects and future research. IEEE Access **9**, 87643–87662 (2021)
21. Guo, S.: An electronic contract management system based on blockchain a case study of technology framework with improved algorithms. In: 2022 Asia Conference on Algorithms, Computing and Machine Learning (CACML), pp. 115–120. IEEE (2022)
22. Du, X., et al.: A low-latency communication design for brain simulations. IEEE Netw. **36**(2), 8–15 (2022)
23. Zhou, Z., et al.: Blockchain in big data security for intelligent transportation with 6G. IEEE Trans. Intell. Transp. Syst. **23**(7), 9736–9746 (2021)

24. Fedorov, I.R., et al.: Blockchain in 5G networks: perfomance evaluation of private blockchain. In: 2021 Wave Electronics and its Application in Information and Telecommunication Systems (WECONF), pp. 1–4. IEEE (2021)
25. Zheng, Z., et al.: Blockchain challenges and opportunities: a survey. Int. J. Web Grid Serv. **14**(4), 352–375 (2018)
26. Du, X., et al.: Scientific workflows in IoT environments: a data placement strategy based on heterogeneous edge-cloud computing. ACM Trans. Manage. Inf. Syst. (TMIS) **13**(4), 1–26 (2022)
27. Monrat, A.A., Schelén, O., Andersson, K.: A survey of blockchain from the perspectives of applications, challenges, and opportunities. IEEE Access **7**, 117134–117151 (2019)
28. Abdelsalam, H.A., Srivastava, A.K., Eldosouky, A.: Blockchain-based privacy preserving and energy saving mechanism for electricity prosumers. IEEE Trans. Sustain. Energy **13**(1), 302–314 (2021)
29. Yan, T., et al.: Handling conditional queries and data storage on hyperledger fabric efficiently. World Wide Web **24**, 441–461 (2021)
30. Du, X., et al.: BIECS: a blockchain-based intelligent edge cooperation system for latency-sensitive services. In: 2022 IEEE International Conference on Web Services (ICWS), pp. 367–372. IEEE (2022)
31. Thakkar, P., Senthilnathan, N.: Scaling hyperledger fabric using pipelined execution and sparse peers (2020). arXiv preprint arXiv:2003.05113
32. Berendea, N., et al.: Fair and efficient gossip in hyperledger fabric. In: 2020 IEEE 40th International Conference on Distributed Computing Systems (ICDCS), pp. 190–200. IEEE (2020)
33. Xu, X., et al.: Latency performance modeling and analysis for hyperledger fabric blockchain network. Inf. Process. Manage. **58**(1), 102436 (2021)
34. Wang, Y., et al.: Improved lstm-based time-series anomaly detection in rail transit operation environments. IEEE Trans. Ind. Inf. **18**(12), 9027–9036 (2022)
35. Alexandridis, A., et al.: Making case for using RAFT in healthcare through hyperledger fabric. In: 2021 IEEE International Conference on Big Data (Big Data), pp. 2185–2191. IEEE (2021)

Microservice-Based Computation Offloading in Mobile Edge Computing

Shengnan Zhang, Hanchuan Xu, Lanshun Nie(✉), and Dechen Zhan

Faculty of Computing, Harbin Institute of Technology, Harbin, China
21S103269@stu.hit.edu.cn, {xhc,nls,zdc}@hit.edu.cn

Abstract. Microservices are an emerging service architecture that, when combined with mobile edge computing (MEC), can offer low latency to nearby mobile users. Several instances of microservices hosted on the server can be started or stopped flexibly to address computational requests from users at various times of the day or night thanks to the characteristics of dynamic deployment, quick start-up, and easy transfer of microservices. from the perspective of the application provider, we need to ensure the quality of service for end-users while minimizing the number of leased edge servers. To enable efficient use of MEC resources and provide reliable performance for mobile devices, we developed an Ant colony Optimization algorithm for computational offloading based on Microservices in MEC (ACO_MMCO). then we simulate the scenario using the simulation program iFogSim2 and real data sets. According to the experimental findings, this method's generated offloading policy outperforms the benchmark method in a number of performance evaluation criteria.

Keywords: microservice · mobile edge computing · computation offloading · Ant colony Optimization · iFogSim2

1 Introduction

Mobile devices running computationally intensive applications can drain battery life and lead to slow response times, negatively impacting the user experience. To address these challenges, it may be more effective to offload computation to a less resource-intensive infrastructure in mobile edge computing [3]. By deploying edge nodes with computing, storage, and communication functions, traditional wireless access networks can provide higher bandwidth and lower latency data services to end users while reducing network load. In the industrial internet, data collection typically involves sensors and cameras. Real-time analysis and processing using AI technology enable intelligent control and monitoring. With the high-speed transmission of 5G, product images can be quickly sent to cloud servers for real-time AI analysis. MEC allows for AI reasoning and policy execution on mobile devices, while services requiring more powerful computing and

Supported by National Natural Science Foundation of China Project U20A6003.

Z. Wang et al. (Eds.): ICSS 2023, CCIS 1844, pp. 505–519, 2023.
https://doi.org/10.1007/978-981-99-4402-6_36

storage capabilities can be deployed to edge nodes or central clouds. This simplifies field devices and improves performance.

In the mobile Internet era, traditional monolithic applications that prioritize peak satisfaction result in significant resource wastage during off-peak periods. Microservices offer a solution with their easily scalable and autonomous characteristics, allowing for flexible starting and stopping of multiple instances across different resource centers [1]. In the industrial sector, applications are based on microservices and modeled based on the capabilities of PaaS-based services. These microservices are divided into groups and combined to form industry APPs. Each microservice performs a specific subtask or service, requiring fewer resources and reducing communication overhead, making it ideal for MEC architecture.

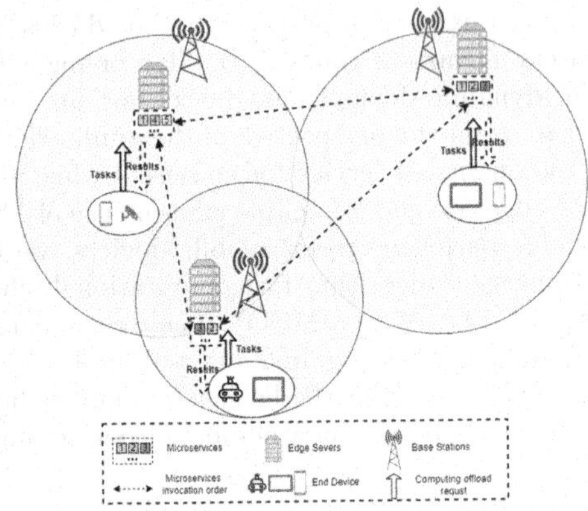

Fig. 1. Mobile edge computing compute offload diagram

Current research on microservices focuses on scheduling and placement methods in cloud-edge collaboration, but there is comparatively less research on computing offloading in mobile edge computing, especially with regards to microservice architecture. We aim to investigate the decision-making process for computing task offloading between edge servers and mobile devices in the Industrial Internet. Figure 1 shows a scenario where end-users with mobile devices provide geolocation information and require different computational tasks involving multiple microservices. The microservices-based edge server handles user requests, but limited resources restrict the number of deployed microservices. Offloading computationally intensive tasks to the server reduces mobile device latency and resource consumption and minimizes the cost of application providers on the edge server. However, it must consider the limited resources of the edge server and invocation dependencies between deployed microservices.

Microservice architectures are widely used in MEC [2], doing research based on this premise is of some value. Specifically, different mobile applications have varying different microservices and their invocations, resource and computation requirements, which may result in computational tasks' data transfer requirements. Additionally, the resources of the edge server are limited, as well as the association with the base station can only handle requests from nearby users.

We model microservices-based MEC offloading as a nonlinear optimization problem to meet latency requirements and reduce application provider costs. Our ant colony algorithm-based offloading method uses multi-objective heuristic information and a feedback mechanism to avoid local optima and find optimal solutions quickly.

Our experimental results show that our approach reduces costs, satisfies latency restrictions, and handles resource limitations, providing a near-optimal offloading method for microservice tasks on edge platforms. The results suggest that our approach can balance the interests of mobile users and service providers effectively.

The rest of this paper is organized as follows. Section 2 discusses related research. Section 3 introduces a mathematical model. Section 4 formulates the optimization problem. Section 5 presents an algorithm to solve it. Section 6 evaluates the algorithm through simulations. Section 2 concludes the paper and discusses future work.

2 Related Work

2.1 Computational Offloading Research

Liang et al. [3] proposed a DDLO algorithm to minimize energy consumption and ensure quality of service in multi-server MEC networks. S. Chu et al. [4] designed a DMCO algorithm to minimize response time and energy consumption, achieving a Nash equilibrium. Pan et al. [5] proposed a joint partial offloading and task priority computation algorithm to minimize time delay and energy consumption, while Lai et al. [9] aimed to maximize the number of assigned end users while minimizing the number of leased edge servers and ensuring quality of service, modeled as the VSVBP problem and solved using lexical goal programming.

However, the edge user allocation problem does not take into account the need for the system to be based on microservice architecture, where each user request consists of an entire monolithic architecture running as a single service.

2.2 Research on Task Assignment for Microservices

Recent research on microservice architecture in edge computing includes: Tian et al. [6] modeled microservice caching as a Markov decision process to minimize fetching latency and proposed a distributed algorithm based on D3QN; L. Chen et al. [7] proposed a method for microservice-based service deployment policy using reinforcement learning and neural networks to reduce average waiting time for IoT devices in a hybrid environment; M. Lin et al. [8] developed a multi-objective optimization model for container-based microservice scheduling and used an ant colony algorithm to solve the scheduling problem.

Several research studies have proposed different approaches to address microservice placement and scheduling challenges in IoT applications. Pallewatta et al. [10] introduced a decentralized placement algorithm for microservices in fog nodes, while Gu et al. [11] studied a layer-aware microservice placement problem to maximize edge throughput. i.-D. Filip et al. [12] designed a hybrid cloud scheduling model for assigning tasks to processing entities in an IoT microservice platform focused on energy-saving scenarios, and discussed relevant scheduling and edge/cloud considerations. M. Alam et al. [13] proposed a scalable architecture based on lightweight virtualization, while Samanta et al. [14] designed a dynamic microservice scheduling scheme to maximize network throughput and QoS. S. Wang et al. [15] investigated the availability of microservice orchestration and proposed dynamic planning-based and reinforcement learning-based algorithms.

Considerable research has been conducted on scheduling and placement methods of microservices in various cloud-edge collaboration scenarios. However, little attention has been given to addressing the challenges associated with computational offloading in MEC. These challenges include the limitations of mobile end devices and deployment of microservices on edge servers.

3 System Model

3.1 System Architecture

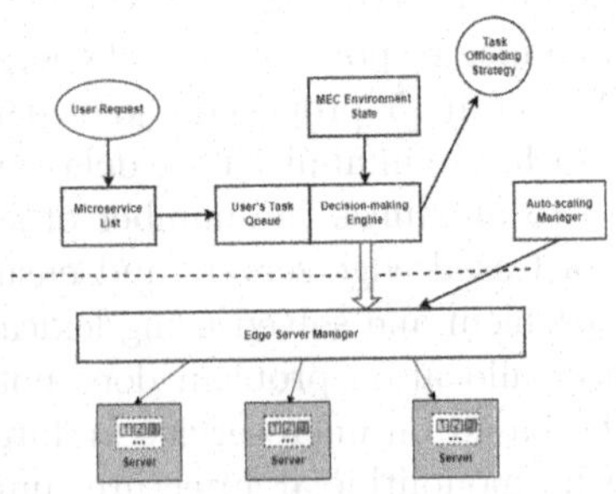

Fig. 2. System Architecture diagram

Figure 2 describes the architecture behind system model. In our architecture, the user agent resolves user-requested applications into a list of corresponding microservices, inputs and outputs, and the order of invocations between multiple microservices. The defined user requests are then added to the task queue. The decision engine begins to understand the user's task and decides how to offload the user's computational tasks based on policies and algorithms that combine resource availability, microservice invocation relationships, scope constraints, and other factors. Depending on the microservice characteristics, the

Auto Scaling Deployment Manager is also included to keep track of available resources and automatically scale microservice instances.

The architectural components of our system include:

User requests: User requests are compute task offload requests, consisting of a combination of microservices executed with specific inputs, and their invocation relationship represented by a chain of invocations.

Microservices: Represent atomic execution units of a task.

Microservice list: Contains the list of microservices that complete the tasks requested by the user. It includes the resources needed to execute microservices located on different servers, etc.

User task queue: The User task queue is a buffer for the decision engine. It contains the task definitions, and the scheduling engine must be aware of changes in mobile devices due to their dynamic nature. The task queue and the decision engine work together as strongly connected modules.

Decision engine: The main responsibility of the decision engine is to solve the offloading problem by applying a given offloading policy and providing a task→edge server correspondence.

Scheduling policy: The pluggable part of our system that defines a set of offloading policies and algorithms for solving the problem.

Edge servers: Provide computing power and resources, and deploy and execute task-related microservices.

When scheduling task, choosing between an edge server or a local edge device is often a consideration. The user tasks can either be processed on their mobile device or by an edge server providing the necessary resources. Typically, the user's task is implemented via microservices, and their task request may involve completing multiple microservices. As the microservices run, they generate a demand for resources, which can be met by the edge server hosting them.

3.2 System Model

The edge server is typically installed on the base station, and the geographic position (x_j, y_j) of the edge server s_j can be determined using the latitude and longitude of the base station, and the geographic location of user u_i at time t is expressed as $(x_{i,t}, y_{i,t})$. If the coverage area of edge server s_j is a circle with a radius of $cov(s_j)$, then each edge server will only be able to service the users inside that area. where $UM_i = \{m_1, m_2, ..., m_a\}$ is the collection of microservices that are supported by task requests for each end-user $u_{i,t}$, and the collection of microservices owned by the edge server s_j is represented as $SM_i = \{m_1, m_2, ..., m_b\}$. The set of d-class resources offered by the edge server in this case, taking into account the resources needed by the microservices and the d-class resources it offers, and the resource required for microservice m_k are represented as $\omega_k = \{\omega_k^1, ..., \omega_k^d\}$.

3.3 Communication Model

The signal-to-noise ratio (SNR) between end device i and edge server (EN) j is defined as

$$\xi_{i,j}(t) = \frac{p_{i,j}(t)\, h_{i,j}(t)}{\sigma^2} \tag{1}$$

where $p_{i,j}(t)$ represents the transferred power between EN j and the terminal device i, $h_{i,j}(t)$ is the channel gain between terminal device i and EN j, σ^2 is the power of the Gaussian white noise. As a result, the terminal device i and EN j's transmission rate between time slot t is defined as

$$\beta_{i,j}(t) = a_{i,j}(t) B_{i,j} \log_2 \xi_{i,j}(t) \tag{2}$$

where $a_{i,j}(t)$ is the computational task offload policy between end device i and EN j, $B_{i,j}$ is the bandwidth between end device i and EN j.

The data transfer time for the task is defined as

$$tran_{i,j}(t) = \frac{p_t}{\beta_{i,j}(t)} \tag{3}$$

3.4 Delay Model

Microservice startup latency is defined as

$$D_i^{spin}(t) = I \cdot X_i \tag{4}$$

I indicates the number of microservice instances required to complete this task, X_i indicates the total latency of starting microservices in a container. Equation (4) indicates the total latency of all microservice instances required for the container to start to complete this task.

Microservice runtime latency is defined as

$$D_k^{ex}(t) = \frac{in_i w_i}{f_{j,k}} + W_k \tag{5}$$

The tasks of end-user u_i can be represented as a triple $< p_i, \tau_i, w_i >$ denotes the input size (in bits) of the end-user u_i task, τ_i denotes the task's deadline (in seconds), and w_i is the computational intensity (in CPU cycles/bit). $f_{j,k}$ denotes the computational intensity (i.e., CPU frequency) of microservice m_k required for the tasks that edge server s_j can assign to user u_i.

Due to the limited computing power of the edge server, there may be some unfinished tasks waiting to be processed. Therefore, the queuing time should be considered. W_j denotes the waiting time of the microservice in the waiting queue.

Let $w_{k,t}^q$ denote the computational intensity of the outstanding tasks in microservice m_k of the edge server, $f_{j,k}^q$ denotes the computational intensity allocated to microservice m_k by edge server s_j. The queuing time can be calculated by Eq. (6).

$$W_k = \frac{w_{k,t}^q}{f_{j,k}^q} \tag{6}$$

Therefore, the delay time of a task request execution is defined as

$$D_i^{total}(t) = D_i^{spin}(t) + \sum_{k \in UM_i} D_k^{ex}(t) + \sum_{j \in \{1,\ldots,m\}} a_{i,j}(t) \cdot trans_{i,j}(t) \tag{7}$$

This equation represents the latency time for the container to start the microservice instance, the microservice execution time, the microservice wait latency, and the user data transfer latency if all microservices needed to complete the task need to be offloaded to the edge server for computation.

4 Microservice Computation Offloading Framework

An end-user selects one or several specific microservices to perform their tasks in a time slot. Denoting the length of the time slot as t, $t \in T$, $T = \{1, 2, \ldots\}$. Here it is first assumed that each end-user will generate a computationally intensive task that needs to be processed in any time slot t. The task offloading strategy for time t is expressed by the following equation.

$$a_{i,j}(t) = \begin{cases} 1 & \text{EN j processes the microservice that user i's request} \\ 0 & \text{otherwise} \end{cases} \tag{8}$$

To optimize the offloading of microservices to edge servers in MEC, a multi-objective optimization model is used, taking into account resource capacity, location constraints, and microservice request constraints. A nonlinear optimization problem is formulated to minimize cost and processing latency for the application provider. When edge servers are unable to handle all required microservices, only certain microservices should be offloaded, with the remaining processed locally on the device.

$$\max |I| \tag{9}$$

$$\min |J| \tag{10}$$

Subject to

$$a_{i,j} = 1, j \in \{j | u_i \in cov(s_j)\}, \forall u_i \in U, \forall s_j in S \tag{11}$$

$$\omega_k^d \leq c_j^d, \forall d \in D, \forall m_k \in M, \forall s_j \in S \tag{12}$$

$$a_{i,j} = 1, j \in \{j | um_i^p \in SM_j\}, \forall u_i \in U, um_i^p \in UM_i \tag{13}$$

$$\sum_{m_k \in UM_i} ins_j^k \cdot \omega_k^d \leq c_j^d, \forall d \in D, \forall m_k \in M, \forall s_j \in S \tag{14}$$

$$D_i^{tot}(t) \leq t_{max} \tag{15}$$

By solving this problem, we can determine the best way to allocate resources and balance processing between edge servers and mobile devices to achieve optimal performance and cost efficiency.

From the perspective of an application provider who chooses to deploy their service to an edge server in order to reduce end-user latency, the goal of the problem is to maximize the number of users assigned to the edge server while ensuring the required quality of service for the end-user (9), as well as to minimize the number of leased edge servers needed (10). In this case, we also need to make sure that the edge server can only handle requests from end users within its coverage area (11), that the microservices deployed on the designated edge server can handle user requests (12), and that there are limits on the size of the microservices (13), as well as resource utilization limits (14), and that the application's response time does not exceed the set latency requirements (15).

5 Algorithm Design

We developed a microservice computing task offloading algorithm based on the ant colony algorithm. Inputs required include task requests for each user, microservice invocation relationships, edge server information, number of ants, and maximum iterations. The main algorithm flow is as follows.
(1) An ant, denoted as k, is randomly assigned to the starting microservice for a user request denoted as i;
(2) Ant k then selects the path (i, j), which represents all microservice request assignments for user request i;
(3) Next, The repeat step (2) for the next user request for the next allocation;
(4) All ants complete the computational task of request offloading policy for all mobile devices, and one iteration covers all microservice request assignments for one user request. The algorithm terminates when the maximum number of iterations is reached.

Combining the two optimization objectives described above, the heuristic information for setting up the computation task offload of microservice request r from user i to edge server j can be described as follows.

$$\eta_{ij}^{k} = \eta_{ij}^{k(1)} \times \eta_{ij}^{k(2)} = |I| \cdot \frac{M}{|J|} \tag{16}$$

The Eq. (17) for updating the pheromone concentration is as follows.

$$\tau_{ij}(t+1) = (1-\rho)\tau_{ij}(t) + \sum_{k=1}^{m} \Delta\tau_{ij}^{k}(t) \tag{17}$$

where

$$\Delta\tau_{ij}^{k}(t) = \begin{cases} \frac{Q}{eval(X^k)}, & if \quad x_{ij}^{k} = 1 \\ 0, & if \quad x_{ij}^{k} = 0 \end{cases} \tag{18}$$

X^k denotes the solution generated by ant k, and $\Delta\tau_{ij}^{k}(t)$ denotes the pheromone added by the current ant along its current path.

Algorithm 1. Ant colony Optimization algorithm for computational offloading based on Microservices

```
Require: task requests $I = \{u_1, u_2, \ldots, u_n\}$;
    user i microservice requests $UM_i = \{m_1, m_2, \ldots, m_a\}$;
    edge servers SERVERs $J = \{s_1, s_2, \ldots, s_m\}$;
    K, $N_{max}$
Ensure: offloading strategy
Initialize pheromone matrix
$t \leftarrow 1$
while do
    Random place K ants to M task requests for mobile users
    for each $Ant_k$ do
        for each $I_i \in I$ do
            for each $ms_r \in UM_i$ do
                for each $edge_j \in S$ do
                    Determine location, microservice, and resource constraints
                    Calculate $\eta_{(i,r,j)}$ by Equation (16)
                    Calculate the transition probability $p_{(i,r,j)}$ by Equation (20)
                    Select the server on which the next microservice for this request will be processed
                end for
                Update the optimal solution best PATH found so far
            end for
        end for
        put $ms_r$ into $Tabu_k$
    end for
    $t \leftarrow t + 1$
    if t ¡ $N_{max}$ then
        Calculate pheromone increment $\Delta\tau_{ij}^k$ by Equation (18)
        Update pheromone matrix $\tau_{ij}$ by Equation (17)
    else
        return best PATH
    end if
end while
```

Ants traverse user requests and their paths provide the solution to the multi-objective optimization problem. The solution quality is assessed using the evaluation function described by an equation to obtain the optimal solution quickly.

$$Eval(X) = |I| \times \frac{M}{|J|} \tag{19}$$

Ants choose their path based on the concentration of pheromones, with higher concentrations leading to higher probabilities. The roulette algorithm is used to calculate these probabilities.

$$p_{ij}^k(t) = \frac{[\tau_{ij}(t)]^\alpha \times [\eta_{ij}(t)]^\beta}{\sum_{l \in a_k} [\tau_{il}(t)]^\alpha \times [\eta_{il}(t)]^\beta}, j \in a_k \tag{20}$$

where α is a pheromone factor, and β is a heuristic function factor.

6 Experiment

6.1 Experimental Setup

The experiment was conducted using iFogSim2 [16] simulation tool on a machine with Intel(R) Core(TM) i7-10510U CPU @ 1.80 GHz 2.30 GHz 8.00 GB RAM. Multiple end-users, equipped with mobile devices that are running microservices-based IoT applications, were considered. The end-users were distributed over a certain area, and the open-source experimental dataset eua-dataset [9] was used, which gathers location information from Australian cellular base stations and end users. Each base station connected to a MEC edge server had a 200-radius circular coverage area and 50 orthogonal radio channels were included for the purpose of offloading computational activities from the edge devices to the edge server. The relevant parameters for this experiment are listed in Tables 1 and 2.

The base stations in the system have a 100 GHz bandwidth, whereas the IoT devices have a 0.7 GHz processing speed. Each mobile device is assigned a task that launches multiple microservices on the edge server, and each end user has unique real-time duties. There are 4 edge servers, each hosting a minimum of 8 microservices. The latency between servers and microservices is set to 1–1.5 ms, with a data size of each microservice task between 300 and 500 Kb. The overall time for offloading computing services by mobile edge devices is randomly distributed between 5 and 10 ms, with an edge device delay requirement of 0.5 to 1 s.

In the simulation experiment, the number of applications based on microservice architecture is 20, and the number of microservices needed for each application is set to 2–3. The user request includes details like the user id, the resources required for the task, and the application id. When a request requires more microservice instances than are available, a copy of that instance is gener-

Table 1. Main Parameters

Parameter	Value
Bandwidth of edge servers	20 MHz
Total number of CPU cycles for the computing task	1000 Megacycles
Resource requirements for computing tasks	[10, 20] MHz
Data size for microservice-based tasks	[300, 500] Kb
Uplink bandwidth	12500000 bps
Downlink bandwidth	12500000 bps

Table 2. Amount of Resources for Different Equipment

Resource Type	Edge Server	Mobile Device
CPU Speed (MIPS)	2500–3000	500
RAM (GB)	16	1

ated based on the scalability of the microservice itself. Each edge server installs microservices to handle the user's computational needs. A resource-constrained MEC network based on microservice architecture is constructed.

6.2 Evaluation Indicators

1. Resource Utilization
   The resource utilization of node j during the interval time Δ is defined as

$$ram\_util(n_j, \Delta t) = \frac{\sum_{\forall s_i \rightarrow n_j}(ram_i \cdot part(runtime_j^i, \Delta t))}{RAM_j \cdot \Delta t} \tag{21}$$

   ram_i denotes the resource request of microservice instance i, RAM_j denotes the resource limit of the server, and $part(runtime_j^i, \Delta t)$ denotes the running time of service s_i running on the node n_j at time Δt.
2. The processing latency
   The processing latency of a computing task D_i^{total} is calculated by adding the task transfer time, the running time, and the start-up delay of the microservices.
3. Request's response time
   Calculate the request's response time, the waiting time from when the device sends the request to when the task is finished and the request is received.
4. Compute task offload rate
   The percentage of compute tasks that need to be processed by the mobile device during this time interval that are instead handled by the edge server.

6.3 Baseline Approaches

Given the limited number of studies that have investigated offloading decisions for computing tasks in microservices-based architectures on both edge servers and mobile devices, we focus on comparing two fundamental approaches.

•Local: Only the local processing of user tasks is considered.

•The random assignment strategy involves choosing at random one of the edge servers that can handle each user's request for a computational task.

•The greedy algorithm traverses each request while utilizing the fewest number of edge servers possible.

6.4 Analysis of Result

For 20, 50, 100, 150, and 200 mobile user requests, respectively, the performance of the random assignment technique, greedy algorithm, and ACO_MMCO was analyzed on various metrics.

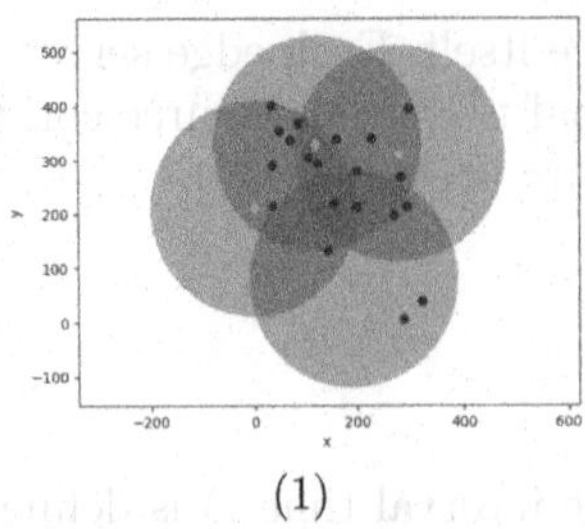
(1)

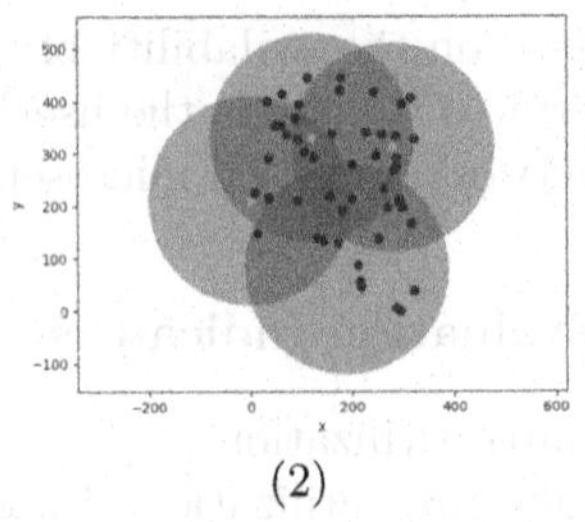
(2)

Fig. 3. Mobile user and edge server location map

Figure 3 depicts the location maps of the edge servers along with their coverage, as well as the location maps of 20 and 50 mobile devices.

The ACO_MMCO algorithm generates the time required to compute the offloading strategy within a range of a few hundred milliseconds to a few seconds, whereas the greedy and random strategies typically take around 100 ms on average. This is due to the fact that the ACO_MMCO algorithm has more iterations, thus taking more time to execute than the random method and the greedy algorithm. In Fig. 4, average response time of different algorithms for request processing is compared. Greedy and ACO_MMCO algorithms can handle all computation tasks when the number of user requests is 20 and 50, but as the number of requests increases to 100, 150, and 200, the edge server resources cannot meet the demand, leading to local processing on mobile devices with longer completion times. ACO_MMCO reduces the average response time of computation tasks compared to the greedy and random policies, even though it cannot offload all tasks to run on the server. The ACO_MMCO algorithm assigns more computational tasks to the edge server for processing, resulting in an average response time 19.6%, 11.3%, 18.3%, 11.04%, 6.33%, lower than that of the random policy and 0%, 0%, 12.9%, 0%, 1.6% lower than that of the greedy policy. Consequently, the response time of user requests corresponding to the ACO_MMCO algorithm is relatively low. Figure 5 compares the offloading rate of computational task requests to the MEC server for processing using

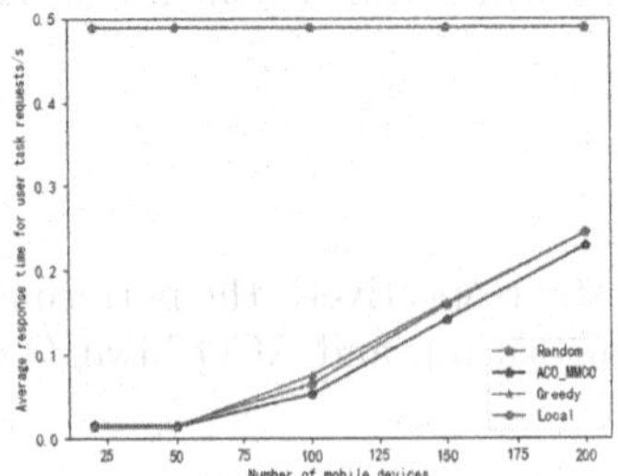

Fig. 4. the average response time of different algorithm requests

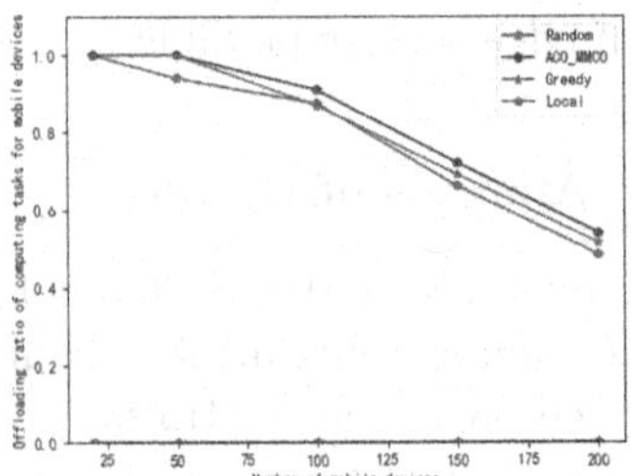

Fig. 5. unloading rate of task requests calculated by different algorithms

various algorithms. At 20 mobile user requests, all three allocation policies successfully offload all computational requests to the edge server. As the number of requests increases to 50, both the ACO_MMCO and greedy policies outperform the random policy in terms of offloading rate. When the requested resources exceed the available resources, the ACO_MMCO can leverage information about the microservices deployed by each edge server to find a more optimal solution by attempting multiple schedules. As a result, the offloading rate of the ACO_MMCO method is higher than the other two methods.

When the number of microservices increases from 50 to 200, due to the resource capacity limitation of the four edge servers, not all requests for computational tasks can be processed on the servers. In this scenario, the ACO_MMCO algorithm achieves a 2.5%, 2.3%, 2.5% higher offloading rate than the greedy algorithm-based strategy, and a 3.5%, 6%, 5.5% higher offloading rate than the random strategy, respectively.

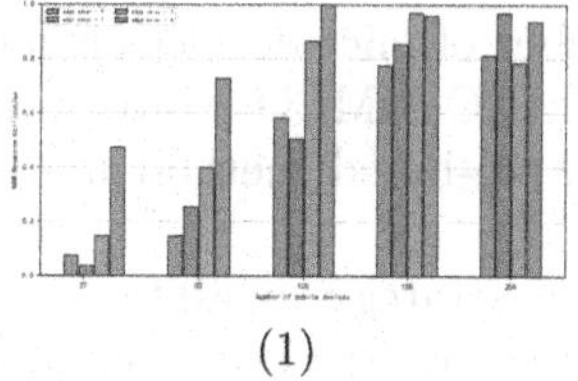
(1)

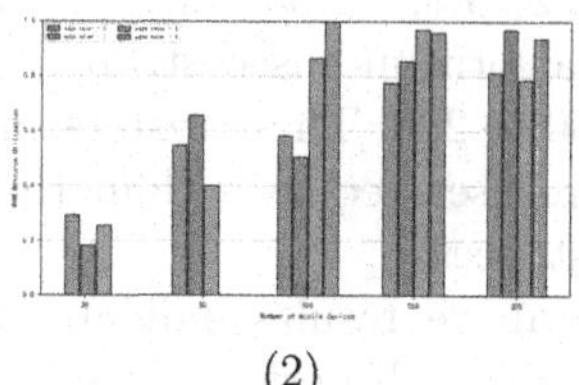
(2)

Fig. 6. Resource utilization diagram of four edge servers for greedy approach

The offloading policies generated by the greedy algorithm vary with different scenarios. Specifically, the deployment of different microservices on the edge servers can lead to different optimization goals, resulting in different offloading policies for the same request.

As shown in Fig. 6 above, when 20 mobile devices generate computational requests, if a task that is simultaneously requested by users in the coverage of multiple edge servers needs to be processed first, the decision on which server will handle it can only be made once, and the greedy policy may not achieve the optimal solution even if the problem optimization objective is taken into consideration.

The average RAM resource use of the four edge servers for various numbers of microservice requests for the three techniques is shown in Fig. 7 and Fig. 8. It is evident that the overall RAM resource utilization of the edge servers increases with the total number of microservice requests.

Due to the increasing number of microservices, the edge server's resources become insufficient to handle all requests simultaneously, requiring more resources. When the total number of mobile devices is 20 and 50, the edge servers' resources are enough to process all requests, resulting in the same RAM utilization for both policies. Thus, server 4 is not required. The optimization goal is to reduce the number of edge servers used, which is achieved by the greedy strategy and the ACO_MMCO algorithm in Fig. 6(2).

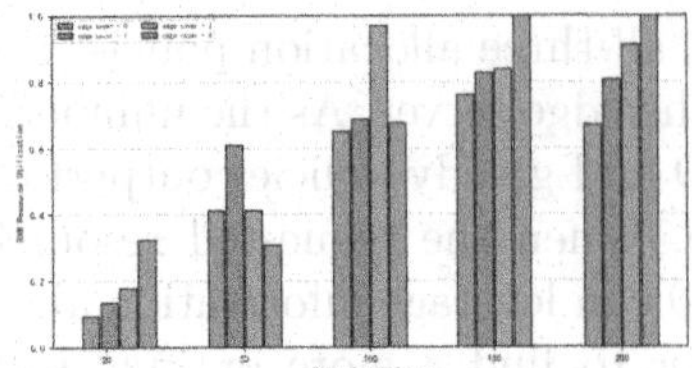

Fig. 7. Resource utilization graph of four edge servers for the random method

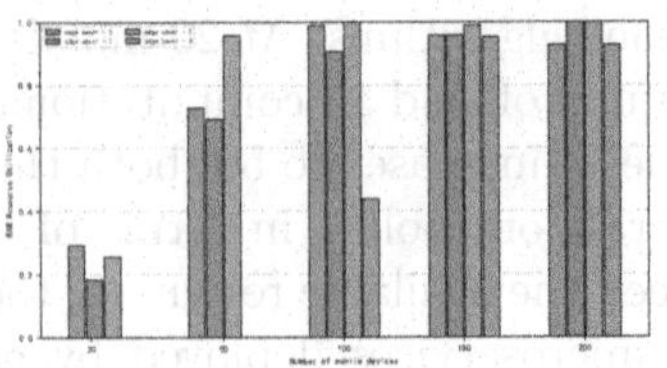

Fig. 8. Resource utilization graph of four edge servers with ACO_MMCO algorithm

When the number of microservices increases from 100 to 150, the average RAM resource utilization is 18.23%, 10.41%, 2.08%, −0.5% higher for the ACO_MMCO strategy than the greedy algorithm-based strategy, and 11.45%, 3.125%, 21.3%, −1.05% higher for the ACO_MMCO algorithm strategy than the greedy algorithm-based strategy when the number of microservices is increased from 150 to 200. These results suggest that the ACO_MMCO strategy can handle more user requests than the greedy algorithm-based method under these circumstances.

The above results indicate that the random strategy exhibits uncertainty and poor overall performance. The greedy strategy, on the other hand, reduces the algorithm's running time but does not guarantee the production of the best solution due to the problem of first selection. The heuristic algorithm, however, repeatedly iterates the optimization process, at the expense of decision time, ultimately yielding a solution with acceptable performance.

7 Conclusion

In this thesis, we address the problem of offloading decision-making for computing task requests based on microservice architecture in MEC, aiming to satisfy users' latency requirements while minimizing service provider costs. We propose an offloading strategy for microservice computing tasks based on the ACO_MMCO. Experimental results demonstrate that the solution is optimized through multiple iterations, ultimately achieving relatively good performance, which surpasses that of the benchmark strategy.

However, in the problem of offloading decision-making for computing task requests based on microservice architecture in MEC, our future work will focus on studying dynamic offloading methods for microservice-based computing, taking into account the mobility of mobile users.

References

1. Tian, H., et al.: DIMA: distributed cooperative microservice caching for internet of things in edge computing by deep reinforcement learning. World Wide Web **25**, 1769–1792 (2021). https://doi.org/10.1007/s11280-021-00939-7

2. Josip, Z., et al.: Edge offloading for microservice architectures. In: Proceedings of the 5th International Workshop on Edge Systems, Analytics and Networking (2022)
3. Liang, H., Feng, X.: Multi-server multi-user multi-task computation offloading for mobile edge computing networks. Sensors **19**, 1446 (2019)
4. Chu, S., Fang, Z., Song, S.: Efficient multi-channel computation offloading for mobile edge computing: a game-theoretic approach. IEEE Trans. Cloud Comput. (99), 1 (2020)
5. Pan, M., Li, Z.: Multi-user computation offloading algorithm for mobile edge computing. In: 2021 2nd International Conference on Electronics, Communications and Information Technology (CECIT). IEEE (2021)
6. Tian, H., et al.: DIMA: distributed cooperative microservice caching for internet of things in edge computing by deep reinforcement learning. World Wide Web **25**, 1769–1792 (2021)
7. Chen, L., et al.: IoT microservice deployment in edge-cloud hybrid environment using reinforcement learning. IEEE Internet Things J. **8**(16), 12610–12622 (2021). https://doi.org/10.1109/JIOT.2020.3014970
8. Lin, M., Xi, J., Bai, W., Wu, J.: Ant colony algorithm for multi-objective optimization of container-based microservice scheduling in cloud. IEEE Access **7**, 83088–83100 (2019). https://doi.org/10.1109/ACCESS.2019.2924414
9. Lai, P., et al.: Optimal edge user allocation in edge computing with variable sized vector bin packing. In: Pahl, C., Vukovic, M., Yin, J., Yu, Q. (eds.) ICSOC 2018. LNCS, vol. 11236, pp. 230–245. Springer, Cham (2018). https://doi.org/10.1007/978-3-030-03596-9_15
10. Pallewatta, S., Kostakos, V., Buyya, R.: Microservices-based IoT application placement within heterogeneous and resource constrained fog computing environments. In: Proceedings of the 12th IEEE/ACM International Conference on Utility and Cloud Computing, pp. 71–81 (2019). https://doi.org/10.1145/3344341.3368800
11. Gu, L., Zeng, D., Hu, J., Li, B., Jin, H.: Layer aware microservice placement and request scheduling at the edge. In: IEEE INFOCOM 2021 - IEEE Conference on Computer Communications, pp. 1–9 (2021). https://doi.org/10.1109/INFOCOM42981.2021.9488779
12. Filip, I.-D., Pop, F., Serbanescu, C., Choi, C.: Microservices scheduling model over heterogeneous cloud-edge environments as support for IoT applications. IEEE Internet Things J. **5**(4), 2672–2681 (2018). https://doi.org/10.1109/JIOT.2018.2792940
13. Alam, M., Rufino, J., Ferreira, J., Ahmed, S.H., Shah, N., Chen, Y.: Orchestration of microservices for IoT using docker and edge computing. IEEE Commun. Mag. **56**(9), 118–123 (2018). https://doi.org/10.1109/MCOM.2018.1701233
14. Samanta, A., Tang, J.: Dyme: dynamic microservice scheduling in edge computing enabled IoT. IEEE Internet Things J. **7**(7), 6164–6174 (2020). https://doi.org/10.1109/JIOT.2020.2981958
15. Wang, S., Guo, Y., Zhang, Z., Yang, P., Zhou, A., Shen, X.: Delay-aware microservice coordination in mobile edge computing: a reinforcement learning approach. In: IEEE Transactions on Mobile Computing, vol. 20, no. 3, pp. 939–951 (2021). https://doi.org/10.1109/TMC.2019.2957804
16. Mahmud, R., et al.: iFogSim2: an extended iFogSim simulator for mobility, clustering, and microservice management in edge and fog computing environments. J. Syst. Softw. **190**, 111351 (2022)

Author Index

Z. Wang et al. (Eds.): ICSS 2023, CCIS 1844, pp. 521–522, 2023.
https://doi.org/10.1007/978-981-99-4402-6

Printed in the United States
by Baker & Taylor Publisher Services

Printed in the United States
by Baker & Taylor Publisher Services